The Extended Family in Black Societies

World Anthropology

General Editor

SOL TAX

Patrons

CLAUDE LÉVI-STRAUSS
MARGARET MEAD
LAILA SHUKRY HAMAMSY
M. N. SRINIVAS

MOUTON PUBLISHERS · THE HAGUE · PARIS
DISTRIBUTED IN THE USA AND CANADA BY ALDINE, CHICAGO

The Extended Family
in Black Societies

Editors

DEMITRI B. SHIMKIN
EDITH M. SHIMKIN
DENNIS A. FRATE

MOUTON PUBLISHERS · THE HAGUE · PARIS
DISTRIBUTED IN THE USA AND CANADA BY ALDINE, CHICAGO

Distributed in the United States of America and Canada
by Aldine Publishing Company, Chicago, Illinois
ISBN 90-279-7590-6 (Mouton)
0-202-90077-0 (Aldine)
Jacket photo by Mike Mauney
Cover and jacket design by Jurriaan Schrofer
Indexes by Society of Indexers, Great Britain
Printed in Great Britain at the University Printing House, Cambridge

Dedication

This volume is part of the work of the Milton Olive III Memorial Corporation, a community organization of Holmes County, Mississippi, committed to "research and services for human welfare, under community control." The Corporation commemorates the grandson of a Black Holmes Countian, Private First Class Milton Olive III, of Chicago, who on October 22, 1965, and at the age of not quite nineteen, gave his life for others. At Phu Cuong, in Vietnam, ". . . Private Olive and four other soldiers were moving through the jungle together when a grenade was thrown in their midst. Private Olive saw the grenade, and then saved the lives of his fellow soldiers at the sacrifice of his own by grabbing the grenade in his hand and falling on it to absorb the blast with his body. . . ." (U.S. Army, General Order No. 18, 26 April, 1966). Private Olive was posthumously awarded the Congressional Medal of Honor.

This volume, in particular, has been prepared in memory of those who committed their lives to freedom and human dignity in Holmes County, Mississippi:

Mr. Ralthus Hayes, b. September 7, 1916; d. December 6, 1967. Community organizer; area teacher for the Southern Christian Leadership Conference; Director for Social Service, Milton Olive III Memorial Program for Children; one of "The Thirteen," Black Holmes Countian men and women remembered for defying White supremacy by first seeking to register as voters on April 9 and 10, 1963, at Lexington, Mississippi;

Mrs. Margaret Montgomery, b. July 4, 1915; d. September 24, 1971. Board Member, Milton Olive III Memorial Corporation; Principal, West Elementary School;

Plate 1. PFC Milton Olive III

Plate 2a. At the FDP shack, Pecan Grove (Lexington), January, 1967

Plate 2b. The rescue on Highway 13, north of Saigon, July, 1972

Plate 2c. Journalism in the field, Kien Hoa Province,
Vietnam, December, 1971

Plates 2a–c. Alexander D. Shimkin

Mrs. Mary Pitchford, b. September 20, 1918; d. February 23, 1972. Board Member, Milton Olive III Memorial Corporation; Member, Health Service Committee; Employee, Holmes County Health Research Program;

Mr. Samuel Friar, b. November 23, 1925; d. March 15, 1974. President, Milton Olive III Memorial Corporation; Principal, Lexington Elementary School; and

Miss Emma Nola Williams, b. June 2, 1930; d. March 25, 1974. Board Member, Milton Olive III Memorial Corporation; Elementary School Teacher.

Finally, *The extended family in Black societies* honors

Mr. Alexander D. Shimkin, b. October 11, 1944; missing and probably captured following an encounter with North Vietnamese troops, while on assignment with *Newsweek*, at Quang Tri, Vietnam, July 12, 1972.

B.A., Political Science (High Distinction), Indiana University 1969. Former associate of Dr. Martin Luther King at Selma, Montgomery, and the Meredith March; Staff Member, Mississippi Freedom Democratic Party; Volunteer worker, Bien Hoa Mental Hospital; Agricultural Specialist, International Voluntary Services; Journalist. On July 7, 1972, the Saigon Press reported Mr. Shimkin's rescue of a seriously wounded Vietnamese soldier, under heavy mortar fire, on Highway 13, north of Saigon.

While observing combat for *Newsweek*, Mr. Shimkin responded to the soldier's distress, ran into the barrage a considerable distance, picked up the soldier, and carried him to safety.

All author's royalties that may derive from this volume have been assigned to the Milton Olive III Memorial Corporation for its humanitarian work.

General Editor's Preface

Since publication in 1871 of Lewis H. Morgan's *Systems of consanguinity and affinity*, kinship as a comparative, historical, and theoretical subject has symbolized cultural anthropology. But not until recent times have systems of kinship been studied in complex and urbanized societies as distinguished from simpler — often indeed called "kinship" — societies. The present volume is part of this new trend. It is also a study of Afro-American culture, which was hardly recognized as a field until about 1950. By coincidence it was my pleasure to write a preface to perhaps the earliest assemblage of papers on American cultures originating in Africa — a book entitled *Acculturation in the Americas* — which resulted from the 29th International Congress of Americanists held in New York in 1949. The present volume becomes the first which combines these two new trends and gives a new perspective to the nature of the Black family in modern society. But it also pioneers a third characteristic: it involves recently freed people in the study of their own family system as part of an effort to improve the physical and mental health of their own community. This kind of "action anthropology" in which scholars help communities to know and to help themselves is only now becoming recognized professionally. It received impetus by the presence at the Chicago Congress of an unusually large number of scholars from the "Third World" countries of Africa, Asia, and Latin America.

Like most contemporary sciences, anthropology is a product of the European tradition. Some argue that it is a product of colonialism, with one small and self-interested part of the species dominating the study of the whole. If we are to understand the species, our science needs substantial input from scholars who represent a variety of the world's cultures. It was a deliberate purpose of the IXth International Congress of Anthropological and Ethnological Sciences to provide impetus in this direction. The *World Anthropology* volumes, therefore, offer a first glimpse of a human science in which members from all societies have played an active role. Each of the books is designed to be self-contained; each is an attempt to update its particular sector of scientific knowledge and is written by specialists from all parts of the world. Each volume should be read and reviewed individually as a separate volume on its own given subject. The set as a whole will indicate what changes are in store for anthropology as scholars from the developing countries join in studying the species of which we are all a part.

The IXth Congress was planned from the beginning not only to include as many of the scholars from every part of the world as possible, but also with a view toward the eventual publication of the papers in high-quality volumes. At previous Congresses scholars were invited to bring papers which were then read out loud. They were necessarily limited in length; many were only summarized; there was little time for discussion; and the sparse discussion could only be in one language. The IXth Congress as an experiment aimed at changing this. Papers were written with the intention of exchanging them before the Congress, particularly in extensive pre-Congress sessions; they were not intended to be read aloud at the Congress, that time being devoted to discussions — discussions which were simultaneously and professionally translated into five languages. The method for eliciting the papers was structured to make as representative a sample as was allowable when scholarly creativity — hence self-selection — was critically important. Scholars were asked both to propose papers of their own and to suggest topics for sessions of the Congress which they might edit into volumes. All were then informed of the suggestions and encouraged to rethink their own papers and the topics. The process, therefore, was a continuous one of feedback and exchange and it has continued to be so even after the Congress. The some two thousand papers comprising *World Anthropology* certainly then offer a substantial sample of world anthropology. It has been said that anthropology is at a turning point; if this is so, these volumes will be the historical direction-markers.

As might have been foreseen in the first post-colonial generation, the large majority of the Congress papers (82 percent) are the work of scholars identified with the industrialized world which fathered our traditional discipline and the institution of the Congress itself: Eastern Europe (15 percent); Western Europe (16 percent); North America (47 percent); Japan, South Africa, Australia, and New Zealand (4 percent).

Only 18 percent of the papers are from developing areas: Africa (4 percent); Asia-Oceania (9 percent); Latin America (5 percent). Aside from the substantial representation from the U.S.S.R. and the nations of Eastern Europe, a significant difference between this corpus of written material and that of other Congresses is the addition of the large proportion of contributions from Africa, Asia, and Latin America. "Only 18 percent" is two to four times as great a proportion as that of other Congresses; moreover, 18 percent of 2,000 papers is 360 papers, 10 times the number of "Third World" papers presented at previous Congresses. In fact, these 360 papers are more than the total of *all* papers published after the last International Congress of Anthropological and Ethnological Sciences which was held in the United States (Philadelphia, 1956).

The significance of the increase is not simply quantitative. The input of scholars from areas which have until recently been no more than subject matter for anthropology represents both feedback and also long-awaited theoretical contributions from the perspectives of very different cultural, social, and historical traditions. Many who attended the IXth Congress were convinced that anthropology would not be the same in the future. The fact that the next Congress (India, 1978) will be our first in the "Third World" may be symbolic of the change. Meanwhile, sober consideration of the present set of books will show how much, and just where and how, our discipline is being revolutionized.

Preface

The extended family in Black societies seeks to describe the nature, functioning, and variations of a widespread and, indeed, fundamental institution of Afro-American peoples in the United States, the Caribbean and Latin America, and Africa. That is the extended family, a multi-household descent group which is the carrier of values, emotional closeness, economic cooperation, child care, social regulation, and other functions in many Black communities.

Our book also deals in considerable detail with individual and family life histories, and with the larger social settings of these families. In this way, the volume contributes to the general understanding of Black culture and lifeways as well as to its more specialized goal.

Our greatest body of data concerns the Black people of Holmes County, Mississippi, who are indeed the originators and controlling figures of this work. They have defined the context of this study, especially in Mr. Eddie W. Logan's incisive Introduction; they have assessed our findings; and they and other Black people struggling for freedom and dignity are the key audience of this volume. It is a volume, therefore, that is not "neutral" but, rather, explicitly committed to a particular point of view and line of action. It is with this caution that we welcome every reader, scholarly or idly curious, friendly or suspicious.

The extended family in Black societies seeks above all to present reliable, candid, and broadly representative information about Black people and their cultures. Many of our authors, such as Mr. Logan, Miss Gloria Jean Louie, Mr. Lenus Jack, Dr. M. Jourdan Atkinson, and Mr. Michel Laguerre, are active members of the societies they describe. Our other sources of primary data all have done extensive fieldwork. Their diversity of background — American, British, Japanese, West African — and of technical training yields, we hope, a scholarly detachment, a professionalism, which can serve as an intellectual foil to the more intuitive views of our basic writers. Several of our authors — Drs. Bert Adams, Joyce Aschenbrenner, Vera Green, and Leonard Borman — have undertaken theoretical, problem defining, or interpretative essays. These must be viewed as initial analyses of a vast set of pure and applied research questions. We feel that the primary findings of our book will last; we know that its scientific interpretations will change. For this reason, we have left a diversity of views and approaches little touched. We have sought to impose no single set of theories or conclusions upon the authors, nor upon readers.

The specific characteristics of this book arise in large measure from its history, which has been an evolution over nearly a decade. Initial work on the Black family in Holmes County, Mississippi, grew out of both operational needs and scientific requirements associated with the formation and conduct of the Holmes County Health Research Project. The involvement of young people — Miss Louie as one of the Holmes Countians studying at the University of Illinois; Mr. Dennis Frate, as an investigator of the nature and significance of geophagy in Holmes County — permitted the undertaking of family studies of considerable depth. Out of this came a joint study which was reviewed by representatives of the Holmes County Black community and presented as the core of a session of the IXth International Congress of Anthropological and Ethnological Sciences at Chicago, on September 6, 1973.

This session consisted of four parts. First were brief substantive presentations by Shimkin, Louie, and Frate on Holmes County, and by Mr. Lenus Jack on an extended family in New Orleans. Second were community evaluations by a panel of Black Holmes Countians. Third were scholarly comments by Drs. Bert Adams, Kiyotaka Aoyagi, Joyce Aschenbrenner, M. Jourdan Atkinson, Leonard Borman, Vera Green, Verena Martinez-Alier, G. K. Nukunya, and Robert Roberts.[1] Finally, Representative Robert Clark, Jr., analyzed the policy implications — from the viewpoint of Mississippi's sole Black legislator — of the study of the Black extended family.[2]

---

[1] Written comments were also submitted by Drs. Henry P. Lundegaarde, John H. Peterson, Jr., Margaret Sanford, and Nancy J. Schmidt. Both the oral and written comments have been considered most seriously in the further development of this book.

[2] In this volume, Representative Clark's comments are the culmination of D. A. Frate and E. W. Logan's chapter on Community Reactions.

The congress provided the basis of a new phase of development in our study. Most of our scholarly commentators were able to contribute chapters. In addition, a number of substantive and conceptual gaps were filled by chapters elicited from Mr. Eddie W. Logan, Dr. Regina Holloman and Ms. Fannie Lewis, Mr. Michel Laguerre, Dr. Esther Goody, and Dr. Victor Uchendu, as well as by some editorial insertions. Throughout this final stage, the editors sought to correlate the many parts and points of view expressed in the volume into a compatible assembly, particularly from the standpoint of format. It is our belief and hope that we violated no contributor's integrity in doing so.

This, then, is how *The extended family in Black societies* came about.

Our entire effort was guided by the Executive Board of the Milton Olive III Memorial Corporation of Holmes County. It has been an integral part of the Holmes County Health Research Project, which has been financed by the National Center for Health Services Research and Development, H.E.W. under Grant HS00422. The initial study of the Black family in Holmes County[1] received support from the National Institute of Mental Health and the Center for Advanced Studies in the Behavioral Sciences, Stanford, California. Our final volume was aided by a grant from the Research Board of the University of Illinois at Champaign-Urbana, and by assistance from Mouton Publishers. To these agencies we give thanks.

Mr. James A. Bier, cartographer, Department of Geography, University of Illinois, has been responsible for the graphic work of the entire volume. We feel our readers will enjoy the artistic layout and skillful execution of his figures.

Mrs. Blanche Gudauskas, University of Illinois Stenographic Bureau, typed the bulk of the manuscript; the editors wish to express their thanks for her accuracy and devotion to the task.

Throughout our work, two persons gave us continual help and encouragement. This volume would not, indeed, have been possible without Dr. Bela Maday of the National Institute of Mental Health, and, especially, Professor Sol Tax, President of the IXth International Congress of Anthropological and Ethnological Sciences. Gentlemen, we are deeply grateful to you both.

DEMITRI B. SHIMKIN
EDITH M. SHIMKIN
DENNIS A. FRATE

---

[1] See "The Black extended family: a basic rural institution and a mechanism of urban adaptation" by Demitri B. Shimkin and G. J. Louie (1971, mimeographed manuscript, Lexington, Miss.: Milton Olive III Memorial Corporation).

Table of Contents

Dedication   V

General Editor's Preface   XI

Preface   XV

SECTION ONE: INTRODUCTION

The Struggle for Black Community Development in Holmes
County, Mississippi: Internal Efforts, External Support, and the
Role of Science   3
by *Eddie W. Logan* and *Dennis A. Frate*

SECTION TWO: THE EXTENDED FAMILY IN HOLMES COUNTY,
MISSISSIPPI AND ITS OUTLIERS

The Extended Family Among Black Holmes Countians: A
Personal Note   23
by *Dennis A. Frate*

The Black Extended Family: A Basic Rural Institution and a
Mechanism of Urban Adaptation   25
by *Demitri B. Shimkin, Gloria Jean Louie,* and *Dennis A. Frate*

Community Reactions and Appraisals: The Extended Family as a
Social Core   149
edited by *Dennis A. Frate* and *Eddie W. Logan*

SECTION THREE: IS THERE A NATIONAL PATTERN IN THE UNITED STATES?

Black Families in the United States: An Overview of Current
   Ideologies and Research   173
   by *Bert N. Adams*

Continuities and Variations in Black Family Structure   181
   by *Joyce Aschenbrenner*

The "Clan": Case Study of a Black Extended Family in Chicago   201
   by *Regina E. Holloman* and *Fannie E. Lewis*

Kinship and Residential Propinquity in Black New Orleans: The
   Wesleys   239
   by *Lenus Jack, Jr.*

Kinship and Friendship in Black Los Angeles: A Study of
   Migrants from Texas   271
   by *Kiyotaka Aoyagi*

Familialism in Texas: A Texan View   355
   by *M. Jourdan Atkinson*

Texas Indeed Is Different: Some Historical and Demographic
   Observations   363
   by *Demitri B. Shimkin*

The Black Extended Family in the United States: Some Research
   Suggestions   379
   by *Vera M. Green*

SECTION FOUR: AFRO-AMERICAN PERSPECTIVES ON THE EXTENDED FAMILY

Persistence, Borrowing, and Adaptive Changes in Black Kinship
   Systems: Some Issues and Their Significance   391
   by *Demitri B. Shimkin* and *Victor Uchendu*

Ticouloute and His Kinfolk: The Study of a Haitian Extended
   Family   407
   by *Michel Laguerre*

Delegation of Parental Roles in West Africa and the West Indies   447
   by *Esther N. Goody*

SECTION FIVE: IMPLICATIONS FOR POLICY

Black Institutions and Potential Social Change in the United
    States   487
    by *Leonard D. Borman*

Biographical Notes   497

Index of Names   503

Index of Subjects   509

SECTION ONE

Introduction

The Struggle for Black Community Development in Holmes County, Mississippi: Internal Efforts, External Support, and the Role of Science

EDDIE W. LOGAN and DENNIS A. FRATE

ABSTRACT

The author of this chapter evaluates *The extended family in Black societies* from his own viewpoint as Director of the Holmes County Health Research Project, and, generally, from that of the Black community of the County. The need for study of the Black extended family grew out of the objectives, both scientific and practical, of the Holmes County Health Research Project.

Following is a review, in the form of a dialog, of the accomplishments and setbacks of the Holmes County Black community from 1962 through 1974. The period from 1962 through 1967 was primarily one of political organization, with the election of Representative Clark to the Mississippi State Legislature in 1967. Also Head Start centers in Holmes and Attala Counties were organized and funded. From 1967 to 1971, in addition to the operation of the Head Start centers, the following programs were set up: the Beef Cattle Project, the Migrant Farmer Program, the Community Health Improvement Program (for maternal care) funded through the University of Mississippi but with good local participation, and the Mississippi Pilot Project for the enrollment of Black students from Holmes County in the University of Illinois. Finally, the Milton Olive III Memorial Corporation was founded, followed by the funding of the Holmes County Health Research Project in 1969.

In the 1971 election, however, the Black community suffered some political defeats, although Representative Clark was reelected. The Community Health Improvement Project and the Head Start operations were taken over by the State of Mississippi. Funding of a health services project which was to have succeeded the research project was denied. A selective buying campaign, organized as a protest against the local White power structure, divided the Black community.

Finally, the author discusses the relationships involved between community people and scientific and technical personnel assisting with community projects.

A STATEMENT OF PROBLEM AND VIEWPOINT

From the standpoint of Black people in Holmes County, Mississippi, *The extended family in Black societies* is primarily a tool for increasing the self-knowledge needed for awareness and good decision making by a community striving for political, economic, and social independence. It is secondarily a vehicle for communicating to possible friends the values, institutions, and survival needs of the County, and of Black people more generally. The idea of the work as an abstract contribution to knowledge is important only to a very few.

The perception of science illustrated in this case is not unique to Holmes County. It is, in fact, clear from my experience as Director of the Holmes County Health Research Project since 1969 that such a perception is a basic fact in *all* work at the community level. Thus, in placing *The extended family in Black societies* in its historical and practical setting, I think that I am bringing out lessons of general importance to the proper use of expertise for developing communities. For a more detailed discussion see Logan and Polk (1974).

The need for a study of the extended family came out of both the political and the scientific objectives of the Holmes County Research Project. On one hand, the creation of an awareness of the nature, the variations, and the ways Black families, especially the extended family, work has helped us to do better planning of our health, social welfare, and other projects. The scientific study helped us understand better why we do what we do. On the other hand, the scientific design of the Health Research Project, which was based by Drs. Adrian Ostfeld and Demitri Shimkin on a "Biosocial Assessment of the Population," anticipated that families would be key institutions to mediate stress (Ostfeld and Shimkin 1967). In fact, one of our key findings in the Hypertension Study could not have been developed without the family research. We found that very significant differences occurred between the blood pressures of heads of households and dependents, with full corrections for age (Schoenberger, et al. 1974).

I have given much thought to the best way of bringing out the important questions of our struggles, the role of external support, and the plan of science simply and clearly. I know my views are biased by living in Holmes County only since 1962, and by my own life. So I have decided to present my views as a personal thing, in the form of a dialog just the way I talk to old friends — with Dennis Frate.

ORGANIZING THE BLACK COMMUNITY: 1962–1967

FRATE: What is the best way to understand how this study of the extended family developed?
LOGAN: The best way to introduce this study is to place it in its proper perspective, as a product of years of organizing and development in Holmes County.
FRATE: How did this all begin?
LOGAN: Well, in the early 1960's, the Black people of Holmes County were inspired to the point of view that they would try to do something about their educational, political, and economic status. Various community leaders in Holmes County were aware of what Black people were doing in other states; they heard of the progress being made in the educational, the economic, and, of course, the political field. The leaders felt that we could do the same things here.

The community leaders set out to try to organize and develop group activities, such as Head Start, along with wanting to improve the overall social and economic status of the Black residents. All of the work was hard at first due to the fact that the White power structure was inclined to fight change, whenever it was change for the good of the Black people.
FRATE: Seeing that the Whites still controlled most of the power positions, how did the change occur?
LOGAN: Some people took it upon themselves to fight their resistance to change. For example, during the early 1960's, the voter registration drive started, and it started by way of a few people in certain localities standing up alone. Henry and Sue Lorenzi have told how it was:

First, they got together and they met. In one sense we can say they started to organize. It must be emphasized very strongly that the very process of meeting and discussing civil rights at this time was a dangerous, a very dangerous, act. It was an alienating act in definite violation of the two-caste system. The first meeting might be excused as a manifestation of curiosity, but any regularity in continuing meetings was engagement in obviously and overtly alien acts. Those who continued to meet and performed the later acts could be called innovators, very bold people who had made a conscious decision to start working toward changing the system. They were in physical danger, harassed by police, and had any and all of their credit cut by White stores, banks, and individual White people. What is significant, however, is that the meetings continued to take place and were not stopped. This in itself was a success.

Another paramount factor was the outside workers. The workers came from outside Holmes County; in the early years they were mainly young Mississippi Negroes who had left their own homes to work in the Movement. This was impressive to the local Negroes for it showed that someone outside cared about them and was sacrificing on their behalf. Further, the workers were bringing in information and telling the community of its rights. In some instances they were teaching new facts; also, however, they were restating, reaffirming by their outside authority, truths that many of the local people already knew were obviously right. The workers also brought some definite, concrete plan of action. So, we see that the outside worker was important as a morale booster, as a source of education and outside information, and as a catalyst for the few people who were ready to act.

A third important factor was that they were undertaking acts which were right — morally, religiously, constitutionally right. Of course, the acts were wrong, alien to the two-caste system under which they lived. Yet the higher or deeper authority of Christianity and "America" gave them a basis for believing in the rightness of their acts. Once they could get some reasonable assurance for believing that they would not get killed outright, then some could undertake the actions. After many meetings and discussions, they decide to act further. It is important here that they are working together, even in their act of meeting, as a group. The group decides to and can undertake acts which possibly no one individual could undertake alone.

Then, they do act, or some do. And, they have a success in the sense that there is no drastic violence at the time at which they perform the act. As a rule they usually do not accomplish what they supposedly were trying to accomplish, like registering to vote, but still they have a success in the important sense that no violence occurs at the time of performance. This sort of success strengthens each individual and binds the groups together. They performed an alienating act and were not stopped.

Usually violence does occur; soon after, perhaps on that same night or within the week. However, this violence is different from the past violence of the lynchings, for, though it may keep some individuals from joining the group, it tends to strengthen the group itself. In the past, the mob violence was directed against a man alone who actually did something on his own or was picked at random as an example to others; there had been no organized undertakings with the man before his lynching, and his lynching caused only the intended fear and frustrated aloneness. However, now in the case of the Movement there has been an organized undertaking, and this violence against one becomes an attack against the whole group and what they have done. There is a group sense and spirit, a group indignation and strengthening of resistance. Even some of those outside the group identify with them and recognize this, all of which strengthens and encourages them in their continuing. Thus violence, though assuredly painful and unpleasant, tended to help and strengthen the Movement.

It can be said that after this first set of occurrences — meetings, outside workers, decision to act, action, success, violence, strengthening — the Movement in Holmes County is in existence. It is very small, but the Movement meetings continue regularly, every week at Mileston with a core of faithful attenders (Lorenzi and Lorenzi 1969: 9–10).

Let me tell you how it was. There was a foreman on the Bonanza Plantation, a Mr. Kimble; he was one of the key figures in the early drive for registering people to vote. Most of the people on plantations were not registered to vote; Mr. Kimble knew this. One day, he was successful in stopping all the tractor drivers, saying, "Look here, we have done our homework, we are going to stop the tractors, and we are going down to City Hall to register to vote." According to Mr. Kimble, the boss man, the plantation owner, got quite mad, but since Mr. Kimble was successful in stopping, I would say, 95 percent of all the people that were working on that particular day, the plantation owner couldn't do anything about it; to fire the whole working crew would mean he would have to shut down the plantation. So Mr. Kimble got away with it even though he was not independent from the White power structure.

FRATE: Was everyone dependent on the White power structure?

LOGAN: Some groups of people were very dependent on the White power structure. Back in the early 1960's, the teachers were one group who were more dependent than a lot of groups. A good case in point, using myself as an example, occurred in 1964 after I first came to the County. Back then the FDP, Freedom Democratic Party, was holding their regular weekly meetings out at Second Pilgrim's Rest.[1] Reverend Gratham and I worked together, he taught math and I taught science, and we heard something was going on out at Second Pilgrim's Rest, but we didn't know exactly what.

This one particular afternoon we learned that someone had tried to burn the church down where the meetings were held. The next night a group of Whites went by and fired off a few shots. We figured that we would go on out and see what they were doing. So we went out, and the very next day when we got back to school we were told by our coworkers, "Look here, Logan, you and Gratham don't know what you are doing. You're going to get fired going out there and messing with those farming folks." So, were the teachers as a group being independent? No, the teachers as a whole played no significant role in voter registration. But a few of the key individuals were teachers; one that really stands out is Bernice Montgomery.

Basically, the people that played the most significant role were the independent landowners. They had their independence from the White power structure. For instance, Reverend Russell, who owns some land, played a big role in getting people to register. And he was one of the thirteen who were the first to register in the County (see also Lorenzi and Lorenzi 1969: 8–9). Except for a few individuals, it was the independent landowners, especially those in and around Mileston in the Delta,[2] who led the way for civil rights in the County.

[1] Second Pilgrim's Rest is one of the older Hill communities, named after the church there, which at one time served as a school and later as a Head Start center. The (Mississippi) Freedom Democratic Party is described in Carmichael and Hamilton (1967: 86–97) and in McDowell and Loventhal (1971: esp. 5–19).

[2] In 1939–1940, the U.S. Farm Security Administration had purchased and resold to 120 Black families the plantations at Mileston, Mississippi. The resulting group of

I guess looking back you could say that before 1962 it was a period of hopelessness.[3] It was more or less a period when Blacks in Holmes County found themselves fenced in. Most of the people who lived on the plantation had to depend upon the plantation owner, and, of course, the sharecroppers were dependent also. They found themselves fenced in trying to make a little money to make things better for themselves.

FRATE: What happened after 1963 when the first signs appeared that the community was coming together?

LOGAN: Between 1963 and 1967 was, I guess, a real crucial period as far as the Black man goes. And of course, during that time, we had a series of violent incidences in Holmes County, and all of this was an outgrowth of the Black people trying to get their equal rights.[4] The trouble occurred in a lot of instances in the Black neighborhoods, but it also occurred in the White neighborhoods. There were a few liberal Whites around, and some of them spoke up for the Black people as far as assisting them to register to vote, and they were looked down upon. In some instances, crosses were burned around their homes or places of business. I guess I can use another example here to illustrate. The White mayor of Durant spoke out a few encouraging words, so far as Blacks go, back in the early 1960's. And, of course, for the next two or three days, crosses were burned on his lawn. These were years of a very, very grim and frightening kind. As far as the Ku Klux Klan goes, I think they showed their faces, well, probably not their faces, but they showed their hoods and were more visible during this period than any other time.

independent farmers has provided important social, political, and economic leadership in Holmes County ever since. Educationally, its high point was reached in 1974 when Mr. Willie Epps received his Ph.D. [D.B.S.]: See also Shimkin 1971: 90.

[3]   In 1939, a religious group led by Mr. A. E. Cox had established a biracial Providence Cooperative Farm with a credit union, consumer cooperative, clinic, and adult education center (Shimkin 1971: 89–90). This effort reached its peak after World War II, particularly from the efforts of a White physician, Dr. D. R. Minter. Cox and Minter were driven away by White terrorism in 1955; Rev. Marsh Calloway, a Presbyterian minister who sought to support them, was also forced out. The publisher of the *Lexington Advertiser*, Mrs. Hazel Brannon Smith, did support Cox and Minter despite bombings, arson, and other assaults. She is still in the County, as are several members of the old farm, notably Mrs. Fanney Booker (see Carter 1959: 148–156). The period between 1955 and 1962 was one of very heavy White oppression in Holmes County.

[4]   On violence in 1964 see Holt (1965: 180, 209, 211, 220–221, 224, 234). The level was held down by the fact that independent Black farmers sheltering civil rights workers were prepared to defend them with arms. An incomplete record of violence and harassment is given by the U.S. Commission on Civil Rights (1968: 73–74, 90–91, 108–111, 121, 130–131). The two most serious incidents are not cited. In July, 1967, Mr. Edgar Love barely escaped being kidnapped from the steps of Tchula's city hall by three White men. On election day, at Ebenezer, the sheriff narrowly held off a firefight in the wake of irregularities at the polls [D.B.S.].

FRATE: Did any outside organizers come into the County during this early period of the civil rights days?

LOGAN: A lot of young White people came into the County in the summer of 1964. Henry and Sue Lorenzi came and stayed for five years. Henry was a big planner and he taught people how to organize and get legal help, projects, and other resources. Sue started work with the small children which led to our Head Start centers. The Lorenzis lived first in the loft of the Mileston Community Center. Later on, when Henry was helping getting the Health Research Project going, they lived in a little house in Balance Due. People used to come and talk with Henry morning, noon, and night.

Another great help was Alex Shimkin. He had been with Reverend King in Selma and Montgomery. Then he became a staff member of the MFDP. He worked out of Jackson all over the State. He was in McComb, Shaw, Natchez, and especially in Quitman County. He did a lot of things. He worked up little books on county government so poor folks could understand about voting. He registered voters. He got jailed quite a few times. And he helped organize projects.

He came to Holmes County in 1966. He worked with Bernice Montgomery and the Lorenzis to set up the Milton Olive III Memorial Program for children, which was a real grass-roots Head Start program. Later on, he and Edgar Love, who used to be a plantation worker, and Mrs. Allie Mae Wright, the midwife, and some others got Black people really registered to vote, even on plantations where they could get shot on sight. When registration started we had 20 Black voters. By election time in 1967 we had 6,332 (U.S. Commission on Civil Rights 1968: 244–245). Alex was Representative Clark's campaign manager in 1967 when Clark became the first Black in the State House since Reconstruction, and he is still the only Black in the House.

Also, at this time, we had come together to look at ways and means of trying to develop things within the community. We were concerned about some kind of mechanism that we could use for the purpose of developing and channeling change. After talking with various people in various states and localities, and with the help of Henry and Susan Lorenzi, and Alex, we decided to develop a nonprofit corporation in Holmes County. The purpose in developing this corporation was to use it as a uniting mechanism to bring forth changes the Black community wanted and needed in the fields of education, politics, economics, and health. In 1967 the corporation, the Milton Olive III Memorial Corporation, was founded.

It was the first of its kind in the history of Mississippi.[5] We tried to put together a program for the purpose of developing a comprehensive health care delivery system. We were told that our chances for getting money for services were slim. But we were encouraged to write a proposal for health research. So with the help of outside consultants, namely Dr. Shimkin and Dr. Ostfeld, a proposal was written for the purpose of looking at the health problems in the County from a research point of view. After documenting the problems, we were then to utilize the data for the purpose of writing a comprehensive health service proposal.

HOPEFUL TIMES: 1967–1971

LOGAN: After 1967 things began to look a little bit brighter. Between 1967 and 1970 we had roughly 8,000 Black people registered to vote, more than the whole White population. And of course, having access to the ballot, we felt that we would be able to change things not with just guns and chains but by way of the ballot. As far as the community goes, the community as a whole felt that we were moving in the right direction. They were gaining a lot of self-assurance.

Politically, we elected Honorable Robert G. Clark, as I stated before. On the County level we were also able to elect one constable and one justice of the peace. So between 1967 and 1970 the outlook was brighter for the Black community. Quite a few projects materialized. During this period the community formed the Milton Olive III Memorial Corporation. They decided to improve health conditions, and, during this period, in 1969, the Holmes County Health Research Project became a reality. We had our own locally operated Head Start centers; we had eighteen centers throughout the County and almost every Black child was enrolled.[6] We also had the Beef Cattle Project, wherein independent small farmers

---

[5]   The chartered purposes of the Milton Olive III Memorial Corporation are
. . . to operate Head Starts and other preschool educational centers; to provide and assist adult educational and vocational training programs and other educational programs . . . to conduct and take part in research into economic conditions and into other matters; to organize and assist in the organization of credit unions, agricultural and other cooperative organizations, and other self-help programs to improve the economic conditions of Holmes and Attala Counties . . . and to improve the quality of health services available to the citizens of Holmes and Attala Counties in the State of Mississippi.

[6]   In 1970, Holmes County had one of the largest programs in the entire Head Start system. In all, 1,130 children were enrolled; they included 966 from Holmes County, 60 at Holmes County Centers but resident elsewhere, and 104 in Attala County (Shimkin and Rice 1971: 46).

were able to get cattle on the farm for a small down payment and quite a few years to pay for the cattle. We also had the Migrant Farmer Program going; the purpose of that project was to try to upgrade the educational status of the migrant farmers. And we had a project in the County that was basically for pregnant women and new mothers. This project was the Community Health Improvement Program, which was funded through the University of Mississippi but with good local participation.

Another project that should be mentioned started during this period, the Mississippi Pilot Project, which was sponsored by the University of Illinois through the work of Alex and Dr. Demitri Shimkin. The purpose of this project was to get Black students from Holmes County with a high degree of ability and place them in college. The University of Illinois took on the job of interviewing and selecting eighteen Black students from Holmes County to attend the University of Illinois.

Now, it is generally felt that one cannot equate a twelfth grade education in Holmes County, Mississippi, with a twelfth grade education in Urbana, Illinois. But I guess the selection process was very successful. I am saying this because the children who went to the University of Illinois as freshmen completed their undergraduate work, with the exception of three. Some of those kids were very successful; one is now in medical school and I think two are in law school. I might also throw this in, Dennis, that four of those eighteen children were former students of mine.

I guess to look back over this period in time, people were feeling optimistic. And of course, the projects themselves provided some additional income for Blacks. Some of these people never had a public job before, and they were all working to better the community. One could say that the County was very enthusiastic; most of the people in Holmes County during those years were very proud of the County. It seemed like everyone was involved. We had meetings every night somewhere in the County. This was really the peak of our organization, participation, and enthusiasm.

Of course, especially during the early 1970's, we really felt we were going places, and going there fast. This was due to the fact that we had accomplished quite a lot by starting the few projects that were going in the County. We also had been successful in getting roughly 8,000 Blacks to register to vote, in comparison to roughly 4,000 Whites. We felt it was time to put on the big political push. So, in the general election in 1971, we selected Black candidates to run for all the political positions that were coming up for election. I believe we had seventeen Black candidates to run, and of course, we were very enthusiastic. We felt that with 8,000 registered Black voters in comparison to 4,000 registered White voters, we would really be able to elect an entire slate of Black officials. Of course, I wouldn't say an all-Black thing is good; I wouldn't say it is bad, but at least we had access to the political process, and we felt that we were going to put our people in office.

As you know, Dennis, things didn't work out as planned. During the course of the campaign most of us who were involved depended upon the margin of registered Blacks to Whites. And we felt (I am one in particular, as I ran for Superintendent of Education), and it was the basic feeling of the FDP (Freedom Democratic Party) group, that we could win. We can put our people in on the basis of the Black vote, *period.* And, of course, not knowing too much about the political process, the old campaign circuit, we really got hung up on, *vote Black, vote Black, vote Black.* I wouldn't say strange things happened, but just to make a long story very short, in the 1971 general election we were not that successful as far as the percentages go, but we did elect some Blacks. We got Representative Robert Clark back and we were able to elect two constables. And that was basically it.

FAILURES AND NEW STRUGGLES: 1971–1974

FRATE: What else was happening in the County around the time of this political defeat?

LOGAN: After the general election, things began to go wrong. Most of the projects we had going began to get into trouble for some reason or other. I guess one project to mention is the Community Health Improvement Project, which was in the County for the purpose of trying to cut down infant mortality.[7] When the project was first organized in Jackson, Mississippi, they centered it around a locally based executive committee, which was more or less an advisory council to the CHIP program. Until the fall of 1971, the local committee played an integral part in defining the policies and hiring people, or what have you, but then something happened. We don't know exactly what, but around 1971 the local Blacks' responsibility for defining policies and running the program —

---

[7]　Maternal and child health was an initial target of the Holmes County Health Research Program, which defined the problem and started services; these services were then taken over by a well-funded program of the State of Mississippi. The same histories are happening to health services for the poor and for hypertension control. In every case, the State and the White doctors have seized control, pushing out the Black community.

well, we were pushed out. The program was completely taken over by the State of Mississippi, the Mississippi State Health Department.

As far as the Milton Olive Head Start project goes, during 1967 through 1970, the centers were pretty completely controlled by Blacks in Holmes County. Then, some very strange things happened with these centers. The project directors and the entire central staff (that was based in Holmes County and was responsible for operating this project) were shipped out to Winona in Montgomery County. So the Head Start project was in grave and great trouble locally. This really kind of killed the hopes and aspirations of a lot of local Blacks, and it took jobs away. I might add that the Head Start program provided employment for three to four hundred local people. Also, the controlling Head Start people started to put extreme measures on the types of buildings you could have for a center. For instance, they wanted centers to have wells and running water. Most of our centers are scattered throughout the County in the boondocks and they use cesspools; this really put an additional strain on the local project and the people.[8]

The Health Research Project was funded for the purpose of bringing a small health care system into Holmes County. The government told us to find out the health needs, and they would fund services. So we preached the project's value, we preached the process of doing research, and we preached to the community people that we needed information and data for the purpose of getting a comprehensive health care delivery thing into Holmes County. We had high hopes that a comprehensive health service project would be funded. After getting the data compiled and analyzed to some extent, we wrote the big proposals which we submitted to the funding agency. Well, as you know, Dennis, we were not funded, to make a long story short. This also was a big setback to the community. After all these things that were so successful, for a few years, you could see the people's smiles; then the agencies didn't care. So, after a period of success, things began to fade out and fade away.

FRATE: How does the community feel now, Eddie, are they pessimistic or optimistic about trying to better things for themselves in Holmes County? LOGAN: Oh, the community is not optimistic as a whole. We had a lot of good things going and, over a relatively short period of time, as I mentioned, they began to fade out and fade away; and budgets from most of the projects were cut, seemingly without any justifiable reason. We thought we had ourselves really moving for the purpose of making things

[8] All of these actions were supposedly to improve efficiency. They ended in total control of the Head Start programs in Holmes County by Central Mississippi, Inc., a six-county, White-dominated organization.

better, but for some reason we were not able to use the projects for the purpose for which they were desired, or we lost community control. So, looking at the community from a Black perspective, we are not optimistic at this point. Now as far as bettering our condition by the political process, it seems very doubtful in the near future. I tend to think that the Black candidates that ran in the general election in 1971 came closer, as a group, to getting elected than we will ever come again in the near future.

FRATE: Do you think the community can pull together again for the next election?

LOGAN: Well, it's going to be very, very difficult. You see we now have two well-defined political groups in the County. For the first time, we have Black groups fighting each other politically. I don't know if this was planned by the Whites to separate us, but I do know that it happened. I might as well give the background to what started the whole thing. A young man by the name of Mr. Young lived out in the Long Branch community, and he had a heart condition. Of course, he was taking his heart medicine. Well, one Saturday night, I guess around ten o'clock, he was picked up by the Sheriff or a highway patrol; I don't know who. He was picked up because he was weaving and bobbing across the highway, and, of course, he was accused of being drunk. He was locked up, and it was found out later that the man was not drunk but rather he was having one of his heart attacks; he kept his pills on him. So, the man was locked up around twelve midnight. And the next morning he was found dead in jail. His wife, his brother-in-law, and some other relatives went to the deputy sheriff's home earlier in the morning before daylight, and they asked the deputy sheriff if they could go up and see Mr. Young to see how he was doing. They told the deputy, "We know the man is sick, because he keeps his pills on him." I don't know the actual reply to their question but they were not allowed to see him. And, of course, the next morning, when the jailer opened the jail he found that Mr. Young had passed away. Naturally the community was inquisitive as to what had happened. It was known that the man didn't drink. This particular man did not drink. I don't think he even consumed liquor prior to his heart condition. Also, he was a very religious man, and at our meetings he would be the one that sang the solo, the hymn; he was very religious.

This death lead to the split of the Black community. See, the community as a whole felt that, okay, we've got to do something. We don't know the cause of the man's death. And, of course, trying to get some response from the local law enforcement officers; well, they didn't want to talk about the man's death — it was top secret. So, what can we do in a case like this to solve this problem? We tried using early civil rights tactics;

that is, we put on peaceful protests. The protests were based on two parts, and first we had a series of meetings leading up to our actions. Now, one thing was decided, which I went along with, and that was that we could at least show our dissatisfaction by way of marching from the church around the jail house, from there around the court house square, and back to the church. After the march we went back to the church, and our various leaders made speeches about jailing a sick man and not allowing his people to see him. The big question after the march was what else we should do; we had to do something. We needed to figure out a way to make the people in the local power structure more responsible. We talked about these things and came up with one of the oldest weapons we have, i.e. we decided to put on a selective buying campaign.

FRATE: A boycott?

LOGAN: Yes, but of course, legally you are not supposed to use this term now, for some reason. Some of the Black leaders really spoke out against the selective buying campaign. Some of them said, "Okay, maybe the man was treated unjust, but if we put on the selective buying campaign we are going to hurt a lot of poor Black people." We had a lot of people that traded with the local White merchants. They get their welfare checks each month, and sometimes the money runs short, and they have to get some credit until the next check. So, if you put on a selective buying campaign you are going to hurt a lot of Black people's credit. But it was decided to put it on anyway. What went wrong when the FDP (Freedom Democratic Party) decided to put on the selective buying campaign was that a group disagreeing with that tactic emerged.

The name of this group is the Voice of the Working People. Another reason why this group was formed is that quite a few Black people work in the stores downtown. Some of the jobs are maybe sweeping the floors, or arranging the fruits and vegetables and the pole beans, but after all each is a job. So it was said: "Look here, if you put on the selective buying campaign, look what is going to happen to some Black people that have jobs." The people who worked at the stores were concerned about what had happened to Mr. Young, but they were concerned with survival too. So it was said that maybe we ought to look at other means of trying to make the power structure more responsive to us, rather than putting on a boycott, I mean, a selective buying campaign. They thought maybe we ought to try to get around the bargaining table and work out something around that table. So, we wind up with the Freedom Democratic Party, that really brought us through the 1960's, running head on with the newly emerged group, the Voice of the Working People.

Then the FDP was sending demonstrators uptown to picket — I'm not saying who was right or wrong, but we had Black folks fighting each other; and in one or two instances, there were threats of shootings, beatings, and mistreatment.

So, considering these things I doubt that the County will come together for the next election. I hope I am wrong, but things look pretty grave. People are split and not optimistic any more; the Whites really played us off against each other. Also, the selective buying campaign was not a success. Quite a few of the leaders were jailed, and I believe there is a big lawsuit pending. I don't know what the charges were, but they had some pretty stiff fines. Bail bonds were hung around their necks. I guess it is anyone's guess whether these people can beat the rap; they may not be able to beat it. A lot of people are angry and it has been said that both groups will be putting up candidates in the next election, splitting the Black vote.

So, again looking at the advancement of any community, let's face it, you have got to get your politics right before you can expect any significant gains as far as economics and education and the whole works go. The situation today looks grim, awfully dark, and looking at inflation, and looking at the length of time a candidate seeking a county position has to run, expenses are going to kill him. Holmes County is roughly 700 square miles, and you are talking about sixty cents per gallon of gasoline. During 1971, through various organizations, the Freedom Democratic Party was able to bring in and receive funds to help candidates buy their campaign literature, get radio spots, etc. Today this organization lacks financial backing and I doubt if very much money will be channelled through the central office. Inflation, White manipulation, and the lack of concern from the outside — well, Dennis, it is really hard to win.

I don't want to present too grim a picture, though. We've come a long way, but we still have a way to go. We have done more than most Black communities, and we will continue to fight. I guess one reason is that we had the expertise available to us. I think the sciences, especially social science, and, of course, the physical and biological sciences, have played a very significant role in getting the community on the right track. You've got to remember that this is a poor community; we were aware of what we wanted, but we did not have the proper expertise, or enough people to really get the project moving, such as Dr. Shimkin — he was one of the pioneer scientists. Social science is more or less the nucleus of the whole scientific operation as far as the project and community goes. Moving toward our goals we have had to look outside the realms of the Mississippi professional structure for the purpose of finding the social scientists, physical scientists, biological scientists, medical scientists, etc., to help the community accomplish its goals. Remember, back in the 1960's, times were dangerous and not too many people wanted to get involved. It is still hard to get people involved.

FRATE: What about the scientists themselves? What kind of people work in a community situation like this?

LOGAN: As far as professional people go, they are not missionaries; when they get involved in community projects, many of them expect something in return. I am not saying that all scientists or professional people that get involved in poor communities are rip-offs, but we have to be mindful of those people and what their involvement will be. We ought to try to figure out exactly what their motives are as far as the Holmes County community goes. Well, most of the professionals that we have worked with have been trustworthy, very decent people, and of course, without the outside expertise we received, we would not have been able to move as far as we have moved.

FRATE: Do you have to watch a professional closely?

LOGAN: Not often. By the way of my nature, I trust people when I get to know them personally. I am not saying that I don't watch them, but in the process of talking with them I get to know them; I have to satisfy my conscience when I am working with a particular person, whether he be M.D., Ph.D., or whatever. I guess that's because there are a lot of people coming to poor communities for the purpose of really ripping off. So, you turn to observing them, trying to analyze what they have to say to us. Remember, we want to think in terms of community control when considering scientific progress, but it is pretty hard to build such controls or to fix really meaningful ones. You must realize your needs, and you must know the particular person you want to interrelate with, in the particular field that this person is knowledgeable in. Washington, of course, has got some hangups about community control projects. So, basically our people have a hard time controlling a project which is scientifically oriented. The only way to make it work is to look at the control from three angles: educate the local executive board, write the policies, and define the policies that the board ought to use for the purposes of control. Also you should get a professional from outside the community, who is willing to take the responsibility of seeing to it that the community controls are working as they should. It takes a lot of training not only for board members but for the actual research staff of local people as well.

The Milton Olive Board came up with some very decent criteria for selecting the original employees of the Health Research Project, and most of the employees worked out, I'd say, real well. So, overall, the idea of community control is good, and I guess back in the 1960's it was an organizing force. But times change and we must be able to change with them. We have to take the time to redefine what the present objectives of the community are. And we should never take for granted what outsiders say they will do for us. That can become the downfall of any group.

You have to be aware of the consultant's competence or incompetence. You have to ask, "What is your particular field? Okay, if your field happens to be anthropology or geology or whatever, I want you to prove to me that what you know will benefit the County." You have to make sure that consultants don't spread themselves too thin, and if they do, question them. The consultants should not be, I hate to say, considered divine — the community should be the boss. Looking back now, most of the consultants or professionals we have worked with understood this, and worked out just fine.

FRATE: Well, Eddie, what has all of the social and health research meant to the community over the years?

LOGAN: As far as facts go, I am sure that the community has benefited from these scientific works that we have involved ourselves in. Although our final goal of health services hasn't been reached, we have benefited in many ways. Remember, we needed hard, cold facts about our health problems to get some health services started. Also, we have learned to understand ourselves and get some community pride. That's why this Black family thing is so beautiful. You know, in general terms, I think one can very accurately define Holmes County, being an area with roughly 18,000 Black people, as one big extended family. The whole corporation thing is built on family concepts.

Let me use myself as an example. Where I grew up, I believe there were about six families. And, of course, we were farmers. Certain times during the year, like during harvesting season, we would help each other out. This still happens; this is how we can survive. So, overall, the Black family research has been good for all of us. You know, you can look at something for a long time without really understanding it. Now we do.

FRATE: Well, Eddie, looking back on everything you've done in the community and your own involvement over the past five years, has it all been worthwhile?

LOGAN: Oh, I think so, Dennis. You know we've come a long way, and, if I had to live my life over again, I doubt very seriously that I would do anything differently. Personally, I don't regret anything. I'm sure the community as a whole doesn't either. Sciences, the Black family, community pride, well, they have all been valuable and in the long run they should help the Black community, not only here, but in other places as well. Let's just hope someone listens for a change. I guess it's all a matter of getting a little at a time.

REFERENCES

CARMICHAEL, STOKELY, CHARLES V. HAMILTON
1967 *Black power: the politics of liberation in America.* New York: Random House.

CARTER, HODDING, III
1959 *The South strikes back.* Garden City, N.Y.: Doubleday.

HOLT, LEN
1965 *The summer that didn't end.* New York: William Morrow.

LOGAN, EDDIE W., ERMA JEAN POLK
1974 "Recruiting, hiring and training of the local staff: a combined effort." Mimeographed manuscript. American Public Health Association, 102nd Annual Meeting, Community Health Planning Section. October 24th. New Orleans.

LORENZI, HENRY, SUSAN LORENZI
1969 "The management of fear by a community: Holmes County, Mississippi — 1963 through 1967," in *Some views on Blacks and Black communities* (mimeographed). Edited by Susan H. S. Lorenzi, 1–23. University of Illinois, Urbana.

MCDOWELL, JENNIFER, MILTON LOVENTHAL
1971 *Black politics: a study and annotated bibliography of the Mississippi Freedom Democratic Party.* San Jose, Calif.: Bibliographic Information Center for the Study of Political Science.

OSTFELD, A. M., D. B. SHIMKIN
1967 "Planning conference on the ecology of migrant populations of the sectional committee on the International Biological Program" (Chicago, March 17–19). Mimeographed manuscript. Washington, D.C.: National Academy of Sciences.

SCHOENBERGER, JAMES A., *et al.*
1974 "Hypertension in Holmes County, Mississippi." Paper presented at the Second International Congress on Hypertension. Chicago: American Heart Association.

SHIMKIN, D. B.
1971 "Black migration and the struggle for equity: a hundred-year record," in *Migration and social welfare.* Edited by Joseph W. Eaton, 77–116. New York: National Association of Social Workers.
1974 "Black problems and potentials in rural development," in *Rural community and regional development: perspectives and prospects*, 53–73. Urbana: Department of Agricultural Economics, University of Illinois (AE-4336).

SHIMKIN, D. B., ANN RICE
1971 *The Black population of Holmes County, Mississippi: a statistical characterization as of January, 1970.* Urbana: University of Illinois.

U.S. COMMISSION ON CIVIL RIGHTS
    1968   *Political participation: a study of the participation by Negroes in the electoral and political processes in 10 Southern States since passage of the Voting Rights Act of 1965*. Washington, D.C.: U.S. Government Printing Office.

SECTION TWO

The Extended Family in Holmes County, Mississippi, and Its Outliers

The Extended Family Among Black
Holmes Countians: A Personal Note

DENNIS A. FRATE

In January, 1971, I moved to Holmes County, Mississippi, to investigate the practice of geophagy or clay eating among the Black people there (Frate 1973). I entered this field situation with a rather limited research background; also, being a White researcher in a Black community presented a number of perceptual limitations. Yet, I had been reared in a somewhat similar environment; my family is second generation Italian-American. I grew up interacting within a large and functioning extended family. As a child, our household at various times had members of the extended family residing with us. Thus, although I was not Black, I was personally aware of the broad institutional form of the extended family. This fact proved soon to be invaluable in my work with the Black family.

My research on geophagy brought me into constant interaction with the Black extended family, which affects every way of life in this community. Working with the "Mitchell" family provided an opportunity for me to observe the form and functions of their extended family on a day-to-day basis. Traveling with the "Mitchells" to family gatherings and to church services and working with them in the fields, I began inevitably to compare them with my own family. Numerous similarities, such as the complex network of communications for arranging social gatherings and solving household economic crises, became readily apparent. The functional distinction between the household as a unit and the family as a unit is also a characteristic feature of both families. And, as within the Black family, relationships in my family center on bilateral descent, as well as draw in numerous fictive kin.

Although these basic similarities were striking, many differences eventually also became evident to me. For instance, the particular practice of fosterage within the Black extended family is absent from the Italian-American family. In contrast to that of Black Holmes Countians, marriage within my family tends to be locally exogamous, creating alliances between not only families but local communities. By observing the "Mitchells" I also became aware of the differences between the roles of men and women in the Black family as compared to my own. In the Black family, the domains of men and women are clearly defined. The woman's position concerning household responsibilities and care for the children is complementary to the man's role in organizing social and work activities. This is not the case in my own family, where behavioral domains and role differentiation are not as rigidly defined.

Although grandparents occupy an important social position within both family types, in the Italian-American family the respect shown the grandparents is often shared by an elderly *padrino*, or godfather. This institution is not found in the Black community of Holmes County, Mississippi.

Another rather interesting difference centers on the relative importance of funerals and weddings. Within the Black extended family, funerals are of extreme social importance. Individuals will travel hundreds of miles to be present to pay their last respects and reinforce family ties. Weddings, on the other hand, are less socially significant.

Within my own family, the opposite is true. Since weddings functionally signify an alliance between two families, they are viewed as important ceremonies where attendance reaches almost one hundred percent. On the other hand, while funerals are not ignored, the number of relatives attending is significantly less.

In all, the similarities and differences between my own family and the Mitchells have influenced the direction of my work and that of my colleagues on the Black extended family. It is indeed an institution psychologically, functionally, and, in part, structurally similar to that found among many other peoples of peasant origin, including my own. But it is also distinctly different with its special rules and behavioral subtleties — a component, I feel, of a particular Black tradition.

REFERENCES

FRATE, DENNIS A.
1973 *Geophagy: a dietary practice in Holmes County, Mississippi.* CAC Document 85 (September). Urbana: University of Illinois at Urbana-Champaign.

The Black Extended Family: A Basic Rural Institution and a Mechanism of Urban Adaptation

DEMITRI B. SHIMKIN, GLORIA JEAN LOUIE, and
DENNIS A. FRATE

ABSTRACT

Since 1967, the Milton Olive III Memorial Corporation, a community organization of Lexington, Mississippi, has been engaged in research on and the development of health services for the Black people of Holmes County. This research has defined an extensive migratory pattern to urban areas, a complex, variable culture unified by common values, and a social system comprising bilateral, multihousehold extended families as major economic, political, and emotional centers. Intensive studies of these families have shown that they have been functionally effective under varying circumstances ranging from systematic migration and upward mobility to local survival on a bare subsistence level. A review of the literature and limited primary studies indicate that quite similar institutions have been characteristic of other Black populations in the rural South, especially the Sea Islands of South Carolina (including migrants therefrom to New York). Although kin networks have clearly been important for many urban Black groups, the relations of these to the institutions of the rural Blacks are not yet clear. At the same time, detailed comparisons with African extended families, notably among the Ewe of Ghana, strongly indicate deep historic roots for the Black extended family in the United States, a presumption which is compatible with a number of important facts in the history of the Southern plantation. Black extended families differ significantly, in structure and function, from upper-class White extended families in the rural South. By the same token, the significances of borrowing and of situational adaptation in the development of the rural Black extended family are believed to be moderate at most. Study of this problem needs to be continued. Above all, the potentialities of the Black extended family, in its variant forms, as a vehicle of social action need careful appraisal.

INTRODUCTION

Since its founding in December 1967, the Milton Olive III Memorial Corporation, an agency of the poor, primarily Black people of Holmes County, Mississippi, has been engaged in basic and applied studies of this area's population, environment, culture, and problems. Technical support for this effort has come from the University of Illinois at Urbana-

Champaign and at the Medical Center, Rush-Presbyterian-St. Luke's Hospital (Chicago), the University of Mississippi College of Medicine, and other academic institutions. Financial support has come largely from the National Center for Health Services Research and Development, U.S. Department of Health, Education and Welfare.

In these efforts, basic research has been utilized as a means of effectively directing limited resources to the practical goals desired by the Black people of Holmes County. It has also provided a mechanism for identifying and developing local skills in interviewing, laboratory work, office management, data processing, and other technical operations. In the programs developed cooperatively between the elected local Executive Committee of the Corporation and its unpaid technical consultants, particular attention has been paid to the forces generating out-migration from Holmes County and to the opportunities and potential courses of action open to the Black community to maintain and strengthen itself, especially in the fields of health, education, and economic growth. Action programs have focused upon major health problems: hypertension, endemic streptococcus infections, parasitoses, infant mortality, etc. Hypertension has been given highest priority as a disease of wide prevalence and severe consequences that is particularly suitable for control via community health operations. Progress to date has been gravely hindered by financial difficulties, engendered in part by local vested interests and by an adverse national climate. The lack of resources has also made possible only limited efforts in expanding college opportunities, even to the talented poor, and in meeting great needs for adult education (Project Grass Roots). Finally, the Milton Olive III Memorial Corporation has developed extensive statistical data and numerous analyses useful for other

This study was financed under Grant HS 00422, National Center for Health Services Research and Development, awarded to the Milton Olive III Memorial Corporation (the late Mr. Samuel Friar, President; Mrs. Bernice Montgomery, Principal Investigator; and Mr. E. W. Logan, Program Director), in cooperation with the University of Illinois, Urbana. This study was prepared, in preliminary form, on a Special Fellowship of the National Institute of Mental Health, at the Center for Advanced Study in the Behavioral Sciences, Stanford, California. Among the many commentators on this initial version, the comments of Profs. J. R. A. Ajayi, B. Farber, and R. Hill have been especially helpful. Generous help from the Center for Advanced Computation and the College of Engineering, University of Illinois, Urbana, in final work on this manuscript is also noted.

Acknowledgement is also due Mrs. Mary H. Williams and Mrs. B. A. Gudauskas of Stenographic Services, University of Illinois, Urbana, who typed the final manuscript of this chapter as a monograph prepared for the IXth International Congress of Anthropological and Ethnological Sciences, Chicago, Illinois, August–September 1973. The figures were drawn by Mr. James Bier, Cartographer, Department of Geography, also at Urbana.

applied efforts within the purview of allied organizations such as the Mississippi Freedom Democratic Party, the Mileston Farmers' Coopera-tive, etc.[1]

In the actual course of developmental, research, and applied efforts since 1966, the critical importance of extended families — groups of related, cooperating households within the Black community — has become evident at many points. The key decisions of the past decade which underlaid Black political struggles and socioeconomic innovations could be implemented only with the united support of the most powerful extended families. Friction between some of these families has, unfortu-nately, also been a cause of factionalism which has hurt the Black community more than once in recent years.

In addition, growing familiarity with the daily problems, the life crises and the aspirations of Black Holmes Countians has revealed the pervasive-ness of extended families as the settings and agencies of economic cooperation, the care of children and the aged, religious practice, conflict resolution, and even political affiliation. Among the economically and educationally stronger families, networks of kin stretching across the United States and even abroad have given information, shelter, and support to their younger members as they sought optimum economic opportunities. Ties to people, cemeteries, and land in Holmes County have provided continuing, cohesive social identities. Among the poorest, least educated families, local networks pooling labor and other resources have permitted survival under extreme adversity. Because of facts such as these, an understanding and exposition of the structures and functions of the extended families became research objectives for the Milton Olive III Memorial Corporation.

This study seeks to provide materials and interpretations yielding an understanding of extended families among Black Holmes Countians at home and, in part, in urban settings. It rests upon five bodies of data:

Spontaneously Given and Elicited Data

The first has been a collection of opinions on social institutions, values, and modal behavior spontaneously given by, or elicited from, Black Holmes Countians. The spontaneous statements have been numerous and from many people, since these topics are of much interest, intellectually and practically, to almost everyone. There are often long arguments about

---

[1] For additional information on these organizations in Holmes County, see Lorenzi and Lorenzi (1969a and 1969b); McCracken (1970); and Eckenfels (1972).

which might be the key Biblical guides to behavior; generally these tend to favor the Old Testament. Again, exotic social ideas, such as the neo-African culture and nationalism espoused by visitors from Detroit, will arouse much curiosity. Characteristically, such ideas find a few, usually short-term, converts but are smothered by the strong convictions or loud skepticisms of the many. Individual achievements and failings are inexhaustible sources of gossip and social evaluation. To what extent is a particular act amusing or reprehensible? Should this person be given political support despite his indiscreet and indiscriminate womanizing? Should that hero of past civil rights struggles — and current ne'er-do-well — be given yet another chance at a good job, in recognition of the past and in regard for his respected mother, or is it time to say "no"? The stream of talk yields rich social data indeed for those included within the Black community's bounds of trust.

The elicitation of data, both formally and informally, took place within narrower limits, mostly from middle-aged and younger people involved in Milton Olive projects. Three levels of inquiry were pursued.[2]

Particular events often needed explanation. Why did so-and-so do that? What was the right answer in this conflict? Who can help in that crisis? Out of this came many specific and general statements, e.g. on the functions of lying as a protection for the weak, the ways that lies might be detected (criteria of probable self-interest), and the best compromise between efficient performance and kinship obligations.

A second level of elicitation was the formal pursuit of terms and criteria. Who were "family"? Why might a biological mother be called "Little Mama"? What distinguished "strong" from "weak" families, and "strong" from "weak" persons? In general, these matters were pursued with several informants on various occasions, until reasonably general usage could be established.

Finally, more complex questioning, based on knowledge of European peasant societies in particular (Thomas and Znaniecki 1927; Shimkin and San Juan 1953; Halpern 1967 [1956]),[3] was pursued with a limited number of more articulate and knowledgeable informants. For example, while the

---

[2]   Special mention should be made of Mr. Howard T. Bailey, Miss Lillie McGee, Mrs. Bernice Montgomery, Mr. Eugene Montgomery, Mr. and Mrs. Oscar Moore, Sr., and Miss Verlean Williams of Holmes County; Mrs. Fannie Lou Hamer of Sunflower County; Mrs. Hazel Meredith Coleman of Attala County; Mr. Robert Stewart of Holmes County and Rush Medical College, Chicago, Illinois; Mr. Charles Williams of Columbus, Mississippi, and the University of Illinois, Urbana; and Miss Shirley Masher, formerly of the Southwest Alabama Farmer's Cooperative.
[3]   The background of serfdom well into the 19th century in these societies gives an important common element with plantation slavery in the United States.

literature on Black communities in the United States gave few suggestions to that effect, comparative evidence indicated the likelihood of fairly stable customary law, folk adjudicators, and legal procedures. This statement evoked prompt responses: the institutions indicated did exist; Mr. Milton Olive, Sr., and certain others were *de facto* judges; and this body of practice derived via patrilineal instruction, personal innovation, discussions with a learned Jewish peddler, and Biblical precepts. On the basis of statements such as these, further elicitations and observations often became possible, thereby developing illustrations and variations in the customs considered and providing leads to still other concepts. At all times, considerable care was taken to differentiate local Holmes County features from those common to other areas in Mississippi and Alabama.

Spontaneously Given and Elicited Data

The desirability of testing spontaneous and elicited opinions and gossip with systematic studies of extended families became clear at an early stage of research. Initial explorations also indicated that extensive and reliable access to data on particular families was more important than sampling adequacy at the probable price of reticence and, sometimes, falsification. In particular, information on two extended families proved to be especially valuable.

Miss Gloria Jean Louie, a student at the University of Illinois, and a native of the Holmes County Black community, undertook a comprehensive survey of the "Bidwell" family in Holmes County, Chicago, Jackson, and other localities during 1969–1970. The study produced much structural and behavioral information, in a systematic framework developed by Miss Louie. She specifically contributed the concepts of "nucleus family" and "subfamily" to describe recurrent, yet unnamed, elements and interrelationships of Black extended families among Holmes Countians.

Dennis Frate, then a graduate student at Louisiana State University, conducted a basic study in 1971 on the prevalence, cultural contexts and content, and nutritional implications of geophagy among Black people in Holmes County (Frate 1972). As a correlate of this work, he also surveyed the membership and interrelationships of an extended family of very poor people, the "Mitchells." This study has shared the frames of reference already described. Mr. Frate, a young White man working within the Milton Olive setting, gained, however, a somewhat different perspective than did Miss Louie.

In general, these two studies are believed to encompass much of the structural and functional variation, of Holmes County's Black extended families. It must be stressed, however, that specific peculiarities characterize every such family.

Statistical Information

The general information on, and the specific studies of, Black extended families rest within an extensive body of statistics on the population, housing, health status, health-care utilization, nutritional status, and other parameters of Holmes County's Black community. These data have been generated by the Corporation's Holmes County Health Research Program on the basis of especially adapted and locally field-tested protocols. The censuses of population and of housing, in particular, developed information, e.g. on household composition, labor force participation, crowding, and health hazards, beyond the details present, even on a sample basis, in the federal censuses. Moreover, the excellent cooperation of the Black people and the painstaking efforts of Mr. E. W. Logan and his staff, supported by technical guidance from Mr. Henry Lorenzi and, later, Mr. Edward Eckenfels, generated coverages much fuller than those of the U.S. Census of Population, 1970. For example, the population estimate for January 1, 1970 gained from these data was 18,100, compared to a U.S. Census figure of 15,743. A preliminary study based on a 2.6 percent simple random sample of the households has been prepared (Shimkin and Rice 1971). A final publication, based on data processing via the Osiris program, is in preparation.

Direct Observations

In addition, the study rests upon a variety of direct observations of behavior and events. These have been important as verifications of informant statements and as expressions of the emotional dimensions of family life, in happiness and in crisis, among Black Holmes Countians. The significance attached, say, to bringing deceased kinfolk back for burial in Holmes County is vividly brought out by seeing thirty or forty people alighting from a predawn train as escorts for the coffin. They are an entire colony recently established in Minneapolis in response to newfound opportunities in the computer industry. Well-dressed, well-spoken, these men, women, and children still are impelled to travel a thousand miles by rail, and perhaps twenty miles by rough country road, to bury an older member in a half-abandoned graveyard.

The imperative nature of hospitality becomes vibrantly clear when a mother must leave her cooking for family and guests to attend her son who had been pinned under an overturned truck. Even in this agony, she first turned over the cooking to a White friend, so that — come what may — obligations would be met.

These and other observations came as events dictated. Thus, while they were invaluable, they were often unpredictable; certain problems could be covered and others not at all.

Sample Study in Chicago, 1969

Finally, three Holmes County students of the University of Illinois, Miss Gloria Jean Louie, Miss Lillie McGee, and Mr. Robert Stewart, conducted a sample study, in the summer of 1969, of Holmes Countians resident in Chicago. Working under the guidance of Dr. Ozzie Edwards, then of the University of Illinois at Congress Circle and now of the University of Michigan, they gathered information on a set of 105 households, extending outward from personal networks of families and friends (see also Shimkin and Rice 1971). These data provide important supplements, especially on household compositions, to the detailed family studies and to statistical surveys of Holmes County.

The materials reviewed provided the facts on the Holmes County setting, the general characteristics of the extended family, and the "Bidwell" and "Mitchell" studies presented in later sections. In general, it is believed that these data are reliable and broadly representative, as of 1969–1970. At the same time, they are subject to several important limitations. Comprising parts of a larger, essentially practical, undertaking, they cover a more limited range of questions and in less depth than would be expectable in specifically academic research. Moreover, the roles of participant–observer characterizing all the authors of this study brought both advantages and restrictions in what could be observed and reported. A fancy-free Black youth might well have quite different impressions on many points. Finally, while Black–White relationships are often of utmost importance, to this day, for even intimate aspects of family life, these relationships could be seen only from one perspective. In Holmes County, race — as socially defined — is still the overriding identity; acceptance by the Black community brings with it corresponding exclusions.

This investigation has sought to place information on the Black extended family in the context of national patterns as well as in the framework of Holmes County culture. The study therefore includes a review of materials on kinship from both rural and urban areas of the United States. These materials indicate the presence of important similarities between Holmes County and other areas, especially the Sea Islands of South Carolina. These exist both in structural features and in urbanization dynamics.

A final topic has been exploration of the evidence that might relate the Black extended family of the United States to African origins, to borrowings from White culture, and to situational factors.

In general, it is believed that this study has been able to provide reliable and fairly extensive materials on the family and allied institutions of a rural Black community. It has brought forth strong indications that similar institutions are widespread in the rural South of the United States but are modified to varied extents in urban localities. It has proposed also that the Black extended family is most likely to be a modified African cultural complex.

It is hoped that this study will stimulate further descriptive and analytical researches in the widening depiction of Black culture in the United States. In particular, there appears to be a necessity for, and a potential fruitfulness of, comprehensive ethnographic investigations of both rural and urban communities. A number of key topics, such as Black customary law, especially need study. For all topics, an emphasis upon comparability between studies would be most important.

Extensive, reliable data on the characteristics, history, and dynamics of the Black extended family and allied institutions would be the basis for a number of significant applications. First, they would facilitate the preparation of popular and primary educational presentations, aiding both pride in Black traditions and understanding of the varied nature of American cultures. Second, these materials would also be important in correcting seriously harmful White misconceptions about the Black family and about Black society in general. A point in case is family reinforcement rather than disruption by the participation of grandparents, uncles and aunts, and other relatives in the care and education of children. Third, the better recognition of Black family values, institutions, and customary law should serve as the basis of appropriate legislative actions: for example, in the rectification of currently biased laws on adoption and fosterage.

Furthermore, it is urged that this study and others that may follow be utilized in the development of more effective social planning.

Thus, as Vernon J. Dixon (1970: 427–428) has emphasized, family values have strongly influenced Black economic behavior. In that behavior, the essential criterion is the satisfaction not of the individual alone but jointly that of the individual and of a number of kinsmen beyond the immediate family. The Black "utility function" is not independent but "interdependent," as a result. Black "marginal costs" include hidden elements, "rents" as it were, owed to members of extended families. In other words, Black earnings of every type are entailed by actual or potential obligations beyond the household. Conversely, the "marginal utility" of goods and services accruing to Black consumers is augmented by this same interconnectedness of households. The result is, that, while the underlying concepts of economics, e.g. the maximization of utility functions, are valid for Black as well as other societies, the applicable calculus differs from the "universal" model of independent economic decision making. It is a calculus under constraints.

Correspondingly, the Black extended family appears to have significant potentialities as a vehicle for managing the growing problems of long-term medical care. The experimental work of Dr. Arnold Golodetz and his colleagues among White families in Boston shows that, with technical support, training, and moderate augmentation of resources, families can cope with serious, including terminal, illnesses, effectively and at less psychological cost to the patient and his kin than can institutional care. The study utilized "responders" who were spouses, children, or parents; given "stable and reliable" relationships, considerable advantages in reducing strains would have come from the use of more distant kinfolk (see Golodetz et al. 1969).[4]

In the field of social welfare, Bert N. Adams' (1970) plea needs to be applied to Black extended families as well as White kin networks:

[Social workers] . . . must therefore be careful not to minimize the importance of kinship among their clients. Caseworkers have been prone to deal with individuals, and more recently with people-in-families, but what Leichter and Mitchell's [1967] findings suggest is that among these Jewish clients — and perhaps among other social groups — the approach should be to try to work with them as people-in-kin-groups. The eventual significance of this suggestion for case work practice, and the further significance of the interplay between kinship systems and the social work institution, remains to be seen (Adams 1970: 592).

And, beyond the programmatic, there exists a need to infuse the fruits of the Black experience in the United States more broadly and effectively into artistic creativity. Just as the tragedies, the horrors, and the human

[4] These materials have also been discussed at length with Count Gibson, Jr., M.D., one of the team members, to whom the authors are grateful.

victories arising out of Russian serfdom contributed to the writings, at once unique and universal, of Tolstoy, Turgenev, Chekhov, and Dostoevski, so too is there a greater portent in the Black experience. An important element of this experience has been the system of loyalties over time encompassed in the Black extended family.[5]

THE WORLD OF THE BLACK HOLMES COUNTIAN

Black people in Holmes County, Mississippi, live in a dynamic world. (Plates 1–16 illustrate various aspects of Black life in Holmes County.) They interact with a diversified physical environment dominated functionally by the contrasts between commercialized plantations and subsistence gardens. Within this physical setting, Black attitudes and behavior have been molded by a number of social forces and institutions: namely, racial relationships, kinship networks, and community support mechanisms, such as the church and the numerous formal organizations. Population dynamics, especially migration, have also had major effects. Many of these physical and social forces influencing daily life in Holmes County are historically based; nevertheless, this continuity has recently been modified and partly broken by the processes of change associated with the rise of the Civil Rights movement, on one hand, and the decline of agricultural employment, on the other.

Physical Setting

Holmes County is located approximately sixty miles north of Jackson in west-central Mississippi (Figure 1). Holmes County experiences a subtropical climate characterized by an annual rainfall of over fifty inches a year, and a mean temperature of 66 degrees Fahrenheit. The temperatures range from over 100 degrees Fahrenheit in the summer months to a minimum of zero degrees Fahrenheit during the winter. The maximum temperatures cause few physical hardships, except for infants, but the few cold periods are a stressful time for the Black population, and it is expectable that one or more families may burn to death each winter from fires started by inefficient gas heaters and wood-burning stoves. In general, the sufficient rainfall and long, warm summers provide a favorable environment for agriculture.

[5] As stated long ago by Langston Hughes (1968: 50) in "The Negro Mother."

Plate 1.　A row cluster of Black homes. This was once the site of a plantation

Plate 2.　A Black home located in one of the rural church communities in the Hills

Plate 3.   A Black community church on the eastern margin of the Delta. The congregation of this church is a mixture of plantation people and subsistence gardeners

Plate 4.   The home of a Black independent landowner in rural Holmes County

Plate 5. A skilled plantation worker in the Delta of Holmes County

Plate 6. A disappearing but still current scene: a subsistence farmer with his mule

Plate 7. An urban scene: Durant, Mississippi, the second largest urban area in Holmes County

Plate 8. A group of young boys exchanging traditional folk tales and improvising stories

Plate 9.   A group of young children in Holmes County with varying physical characteristics

Plate 10.   Two children and an infant in front of one of the County's newer and better houses made of concrete blocks

Plate 11. A scene from one of the twenty Head Start centers in Holmes County

Plate 12. The present center of the Freedom Democratic Party in Holmes County. Its main office is located in Lexington, Mississippi

Plate 13. The two daughters of a Black sharecropper in rural Holmes County

Plate 14. A Black family's home and subsistence garden in a rural church community in the Hills of Holmes County

Plate 15.   Two young children of a Black sharecropper in the Hills of Holmes County

Plate 16.   A multiple-generation household in rural Holmes County, Mississippi

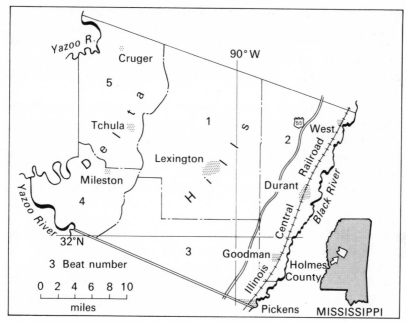

Figure 1. Holmes County, Mississippi.

Holmes County is bordered by the Black River on the east and the Yazoo River on the southwest. The 769 square miles of the County span two distinct physiographic and cultural units: first, the Mississippi – Yazoo River alluvial flood plain, and second, the Hills, which are part of the larger coastal plain of the Southeastern United States. This geographic location presents two contrasting, diversified environments (Figure 1).

Approximately one-third of the County's 769 square miles is covered by the Mississippi–Yazoo River floodplain, or, as it is locally referred to, the Delta region. The Delta is characterized by uniform topography as elevations reach only from near sea level along the Mississippi to 115 feet above sea level on the edge of the Hills, 50 miles to the east. The Delta was formed by the flooding of the Mississippi and Yazoo Rivers, and numerous abandoned stream channels from the Yazoo are still discernable. These oxbow and horseshoe lakes are where settlements occur, and the lakes, which are extensively fished, also provide an important food source for many Black residents. The alluvial soils of the Delta are very fertile and currently are intensively cultivated. The development of the Delta, which occurred after the Civil War and in part since the 1930's, was relatively very late compared to that of the rest of the County; poor drainage and dense forests long hindered agricultural development. Today, despite frequent inundations, most of the Delta is under cultivation. The Delta is characterized by large, White-owned commercial farms, or plantations, except in the southern part near Mileston, the site of a community of Black landowners, where smaller family farms predominate.

Flatness, extensive cultivation, and domination by plantations give an illusion of uniformity to the Delta, which actually comprises a variety of local population and sociocultural patterns. These range from tiny, isolated hamlets, hidden in waters-edge vegetation and heavily dependent upon subsistence gardening and fishing, to the complex cooperative economy and social structure of the Mileston community, and to varying patterns of plantation settlement and operation. Depopulation and local movements, especially to the outskirts of Tchula, a town of some 1,700 persons, have been the consequences of progressive land clearance, mechanization, and expulsions from plantations.

A nearly continuous bluff separates the Delta from the remaining two-thirds of the County, the Hills. The bluff runs north and south across the county with a local relief of 80 to 100 feet. It sharply divides these two diverse regions.

In contrast to the Delta, the Hills, characterized by gently rolling land, have been dissected by numerous streams and erosion. Elevation reaches about 400 feet above sea level in this region, with local relief peaking at about 100 feet in the forested, north-central section of the County and gradually lowering to an almost flat plain in the south-central area.

A belt of loess covers the western half of the Hills (Figure 2). Loess, a fine-grained, deposited soil, is fertile and easily cultivated. It reaches depths of twenty feet or more atop the bluff, extending eastward for ten miles, gradually thinning until it merges with the clays of the red-yellow podzolic soils (Figure 2).

Widespread cultivation of the Hills occurred even before the Civil War as the pines and mixed hardwoods were cleared. Deforestation, intensive cultivation, and poor farming methods have contributed to rampant soil erosion. Erosion has generally influenced the character of the landscape, and the gullying of fields still occurs today. Consequently, intensified agriculture is decreasing in the Hills and being replaced by less demanding uses of the land, such as cattle raising.

The Hill section of the County is generally more "urban" than the Delta. Two communities had total 1970 populations of over 2,500: Lexington with 2,753, and Durant with 2,697. However, the dominant settlement pattern in the Hills is the small, rural church community.

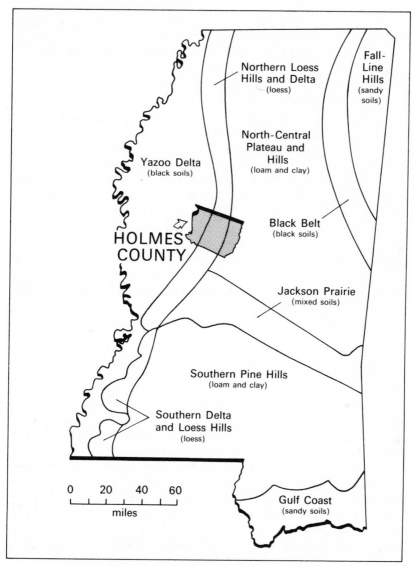

Figure 2. Physiographic regions and soil types.

These numerous communities, centered on churches and burying grounds, vary in size from 50 to 500 individuals; many are all Black, a few, like Coxburg in south-central Holmes County, are all White, and a few, like the Howard community west of Lexington, are mixed. Many of these communities are old settlements dating back over a century; a few are recent. These communities are usually dominated by a few extended families, which in the Hills tend to be more independent social units than their Delta counterparts, among whom the plantations retain important influences. In contrast to the Delta, the Hills are mainly composed of smaller family farms, both Black and White.

The poor road system in the Hills has contributed to a general isolation of these communities. The roads, mainly compacted dirt-gravel, become impassable during heavy rains or winter ice storms.

Though there is isolation within the County, it is tied to the larger society by the Illinois Central Railroad. The Chicago to New Orleans route of the Illinois Central runs directly through Holmes County with a depot in Durant (see Figure 1). This transportation outlet has contributed to the heavy out-migration that characterizes the Black population. The County is also linked to the outside by a few poorly paved roads, but this pattern will soon change with the completion of Interstate 55. This highway will directly link Holmes County with Jackson to the south and Memphis to the north; this route, which permits easy movement as far as New Orleans and Chicago, will undoubtedly have a great impact on the Black population.

Economy

Despite erosion and rapid soil depletion in the Hills, agriculture is still the main industry in the County. Contrary to popular belief, the agricultural system in the County has been marked by constant change. The Hill region in Holmes County was once a center for orchard crops; the mixed fruits found markets not only in the South but also in northern urban areas. Changing market relationships and crop failures prior to World War II marked an end to the orchards. During World War II, with increased demand for cotton, it completely dominated as the cash crop in the whole County. But with the development of synthetic fibers and the continued depletion of land resources, cotton, though still the main cash crop, has decreased in importance except on prime land. Presently, a shift is underway toward the raising of cattle. This change of agricultural priorities was due to the excellent market for beef and a growing emphasis upon pasture as both productive and conserving of diminished soil resources.

Throughout the economic history of the County two major phenomena have had critical influences on the Black population. First, though the main control of land is by a few White landowners, there has been a large group of independent Black farmers. Second, the gradual mechanization of farming among both Whites and Blacks and the paucity of occupational alternatives have left a large percentage of the Black labor force unemployed and all but destitute. Although some relief has been given the very poor by federal programs such as the Food Stamp Program, Old Age Assistance, and Head Start, recent economic changes have also, paradoxically, revived the significance of subsistence gardening and fishing.

In 1970, according to Mr. H. T. Bailey of Mileston Farmers' Cooperative, some 650 Black households were engaged in independent farming, including some 300 full-time farm families. The actual percentage of Black-owned land approximates 23 percent of the County's total farming acres. Though this percentage may appear small, the Black people in Holmes County own a larger proportion of farmland than the Blacks in any other county in the state.

A large proportion of the Black landowners is concentrated in the Delta community of Mileston, which was created as a resettlement project under the Bankhead-Jones Farm Tenant Act of 1937 (Morgalla 1969: 16). This project made loans to sharecroppers to enable them to purchase land and thereby gain independence. The project was a success, and created a core of independent Black farmers who have not only affected the economics of the County but have also been social innovators, thanks partly to their freedom from White economic control.

In January, 1970, approximately 4,250 Blacks were in the labor force, defined as including those employed, or unemployed and seeking work (Shimkin and Rice 1971: 37). Unemployment is subject to seasonal variation as demands for labor in agriculture and construction vary. The percentages of the Black labor force unemployed by season are as follows: June, 23 percent; August, 29 percent; and December, 45 percent (Shimkin and Rice 1971: 40). These high unemployment rates are the result of the reduction in farm wage labor by two-thirds between 1960 and 1970. The few remaining agricultural workers are the skilled operators of farm machinery. Coupled with this mechanization was the decline of employment in manufacturing, in lumbering and milling, and with the Illinois Central Railroad.

There have been three main responses by Blacks to the economic situation in Holmes County: first, there has been an increase in migratory farm labor; second, many Blacks, especially males, have left the County, seeking employment; and finally, for those remaining, it has created impoverished living conditions and dependence upon subsistence gardening, fishing, and the welfare system.

The Federal Government has been responsible for the only recent development in new employment and for partial economic betterment. Approximately 10 percent of the labor force of 4,250 was employed in 1970 by the Federal Government. This employment included persons working for the local Head Start program, a Health Research Project, a Beef Cattle Project, and other Federally funded projects. As mentioned earlier, programs such as the Food Stamp Program, Old Age Assistance, and Medicare have also eased the economic burden of many Black families. Yet, though these programs have been beneficial, they have offset the effects of massive unemployment only to a modest degree. Thus, pressures toward out-migration are ever present.

Though the future appears dim, there is, however, potential for economic development in Holmes County. Labor force capabilities have rapidly changed in the County, with the young people now averaging eleven years of schooling and management skills developed from practical experience in the Head Start and other Federal programs. Also, with the completion of Interstate 55, the presence of a natural gas pipeline, and the increased sophistication of the Black labor force, the components needed for industrial development are present in Holmes County. The actual course of development will, however, be deeply influenced by race relationships and the political climate locally and nationally.

Population and Population Dynamics

The State of Mississippi was settled by Whites migrating from Alabama, Georgia, and the Carolinas in the late 1700's (Lynch 1943: 315). Traveling up the Mississippi River, these settlers, along with some Black slaves, moved eastward into the Mississippi alluvial plain. Holmes County, located at the eastern margin of the Mississippi–Yazoo River floodplain, was settled in the mid-1800's, with the first farms in the Hills started around 1826. The majority of slaves in Holmes County were brought from more southerly Delta plantations or transferred from old tobacco areas in Virginia, North Carolina, and Maryland (Lynch 1943: 321). Many Blacks in the County can still trace their origins to these areas.

According to the results of an independent population census conducted by the Black community operated Holmes County Health Research Project, the Black population in the County in 1970 was 18,081 (Shimkin and Rice 1971: 5). This was a decrease from 1960, when the U.S. Census reported 19,488 Blacks in the County (U.S. Bureau of the Census

1963: Table 28). The Health Research Project's census did not ascertain the White population of the County, although the 1970 United States Census listed 7,345 Whites as residents. Consequently, over 70 percent of the County's population is believed to be Black. Such a numerical majority of Black occurs in only three other Mississippi counties: Tunica, Claiborne, and Jefferson.

The Black population of Holmes County can be characterized as predominantly rural. In 1970, only three incorporated areas in the County had a total population of over 1,500: Lexington, with 2,753; Durant, with 2,697; and Tchula, with 1,721 persons. Four additional incorporated regions have populations below 1,500. In all, approximately 40 percent of the Black population resides in incorporated regions while 60 percent live in a fully rural setting.

Regionally, the majority of the Black population resides in the Hills. Thus, although the Delta region covers nearly one-third of the County's total area, it contains only one-fourth of the population. This local population distribution is tied to the land use patterns of the large Delta plantations which, coupled with recent mechanization, have pushed down the population density. This was, in part, a forced movement accelerated by White reactions to the civil rights efforts of the 1950's and 1960's, and to minimum agricultural wage legislation which favored small, skilled and stable work forces on the plantations. Consequently, the Black population density in the Delta approximates eighteen persons per square mile, while in the Hills it reaches twenty-five persons per square mile.

A breakdown of the Black population by age and sex reveals three conspicuous demographic divisions: the 30–49 age group, the 50–64 age group, and the over-64 age group. For the younger adult population it is clear that net out-migration during 1960–1969 was clearly even more selective, by age and sex, than that in 1950–1959. In consequence, the sex ratio (or proportion of males to females) in the age group 30–49, numbering about 2,339 in 1970, fell from an already low level of 72:100 to a truly grave one, 43:100. In other words, nearly five black women are resident in the County today for every two Black men in this age cohort of prime importance for income generation and family development. The in-migration and return migration of older, often retired men is evidenced by the increase of sex ratio for the age group 50–64: from 88:100 to 103:100. The total number in this age group was approximately 2,534 in 1970. In small part, these older men fill the demographic gap; November–May marriages are frequent among the Black people of Holmes County.

The lowered sex ratio for the years 65 and above (94:100 in 1960,

67:100 in 1970), numbering about 2,534 individuals in 1970, is also probably significant. Its most plausible explanation is heightened male mortality during the hard years of civil rights struggle and hunger in the mid-1960's. Differential in-migration at these older ages may be a lesser factor involved.

Finally, the very young median age of the male population — the average Black Holmes Countian is in high school! — adds to the shortage of men in generating problems of socialization, social control, employment patterns, and economic viability for the community.

The present pattern of household and family compositions in the Black community of Holmes County reflects the modification of social traditions by extreme poverty and high in- and out-migration. This is best shown by comparisons with the Holmes Countians in Chicago; the scanty data from the U.S. Census of 1960 (U.S. Bureau of the Census 1963: 83–203) permit only a few observations (Table 1). Over the decade 1960–1970, the decreasing availability of younger men was the evident cause of the decline in the proportion of husband–wife families among all families — from 75 to 66 percent. Families with husbands younger than 45 years of age diminished from almost a quarter of all households to one-seventh. With the great scarcity of men and the somewhat better survival of couples over the decade may also come a reduction in the frequency of single-individual households.[6]

The current pattern of residential units in the Black community of Holmes County is marked by a high frequency of multiple-generation and other complex families, of both husband–wife and woman-headed type. These constitute almost half of all the families; the corresponding proportion among Holmes Countians in Chicago is 30 percent. This contrast reflects differences of age composition (the frequency of households with persons aged 65 or over is 5.5 times as great in the former area),[7] plus adaptations to increased social and economic viability. Nevertheless, barely half of the County's Black households, comprising some 60 percent of the population, have any employed member. It is little wonder that in

[6] Another factor possibly reducing the frequency of single individual households is the recent development of homes (group quarters) for the Black aged, in Holmes County and neighboring areas. However, these data are tentative; single-person households which are highly affected by seasonal migration may well be underenumerated in the Holmes County census.

[7] This statistic is highly provisional since the age composition of the Chicago group studied is appreciably younger than expected from the calculated distribution of net Black out-migrants from Holmes County. To what extent this reflects a sampling bias, secondary migration from Chicago (e.g. to Minneapolis or California), or unsuspectedly high mortalities is not as yet known.

Table 1. Household and family compositions among Black Holmes Countians in 1960 and 1970, and in Chicago, 1969

Household type and characteristic	Holmes County, 1960		Holmes County, 1970		Chicago, 1969	
	Frequency (percent of total)	Average size (persons)	Frequency (percent of total)	Average size (persons)[a]	Frequency (percent of total)	Average size (persons)
All households	100.0	4.37	100.0	4.56	100.0	4.14
Families	86.2	4.91	92.0	4.86	93.3	4.64
Husband–wife	64.3	n.a.	61.0	4.77	81.8[c]	4.50
Conjugal couple	n.a.	n.a.	14.0	2.00	14.3	2.00
Couple with children only	n.a.	n.a.	22.0	5.90	42.9	4.80
Extended:[b]	n.a.	n.a.	25.0	5.39	24.8	5.42
Single generation	n.a.	n.a.	4.0	3.19	3.8	3.25
Two generation	n.a.	n.a.	11.0	4.47	16.2	5.35
Multiple generation	n.a.	n.a.	10.0	7.37	4.8	7.40
Woman-headed	n.a.	n.a.	28.0	5.23	10.5	3.45
Mother–children	n.a.	n.a.	9.0	3.60	7.6	3.50
Grandmother–children–grandchildren	n.a.	n.a.	6.0	7.21	1.9	4.00
Other	n.a.	n.a.	13.0	5.44	1.0	2.00
Male-headed	n.a.	n.a.	3.0	3.60	1.0	3.00
Single individuals	13.8	1.00	8.0	1.00	6.7	1.00
Age characteristics[d]: Households with:						
Persons over 64	n.a.	n.a.	42.0	3.23	7.6	3.63
Husbands under 45	23.6	n.a.	14.0	6.67	61.9	4.42
Children under 18	43.5[e]	n.a.	56.0	6.48	67.6	5.00
Children under 6	27.6[e]	n.a.	35.0	7.50	46.7	5.12
Economic characteristics						
Retirement households[f]	n.a.	n.a.	13.0	1.66	1.0	1.00
Households without employment	n.a.	n.a.	35.0	4.75	n.a.	n.a.
Employed households	n.a.	n.a.	52.0	5.16	n.a.	n.a.

Notes: *n.a., Data not available.*
[a] In all cases the raw data have been multiplied by a coefficient of 0.983 to correct for sampling bias.
[b] Extended families include relatives other than children, and, in some cases, nonrelatives.
[c] Of these husband–wife families 7.0 percent (or 5.7 percent of all households) are consensual.
[d] More than one characteristic may be applicable, so the sum of households exceeds 100 percent.
[e] "Own children" only; thus, slightly incomparable with the 1969–1970 data.
[f] Households all members of which are 65 years old or older.

June, 1969, 7,209 persons in Holmes County were depending on nutritional aid via U.S. Department of Agriculture foodstamps.[8]

The proportion of woman-headed families in the County is nearly three times as high as in Chicago where, however, consensual unions make up 7 percent of the conjugal families. The frequency of households which either have female heads or consist of women with children but without husbands is 48 percent in Holmes County and 19 percent among the Holmes Countians in Chicago. Premature male deaths, brittle marriages, and consensual relationships underlie these patterns which both derive from and contribute to intense poverty.

In the great bulk of marriages, both spouses have been born in Holmes County, although the marriage of traceable relatives is avoided. In the Black population of Holmes County, 16.4 percent of all current marriages are between natives of other areas (especially adjoining counties in Mississippi); in 23 percent of the marriages, one of the spouses is a native of Holmes County, while in the remaining 60.6 percent of the cases both partners are native Holmes Countians. Thus, 86 percent of the Holmes Countians marry other Holmes Countians — a frequency identical for men and for women. Virtually the same endogamy persists in Chicago, where 84 percent of the spouses are from Holmes County. This endogamy is an important factor in maintaining sociocultural continuity despite physical dispersals and new economic patterns.

Yet conservative changes are observable: in both Holmes County and Chicago the relative ages of husbands and wives vary greatly, but the average difference is less in Chicago. There, the age of the husband is 4 ± 5.7 years greater than his wife's, while in Holmes County it is 7.3 ± 8.3 years greater. This variability has an adaptive value, tending to separate status and age in a society with a highly irregular composition by age and sex.

Three main processes continuously affect this population: fertility, mortality, and migration. These processes and their effects have become structurally embedded in the social values of this community.

The fertility rates among Black women in Holmes County have altered only slightly in the past ten years. The reported or estimated crude birth rates dropped from 32.8 births per 1000 persons in 1960, to 29.5 births in 1969 (Shimkin and Rice 1971: Table 5). There has been a slight reduction in fertility among young women aged 10–24 possibly due to increased

[8] The *Lexington* (*Mississippi*) *Advertiser*, July 31, 1969. The proportion of White recipients in this group is unlikely to exceed 20 percent. In 1960, 83 percent of the families earning under 3,000 dollars and 92 percent of those earning less than 1,000 dollars during the previous year were Black (U.S. Bureau of the Census 1963: 196).

education, but its effects have been offset by the high fertility of women 25–39 years of age and of the unmarried mothers, bringing into focus the continued value placed on children.

In Holmes County, children are desired and parenthood gives prestige. The acute shortage of men has made consensual marriages and liaisons more acceptable than formerly, even in the more permissive Delta areas. The distinctions between firm or shaky legal marriages, consensual marriages, and liaisons are gradations differing in the status accorded, not sharp cleavages between moral and immoral domains. Even in the case of liaisons, little secrecy prevails; with few exceptions, fatherhood is not only known but acknowledged, sometimes through periodic gifts to the child and sometimes through adoption into the father's family.

In this setting, it is not surprising that almost 23 percent of the County's Black mothers are unmarried. Among the unmarried women aged 20–49, 60 percent are mothers; the proportion of married women who are mothers in the same age group is 83 percent. The average unmarried mother is twenty-seven years old, has had ten years of schooling and has three children. She differs from wives (both with and without children) primarily in age — the average for the latter being thirty-seven years. The slightly lower educational attainment of the wives (eight years) and the larger average number of children per married mother (4.5) are correlates. These factors give impetus to the idea that illegitimacy is an external concept of low functional relevance to this community.

From 1963 to 1967 the crude death rate among the Black population is estimated to have averaged 13.5 per 1000 persons (Shimkin and Rice 1971: Table 5). This can be compared to the average death rate in the United States as a whole, of 9.8 per 1000 persons. Infant mortality, almost certainly underenumerated, averaged 49.1 per 1000 births over this period. For total mortalities, crude death rates can be transformed to standardized mortalities by dividing the crude rates by the death rate expectable at the age and sex composition of each population, given the age-and-sex specific mortality expectations (Mx) of the 1959–1961 White Life Table for the Southeastern United States (U.S. Department of Health Education and Welfare 1965: Tables 21–24). Under this conversion, the death rates of the Black population of Holmes County are 1.5 to 1.6 times higher than those for the southern White population. The elements contributing to high death rates are varied but generally reflect the poor environmental health conditions of the County — poor nutrition, endemic parasitoses, hyperendemic streptococcus infections, severe hypertension, and high accident rates.

In general, death is a constantly present part of life for Black Holmes Countians. The deaths of infants and children evoke, however, far less grief than do those of the mature and elderly. The loss of parents is particularly traumatic; the support of family members, the help of ministers, and the catharsis of public wakes and funerals mitigate the profound feelings that are thus aroused. Correspondingly, attendance at funerals, in proper clothing, is a deep-felt obligation even among the very poor.

Migration has been a dominant element for the Black population of Holmes County since World War I. The basic forces contributing to out-migration have been economic and social deprivation, from both poverty and denials of civil rights (Shimkin 1971). The estimated gross number of out-migrants over the period 1960 to 1970 for those now aged 16 to 74 years is 5,063 (Shimkin and Rice 1971: 28). On the basis of lists of relatives in obituaries published in the *Lexington* (*Mississippi*) *Advertiser* in 1969, and of family studies, it is estimated that about 12,000 Black migrants from Holmes County, or some 40 to 45 percent of those living, resided in Chicago at the end of 1969. Besides Chicago, cities such as St. Louis, Detroit, Los Angeles, Jackson, and New Orleans have been significant destinations.

The pattern of out-migration is one of predominantly (55 percent) individual movement: five out of six in this group are men and women aged 16–29 coming to live with relatives or friends who migrated earlier. Families with a wide range of ages represented, including some 36 percent under age 10, make up 27 percent of the migrants, with young couples — generally recent high school graduates or dropouts — making up the remainder. Overall, the age distribution of the out-migrants of 1960–1969 in midsummer 1969 was 0–9, 11.4 percent; 10–15, 3.0 percent; 16–19, 17.4 percent; 20–29, 59.1 percent; 30–39, 5.3 percent; 40–49, 2.3 percent; and 50–64, 1.5 percent (Table 2).

The in-migrants to Holmes County, resident there on January 1, 1970, made up 17.2 percent of the Black population, or some 3,118 persons. The date of their in-migration, if prior to 1969, was unfortunately not asked, but the age distribution of migrant individuals and families indicates that at least 974 had come during the past decade. The units of migration and the age of distribution of these in-migrants differ substantially from those of the out-migrants. Almost half came in families, both conjugal and woman-headed. Individual migrants (38 percent) and couples (12 percent) covered a much wider gamut of ages. The high number of children aged 0–9, about 468 or nearly half of the decade's in-migrants, is striking.

The contrast in the patterns of out- and in-migration seemingly reflects

Table 2. Black Holmes County migrants to Chicago: by sex and age in 1969, by sex and age at migration, and by migration unit and age (percent distributions)

Category	Distribution by age									
	All ages	0–9	10–15	16–19	20–29	30–39	40–49	50–64	65–74	75 & over
A. By sex and age in 1969										
Total	100.0	5.9	3.4	11.0	40.5	18.1	11.4	5.9	2.1	1.8
Males	100.0	7.0	4.3	11.3	43.5	13.0	13.0	5.2	1.7	0.9
Females	100.0	4.9	2.5	10.7	37.7	23.0	9.8	6.6	2.5	2.5
Males as percent of total	48.5	57.1	62.5	50.0	52.1	34.9	55.6	42.9	40.0	25.0
B. By sex and age at migration										
Total	100.0	11.9	10.2	39.4	28.8	5.1	2.1	1.7	0.8	—
Males	100.0	13.0	9.6	35.7	32.2	6.1	1.7	0.9	0.9	—
Females	100.0	10.7	10.7	43.0	25.6	4.1	2.5	2.5	0.8	—
Males as percent of total	48.5	53.6	46.3	44.1	54.4	58.3	40.0	25.0	50.0	—
C. Migration unit and age at migration										
Total	100.0	11.9	10.2	39.4	28.8	5.1	2.1	1.7	0.8	—
Individuals	100.0	3.8	7.7	55.4	28.5	0.8	1.5	0.8	1.5	—
Couples[a]	100.0	—	9.5	31.0	45.2	9.5	4.8	—	—	—
Families[b]	100.0	35.9	15.6	12.5	18.8	10.9	1.6	4.7	—	—
Individuals as percent of total	55.1	17.9	41.7	77.4	54.4	8.3	40.0	25.0	100.0	—
Couples as percent of total	17.8	—	16.6	14.0	27.9	33.3	40.0	—	—	—
Families as percent of total	27.1	82.1	41.7	8.6	17.6	58.4	20.0	75.0	—	—

Notes: —, No cases.
a Husband and wife.
b Husband and wife plus other relatives, or two or more other relatives.

important motivational differences in these two movements. Black out-migration from Holmes County is predominantly a search for economic opportunity by young people, with the flight of dispossessed families also being appreciable. The in-migrants are, in part, families and individuals from even more disadvantaged areas than Holmes County; some were forced off plantations into refugee hamlets, especially in the environs of Tchula. Also, it appears that children have been transferred from other areas to relatives in Holmes County, almost certainly in response to the excellence of the Head Start programs there. Finally, retirement couples form a distinct part of this inflow. It is only recently that substantial numbers of out-migrants from the Black population of Holmes County have reached the age of forty or more. This fact is of basic importance for evaluating future trends in Holmes County, which might well become an important retirement area for the 20,000 or more migrants of 1940–1960. In-migration from nearby counties is likely to continue, with the inflow of children making up for much of the decreasing number of births. Decreased mortalities, especially at ages 50–64, are also expectable.

In all, it is likely, even without major socioeconomic changes in Holmes County, that the decline in the Black population will be reversed during the coming decade. But the population under such circumstances would continue to be woefully short of young adults. Serious disproportions in sex ratios would continue, with profound consequences for family formation and maintenance. Only the advent of a much stronger economic base adequate to attract young people could remedy these structural weaknesses, which in turn contribute heavily to the perpetuation of poverty.

Migration also has had more direct social effects. In addition to the profound changes in age-and-sex and household composition already reviewed, migration brings with it a broadened perspective and a more purposeful life strategy for young people. Movement to areas of possible residence long antedates final departure; communications with potentially important relatives and friends are correspondingly cultivated. At the same time, both the young people and the established migrants have become aware of, and increasingly capable in, alternative rural and urban behavioral styles. This switching, an aspect of the larger pattern of role playing characteristic of Black Holmes Countians, often takes place among the same group as contexts change: one moment it is ghetto talk; the next it is pure Delta dialect.

One aspect of the social effects of in-migrants from other counties and of the return migration of the retired is noteworthy. These people tend to be social isolates, with little knowledge of County institutions or events.

Often they are both illiterate and politically inert. Thus, they constitute an important problem in social integration for the Black community of Holmes County (see also McCracken 1970).

In sum, fertility, mortality, and migration determine the population dynamics in Black Holmes County. These factors, coupled with still critical racial relationships, economic deprivation, inadequate housing, poor nutrition, and a general low health status have helped to mold many of the social institutions and values shared by the Black population of Holmes County. These can now be considered briefly.

Social Institutions and Values

Black society in Holmes County is characterized by a number of inter-related structural features: interracial relationships, kinship networks, residential units, occupational groups, age cohorts, sex divisions, religion, and status gradations.

One of the most critical social forces that has influenced the behavior of Blacks in Holmes County is the complex of relationships with Whites. For years Black–White relationships have been dominated by the principle of White superiority in status and by the reality of White political and economic control. Fear of violence from the White community and management of that fear became a definitive element in the lifeways of Blacks (Lorenzi and Lorenzi 1969b: 1). This fear has now more or less disappeared as the Blacks in Holmes County have become politically organized. One main factor that contributed to this change was the presence of Black landowners, a group not tied to White economic control.

Though fear has diminished and numerous visible changes have occurred, such as Black voter registration, political organizations, the election of Blacks to County and even state offices, the free use of the County courthouse, and better police behavior, the actual underpinnings of racial relationships have changed little; this is especially true for the segment of the White population economically controlling the County. Consequently, although some alterations have taken place, it must not be forgotten that the last attempted lynching occurred in Holmes County in the summer of 1967 and that the possibility of armed confrontation, although much reduced, is still real.

The kinship network, especially the extended family, is a critical social unit enhancing survival in the County. The family is a genealogical concept which is primarily built on a bilateral descent and secondarily on ties of marriage and fosterage. Through these established links an individual realizes a kin network that delimits his social resources and obligations. The Black family, especially in the Hills, has a long continuity which tends to breed strong group identification and solidarity. Consequently, since such a strong identification fosters in-group loyalties, feuds between such families are a potential reality even today. The family is also the functioning economic unit in the County. In many Black families economic survival is tied to household cooperation and joint economic pursuits.

The basic residential unit of the Black rural population in Mississippi is the County. When residents of two different counties meet, the County rather than the town or village is given as a means of identification. Within Holmes County, the first-level residential division is the Delta–Hill dichotomy. Certain characteristics are attributed to the two regions, such as the larger extended families for the Hills and plantation lifeways for the Delta.

Though these two large residential divisions are employed as social indicators, the dominant residential unit within the County is actually the small church community. These communities center on a church and cemetery, number between 50 and 500 individuals, and are usually dominated by one or two extended families. Some of these communities, such as Mt. Olive, north of Lexington, are over a century old, while others, such as Balance Due and Pecan Grove in Lexington itself, are of recent origin. Even though these communities may be located within a larger social context, such as urban Lexington, they are well-delimited localities with corresponding residential identification and sentiments.

Whereas a family may dominate one residential unit, occupational groups crosscut communities and families. These occupational groups do not involve every job type in the County but are large categories that are ranked by Black people according to social prestige. The highest status within the occupational rankings is occupied by the Black landowner. Such an individual is generally well respected and considered a source of leadership within the Black community. This has been especially true since the rise of the Civil Rights movement in 1963–1967, for it was the Black landowner that assumed political leadership in the County at that time.

While the Black landowner occupies the highest position on the status continuum of occupational groups, the domestic worker is located at the opposite end of the continuum. The domestic worker's low status is mainly due to the direct tie with the White community and dependence upon it. The plantation worker at one time may have occupied the lowest occupational status position, but recent farming mechanization has left only a skilled residual force on most plantations. Subsistence farmers, although recognized as conservative elements of the society, have a collective significance as "grass-roots people" — the basic constituency of the County's new political and social organizations.

Four other main occupational groups positioned between the independent landowner and the domestic worker are small businessmen, independent craftsmen, school teachers, and midwives. Shopkeepers and, especially, skilled craftsmen have statuses approaching those of the independent landowner. The Black school teacher is generally considered as occupying a high status position when defined by the educational level and amount and stability of income. However, his continuing subordination to White leadership and consequent frequent social timidity is an adverse factor. Teachers too are highly vulnerable to social criticism for peccadillos tolerable among other occupation groups. Health workers, Head Start instructors and other new white-collar workers tend to be assimilated into this general category of teachers.

School teachers in Holmes County have unusually close relations, in many cases, to the rural "grass-roots" people. The Black school system in Holmes County has had a dynamic history. During the 1920's and 1930's, numerous one-room schoolhouses were scattered throughout the County. Not only did these schools provide a basic education but they functioned as social centers for the various communities. Many community activities such as picnic dinners were held at the school. School fairs raised money; the celebration of "Children's Day" provided outlets for budding skills. During the 1950's, the Black schools were consolidated and professionalized under pressure from the Federal Government. In 1967, the organization of Head Start programs reintroduced the community-school concept to the Black population of Holmes County. And with this new school system came a renewal of community participation in local centers.

The Black midwife has long held a respected social position in the County. The midwife not only delivers babies but is a respository of genealogies. The Black midwife is not tied solely to the Black community, as her services generally were, and at times still are, sought by Whites. Thus, she becomes an important link between races. This occupational group is gradually disappearing from the County due to the introduction of federally funded programs promoting hospital deliveries. Consequently, though seventeen midwives were licensed and actively practicing in Holmes County in 1967, today only two Black midwives are currently licensed by the State of Mississippi.

Age grades and sexual divisions are two additional coordinating social units superimposed on the Black community that define a person's behavior relative to other community members. There are four basic age grades that are recognized by Blacks in Holmes County: elders, adults, young people (children), and infants.

The elders occupy a respected social position in the community and are often sought for advice and counsel. The age responsible for economic input, family rights and duties, and community leadership is that of the adult members of the community. Young people or children should generally be obedient to their elders, especially family members, and are given a number of responsibilities. The actual division between adulthood and this lower age grade is not dependent upon one single element. Many factors such as marital status, community involvement, and maturity are individually weighed. Consequently, entrance into adulthood may at times be deferred until the early or mid-twenties. This is a relatively formal act; it is the point, for example, at which a person may speak at political meetings without asking leave. Infancy is a general period of no responsibilities and family affection. Grading from infancy to childhood is not sharp and may occur gradually.

The social behavior ascribed to males and females of the Black community is in contrast not only to the behavioral divisions found in the White community but also to those often attributed to Black people. The female dominance in all social spheres that is frequently attributed to the Black population is not a reality in Holmes County. Males dominate both the political and the religious arenas. In the political sphere, male dominance is general. Female leadership does occur but usually within lower staff positions. And, at times when women do exercise political influence, male resentment of nontraditional behavior is often openly expressed. Female religious participation does occur in roles such as that of the "church mothers," but even this position may depend upon whether husbands are deacons.

Politically, Holmes County has the most highly organized Black community in Mississippi. Numerous groups promoting not only political, but economic and social advancement as well, are present. The Mississippi Freedom Democratic Party, formed in the summer of 1964, has been responsible for the main Black political thrust in the County. Other organizations promoting political, economic, and social betterment include the Milton Olive III Memorial Corporation, the Milton Olive III Memorial Program for Children, Community Action Program, the Robert Francis Kennedy Civic Association, and the Mileston Farmers' Cooperative.

Coupled with these formal organizations are a number of fraternal organizations, societies, and clubs. These organizations promote in-group feelings and often offer mutual aid and recreation. These groups may be exclusive, but the criteria of selection tend more toward sex, age, and conviviality than toward social characteristics. One of the more prominent fraternal organizations is the Masons.

Religion for the Black people of Holmes County is the very foundation of social cohesion and moral strength. Religion is a dual phenomenon: the church and religious faith. The many churches of Holmes County are, in general, fundamentalist in persuasion. The core of each is the set of families who support the church and who provide its deacons and "church mothers." Basic to church services are prayers, with congregational participation, and singing by the congregation, generally without accompaniment. Ministers rotate between churches, leading services at each place, perhaps monthly; their services and their religious and emotional management of crisis ceremonies, such as baptism, revival meetings, and funerals, are important social regulators. Ministers, who are generally self-trained, are largely part-time specialists; they are esteemed for the capacity to provide comfort, to speak with power and grace, and to exercise good social judgement. Politically and socially, the Black ministers of Holmes County have varied from deep conservatism to dangerously courageous involvement in the struggle for civil rights. Correspondingly, their services have ranged from denunciations of women's flaunting of "bad" natural hair to deep concern with social and moral problems. While ministers are, at most, but nominally paid, their congregation will provide them with fine suits and even a car, particularly at periodic "appreciations" (see fn. 11) and when church conventions are in the offing.

Religious faith provides the ultimate reservoir of courage, the deepest social bond, and the most constant touchstone of moral rightness to Black Holmes Countians. It was on the basis of religious faith that the terrible risks of the 1960's were assumed — initially by a middle-aged brother and sister. It is on the basis of Biblical precept that grave judgements, such as the potential expulsion of a strong yet erratic leader from the high political councils of the community, are decided. No meeting is considered truly valid without prayer and song. And, correspondingly, the characteristic service of worship is structured as an inward-facing ring of participants, rather than an attendance upon an external altar.

Religious leadership in the churches, in community activities, and in the home is a man's task. The saying of grace before at least one meal is still an important practice in Holmes County. In general, within the home, male–female roles become merged with parental ones. But, once again female dominance, or the "matriarchy," is not a prominent feature, since rights and duties are individually defined. While spouses' interests and activities tend to be parallel rather than fused, a switch in duties, such as the husband caring for the children and the wife working in the fields, is common. In general, a woman's economic independence is encouraged. And both husband and wife may retain some separate resources. Consequently, it is not uncommon for incomes to be separate, with the wife's going toward immediate household needs (such as food and clothes), while the husband's may be used for the purchase of fodder or farm equipment.

In broadest terms, Black society in Holmes County is not stratified into essentially isolated classes, on the order, say, of the social structure of Columbus, Mississippi or Selma, Alabama. Rather, it consists of a large, interrelated, partly cooperative, partly factionalized core of social groups within which social adults have multiply defined statuses. These statuses combine social centrality with marginality, acceptability with ostracism, and power with dependence. They rest in part on ascribed factors, such as occupational group, education, the reputation and the power of one's extended family, and visible wealth. But they rest even more upon personal attributes and behavior: here, an important element of Holmes Countian and, in general, Black social regulation must be recognized.

Holmes Countians admire an aggregate of desirable "strong" traits, such as athletic skill, oratorical ability, courage, honesty, and moral correctness. Men and women who combine traits such as these are respected and influential regardless of other attributes, such as poverty or lack of education. At the same time, Holmes Countians realize the prevalence of failure, particularly under the traditional burdens of racial oppression and chronic poverty; for many, alcohol is the terminating comfort. Gambling and wenching are commonplace. But the community needs its people; only the truly dangerous can be ostracized, expelled, or even killed as "crazy niggers." For the rest there is the tolerance, the resigned acceptance of "weakness." This tolerance also moderates the intensity of rivalries; the fights for ultimate prestige may be severe, but few lack compassion and some support for those former leaders who are no longer "strong."

Daily Life: Continuity and Change

While the daily life of a Black person in Holmes County represents a mixture of work and social relationships, it also reflects contrasting processes of continuity and change. The social isolation and economic deprivation present in Holmes County promote the continuation of many traditional values and lifestyles. In fact, in some areas of the County, few if any modernizations have yet made their impact. In many families, piped-in water and such items as an indoor toilet or even a privy are nonexistent. To these people, wells and a water supply become critical factors of survival. Many Black families are dependent upon subsistence gardening, the raising of a few animals, such as chickens and sometimes pigs, and fishing for survival. Hunting is still a source of food but has recently diminished in importance as land clearance has reduced game.

Another area of traditionalism is the perpetuation of folk crafts within the Black population. A few of these folk crafts, such as sewing and quilting, are very widespread; others, such as blacksmithing, basketry, and pottery making, are today practiced by only a few individuals.

To an important degree, the home is still a center for folk education and recreation. From the ages of perhaps five or six, girls are charged with supervising babies, while boys' chores include hoeing gardens and feeding animals. While many homes have record players and even TV sets, books are found in only a few, and traditional recreations are still important. For example, almost all children in the Head Start programs are well acquainted with many folktales, especially ghost stories.

Traditionalism correspondingly still affects much adult life. Geophagy is widespread. Many farmers still regulate their activities by the moon. And outlandish ideas are often rejected; many people, perhaps most, are highly skeptical of reported U.S. landings on the moon. Both folk wisdom and cynical assessments of White folks' propaganda are grounds for disbelief.

Yet with traditionalism there has also been profound change over the past decade. Most obvious and widespread have been the shifts from the omnipresent past, the obsessive involvement with the terrors of lynchings and feuds, to concern with the future; and from a self-image of "colored and subordinate" to one of "Black and equal." Unfortunately, while younger urban Whites in Mississippi have made corresponding shifts, the old White leadership in Holmes County is locked into the past.

The conditions predisposing to new racial relationships and identity were the founding of the numerous political organizations in the County. As a consequence of these organizations, Black people have become skilled at sociopolitical action.

Along with the increases in organizational networks have come opportunities for more education. Consequently, education levels in the County are rapidly rising. In 1970, about 44 percent of the individuals in the 16–29 age bracket had nine to twelve years of formal education. In the 30–49 bracket, only 22 percent had reached a similar education level, while in the 50–64 and 65–74 age brackets the percentage of those with nine to twelve years of schooling was about 10 and 3 percent respectively (Shimkin and Rice 1971: 45).

With the rise in educational levels and the advent of the federally funded programs, a small segment of the Black population has entered a period of economic betterment somewhat resembling the White middle class in terms of modern housing and technological consumption patterns.

One of the most critical parallel changes in recent years has been the betterment of communications between individuals and communities. The need for a better communications system was felt in the days of the Civil Rights movement. Today, communications advancements in the Black population are mainly represented by an increase in the number of automobiles and in the use of telephones; approximately 50 percent of the Black households have the use of a telephone.

In summary, although Holmes County can generally be characterized as poverty stricken, the Black population should not be considered as an economically or socially homogeneous group. Variations within the Black population occur and within these variations, the interplay of traditional and contemporary features gives the Black culture of Holmes County a dynamic character.

Holmes County and Black Mississippi

Holmes County is distinguished among the counties of Mississippi by the strength of its Black political organizations and by the high proportion of land — almost a quarter — in Black possession. Culturally, the County shares the basic traditions of central and northern Mississippi, in which old frontier patterns (including significant Choctaw and Chickasaw Indian elements) are found in the loess hills and clay plains, while the bottom lands are dominated by substantial plantations. French culture, including Catholicism, which is a feature of southwest Mississippi, is absent here.

In terms of socioeconomic characteristics, Holmes County is very deprived in relation to the State of Mississippi as a whole, but is close to the median for the seventeen counties (out of 82) which, in 1960–1970, were 60 percent or more Black. These include Tunica, Coahoma, Quitman, Tallahatchie, Leflore, Sunflower, Bolivar, Holmes, Humphreys, Sharkey, and Issequena Counties in the Delta; Claiborne, Jefferson, and Wilkinson Counties in southwest Mississippi; and Madison, Noxubee, and Marshall Counties in central and northeastern Mississippi.

For example, while only 13.3 percent of the Holmes County population enjoyed private and public wage or salaried employment, in comparison to 21.5 percent for the State as a whole, the corresponding median figure for the seventeen Black counties was 14.5 percent. Per capita annual earnings were, correspondingly, 834 dollars for the State, 378 dollars for Holmes County, and 421 dollars for the Black-county median. For the State as a whole, only 8.2 percent of those employed were in agriculture, compared to 33 percent in Holmes County, and 35.7 percent for the median of the seventeen Black counties. In 1970, 33.9 percent of the Black-occupied housing units had plumbing and were uncrowded, with less than a single person per room. The corresponding figures for Holmes County and the Black-county median were 22.9 percent and 19.5 percent, respectively. In 1966, there were 1,417 persons per physician in Mississippi, but 3,863 persons per physician in Holmes County, and 2,990 persons per physician as the median for the seventeen Black counties. The death rates of the Black people, when adjusted to a constant age-and-sex pyramid, averaged, in 1963–1967, 47.4 percent higher than if 1959–1961 White southeastern U.S. life expectancies had prevailed. The slightly higher figure for Holmes County was the Black-county median. Although Black infant mortality data for Mississippi in 1963–1967 are very unreliable,[9] those of Holmes County appear also to have been close to the State average and Black-county median.

In sum, while local variability in Mississippi and throughout the South is high, the findings for Holmes County may be tentatively applied to a considerable number of other primarily rural, predominantly Black counties.[10]

[9] Marked undercounting has been noted in these figures. Two practices contribute to such an underenumeration: a fair number of infant and child burials take place privately, in family plots; also an appreciable proportion of deaths of County residents take place in other localities, such as hospitals in Jackson (see Shimkin and Rice 1971: 21).

[10] The sources used directly or for lineal interpolation to about 1965 were as follows: for 1960 populations by race, sex, and age (U.S. Bureau of the Census 1963); for 1970 population by race, sex, and age (U.S. Bureau of the Census 1971b); for farm employment and payrolls in 1964 (U.S. Bureau of the Census 1967: Table 5); for private nonfarm employment and payrolls in 1959 (U.S. Bureau of the Census 1960: Table 3); for private nonfarm employment and payrolls in 1969 (U.S. Bureau of the Census 1969); for government employment and payrolls (U.S. Bureau of the Census 1970a); 1970 housing data (U.S. Bureau of the Census 1971a); data on the number of physicians, by County, in 1966 (American Medical Association 1967: 2176–2190), with those aged 70–79 counted as half-time and those aged 80 or over assumed to be related; data on numbers of deaths (Mississippi State Board of Health 1963–1967) were related to age and sex compositions and to White life expectancies (U.S. Department of Health Education and Welfare 1965).

THE BLACK EXTENDED FAMILY IN HOLMES COUNTY: GENERAL CHARACTERISTICS

At the present time, race and family are the fundamental bases of social identity and behavior among the Black people of Holmes County. Age, community of origin, residence, class, county, and new sociopolitical institutions such as the Freedom Democratic Party are of auxiliary importance.

The Concept of "Family"

"Family," in the social theory and practice of Black Holmes Countians, is a genealogical concept built primarily on bilateral descent and second- arily on ties of marriage, fosterage, and adoption. The scope of "family" is variously defined according to purpose. The network of kin extending out from oneself delimits a person's social resources and obligations. Corporate units are established by common surnames and by links to an honored ancestor or other relative, male or female; they are also bounded by choices of affiliation, especially when conflicts arise. Persons who are distantly related to, or allied with, more than one extended family may make choices between competing factions in the community by a selective recognition of ties.

The genealogical relationships which underlie the concept of "family" among Black people in Holmes County are, in the first instance, an important and often refreshed part of the information kept and supplied by older persons, both male and female. At extended-family gatherings, for example, a female elder may place a young returned migrant or visitor for the entire group by specifying her relationship to a senior kinswoman: "She's Sally's daughter." At such gatherings, also, the sequence of food service, deferential greetings between younger and older, and the clustering of peer groups provide markers of relative seniority and affiliation within the family and its allies.

There are few secrets of parentage, including links with the White community, that are not widely known, particularly by the midwives. In general, most adults know their own and each other's ancestry, bilaterally, for three or four generations past. Beyond this are found more general traditions: the Bailey family comes from Tidewater, Virginia; one branch of the Montgomerys comes from Starkville in eastern Mississippi, while another, not directly traceable in its links to the first, comes from South Carolina; members of the Clark family were distinguished refugees from

White threats in Hinds County (Jackson), Mississippi, at the end of Reconstruction; and so forth.

Oral traditions are reinforced by family and community church records which are validated and publicized as parts of funeral observances; data on the various relationships and addresses of relatives of the deceased have also been published, in recent years, in the *Lexington Advertiser*. Other ceremonial occasions, such as "appreciations"[11] for ministers or prominent family members, likewise serve to mark far-flung ties. It is expected that older men of high status should acknowledge distant relationships by marriage as well as blood, with attendance at the funerals of remote kin being a typical expression of family solidarity. In times of crises, high-status men may reach out for kinsfolk even across racial boundaries.[12] This has served to avert large-scale violence on at least one occasion still well remembered in Holmes County. It is also meritorious for men to acknowledge illegitimate offspring, publicly through visits and gifts, or at least privately through the payment of burial insurance.[13]

Within extended families, ties of friendship and cooperation are sometimes accentuated by upgrading known kinship links; an actual first cousin once removed with whom a person visits and who is otherwise emotionally close often becomes an "aunt." A wife's male cousin with whom one cooperates in farming may be termed "brother-in-law." Child fosterage and adult adoptions also create ties with both relatives and nonrelatives which intensify or even generate many rights and obligations. These ties may incorporate a former stranger into the family network. They serve, in addition, to establish bonds between families. An illustration is the adoption of a young man by a childless couple. The young man, visits to his adopted parents apart, remains with his own family. He gains, however, the patronage of his adopters, and may become their heir in part. In return, he owes deference, small courtesies, and perhaps care in old age to the adopters. The two families express solidarity in, say,

---

[11] An "appreciation" is a ceremony in which a congregation, family, or other group brings gifts, such as money or clothing, or other tokens of esteem, to a highly respected person. Such "appreciations" often take place before church conventions and are a means both of reward for services, including prestige brought to a group, and of display of the group's economic resources.

[12] Tacit recognitions of relationship, including transfers of property and some visiting, between White and Black descendents of prominent Whites were apparently in existence in Holmes County in the 1930's and earlier. By the mid-1960's this was only a memory, in contrast to the continuity of these observances in at least one southern Mississippi town (Dollard 1957: 142).

[13] While babies and young children are often buried by their families in private burying grounds or even gardens, the proper public burial of adults is a matter of great social and emotional importance for Black Holmes Countians.

political decisions, within the larger community. Naming a child for a respected relative or nonrelative is another means of signalling family solidarity and interfamily alliances.

In general, the identification or establishment of family relationships determines in large part how people will behave toward each other.[14] For this reason, strangers meeting, for example, on trains, will seek to identify each other's county of origin and then to elicit possible ties by blood or marriage, even if they are very remote. If such ties are discovered, the nature of the conversation and the probability of such friendly acts as food sharing are greatly changed. Moreover, family ties establish claims to rights and obligations which may be truly categorical according to Black people's customary law in Holmes County. Blood feuds between the great extended families still remain as potential threats. Thus, as late as 1968, William (pseudonym), a low-status member of a powerful family, defended the reputation of a high-status member during a bitter quarrel with a member of a hostile family.[15] "If anybody told me that, I'd get my .45," he said. The opponent, alarmed by William's remark, sought to place him under a crushing peace bond. William then turned anxiously to the senior members of his extended family in a formal and binding appeal for help, which brought the family's weight to bear on ending the quarrel.

Rights and Obligations Associated with Family Membership

The gamut of rights and obligations associated with family membership is extensive. It runs, in general, from pressures for solidarity in public decisions and feuds to attendance at funerals, cooperation in work, aid in job hunting, coresidence privileges, child fosterage, care in old age, the rental of land on nominal terms, and gifts and inheritances. Marriages, sexual relationships, and even adolescent dating between blood relatives of any degree or between persons bearing the same surname, even if unrelated, are strongly disapproved of.

In most cases, the number of relatives with whom it is possible to

---

[14]   For the Pruitt-Igoe housing development in St. Louis, Rainwater writes, ". . . kinship ties are normatively defined as involving heavy reciprocal obligations. The sense of deep gratefulness which the respondents expressed as they described the help they received reinforces this interpretation. Similar feelings were expressed about friends and neighbors who proved helpful, but these friends 'didn't really have to' help, there was not the same obligation that exists among kinsmen" (Rainwater 1970: 69).

[15]   The slur in question was relatively mild. Obscene vituperations of the kind reported by Rainwater (1970: 205) would result in immediate violence, if not a killing, in Holmes County.

establish reciprocities is far greater than is practically feasible or personally rewarding. The choices made reflect personal likes and calculations of advantage within a broad hierarchy of social distance. A basic customary law, recognized even by the most oppressive planters, is that farm workers must be allowed time off to attend the funerals of "father and mother, brother and sister." To bury these close relatives properly, and to be decently attired at their funerals, is one of the truly imperative requirements of Holmes County Black society, even among the very poor. Correspondingly, the obligations of mutual aid, respect, and care for these relatives are intensely felt, throughout life. Unreconciled conflicts within this familial core are likewise exceptionally bitter; characteristically, they are fights involving property.

The relations with parents are by no means uniform. Generally, both boys and girls are more demonstrative with, and more subject to the direct authority of, their mother. This is true even for adult children. The father, particularly if he is older, is a remoter figure; his responsibilities are most evident in the organization of outdoor work, on trips, in family religious observances (especially the saying of grace), in the settlement of family disputes, and in the family's public life. The father and other males receive certain acts of deference; in large families, they eat before the women.

Whenever the parent or parents remain part of a larger extended household, or whenever a child is given for fosterage to other relatives, an important variant of the child–parent relationship develops. In such instances, clear distinctions arise between the social and the biological parents. The former, with whom the ties of affection and obligation are far more intense, are terminologically distinguished from the latter. This may be variously done: "Big Mama" or "Big Daddy," versus "Mama" or "Daddy"; "Mama" or "Daddy," versus "Little Mama" or "Little Daddy," etc.[16] The distinction in status and feeling is lifelong; one middle-aged man recounted, for example, how his grandfather rather than his father was his primary mentor in customary law. He grieved deeply at his death. In another instance, a granddaughter gave up work to give day-and-night care to her grandmother throughout an extended last illness.

After the early years of cuddling and spanking, children are quite independent. They contribute significantly to the family economy by

[16] Powdermaker's study of a Mississippi Black community in the 1930's reports similar distinctions. In two cases, the social mother was termed "mother," while the biological mother was called by name. In the third instance, the ellided form "mother-dear" was used for the biological mother (Powdermaker 1966 [1939]: 202).

baby-sitting and gardening from early ages on; almost all seek summer work in the cities, once they are fifteen or sixteen. In contrast to old-time practices, their earnings are now their own, although moral obligations to help widowed or single mothers are particularly felt.

Adolescent and grown children expect, on their part, to be backed by parental loyalties and by such parental aid as is feasible. A young woman was much upset on learning that her father had passed on civil rights confidences to his employer, a White planter.[17] Considerable bitterness may develop if young people sense a lack of generosity, rather than of means, in helping their own strenuous efforts to earn money for education. Whenever adult children remain at home rather than migrate, and where sharp differences in racial attitudes occur between generations, property disputes can precipitate major quarrels. A woman working as a domestic for a White family had her militant, bitter, and jobless son arrested for the alleged theft of eleven dollars. The testimony of a small child, his nephew and her grandson, was the basis of the man's conviction in the White court.

The relations between brothers are ideally those of lifelong companion-ship, economic cooperation, solidarity in conflict, and mutual concern. Conflicts between brothers are rare. Brothers-in-law (real or extended) may be as close to each other as brothers. In such cases, the intervening marriage is likely to be exceptionally strong and enduring. Sisters too are close, and cooperate particularly in the care of children and aged relatives. Conversely, the relations between sisters-in-law are not especially close. Those between brothers and sisters are often ambivalent; older brothers especially may be figures of authority more than of affection. In stricter families, particularly in the Hills, they may chaperon their sisters during prolonged courtships. In the cities, brothers seek job opportunities for sisters as well as for brothers. They may take a father's place at weddings and other family ceremonies. If mothers die, older sisters often help rear the younger children. Sisters may sacrifice heavily for the advanced education of their brothers or give up their own life chances to take care of aged parents. In general, the heavy dominance of obligations over voluntary sentiments in brother–sister relationships leads to strains which may be long suppressed but are likely to be manifested in disputes over property, particularly land, when parents die.

[17]   The White community devotes much effort to developing information on Black people, especially to identify and, if possible, to destroy Black leadership. This is an old practice. Davis et al. (1941 : 406) write, for rural Mississippi in the 1930's, that "One of the strongest bonds between colored tenants and white landlords is the 'grapevine,' or the practice of 'tellin' the white folks.'" These authors also note Black resentment of such practices (Davis et al. 1941 : 446–447).

The fundamental relationships of "father and mother, brother and sister" dominate other, especially marital, ties, in sharp contrast to the ideal model of the family in White America (e.g. Schneider 1968: 49).

The Nature of the Marriage Tie

In Holmes County, and among out-migrant Holmes Countians in Chicago, five out of six marriages are between Black natives of the County (Shimkin and Rice 1971: 13–14). They are between members of the same local community[18] who have known each other for years, or the outcomes of courtships, sometimes of several years' duration, or the unions of more mature persons. Few develop from liaisons or consensual relationships, which may, however, be quite stable as such.

Marriages are the cooperative relationships of two persons in the business of life, especially economic cooperation, companionship, and the care of children and other dependents. The spouses' interests and activities tend to be parallel rather than fused.[19] Women often work in the fields, drive tractors, and herd cattle; men may care for children and share in housework. In the community churches, men are deacons and their wives are church mothers. Yet both husbands and wives have many separate economic and social activities; only rarely does a man feel embittered by his wife's independence as a seamstress, midwife, or Head Start cook. Men circulate widely for business and gossip; women also visit widely, especially with their blood relatives. Both husband and wife retain some resources of their own. Nevertheless, there are many close, lasting, and affectionate marriages, marked publicly by mutual respect and consideration. Displays of endearment are very restrained; even pet names for wives, such as "Bunny" or "Rie," are mentioned only in fairly intimate circles. The strongest marriages are those reinforced by other ties, especially good relationships with in-laws on both sides, and by mutual fidelity and sobriety.

[18] "Communities" are small, named localities centered on churches and burying grounds and dominated by a few extended families. Out-migration has greatly reduced the population of the average community, from 500–1,000 to 200–500. Some of the old communities, such as Mt. Olive, north of Lexington, are over a century old; others, such as "Balance Due" and "Tin Cup" in Lexington, are of recent origin.

[19] A wife married thirty years denied involvement in certain disputes of her husband's family, which she felt to be the business of his patrilineage, not hers. A pattern of marital relations among Black workers in Detroit very similar to that in Holmes County has been reported by Blood and Wolfe (1969: 59–64).

Family involvement in marriages also has its adverse aspects. The ready availability of refuges from marital quarrels for contesting spouses and their children in their respective families of procreation aids in the dissolution of marriages. Also, grown children often keep widows and widowers from remarrying, and even unmarried mothers from marrying, because of objections to possible disturbances of established networks of relationships, especially property rights.

Apart from regular marriages, a wide range of sexual relationships, from casual liaisons to stable consensual "keeping," is recognized by Black Holmes Countians. Such relationships, in contrast to marriages, are highly individual and private matters.

Parent–Child Relationships; Fosterage

The relationships of parents to children are, essentially, intensifications of the general relationships of family elders to those younger. Both sexes feel an obligation to provide babies with physical affection, while contingent responsibility for the protection, care, instruction, and discipline of all children is diffused among related adults and, indeed, all adults. Whether the relationships are actually centered in the biological family depends upon circumstances and personalities. Children are readily transferred from the care of an unmarried mother or immature parents, say, to that of grandparents or an uncle and aunt. Less crowding in one household than in another, the availability of Head Start, or better schooling may motivate such adaptive shifts. These are designed for the children's welfare and may, in fact, be initiated by them. Often characterizing the behavior of strong and cohesive extended families, such fosterages are not abandonments of parental responsibility but rather sharings in the deep satisfactions felt by Holmes Countians in child rearing. Although child neglect is not unknown, and children are often burdened with the care for those younger, the truly unwanted child in one household finds a welcome home in another. Thus, while the intensity of parent–child relations found in the White nuclear family under some circumstances is uncommon in Black Holmes County, so too are the savage angers expressed in the "battered child" syndrome so common among lower-class Whites.[20]

---

[20] Rainwater (1970: 225) reports for the Pruitt-Igoe development, where fosterage is apparently less common than in Holmes County, that some women who feel "over-run with children" are afraid to discipline them for fear that they will go too far and seriously hurt them.

The Extended Family as a Corporate Body

As corporate bodies, extended families are identified by numerous features. Critical is the presence of a group of sociological adults, male and female, who are siblings or siblings-in-law, and who are the centers of economic activity, decision making, and care for children and dependents. Also important is a relatively permanent local base, where many members live, own homes and perhaps farmland, participate in a common church, and are buried in its cemetery. Economic cooperation in farming and logging is characteristic; sometimes, there is a joint economic enterprise, such as a café. In other cases the pooling of labor and the exchange of goods are elaborately developed as systems of obligations and equities, guided by joint decision making. There is much reciprocal visiting and communication; the reassembly of dispersed extended families at the funerals of adults, including the burial in Holmes County of those dying in cities, is particularly important. Members of extended families recognize obligations for mutual aid in job-hunting, housing, and the care of children and the ailing. Often a particular member of the family is recognized as its senior spokesman; thus, in 1967, the basic decisions to engage in a community health-research and health-care effort were formally and publicly affirmed by the spokesmen of all the major extended families. Formal meetings of the adult members of an entire extended family are also not uncommon. Among some families an annual meeting has been the custom. These representative mechanisms aid in the internal settlement of family quarrels and in the formation and conduct of common family positions in relation to White people, County politics, and other Black families. All families have distinctive public reputations.[21] Neither extended nor nuclear families are property-holding units as such; land may be rented or sold as well as given between father and sons or between siblings. (However, the voluntary sale of land to Whites is regarded as despicable.) Finally, while some degree of economic sharing is expected throughout extended families, a common budget absolutely controlled by a single person is exceptional today even within a household.[22]

Structurally, the typical extended family of Holmes County includes four kinds of component elements — *elderly persons* who are the objects

[21] Some of these are stereotypes; families with substantial proportions of Indian blood are stated to be somewhat "peculiar," especially reserved and moody. Frazier has noted similar stereotyping (Frazier 1966: 188–189).
[22] In this regard, the "patriarchal" family noted by Frazier, Davis, and others for the 1930's and earlier is an institution of the past in Holmes County. Compare Frazier (1966: 127–141), and Davis et al. (1941: 411–412).

of common orientation and respect, "founders" as it were; a group of *middle-aged siblings* (and sometimes cousins) and their spouses who serve as the "nucleus" families; the *married offspring* and grandchildren of these "nucleus" persons, who form independent households, often in different localities, but who are felt to be "subfamilies" of each "nucleus" family; and a varying assortment of *mobile individuals*, children, adolescents, young adults, and a few older ne'er-do-wells, who shift between households within the extended family in response to personal needs and pressures. The senior men of "nucleus" families and old "subfamilies" are commonly deacons in the same community or urban neighborhood church; the senior women are, correspondingly, church mothers. The "subfamilies" may also be united, especially in cities, through membership in family social clubs.

The Concept of "Strong" and "Weak"

Families have reputations and, in large part, self-identifications as being "strong" or "weak." Strong does not necessarily mean "respectable," which, as Mrs. Hamer has observed in conversation, is for today's Black people a class term meaning "acceptable to Whites."[23] And certainly it does not connote a "patriarchal" dominance. Rather, "strong" is a subtle concept.[24] It expresses a common striving for moral rightness, mutual concern, and economic betterment ("improving") maintained despite the inevitable adversities, the surface compromises, the humiliations, and the periodic human failings of Black life in a savagely hostile White world. Its foundation is, for many Black people in Holmes County, explicitly Old Testament; middle-aged men particularly regard Moses as the ultimate role model.[25] Family strength means not an absence of internal conflicts

---

[23] The discussion in Bernard (1966, esp. 27–30) in regard to "respectability" is very dated.

[24] An insightful discussion of the nature of "strong" families is given in Billingsley (1968: 97–101).

[25] In general, the role of religion in the life of Black Holmes Countians is multiple and complex. It is, however, intimately related to family structure and behavior. The preacher is felt to be most important as a leader in ritual, leading to emotional release in times of crisis. Because of this, while political sagacity, oratorical capacity, and learning add greatly to the respect in which a preacher may be held, even nonintellectual preachers with, say, irritating ideas about "naturals" in church, may still be accepted as ritual leaders. Respected men tend to drift into preaching in middle age; trained ministers are very few.

The religious substratum of Black social behavior was brilliantly delineated, long ago, by W. E. B. DuBois (1965) in "The souls of Black folk."

and behavioral lapses, but a capacity for reconciliation and self-control: family discipline, a taking care of one's own, a guarding of family privacy. The fruits, the ultimate criteria, of a "strong" family are the quality of its children and the security of its aged members.

Family strength is aided by the presence of stable marriages, by property holding — independent farms in the South, home ownership in the North; by membership in churches, fraternal groups, and other agencies of mutual aid; and by education. The mother's engagement in respected activities — as a midwife, a teacher, a participant in church or community affairs — is, in most instances, a definitely positive factor.

Yet this does not identify "strength" with "middle class." There are families, for example, among teachers, with good incomes and formal stability that have widespread reputations for "weakness" engendered by a spouse's alcoholism, reckless gambling, and outrageous philandering (see also Frazier 1966: 137–333). There are also families on welfare headed by widows or unmarried mothers that have reputations for great strength and integrity, notwithstanding occasional lapses. In such families, a defining feature is sons of character who often go into military service (since mobility through higher education is economically not possible for them), contribute to their mother's support, often buying her a house, and themselves form stable husband–wife families.

Correspondingly, the contrast between the strict rules of independent farmers and craftsmen and the extreme permissiveness of plantation workers and domestics has some basis in fact (Rushing 1969). Nevertheless, these social categories are not airtight. A family that once owned land may feel its status as "plantation folk" is only a passing misfortune. It seeks then, perhaps vainly, to maintain behavioral standards appropriate to its past. Moreover, planter paternalism is not altogether a myth, save in the agribusinesses largely owned by Northern corporations. Respect for Black family integrity, aid in crises, and even financial assistance to Black people in buying farms occur not infrequently.

In sum, family "strength" is manifested by behavior, not socioeconomic class or status. And it depends far more on the vitality of the basic consanguineous ties, "father and mother, brother and sister," than it does on those of marriage. Families can withstand the dissolution of marriages, let alone informal liaisons. They terminate when parents and children, brothers and brothers, sisters and sisters, brothers and sisters, are lastingly alienated.

To summarize: extended families, namely, corporate bodies of a few to many households unified primarily by descent and exogamy, are fundamental elements of Black society in Holmes County, Mississippi. These institutions are objects of much customary law, particularly in regard to obligations toward parents, grown siblings, and dependent children; and in the regulation of relations between extended families. They are normally reinforced by propinquity in local "communities," by membership in the same local church, and by burial in the same graveyard. Within extended families, dependent and mobile members are readily transferred between households, so that the entire family acts as one system of mutual support. Marriage, adult adoption, and births recruit members; the breakup of marriages and liaisons and the long-term departure of migrant members loosen ties. However, recognitions of fatherhood, attendance at the funerals of kinsfolk, and marriage with other Black Holmes Countians at home or in migratory destinations are ultimate signs of family membership that are but slowly relinquished.

These general features encompass a large range of specific behaviors and attitudes, which are sometimes the distinctions of a particular extended family. This range can be indicated, albeit in a fragmentary way, by the sketches of two extended families of contrasting history: the Bidwells and the Mitchells.

A MIGRATORY UPWARD-MOBILE FAMILY: THE BIDWELLS

Out-Migration from Holmes County

Since the start of substantial out-migration from Holmes County during World War I, over 35,000 Black Holmes Countians have moved to other, primarily urban, localities. In fact, it is estimated that almost two-thirds of the living Black natives of Holmes County are now resident elsewhere. Chicago has been the most important destination, the home of perhaps 40 percent of the out-migrants. Other important destinations include Detroit; St. Louis; Waterloo, Iowa; New York City; Los Angeles; Memphis; and Jackson, Mississippi. Service in the Armed Forces, including long-term service in the Army and Air Force, has also been significant (see Shimkin 1971 for a fuller analysis).

The Holmes County migrations have resulted in the formation of extensive networks of relationships, maintained by much communication and return visiting, that serve today to direct individual movements and the formation of new colonies toward favorable opportunities. The process is highly dynamic; established colonies, such as those in Chicago, are not only the targets of migration but also the sources of secondary movements, for example, to Minneapolis and smaller cities in Illinois where jobs appear plentiful and housing and schooling conditions better.[26] In fact, a statistically measurable return migration of adolescents back to Holmes County has recently developed in consequence of parental and, indeed, young peoples' fears of ghetto disorganization. This has augmented an earlier trend, the return migration of retired individuals and couples (Shimkin and Rice 1971: 21–25).

The networks governing migration are primarily those of individual extended families, cross-connected by friendships and exchanges of information in Holmes County and, to a lesser degree, by message centers (especially, particular cafés), churches, and migrant associations in the larger colonies.

The Bidwell Family as a Migratory Network

The Bidwell family constitutes such a network (see Tables 3 and 4).[27] In general terms, this extended, patrilineal family of independent farm origins is strong and cohesive, with few broken marriages and unmarried mothers. It includes five generations, the issue of two couples, grandparents of the young adults who are actively in the processes of physical and social mobility. In this generation (III), lateral relations extend to first cousin; second-cousin relationships are maintained among their children. Although the fertile years of this generation still continue, the number of children per woman (less than one) is strikingly less than in generations I (6) and II (4).

In Holmes County, the Bidwells have been vigorous participants in the Civil Rights movement since the early 1960's. Everywhere in this family, considerable strivings toward stable employment, better education, and home ownership have been evident. Church activities have provided important foci for the family's social life. Economically, most of its members have yet to attain security; in Holmes County, they are perhaps in the upper third of the Black community. In Chicago, they reside mostly

---

[26] For an extremely perceptive and careful account of the flight of a family from Mississippi to residence in Springfield, Illinois, see Ben H. Bagdikian (1967) "The new immigrants." The family in question had come earlier from Holmes County to Bolivar County, whence it fled White threats in 1967.
[27] All names and localities other than major cities mentioned in connection with the Bidwell Family are pseudonyms. In addition, a few minor facts that would otherwise closely identify individuals have been altered.

in areas of the "upper poor."[28] Only one of the nucleus families is definitely affluent; at least one household is very poor.

More specifically, Gloria Jean Louie, beginning with Nucleus Family VIII (see Table 3), identified a body of 101 Bidwell kinsmen, whose 93 living members interact, at least periodically, and who express feelings of reciprocal obligation to form the Bidwell family and its allies. As of 1969, only 58 of the living members had been born in Holmes County, and only 17 of the Holmes County natives were still resident there. Twenty-five of the remaining 41 were in Chicago; seven in Jackson, Mississippi; five in Detroit; two in New York; one each in St. Louis and the Armed Forces. Thirty-five children and spouses born elsewhere have been identified. Twenty-two of them were in Chicago, eight in Jackson, Mississippi, and one each in Detroit and the Armed Forces. The current residences of three were unknown, although none lived in Holmes County. In sum, while the Bidwell family is of Holmes County origin, and while its culture and social identity are as yet profoundly rooted in the County, only 18 percent of its living members resided there in 1969, compared to 50 percent in Chicago.

This redistribution of population began, not with the earliest waves of Holmes Countian migration north during World War I, but in the mid-1930's when Eddie Bidwell and his family moved to Detroit in search of work. During the early 1940's, a period of intense out-migration among Black Holmes Countians generally, three more families and two individuals became established in Detroit, Chicago, and Jackson, Mississippi. Between 1949 and 1952, these were joined by a couple and a family in Chicago and by another family in Jackson.

Since 1955, a markedly different pattern of migration has developed. In the earlier period, six families, one couple, and two individuals had moved. The migrants included persons in their teens and twenties to late thirties and young children; the adults were poorly educated farm people who sought, at least initially, whatever blue-collar jobs might be available.

In the later period, 1955–1968, the migrants included seven individuals, three couples, and only one family. They averaged 18–22 years of age, and had high school educations. Guided by advice from relatives, they have known where and how to seek jobs or further education; these relatives have also provided them with shelter and emotional support. Moreover, while the young migrants have had strong desires for families and homes

[28]   These areas and their socioeconomic evolutions are taken from M. Lepper and J. Lashoff (1969) *Preliminary report on patterns of medical and health care in poverty areas of Chicago*. The basic socioeconomic data used were for 1960 and 1964; this study has generally tended to understate the intensity of poverty currently present in these areas.

Table 3. Components of family structure: the Bidwells[a]

Generation		Persons			Living in 1969	Marriages			Separations[b]
Number	Designation	Total	Male	Female		Total	Formal	Consensual	
I	"Founder"	4	2	2	2	2	2	0	0
II	"Nucleus"	19	9	10	16	8+d	8+d	0+d	1
III	"Subfamily"	56	30	26	53	14+d	13+d	1+d	2+d
IV	"Subfamily dependent"	21	9	12	21	1	0	1	1
V	"Subfamily grandchild"	1	0	1	1	0	0	0	0
All generations		101	50	51	93	25+d	23+d	2+d	4+d

Span of Relationships

Generation		Offspring		Siblings[c]		1st cousins		2nd cousins	
Number	Designation	Sets	Persons	Sets	Persons	Sets	Persons	Sets	Persons
I	"Founder"	2	12	n.a.[f]	n.a.[f]	n.a.[f]	n.a.[f]	n.a.[f]	n.a.[f]
II	"Nucleus"	9	42[e]	2	12	0	0	0	0
III	"Subfamily"	9	21	9	42	9	42	9	21
IV	"Subfamily dependent"	1	1	6	18	7	18	0	0
V	"Subfamily grandchild"	0	0	0	0	0	0	0	21
All generations		27	76	17	72	16	60	9	21

Notes: [a] Compiled by Charles Williams and Gloria J. Louie; see also Table 4.
[b] No formal divorces recorded.
[c] No half siblings recorded.
[d] Additional cases indicated but not verified.
[e] Includes 2 adult adoptions; see text.
[f] Data not available.

Table 4.   The Bidwell family and its allies in late 1969

Legend:

Gen. ....Generation	Y .....Yes	
F ("Founder" family)............Grandparent	N .....No	
N ("Nucleus" family) ....Parent	M .....Male	
S ("Subfamily") ....Child	F .....Female	
SD₁ ("Subfamily" dependents) ...Grandchild	() .....Approximate age	
SD₂ ("Subfamily dependents") ...Greatgrandchild	Loc'n..Location	
Index numbers	AF .....Armed Forces	
	Ch .....Chicago	
A ....Family/household unit	D .....Detroit	
	HC ..Holmes County	
B ....Person	J .....Jackson, Miss.	
	NY ...New York, N.Y.	
Family member's name ....Jeff Bidwell	SL ....St. Louis, Mo.	
Ally's name ....*Bill Walker*		
Data not available XX	9a .....Adopted	
Item inapplicable or lacking ....—	7x .....Separated	

Index number		Name		1969 Status				Relationships				
Gen.	A	B First	Last	(Maiden)	Sex	Alive	Age	Loc'n	Parents	Siblings	Spouse	Children
F	I	1 Jeff	Bidwell		M	Y	87	HC	XX	XX	2	5-14
	I	2 Jane	Bidwell	(XX)	F	N	—	—	XX	XX	1	5-14
	XII	3 *Charles*	*Walker*		M	N	—	—	XX	XX	4	15, 16
	XII	4 *Aretha*	*Walker*		F	Y	67	HC	XX	XX	3	15, 16
N	I	5 Sylvia	Peters	(Bidwell)	F	Y	67	Ch	1, 2	6-14	17	25, 26

Table 4 (cont.)

Generation group markers (far-left "Gen." column): **II** aligns with index 6; **N** brackets indices 7–24.

Gen.	A	B First	(Maiden) Last	Sex	Alive	Age	Loc'n	Parents	Siblings	Spouse	Children
II	6	Carmilla	(Bidwell) Crane	F	Y	65	J	1, 2	5, 7-14	18	27, 28
III	7	Eddie	Bidwell	M	Y	(64)	D	1, 2	5, 6, 8-14	19	29-31
IV	8	Dorethy	(Bidwell) Jones	F	Y	(63)	Ch	1, 2	5-7, 9-14	XX	32-4
V	9	Nathine	XX	F	Y	(62)	D	1, 2	5-8, 10-14	XX	XX
VI	10	Ben	Bidwell	M	Y	(60)	HC	1, 2	5-9, 11-14	20	35-9, 41a
VII	11	Bob	Bidwell	M	N	—	—	1, 2	5-10, 12-14	21	43-8
VIII	12	Lorenzo	Bidwell	M	Y	52	HC	1, 2	5-11, 13-14	16	50-8, 64a, 65a
IX	13	Mary	(Bidwell) Cute	F	Y	48	Ch	1, 2	5-12, 14	22	66-8
X	14	Shelia	(Bidwell) Curtis	F	Y	45	J	1, 2	5-13	23	71-5
XII	15	*Bill*	*Walker*	M	Y	52	HC	3, 4	16	XX	XX
VIII	16	*Viola*	(*Walker*) Bidwell	F	Y	51	HC	3, 4	15	12	50-8, 64a, 65a
I	17	Jessie	Peters	M	N	—	—	XX	XX	5	25-6
II	18	Michael	Crane	M	N	—	—	XX	XX	6	27-8
III	19	Carmilla	(XX) Bidwell	F	Y	(58)	D	XX	XX	7	29-31
VI	20	Alma	(William) Bidwell	F	Y	58	HC	XX	XX	10	35-9, 41a
VII	21	Sue	(Stone) Bidwell	F	Y	49	HC	XX	XX	11	43-8
IX	22	John	Cute	M	Y	55	Ch	XX	24, XX	13	63-5
X	23	Bill	Curtis	M	Y	53	J	XX	XX	14	71-5
XI	24	*Alex*	*Stone*	M	Y	XX	NY	XX	21, XX	XX	XX

Table 4 (cont.)

Gen.	Index number		Name		1969 Status				Relationships			
	A	B	First	(Maiden) Last	Sex	Alive	Age	Loc'n	Parents	Siblings	Spouse	Children
S	I	25	Fannie	Peters	F	Y	42	Ch	5, 17	26	—	—
	I.1	26	Cynthia	(Peters) XX	F	Y	XX	Ch	5, 17	25	XX	XX
	II	27	Melvin	Crane	M	Y	29	J	6, 18	28	—	—
	II	28	Ed	Crane	M	Y	23	J	6, 18	27	—	—
	III.1	29	Rebecca	(Bidwell) XX	F	Y	(40)	D	7, 19	30, 31	XX	XX
	III.2	30	George	Bidwell	M	Y	(35)	D	7, 19	29, 31	XX	XX
	III.3	31	Tom	Bidwell	M	Y	(30)	D	7, 19	29, 30	XX	XX
	IV	32	L. C.	Jones	M	Y	19	Ch	8, XX	33, 34	—	—
	IV	33	James	Jones	M	Y	(17)	Ch	8, XX	32, 34	—	—
	IV	34	Herbert	Jones	M	Y	(15)	Ch	8, XX	32, 33	—	—
	VI.1	35	Lydia	(Bidwell) Bowman	F	Y	40	Ch	10, 20	36-9, 41a	40	—
	VI.2	36	Pearlie	(Bidwell) Neill	F	Y	—		10, 20	35, 37-9	41	80, 81
	VI	37	Warrine	Bidwell	F	N	—	—	10, 20	35-6, 38-9	—	—
	VI.3	38	Ken	Bidwell	M	N	33	—	10, 20	35-7, 39, 41a	XX	XX
	VI.4	39	Normann	Bidwell	F	Y	31	Ch	10, 20	35-8, 41a	—	—
	VI.1	40	Sylvester	Bowman	M	Y	41	Ch	XX	XX	35	80, 8
	VI.2	41	Leslie	Neill, Sr.	M	Y	(40)	HC	10a, 20a	35-9a	36	82
	VII.1	42	Betty	Bidwell	F	Y	27	SL	11, 21	43-48	49	—
	VII.2	43	Stewart	Bidwell	M	Y	(24)	Ch	11, 21	42, 44-8	—	—
	VII	44	Franklin	Bidwell	M	N	—	—	11, 21	42-3, 45-8	—	—
	VII.3	45	Lee	Bidwell	M	Y	21	AF	11, 21	42-4, 46-8	—	—
	XI	46	Diane	Bidwell	F	Y	19	NY	11, 21	42-5, 47-8	—	—
	VII	47	Grace	Bidwell	F	Y	16	HC	11, 21	42-6, 48	—	—

Table 4 (*cont.*)

Gen.	Index number A	Name B First	(Maiden) Last	Sex	Alive	Age	Loc'n	Parents	Siblings	Spouse	Children
S											
VII	48	Millie	Bidwell (XX)	F	Y	11	HC	11, 21	42–47	—	—
VII.2	49	Bess	Bidwell (XX)	F	Y	(21)	HC	XX	XX	43	82
VIII.1	50	Yolanda	Rudolph (Bidwell)	F	Y	32	Ch	12, 16	51–58, 64a, 65a	59	83–9
VIII.2	51	Ruthann	Patterson (Bidwell)	F	Y	29	Ch	12, 16	50, 52–8, 64a, 65a	60	90–2
VIII.3	52	Barbara	Wilson (Bidwell)	F	Y	26	Ch	12, 16	50–1, 53–58, 64a, 65a	61	93–4
VIII.4	53	Shrom	Smith (Bidwell)	F	Y	23	Ch	12, 16	50–2, 54–58, 64a, 65a	62	95–6
VIII.5	54	Catherine	Jackson (Bidwell)	F	Y	21	Ch	12, 16	50–3, 55–58, 64a, 65a	63	—
VIII.3	55	Veevee	Bidwell	F	Y	19	Ch	12, 16	50–4, 56–58, 64a, 65a	—	—
VIII	56	Larry	Bidwell	M	Y	16	HC	12, 16	50–5, 57–58, 64a, 65a	—	—
VIII	57	Belinda	Bidwell	F	Y	14	HC	12, 16	50–6, 58, 64a, 65a	—	—
VIII	58	Irene	Bidwell	F	Y	10	HC	12, 16	50–57, 64a, 65a	—	—
VIII.1	59	Alex	Rudolph	M	Y	37	Ch	XX	XX	50	83–9
VIII.2	60	Dan	Patterson	M	Y	30	Ch	XX	XX	51	90–2
VIII.3	61	Bob	Wilson	M	Y	29	Ch	XX	XX	52	93–4
VIII.4	62	William	Smith	M	Y	24	Ch	XX	XX	53	95–6
VIII.5	63	Allen	Jackson	M	Y	22	Ch	XX	XX	54	—
XX	64	David	Henry	M	Y	(25)	XX	12a, 16a	50–58a, XX	XX	XX
XX	65	Jack	Williams	M	Y	(25)	XX	12a, 16a	50–58a, XX	XX	XX
IX.1	66	Hattie	(Cute) Brown	F	Y	29	Ch	13, 22	67–8	69	XX
IX.2	67	Bernice	(Cute) Cooper	F	Y	26	Ch	13, 22	66, 68	70	XX

Table 4 (cont.)

Gen.	Index number A	B	First	(Maiden) Last	Sex	Alive	Age	Loc'n	Parents	Siblings	Spouse	Children
S	IX.3	68	Booker	Cute	M	Y	23	AF	13, 22	66–7	—	—
	IX.1	69	Willie	Brown	M	Y	XX	Ch	XX	XX	66	XX
	IX.2	70	Ralthus	Cooper	M	Y	XX	Ch	XX	XX	67	XX
	X	71	Alvin	Curtis	M	Y	26	J	14, 23	72–5	76x	—
	X.1	72	Charles	Curtis	M	Y	24	Ch	14, 23	71, 73–5	77	XX
	X.2	73	Geraldine	(Curtis) Byrd	F	Y	23	J	14, 23	71–2, 74–5	78	97–8
	X.3	74	Yvette	(Curtis) Ford	F	Y	21	J	14, 23	71–3, 75	79x	99
	X.4	75	Vanita	Curtis	F	Y	18	J	14, 23	71–4	—	100
	XX	76	Mary	(XX) Curtis	F	Y	XX	J	XX	XX	71x	—
	X.1	77	Charlean	(Miller) Curtis	F	Y	22	Ch	XX	XX	72	XX
	X.2	78	Bolivar	Byrd	F	Y	XX	J	XX	XX	73	97–8
	XX	79	Sam	Ford	M	Y	XX	XX	XX	XX	74x	99
SD₁	VI	80	Leslie	Neill, Jr.	M	Y	(18)	HC	36, 41	81	—	—
	VI	81	Sandra	Neill	F	Y	(15)	HC	36, 41	80	—	—
	VII.2	82	Stewart	Bidwell, Jr.	M	Y	4	Ch	43, 49	—	—	—
	VIII.1	83	Debra	Rudolph	F	Y	16	Ch	50, 59	84–9	—	101
	VIII.1	84	Albert	Rudolph	M	Y	14	Ch (HC)	50, 59	83, 85–9	—	—
	VIII.1	85	Tony	Rudolph	M	Y	12	Ch	50, 59	83–4, 86–9	—	—
	VIII.1	86	Peter	Rudolph	M	Y	11	Ch	50, 59	83–5, 87–9	—	—
	VIII.1	87	Ann	Rudolph	F	Y	9	Ch	50, 59	83–6, 88–9	—	—
	VIII.1	88	Judy	Rudolph	F	Y	8	Ch	50, 59	83–7, 89	—	—
	VIII.1	89	Virginia	Rudolph	F	Y	7	Ch	50, 59	83–8	—	—

Table 4 (*cont.*)

		Name		1969 Status				Relationships			
Gen.	Index number A	B First	(Maiden) Last	Sex	Alive	Age	Loc'n	Parents	Siblings	Spouse	Children
	VIII.2	90 Joann	Patterson	F	Y	10	Ch	51, 60	91, 92	—	—
	VIII.2	91 Belinda	Patterson	F	Y	8	Ch	51, 60	90, 92	—	—
	VIII.2	92 Lorraine	Patterson	F	Y	6	Ch	51, 60	90–91	—	—
	VIII.3	93 Doris	Wilson	F	Y	7	Ch	52, 61	94	—	—
	VIII.3	94 Bruce	Wilson	M	Y	4	Ch	52, 61	93	—	—
	VIII.4	95 Reba	Smith	F	Y	5	Ch	53, 62	96	—	—
	VIII	96 Luther	Smith	M	Y	4	Ch (HC)	53, 62	95	—	—
	X.2	97 Jeff	Byrd	M	Y	6	J	73, 78	98	—	—
	X.2	98 Dorethy	Byrd	F	Y	3	J	73, 78	97	—	—
	X.3	99 Josephine	Ford	F	Y	2	J	74, 79	—	—	—
	X	100 Author	Curtis	M	Y	1	J	75	—	—	—
SD₂	VIII.1	101 Lois	Rudolph	F	Y	0	Ch	83	—	—	—

of their own, almost all have exercised birth control to delay or limit births until adequate resources could be amassed. For five of the migrants, military service has been a mechanism of mobility. In consequence of all these advantages, the younger migrants are gaining both skilled industrial jobs, especially in steel manufacturing, and white-collar ones: clerk, dietician, teacher.

The average member of the Bidwell family today (1969) is a young man or woman in his early 20's. Only one member of the very aged, Mr. Jeff Bidwell, survives; in fact, only eight are above sixty — tragic testimony to the hardships of Black life in contemporary America. Children under ten number 15. Most important, 52 family members out of 93 are in the ages of 20–59. Thus the Bidwell family, in sharp contrast to the resident Black population of Holmes County, has an economically favorable age composition. Moreover, within the ages of 20 and 59, the men outnumber the women, 28 to 24, a truly dramatic contrast with Holmes County, where only 60 men are to be found for every hundred women in this age group. In sum, the Bidwell Family, like other dispersed, migratory, extended families based in Holmes County, has far greater socioeconomic capacity than is evidenced in rural Mississippi alone.

Structurally, the center of family identity remains in Pleasant View community, near the edge of the hills in Holmes County, where Bidwells still hold land and where the Jerusalem Baptist Church is served by Bidwell deacons and church mothers. Here Bidwells dying locally or, in some cases, in distant cities, have been laid to rest for generations. Here also lives the widower, Jeff Bidwell, whose frailty and loneliness find relief in the respect and care of his family, especially his middle-aged sons and daughters.

Of the nucleus families, five — Ben Bidwell's (VI), Bob Bidwell's (VII), and Lorenzo Bidwell's (VIII) in Holmes County, John Cute's (IX) in Chicago and Bill Curtis' (X) in Jackson, Mississippi — have been particularly strong and cohesive elements of the Bidwell family as a corporate body. Eddie Bidwell (III) in Detroit has been more remote, while the other nucleus families are those of widows and unmarried women. At the same time, important roles in the fosterage of Bidwell children and in other aid have been played by allied families, notably those of Aretha Walker (F II) and Alex Stone (XI) (see Table 4). Sub-family development has been especially evident in Chicago.

Bidwell Family Lifeways

Below are sketches of varying length and scope on the lifeways of the Bidwells. Such unevenness is inherent in the observation and elicitation of personal information during relatively brief fieldwork.

Nevertheless, these sketches illustrate in lively fashion many of the points discussed in the previous section, such as mutual aid among sisters, visiting patterns, and the drive for educational improvement. The aggregate picture of a stable, hardworking, and hopeful group is profoundly different from the stereotype of Black family life available from the literature. It is believed, however, to typify the "stronger" Holmes County families and a great many other families throughout Black America.

The sketches cover about two-thirds of the Bidwell family; they are grouped by nucleus family and related subfamilies (see also Table 3).

NUCLEUS FAMILY I. Mrs. Sylvia Peters (5), the oldest child of Jeff (1) and Jane (2) Bidwell, is sixty-seven years old. She was born and raised in Pleasant View. Her late husband, Jessie Peters (17) who died in 1966 at the age of seventy-five, came from a Delta community five miles away, Plum Creek. When he was young, it numbered a thousand people but it is now very small.

When they were married, the Peterses moved to Plum Creek, where Jessie bought a small house. Their two children, Fannie (25) and Cynthia (26) were born here. Just before World War II, Jessie Peters was able to get a steady job as a workman on the Illinois Central Railroad. In 1942, when labor was short, Jessie was transferred to a better railroad job in Chicago, where he worked until retirement.

During World War II the Peterses saved their money, and in 1950 they moved to their present home, which has two flats and a basement apartment. A year later, Sylvia Peters's sister, Mary Cute (13) and her husband John (22), joined the Peterses. The two families have since been able to buy the building. They rent the basement apartment to their nephew Stewart Bidwell (43), the oldest son of Bob Bidwell (11), and his family.

The Peterses' older daughter, Fannie (25), now aged forty-two, has never married and still lives with Mrs. Peters in the second-floor flat. Earlier, the Peterses had "adopted," i.e. fostered, their nephew L. C. Jones (32). Sylvia Peters's sister, Dorethy Jones (8), had been abandoned by her husband and had had a hard time raising her three boys by herself. L. C. is now living with his mother, while Dorethy's youngest boy Herbert (34) is visiting with the Peterses.

Mrs. Peters's church is a block from her apartment. She and her sister Dorethy (8) are both church mothers there. Although Dorethy lives only four blocks away, she doesn't always have a chance to visit with her sister, but they always get together at church.

Mrs. Peters visits home every year; sometimes she stays three weeks or a month. She goes home to be around her father, Jeff (1), cooking and cleaning house for him. She also visits her other relatives in Holmes County and Jackson, Mississippi.

NUCLEUS FAMILY II. Carmilla Crane (6), the second daughter, is sixty-five years old and also a widow. Her late husband, Michael (18), was a fellow Holmes Countian. They moved to Jackson, Mississippi, in 1942, where Mr. Crane died twelve years later. Carmilla was left with two boys, Melvin (27), then fourteen, and Ed (28), then eight years old. But she held her family together and insisted that the boys finish high school. At first, after her husband's death, she tried to live in Holmes County, but after two years returned to Jackson where jobs were more plentiful.

After high school, Melvin went into the Army. When he was finally discharged he used his veteran's rights to go to City State College, which he is still attending. Melvin and Ed live with their mother; neither has married.

NUCLEUS FAMILY III. Eddie Bidwell (7), Jeff (1) and Jane (2) Bidwell's oldest son, was born and raised in Pleasant View, a Hill community of 300 people today. Eddie only graduated from the fifth grade, but was ambitious to improve himself.

When he married Carmilla (19), he moved to a small community, Paul Williams, three miles from Pleasant View. But the depression ruined him, and he and his wife made a bare living as farm workers, chopping and picking cotton. In 1934, they and their little girl Rebecca (29) made their way to Detroit, where Eddie found a job with a coal dealer.

Eddie was a hard and faithful worker. As a result, when the coal dealer retired, he gave his business to Eddie.

The Eddie Bidwells are homeowners and well off. They have three children: Rebecca, and two sons born in Detroit. All are married and visit with their parents only occasionally.

Major emergencies alone bring Eddie Bidwell back to Holmes County.

NUCLEUS FAMILY VI. Ben Bidwell (10), still lives and farms in Pleasant View, where he was born sixty years ago. Forty-three years ago, when he had finished the sixth grade and Alma William (20), then fifteen, had finished the seventh grade, they were married. At first they lived with his father, Jeff Bidwell (1), but later Ben bought his own land and rented more from his father.

The Ben Bidwells have had five children. The oldest, Lydia Bowman (35), is now forty, married, and living in Chicago; one, Pearlie Neill (36), died during childbirth; another, Warrine (37), died of sickness at an early age; the two youngest, Ken (38), a son aged thirty-three, and Normann (39), a daughter aged thirty-one, are in Chicago.

Ben Bidwell is a farmer, but his health isn't good enough now for him to do a lot of hard work. His wife Alma helps him. She also looks after her father-in-law, Jeff Bidwell (1), and sees that he gets his meals every day. The Ben Bidwells are buying a new house which they had built in 1968. Living with them are two grandchildren, Leslie Neill, Jr. (80), and Sandra Neill (81). Young Leslie, now eighteen, does all the cultivating on Ben Bidwell's land; Lorenzo Bidwell (12) and his son, Larry (56), have also helped in the spring planting for the past two years. Before that, Ben and his late brother Bob (11) used to work together. Sandra Neill, now fifteen, goes to school full time. The Ben Bidwell's son-in-law and adopted son, Leslie Neill, Sr. (41), often spends the night with them.

The Ben Bidwells attend the Jerusalem Baptist Church in their community. They read mostly farm magazines and the *Lexington Advertiser*. They study mail-order catalogues closely to buy well.

Subfamily VI. 1. Lydia (Bidwell) Bowman (35) and her husband Sylvester (40) were both born in the Pleasant View community of Holmes County. They attended a little elementary school in the community, but neither went to high school. In 1949, when he was twenty-one and she was twenty, they married and went to Chicago. They have worked hard and moved to a nice place on the South Side four years ago. They have no children.

They visit Mississippi about every two years, and in emergencies.

Subfamily VI. 4. Normann Bidwell (39) lives at the same address as the Bowmans (35, 40) but in a different apartment. She left Holmes County when she was seventeen, after finishing the eighth grade. Still single, she has had a hard time since 1955. She is now taking up a trade and trying to finish her high school education by going to night school.

She is not a regular member of her cousins' social club (see Subfamily VII.2), but she comes in once in a while. Every two years or so she visits Mississippi.

NUCLEUS FAMILY VII. The late Bob Bidwell (11) was fifty-five when he died two years ago; his widow, Sue (21), is now forty-nine. Bob lived in Pleasant View all his life. He graduated from the sixth grade and then had to go to work to help his family. All his life he was a farmer, cultivating land he rented from his father.

When Bob was twenty-four, he married Sue Stone (21), who was then sixteen and had graduated from the eighth grade. They settled in Pleasant View and had seven children, one of whom, Franklin (44), died of heart disease. Of the other six, Betty (42) is in St. Louis, Stewart (43) is in Chicago, Lee (45) is in the Army, and Diane (46) is in New York. Only the two youngest children are at home with Mrs. Bidwell; they are Grace (47), now in the tenth grade at age sixteen, and Millie (48), in the sixth grade at age eleven.

When Bob Bidwell died, Sue Bidwell could no longer operate the farm, so she moved to Oldtown where she got a job as a secretary with a federal program. She really enjoys her work very much. It only takes her about ten minutes to get to work, and she works only days. The federal program staff wanted her to finish high school, and she has been able to do so by attending classes in the evening. Sue misses Bob greatly, but she and the children are making it.

Subfamily VII.1. Betty Bidwell (42), and Bob and Sue Bidwell's oldest child, graduated from Lake Port Vocational High School at eighteen. She then moved to Jackson, Mississippi, where she stayed with her father's sister, Shelia Curtis (14). She worked in Jackson for a year, but felt that she could do better in Chicago. After a short time there, she was able to get a still better job in St. Louis, where she now lives. She has her own three-room apartment; she is still single at twenty-seven.

Betty visits Mississippi about once a year, staying there for two to three weeks.

Subfamily VII.2. Stewart Bidwell (43), Bob and Sue Bidwell's oldest son, also grew up in the Pleasant View community. Just like most young men from the Hill area of Holmes County, he met his wife, Bess (49), at church; church is the regular meeting place for Blacks in Mississippi. Bess is also from Pleasant View, but Stewart did not know her well until they started courting.

They got married in 1965, when they left school; their son, Stewart, Jr. (82) was born in 1966. They knew that jobs for young people were hard to get in Holmes County, so they moved to Chicago. Here they live in the basement apartment of the house owned by Stewart's aunts and uncles, the Peterses (Nucleus Family I) and the Cutes (Nucleus Family IX). Both Stewart and Bess work; they are trying to save money to buy a house before having any more children.

The Stewart Bidwells communicate a good deal with other young Holmes Countians in Chicago. Stewart is a regular member of a social club limited to Holmes Countians, to which William Smith (62, Subfamily VIII.4) also belongs. The club members are almost all in their early twenties. Whenever they give any type of entertainment the people who attend are 90 percent Holmes Countians. They don't have Illinois people in the club because they do not know them as well and they feel that "outsiders," as they call them, may bring confusion.

The Stewart Bidwells try to visit Holmes County once a year, when they both have vacations. Otherwise, just Bess and the baby visit, for two or three weeks. In this, as in most other Bidwell families, the women do most of the visiting.

Subfamily VII.3. Lee Bidwell (45) only went through the eleventh grade. He did not want to continue in school, which he felt was a waste of time. In the summer of 1966, when he was eighteen, he went to Chicago to look for work. He could not find what he wanted to do for quite a while, but he was then drafted into the Army. He has done well and reenlisted since.

Lee visits home every chance the Army gives him, which is about twice a year. He is still single.

NUCLEUS FAMILY XI. Diane Bidwell (46) graduated from high school when she was seventeen. Her father died, but she wanted to continue her education and so needed to make money. She found she could do both in New York, where she is now living with her mother's brother, Alex Stone (24) and his family.

Diane hasn't returned to Holmes County since she left in August of 1968. However, she does write regularly to her mother and other relatives in Mississippi.

NUCLEUS FAMILY VIII. Lorenzo Bidwell (12) grew up and went to school in the Pleasant View community, finishing the sixth grade. When he was nineteen, he married Viola Walker (16) who was a year younger and had finished the eighth grade. Viola came from the Fox Run community, which is now very small but used to be almost as large as Pleasant View, from which it is separated by only a bridge.

At first, Lorenzo and Viola lived in Pleasant View, where he farmed land rented from his father. Part of the time he travelled all over the

South, working gravel pits. Although their family was growing, Lorenzo and Viola were able to start buying a house and farm of their own in 1948, in the Strongheart community. This was closer to Viola's parents' home; the community, although numbering less than 200 people, was almost all Black; and the farm had rich, fresh soil.

The Lorenzo Bidwells have had nine children, five of whom are married and living in Chicago; another is in college, and three are still in school in Holmes County. They include Yolanda Rudolph (50), aged thirty-two; Ruthann Patterson (51), aged twenty-nine; Barbara Wilson (52), aged twenty-six; Shrom Smith (53), aged twenty-three; all but one are high school graduates. Veevee Bidwell (55), aged nineteen, goes to Prairie College, but also spends a lot of time with her sister, Barbara. Larry (56) is only sixteen but has been working on his father's and his uncle Ben's (10) farms for the past three years. He is in high school. Belinda (57), who is fourteen, is in junior high school; Irene (58), the youngest child, is ten and in grade school.

The Lorenzo Bidwells have two adopted sons, both former civil rights workers.

This is how it came about: In 1963, Mr. Robert Moses of SNCC came to Greenwood in Leflore County to tell people they should seek their rights as voters and citizens. Two people from Holmes County, a middle-aged brother and sister, heard him and felt he was right. They talked to other people, including some in the Strongheart community, and they agreed. They met and talked for months before trying to act, for this was very dangerous, as they well knew.

Then in the summer of 1964, SNCC and other groups brought a lot of young people to help register voters, educate people, build community centers, and set up kindergartens, libraries, and health centers. The Black people of Holmes County took these young people into their homes and protected them against the Ku Klux Klan. Many times, Lorenzo Bidwell and others were up all night with their guns on their laps. There was some trouble, but the Klan learned that, while Holmes County Black people would start no fight, they were ready, and would and did shoot back if attacked.

David Henry (64) was a young Black man from the Delta in Mississippi, but already an experienced civil rights worker when he came to live with the Lorenzo Bidwells. He stayed for two years before he married a girl from another family in the Strongheart community. David really got involved in the Bidwell family by his great attention to the younger children.

He helped them with their homework, played games, and helped with work around the farm. Separated from his own family, he was lonesome. One time he asked Mrs. Bidwell if he could call her "Mom"; he heard the word "Mother-dear" around the house all day. At first, the children objected to his calling her "Mom," because they did not feel that someone not related by blood should do so. But then they felt he had really become their brother.

Jack Williams (65), a Caucasian, came from Iowa to Mississippi a little later than David did in 1964. He stayed with the Lorenzo Bidwells a year and a half. Jack helped the children with their homework regularly. He had graduated from college; therefore, he was able to help even more than David in explaining materials. He too became the children's brother.

Raising and educating children keeps the Lorenzo Bidwells busy. Mr. Lorenzo Bidwell is a farmer who works days and nights. A person who owns a farm has to work whenever he can. Sometimes, especially during tilling season, it rains a lot, and little is done. Later on, lost time needs to be made up, in order to plant on time. And farmers have to work together. Larry (56) does most of the cultivating for his father. He and his father also help back and forth with Bill Walker (15), Lorenzo Bidwell's brother-in-law, and his son, during planting and harvesting. They rent a cotton picker from the Black farmers' co-op to pick their cotton.

During his leisure time, Lorenzo Bidwell fixes electric and hand pumps.

Mrs. Viola Bidwell has a garden where she raises all types of vegetables; these are then canned. Generally every summer one of her daughters from the North comes down to help her in this work. Mrs. Bidwell is also a Head Start teacher. When Head Start was first organized by the Black people of Holmes County, very few of the college graduate teachers would help. So grass-roots people had to learn to teach. One of them was Mrs. Bidwell, who has worked hard; she has finished high school through night classes. She and her family read a good deal: *the Lexington Advertiser, Farm Report*, the General Electric newspaper, and different kinds of magazines. Also, they get mail-order catalogues to be able to buy well.

The Lorenzo Bidwell family attends the Strongheart Baptist Church, which is four miles from their farm. When they had just arrived in the community, they used to walk there. It was only years later that they could buy a car. Today, Lorenzo Bidwell is a deacon and Viola Bidwell a mother of the church. Lorenzo and Viola also remain active in County affairs; every third Sunday of the month, they join with people in their own and other communities in the countywide meetings in which Black people find out what is going on and decide together what they should do.

Subfamily VIII.1. Yolanda Rudolph (50) grew up in Sequoia community, in the Delta area of Holmes County. When she was little, her mother's parents, Charles (3) and Aretha (4) Walker, asked to have her live with them, since both of their own children were grown and married. When she was only fifteen, she married Alex Rudolph (59), a young man of twenty, from the town of Moundville in Holmes County, who had just returned from army service.

Shortly after they were married, they moved to Chicago. At first they lived in the basement apartment of the Peterses' (Nucleus Family I) and the Cutes' (Nucleus Family IX) house. Later they moved to an apartment of their own; since 1963, they have rented the same place, in a large and crowded building.

Life is hard. Alex works at the United States Steel Corporation, which takes him thirty to forty minutes by bus to get to; the family does not own a car. Yolanda works at a cleaners' as an assistant manager in the clothing take-in department. It takes Yolanda thirty minutes to get to work. She works days, while Alex works nights, so that someone is always home with the children. They have seven children, all in the public school.

Debra (83), aged sixteen, is in high school. She has a baby, Lois (101) who is eight months old; Yolanda Rudolph cares for Lois when Debra has to go to class.

Albert (84), aged fourteen, has been going to school at Moundville High School, where he is a freshman; he lives with Alex Rudolph's mother. He did not want to attend school in the North. He said that in the South you did not have to worry about standing on the street corner waiting for a bus, nor did you have to worry about the gangs. He also said that he could get along with the children in Holmes County better than he could with those in the North.

The other children are Tony (85), aged twelve and in the eighth grade; Peter (86), aged eleven and in the sixth grade; Ann (87), aged nine, and in the fifth grade; Judy (88), aged eight, and in the third grade; and Virginia (89), aged seven and in the second grade.

The Rudolphs are proud that their children are doing well in school. They too try to keep up; *Jet, Chicago Today* and the Chicago *Sun-Times* are great favorites in this household.

Yolanda, like her sister Ruthann (51), likes to cook. Occasionally, Alex and she attend movies. She likes to dance, but he does not. The Rudolphs are members of the same Holmes Countian social club as Stewart Bidwell (see Subfamily VII.2). The family's church is a half-block from their apartment; a few of the congregation are also from Mississippi, but none from Holmes County.

The family visits home once a year, either in summer or at Christmas. In case of emergency, Yolanda or Alex returns to Mississippi alone. Yolanda Rudolph does all the letter writing and calling back to Mississippi.

Subfamily VIII.2. Ruthann Patterson (51) was married to Dan (60) in 1958. He lived less than a mile away from the Lorenzo Bidwell farm in the Strongheart community. She was eighteen and he nineteen; they had both just finished school.

Soon after the marriage, they came to Chicago, where they stayed with a cousin of Dan's, who also helped him get a job driving a truck. Ruthann worked part-time at a cleaners' but then quit work to go South to have her first child, Joann (90), a year later. Joann is now ten and in the fifth grade.

Dan was a steady worker, so he was able to get a four-room apartment in a high-rise building on the South Side. He then sent back for his wife and child. Two years later, the Pattersons had their second child, Belinda (91), now eight and in the third grade. Lorraine (92), their third child, was born in 1963; she is now in the first grade.

Dan and Ruthann's life was at first upset when he was laid off his truck driver's job. But he was very lucky, for two days later he was able to find a job with Union Steel Company, where he still is. What had happened was that his brother-in-law, Bob Wilson (61), also had lost his job a little earlier. Bob drove around, looking for work, and after a while found that this steel mill was hiring workers. Bob went to the employment office, signed an application, and got the job the same day. Bob called Dan and told him of the opportunity; Dan's application was also accepted. Since then, both Bob and Dan have been promoted several times. The two brothers-in-law really help each other in times of hardship or need.

In 1967, the Head Start programs started up in Chicago. Ruthann, with her children in school or in Head Start, was able to work there as a teacher. Since she was a very good worker, she was sent for further training, first to Central Junior College and later to Eastern University.

With both Dan and Ruthann working and saving, they began to look for a house of their own. Their high-rise building was too crowded. They did not know their neighbors. Their children were not free to go outdoors to play without danger of being hurt. An adult always had to be around to see that no one got into a fight. And they were paying rent which could go into paying off a mortgage.

In the late summer of 1969, they found a home outside the poverty areas, on the deep South Side, that fitted their budget. The children were upset about leaving their friends at school. Here the mother played the role of persuader. She explained to them that a home of their own was very important, a place where they could always stay, and also that they would not have to worry about getting the manager to fix anything in the house. Moving into a new atmosphere, the children could meet new friends.

After moving, the children liked their new place. Their school was not crowded, and the teachers were better. Dan is closer to work now, only a fifteen-minute drive. But Ruthann has a great distance to travel, approximately eighty blocks.

The Pattersons still attend the Baptist church in their old neighborhood. Dan does not attend church as regularly as Ruthann and the children because he has to work on some Sundays. The children now also go to the Wilsons' church, although it is Methodist, whenever there is children's program. The children like the Methodist church better because they can participate more in it than in the Baptist one.

Dan likes sports. He is also a great reader; there are always novels and other books by writers such as Reverend King, John Kenny, Richard Wright, James Baldwin, and Warren Miller around the Patterson house. The Pattersons subscribe to *Jet* and *Look* magazines, and the Chicago *Sun-Times* and *Chicago Today* newspapers. They do not subscribe to any Black paper because they are not available in the community in which they now live. However, Dan occasionally picks up a Black paper whenever he is in the neighborhood where they are sold.

Ruthann likes to cook and sew. She makes most of her daughters' clothes. She is also in a social club (see also Subfamily VIII.4). She does most of the family writing back to Mississippi to both her parents and Dan's. Sometimes she lets the two older girls write. Whenever they are all so busy that they do not have time to write, they call home.

As a family, the Pattersons visit Mississippi once a year. During the summer, Ruthann and the children visit home to get vegetables and help her mother can fruit. She brings some back North to use. Sometimes Dan drives the children to Mississippi on a weekend and picks them up later. The children stay with both sets of grandparents, who live about three-fourths of a mile from each other.

Dan is highly thought of by the Lorenzo Bidwell family. When the two younger sisters, Shrom (53) and Catherine (54) were married in Holmes County, Mr. Bidwell could not be there. One wedding was held in the spring when he was tilling the land; the other was held in the fall when he was harvesting. Dan then acted as the father. The oldest sister, Yolanda (50) played the role of the mother. She and Ruthann (51) organized everything for each bride.

Subfamily VIII.3. Barbara Wilson (52) is the only one of her family, thus far, who has married outside of her county. Her husband Bob (61) is from Hill County, seventy miles away from the Strongheart community.

Barbara left Holmes County in 1961, when she was eighteen and had just graduated from high school. There were no jobs to be had at home, so she went to Chicago with her uncle and aunt who had been visiting Mississippi. She hated Chicago when she first arrived. It was her first time away from home. Most frightening was the difference between a small country farm and a big city like Chicago. And staying with her aunt and her aunt's family was hard; they were too old and different. Every night she cried in bed.

After a week and a half, she moved to live with her sister Yolanda (50) and her family, where it was much more crowded but where she was happier. There she stayed until she got married. She also found a job at Spiegel Catalog Company.

Barbara met Bob at a shoe store in Chicago, where he was working as a part-time salesman. Barbara had always thought she would marry someone she knew in high school, but Bob courted her and convinced her otherwise.

After getting married, she and Bob moved into an apartment of their own in South Chicago. Bob found a job with Union Steel Company and did very well, being promoted several times. Barbara continued working for a while, but when the children came she was sick regularly. Bob felt it would be safer for her to stay home and manage the household.

Bob has done well enough so that, in the summer of 1969, the Wilsons moved into a house they are buying, in the far South of Chicago, near the Pattersons (Subfamily VIII.2). It now takes Bob only fifteen minutes to get to work. Bob works a split shift, sometimes at night, then again during the day.

Bob and Barbara have two children, a girl and a boy. Doris (93) is seven and in the second grade. Bruce (94) is four, and does not attend school. He is often brought back to Mississippi by his aunts and uncles, Bob's and Barbara's sisters and brothers, because he is not yet in school. Often, Barbara's younger sister Veevee (55), a student at Prairie College, comes to stay with the Wilsons.

Bob is a young deacon in a Methodist church near the apartment where they used to live; he also sings in the choir. Originally, Barbara was a Baptist, but after she married Bob she changed her faith to that of her husband. Barbara works with various church auxiliaries. Their children are members of the intermediate choir.

The Wilsons' social activities are very casual; they attend movies, church, and church concerts. They like just riding around. When friends come over they listen to music and play cards. On the Fourth of July and Thanksgiving, Barbara and her sisters fix a "family get-together" dinner. They also like to picnic.

Barbara likes to read novels and clean house. Unlike Ruthann, she does not like to cook, accepting it as a job. Homemade biscuits are never made in this family; the bread is always bought from the supermarket. But Barbara does go with her sisters to buy fresh vegetables from a farm near Chicago. Since Barbara participates in the church a great deal she has no time for social clubs, but she does attend some of their activities (see also Subfamily VIII.4).

The Chicago *Daily News* and Chicago *Sun-Times* are very popular in this household.

Both Barbara and Bob write back to Mississippi. Whenever Barbara does not feel like writing, Bob does it. On special holidays — Christmas, Easter, Mother's Day, etc. — they send cards to their parents and other relatives. Bob and Barbara hope to return to Mississippi in ten years, to stay. By then, they hope that Holmes or Hill County will have better paying jobs. The Wilsons feel that the city is too crowded, that their children cannot play and live as they would in Mississippi.

Subfamily VIII.4. Shrom Smith (53) is now twenty-three. She was born in Pleasant View and then lived with her parents in Strongheart. When she was twelve, her mother's parents, the Walkers (3, 4) asked to keep her as they had kept her sister Yolanda before she married (see Subfamily VIII.1).

Shrom stayed in the Sequoia community from the seventh grade until she finished high school, returning to Strongheart to visit or spend the weekend. She met William Smith (62) in the Sequoia Baptist Church, which she attended with her grandparents. Bill, who grew up in Sequoia, was also in school with her, but a grade ahead.

Shrom finished high school and left Holmes County for Chicago in 1964; there she stayed with her sister Ruthann (51). She got a job as an order clerk with Spiegel Catalog, where Barbara Wilson (52) had also worked. A few months later she married Bill Smith, who had enlisted in the Air Force.

Bill (62) was first assigned to Omaha, Nebraska, where they moved. Later he was sent to Vietnam. Before he left for Vietnam, he brought Shrom and the children — Reba (95), now six, and Luther (96), now four — back to Mississippi. But Shrom returned to Chicago, to stay with her sister Ruthann, after only two months in Holmes County.

When Bill returned from Vietnam and received his discharge, the family moved to Bay City, Michigan, where his father lived. Shrom got training and a job as a dietician at the hospital there. But there was no one there she could be close to, only Bill's father and his relatives.

So they moved back to Chicago, where Bill's mother lives, as well as Shrom's sisters. She is now a dietician at University Hospital, only fifteen minutes away. She works days and Bill works nights. It takes him thirty minutes to get to work. They live in his mother's house, paying her rent. At the same time, they are buying a house in Bay City; every so often they return to Michigan to check it.

Their daughter Reba has been attending a Head Start school. On Sundays she goes with her mother to church. When Shrom has to work on Sunday mornings she sends Reba to church with her aunt Yolanda (50). The Smiths attend the same church as the Rudolphs.

William Smith does not like to attend church; he rarely goes since he has been living in Chicago. He is in a social club with several other migrants from Holmes County, both men and women (see Subfamily VII.2). Both Shrom and William like dancing, movies, and playing cards. Shrom also belongs to a social club just for housewives; all her sisters except Barbara are also members.

Chicago Today and *Jet* are popular in this household. The Smiths do not subscribe to any Black papers, but they buy them occasionally.

The family visits Mississippi once a year, during the summer months when Shrom is on vacation. Luther, their boy, is now in Mississippi with Shrom's parents, the Lorenzo Bidwells (Nucleus Family VIII). Mr. Bidwell had visited the Smiths during the Christmas holidays, and they let him take Luther back with him. Luther is now going to Head Start in Holmes County.

In between visits, Shrom, like her sisters, writes and calls her family at home.

Subfamily VIII.5. Catherine Jackson (54) is only twenty-one, but she has been traveling a lot ever since she was fifteen. Her first trip was to Atlanta, Georgia, where she worked for the Southern Christian Leadership Conference teaching people how to register as voters. Because of this she was forced to leave Moundville High School and finish at a private Black school. Then she entered Mississippi Liberal Junior College, majoring in secretarial science. Returning to Holmes County, she worked in the Head Start program then getting under way. One of the ladies at the Head Start center introduced her to her son, Allen Jackson (63). He was a fellow Holmes Countian visiting from Chicago, where he had moved in 1965.

In the summer of 1968, Catherine went north to attend summer school at Central Junior College (where Ruthann had gone; see Sub-family VIII: 2). There she met Allen Jackson again.

Soon he was visiting her at her sister Ruthann's apartment, where she was staying. Then he called her parents to ask for her. He said that asking through letters would take too long, that Mr. Bidwell might never give him an answer. Allen and Catherine were married in March, 1969.

There are only the two of them now. They do not want any children yet; they want to wait until they are able to move out of their apartment. The apartment building is quiet, but the neighborhood is not good for rearing children. There are no adoptions in the family, but their nieces and nephews generally spend weekends with them. Whenever Catherine has a couple of days off during the week, she picks up her twin godchildren and keeps them until she goes back to work.

Catherine had worked at Spiegel's (see also Subfamily VIII.3) as a file clerk; now she is a secretary in charge of ordering at a small department store. It takes her about twenty minutes to get to work when Allen drives her; when she has to take the bus, it takes her about thirty-five minutes. Allen often works nights while she works during the day.

Catherine likes to sew and to cook; Allen especially likes to follow sports. The Jacksons like a lot of recreation; dancing is one of their favorite hobbies. Allen is not in any kind of social club, but he does attend Catherine's. They read the Chicago *Daily News*.

They attend church regularly; their minister is from Mississippi. Their church is like a Black church in the South; the choir sings really well.

Since they married, Allen and Catherine have been back home to Mississippi together once; she has also come back by herself. The youngest to be married, she misses home.

NUCLEUS FAMILY IX. Mary Cute (13), the second-youngest daughter of the Jeff Bidwells (1, 2) is now forty-eight. She grew up in Pleasant View, a community which numbered 800 people when she was young. Now it is 300 or fewer, and 25 percent of those living there are children, perhaps 20 percent are in their thirties and forties, and the other 55 percent are in their late fifties and up.

John Cute (22) comes from the Sequoia community (see also Subfamily VIII.1), which used to have 200 people but now numbers only 55 — half children, half old people. Black people feel that children reared under the direction of their grandparents are very smart. Grandparents, they think, tend to be harder on children then parents.

The Cutes left Holmes County in 1940 because they did not want to farm anymore and felt they could progress more in the city. John Cute was twenty-six and had graduated from the seventh grade; Mary Cute was nineteen, and she had finished the eighth grade. They had a small baby, Hattie (66).

When the Cutes arrived in Chicago, they stayed with his relatives. In the years since, they have worked hard. John Cute is a laborer and a part-time barber. Mary Cute is a maid, working for a rich Caucasian family. Even though they have never made much money, they have joined with the Peterses (Nucleus Family I) in buying a house, where they have lived nearly twenty years. The Cutes live on the first floor; the Peterses on the second; the basement apartment is rented to their nephew, Stewart Bidwell (43, Subfamily VII.2), and his wife and son.

The Cutes have raised three children: Hattie (66), now twenty-nine; Bernice (67), now twenty-six; and Booker (68), now twenty-three. Both of their girls are married and live in Chicago; Booker is in the Army. All of their children have graduated from a Catholic high school, which the older Cutes felt gave a better education than the public schools. Since their children attended Catholic school, they have accepted that faith, but their parents remain Baptists.

Now that their children are grown, the Cutes can think more about themselves. They take the Chicago *Sun-Times* and the Chicago *Daily News*. And, since there are only the two of them, they hope to move to the far South Side, where the neighborhood is better.

The Cutes visit Mississippi about once a year. They usually drive. Mary Cute usually stays two or three weeks with her father; John Cute must often return earlier by himself.

NUCLEUS FAMILY X. Shelia Curtis (14), the youngest daughter of Jeff and Jane Bidwell (1, 2), is now forty-five. When she was sixteen and had finished the eighth grade, she married another Holmes Countian, Bill Curtis (23), who had a seventh-grade education. Bill, however, was drafted into the Army during World War II and trained as a medical corpsman. After the war, he was able to qualify as a male nurse in a hospital in Jackson, Mississippi, where he and his family moved. He is also a part-time carpenter. Shelia Curtis is a maid.

Shelia and Bill Curtis have five children: Alvin (71), now twenty-six; Charles (72), twenty-four; Geraldine Byrd (73), twenty-three; Yvette Ford (74), twenty-one; and Vanita (75), eighteen. Alvin and Vanita stay mostly with their parents; Geraldine and Yvette also live in Jackson, while Charles has moved to Chicago. Vanita's baby boy, Author (100), is cared for by the older Curtises; other grandchildren also visit them.

Shelia and Bill Curtis lead a quiet life. They are good Baptists; their church is only two blocks away from their house. They like to read, especially the Memphis *Commercial Appeal, Ebony,* and *Jet.* Shelia visits Holmes County regularly. Since her mother is deceased, she visits back to see how her father is getting along because he lives alone.

When Alvin Curtis (71) was in his teens, he used to visit his uncle Lorenzo's farm (Nucleus Family VIII) in Strongheart and help him harvest his crop. Alvin was not very good, but he tried hard. Alvin married Mary (76), a girl from Jackson, right out of high school. The marriage did not work out; they lived in a rented place ten blocks from the Curtises and used to visit them regularly. They had no children. Alvin could not find regular work. Finally they separated. Mary is now living with her parents and he with his; they have not gotten a divorce.

Subfamily X.1. Charles Curtis (72) is now twenty-four and living in Chicago. When he was a teenager, he used to stay during the summer with his grandparents, Jeff and Jane Bidwell (1, 2) in Pleasant View. There he met Charlean Miller (77), whose family had moved to Pleasant View from Sequoia community (see also Subfamily VIII.1). The dating period was about five to six years before they got married.

Charles and Charlean lived with his parents in Jackson for a year. Then in 1967, they moved to Chicago, searching for better jobs. At first they lived with relatives; now they have an apartment of their own. They have two children.

The Curtises visit Holmes County and Jackson but once a year. Sometimes Charlean visits twice; each time she comes, she visits his parents as well as hers. She does all the calling and writing back to Mississippi.

Subfamily X.2. Geraldine (73), the oldest daughter of Bill and Shelia Curtis (14), is now twenty-three. She graduated from high school and then attended City State College for about a year before marrying Bolivar Byrd (78). Although he graduated from the same high school as she, they met only later.

When they were first married, they stayed with his parents and hers; later they got a place of their own. Bol has a steady job, and they now have two children, Jeff (97), aged six, and Dorethy (98), aged three. Jeff is in the first grade, while Dorethy remains at home. There are no adoptions in the family.

Since they live in the same city as their parents on both sides, Geraldine and Bol visit them regularly. They come to Holmes County to see her grandfather, Jeff Bidwell (1), about once a year.

Subfamily X.3. Yvette Ford (74) married a young man, Sam Ford (79), also from Jackson, but they separated shortly afterwards. In 1968, she went to Chicago, where she stayed with the Peterses (Nucleus Family I) until she could get a place of her own. Her little daughter Josephine (99) lives with her.

Yvette visited Mississippi for the Christmas holidays in 1969.

A FAMILY OF SEDENTARY SUBSISTENCE FARMERS: THE MITCHELLS

In contrast to the Bidwell family, the Mitchell family[29] represents a corporate group bounded almost entirely within Holmes County. The Mitchells represent an aggregate of individuals occupying one of the lower socioeconomic positions in this impoverished region. This position is defined by the fact that no household in this family owns any land or receives any stable income from wage labor. The Mitchells' livelihood depends upon sharecropping and subsistence farming. They occupy a precarious economic position, and this position has influenced the structure and functions of their extended family. At the present time there are ninety-one members in fourteen households identifying with the Mitchell extended family.

The Mitchells have been long-term residents in the County. They can trace their family movement into the County from a large southern Mississippi plantation back to the days immediately following the Civil War. From their initial movement into the County, the Mitchells have been structurally centered on the Tipton community. Though once a thriving community, Tipton is presently little more than a rural church site, where the Mitchells are one of two extended families numerically dominating the area. Tipton is located in the uplands of the County and is an agricultural region owned mainly by White farmers.

Only twice since entering the County has the Mitchell extended family not been centered entirely in and around Tipton. The first family split occurred approximately in the late 1930's when two households of Mitchells moved to the Delta region in Holmes County and worked on one of the large plantations. These two households remained on the plantation about two years, after which they returned to the Tipton area. No specific reasons are known for the move or the subsequent return. The second split occurred in 1969, when two households of Mitchells moved to Mount

[29] All proper names in this section are pseudonyms.

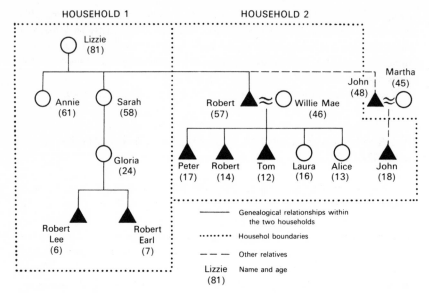

Figure 3. Genealogical relationships of the Lizzie and Robert Mitchell households

Eaton, a small, rural church community located in the uplands about fifteen miles from Tipton. At the present time these two Mitchell households continue to reside in Mount Eaton.

The majority of research on this Black extended family was conducted with the two households of Mitchells in Mount Eaton and was collected as an offshoot of another research project. Consequently, some data are lacking, limiting the range of comparisons with the Bidwell family. The field research with the Mitchells was conducted from February, 1971, to August, 1971, though occasional visits have been made since that time.

Mitchell Family Relationships

Two households of Mitchells moved to Mount Eaton in 1969. The biological relationships of the thirteen members of the two households are illustrated in Figure 3. These two households left the family region of Tipton when Robert had the opportunity to lease about forty acres of land. This tract of land was too large for Robert's household to hand-cultivate unassisted. Consequently, Lizzie's household also decided to make the move to Mount Eaton to assist Robert in farming. The two households are located on the leased land about fifty yards from each other. The houses are in poor condition and only Robert's house has electricity.

There are seventy-eight members of the Mitchell extended family residing in twelve households in Tipton. Six of the twelve households are located in close proximity to each other near the family church. The remaining six households are scattered around the Tipton area but identify with Tipton as their home community.

The average household size in the Mitchell family, 6.5 persons, is significantly higher than the average for the Black population of the County, approximately 4.5 persons. One main factor possibly bearing on the difference in household size is the marginal economic conditions faced by the Mitchells and the resultant strategies for survival.

Resource Base of the Mitchell Family

As stated previously, the Mitchell family is one of the poorer families in Holmes County. The main occupational pursuit is farming, with share-cropping and some land leasing as the two modes. No Mitchell household presently owns any land or intends to purchase any in the near future, but the family once jointly purchased a small piece of property. Back in 1959, the Mitchell family consolidated their money in order to buy some land from a White landowner in Tipton. They did buy a small tract, but property taxes and a foreclosure on some newly purchased farm equipment forced them to sell the land back to the previous owner at a considerable loss. This failure has had a direct influence on their outlook on property ownership and control. Their sentiments on land ownership were summed up by Lizzie. "We just can't own land. It is too much trouble. It's better to take what you can from it. That way when the land is no good anymore you can leave it." This attitude has effectively created a barrier to any socioeconomic advancement. They have accepted their marginal economic position, but' in doing so they have created an economic strategy maximizing chances of survival.

The resource base of every Mitchell household is marginal. The land available to them is the poor and eroded land considered unproductive by the White landowners. To compensate for their lack of economic resources the Mitchells have structured a complex set of economic inter-relationships stressing cooperation and sharing. Though once common-place, this cooperative economic structure employed by the Mitchells appears to be rare today in the County. This corporate system consolidating a minimal resource base serves to increase the number of alternatives open to every household; thus, it enhances the chances of survival of each on a minimal level. Furthermore, it is doubtful whether any single household of the Mitchell family could, as a separate economic unit, continuously produce a standard of living comparable with that resulting from cooperation.

The corporate system among the Mitchells is based mainly on economic unit specialization and nonreciprocal, circular sharing. Since no one household contains enough resources to survive alone, each household or set of joint households constitutes an economic unit which contributes some component of the family's aggregate economic output. Each economic unit is the production mechanism within the extended family responsible for one specific economic task. This creates a highly effective work system with clearly defined rights and obligations assigned to each unit. Depending upon the economic task and resources in question, the economic unit may be one or two households.

The major contribution to the family economy made by the two households in Mount Eaton is production of sweet and white potatoes (see Table 5). These two households have joined together to form one economic unit, since all cultivation is done by hand, and planting, weeding, and harvesting are very time- and labor-consuming. Consequently, each adult member of the two households, except Lizzie, works the fields. Robert is in charge of organizing the necessary work to successfully operate the forty-acre farm. Even though it is their staple, the Mitchells in Mount Eaton grow many more potatoes than their two households can consume. The surplus potatoes are given to the remaining family members in Tipton.

In Tipton, six of the twelve households specialize in raising livestock, usually pigs and a few cattle. These six households form five economic

Table 5. Household and economic relationships of the Mitchell family

Location	Economic unit	Number of households	Functions
Mount Eaton	1	2	Potatoes
Tipton	1	2	Livestock
	1	1	Livestock
	1	1	Livestock
	1	1	Livestock
	1	1	Livestock
	1	1	Potatoes
	1	1	Mixed vegetables
	1	1	Labor
	1	1	Labor
	1	1	Labor
	1	1	Labor
Total	12	14	

units, as two households share pasture lands and jointly buy additional fodder (see Table 5). These five economic units supply most of the meat consumed by the members of the remaining eight households. Growing feed and paying for additional fodder are the responsibility of the economic unit raising the animals. Butchering is usually a family activity in which everyone gathers to help and to take his or her share of the meat home. Although all fourteen households of the Mitchell family participate in the Food Stamp Program, they do raise most of the meat consumed by the family. This, in turn, allows the various households to use their food stamps for other necessary food items.

The remaining six households in Tipton not raising livestock contribute a variety of goods and services to the family economy and comprise six distinct economic units (see Table 5). One household raises both sweet and white potatoes; another grows the largest mixed vegetable garden in the family. The remaining four households have no access to any cultivable land; consequently, they contribute their only asset: labor. These individuals contributing labor will assist the other households in planting, feeding, harvesting, and butchering, shifting from one household to another whenever needed. Their activities center on Tipton for it is too difficult to continuously assist the two households in Mount Eaton due to the family's lack of transportation. Even though their input may appear minimal, their contribution is critical to the family's economic stabilization, and, accordingly, they reap equal benefits.

Although each household specializes in one major activity that contributes to the family economy, each household also maintains its own separate vegetable garden and welfare income, plus any possible small income from occasional wage labor. These economic endeavors are separate from the family pursuits. Consequently, even though economic cooperation is the dominant feature, no one family nor household controls the joint family income, nor is money shared among the Mitchells. These separate economic pursuits help to illustrate that a division between household activities and extended family activities is structurally recognized by the Mitchells.

The goods and services produced by each economic unit are exchanged with every household that contributes to the family economy. Thus, even though economic input is not always household-based, the goods produced are distributed to each household. The economic exchanges are asymmetrical, as exchanges occur at different intervals throughout the year and usually without any immediate reciprocity. Work input and economic output are not balanced among the various economic units. Yet there is little attention given to the fact that one economic unit contributes more than another since every contribution is viewed as critical to the aggregate family economy.

Communications Patterns

To keep this corporate economic system operating efficiently, communication links among the various households must be kept open and constantly maintained. It has already been mentioned that reciprocal visiting and social gatherings are characteristic elements of the Black extended family. With the Mitchells, social gatherings not only serve to extend the normal social obligations of the extended family, but also function as a time to organize, operate, and maintain the cooperative economic system.

The most frequent opportunity for communication occurs at a monthly church service in Tipton. A majority of the adult family members, especially the nucleus families, usually attend the service. Although church services take place every Sunday and a good portion of the Mitchells are in attendance, one Sunday a month is specifically set aside by the family for such a gathering. These gatherings usually take place over the whole day, with the family members all going to one household when the church service is completed. At these gatherings, information will be exchanged about the economic status of the family. If a specific economic task is anticipated, the economic units contributing labor will be asked to assist. Other events of family interest, such as illnesses and romances, will also be discussed.

Other visits occur among the various households during the week, but the monthly gathering is the best medium of social communication. The weekly visits tend to be more female dominated than the monthly gatherings, which both sexes attend. Communication among the Mitchells may not be as frequent as in other extended families, due to their lack of resources. Only three Mitchell households have telephones and only eight of the fourteen households have automobiles; consequently, the gatherings have to be carefully planned.

As stated previously, the Mitchell family, in contrast to the Bidwell family, does not operate as a mechanism facilitating migration. Family members occasionally do leave the confines of the County, but they are then no longer considered effective members of the extended family by the remaining Mitchells. These migrant individuals are still considered biologically related, but a critical component of social interdependence is no longer present. Consequently, contact with individuals who have left the County occurs only on a minimal level with nuclear relatives. Bitter feelings are not fostered when someone leaves the family, but it should be stressed that family membership is closely tied to participation in the corporate economic system. The economic resource base is so marginal that few individuals can accumulate enough resources to leave. Those that have managed to leave permanently have broken the social obligations imposed and extended by the economic structure; thus, they no longer share the extended family's network of equities. This distinction became apparent when Lizzie distinctly separated "family members" from what she termed "other kin."

The Household–Family Dichotomy

This process of breaking family ties with migrant individuals is closely associated with the household–family dichotomy. As previously mentioned, some economic division exists between the household and the extended family. Identification with the Mitchell family is closely tied to the social bond, the biological relationships being secondary. But within the household, the biological relationship overrides the social component. Consequently, when an individual leaves the County he only severs the extended family tie, based on the social relationship, but he cannot break the biological relationship with his household or nuclear relatives. Thus, communication and recognition continue but only on the household level.

Communication patterns are tied closely to social relationships within the family. The nucleus families have prime responsibility for input into the extended family's economic system. Their attendance at social gatherings is a functional representation of their position. The only other family component expected to attend all social gatherings is the "founder." In the Mitchell family, this position is occupied solely by Lizzie. She occupies a critical social position since she is the oldest living member of the family and the only representative from her generation. This position gives her special recognition in terms of social status and interaction. Her position within the family is best illustrated by the effort made by other family members to assure her presence at family gatherings. Since she is presently eighty-one years of age, she is catered to by the other family members and is generally the center of attention. Another indicator of her social status within the family is the name used by family members when addressing or referring to Lizzie. The name, "Mama Lizzie," is used by all family members regardless of generation or sex. The name is a term of endearment that emphasizes her unique position within the family as "founder," and this name, as well as her social position, is unique within the family.

While the economy is more family oriented, child rearing generally centers on the household. Before moving out to establish her own household, Gloria lived with her two young sons in Lizzie's household. Although three older women resided in this household, child rearing was left up to Gloria. She was responsible for care and direct discipline. Of course, Lizzie, Sarah, and Annie did assert some authority whenever Gloria was absent or when she was unaware of misbehavior by the children. In addition to Gloria, one other individual figured prominently in child rearing: Gloria's uncle, Robert. Although he had five children of his own plus his nephew John at home, Robert took an active role in the socialization of Gloria's children. Besides taking the boys fishing and to town, he was once called over to discipline one of the boys who had been "talking back" to his mother. No direct force was used, as Robert's presence quickly ended the child's misbehavior; consequently, it appears as though Robert's authority was frequently applied and thus recognized without question by the children.

In Robert's household, child rearing and minor discipline are handled more by the mother. Robert's role is one of a remote figure, however, but one clearly defined, with specific duties and obligations. The definition of his role can be inferred from observing his participation in handling severe disciplinary problems with the children, organizing outside work, and taking an active part in deciding household issues, such as setting curfew times for the girls. His activities with the children contrast with those of his wife. Besides minor discipline, her responsibilities include normal child care and work organization within the house.

Child and Adult Fosterage

An interesting characteristic of the Black extended family is child and adult fosterage. Within the Mitchell family, one case of child fosterage and four cases of adult fosterage have been observed and documented.

The practice of *child fosterage* involves the transferring of children from one household to another and occurs for a variety of reasons including overcrowding, maltreatment, economic deprivation, and the distance from schools. A clear case of child fosterage occurred within Lizzie's household. Gloria left Lizzie's household to establish her own; basically, Gloria indicated a desire to be autonomous and now had an opportunity to move into a low-rent house. But Lizzie's household is located within walking distance of a Head Start school, which one of Gloria's children attended. Gloria's new location is about four miles from the school. Consequently, her move created problems for her son's attendance. In order for her son to attend school on a regular basis, Gloria felt it was necessary for him to remain in close proximity to that school. Also, since this son is considered by the family to be "a trouble-maker," leaving him in Lizzie's household left him near Robert. This action of leaving her son with Lizzie and her mother, Sarah, was taken after long deliberation; although Gloria discussed it with Lizzie, Sarah, Annie, and Robert, she made the final decision.

After the fosterage occurred, the relationship between mother and son did not change. The parent–child relationship is still stable and can be characterized as affectionate. The accessibility of an educational facility was the determining factor, just as the child's development was the prime consideration. One interesting characteristic of this fosterage is that on weekends Gloria will usually return to Lizzie's household rather than have her son go to her home. This pattern of visitation reinforces the idea that this move constituted an actual beneficent fosterage.

Adult fosterage appears to be structurally somewhat different from child fosterage in the Mitchell extended family. Four cases of adult fosterage were noted among the Mitchells, and all four cases seem to center on the need for additional labor. One of Robert's nephews, John, moved permanently into Robert's household. John is not much older than Robert's oldest child, but his social position is that of an adult, not a child. The reason given for John's move was the need for additional labor in the fields, and there was no indication that any other circumstances were related to the move. The household John moved from had eight members. One interesting factor to note is that this household is an economic unit contributing labor to the Mitchell family as a corporate system.

The other three cases of adult fosterage involve three young men of no biological relationship to the Mitchells. These three men have been taken into the family, each in a separate household. The three men participate in and receive the benefits of the extended family. Background information on these young men is lacking, and the only reason stated for taking them into the family was the need for additional labor. Since little is known about these three individuals it is unknown if any social ties and obligations were extended to their families of orientation; it is known that all three young men came from families residing in Holmes County. Both child and adult fosterage among the Mitchells represent a highly functional institution that may erase adverse social conditions while also operating as a mechanism for family recruitment.

Social Interaction

Most social interaction among the Mitchells is confined to the family itself. The Mitchells participate little in formal community activities, such as religious leadership and political organizations. Their lack of community interaction may be tied to their limited economic resources and the family's consequently demanding social structure. The cooperative economic system, including the network of communications necessary for its operation, dominates the lives of every member of the family. Thus, anything outside the realm of economic survival is considered nonvital to the perpetuation of the family. Their lack of community involvement was even evident during the hectic civil rights days of the early 1960's. In fact, at the present time no Mitchell in Mount Eaton is registered to vote, and, although complete data are lacking, it appears that few if any of the Mitchell family members in Tipton are registered either. Also, none of the adults regularly attend any of the numerous political meetings held throughout the County. This lack of political participation does not mean they have a corresponding lack of political consciousness. They are aware of the Black political structure that now dominates the County but find little time to take an active role.

Another community-wide social institution than can demand a certain amount of individual participation is the church. As stated previously, the church in Tipton is regularly attended by most adult Mitchells. Although they attend regularly, their participation is minimal in the realm of religious leadership. At the present time no adult male in the Mitchell family is a deacon in their church, though according to Lizzie her late husband's brother was once a deacon in Tipton. The lack of religious involvement may again be due to their marginal economic position and the corresponding drain on time. The limited resource base available to the Mitchells has structured their lifeways. And their economic corporate system defines not only the structure and functions of their extended family but also the amount of participation in community organizations.

BLACK EXTENDED FAMILIES AND KIN NETWORKS IN THE RURAL AND URBAN UNITED STATES

Studies of Black cultures in the rural and urban United States have been undertaken — unsystematically — for some eighty years. These studies have varied greatly in their underlying assumptions, topics of inquiry, and methods of research. In consequence, very few features of the Black cultural heritage and its adaptive development can be traced with certainty to this day. Some regions, such as Texas and the Southwest, remain almost totally unknown.

A review of published and, in part, unpublished research on Black kinship beyond the level of the household can, given these circumstances, only be indicative. It is almost certain, however, that Black extended families as true corporate bodies have been characteristic of the South Carolina Sea Islands, rural Mississippi, and other parts of the rural Southeast. Bounded kin groups less closely related to propinquity, church, and political cohesion have been identified in the town of "Kent" in the Carolinas. They may represent a variant tradition. Both types of structure have been clearly operative in migrations to the North.

There is also little doubt that kin networks are important elements of the social environment of both poor and upwardly mobile Black people in most northern cities. They are also present among the old elite strata of Black society. The degree to which these various networks are extended families which retain or develop structural and normative features differentiating their members from the outside world remains largely unstudied. Finally, recent migrations to California and affiliation with the Black Muslims appear to be highly disruptive, at least initially, of kin networks and perhaps of true, corporate, extended families.

The literature supporting these impressions is summarized below, generally in chronological order, and moving from the rural South to California. A few remarks concern the Black Muslims and other isolating groups. In several cases, the author's assumptions have been presented as a guide to the interpretation of his data.

The scientific study of the Black family and, indeed, of Black culture generally was initiated by the great scholar, W. E. B. DuBois. He was guided, however, by a pattern of assumptions which arose from the stereotypes of his day. Moreover, as a highly educated Northerner, he lacked access to many deeper facets of southern, rural Black society. He thus espoused a theory of extreme cultural loss for the U.S. Black population:

The plantation organization replaced the [African] clan and tribe, and the white master replaced the chief with far greater and more despotic powers. Forced and long-continued toil became the rule of life, the old ties of blood relationship and kinship disappeared, and instead of the family appeared a new polygamy and polyandry which, in some cases, almost reached promiscuity (DuBois 1965: 341–342).

In his study of the Black family, DuBois emphasized that:

The essential features of Negro slavery in America was [sic]:
1. No legal marriage.
2. No legal family.
3. No legal control over children.
. . . Slavery gave the monogamic family ideal to slaves but it compelled and
desired only the most imperfect practice of its most ordinary morals (DuBois
1970 [1909]: 21–22).

Yet this very same study quoted indications of the maintenance of
strong family sentiments among slaves (DuBois 1970 [1909]: 23–25),
cautions that (even in the Black belt of Mississippi), "the indictments
brought against the race now have never been fully true" (DuBois 1970
[1909]: 40–41), and shows evidence of considerable genealogical reckon-
ing:

On the father's mother's side the descent is direct from Africa, without any
mixing of blood, on the father's father's side there has been an intermingling of
white blood somewhere which makes the father a shade between black and light
brown, or a ginger-cake color. On the mother's side the grandfather was a white
man and her father was yellow. The mother's mother had a strain of Indian
blood in her, making her dark red. This makes the mother yellow. Both sides
were in slavery except the mother's grandfather (Dubois 1970 [1909]: 140).

The study noted the presence of many "village communities" among
southern Black folk. Few details are given, but for Covington, Georgia,
Dr. DuBois specifies: "In the surrounding country there are many small
communities composed entirely of Negroes, which form clans of blood
relatives" (DuBois 1970 [1909]: 56). Important interrelations between
community, church and family are also hinted:

. . . the Negro population of the United States is virtually divided into church
congregations which are the real units of race life. . . . The typical Negro country church stands at some cross-roads and holds services once or twice a month.
These meetings are great reunions and are the occasions of feasting, country
gossip and preaching. The people gather from 9 A.M. to 1 P.M. and remain
usually till late in the afternoon. Christenings and baptizing take place at this
time . . .
The only distinctly family festivity is the wedding. This is celebrated with
varying emphasis, being a ceremony only a generation old in the country districts. In the newer Southwest it seems to be more of a general occasion of
rejoicing. A correspondent says: "The two things that interrupt our community
life more than anything else in the way of home duties are the weddings and the
funerals, both of which seem to give the people more actual happiness and joy
than anything they enter into during the whole year" (DuBois 1970 [1909]:
130–131).

Finally, DuBois' classic study of the Philadelphia ghetto indicated the presence of both complementary functions between rural and urban households and a variety of conjugal ties.

The size of families in cities is nearly always smaller than elsewhere, and the Negro family follows this rule; late marriages among them undoubtedly act as a check to population; moreover, the economic stress is so great that only the small family can survive; the large families are either kept from coming to the city or move away, or as is most common, send the breadwinners to the city while they stay in the country (DuBois 1967 [1899]: 165).

Elsewhere, he notes that, in addition to formal marriage,

Cohabitation of a more or less permanent character is a direct offshoot of the plantation life and is practiced considerably; in distinctly slum districts, like that at Seventh and Lombard, from 10 to 25 percent of the unions are of this nature. Some of them are simply common-law marriages and are practically never broken. Others are compacts, which last for two to ten years; others for some months . . . (DuBois 1967 [1899]: 192–193).

In sum, DuBois' observations illustrate an institutional complexity for the Black family difficult to ascribe solely to social inventions after 1863 or to distorted borrowings from White practice. The details, in so far as they are available, seem to be compatible with the data from Holmes County.

T. J. Woofter, Jr.'s study of the island of St. Helena, off the coast of South Carolina, provides not only confirming materials but added dimensions on social history, social controls, and the effects of migration (Woofter 1930: 291). Woofter indicates that, in contrast to conditions in many localities, planters on St. Helena

. . . exercized as little supervision as necessary over the social life of their people. . . . When the task was finished, the rest of the day was theirs to spend as they chose. Then, living began in the slave street. This was the time for marriaging, housekeeping, gardening, funeralizing, praising, and pleasuring (Woofter 1930: 34).

Freedom brought with it expanded Black land ownership, rapid population increases, and the later out-migration of young adults, especially to Savannah, Georgia; Philadelphia, New York and Boston. At the same time, the old plantations defined social units; in the 1920's each was ". . . a larger extension of several families which have intermarried. . . . a face-to-face neighborhood where relationship is complicated but well recognized" (Woofter 1930: 213). Within the plantation

. . . the praise house is essentially a community organization. Here there is a face-to-face gathering of neighbors for the purpose of worship and the promo-

tion of community solidarity. It is the unit on which the church is built. . .
Here the community in simplest form initiates its business and promotes law
and order (Woofter 1930: 238).

The church and praise house have a definite organization for settling disputes
and thereby preventing crimes of violence. When a dispute arises among them,
it is referred to one of two committees appointed for that purpose. If these are
unable to compose the difference, the matter goes to the church council which
is made up of a leader and a deacon from each praise house. Finally, the matter
may be debated before the membership of the church as a whole (Woofter
1930: 239).

The normal family — man, wife, and children — is the fundamental social
organization . . . (Woofter 1930: 250–251). Marriage is a solemn affair with the
Islanders. . . . Weddings, while presided over by the preacher and always sanctioned by the church, are not held in the church but in the residence of the
bride. . . . Then the young couple moves off down the road to an unoccupied
piece of land belonging to some absent relative and the new home is started.

This comes after a conventional counting which follows the customs usually
prevailing in the country. . . . That the counting is not always so conventional
is indicated by the fact that 30 percent of the births are illegitimate (around
forty per year). . . . Many of these couples marry afterwards. . . . Sex irregularity
after marriage is, however, not noticeable. The social pressure toward sex
morality is applied by the church . . . (Woofter 1930: 205–207).

The family and the household are practically synonymous as there are only a
negligible number of young couples living with their parents. The usual household includes a father, mother, and their own children, or widow and her
grandchildren or nephews. Quite a number of households have adopted members of the family, but practically none have lodgers (Woofter 1930: 213).

Authority for making decisions in the family is usually divided, the woman
governing the household and, to a large extent, the children, the man governing
the farm and finances. Occasionally a strong personality will exert more influence than tradition has decreed for his or her sex.
    Women do not hold official positions in the church, but are unofficially
powerful in its organization and in the affairs of the praise house. The lodges
and societies are usually separately organized for men and women (Woofter
1930: 211–212).

In general, families value their holdings far above the money price which the
lands will bring. They may scatter to different cities or cease cultivation of the
major part of their tract but they usually scrape up tax money to hold their land.
Often they return for short periods of residence, and always, if possible, they
wish to be buried in the plantation burying grounds. Almost every month sees
several of them brought back on their last journey from Savannah or Charleston
or even New York or Philadelphia to their final rest beneath the moss-grown
oaks (Woofter 1930: 136).

Woofter's student, C. V. Kiser, enriched the original investigation of St. Helena society with important new materials (Kiser 1932). In St. Helena, as in the Mileston community of Holmes County, some seventy years later, federal action giving Black families access to land ownership served as a social stabilizer.

Negro ex-slaves were given an opportunity to buy small parcels. This came by virtue of instructions issued in 1863 by the President; namely, that parts of certain tracts be divided into small parcels and sold to "heads of families of the African race, one only to each, preferring such as by their good conduct, meritorious services, or by exemplary character, will be examples of moral propriety and industry to those of the same race, for the charitable purpose of providing homes for such heads of families." By 1865 . . . 347 purchases had been made by Negroes in St. Helena (Kiser 1932: 62–63).

Kiser emphasizes the importance of "praise house" meetings in social control. As in Holmes County, public opinion deplored bringing Black folks' problems into White courts.

If, for instance, two natives became involved in an altercation, or if one commits a minor offense against another, the affair is settled in a church trial. Unless the offense is a serious one, the county court of Beaufort rarely hears of it. Public opinion would condemn the plaintiff's reporting to civil authorities any offense of a minor nature. If settlement can be secured in the church with which the Islanders are familiar, why go to the trouble and expense involved in paying court fees and attending court? Civil law is dreaded and is generally spoken of as the "unjust law" as contrasted with the "just law" of the church (Kiser 1932: 80).

At more informal levels, family members and neighbors shared implicit responsibilities to control behavior, again as in Holmes County:

On the Island domestic and work life form an inseparable whole. Members of the family are constantly together in their work-a-day activities. . . . There are few evening activities and even courting is confined to Saturday evenings and Sundays. . . . In such an environment the family is a strong agency of social control. . . . The neighborhood environment, too, is conducive to the proper rearing of children. Mischievous deeds are reported to the parents by observing neighbors and unless punishment ensues there will be neighborhood gossip to the effect that the children of the particular parents concerned are only "half brought up" (Kiser 1932: 201–202).

Here too, substantial economic differences were observable between households:

Among the owners of the larger farms will be found some who live well whether or not they are able to show much in the way of cash returns at the end of the year. They have learned that the chief function of the farm is to feed the family and the farm animals.

Their large farms have been acquired by outright purchase of surrounding tracts, through inheritance and marriage. Many of the male heads of such families have had instruction in farm work at Penn School. A few have gone to Tuskegee and Hampton and have returned to put their knowledge into practice. To the provision of vegetables, home grown meat, hay, and forages they have given as much thought as to "money crops." Side incomes are often derived from seasonal work in Savannah, from the operation of small grocery "shops" and from the sale of miscellaneous produce (Kiser 1932: 66).

At the other end of the scale are the few families who are eking out an existence on holdings less than ten acres in size. In this class will be found old widows living alone or perhaps with a "drift" — an adopted child. Most of the farm labor on these extremely small plots is done by hand. . . . The interiors of their one-room or two-room houses generally express stark poverty. From friends and relatives, however, the poorest secure help in the form of food and clothes. In some instances a son or daughter in the city occasionally sends small amounts of money, especially when the tax payments are due (Kiser 1932: 67).

Beginning in the 1890's, St. Helena had been a source of out-migration to sea-based cities, especially Savannah in the South, and New York, Philadelphia, and Boston in the North. Characteristically, the migrants were young single people, with the departure of entire families being much rarer. Advice from friends and relatives influenced migrant decisions and destinations. Surprisingly,

In relatively few cases, however, have migrants gone from their homes mainly for the purpose of being with particular individuals. The few parents who joined migrant children, the individuals who "left mainly on love affair," and some of the children sent to the homes of city-dwelling relatives are the most important examples of those interested in proximity to certain individuals in the cities. . . . Approximately one-fourth of the 223 individuals interviewed in New York left home shortly after the death of a member of the family. Almost half of those who left under such conditions were dependent children whose relatives in the cities provided houses for them. Disruption of family life often crystallizes the desires of older children to leave home in search of work (Kiser 1932: 134–135).

Kiser characterized the behavior of the migrants in essence as follows:

A large part of the migrants begin their city careers as lodgers. Some live in the houses of relatives. Others continually drift from one rooming house to another. Two or more unmarried individuals often take an apartment together. It would seem that the more normal home life afforded by marriage facilitates adjustment to urban conditions. . . . Fertility is significantly reduced by migration. Marriages are later and apparently less permanent in the city. Island migrants have expressed the belief that in St. Helena practically no use is made of contraceptive devices, whereas such are used to some extent among those who have come to the cities . . . (Kiser 1932: 204–205).

In all the cities the Islanders are a more or less interrelated group. There are few who do not have close relatives in the city and manage to keep in touch with them. . . . The tendency for St. Helenians in New York to care for unemployed relatives during the present [1930's] depression is another indication of the cohesiveness of the migrants. Still another illustration might be found in the surprising frequency of intra-marriages among Islanders after they leave home. In New York, among sixty-one females who married after they left St. Helena, almost half (twenty-seven) married Island-born males. Most of the exogamous marriages were contracted with Negroes from other parts of South Carolina and from Georgia (Kiser 1932: 210).

Kiser confirmed, finally, Woofter's observations on the strong ties of migrants with St. Helena:

In spite of the radical changes of experiences encountered in coming to New York, the home ties of migrants are very strong in many instances. Visits from New York to St. Helena are made every year by a few and somewhat less frequently by many others. . . . Often the funerals in St. Helena are delayed until sons or daughters from far-away cities arrive. Since several days are frequently required, the corpse is sometimes "buried shallow" and taken up again for the regular funeral and final interment. . . . Almost invariably, Islanders in New York expressed the desire of being returned to St. Helena for permanent resting (Kiser 1932: 83–84).

In general, the data on St. Helena indicate the presence of customary laws, kinship systems and behavior, and dynamic adaptations profoundly similar to those of the Black Holmes Countians. Gaps in information leave the comparisons incomplete, but the data reported for two societies eight hundred miles and forty years apart appear to be samples drawn from a single basic pattern.

The studies of Southern Black and White society in the 1930's were primarily focused upon race relations and their effects upon behavior and personality.[30] None of these studies undertook a true ethnography; none used models of Old World and Latin American peasant-and-landlord cultural configurations as bases of research. Nevertheless, some of these investigations did develop useful generalizations about the Black extended family and its component households. Most noteworthy are the Davis et al. (1941) observations for the Natchez area of southwestern Mississippi:

[30] See especially Davis, Gardner, and Gardner (1941); Johnson (1934, 1967 [1941]); Dollard (1957); and Powdermaker (1966 [1939]). The case material on urban Black children in Natchez and New Orleans presented by Davis and Dollard: *Children of bondage* (1940: 267, 275) is very difficult to use analytically. It does include some important generalizations — e.g. on the widespread use of physical punishment among "lower-class" but not "middle-class" parents, but these are difficult to relate to their factual bases.

. . . it is interesting to note the extension of the kinship bonds among rural families. Six of the largest colored rural families in Old County counted from forty to seventy-five members, most of them living in the county. Kinship by blood and by affinity was recognized as far as "third cousins" and "daughter-in-law's aunt." The most extended kinship relations were not only defined by terms but were recognized by the performance of services. One tenant-manager in Old County, for example, sold the cotton, paid the taxes, and performed many other services for extremely distant blood and collateral kin, who depended upon him for technical aid in such business matters. They, in turn, supported him in his management of church and lodge affairs. A member of the largest extended family counted twenty-three children, many of whom were illegitimate. Although the extended family seldom farms as a unit, the organization of large kinship groups by visiting, performance of mutual services, and by church and associational solidarity undoubtedly was instrumental in keeping large numbers of tenants on the plantation.

Immediate family — The immediate family of father, mother, and children, however, is a productive unit, and every effort is made to keep it intact by both tenant and landlord . . .

The patriarchal family — The best examples of the integrated and stable tenant-family, however, were those of tenant-managers. All of the eight colored managers who were interviewed had married sons working with them, or renting from them, on that part of the plantation which the manager himself rented. . . . Another tenant-manager had three married sons and their wives working with him. The communal division of labor extended even to the wives, each of whom had an established round of duties for each day in the week. A third tenant-manager had been able to buy a farm through the combined work of an extended family, including a nephew and a son-in-law, in addition to his own children . . .

Matriarchal family — One-seventh (14.1 percent) of the autonomous cotton-farmers in Old County were women. Most of these were colored tenants. The solidarity of these matriarchal families as production units rivaled that of the patriarchal families cited above (Davis et al. 1941: 410–412).

The strong central authority of the father or mother, reinforced by religious and moral sanctions, organizes all members of the family into a single productive unit, which often includes married sons or daughters and their families (and, in the case of aged tenants, children whom the tenant has adopted to help him on the farm after his own children have left him). The social authority of the family head, in turn, is greatly strengthened by his economic and technical power as head of the family's productive system (Davis et al. 1941: 413).

Without exception, the authors of the late 1930's and 1940's considered Black family structure and behavior to be strongly affected by class level — lower, middle, or upper. Yet while both class structures (associated with color, education, and income) and variant family patterns can be accepted as facts, the degree to which these were actually correlated remains open. The authors of *Deep South* found great continuity, from one status to another, in the spectrum of informal social clubs ("cliques");

they also found that socioeconomic positions and excellence of reputation were by no means closely correlated (Davis et al. 210–214; 230–232).

In her study of Sunflower County, Mississippi, Hortense Powdermaker (1966 [1939]), in contrast, developed an elaborate formulation:

Socially, the upper class, like the white aristocracy, constitutes an exclusive and revered minority. . . . The most constant class indication among the Negroes has to do with the acceptance of certain modes of behavior formerly restricted to Whites, particularly those which center in marriage and sex life, family life, education, occupation, and forms of religious worship (Powdermaker 1966 [1939]: 60–61).

As a result of the insistence upon legally sanctioned and monogamous marriage, the upper class has developed a family life more stable than that of the others. It is also the one class in which the structure of the family is patriarchal rather than matriarchal. The greater stability and cohesion of the family has made for a stronger growth of family traditions: as a rule upper-class persons know more about their parents and grandparents than do their social inferiors (Powdermaker 1966 [1939]: 63).

Limited reinquiries in Sunflower County cast much doubt on these generalizations. Widespread networks of kinfolk are ubiquitous today in Sunflower County at all levels. For example, Mrs. Fannie Lou Hamer, a former plantation day laborer, numbers over 150 persons (including relatives in Memphis and other cities) in her active family relationships. Much the same must have been true a generation earlier. And while family disorganization, sexual license, personal abusiveness, and other failings are, of course, found among Black people in the County, few would correlate reputations of virtue with social class. To identify the "upper class" as revered paragons of virtue would indeed startle many Black people in Sunflower County.

Overall, the data on the rural South, although developed for other purposes and somewhat subject to theoretical bias, do confirm the presence of the Black extended family as a widespread and rather homogeneous institution. It is clear, furthermore, that many recent migrants from the rural South to the urban North have retained the extended family. Carol Stack's careful study of a ninety-six-person network dispersed between Arkansas, Illinois, Michigan, Wisconsin, and California describes a group unified by common occupations in migratory farm work and a resulting mobile life.[31] The extended family, although apparently lacking in much fixed property, is a basic system of economic information and cooperation, within which households are formed and reformed. The

[31]   Carol Stack ("The kindred of Viola Jackson", 1969) has completed a greatly expanded version of this study as her doctoral dissertation.

cooperation of adult siblings is more persistent as a basis of household formation than are marriages, which tend to be brittle. "Adoptions," i.e. fosterage, is widely practiced by adults on both the male and female sides. Conversely, grown children exercise considerable control over the movements of the aged.

Bagdikian's sketch illustrates similar phenomena of cooperation and coresidence in the movement of the "Austin" family from Bolivar County, Mississippi, to Springfield, Illinois. The conflicts of the 1960's were prime movers for this flight. Ultimately, thirty-six "Austins" resided within a half-mile of each other in the latter place (Bagdikian 1967).

Virginia Young's study of Black families, and childhood among first-generation migrants to "Georgiatown" in 1961–1966 reveals patterns similar to the stereotypes of Delta families in Holmes County (Young 1970, 1971).

In family behavior, men are usually accorded or assume authority in the house. Women act as though their husbands had authority, and children are respectful of them. . . . The grandmothers who supervise large households of children, grandchildren, and great-grandchildren all have husbands supporting them.

Since men head a large proportion of households, it is not surprising that illegitimate and orphaned children are often cared for in the households of male kinsmen — the paternal grandfather, a paternal uncle, a maternal uncle, and a maternal great-uncle in cases known. Responsibility for a son's illegitimate children as well as a daughter's may be assumed by older stable couples. . . . Thus family ties through men and emotional ties of men to their kinsmen are socially important in this town, as well as mother–daughter ties (Young 1971: 197–198).

Illegitimate births are especially common before the first marriage. Of forty-four women who gave life histories, at least twenty-one had one or more children before marriage. The unwed mother almost never forms a separate household, but remains with her own childhood family, sometimes working and relying on her family for child care. Having children out of wedlock is not approved, even though it is so common. . . . The child probably does not suffer from its illegitimacy. His mother shows the immense pride in her baby that is typical of all births in this community. . . . Sometimes the father of the illegitimate baby helps support it and, as it grows, sends for it to visit him. The child usually has two or even three households where he has a berth — the paternal and maternal relatives who helped raise him and his own mother's house after she marries (Young 1971: 199).

Marriage is thought of as a relationship concerning only the couple and neither the community nor individual families attempt to regulate marriage beyond a qualified adherence to an ethic of obligations between mating couples. Adolescents are free to engage in sexual behavior, but marriage as an acceptance of enduring obligations and as an economic arrangement comes about with more maturity and primarily as a matter of choice and with a minimum of social pressure. In the family, husband and wife both contribute economically, both have authority, both can take the initiative to bring about separation, and both may find separation advantageous. Although many marriages dissolve, re-marriage is usual, and middle-aged persons not living in a married state are uncommon. In contrast to the two-generation White nuclear family, the Negro family maintains strong ties over three or four generations . . . (Young 1971: 200–201).

At the same time it is not clear whether the same type of Black extended family is really characteristic of the urban as well as of the rural South. Hylan Lewis's study of the Black community in a Carolina Piedmont mill town (which was apparently done in the early 1950's) brings out some features similar to those of Holmes County society (Lewis 1955). For example, while a well-defined class system was absent, the good or bad social reputations of families and individuals were sharply delineated. Their basis was conduct, with the standards of propriety being raised with increasing education or economic status. The independent farmer, the artisan, the teacher, and the undertaker were more secure in their status than the preacher (Lewis 1955: 223–256).

As in Holmes County, the households were of varied type, with nuclear families constituting only 40 percent of the total and the fosterage of children being a commonplace (Lewis 1955: 93–103). Family functions included

. . . crisis aid and protection, transmission of work skills, support in design for upward mobility via education, limited ascription of status, definition of role vis-à-vis whites and provision of techniques of survival and getting along.

Innumerable crisis situations are a part of the normal routine of life for most Kent families. Whether prepared for or not, these situations tend to be part of the normal expectancy in this setting and they usually involve some mobiliza-tion of relatives. The type of aid ranges from sympathy and moral support through various degrees of material or physical support . . . (Lewis 1955: 103–104).

Even in the most loosely organized or disorganized families, there tends to be some recognition of the support and protection demands of kinship. There is particular sensitivity to the outside attack or supposed insult. This ties in with the oft-expressed creed: "I minds my own business; other folks is supposed to mind theirs" (Lewis 1955: 104–105).

The transmission of work skills from father to sons is particularly noticeable. A great premium is placed upon the male's being able to do something with his hands, and the average male possesses a mechanical skill or ability.

In this setting, a greater premium has been placed on the higher education of girls than boys.... These are the ways in which independence — working for one's self in the case of the male and "getting out of the white folks' kitchen" in the case of the female — has been defined in practical terms (Lewis 1955: 105–106).

"Kent," like Holmes County, is a source area for migration, in this case to New York City, Philadelphia, and Washington. This does not break ties.

Many migrants follow the custom of the annual vacation visit to family and friends. Death and illness in the family are other important reasons for the temporary return of the migrant. A small number of persons return to Kent to live out the remainder of their lives after having spent many years away. For the most part such persons are older men and women who have no conjugal families of their own who return to live with sisters or brothers or to set up their own households (Lewis 1955: 35).

Yet with these similarities, important differences can be noted. Although courtship prior to marriage was customary, the marriage ceremony in "Kent" was both civil and private (Lewis 1955: 92–93). Families tended to be small; children were often insecure. Religion did not appear to be significantly a family affair; numerous voluntary organizations on the one hand and sharply felt individualism on the other were more important than kinship in determining behavior (Lewis 1955: 94, 256–285, 322–325). Above all, extended families did not appear to be strong sociopolitical entities, nor to be specifically reinforced by religion. A few families ". . . differentiated by property, enterprise or artisanry, education of children, public morality, and the symbols of family unity and loyalty . . ." were "ascribed a certain place in the status or success hierarchy," yet they were essentially passive retainers of prestige (like many upper-class White families in the South) rather than dominant actors in their community. "Although there is some intermarriage among these top families, there is a minimum of social commingling, and there is no evidence of clique behavior among them. They tend to be proud isolates each with a certain amount of disdain for the other" (Lewis 1955: 107). Whether such families are endogamous or exogamous Professor Lewis does not make clear.

To this day, the data on the extended families and kin networks of Black people in northern cities are fragmentary. The excellent early studies of Chicago, which are centrally concerned with social ecology, sexual behavior, and delinquency, unfortunately fail to provide enough specifics to substantiate or to disprove the presence of significant kin networks beyond the household level. (See, for example, Frazier 1932; Warner et al. 1941; Drake and Cayton 1945.) However, a general indication is given by Mueller and Ladd's (1970) survey of 2,406 White and 263 "non-White" families which constituted a probability sample of all families living in private dwelling units in the coterminous United States. These authors found that

The ties of the Negro to the community seem to be to an important extent family and friendship ties. . . . even though only one-third of Negro adults are still living in the county where they were born 59 percent have all or most of their relatives living near them now in the same community. Most of the remaining Negro families reported that "some" relatives are living in the same community where they are. The survey shows that only 6 percent of Negro families, in contrast to 21 percent of white families, have no relatives where they are now residing.

When a family does decide to move, relatives may play a further role in facilitating and guiding the move. In discussing their most recent move across family lines, most Negro as well as most white families mentioned job or economic factors as the primary reason for moving. However, among Negroes who were born in the South and have moved North or West, family reasons were mentioned with considerable frequency. A third of the group said that they moved in order to be closer to a relative who had moved earlier. A closer look at cases of recent Negro migrants in the survey suggests that job and family considerations tend to be inseparable in many instances, since relatives are the major source of job information and often help the migrant find work (Mueller and Ladd 1970: 111).

Beyond the level of generalizations, the data are often equivocal. For example, a great deal of study has been done on the corrosive effects of current welfare practices and high-density public housing on many aspects of the Black family. Yet, even in this context, it is easy to overstate the degree at which social atomization and disorganization proceed. Illustrative is Rainwater's study of the highly unsuccessful Pruitt-Igoe housing development in St. Louis, which isolated a project with 62 percent of the families female-headed; 69 percent of the population, minors; and less than 9 percent of the population, adult males. In only 45 percent of the households was employment the sole source of income, while 38 percent included no employed person (Rainwater 1970: 13–14). Associated with these anomalies were a number of apparent social changes. Parent–child relationships involved much open conflict, including the beating of wives and children by husbands (Rainwater 1970: 163) but also a shift to a "peer" relationship which

. . . is much easier with female than with male children; an almost sister-like relationship often appears even between early teenage girls and their mothers, but boys can come to feel very much like strangers in their own homes.
The peer basis of parent–child relations is important for preserving the solidarity of the family because it makes it possible to avoid and underemphasize issues of parental control . . . (Rainwater 1970: 68).

Each of the different fathers recognizes obligations in most cases only to his own child, although this often involves "an underlying sense of vulnerability and discreditability, subtly affecting the child's ability to build and maintain a sense of common family membership and solidarity" (Rainwater 1970: 217). In general, in contrast to the self-sufficiency of rural Black families, those at Pruitt-Igoe have been

... quite open to penetration by the outside world. . . . The family is held together by a set of expressive and instrumental functions parents perform for their children and to some extent children for their parents. But the boundaries of the unit are readily broken by any member who feels he needs to bring in outsiders or take the resources of the family away for his own use . . . (Rainwater 1970: 233).

Nevertheless, even this tortured population retains more general Black family norms: wives are completely in charge of households; husbands are expected to exercise fidelity and to provide financial support; blood relatives are looked to as sources of help; visits with blood relatives are a major part of adult social activity, and the kinship network is widely expandable (Rainwater 1970: 68–69, 111, 162, 170). Finally, it is possible that Rainwater and his associates, concentrating particularly on social pathologies, may have underestimated residual strengths in conjugal relations and male roles. This is indicated by Moore's study, apparently of the same population (Moore 1969: 34–35, 70–110).

In one of the few studies published on middle-class urban Black people, John H. Scanzoni (1971) examined the characteristics of 400 conjugal families married at least five years in all-Black neighborhoods of Indianapolis. This design clearly introduced biases into the sample so that Scanzoni's results must be viewed as perhaps exceptional. For example, 86 percent of the respondents had lived with only their nuclear families during adolescence (Scanzoni 1971: 134). Moreover, 69 percent denied and only 28 percent affirmed that relatives beyond the immediate family had helped them get ahead in life in their earlier years (Scanzoni 1971: 135).

This possible evidence of familial fragmentation is in contrast to the indications available for the old elite elements of Black society. A special study of this subject, by Dr. Horace M. Bond, is unfortunately available only in brief summary. Essentially, this authority estimates that the 550,000 free Negroes in the United States in 1860 represented about 5,000 extended families. In his opinion, three-fourths of the "leading" Negroes have come from about 400 of these families and from about another 100 slave families issuing from ancestors of exceptional ability and status, especially domestic slaves. Crucial in the emergence of "leadership" has been, not White blood, but rather some favorable event which gave the striving family an advantage in money and education. Family discipline and cohesiveness presumably have consolidated such initial advantages into traditions of "leadership" (Billingsley 1968: 118).

Much needs to be added to these tantalizing suggestions. What were the interrelationships between kinship and other reinforcing mechanisms for the elite — church leadership, fraternal orders, secluded vacation spots? To what extent has the old elite been able to absorb newcomers? Is it still a unitary body, with a common value and status system? Or is it only a dying memory? (See also Frazier 1964: 29–46; Coombs 1964: 24–31.)

Whatever the general questions may be concerning the effects of upward mobility or high status upon Black kinship norms and behavior, there is little doubt that the post-World War II migrations from the South and East to California have had great effects. These, in general, have weakened extended kinship ties. Mr. Jerry Wright, a young Black graduate student from California, summarizes the basic facts as follows:[32]

Most of the Blacks who arrived in the 1940's were from Negro communities in the Midwest; most had already begun the process of urbanization. Most of them had eighth-grade schooling, while a fifth had finished high school. . . . Few older people ventured so far — the average couples were in their lower or middle twenties and had one child.

When migration to California was new, and the migrants knew no one in the area, the husband usually came alone and sent money to his family. When the savings were sufficient, the family then moved to the area. There was and is little of the Chicago–Detroit phenomenon of children remaining in the South with relatives. The reasons are that, until of late, the streets were safe and the problems that lead to delinquency and crime were just not that prevalent. The weather was fairly constant in Southern California, so parents did not have to worry about children freezing in the winters or setting the house afire, although there were problems of housing, transportation, schooling, and employment.

The pattern of finding jobs and providing lodging and food for kin (not always blood kin, but often people from the same home town, who often will assume a fictive kinship) was and is still commonplace. I know of a married couple who lived as neighbors of my parents for some years and who sponsored either financially or otherwise the immigration of some twenty-five family members from Arkansas to Los Angeles.

Contrary to the free movement of Blacks between Chicago, Detroit, and New York, and places in the South, most immigrants to California were rather confined because of distance to the West Coast. There is an exception, and that would be the large number of migrants who came from Texas, Arkansas, and

---

[32] Department of Anthropology, Harvard University; personal communication used by permission.

Louisiana, for whom treks back and forth between their original home and California became commonplace.

Migration has had some effect on the family life of Blacks in California. Perhaps most important has been the breaking up of the southern extended family, or its facsimile as it has continued in the Midwest. It is true that many people sponsored other members of their family to come to California, but most did not. It was the young who came, and as a result the nuclear family became extremely important. The extended family is only of recent occurrence in California, found among the original migrants, their offspring and their sibs. Fictive kinship has served as a substitute.

Age-status as described in the South and in Chicago is almost non-existent. Primarily, this is due to the fact that so few older people migrated. The offspring of the original migrants are so urbanized that they regard the whole affair (of age-status) as old-fashioned. Many of the original migrants (grandparents in their late forties) speak of the "old days at home" when the children behaved and "minded" their parents. It is not uncommon to hear, "Boy, if you had been my father's son, he would have killed you years ago for talking back."

Perhaps one of the vestiges of age-status is the "long childhood" stage. Young people are regarded as children by kin and community until they are sometimes in their twenties. A vivid yet usual comment is, "I don't care how old you are, you'ar still a child to me." As in the South, sexual escapades and illegitimate births are often excused on the grounds that a person is "young and crazy." The child's view of the adult is one of respect but not necessarily, recognition of a higher status. It is very apparent that adults could have never played the part in Black organizing (e.g. Black Panthers, etc.)[33] in California the way they did in Mississippi.

Social clubs that are geographically founded are common, but this appears to be very middle-class or upper-class oriented . . .

The church is very important to most older migrants and to young people for a while. The church is sought by denomination. Methodists and Episcopalians view Baptists as being much too primitive and emotional, and Baptists have a similar view of the more fundamentalist groups.

The church seems to serve as a point of social adjustment for younger people. After they have learned the "ropes" of how to maneuver in the urban setting, they usually leave the church. They have a suspicious view of preachers . . .

The church does provide more than just a religious outlet for the new migrant; it also fills a social gap. Often it is through the members of the church that the new migrant learns of jobs, how to transport himself around the town, and how to get on welfare, if that is necessary. Often the members of the church will provide support for the new family. Sometimes the church offers the new migrant his first real opportunity to see other parts of the city when members visit other churches.

The return of deceased members of a family to ancestral burial plots in the South is slowly dying out among California Blacks. Besides its being very

---

[33]   This refers to the original Black Panthers of the rural South and not to the rather different and later urban organization. Even more significant have been the Deacons for Defense, largely mature men including many veterans, who banded together to resist attacks by the Ku Klux Klan [D.B.S].

expensive, it is seen as of no worth by the young people. Many of them have never been to the South and unless the deceased requested it, the usual pattern is burial in California. But this does mean that close relatives in the South sometimes will come out for the funeral.

Affiliation with the Black Muslim faith has been, even more than migration to California, disruptive of kin ties. Social reconstruction through religion has been an old element of American culture from the days of the Shakers and Mormons onward. Within Black society, however, it became significant only after World War I, especially in conjunction with the activities of Father Divine. This religious leader developed a biracial religious community, previously in Philadelphia, which sought to absorb the total interests and resources of its devotees. Sexual relations, even between man and wife, were supposedly forbidden (Frazier 1966: 59). Kinship existed only in relation to Father Divine.

The tenets of the Nation of Islam, according to Harry Edwards's (1968) pioneer study have furthered not an abandonment of families but rather their profound reconstruction as vehicles of the Faith. Within the household, sex roles have been redefined. The men are strictly income producers; their wives are homemakers. Contraception is forbidden. Drinking, smoking, and idling are prohibited; neither hair straighteners nor makeup are permissible for women, among whom modest dress and behavior are compulsory; the dietary prohibitions are also extensive. These norms are, in principle, developed and maintained through intense religious education; physical chastisement of children is to be used only when all else fails.

In general, the rigid behavioral norms of Black Muslim families conflict sharply with the traditional behaviors reviewed in previous pages. In consequence, the ties with Christian kin are minimal, if maintained at all. What ties develop within the body of Muslims is yet to be studied.

To summarize: the available materials on Black extended families and kin networks in the rural and urban United States suggest that the Holmes County data are representative of a widespread pattern. The materials from the Sea Islands of South Carolina are particularly suggestive. Research covering points not specifically established, such as the formal corporate activities of extended families, as well as the bringing up to date of Woofter's and Kiser's classic investigations, is urgently needed.

In general, the other findings are tentative indeed. Rigorous comparative research is essential. It is hoped that such research will include family histories using combinations of memory, family records, church records, and information from social specialists, notably ministers, folk judges, and midwives. Attention needs to be paid both to expressed norms and to observed or reported behavior. The structures and functions of extended families need to be studied in detail at the community level as well as in relation to the household. The interrelationships of extended families and networks with other institutions — churches, fraternal orders, youth groups, etc. — need to be defined. And the support and disadvantages offered by these institutions to their members need to be examined with care.

HISTORICAL CONTINUITY, BORROWING, AND SITUATIONAL ADAPTATION IN THE BLACK EXTENDED FAMILY

Although the characteristics of Black extended families and kin networks in the United States are known only approximately, an exploratory effort to place these data in a processual framework appears to be worthwhile. At the very least, such an examination indicates areas for future inquiry.

The subject of African antecedents for Black family structure and functioning in the United States has received a preliminary review by M. J. Herskovits (1971 [1941]). He discerned African origins for a number of features:

The "common-law relationship" is merely a phrase for the recognition of the fact that matings not legally sanctioned may achieve enough stability to receive equal recognition with regularly performed marriages. In Africa, and in the West Indies where Africanisms persist, marriage is not a matter requiring approval of the state or any religious body. Only consent of the families concerned is needed, while marriage rites depart from the secular only to the extent that they are directed toward obtaining the benevolent oversight of the ancestors. Therefore Negro common-law marriages in the United States conflict in no way with earlier practices, while in so far as they require the approval of the families of the principals, they are, indeed, directly in line with African custom.

The "competent, self-sufficient women" who wish to have no husbands are of especial interest. The social and economic position of women in West Africa is such that on occasion a woman may refuse to relinquish the customary control of her children in favor of her husband. . . . The same traditional basis exists for "children by the way," those offspring of women, once married, by men other than their husbands (Herskovits 1971 [1941]: 38).

It cannot be regarded only as coincidence that such specialized features of Negro family life in the United States as the role of women in focusing the sentiment that gives the family unit its psychological coherence, or their place in maintaining the economic stability essential to survival, correspond closely to similar facets of West African social structure. . . . Though everywhere the father has his place, the tradition of paternal control and the function of the father as sole or principal provider essential to the European pattern is deviated from . . . (Herskovits 1971 [1941]: 45).

In both West Africa and the West Indies the women, holding their economic destinies in their own hands, are fully capable of going their own ways if their husbands displease them; not being hampered by any conception of marriage as an ultimate commitment, separation is easily effected and a consequent fluidity in family personnel . . . results (Herskovits 1971 [1941]: 46).

The African immediate family, consisting of a father, his wives, and their children, is but part of . . . the "extended family," while a series of these extended families, in turn, comprise the matrilineal or patrilineal sibs, often totemic in sanction, which are the effective agents in administering the controls of the ancestral cult (Herskovits 1971 [1941]: 47).

Later in this work, Herskovits, reviewing the characteristics of an extended Black family in Virginia, found specific resemblances to the corresponding institution in Dahomey:

In such matters or the inheritance of headship from the eldest sibling to his next in line, in the retained identity of the family land as a part of the mechanism making for the retention of identity by the relationship group itself, and in the relatively small proportion of members who leave their group, immediate correspondences will be discerned (Herskovits 1971 [1941]: 48).

In the posthumous summary of his work, Herskovits (1966) evaluated Black social organization in the United States as "somewhat African"; "very African" social organization he limited, in the New World, to the Bush Negroes of Guiana (Herskovits 1966: 53). Y. W. Blassingame's recent analysis of Black slave life on U.S. plantations deals at length with African elements in languages, dance, music, folk tales, and religion, but not in kinship or other elements of social organization (Blassingame 1972: 1–40).

The significance of suggestions of African affiliations can be increased by other direct comparisons and by consideration of the possible mechanisms of transfer and continuity. At the same time, it must be emphasized that contemporary similarities can provide only clues to transfers of 100 to 300 years ago; firm conclusions would require detailed ethnohistorical research yet to be done.

Two levels of comparison can be added to those presented above. The first is to place the characteristics of the Black extended family, particularly as found among Hill people in Holmes County, the Sea Islands of South Carolina, and other areas of the rural South, into the general pattern of African family and marriage as propounded by L. P. Mair (1953: 1–8). Both similarities and differences may be noted. Among the former, the most significant are shown in the following citations:

... cooperation in tilling the fields and herding the cattle is provided by a group of people bound by the obligations of kinship and marriages and not by the relationship of wage-earner to employer (Mair 1953: 1).

A child grows up in a household where there are a number of adults and many other children. When he is small any of the women may take temporary charge of him, and as he gets older any of the adults may admonish him (Mair 1953: 2).

Divorce is often thought preferable to inability to live in amity, partly because quarrels lead to violence and bad feeling, and bad feeling is believed to lead people to practice sorcery. . . .

Every marriage requires the consent of some senior person, sometimes not even the nearest male relative but the lineage head. Individual choice is limited by prohibitions against marriage with related persons, the extent of which varies from tribe to tribe but is nearly always much wider than in the Western world . . . (Mair 1953: 4).

Again the African husband jealously retains his own property rights even in household objects provided by himself. But his wife too is usually entitled to independent control of any property that she may acquire by her own efforts . . . (Mair 1953: 7).

Basic differences between the U.S. Black rural and the African patterns are the prohibition of polygynous marriage and the absence of bride price, child betrothal, and the levirate among the former. The extensive mechanisms of fosterage and adoption found among Black Americans have parallels in limited parts of Africa. And, of course, several of the common characteristics have only limited distribution and, often, conditional expression in the United States.

Under the direction of Professor Donald Vermeer, Dennis Frate has identified an elaborate complex of geophagy among the Black people of Holmes County (Frate 1972). Substantially similar practices are known for the Ewe of Ghana (Vermeer 1971). The traditional economic activities in Holmes County are remarkably similar to those of the Anlo Ewe: farming, poultry raising by women and children, fishing; weaving of cloth, mats, mattresses, and wicker baskets; pottery making; and blacksmithing (Nukunya 1969: 7). (The absence in Mississippi of significant women's trading enterprises is, however, a noteworthy contrast attributable to prohibitions against trading by slaves.)

Given these special similarities, the presence of particular resemblances in kinship deserves attention. The Anlo Ewe clan, like the Holmes County extended family in the recent past, had vengeance obligations and obligations to help offended kinsmen (Nukunya 1969: 23). Membership in a clan is associated with a stereotyped reputation, e.g. "being notably wicked, even-tempered, violent or even fecund" (Nukunya 1969: 24). The lineage head, like the "founder" of a Holmes County extended family, is usually its oldest surviving member in terms of both generation and age. The head's influence increases with age; no undertakings of importance for the group or a member are taken without consulting this head (Nukunya 1969: 26). Lineages are associated with a particular locality where its members reside, have a ceremonial center, and are buried. However those out-migrating retain membership in the lineage; they return to the home locality for important meetings and ceremonies and are buried there (Nukunya 1969: 28–29). Father–son relationships are reinforced by coresidence and cooperation in work, but are essentially those of authority and deference (Nukunya 1969: 39). In addition, it appears that some terminological pecularities in Holmes County may have explanations in earlier classificatory usages; thus, among the Anlo Ewe, the father's brother is called "Big Father" or "Small Father" depending upon his age relative to the actual father (Nukunya 1969: 40). Again, in both Holmes County and among the Anlo Ewe, the ties between adult brother and sister may often outweigh and strain marital ones (Nukunya 1969: 118). Finally, in both areas, a substantial proportion of the households are female-headed; in both, households with daughters' children greatly exceed those with sons' children in frequency (Nukunya 1969: 130–132).

Granting that the resemblances marshaled thus far suggest some historical connections, the question of possible mechanisms of transmission and retention becomes paramount. Here, only the outlines of an argument can be proposed.

In the first place it should be noted that slave imports from Africa to the United States continued on a substantial scale — perhaps 15,000 persons per year — up to the Civil War (DuBois 1970 [1896]: 162–167, 178–183; Weld 1969: 18–24). The coasts of Georgia, Florida, and Texas were the primary landing areas; however, according to Stephen A. Douglas's personal observations in the 1850's, Africans were transshipped as far inland as Vicksburg, Mississippi, and Memphis, Tennessee (DuBois 1970 [1896]: 181–182). In 1860, four slaves from the notorious slaving ship, the "Wanderer," were sold in Marshall County, in north-central Mississippi (Sydnor 1933: 142). In short, infusions of African culture continued into the American South throughout the years of slavery.

Second, slavery in Virginia, which state accounted for half of the entire Black slave population throughout the eighteenth century and about a quarter of the total as late as 1830, was based on the binding of slaves to land according to the Code of 1705 (Weld 1969: 8; Talpalor 1960: 331–

333). This annexation of slaves, "together with all their future increase" (Talpalor 1960: 331), to particular tracts of land set up a demographic basis for extended family retention and development, notwithstanding the sexual predations of White masters and the export of surplus slaves to other states. It reinforced, moreover, the close relationship between land and family which was part of the African tradition.

Third, the proprietory ideal developed on the Virginia plantations of the seventeenth century and central to the concept of the southern planter to this day was that of a self-sufficient and self-perpetuating manor managed by paid overseers for the benefit of often-absent owners.[34] The overseers, in turn, were concerned with extracting a maximum cash return from the plantation via the sale of cotton, tobacco, rice, indigo, and other crops, and via the sale or hiring out of slaves. The foundation of the entire system was a highly organized slave labor force, including field gangs under slave "drivers," slave craftsmen of various types, slave midwives and nurses, and perhaps other specialists, such as community cooks. (See Olmsted 1970: 47 for an example.) The origins of this complex labor force appear to have been largely from indigenous skills brought by the slaves and transmitted to their offspring. Only rarely is there evidence that planters or overseers consciously trained their slaves; clearly, a ratio of one manager and four overseers to five hundred slaves, which character-ized many large estates (e.g. Sydnor 1933: 68), was totally inadequate for such tasks.

Fourth, while an extensive system of surveillance over slaves, prohibi-tions against slave gatherings, and rigid controls on the movements of slaves were basic features of southern society from the early eighteenth century onward, its effectiveness was highly variable. It was least func-tional in the malarial areas of South Carolina and Mississippi and most effective against urban slaves (see Henry 1914; Wade 1964). It was, in general, a force tending to make slave society covert, rather than one capable *per se* of destroying manifold, functional relationships.

Fifth, while acculturation was undoubtedly extensive in the cities, among domestic slaves, and on the small slave holdings of the frontier farmers, large plantations (with some exception) discouraged literacy, Christian indoctrination and the quasi-legal recognition of marriages. This is well discussed in the literature on the large plantations of Missis-sippi in the 1850's (see Olmsted 1970: 21–23 56, 64, etc.). The social

---

[34]   For other discussions, see Talpalor (1960), Sydnor (1933), and Johnson (1930). Skrygley's autobiography states that minor adjudications and punishments were some-times delegated to "a sort of court among the negroes," albeit "under the jurisdiction and general supervision of the master himself" (Skrygley 1893: 272–274).

isolation of field slaves from their owners and overseers, punishments and sex apart, is characterized by Olmsted (1970: 71) as follows:

Even the overseer had barely acquaintance enough with the slaves individually, to call them by name; the owner could not determine with confidence if he were addressing one of his own chattels, by its features. Much less did the slaves have an opportunity to cultivate their minds by intercourse with other White people . . .

Sixth, the dispersion of the slave population from the old centers on the East Coast to the new cotton lands of Mississippi largely took place in the 1830's and, in considerable part, through the reestablishment of entire plantations. In consequence, while heavy deculturation and indeed loss of life marked the activities of domestic slave traders (or "soul drivers"), and while some planters literally worked their slaves to death, Mississippi plantation society was essentially a transplant rather than a new tradition. (See Sydnor 1933: 131–202; Weld 1969: 12–18, 44–87.)

And seventh, the Black extended family as described for the Sea Island slaves and for Holmes County, Mississippi, differs basically from the extended family of White planter society. The latter, as known from early Virginia, South Carolina, and rural Mississippi, is marked by endogamy at the second-cousin level, sharply hierarchical ordering, rigid require-ments of legitimate descent, strong property and status orientation, secularism, social equivalence of husbands and wives (rather than sib-lings), and emphasis upon discipline rather than nurture as basic responsi-bilities toward offspring. (Bruce 1907; Talpalor 1960: 126–168; Johnson 1930: 103–123; Davis et al. 1941: 84–99.)

The arguments for historical continuity in the rural Black extended family must be balanced by a recognition of many clearcut borrowings from White culture. Under slavery, the domestics who were often their master's kin, urban slaves, the slaves of small holders, and the free population were especially subject to imposed acculturation. In conse-quence, it is probable that the extended families and kin networks of older southern cities such as Charleston, South Carolina, or "Kent" may be far more influenced by White antecedents than the societies discussed above. Moreover, it is important to note that, even in Mississippi, the egalitarian-ism of the frontier sometimes transformed slavery. Olmsted (1970: 139–151) described a hamlet in northern Mississippi all but run by the slaves, who had taught themselves to read, were avid purchasers of both religious books and novels from peddlers, and had become active Baptists.

During the Civil War, imposed changes accelerated. A notable effort was that undertaken by the Federal Government and the Freedman's

Relief Association of New York in the Sea Islands of South Carolina (Johnson 1930: 154–190). The effort included family education and administrative compulsion; the superintendent issued orders "requiring that all marriages among the people be regularly performed by a minister according to law, and he strictly forbade a couple's living together until the ceremony had been pronounced" (Johnson 1930: 178). As mentioned previously, opportunities to buy land provided incentives to consolidate he social innovations.

In general, much research is needed to define the interactions between Black, White, and, indeed, Indian systems of kinship and marriage. Apart from a series of unequivocal loans, ranging from kinship terms to family prayers at meals, White influences probably reinforced some antecedent Black patterns, such as feud obligations and major funeral rites. Other features such as polygamy and the levirate were suppressed. Although borrowings apparently slowed down after Reconstruction, truly profound assimilations may now be underway in some localities, as is suggested by Scanzoni's study (1971) of middle-class Black families in Indianapolis.

Persistence, borrowing, and spontaneous changes in Black kinship systems have taken place under a wide array of social situations both during and since the days of slavery. Nevertheless, a continuing feature has been the combination of high economic and demographic risks with limited, insecure holdings of property or vested statuses. The minute level of Black proprietorship even today needs emphasis. In 1969, Black-owned firms constituted only 2.2 percent of all firms in the United States and generated only *0.3 percent* of the business receipts (U.S. Bureau of the Census 1972: 471). Even in the few industries where Black capital has developed modest successes, the future is gloomy. Quoting Andrew Brimmer (1971: 33–34),

Essentially, the difficulties arise from the thinness of capital and managerial resources in the Black community. . . . The circumstances from which the present uncertainties arose can be readily understood. In the typical cases, a few men (frequently a single individual) had the vision to see the need for financial services in the Black community. With a venturesome spirit — but with little capital — they took the risk and nurtured the enterprise through many years of slow growth and modest progress. . . .

Because of these survivals, we have a small — but strategically important — network of Black-owned financial institutions today. There are 26 Black-owned commercial banks, 43 savings and loan associations, and 50 life insurance companies. . . .

As I survey the scene, I think a much greater effort must be made to ensure that the existing institutions can survive and prosper. In several cases, one or more important stockholders may find it necessary (because of age, family, or other reasons) to sell their holdings before many more years have passed. If this prospect materializes anytime soon, it is my impression that few buyers could be found in the Negro community. Thus, there is a real risk that ownership and control of some of the most prized of the existing businesses might pass from the Black community.

In general, poverty and discrimination against Black people have necessitated an interdependence and, conversely, generated internal conflicts that are substantially different from those of the White majority. For this reason, findings from studies of kinship in contemporary White society can be used to a limited extent in evaluating the adaptive problems of Black people. While common elements do, of course, exist, the more acute needs and the much more limited resources and alternatives characteristic of Black life in the United States impose major differences. In particular, imperative economic and personal-security demands permit less development of "friendship" features, just as these very needs and the lack of resources limit parental aid to adult children even where traditional views on the primacy of "mother and father, brother and sister" have been replaced by majority attitudes (compare Adams 1970).

Methodological problems also arise because of the interpretation of functional relations and attitudes from a parochial cultural viewpoint. Blood and Wolfe's (1969) study of blue-collar families in Detroit is a revealing mélange of preconceptions and observations on Black kinship. Emphasizing largely nonsignificant difference in wives' "marital satisfactions" and clear contrasts in the intensity of "informative companionship," these authors minimize the greater roles of Black wives in family decision making and the high importance these wives attach to the management of family resources.[35] Hence their negative appraisal of Black families. How different Herskovits's analysis would have been! To state, finally, that "the Negro husband is not so much henpecked as segregated" (Blood and Wolfe 1969: 62) tells little about Black people but much about Blood and Wolfe's flippant research perspective.

With these basic reservations in mind, comparative data on kinship as a mechanism of social adaptation can be utilized. The work of Eugene Litwak is particularly valuable in this regard. His theoretical paper on the continuing functions of the extended family (Litwak 1959–1960) not only indicates the importance of this institution in assisting migration through pooling information and economic resources, but its capacity, through internal deference, to accommodate to economic and occupational differences among kin. (See also Blumberg and Bell 1958–1959; Brown et al. 1963.) These findings are fully compatible with Holmes County norms.

[35] It would be of considerable value to duplicate Reuben Hill's (1962–1963) studies of family resource management among rural and urban Black families.

Litwak and Szelenyi (1969) have further differentiated the relative functional capacities of kin, neighbors, and friends in modern societies. These findings are particularly relevant to Black people, for whom the apparent homogeneity of the ghetto often masks marked fragmentation and conflict between migrants and old residents, householders and youth gangs, poor and middle class.[36]

Also significant have been many empirical studies of kin relationships and dynamics which appear to have cross-cultural significance. An example is Sweetser's (1970) study of the nature of relationships among adult siblings in Finland. She established that, for this population at least, the widespread predominance of females in kin activities (see also Adams 1970: 580) correlates with the separation of men's work from a family setting. Among children of farmers, "the brother-brother communication was sufficiently great to produce a curvilinear relation between sex of siblings and communication" (Sweetser 1970: 56). The correspondence to findings among Black Holmes Countians is marked. The comparative study of families and kin as service networks is also promising.

In general, the functionality of kin networks and perhaps even more formally corporate extended families in American and other urban societies appears to be well established. At the same time, it must be stressed that this functionality has essentially meant the *persistence* of much older institutions, with some losses and many reinterpretations. Evidence has not come to light of structural innovations or new codes and symbols arising from urban experiences.

For the Black extended family and kin networks specifically, the basic and alternative structures and the associated behavioral codes brought from Africa, which were modified by Christianity and tempered by the plantation, have proved capable of coping with the stresses of both minimal rural survival and urbanization. The studies on the Bidwell and Mitchell families give extensive evidence to this effect. To date, extreme and supposedly pathological changes, such as are suggested by Moynihan (1965) and others, appear to be localized and temporary catastrophes, or else pragmatic, nominal adjustments to the demands of welfare law. The Black extended family is, indeed, a source of strength, a basis of pride, and a cultural distinction of American Blacks.

[36] Apart from the relevant materials on the Bidwell family, see Reid's classic work on West Indians in U.S. cities (Reid 1939: 215–232).

CONCLUSIONS: THE BLACK EXTENDED FAMILY AND BLACK CULTURE IN THE UNITED STATES

1. Holmes County, Mississippi, is the origin of a migratory Black population, two-thirds of whom are now residents of urban areas, especially Chicago, Illinois. Geographically, the County is divided into two distinct environments, which also have major economic and cultural correlates. The Hills, the residence of three-fourths of the County's 18,000 Black people, are dominated by communities of independent farmers and subsistence gardeners. The Delta is primarily a plantation area, with an enclave of independent Black farmers. Both areas contain small towns. Holmes County's Black culture and society are complex, with both modern and traditional features evident. Among the former, the political and service organizations developed over the past decade, medium-scale farming, high-school educations for the young, and changing self-images are prominent. Among the latter are economically and socially active extended families, subsistence economies, various handicrafts, and many aspects of household life. A common system of values, including strong religious faith, unifies the society, notwithstanding some factionalism and much isolation among marginal families. In general, while Holmes County is unusual (but not unique) in the rural South because of the extensive sociopolitical organization of its Black population, its culture, adaptive problems, and pattern of migration are broadly representative of the poorer Black counties of Mississippi.

2. A basic social institution of the Black community of Holmes County, Mississippi, is the genealogically defined, bilateral extended family of some 50–200 members, including spouses and adopted members. This institution defines social resources and obligations for its members, the most critical of these being each person's relations with parents and siblings. All adults in the extended family have general obligations of care for the family's children; hence, fosterage and other transfers of small children and adolescents are important adaptive features. As a corporate body, the extended family is associated with a community of origin and, generally, a family-dominated church and burial ground. Differences in reputation distinguish "strong" and "weak" families. Structurally, extended families include founder elements, nucleus families led by middle-aged siblings, subfamilies stemming from the nucleus families but maintaining independent households, and individuals, both children and adults, moving between the more stable units.

3. The extended family has been basic not only as a socioeconomic mechanism for rural life but in the facilitation of migration and urbaniza-

tion as well. It has been compatible, as is illustrated by the examination of the "Bidwell" family, with the educational and economic advances of its members. Although four-fifths of the members of that family are now urban residents, their orientation is still heavily Holmes Countian. Five-sixths of the marriages of the migrants are with other Holmes County natives; social clubs and church affiliations, but not economic relationships, tend to be heavily with other Holmes Countians, or, at least, Mississippians.

4. Similarly isolated migrant groups centered in other counties are found at least in Chicago and Detroit. These isolates tend to compartment Black ghettos not only by class, as has been previously stated by other writers, e.g. Drake and Cayton (1945), but between old and new residents and by place of origin of migrants. Ghetto institutions, such as the Woodlawn Organization, the Black P Stone Nation, and Operation Breadbasket, cut across these internal boundaries, but only to a limited degree.

5. The bilateral extended family can adapt to extreme social and economic marginality; for example, by forming corporate economic systems such as those of the "Mitchell" family. Here, household cooperation and nonreciprocal sharing are basic principles. Social relationships and patterns of communication are directly tied to the economic survival of the family as a whole. Since the critical functions of this type of extended family so completely involve its members in joint economic pursuits, family identification is closely tied to participation in its corporate economic system. Once participation ceases, recognition as an active family member and equities in corresponding economic benefits also cease.

6. Extended families very similar in structure and in functioning in rural and urban environments to those of Holmes County have been described among Black people of the Sea Islands of South Carolina, at home and in cities such as New York. In general, while much of the literature is equivocal, it is believed that bilateral extended families are a *basic* institution of Black people in the rural South and, in considerable measure, the urban North. Observer preconceptions and inadequate observations have been important in the neglect of this institution in the published literature. The reluctance of informants to discuss problems of partly covert structure in both rural and urban areas has contributed to this deficiency.

7. At the same time, the bilateral extended family is not believed to be either universal or uniform among Black Americans. Extremely disorganized environments, such as the Pruitt-Igoe housing complex in St. Louis,

studied by Rainwater and his associates, do bring in matrifocal biases and fragmentation. In many older southern cities, such as Columbus, Mississippi, and Selma, Alabama, sharp class stratification generates separate middle-class and lower-class structures with different behavioral codes. In California, the recency of mass migrations and the youthfulness of the population have provided few structural means, as yet, for extended-family formation. Voluntary associations, such as the Muslims and the Panthers, and fictive kin appear to be partial replacements.

8. Extended families are prominent among other segments of the American population, such as the Mexican-Americans and the east Kentuckians. However, while these extended families share some features, e.g. explicit rural bases or "home places," with Black institutions, they appear to manifest many differences in detail. For example, in many rural White extended families blood kin intermarry rather than being rigorously exogamous; they are, conversely, more prone to be exogamous in regard to place of origin than are Black families.

9. In contrast, West African extended families manifest broad similarities with the patterns described for Holmes County and rural Georgia and South Carolina. Comparative research on structure, family law, patterns of kin attitude and behavior, and adaptation in urban environments is badly needed both to evaluate highly probable genetic relations and to understand the comparative dynamics of the Afro-American world.

10. Even more basically, the necessity for a new approach to the study of Black communities in the United States appears clear. Black cultures are entities with historical traditions and functional integrity; the old, inherently derogatory concepts of simple borrowings from White culture or overwhelming situational determinations whether by slavery or poverty, need to be buried once and for all. At the same time, the understanding of American Black cultures in Black terms can be aided by hints from both African data and from other cultures, such as those of Latin America and Russia, in which serfdom and peasantry have been prominent. Such comparisons are valuable in asking needed questions, for example, on family law.

11. Above all, researches on Black communities can be most fruitfully undertaken as a part of community goals and programs of self-realization. They are valuable because they strengthen self-identities and because they highlight social mechanisms important not only in traditional circumstances but as bases for new adaptations. They are effective when they integrate community people, including both "grass-roots people" and young educated members, with formally trained social scientists, in a common search for bases of identity and social action.

12. Finally, those in power need to be educated to understand that Black cultures are valid and effective bases for public programs. Child care, community health, and many other areas of action can be integrated with viable Black institutions far better than they have been in the recent past. In all of this, there needs to be a realization of Black social strengths as well as weaknesses. White people may feel keenly that marital instabilities and the acceptance of human frailties are signs of Black failure. Blacks feel as keenly that the inadequacies of White care for "father and mother, brother and sister," White favoritism among children, and White indifference to the needs of distant kin are even more profound weaknesses. Recognition and tolerance of cultural differences and the use of those differences in the strategies appropriate to a pluralistic society are essential preludes to building a truly just and stable social order in the United States.

REFERENCES

ADAMS, BERT N.
   1970   Isolation, function, and beyond: American kinship in the 1960's. *Journal of Marriage and the Family* 32: 575–597.
AMERICAN MEDICAL ASSOCIATION
   1967   *1967 American medical directory*, part three: *Geographical register of physicians of the United States* (twenty-fourth edition). Chicago: American Medical Association.
BAGDIKIAN, BEN H.
   1967   "The new immigrants." *Saturday Evening Post*. July 15.
BERNARD, G.
   1966   *Marriage and family among Negroes*. Englewood Cliffs, N.J.: Prentice-Hall.
BILLINGSLEY, ANDREW
   1968   *Black families in white America*. Englewood Cliffs, N.J.: Prentice-Hall.
BLASSINGAME, JOHN W.
   1972   *The slave community. Plantation life in the antebellum South*. New York: Oxford University Press.
BLOOD, R. O., D. M. WOLFE
   1969   Negro-white differences in blue-collar marriages in a northern metropolis. *Social Forces* 48: 59–64.
BLUMBERG, LEONARD, ROBERT R. BELL
   1958–1959   Urban migration and kinship ties. *Social Problems* 6: 328–340.
BRIMMER, ANDREW F.
   1971   "Economic agenda for Black Americans." *The Black Politician*. January: 12–14, 32–37.

BROWN, JAMES S., *et al.*
   1963   Kentucky mountain migrations and the stem-family: an American variation on a theme by LePlay. *Rural Sociology* 28: 48–69.
BRUCE, PHILIP A.
   1907   *Social life of Virginia in seventeenth century. An inquiry into the origin of the higher planting class, together with an account of the habits, customs, and diversions of the people.* Richmond Virginia: Whittet and Shepperson.
COOMBS, ORDE
   1964   "Soul in suburbia." *Harper's Magazine.* January: 24–31.
DAVIS, ALLISON, JOHN DOLLARD
   1940   *Children of bondage.* Washington, D.C.: American Council on Education.
DAVIS, A., B. B. GARDNER, M. R. GARDNER
   1941   *Deep South.* Chicago: University of Chicago Press.
DIXON, VERNON J.
   1970   The di-unital approach to "Black economics." *American Economic Review* 60: 424–429.
DOLLARD, JOHN
   1957   *Caste and class in a southern town* (third edition). Chicago: Anchor.
DRAKE, ST. CLAIR, HORACE CAYTON
   1945   *Black metropolis.* New York: Harcourt, Brace.
DUBOIS, W. E. B.
   1965   "The souls of Black folk," in *Three Negro classics.* Edited by John H. Franklin, 207–289. New York: Avon.
   1967 [1899]   *The Philadelphia Negro.* New York: Schocken.
   1970 [1896]   *The suppression of the African slave-trade to the United States of America, 1638–1870.* New York: Dover. (Originally published 1896 in the Harvard Historical Series, volume one. Cambridge, Mass.)
DUBOIS, W. E. B., *editor*
   1970 [1909]   *The Negro American family.* Cambridge, Mass.: M.I.T. Press.
ECKENFELS, EDWARD J.
   1972   "Progress report: community control of hypertension in Holmes County, Mississippi." Mimeographed manuscript. September. (Obtainable upon request from Milton Olive III Memorial Corporation, Drawer D., Lexington, Mississippi 39095.)
ECKENFELS, E., K. NELSON, D. B. SHIMKIN
   1971   "The status of research and program development as of January, 1971." Mimeographed manuscript. (Obtainable on request from Milton Olive III Memorial Corporation, Drawer D., Lexington, Mississippi 39095.)
EDWARDS, HARRY
   1968   Black Muslim and Negro Christian family relationships. *Journal of Marriage and the Family* 30: 604–611.
FRATE, DENNIS A.
   1972   "The ecology of geophagy in the Black community, Holmes County, Mississippi." Mimeographed M.A. thesis, Louisiana State University, Baton Rouge. (Obtainable on request from D. A. Frate, Department of Anthropology, University of Illinois, Urbana.)

FRAZIER, E. FRANKLIN
  1932   *The Negro family in Chicago*. Chicago: University of Chicago Press.
  1964   *The Negro church in America*. New York: Schocken.
  1966   *The Negro family in the United States* (revised edition). Chicago: University of Chicago Press.
GOLODETZ, A., R. EVANS, G. HEINNITZ, C. D. GIBSON, JR.
  1969   The care of chronic illness: the "responsor" role. *Medical Care* 7: 385–394.
HALPERN, JOEL M.
  1967 [1956]   *A Serbian village*. New York: Harper and Row.
HENRY, H. M.
  1914   "The police control of the slave in South Carolina." Unpublished dissertation, Vanderbilt University (Nashville), Emory, Virginia.
HERSKOVITS, M. J.
  1966   *The New World Negro*. Edited by Frances S. Herskovits. Bloomington: Indiana University Press.
  1971 [1941]   "On West African influences," in *Black matriarchy: myth or reality*? Edited by John H. Bracey, Jr., et al., 34–51. Belmont, Calif.: Wadsworth. (Originally published 1941 in *The myth of the Negro past*, 167–186. New York: Harper and Row.)
HILL, REUBEN
  1962–1963   Judgment and consumership in the management of family resources. *Sociology and Social Research* 47: 446–460.
HUGHES, LANGSTON
  1968   *I wonder as I wander*. New York: Hill and Wang.
JOHNSON, CHARLES S.
  1934   *The shadow of the plantation*. Chicago: University of Chicago Press.
  1967 [1941]   *Growing up in the Black Belt*. New York: Schocken.
JOHNSON, GUION G.
  1930   *A social history of the Sea Islands*. Chapel Hill: University of North Carolina Press.
KISER, CLYDE V.
  1932   *Sea island to city: a study of St. Helena islanders in Harlem and other urban centers*. New York: Columbia University Press.
LEICHTER, HOPE J., WILLIAM E. MITCHELL
  1967   *Kinship and casework*. New York: Russell Sage Foundation.
LEPPER, M., J. LASHOFF
  1969   *Preliminary report on patterns of medical and health care in poverty areas of Chicago*. Chicago: Presbyterian-St. Luke's Hospital.
LEWIS, HYLAN
  1955   *Blackways of Kent*. Chapel Hill: University of North Carolina Press.
Lexington Advertiser
  1969   Article in *Lexington Advertiser*. July 31. Lexington, Miss.
LITWAK, EUGENE
  1959–1960   The use of extended family groups in the achievement of social goals: some policy implications. *Social Problems* 7: 177–187.
LITWAK, EUGENE, IVAN SZELENYI
  1969   Primary group structures and their functions: kin, neighbors, and friends. *American Sociological Review* 34: 465–481.

LORENZI, HENRY, SUSAN H. S. LORENZI
1969a "On research and development operations in Holmes County, Mississippi, 1968–1969." Mimeographed manuscript. September. (Available on request from Milton Olive III Memorial Corporation, Drawer D, Lexington, Mississippi 39095.)
1969b "The management of fear by a community: Holmes County, Mississippi — 1963 through 1967," in *Some views on Blacks and Black communities* (mimeographed). Edited by Susan H. S. Lorenzi. University of Illinois, Urbana.

LYNCH, WILLIAM O.
1943 The westward flow of southern colonists before 1861. *Journal of Southern History* 9 (3): 315–327.

MAIR, L. P.
1953 "African marriage and social change," in *Survey of African marriage and family life*. Edited by Arthur Phillips, 1–172. London: Oxford University Press for the International African Institute.

MCCRACKEN, HUGH THOMAS
1970 "Guidelines for establishing literacy projects utilizing agencies in a university and a rural community." Mimeographed Ph.D. thesis, College of Education, University of Illinois, Urbana.

MISSISSIPPI STATE BOARD OF HEALTH
1963–1967 *Vital statistics, Mississippi.* Jackson, Miss.: Mississippi State Board of Health.

MOORE, WILLIAM, JR.
1969 *The vertical ghetto.* New York: Random House.

MORGALLA, MICHAEL M.
1969 "Black ownership of farmland in Holmes County, Mississippi: a preliminary study." Mimeographed manuscript, Department of Anthropology, University of Illinois, Urbana.

MOYNIHAN, DANIEL P.
1965 "Employment, income, and the ordeal of the Negro family," in *The Negro American*. Edited by T. Parsons and K. B. Clark, 134–159. Boston: Houghton Mifflin.

MUELLER, EVA, WILLIAM LADD
1970 "Negro-White differences in geographic mobility," in *The family life of Black people*. Edited by Charles V. Willie, 102–114. Columbus, Ohio: Charles Merrill.

NUKUNYA, G. K.
1969 *Kinship and marriage among the Anlo Ewe.* London School of Economics Monographs on Social Anthropology 37. London: Athlone.

OLMSTED, FREDERICK L.
1970 *A journey in the back country 1853–1854.* New York: Schocken. (Originally published 1860.)

POWDERMAKER, HORTENSE
1966 [1939] *After freedom.* New York: Russell and Russell. (Originally published 1939.)

RAINWATER, LEE
1970 *Behind ghetto walls.* Chicago: Aldine.

REID, IRA DE A.
1939   The Negro immigrant. His background, characteristics, and social adjustments, 1889–1937. Studies in History, Economics, and Public Law 449. New York: Columbia University Press.
RUSHING, P. V.
1969   "The Black rural migrant: three groups of agricultural workers from Holmes County, Mississippi," in Some views on Blacks and Black communities (mimeographed). Edited by Susan H. S. Lorenzi. University of Illinois, Urbana.
SCANZONI, JOHN H.
1971   The Black family in modern society. Boston: Allyn and Bacon.
SCHNEIDER, DAVID M.
1968   American kinship: a cultural account. Englewood Cliffs, N.J.: Prentice-Hall.
SHIMKIN, D. B.
1971   "Black migration and the struggle for equity: a hundred-year survey," in Migration and social welfare. Edited by Joseph W. Eaton, 77–116. New York: National Association of Social Workers.
SHIMKIN, D. B., ANN RICE
1971   "The black population of Holmes County, Mississippi: a statistical characterization as of January 1970." Mimeographed manuscript, Milton Olive III Memorial Corporation, Lexington, Mississippi.
SHIMKIN, D. B., PEDRO SAN JUAN
1953   Culture and world view: a method of analysis applied to rural Russia. American Anthropologist 55: 329–348.
SKRYGLEY, F. D.
1893   Seventy years in Dixie. Nashville, Tenn.: Gospel Advocate.
STACK, CAROL B.
1969   "The kindred of Viola Jackson: residence and family organization of the urban Black American," in Some views on Blacks and Black communities (mimeographed). Edited by Susan H. S. Lorenzi. University of Illinois, Urbana.
SWEETSER, DORRIAN APPLE
1970   The structure of sibling relationships. American Journal of Sociology 76: 47–58.
SYDNOR, CHARLES S.
1933   Slavery in Mississippi. New York: Appleton-Century.
TALPALOR, MORRIS
1960   The sociology of colonial Virginia. New York: Philosophical Library.
THOMAS, WILLIAM I., FLORIAN ZNANIECKI
1927   The Polish peasant in Europe and America, two volumes. New York: Knopf.
U.S. BUREAU OF THE CENSUS
1960   County business patterns. Mississippi (1st Quarter, 1959). Washington, D.C.: U.S. Government Printing Office.
1963   Census of population: 1960, volume one: Characteristics of the population. Mississippi. Washington, D.C.: U.S. Government Printing Office.
1967   Census of agriculture, 1964. Statistics for the states and counties. Mississippi. Washington, D.C.: U.S. Government Printing Office.

1970a   *County business patterns. Mississippi*. CBP-69-26. Washington, D.C.: U.S. Government Printing Office.

1970b   *1970 census of housing*. Washington, D.C.: U.S. Government Printing Office.

1970c   *1967 census of governments*, volume seven: *State reports. Mississippi*. Washington, D.C.: U.S. Government Printing Office.

1971a   *1970 census of housing. General housing characteristics. Mississippi*. HC(VI)-26. Washington, D.C.: U.S. Government Printing Office.

1971b   *1970 census of population. General population characteristics. Mississippi*. PC(V2)-26. Washington, D.C.: U.S. Government Printing Office.

1972   *Statistical abstract of the United States: 1972* (ninety-third edition). Washington, D.C.: U.S. Government Printing Office.

U.S. DEPARTMENT OF HEALTH, EDUCATION AND WELFARE

1965   *Life tables for the geographic divisions of the United States: 1959–61* 1 (3). Washington, D.C.: National Center for Health Statistics.

VERMEER, DONALD E.

1971   Geophagy among the Ewe of Ghana. *Ethnology* 9: 56–72.

WADE, RICHARD C.

1964   *Slavery in the cities. The South 1820–1860*. New York: Oxford University Press.

WARNER, W. LLOYD, H. JUNKER BUFORD, WALTER A. ADAMS

1941   *Color and human nature*. Washington, D.C.: American Council on Education.

WELD, THEODORE D.

1969   *Slavery and the internal slave trade in the United States*. New York: Arno Press. (Originally published 1841 as *The report of the British and Foreign Anti-Slavery Society*. London: Thomas Ward.)

WOOFTER, T. J., JR.

1930   *Black yeomanry*. New York: Henry Holt.

YOUNG, VIRGINIA H.

1970   Family and childhood in a southern Negro community. *American Anthropologist* 72: 269–288. (Reprinted 1971 in *Black matriarchy: myth or reality?* Edited by J. H. Bracey, et al., 195–217. Belmont, Calif.: Wadsworth.)

Community Reactions and Appraisals: The Extended Family as a Social Core

DENNIS A. FRATE and EDDIE W. LOGAN, editors

ABSTRACT

All research undertaken in Holmes County, Mississippi, on and with the cooperation of the Black community, rests on the basic principle of *public accountability*, both in the inception of research and in the dissemination and publication of results. The following comments on the extended family as an institution in the Black community of Holmes County were made in two workshops, the first held in the County in July, 1973, and the second at the IXth International Congress of Anthropological and Ethnological Sciences, in Chicago, on September 6 and 7, 1973. Of the seven reviewers, six reside in the County and the seventh, originally from Holmes County, now lives in Chicago. All have been community leaders and have widespread kinship ties.

The first workshop dealt with the religious perspective on the extended family and Holmes County Black society generally. The importance of mutual aid and sharing among related households and neighbors, especially in crisis situations, and among migrants from the County was emphasized. The role of religion has seemingly diminished because of the development of secular community centers. The roles of husband and wife apparently continue to be traditional, with the women controlling the household and children and the men working outside as providers but retaining ultimate family authority.

The comments in the second workshop can be summarized in the following points. "Strong" extended families and religious faith have been key elements of survival. Education and migration have been the means to upward mobility. Even among the upwardly mobile and in urban centers far from Holmes County (for instance, Chicago), however, emotional and economic loyalties to relatives survive and are valued. Finally, it is necessary for the White community to have an understanding of the Black extended family for legal reasons. These include recognition of its functioning in the areas of family care for the ill and aged; a greater flexibility in the definition of the terms "dependents" and "immediate family" for tax purposes, as well as recognition of *de facto* adoption of children through fosterage; and stronger protection for the rights of children, including restoration of compulsory school attendance in the state of Mississippi.

Linguistic notes by Demitri B. Shimkin.

EDITORS' INTRODUCTION

Public accountability is a basic principle of all research undertaken in Holmes County on, and with the cooperation of, the Black community. This accountability takes place at two stages: when research is proposed and when research results are ready for publication or other distribution. Both technical consultants and community representatives participate in these reviews, which seek to help the researchers relate their efforts closely to community problems and goals, to communicate their findings in "poor people's language"; and, from time to time, to correct mistakes. Such reviews have proved to be particularly important in studies within the sphere of Black culture, many subtleties of which escape even careful investigations.

We organized and conducted the review of the Shimkin, Louie, and Frate manuscript with Black Holmes Countians in two workshops. One was in July 1973, in Holmes County; the other was on September 6 and 7, 1973, at the IXth International Congress of Anthropological and Ethnological Sciences, in Chicago. Our reviewers — Rev. L. E. Robinson, Mrs. L. E. Robinson, Mrs. Fanney Booker, Mrs. Nadine Randle Jones, Mrs. Matilda Burns, Rev. Philip Rushing, and Representative Robert Clark, Jr.,[1] — are known as thoughtful and articulate people, better educated than many in the County but in good communication with "grass-roots" people, and long active participants in civic affairs. All but Reverend Rushing, who is now a resident of Chicago, live in Holmes County; everyone has widespread ties of kinship.

Below, we present the substance of the two reviews, a little shortened but not otherwise changed. These texts may seem at first to be somewhat elliptical, only tangentially related to the content and the issues of the Shimkin, Louie, and Frate report. But they need to be read in context. On the one hand, we and our panel shared a knowledge of the report, and our reviewers were largely interested in reexamining the data from the standpoints of their own philosophies and experiences. On the other, all of us were aware of the way Black Holmes Countians usually discuss issues — not in terms of abstract sequential arguments but rather obliquely. Reasoning commonly proceeds through the presentation of concrete opposing or reinforcing cases, with Biblical references, or anecdotes, or even songs and animal tales as ultimate allegorical tools of critical definition. The intervening logic is implied.

---

[1] See also the authors' biographical notes.

THE EXTENDED FAMILY AND HOLMES COUNTY SOCIETY IN RELIGIOUS PERSPECTIVE

Our first workshop was dominated by the Rev. L. E. Robinson, with Mrs. Fanney Booker, Mrs. Matilda Burns, and the two of us also present.

LOGAN: We want to look at the Black extended family relative to different points in time . . . And how they stick together under stresses and crises.

FRATE: Dr. Shimkin and Miss Louie wrote about . . . how the family helps migration to cities . . . how the people of Chicago help the Holmes Countians to find a place to live and to get a job. Now the family I wrote about: they're too poor to leave, they've got no money. So we are going to look at both ends — helping migration; and who goes, and who stays. . . . Now the family that I know, they were too poor . . . they had to join together. One [household] would raise potatoes, another one would raise pigs, and they would exchange the food. That was the only way they could survive. . . . They formed a union, as one family [of 14 households].
Maybe you know similar cases? . . .

ROBINSON: The rural sections has that more than any other section of the County. I remember an occasion when a fellow's barn would burn, and his corn and grain[2] would be destroyed; his house would burn and his entire furniture[3] would be destroyed. He would receive more quilts from the burning of the furniture and the house than he had in the beginning. The people would come by and give it to him. Then, if the barn was burned, they would give him corn and would contribute whatever necessities that he needed. . . . Those days brought the Black family to the realization of depending upon one another. And they are closer together than the inner city. And the simple fact is that they have learned: what one can do, it can always be done better by one or more.[4] . . . Which really is the survival of the fittest in the beginning, but it ended up with the community action that we all depend upon each other.
Fire in the County — and they would all line up with buckets. They didn't have any way to fight the fire but with sand to put it out.[5]

---

[2] I.e. human food and animal fodder.
[3] I.e. household furnishings, therefore including quilts.
[4] I.e. more than one.
[5] Fire is still the deadly scourge of the Black countryside, especially in winter, which rarely passes without a fatal fire caused by overheated stoves in flimsy "shotgun" houses.

They would make up[6] at the church and raise collections, and bring it to families that had been somewhat crippled by wind, water, and whatever fell against that family. It was in the hands of the community so the Black family there learned to survive by holding together, by sticking closely together. The Black family not only seem[7] isolated at times, but they do have that ingenuity that causes them to hang on. That may be something to think about.

FRATE: That is the kind of comment that we want; you know, how you see it. We are writing about your community. But this is through our eyes, and we want to reinterpret it back through your eyes. If we say something, we may be completely wrong. If we are, we want you to tell us. . . . You know, we may have talked with atypical families. . . . Maybe you can say that. This is one thing we cannot say.

ROBINSON: I know one thing that we can say and that is about the Black family. I have known people cannot be[8] on the welfare and were not able to receive commodities at the time they were giving out a little food. And they were not accepted for some reason as poor enough as other people were; for some reason the administration that was handling the foodstuffs didn't, they didn't meet their favor; and there would be Blacks that would have more and would share with them. And they would give what they had, divide with them, what they got from the welfare, the commodity help. I think it would be nice to show the cooperative spirit could not compete maybe[9] with their neighbors at all times — they[10] were able to stay close enough together to survive.

BOOKER: You let Mrs. Wright[11] tell you how she, when she was attending the clinic for the expectant mothers, how she would wear the shoes this week, and next week it would be another neighbor that takes care of the family, and she would wear the same shoes. So consequently you know they were more neighborly; that is the way it should be.

FRATE: This is the kind of thing that we are talking about. . . . Now what about helping the migrants? Helping the people moving to Chicago, or wherever they move?

---

[6]   I.e. gather.
[7]   I.e. only seemingly.
[8]   I.e. who could not be.
[9]   I.e. to those who maybe could not compete.
[10]   I.e. the helped and the helpers.
[11]   Mrs. Willie Mae Wright, the senior of the eighteen Black midwives formerly delivering most of the children in Holmes County; now virtually displaced.

ROBINSON: I would say to you in the 1930's and then through 1940 and 1943 again, they were migrating and someone up there would get a job and work awhile. And then he would talk to whoever he worked for about another fellow he knew in the South that did this, and would like very much for you to give him a chance, and if you will hire him, then I will send for him to come. And this man wouldn't have money to come, and sometimes they would send for him to come and would send the money.

BOOKER: My brother is in Vancouver, Washington, today because a friend of his talk to a man about a job out on the road he sent for him.[12] My brother moved up there and then sent for his family.

ROBINSON: Yes, it is families that do it quite a bit. But it is done more than in families, also friends. That is right.

LOGAN: . . . the family that has migrated to Louisiana or California . . . sends for people back home . . . in this way, families remain allied to each other.

ROBINSON: And I know about a song that may have[13] some benefit when people were migrating, that they tell me:

Chicago, Illinois or whatever State you wanted to go
That the colored people, that is what they said,
They were flocking there because they had better pay.
I don't know how true it is but I'm certainly going to try.
When the sun goes down in the west,
    I'm going to bid Mississippi goodby.
Wherever you are, and they think of their brother,
    And it is just about true — get better pay.

We feel now that most of them go North, not necessarily because they like the North so well, but they are there because they get better pay, better treatment, and everything. . . . But migration is mostly done by families getting away and seeing how good it is and calling for their people to come. Sending them money: "Come on up here, man, this is the land of milk and honey Moses was talking about. . . ."

[The discussion then turned to the Black family and religion.]

ROBINSON: [Blacks] are religious people . . . mostly of the Christianity[14] in the South; there are a few Catholics in the South but they are in small

---

[12]   I.e. talked to a man about a travelling job, who then sent for him.
[13]   I.e. may have had.
[14]   I.e. various Protestant denominations.

numbers in comparison to the others. . . . Three major churches — that is, Baptist, Methodist, and the Church of God in Christ — they seem to be the leading churches now.

. . . very few have left for religious purposes. . . . We find this: that most of our people who were deeply religious here, lot of our people when they get North, they are not so religious. They lose some of that fervor they felt there. And I think the reason for that is that I think it is hard to sell a man religion that is doing real good.[15] It is hard to sell a person religion that is very prosperous.

LOGAN: But would you agree with this: say, twenty years ago, if you would go to most country churches, the church would be packed, and if you go to some of those same churches today — they don't necessarily have to be country churches — the church might be just one-third of capacity?

ROBINSON: Now that is true in a lot of cases; we only have to find[16] sections now where the churches respond as they use to do. Now we don't have night services. Night services are going out in all phases of the church, I don't exactly understand why. . . . Now we had night service last night with just a few, and Sunday morning had a good crowd. At night, you know, they are a little afraid to go to church.

LOGAN: What about the community churches[17] — don't you think the style has caused a lot of this?

ROBINSON: Oh sure, a lot of various;[18] a lot of change. As you say, . . . there was a time in the history of the Blacks when the church was the community center. Now since that time, they have been buying and building [secular] community centers that of itself[19] the church doesn't have the hold on the community that it used to have. And at these centers you can dance and you can drink a little bit — and that makes a big difference, I suppose. That makes the church here not as effective as it ever was.[20]

And [yet] it will continue to be effective as long as it is a church, but there is a falling away with some of the things and education has done a

[15]   I.e. to sell religion to a man who is doing very well.
[16]   I.e. find only [a few] sections.
[17]   I.e. chapels maintained by local communities from which the deacons and church mothers are drawn. Rotating pastors conduct services in a number of such churches, usually once a month. At other times, these chapels are used for a variety of public functions.
[18]   I.e. much variation.
[19]   I.e. so that of itself.
[20]   I.e. as it used to be.

good deal. Educated ministers have been able to invade the flock, and play down the emotional strength of the church as though it was something cursed and that has a lot to do with confusing the people — with changing their mood a lot. But . . . without mentioning religion, you would have to leave out all of the Blacks. Because whether he preaches religion right or not is one thing, but he has another [level of belief], and he is proud of it, and if you want to win him you have to win him through his religion.

But the young Blacks they don't care much for religion or anything else. In the time of Civil Rights movement it was a struggle that they thought it was something else[21] to supplement or replace the church. So they got out of the church and got into the Movement. . . . Now they are finding out that there is no answer, that there is no substitute for the church and Christianity, and gradually that group is coming back to the church. . . .

FRATE: . . . There has been a lot of writing . . . that the Black family is run by females . . . and I am wondering about this. . . .

BURNS: Sometimes, like in our area [the Delta region of Holmes County, dominated by plantations], the men have to leave. They have to provide in more ways than just their family — so they have to go out a lot, leaving the females to manage because the man is out looking for work.

ROBINSON: One of the things that should be explained along that too: it isn't in all families but it is the law of averages . . . the woman have charge of the children, and everything they receive; the father is never mentioned no matter how long he stay out in the field. . . . She is the one they receive it from, and by not mentioning him the children believe Mamma gave me all of this. That is the fact that probably exits[22] — in every family. . . . I have noticed in times[23] that when my boy ask me, "When are you going to give me some money?"

I say, "I thought I gave you some already."

And he say, "Mamma gave me that." See, he believed that his mother gave him the money.

Well, she cleared it up and said: "Now, well, son, I didn't give you that; your Daddy gave it to me to give it to you." Now if she hadn't of[24] mentioned that then he would always have believed she gave it to him.

---

[21] I.e. was a struggle which they thought to be something . . .
[22] I.e. exists. Consonantal clusters are often contracted, e.g. "Alanta' 'for "Atlanta" or else decomposed by inserting an epenthetic "s" — as in "Brumsby" for "Brumby."
[23] I.e. at times.
[24] I.e. had not.

But she had to mention it to keep herself out of trouble, and so she mentioned that his daddy makes the provision.

Now some families, the women do rule, she does, because the average man sometimes — being a man it is kind of hard to say it, but it is the truth — sometimes women have a little more common sense and judgment and managerial sense than a man. That is true. Sometimes there are men that can't save money. He can't provide, he can't buy; if he go downtown, he buy nonessentials. . . . But she generally buy what she wants. Now I've made mistakes too, trying to buy like she buy, and I buy something just something to eat now. But she buy something that will last, something that will last across the week. If I had to buy it today, I'd probably buy a steak and an onion and maybe a package of rice, and if I didn't have flour, I'd buy a two-pound package of flour: that is just for that immediate circumstance. But she will buy to last across the week.

So that is a difference there in the house too that she is the little Caesar. And we kind of appreciate them and we like to have her there.

Then, some women just take over. They find a man that is dumb, and it goes to their head, but it isn't the law of averages.

LOGAN: I don't know how it is now, but a few years back I found that men tend to be more wasteful.

[Feminine comment]: That's right.

ROBINSON: It is just the same thing now. It isn't as bad[25] because the Lord wanted it that way.

You have something there that comes against the family and especially the Black rural family — well, the city family too, and that is the women's lib. They are having quite a bit of problem with that.

You [White] fellows have a problem with that, I notice. But it has seeped down into the Black family. I know so.

I know some husbands that are having tremendous problems because the women say: "What I do is because you don't consider me doing good because I am a woman but I am your equal." [People] I have worked with — in [pastoral] consultation, four times in less than a month . . . they are in this way. That kind of hurts the Black family a little bit, because we are not insecure.

I've always asked my wife practically everything: "Would you get up and fix breakfast or shall I fix it?"

Well, she says she'll fix it.

Well then, "Are you going to church with me, or shall I go alone?"

"Well, I'll go."

[25]   I.e. so bad.

That's about all. That at the close of the day I say, "Shall I use the rest room first or shall you?"

Well, I am still asking questions. Well, then you go ahead and then, instead of asking, get in bed without even asking — and that makes a big difference.

No, no, no, I'm not a male chauvinist. I tell the truth. I think it [Women's Liberation] is mostly a thing that they have read up on . . . because after all the Law — now you get me in religion again — the Law never states the woman as the equal of the man. We put her there and the liberation movement has placed her — there. You see, in the Law, God said to her: "Woman obey your husband, for this is right."

BURNS: . . . The middle-class White ladies that want liberation want an equal share with her mate. The Black lady has always had responsibility, equal jobs. I agree.

ROBINSON: You see when you mention the thing of responsibility, those Black women aren't looking for responsibility. They have that, what they are looking for is a way to keep from carrying out that responsibility. And whenever a Black talks about the liberation and sharing, she borrowed that from the society in which she live as part of the Western culture because she know she has always had a way to do most of the things that she wanted to.

Of course, I know I don't argue with my wife over little things. And me, and my father and grandfather did, we always spoke but this I say:[26] "We put too much on them[27] to make take care[28] of us, and all that kind of stuff."

I think that is where we should draw the line. I am responsible for my family eating, and whether she work or not is up to her. She tells me that is my responsibility and I accept that responsibility with honor, for I'd rather be a man working for my family than sitting at home.

Editors' Summary

In summary, this workshop brought out six major points partly confirming, partly expanding and modifying, the findings of the Shimkin, Louie, and Frate study (this volume):

[26] I.e. this is what I say.
[27] I.e. we regard them too highly.
[28] I.e. to make them take care.

1. All participants stressed the great importance of the ethic of mutual help and sharing among related households and neighbors in case of disaster, need, or windfall.

2. All also agreed on the allied ethic of mutual aid among migrants in locating work for relatives and friends, in communicating back this information, and in helping new migrants financially.

3. The perception of migration is also that of a largely voluntary act, in response to economic incentives. It is curious that forced migrations and the strength of ties with home and community were not mentioned.

4. Seemingly, the role of religion has diminished over the past twenty years in Holmes County as well as in the North. This trend, of as much importance to the Black family as other aspects of society, appears to have come about through the development of secular community centers with less puritanical rules than the churches; the reduced role of churches as vehicles of emotional expression[29] with the advent of more educated and restrained preachers, and the competition of the Civil Rights movement as an idealistic center — the last being of diminishing importance.

5. The relative roles of husbands and wives in today's Holmes County families appear still to be governed by tradition: women controlling the household and children; men working outside, providing support, and having ultimate authority. They are also much influenced by the relative competence of each spouse in household economics and by the relative strength of personality of each. Politeness between spouses is seen as an important contributor to family harmony.

6. The concept of women's liberation — explicitly, feminine equality — has reached Black Holmes County and may be generating conflicts in families. It has inspired religious opposition.

THE FUNCTIONALITY OF THE BLACK EXTENDED FAMILY: CASES AND IMPLICATIONS FOR POLICY

Our second workshop, in Chicago, elicited two kinds of reactions from the Holmes County evaluators. The first were case materials from personal experience that brought out further the importance and many functions of the extended family. The comments of Mrs. Fanney Booker, Mrs. L. E. Robinson, Rev. L. E. Robinson, Mrs. Nadine Randle Jones, and Mrs. Matilda Burns were primarily of this type. Comments inter-

[29]   The release of ecstatic emotions through "shouting" is both a major reward of church attendance and a source of discomfort to "modern" clergy in the Black community.

relating the extended family with external, White institutions and pointing out the issues of law and equity that arise from this were made by Rev. Philip Rushing and, especially, Hon. Robert G. Clark — the Black people's sole representative in the Mississippi legislature.

BOOKER: When I was asked to participate on this occasion I began to wonder on my participation and the overall purpose. I am not a well-read educator on the Black family. However, I do know something about my own family, and about many families in Holmes County . . . relating a little about my experience of a very large Black family, and about the Fannye Booker Home for the elderly people, I was do[30] what I could and that is the reason I am here.

To the best of my recollection my family tree started when Emily Saffold was for sale from Virginia. She was sold by her slave master to a Holmes County slave master. And, with a plea, they gave her permission to bring her daughter, Del Saffold, my grandmother. "The plea for not separation," she said, "was very great, in her struggle . . . to bring her with her." My mother, Connilus Thomas[31] — Del Saffold, in other words — was married to Joe Thomas. Then my [real] mother was born. My father was Isaac Stewart.

My paternal family was a strong group of people. They placed a high value on work. They believed in an honest living; they believed in the household working. Joe Thomas, my grandfather, was particularly enterprising. During his life, under a great strain, he was able to purchase 360 acres of land, of which, in his will, he had it so fixed that, as long as a Thomas lived, it would not be sold. It would be for the rest of the Thomas family. And as long as I live, it will not be.

I had an uncle, migrated from home at an early age, he settled in Waterloo, Iowa.[32] He was successful in accumulating land and money. He returned home later for a family reunion. He was so sold out in what is happening[33] that he has already planned, and has already set up, to sell out what he have in Waterloo, Iowa, and return home and help the struggle in Holmes County.

On September 2 [1973], the family reunion for the Thomas family was in Lexington, Mississippi — Holmes County. Of which we had 211 come

---

[30] I.e. was to do.

[31] I.e. My mother was Connilus Thomas. Note this application to an actual grandmother.

[32] This city, on a branch of the main migratory route, the Illinois Central Railroad, has a tractor factory which was the destination of a significant stream of Black Holmes Countian migration as early as World War I.

[33] I.e. so completely convinced by what is happening.

from six different states, believe it or not; 82 of them was from Chicago. They all came home, to celebrate homecoming. There was we who left,[34] like the father was when the son went away, killed the fatted calf, and we had a feast, which made all of us very, very happy.

I think this[35] is particularly true in regard to the Fanney Booker Home. For some time I had observed older people who was left alone with none to care for them — some had children, some did not, some had migrated away from home for work. And these people were left on lonely roads without telephones. . . . I've known these peoples all of my life. I pulled together my little savings that I had and built this home, the Fannye Booker Home for the Elderly. In the eight years' time, I have had 86 peoples, old peoples, to come by and live in this home.

Today we are happy to continue to do whatever we can for the peoples of Holmes County, Lexington, Mississippi. And maybe I will close with this thought.

MRS. ROBINSON: The extended families and economics — this has to do with self-help. Also, it has to do with problems that arose in the yester-years, and the solutions for survival.

I am reminded at this particular time of the Black schoolteacher's salary. When it was fifteen dollars a month, and they were told by the superintendent that that was all the money that was allocated in the County's budget for that specific purpose. But there was money in the County budget to bus the White children, and they passed by my door. We had to walk. There was no fuel or lighting system, and sometimes there was no building provided — the church was utilized. Here the Black families would combine their forces with whatever they could afford, such as wagons, mules, saws, and axes, and went down in the boondocks to cut down and to haul wood to the school, for survival.

ROBINSON: This evening, as we come to talk about religion and the Black extended families, we wish to speak of it in the terms of which our people were so dedicated to — the signs of religion. There were times when there were nothing else and these extended families that they had to hold to.[36] And they had to live together in order to survive.

I think it was their religion that gave them the great courage to survive, and to save not only the family but the race. For in those days of darkness had it not been for the light of religion, they would have perished. Because they could find no comfort and no happiness anywhere else. And

[34]   I.e. we who were left.
[35]   The antecedent is unclear. The reference is apparently to the Black family.
[36]   I.e. the Black people had only religion and their families.

so the church was the first community house. As we know, the home was the first school — and then they were rushed off to the church. In the church they were able to find strength to find courage to continue on.

We find that in that age the preachers were what we would call scholars of that day. And they didn't know much, and neither do we know much today. But they had one thing in leading the people to a higher ground, to believe in the rudiments of Christianity and of Christ.

We speak[37] of religion doesn't mean that we are trying to tell you a religion to accept, for there are many of them. But imbedded within the Black man — the family that always praised [with] religious fervor.[38] And that being so, we believe in these things we survived upon. For the church and the schools were the only places we could go. We had no recreational centers but the schools. We find ourselves playing on the school grounds and other places, swimming in the creek, ponds, or what have you. But all of that was to make the race better, to make the Black family realize their importance of being strong. And so we survived by our religious fervor.

I know that there are others that would think religion[39] as just an opiate for some of us, but it is more than that to those people that had to trust in it. It is a strange thing that a man doesn't have[40] a friend no more than[41] family to go on, and then all of a sudden someone tell him that there is a friend that sticketh closer than a brother, there is a friend that loves you and willing[42] to do his part that you might survive if you will turn to, that man will turn to religion in their darkest hours. And I am sure that you can say that these that are presented to us[43] are in the very darkest hour.

And we find comfort and joy in realizing the great need for a family. Some would go North, and traveling North they would send back for their brothers, and they would come, and they would have a job already for them. They would come and send back for his sister. And that spirit of migration lasted for quite a while.

And then there are those that believe that the Black family had broken down. And we are here to tell you that the recovery of the Black family has been the recovery of respect and the recovery of identity that maybe once was lost, but now can be seen in the face and the hearts of those that

---

[37] I.e. That we speak . . .
[38] For syntax see note 31. "Praised," i.e. prayed with exhortations of praise, as in the South Carolina Black usage, "praise house," for church.
[39] I.e. think of religion.
[40] I.e. man who doesn't have.
[41] I.e. other than.
[42] I.e. and who is willing.
[43] I.e. Black preachers.

love the Black family. We want to say one thing — that it[44] was so rich that it caused us really to seek our identity. So many of our Blacks today, you may find them with long beards and long hair, they are only seeking their identity and they are not ashamed of that — they are not ashamed of anything that caused them to come this far, knowing they were a part of the Black extended family.

Thank you very kindly, and may God bless you.

JONES: I [want] to speak about growing up in Holmes County as it relates to extended families.

I am the second of four children. My father was a small, independent farmer who was a descendant of one of the largest families in Holmes County. . . . My mother migrated into Holmes County because she had to leave her base home to finish high school.

We live in one of the largest communities in Holmes County. Most of the residents in this community are Randles or descendants of Randles. Branched from this community is another we call "Randletown." That is a cluster of about twenty-five or thirty families living in an area, and they are all Randles, or cousins of Randles, or children of Randles, or sisters or brothers of Randles. In this cluster, just like the community that I live in, we share everything. We live within calling distance — I don't mean by telephone — I mean yelling from one person's house to the other. We share things like vegetables that we grow in our gardens; we milk cows, and we share buttermilk; and we share clothing. When my clothes get too small there is always a little cousin in the community that I would give my clothes to.

And this type of family relationship has a great influence on me and the kind of life that I lead now. When I was four years old, I enrolled in school, and I graduated from high school when I was sixteen. This was because this local school in the local community had no particular age limit then, and peoples had to go to fields then. So when they get the children trained they start them to school.

Holmes County now is a lot different from what it was when my parents were children. It is different in that I have self-respect and dignity, and a Black person in Holmes County, regardless of how large the family was, didn't have that then. I walk down the street with my head up — so does everybody else.

So that is how it is being from a large, Black extended family, as I see it.

---

[44] I.e. the Black family.

BURNS: I became interested in the Black extended family mainly because the more I heard about the family the less I knew about my own. If I participate in the program today I felt I would be able to learn about other families plus finding my identity with my own.

I was born in Leflore County[45] in Mississippi. My father is the son of a small independent farmer in Madison County [due south of Holmes County, halfway to Jackson]. The Griffin family was a very small family. He had only three sisters. After serving a set time in World War I, he returned to Greenwood, Mississippi, to use his savings from [military] service to buy a small home. He continued to work in the Leflore County area. After which he sold the small home there, and purchased a home plus land in Humphreys County,[46] Mississippi.

My mother was the daughter of a sugarcane grower in Louisiana.[47] After finishing high school, she began to teach. She taught in the Leflore County and Humphreys County for several years. She continued to work until ill health and death. She died after giving birth to five children; she died in 1952.

Both parents were practical people: strong belief, strong values in education. They taught us to take care of what we have, place strong values in education. There was something good in education. They tried to do their best to provide a college education for all.

After the death of my mother, my maternal uncles and aunts began to visit and write to help with the other children. At this particular time, they were living in various parts of the country. At that time, we had two uncles overseas. They wanted us to spend more time with them, but my father decided that the family of five children would stay together. He did not permit us to visit outside of the state.

My paternal uncles and aunts were not as close as my maternal uncles and aunts.

My education is not a typical Mississippi Delta Black education. The reason for these differences are that my father happened to own his own land; he was a small cattle owner; he had to work for himself. My mother taught school. That was some income besides what was done on the farm. The resources were meager, but they were far better than the share-

---

[45] Leflore County is in the rich, low Delta area, dominated by large plantations. Its county seat, Greenwood, fifty miles northwest of Lexington, the seat of Holmes County, has long been a source of social influence upon the surrounding region. The thrust for Black voting rights originated here in 1963; and to this day, its powerful Ku Klux Klan remains notorious.

[46] In the Delta, west of Holmes County.

[47] Ties between central Mississippi and Louisiana have long been maintained on the basis of seasonal migration from the former to the latter area for sugarcane harvesting.

croppers' families. Indeed, children of these families had very little opportunity for education. And these are some of the reasons: number one, the school building — it was a typical one-room school; one teacher for grades one through eight; children had to walk a long distance to school; buses were not provided until 1951. Number two, incentive: the landlord did not permit children to go to school until the crops were harvested; you did not stop in the spring, or you had to stop school to start the crops. The school year was only eight months. This was the typical Delta-type education because of the farm season. The result of that was more children wanted to go [away] to school to get a better education. Home education was provided by the parents, and even with meager resources, it was [somewhat] successful.

RUSHING: I used to work for the Chicago Housing Authority. The management assistant called us into the office and had us to analyze why, in some months, unpaid rent went up.

We began to go through the files and examine the reasons that people gave. It was because on the Fourth of July and Thanksgiving and Christmas they would take part of their rent money and send it back to their relatives in Holmes County. Whenever someone would die there, the same problem would result. They would take their rent money and would finance transportation down to the funeral.

And as the landlord, we attempted to apply pressure on them, emphasizing that the prompt payment of rent was a condition of the lease. And they could not understand how we could conceivably be so misunderstanding. How could we demand payments of rent when the family's crops down home did not produce? Or when someone was dead? And to them, the most important thing was assisting in the provision of needs for the family.

Later on, I talk to Dr. Shimkin and some other peoples who were interested in this aspect of the Black family. I subsequently began to pay more attention to it and, in the process, to identify many expressions of concern for the extended family. I know that many times we have had to threaten to evict residents, because in the Chicago Housing Authority you could not have unauthorized people living in the apartments. And peoples would come from the South, and sometimes you would get four or five families living in one apartment. And this would create a real problem for the housing management. I think the point I am trying to make is that the commitment to the family, even the extended family, is very straight.[48] And it operates with such force that sometimes it makes people take risks

---

[48]   I.e. straightforward, overriding.

even with respect to their ability to provide food and clothing for their children. This is indeed a strong value among the Black people here in the city.

One of the things I would like to say before I stop is that — what I said here, and I think what all of us might be saying — we would not want anyone to deduce from our statements a monolithic type of perception that characterizes all these Black families. Now, as a Black family — my observations in Chicago indicate — as they move farther up the continuum of education and income, they adopt the habits (I started to say, the corrupt habits) of the Whites. As they get more money, they want to put their older relatives away from them. And also, one other thing, the Black commitment to the extended family is not so much an inherent tradition — I think it does have its genesis in Africa — but[49] it survive in this country as a technique of enabling the Black family to cope with the oppressions that were levied at it by the major society. And it was one of the ways that they could protect themselves. There was no welfare system, and even the early forms of charity were organized not to serve the poor Blacks but poor Whites. And so it was only in this commitment of the family set[50] to its kindred but[51] served as the early form of welfare. Now we notice here in Chicago where the welfare system is a real threat to the continuation of this commitment to the extended families. And sometime I begin to wonder if many White people's inability to understand the structure and viability of the Black family — if they really aren't saying, "We can't understand how it happened when we have done everything we could to destroy it."

CLARK: I'm here, just a country boy from Holmes County, Mississippi. And if any of you saw the report by Shimkin, Louie, and Frate, the place where I live is so large it was left off that map [see Figure 1, page 43]. It is directly south of Lexington and west of Pickens on that particular diagram.

I came here because I am interested in the extended family. Now we asked the brother here from the University of Wisconsin [Dr. Bert Adams] . . . about the legal side of it. And that is the part I am interested in. Now, we could talk all night about social legislation for minorities, but I think this session is more or less directed toward the extended family. . . . Now, from what has been said here today, we see we do have a very strong structure; we see we do have a very strong institution. It might not be the

---

[49]   "But" here is emphatic "but indeed."
[50]   I.e. made.
[51]   I.e. that indeed. See also note 49.

type of institution that is commonly defined as a family but I hope, as has been said earlier, that some of these terms and definitions have been put to rest. I hope that we are convinced and will convince other people that the Black extended family is important and needs supporting legislation.

I live at home now, the same place where some of my folks were slaves. And other foreparents of mine were slave masters in the same spot I am living now. And when I was young I didn't want to be there. But I am proud that I am there; I am proud that I stayed there. But I stayed there when I was young because I was the youngest of a group of grandchildren, our elder grandmother and grandfather, and two or three unmarried aunts. And it was a kind of consensus of the family that I would kind of stick around home, and see about all of my people when they got old, and kind of see after the family land, and carry it on. But, at the time, you know I didn't want to stay there — I stayed there out of sheer necessity. It is customary among us for a grandchild to live with the grandfather, to see after the grandfather and grandmother. No matter where the mother might live, or the father (they might be in Detroit, Chicago, or elsewhere), when the grandparents are kind of old the child comes back to Mississippi to live with them.

Now, when we begin to talk about these things, we can see that the Black culture discussed here is not allowed for in American society. I can give you an example from our schooling.

Several years ago, we had a law passed in Mississippi, about two weeks before school started, that if you did not live with your parents you could not enter school. I was in the public school system at the time, and at least one-third of the children in the average school in Holmes County could not enroll because of this. Well, being a coach at that particular time, I was interested in all students but mainly looking out, you know, for my athletes. And I had only one center on the football team, and he had lived with his grandfather all his life. His grandfather was kind of an elderly person and, at that particular time, his grandfather was sick. Well, in order for my center to enroll in school, since the school officials knew the boy's grandfather but didn't know his uncle, I had to travel to the county south of Holmes County and get the boy's uncle to pretend to be the boy's father.

We don't have a compulsory school law in Mississippi,[52] and we have children having to leave home and go see after their grandparents. Now, it may be absolutely necessary for the child's parents to work for a livelihood. But grandparents are a responsibility for the family and, if push comes to shove, it has to fall on the child. But there is no reason that

[52] Compulsory schooling was abolished in Mississippi in 1956.

some kind of legislation should not be introduced and enacted so that these children would not have to stay out of school to see after grandparents.

Many of our elderly people are not getting the medical attention that they need because they are not able to go into nursing homes. We have very few, even though we are fortunate to have Mrs. Booker in Holmes County. And because the elderly are not able to go on into such homes, they have to go into the home of a niece or a nephew, a daughter or son. But there is no reason that the same benefits that are allowed nursing homes should not be allowed to the families where these elderly people have to go. And if the nephew or niece does not have the proper training, why not use these finances for that purpose?

Several years ago, it was necessary for my nieces and nephews to live in my home. (And this is no exception, as you read the Shimkin–Louie–Frate report, you see that it is necessary, quite a few times, in the Black community.) Also, it was necessary for me to live with my father before he deceased. Yet I had all kinds of trouble in the world trying to get income tax credit for him. I had to show what I spent on him. But, in the meantime, when I went downtown and bought a sack of flour, I didn't buy a sack of flour for my father, and another for my nieces and nephews — I just bought a sack for the whole family. It was difficult with this type of family to show what I actually spent on my father, and what on my nieces and nephews. Most of the time, I wound up with a large family of seven or eight. But at that time I wasn't married and was getting tax credit for only one person.

I have run into all kinds of housing problems, particularly with the Farmers' Home Administration which prevails in our area. If it is necessary for the elderly people to live with their children and the children apply for a house (let's say they have a family of eight or nine, and the FHA will have a certain financial standard for housing a family of that size), if they bring one or two elderly people without income into the house, then the family increases but not its income and this, in many instances, makes the family ineligible for a home through FHA.

The Holmes County Health Research Program and our other Black organizations have done much research about the number of unemployed Black people. These reports are very different from the official statistics. Some show that at least one-third of the Black people in Holmes County are unemployed at one time or another during the year. At times, 60 percent are unemployed or sick or retired. Because of this, welfare and food stamps are important.

As one case, I'm thinking here of a particular family, that of a retired teacher named Estelle Redman. All of her brothers worked to put her through school. And when they had put her through school, she got a teacher's job starting at fifteen dollars a month, as you heard Mrs. Robinson mention earlier. And she used that fifteen dollars a month to help her brothers on the farm when things were pretty tough. So her brothers saw after their father until he died. Then after their father died, she being single and elderly, one brother took her into his home to see after her. Now, her brother has deceased, and she lives with his widow. On the very meager income that she has, she and her brother's widow need each other. Miss Redman was old and couldn't live by herself. But her brother's widow, because she had opened her door to Miss Redman, was not eligible for food stamps. This is a typical example of how the laws do not fit the needs of the extended families in Holmes County.

We can give other examples. The insurance laws of the State of Mississippi do not allow for the extended family. If you have a grandchild living with you, many insurance policies will not include this child as an immediate member of the family; nor a grandmother living with you. We have mentioned the importance of going home to funerals and seeing after elderly people when they are sick, but with the leave laws we have in the State of Mississippi you are not able to take days off for leave for members of the extended family. By the legal definition, these individuals are not a part of the family.

We see these many problems. And we are hoping that, as a result of this study, we will be able to do something in the Mississippi legislature to enact laws relevant to Black people and their extended family.

Thank you.

EDITORS' SUMMARY

In general, the community review of the Shimkin–Louie–Frate report (this volume) clearly emphasized the importance and characteristics of "strong" extended families as the environments of personal capacity among Black Holmes Countians. Great-grandparents and grandparents were significant as role models defining family styles. Ideally, they would be independent farmers holding land in continual trust for their descendants. Extensive mutual aid among family members and religious faith have been key elements of survival; education and migration have been the paths to upward mobility. Even in Chicago, ties of loyalty to relatives in the South have great force: remittances to aid kinsfolk in great need or to attend funerals override the payment of rent as obligations. Leases are endangered in this way and by overcrowding with illegal guests — new migrants or visitors from the South.

Within this pattern, the participants added many variants to those discussed in the Shimkin–Louie–Frate study. At one extreme, large size, close propinquity and extensive sharing can be found (Randles); at the other are small families, physically and socially mobile, which are loath to use the aid of uncles and aunts at the price of weakening nuclear cohesiveness (Griffin). Among some, the extended families have become symbols of a newfound Black identity; among others, felt obligations have weakened with upward mobility.

Nevertheless, the conclusions drawn by Representative Clark, that the Black extended family is today a "very strong institution" deserving legal protection and support, need to be stressed. His indications of key areas in which the span of obligations is well defined in Black customary law but not in Mississippi — or other U.S. — legislation provide significant starts for remedial efforts. In particular these include:

1. Adequate assistance and housing facilities for the Black aged, so that the use of family resources is an option rather than a necessity often managed only at great sacrifice.

2. Funding provisions to permit family caretakers of the aged and chronically ill to receive compensation on the same basis as nursing homes and allied institutions. Such funding would include provisions for the proper training of family caretakers.

3. Greater flexibility in the legal definitions of "dependents" and "immediate family" from the standpoints of tax benefits, insurance, emergency leave, and allied rights, to acknowledge the broad span of fosterage practiced by Black families, as well as the considerable outreach of relatives (e.g. sisters-in-law) for whom obligations accrue.

4. Stronger protections for the rights of children, particularly the restoration of compulsory school attendance in Mississippi.

Is There a National Pattern in the United States?

Black Families in the United States: An Overview of Current Ideologies and Research

BERT N. ADAMS

ABSTRACT

The author first reviews the two tendencies in the study of the U.S. Black family which were prevalent until the mid-1960's: either to ignore its existence altogether, or to treat it as a social problem. The latter view was especially emphasized by Frazier and Moynihan. Billingsley, Heiss, Jackson, Lopata, and Scanzoni, publishing in the late 1960's and early 1970's, challenged Moynihan's "tangle of pathology" characterization. The papers in this volume present a third viewpoint: that the Black family is a culturally unique institution in U.S. society. (Staples and Ladner also take this view.)

The extended kin networks described in the chapter by Shimkin, Louie, and Frate detail family values, institutions, and customary law which need recognition by U.S. White society. Whether or not the unique Black family culture described by contributors to this volume is a passing phase, as a cultural contribution it can and should remain a source of pride to the U.S. Black population.

Until the mid-1960's there were two tendencies in the study of the U.S. Black family: one was to ignore it altogether; the other was to treat it as a social problem. The classic statement of this latter approach is found in the work of E. Franklin Frazier. Prior to Frazier's writing it was felt, within the White community of scholars, that slavery did no real damage to Blacks. Thus, Frazier's view of the disorganizing effects of the slavery and postslavery periods upon Black personality and society was a liberal perspective when propounded. Slavery weakened family life, and the postslavery period saw the disruption even of those ties which were anchored in the plantation system. Frazier put it thus:

When the invading armies disrupted the plantation organization, thousands of Negroes were set adrift and began to wander footloose about the country. Not only were the sentimental and habitual ties between spouses severed, but even Negro women often abandoned their children. Among the demoralized elements in the newly emancipated Negroes promiscuous sexual relationships and frequent changing of spouses became the rule (Frazier 1957: 313).

The result, then, was anarchy in the Black community, which helps to explain many of the problems Blacks are facing today, Frazier felt. This "liberal" perspective, however, was easily adapted to the ideological need to blame the victim. The internal disorganization of the Black community, this view says, is *still* thwarting Black attempts to move into the mainstream of U.S. society. Life for urban Negroes today is casual, precarious, and fragmentary:

It lacks continuity and its roots do not go deeper than the contingencies of daily living. . . . Without the direction provided by family traditions and the discipline of parents, large numbers of Negro children grow up without aims and ambitions (Frazier 1957: 636).

Frazier's characterization of the Negro family gained wide attention when it was repeated and programmed by Daniel P. Moynihan:

The evidence — not final, but powerfully persuasive — is that the Negro family in the urban ghettoes is crumbling. . . . In a word, a national effort towards the problem of Negro Americans must be directed towards the question of family structure. The object should be to strengthen the Negro family so as to enable it to raise and support its members as do other families (Moynihan 1965: 47; abstract).

Proponents of this view are likely to feel that the key problem with the Black family is the lack of a male head of household. A father in the home is necessary for the child to develop "aims and ambitions," as Frazier expressed it. Greater opportunities for Black males in the economy are necessary for these males to become stable members of households; in turn, economic and family stability are necessary for Black people to escape the disorganization which is rampant in their communities today.

The assumptions of this perspective are thus complete: (1) Slavery and the postslavery period resulted in anarchy among U.S. Blacks. (2) That anarchy is still found today, especially among urban Blacks. (3) One focal point of that anarchy is the Black family, which is disorganized and is dysfunctional for the raising of achieving and successful offspring. Therefore, (4) the disorganization is self-perpetuating and will continue until Black families are strengthened, primarily by stabilizing the position of adult males within them. Essential to this view is the assumption that Black families are weak and disorganized.

The first response to Moynihan's "tangle of pathology" characterization of the Black family is found in works such as Andrew Billingsley's *Black families in White America* (1968). The Black family, Billingsley feels, is not that disorganized, not that unstable, not that pathological. The vast majority of Black families — even in urban ghettoes — are male-headed. They have, if anything, shown amazing strength in withstanding the oppression and prejudice of the dominant society. Even illegitimacy statistics, often used to show the greater disorganization of Black people, are fallacious to some extent, and are an artifact of reporting techniques and of the differential treatment of Black and White unwed mothers.

This response, then, is that Black families are very much like White families, with the "pathology" view having arisen due to two factors: (1) the confusion of social class with race, and (2) the ideologies of writers and researchers. Much research of the late 1960's and early 1970's was aimed directly at the Frazier–Moynihan view. This research sought to show that Black families are not all that different from White. Jerold Heiss, for example, finds no evidence that parental marital instability among Blacks is transmitted to their offspring, thus denying that such "pathology" is self-perpetuating (Heiss 1972: 82–92). Jacquelyne Jackson, looking at husband–wife roles and power among aging Blacks, reports that males take a major role in decisions. She finds that matriarchy is not even true among her Durham, North Carolina, couples in terms of power and decision making (Jackson 1972: 21–27). Helena Lopata adds that, contrary to the assumption that older Black widows live full and rich lives surrounded by kin, they are just as isolated as elderly White widows (Lopata 1963: 1003–1010). Finally, John Scanzoni (1971) finds great similarity between middle-class Blacks in Indianapolis and their White counterparts.

One of the problems with these two characterizations of the Black family, i.e. "pathology" and "similarity," is a semantic and statistical one. Terms such as "larger numbers" and "a large portion" are likely to be automatically interpreted as meaning "typically" or "in general." (And often this is the interpretation which the writer wants his readers to draw.) However, the great variety of Black families makes it dangerous to generalize apart from the appropriate statistics and has made it possible to "ideologize" without relying upon hard data. The present volume is one step in the direction of replacing ideology with research.

But what do the papers in this volume show? Do they agree with the *"pathology"* or the *"similarity"* perspective on the Black family and its kin network? To a great extent, they agree with neither, but with a third perspective which has arisen in the 1970's. This perspective says, very simply, that the Black family is not "just like the White" when socio-economic status is controlled, but that does not mean it is "pathological." It means that there is cultural *uniqueness* and validity in the Black model — a model which other members of this society must come to understand and from which, moreover, society can learn. This view of the Black family has arisen in conjunction with two developments within the Black community: (1) concern about origins and African identity; (2) concern with contemporary ethnic identity, with the intensifying "we-feelings" of Blacks in the U.S. The former has reintroduced the old debate about cultural survivals and is epitomized by Alex Haley's *Roots*, an exciting account of his search for, and discovery of, his ancestral home in the Gambia River valley of West Africa. My personal feeling is that, though this issue is not broached by Shimkin et al. and other authors in this volume, a distinction should be made between the individual's need for identification with his ancestral origins and the scholarly necessity for establishing such ties. On the individual level, such a search is important in the intensification of ethnic solidarity. However, the issue of survivals is a difficult one to resolve, and seems of considerably less import than establishing the dimensions and significance of ethnic identity today. The latter, to which the papers of this volume contribute, seems to this author to be an important step in the movement of the Black people away from being a minority to being an *ethnic* minority, and eventually just another ethnic group in this society.

Three important statements of the cultural uniqueness view of the Black family have appeared thus far in the 1970's. These are found in Robert Staples' (1971) decade review for the *Journal of Marriage and the Family*, Joyce Ladner's (1971) report on the Black woman, entitled *Tomorrow's tomorrow*, and in the papers presented at the International Congress of Anthropological and Ethnological Studies, September, 1973, which have been extended and expanded in the present volume (Shimkin et al., this volume).

Staples comments that Billingsley, though sympathetic, does not penetrate Black families but sees even their strengths through middle-class eyes. Instead, such divergences as the greater sexual permissiveness of Black people should not be downplayed but should be seen as reflecting the absence of a double standard of sexual conduct among Blacks. They can thus avoid the sex role conflicts and guilt which plague the White community. Therefore, sex relations both before and after marriage have "a much more positive meaning in the Black community" (Staples 1971: 134). Among Black women, he adds, children are a value in themselves, regardless of marriage. Along these same lines, Ladner asserts that a child has the right to exist, motherhood is the fulfillment of womanhood, and thus neither childhood nor motherhood should be degraded by artificial legal statuses. Blacks, she affirms, must "decolonize," i.e. free themselves from White middle-class definitions of the "good" and the "right." Their structures and values are good in themselves, and a few additional examples may help to make clear her position. Black women are strong but are not pathologically emasculating. Any emasculating of Black men that has been done, has been done by White society. Black self-esteem is not low, but has been -strengthened and clarified in the struggle for survival. Black marriage is not idealistic or romanticized, but realistic — a stance which might help Whites as well. Black women are now role models for many White women, who are questioning the double sexual standard, traditional marriage, "legal illegitimacy," that is, the legal disabilities imposed upon children born out of wedlock, and other factors which in the Black community have been defined as deviant by White middle-class morality (Ladner 1971). So goes Ladner's often compelling argument, based upon interviews with teenage girls when she was a part of Rainwater's Pruitt-Igoe research team.

Thus far, the most convincing research acclaiming Black cultural viability and uniqueness has been Shimkin, Louie, and Frate's continuing study of Black extended families in Mississippi and Chicago. Black extended kin ties are not based upon female dominance and are important to both survival and social mobility. These extended families may number 100 or more, sometimes clustered in one county and sometimes scattered from Mississippi to the great cities of the North. Shimkin's picture of the extended kin network, it should be added, has been corroborated in an entirely different research setting: a small Midwestern city. There Hays and Mindel (1973) have found both more kin visiting and a higher value placed upon kin among twenty-five Black couples than among a matched sample of Whites.

Blacks in such families and networks, Shimkin et al. feel, can be deservedly critical of the shortcomings of the White middle-class model and the dominant legal system.

White people may feel keenly that marital instabilities and the acceptance of human frailties are signs of Black failure. Blacks feel as keenly that the inadequacies of White care for "father and mother, brother and sister," White favoritism among children, and White indifference to the needs of distant kin are even more profound weaknesses (Shimkin et al., this volume).

Thus, value ethnocentrism should be a two-way street, and, as the authors state in their introduction, it is time for cultural pluralism to be recognized by society's legal structures:

. . . the better recognition of Black family values, institutions, and customary law should serve as the basis of appropriate legislative actions for example, in the rectification of currently biased laws on adoption and fosterage (Shimkin et al., this volume).

Other authors have tried to account for the uniqueness of Black culture, some by tracing African roots, some by noting the greater and more lasting prejudice and discrimination faced by Blacks than by the European ethnic groups. But the basis for that uniqueness is not the key issue confronting the spokesman for this view of the Black family. Rather, the issue is: is this Black family culture a passing phase, or will it make a continuing contribution to the U.S. experience? That is, is ethnic minority status, and the resulting view of the Black family as unique and good, merely a phase through which Blacks must pass on the way to societal equality and success — in middle-class terms — or is it a permanent part of the cultural pluralism of the U.S.? Shimkin clearly manifests the dilemma confronting those holding the "uniqueness" position:

As more urbanized Blacks ascend the ladder of success . . . the tendency will of course be toward a more viable nuclear household. That appears to be a concomitant of much of modern urban life and is probably inevitable. But younger Blacks, in particular, should always remember that what they are leaving is not something to be ashamed of. It is not something that is reflective of some deficiency in their culture. And it should not be disparaged (Shimkin as quoted in Bims 1974: 125–127).

If the specter of the "pathology" view were not still hanging over us the final three sentences would be unnecessary. But what of the issue of whether Black extended family strength — so apparent in this volume — is a passing phenomenon? Shimkin et al. (this volume) describe the Mitchells, an economically corporate kin unit in Holmes County, Mississippi, which functions for survival, for the pooling of resources, for living together, sharing, and ritual. They then refer to the Bidwells, a scattered but psychologically close network of kin who come home for visits and for burial, and who remain in contact despite being scattered. In their literature review they describe Scanzoni's study of middle-class Black families in Indianapolis and Wright's study of Black nuclear families in California, among whom there has been a breaking up, says Shimkin, of the southern and midwestern extended family. One cannot help but wonder whether such types are parallel and relatively permanent or whether they are stages in a historical sequence from the unique Black extended family to the urban nuclear family which characterizes so much of the dominant society. Is "nuclearization" the inevitable price which the Black family system will have to pay for eventual ethnic status, for societal success? Ladner would very likely say "no," or at least that in the interim the larger society will learn much from the Black experience and model. Regardless of one's personal view on this matter, the data contained in this volume go a long way toward dispelling the myths that Black family and kin networks are either disorganized or else just like those of Whites.

Is it possible for one to hold both the "similarity" and the "uniqueness" stances regarding the Black family in the U.S.? To this writer, the answer would seem to be "yes." The Black family is not as different as the Frazier–Moynihan position would have us believe, and increasing opportunity and success may change many Black families and their structures, perhaps toward the nuclear type. This, however, will not destroy the unique Black cultural contribution, described so positively at so many points in the present volume. Nor will positive changes take place as a result of programs geared at strengthening so-called "disorganized" Black families. They will result from (1) the recognition, *legal* and otherwise, that there are ways to organize people in families other than in nuclear units;[1] and (2) a change in institutionalized discrimination and prejudice on the part of the dominant society. Both of these are slow and painful processes, because the dominant members of society do not relinquish their prerogatives and ideologies easily, but these processes are in motion. The papers in the present volume will contribute to breaking down the lingering stereotype of Black family disorganization, and to achieving recognition of the strength and uniqueness of Black families and kin relations in U.S. society.

REFERENCES

BILLINGSLEY, ANDREW
   1968   *Black families in White America.* Englewood Cliffs, N.J.: Prentice-Hall.
BIMS, HAMILTON
   1974   The Black family: a proud reappraisal. *Ebony* 5 (March): 118–127.
FRAZIER, E. FRANKLIN
   1957   *The Negro in the United States.* New York: Macmillan.
HALEY, ALEX
   1976   *Roots.* New York: Doubleday.
HAYS, WILLIAM C., CHARLES H. MINDEL
   1973   Extended kinship relations in Black and White families. *Journal of Marriage and the Family* 35: 51–57.
HEISS, JEROLD
   1972   On the transmission of marital instability in Black families. *American Sociological Review* 37: 82–92.
JACKSON, JACQUELYNE JOHNSON
   1972   Marital life among aging Blacks. *Family Life Coordinator* 21: 21–27.

---

[1]   On the need for legal recognition of the viability of family forms which diverge from the nuclear, see Representative Clark's discussion in Frate and Logan, editors, this volume.

LADNER, JOYCE A.
  1971 *Tomorrow's tomorrow: the Black woman.* Garden City, N.Y.: Double-
         day.
LOPATA, HELENA ZNANIECKI
  1973 Social relations of Black and White widowed women in a northern
         metropolis. *American Journal of Sociology* 78: 1003–1010.
MOYNIHAN, DANIEL P.
  1965 *The Negro family: the case for national action.* Washington, D.C.:
         U.S. Government Printing Office.
SCANZONI, JOHN
  1971 *The Black family in modern society.* Boston: Allyn and Bacon.
STAPLES, ROBERT
  1971 Toward a sociology of the Black family: a theoretical and methodo-
         logical assessment. *Journal of Marriage and the Family* 33: 119–138.

Continuities and Variations in Black Family Structure

JOYCE ASCHENBRENNER

ABSTRACT

Contemporary literature on the Black family in the United States has been characterized by two basic approaches — the "pathological" and the "adaptive." A third view, which might be called the "institutional," examines the Black family in the context of a Black cultural tradition, stressing continuity under varying conditions.

Within the context of the institutional approach, the author presents structural characteristics of Black family organization based on her own observations, in conjunction with the literature on the subject. Emerging from this evidence is a model of a bilateral extended family, characterized by high interaction, cooperation, loyalty, and residential propinquity, in which consanguineous ties may carry as much weight as, or more than, do conjugal ones.

The functioning of the Black extended family is further examined in varying contexts: southern rural, southern small town, and southern urban; northern urban; and among different socioeconomic groups. These data confirm that the model of the bilateral extended family referred to above, allowing for some individual variations, applies in both the South and the North. There emerges a family organization based on a communal sense of social responsibility, permitting not only survival but also the maintenance of a sense of individual dignity among Black Americans.

INTRODUCTION: THREE BASIC APPROACHES TO THE BLACK FAMILY

In the growing literature on the Black family, two basic approaches have emerged which may be characterized as the "pathological" and the "adaptive." These perspectives, developed by American observers of their own society, share an assumption of an underlying social and cultural uniformity in U.S. society, to which Black social life — in particular, the Black family — is compared and from which it is seen to deviate. According to the "pathological" approach, the Black family is disorganized, with some exceptions, as a result of "deculturation" during slavery and subsequent social and economic deprivation. This position, developed in the work of E. Franklin Frazier (1939), Lee Rainwater (1970), Daniel P. Moynihan (1965), and, more recently, John Scanzoni (1971), as well as by less well-known scholars, can be regarded as the prevailing view in the sociology of Black family life. According to the second, "adaptive" view, the Black family is essentially an adaptation to the social and economic conditions in which Blacks find themselves as members of a deprived minority. This view, developed primarily by anthropologists, stresses the adaptive nature of the Black family, mainly in northern and urban settings.

A third, different viewpoint, which might be called the "institutional," as presented in this volume, examines the Black family in the context of a Black cultural tradition. It stresses continuity under varying conditions. While adaptable to a wide variety of environments, the Black family is seen in the framework of fundamental concepts and values which differ in certain crucial respects from those of other peoples in U.S. society and are part of a distinctive heritage.

The basic difference between the third, or "institutional," viewpoint and the others is that in the institutional or cultural approach, the Black family is described independently of a (real or imagined) "prevailing" U.S. family system (though not, it should be noted, of the U.S. economic system), using descriptive terms and concepts that have been developed in cross-cultural studies. In the "pathological" approach, an ideal model of U.S. family life is postulated, to which Black families are compared and in terms of which they are judged as to "stability" and organization; in the "adaptive" view, differences from a "dominant" family structure are explained in terms of adaptation to unfavorable economic and social conditions. In these latter approaches, little or no scope is granted to value differences, apart from those of economics or social mobility, and the Black family is viewed as essentially a creature of the American economy.

As Billingsley (1968) has stated, the "pathological" perspective deals not so much with the Black family itself as with the effects of poverty and racism on human behavior. This results in an emphasis on negative traits, held to be characteristic of Black families. For example, a major concern has been the reputed lack of "deferred gratification" among lower-income Black families; this is viewed as a sign of family or personal disorganization rather than as a natural concomittant of long-term economic and political deprivation. Likewise, marital instability, illegitimacy, the absent father, a lack of control over children, or a lack of supportive behavior toward children are cited as evidence for the fundamental pathology of Black families rather than as problems with which they must deal or as possible indicators of a different type of social organization. The model of a "happy family life" held up as a standard for Blacks (and the rest of us) is clearly expressed in the following quotation:

The more reward elements a male provider has, the more integrated, or articulated he may be said to be with the opportunity system. And the more articulated (the more he is part of the opportunity structure), the more rewards he provides to his wife (and children, usually *via* her), and the more positively both spouses experience greater feelings of solidarity about their relationship, greater cohesion of the family as a social system exists, reducing the likelihood of marital dissolution (Scanzoni 1971: 200).

Thus, those of us who are not "articulated" into the "opportunity system" are doomed to an unhappy family life, and the American Dream of a fine house and two cars also apparently assures family solidarity and domestic bliss. Those Blacks who have attained economic security, then, may have "stable" families and share the virtues of American family life; those who do not are doomed to pathology and disorganization. Here is a clear statement of economic determinism, and, like all simplistic views, it is not wholly supported by the facts. The increasing divorce rate among business and professional people, the extensive use of drugs and alcohol among children and parents in affluent families, the problem of the "absentee" father in many business and professional homes, the lack of communication cited by children and wives, and the high rate of suicide reported among middle-class housewives all throw doubt on the automatic benefits of economic opportunity to family living.

In the "pathological" view, we are told that poor Black families are involved in a "cycle of pathology": that because they are not integrated into the opportunity structure, they are disorganized and therefore unable to socialize their children into that system. The true situation, however, is that they do not socialize their children into the "opportunity system" because they are not a part of that system, not because they are disorganized. In this view there is no concession that families may be organized in different ways from the preferred stereotype. Further, there is little attempt to discover *why* children are socialized in a particular manner; while the methods of rearing children in Black communities may appear to hold them back, according to accepted theories of child rearing, these methods may only reflect the realities of the Black situation.

Significantly, the extent to which extended-family relationships are recognized and utilized in Black communities, documented by many observers, is largely ignored by those who take the "pathological" approach. Such relationships are irrelevant when there is focus on marital stability and illegitimacy as indices of family strength. The issue of matriarchy and matrifocality, on the other hand, is a dominant theme. Blacks often see in the preoccupation with this topic, rightly or wrongly, an implied criticism of Black "manliness" and "femininity" (see Staples 1971). Again, here an economic situation is confused with family structure; the prevalence of female-headed households among the urban poor generally and Blacks in particular reflects a low sex ratio and lack of permanent well-paying jobs for Black men, rather than a tendency toward female dominance or the irresponsibility of men. The consideration that Blacks prefer two-parent households should not, however, be cited as evidence that Black families are merely imperfect reflections of "stable" White families. As documented below and elsewhere (Aschenbrenner 1973), in the context of the Black extended family, matrifocal households and other part-families do not carry all the disadvantages of the "broken home" in the isolated conjugal family setting, but generate instead various types of support from adult men and women in a number of kinship and friendship roles. Further, studies have shown that disadvantages suffered by children in one-parent homes are cancelled out in higher-income families, whether Black or White, indicating that it is not family structure *per se* that is crucial to the economic success of family members but economic opportunity.

The much-discussed domestic power of the Black woman is often invoked as a sign of a weakened male role. As cross-cultural data show, in a bilateral kinship system in which ties beyond the nuclear family are strong, a woman's domestic power is typically greater than that of her spouse (Liu et al., 1972). Since women generally tend to be more active in kinship matters, matrilateral ties tend to be stronger than patrilateral ties; the interactive power of woman in the home is strengthened and reinforced by her consanguineous relationships, i.e. ties with mother, sister, brother, maternal aunts and uncles, grandmother. In a patrilateral system, such ties are discouraged and the woman's domestic role is somewhat weakened. However, in either system, an extended-family organization is often accompanied by a "segregated" rather than a "joint" conjugal relationship, in which husband and wife operate in different spheres of activity (Liu et al., 1972). It is probably this characteristic of the conjugal relationship that leads some observers to the view that Black men take little interest in the home; while on one level this may be true, on another level we often find the Black man to be highly conscientious in his domestic role as it is defined by his cultural values, taking responsibility for children who are not his own, contributing to a number of households, including perhaps his mother's or an aunt's, satisfying his mate's needs for attention and love, and instructing children in the ways of the world. While a wife may complain because her husband does not take more interest in the home, in actuality she may rigorously resist his efforts at influence in that sphere, defined as her own. Further, a woman's domestic interest may lead her to be active in community and political matters without seriously threatening the security of her husband, who finds his own social supports elsewhere; thus, husband and wife are not competing in the same arena.

The studies by Bott (1957) and Rainwater (1970) among working-class and lower-income groups have led the latter to the view that role segregation is a lower-class or working-class phenomenon (Rainwater 1970); while it is probably the case that lower-class and working-class male and female roles share similarities across cultures, reflecting economic imperatives and conditions, there is evidence that, as in extended families, a segregation of male–female roles is not uncommon among "upper-class" families, e.g. the Roosevelts, the Kennedys, the Rockefellers, the English royal family; it is also found in most other societies in the world. The "joint" husband–wife role is probably, like the isolated conjugal family, primarily a bourgeois northern-European–American specialization.

According to the "pathological" view, because only relatively affluent Black families can achieve stability (here defined as permanency of the conjugal tie, a high degree of shared activities between spouses, and the fact that the roles of "social" and "biological" father are filled by the same person), there are, in this view, two types of family institutions among Black people: respectable families and disorganized families, depending upon whether they achieve the norm. These family types have little in common: the latter are seen in terms of "a tangle of pathology" with their own misguided beliefs and practices, while the former conform to the ideal family type of American society. White investigators who study lower-income families are criticized by Black professionals, who feel they are generalizing from lower-income families to all Blacks. However, it is the *negative image* of lower-income and working-class Black families as seen through the eyes of American social scientists that they are objecting to, as well as the confusion of economic conditions with family organization. The resemblance between White and Black middle- and upper-income families may be largely superficial, reflecting equality of economic status more than similarity of social organization. For example, stable marriages may represent, in both White and Black upper-income families, congruence of economic interests of husband and wife rather than a solidarity of marital relationships. There is evidence, introduced below, that middle- and upper-income Black families share some characteristics with Black lower-income groups that do not occur in many White families of comparable economic status, suggesting the existence of a Black family institution that transcends economic, as well as geographic, boundaries. Once we have established the idea that economic deprivation does not necessarily imply cultural deprivation and social disorganization, the possibility of the existence of more than one valid type of family organization in United States society, crossing economic lines, is greatly increased.

The view of the Black family as an adaptation to the urban ghetto is an improvement over the "pathological" view since it does not apply to the Black family an ideal model that has been developed in studying other groups in our society. However, in this approach, the view of the Black family as a cultural institution is avoided through fragmentation, i.e. looking at the Black family in the urban North as an adaptation to specific conditions, either ignoring Black family organization elsewhere and historically, or regarding it as adaptive to other specific conditions. The basic assumption by those who stress adaptation appears to be that, collectively, Blacks are not creative in the development of social institutions, although they are granted individual and expressive creativity, that is, adaptive and artistic ability. Black lifeways are seen to reflect primarily the exigencies of their environment; thus, extended kinship networks are ego-centered, so that the individual can maximize his advantage (Stack 1972); children are fostered by a wide group of friends and relatives so that mothers can work (Stack 1975); men leave home so that women can draw welfare checks; households are variable so that family members can take advantage of job opportunities and adjust to loss of job. While many of these explanations are no doubt valid, as far as they go, together they add up to a view of a pragmatic, unstructured family system in which social behavior directly reflects individual needs, unmediated by cultural values or social structure.[1] Taking a less materialistic and individualistic viewpoint we can reach deeper levels of explanation; thus ego-centered kin networks are seen as based on a *series of kinship groups* to which an individual may choose (or is led) to belong, each carrying its own responsibilities and obligations, as well as advantages; we observe a consistent pattern of community and kinship concern for children throughout Black history, and a tradition in which men contribute to a number of households in which they have kinship and friendship obligations, while they may not be entirely supporting one household. Finally, since "family" and "household" in Black communities often do not coincide,

---

[1]   In her book, *All my kin* (1974), published since this article was written, Stack presents a clear picture of the Black family as an institution with distinctive values and organization. She does not, however, explicitly adopt the viewpoint that is presented here, nor does she employ the concept of "Black culture."

a variation in household makeup is seen not as an *adaptive change*, but a basic household *adaptability* present in all extended-family systems.

STRUCTURAL CHARACTERISTICS OF THE BLACK EXTENDED FAMILY

Adopting this latter, institutional approach to the Black family, I will present some structural characteristics of Black family organization which I have observed, many of which were also observed by Shimkin et al. in Holmes County (Mississippi) and by Jack in New Orleans, as described in this volume. These characteristics will be discussed in relation to various ecological settings and among a number of social and economic groups as presented in a variety of literature on the Black family. The characteristics are (1) the relative strength of parent–child and sibling ties in Black families; (2) a high degree of visiting, contact, and various types of economic and social support among relatives beyond the nuclear family; (3) a bilateral orientation, but with the matrilateral kin often given more weight; (4) extended kin groups existing in a social environment in which primary-type relations are extended into the larger community; (5) a high degree of residential propinquity among related households; (6) a high value placed on children and motherhood; (7) responsibility to children diffused throughout extended families; (8) frequent fosterage of children with relatives or neighbors; (9) care for dependent and highly mobile family members, adult or children; (10) emphasis on respect for elders; (11) dependence of the strength of marital ties on certain conditions, e.g. social support by in-laws and a strong economic interdependence between husband and wife; (12) the possibility of the undermining of a marital tie when it conflicts with another kinship loyalty; (13) a "segregated" husband–wife relationship; (14) the existence of, on the one hand, marital relationships with strong public sanctions and economic bases, and on the other, a number of private liaisons between men and women.

In addition to these structural characteristics, which are interrelated, there are some other values and activities characteristic of Black families: (15) an emphasis on family occasions and rituals, particularly birthdays and funerals; (16) a religious orientation; (17) a high evaluation of family and individual moral "strength" as a human quality; and (18) a lack of complete correlation between "strength," and respectability and economic achievement.

The picture emerging from these listed characteristics is that of a social organization in which the bilateral extended family, characterized by high interaction, cooperation, loyalty, and residential propinquity, is a basic institution in the lives of Blacks. Within this institution, consanguineous ties may carry as much, or more, weight as conjugal ties; the strength of the latter depend more upon specific economic and social conditions than on legality or social sanction, and, therefore, a marital tie may be undermined either by close consanguineous relationships or by external influences. Within the extended family, children and other dependents are cared for; in addition, kinship obligation is extended into the larger community through fictive kinship and other "primarylike" relationships. Finally, the strength of family relationships influences the social and ethical orientations of Blacks, who measure human qualities in other terms than those of materialistic or occupational achievement, and whose social mores stress responsibility towards family and neighbors.

In order to determine if this ideal type can be useful in looking at Black families generally, we need to consider them in several settings, namely, southern rural, small town, and urban; northern urban; southern and northern upper and middle class, working class, and poor.

BLACK FAMILY ORGANIZATION AND FUNCTIONING IN THE SOUTH

In the Holmes County study in this volume, Shimkin et al. describe Black families as exhibiting many of the above characteristics; they characterize the family system as "extended," and as integrated into the community through kin-type relationships. In their study of a small-town southern community, Kunkel and Kennard (1971) describe matrilateral extended families which link together a number of households. Although they state that most households are nuclear-conjugal, they indicate the importance of kinship beyond the household, particular ties between parents and children. Relationships between husband and wife appear to be egalitarian, with segregated roles, and "rarely conform exactly to conventional models" (Kunkel and Kennard 1971: 46).

In the Davis, Gardner, and Gardner study, *Deep South* (1941), reference is made to extended kinship relations among tenant farmers:

The most extended kinship relations not only were defined by terms but were recognized by the performance of services. . . . Although the extended family group seldom farms as a unit, the organization of large kinship groups by visiting, performance of mutual services and by church and associational solidarity undoubtedly was instrumental in keeping large numbers of tenants on the plantation (Davis et al. 1941: 410).

Among the tenant managers, socially higher than the tenant farmers, "patriarchal" extended families were found; matrifocal or "matriarchal" families, often including married sons and daughters and their families in a household, were more common among tenant farmers (14.1 percent). In all of these families, the strong central authority of the male or female head guaranteed the productiveness of family members.

Charles Johnson's study of tenant farmers in Macon County, Alabama, also depicts both male- and female-headed households, over half of them having other relatives in the household (Johnson 1934: 29). Adoption of children of relatives and neighbors is easy and frequent, and mothers often do not distinguish between own and adopted children. He finds "stable families with family traditions," close family relationships, and "moral sensitivity" in varying degrees among the educated, the uneducated, owners, tenants, and sharecroppers (Johnson 1934: 33).

E. Franklin Frazier describes "patriarchal families" among landowning Blacks in which sons and their families remain in their father's house and farm jointly (Frazier 1939). He also emphasizes the strength and importance of the roles of mother and grandmother in the history of Black families in America.

Several of my informants in Chicago who had migrated from the South described family organizations similar to those characterized by other authors. A woman from a small southern city described her mother's family as concentrated in the same neighborhood and in a nearby small town, where the entire family went to church every Sunday. She grew up playing with her cousins, and when she was in high school, spent a year with her father's extended family, located in a neighboring state. When she moved to Chicago, she stayed for a while with her mother's sister, who had moved earlier, and also maintained contact with her mother's cousin and her daughters in Chicago, whom she referred to as "cousins." Numerous relatives from the South visited her continuously in Chicago, and her oldest sister came up for a week or two every year, bringing her youngest children. My informant visited her family in Mississippi at least every second year, and, in addition, traveled there on important occasions, such as her grandmother's funeral. On that occasion, several carloads of Chicago relatives traveled to Mississippi for the funeral of the old matriarch.

An older woman in my sample, a widow, was descended from a landowning family in Georgia; her father had inherited his land from his father, and several of his brothers owned and farmed contiguous land which they had also inherited. The family had maintained a "genteel" tradition, and my informant, who was light skinned and exuded southern charm, missed the amenities of her southern background. She moved North with her husband; others in her family had moved to Chicago, and she had raised some of the younger ones; presently, she headed a "matriarchal" family, including her son and daughter and their families.

Hortense Powdermaker characterizes the typical Black family in the South as "matriarchal and elastic" (Powdermaker 1939). She describes various households as "loose" in structure, including many types of relatives and "adopted" children. The upper and some upper-middle-class families are patriarchal, but here households also frequently include relatives beyond the nuclear family. She speaks of the "very real love" for children, and "a great joy in having them about . . . often there seems to be no other reason for wanting them or adopting them" (Powdermaker 1939: 200). Adoption is frequent, seldom legalized, and referred to as "giving the child away" (Powdermaker 1939: 201).

In his study *Blackways of Kent*, Hylan Lewis remarks that young people maintain a respectful and kind attitude toward the aged, and that among all socioeconomic groups there was a "marked filial respect and obedience" on the part of the young (Lewis 1955). He also finds households made up of extended-family members, with frequent "adoption" of children of relatives (Lewis 1955: 23). He concludes that the Black family has an *ad hoc* character, probably on the basis of variable household makeup (which, we may recall, also leads Powdermaker to speak of a "loose" structure); a less biased conclusion is that the Black family is extended in character, as reflected in a variable household makeup. Lewis describes seven household forms; however, they can be reduced to two basic types, based on a conjugal tie and on consanguineous ties (sibling and mother–child) respectively. Extended-family members, including more than two generations, as well as adopted children, are often present in both types as described by Lewis. Higher-status families may be of either type, as may less "respectable" families; however, the conjugal household with both parents present is more common among the former

Virginia Heyer Young speaks of a "secure" family organization in southern Black families, with positive acceptance and care for children by both male and female relatives, as well as by father and mother, and an active role of grandparents in socialization (Young 1971 [1970]). Mother is the center, but not the main support or authority:

In contrast to the two-generation White nuclear family, the Negro family maintains strong ties over three or four generations. It is not organized as a multi-generational household, but the grandparental tie is easily involved in a variety of arrangements (Young 1971 [1970]: 201).

The evidence from these accounts of southern families supports the view that the model most applicable to the Black family is that of the bilateral extended family, with households variable in form but falling into two basic patterns, based on conjugal or consanguineous ties. We can assume, then, that the particular type of household depends on the relative strength of a marital tie, and that this in turn depends on other considerations, such as the ability of a man to support a household, as well as the reinforcement of the marital tie by consanguineous kin. The fact that conjugal-nuclear households are more frequent in upper-income groups merely reflects this economic fact, rather than a different concept or type of family. Further, the idea that "family" and "household" are not necessarily synonymous indicates the necessity to investigate kin relationships beyond the household before making assumptions about family type.

DOES THE BLACK EXTENDED FAMILY MODEL APPLY IN THE NORTH?

We are now faced with the question of whether the extended-family model can be applied to Black families in northern cities. On the whole, accounts of northern Black families have adopted the "pathological" view, stressing poverty, disorganization, and the attempts by "middle-class" Blacks to emulate White ways. Actual description of family organization itself is rare, except for the emphasis on household makeup, whether conjugal or matrifocal.

In her study of women in poor Black families in St. Louis, Joyce Ladner emphasizes the experiences and problems of young women but refers to the extended family as an important source of security for the Black child (Ladner 1971). Motherhood is characterized as of great significance to young Black women, with or without marriage, and children are readily taken in by extended-family members.

Carol Stack (1970) identifies functioning kinship networks and speaks of the importance of the kinship idiom in a northern Midwest city. She stresses the functionality of urban kinship-based domestic units in the location and adjustment of immigrants from the South, as well as in assuring the care of children. According to Stack, "shared parental responsibilities among kin" are the response of Black families to poverty conditions (Stack 1972).

Raymond T. Smith compares West Indian and American lower-class Afro-American family structure, concluding that in neither instance is the normative nuclear family a productive model for the study of family organization. He notes the tendency to keep open as many kinship links as feasible and much reciprocal visiting, temporary boarding, and "the maintenance of close affective relations between people who may be geographically separated" (Smith 1970: 68). He states,

The dominant impression [among low-income families in the Caribbean and in North American cities] is of people helping other people, whether it be by lending, by looking after a child, by giving gifts of various practical kinds, or by transfers of money. These transactions are by no means confined within the limits of a given household, much less within the bounds of a nuclear family unit (Smith 1970: 69).

He characterizes conjugal relationships as "segregate" rather than "joint," and points out that even when he has a steady job and income a man does not necessarily establish a "normative nuclear family," but may provide support for a woman and her children, acting as father to the latter whether they are his or not. The stress on the mother–child relationship in these families results in the existence of clusters of close female kin, "constituting solidary and cooperating groups" (Smith 1970: 66).

In his comprehensive study, *Black families in White America*, Billingsley (1968) describes several family types: "nuclear," "attenuated nuclear" (including matrifocal), "extended," and "augmented," the latter including nonrelatives. If the word "household" is substituted for "family" in Billingsley's analysis, we see that in each household type, either marital or consanguineous relationships, or both, are stressed. The frequency of "extended" and "augmented" households is indicated by census data: in 1965, nearly 15 percent of all Black families reported that they had one or more minor relatives living with them who were not their own children, and more than one-fourth of all Black families had at least one relative living with them, and in more than one kinship role or at more than one generational level (Billingsley 1968: 20). This is indeed significant evidence for the weight given to extended-family relationships. Billingsley characterizes the Black community as an "ethnic subsociety" and speaks of the "sense of peoplehood" among Blacks. He states,

The importance of social class does not mean, as a number of social scientists still hold, that middle class Negro families have more in common with middle class white families than they do with lower class Negro families. Some liberal social reformers even hold that lower class Negro families have more in common with lower class white families than they do with middle class Negro families. Such naive analyses — on which programs are often based — are possible because of a failure to make distinctions between different types of identity people share (Billingsley 1968: 9–10).

Billingsley describes "patriarchal" (though vanishing), "matriarchal," and "equalitarian" authority patterns among lower-income families, noting that the last named are becoming more common among lower- and higher-income families alike. Among lower-income families, "segmented" husband–wife roles are more common; however, he indicates that "role flexibility" and "mutual cooperation between husband and wife in meeting the instrumental needs of the family in both the external world and within the family" are increasingly common (Billingsley 1968: 144).

It should be noted that he contrasts this type of role relationship with the "traditional" division of labor — men the providers and women the housekeepers; as we have noted above, role segregation between husband and wife does not necessarily imply a sexual division of labor along traditional lines. It is perhaps the *egalitarian* nature of the marital relationship rather than its "joint" character (typically with males in instrumental, females in primarily expressive capacities) that is increasingly characteristic in Black families.

Most studies of Black families stress the relative weakness of the marriage tie, except in upper-income families. This confirms the view that the conjugal relationship is dependent upon economic factors; further, in my own investigations in Chicago and southern Illinois, consanguineous relatives, especially mother, siblings, and maternal relatives, were observed to exert influence on whom one married and even on how a marriage worked out. In an upper-middle-class family a maternal aunt regularly "passed on" (approved) prospective spouses of nieces and nephews; in other families, "interference" by siblings was strongly resented by spouses, especially wives, and husbands frequently complained of the influence of their wives' mothers. Marriages which were not on firm ground economically, or were opposed by other family members, were precarious; this was frequently the case in first marriages, but also in later marriages, especially if one or the other spouse had been contributing significantly to another household. Further, private liaisons or "affairs" are a continuous potential threat to marital stability; however, if the economic arrangements are satisfactory to both spouses and a marriage is not actively opposed by other family members, a marriage may be little affected by such relationships "on the side."

My work in Chicago indicated a bilateral extended family system, often with more stress on matrilateral kin, but with men frequently active in kinship roles of father, husband, stepfather, grandfather, and maternal or paternal uncle. A man may be father to his stepchildren, treating them in the same manner as his own biological children. On the other hand, he may have little or no social relationship with his biological children, but be in a supportive role in relation to his sister's or brother's children, while another man is social father to the children of the first man. In one Chicago family, a man was instrumental in keeping together his own extended family — although they lived in different cities — as well as his maternal uncles' stepfamily, through sponsorship of frequent reunions.

Households were based on either a mother–child or a husband–wife tie. A family in the Chicago study, which owned two taverns and was economically stable, was primarily based on conjugal households, while other families showed matrifocal tendencies. In the latter, consanguineous ties apparently often outweighed marital ties, even though in some instances there was relative economic stability, i.e. a husband with a steady job. A woman who had lived by herself with her children since leaving her husband bemoaned the fact that her daughter was doing the same thing; however, she recalled that three of her maternal aunts had left their husbands and lived for many years with their mother. In this family, there appeared to be a tradition of matrifocal households, although there were also stable conjugal households and even "polygynous" households (i.e. in which there were known second "wives" and families).

Kinship relationships were extended into the community through fictive kin relationships, termed "play-relative" or "godparent" ties. Although such relationships were not specifically named in the southern studies cited, Shimkin et al. and Jack, in the present volume, mention close ties with nonrelatives through adoption and propinquity; and the frequency of adoption of neighbors' children described in many of the studies of southern communities confirms the wide acceptance of family and social responsibility. Historically, Rawick speaks of the plantation system under slavery as a "generalized kinship system," with adults assuming responsibility for all children (Rawick 1972: 93). That this type of bond extends beyond childhood is indicated by the relationship described as "go for brother" (or sister or cousin) by Liebow (1967), as well as other fictive kin relationships mentioned by Stack (1972) and described by myself (Aschenbrenner 1973). In a southern Illinois community, 65 percent of a sample interviewed had active "play-kin" relationships. While these relationships involve economic reciprocity in Black communities, the motivation for entering into them is rarely economic in a narrow sense. A Chicago woman had adopted a "play-sister" in response to a close relationship between her biological sister and her "play-sister's" biological sister, who was brought up by her parents. Other types of "play-kin" relationships (parent–child, grandparent–grandchild) involve economic gains for children — primarily gifts of clothing, although rewards in terms of social support and socialization for the children, and emotional satisfaction for the adults, are equally important.

The observance of ritual occasions, such as birthday celebrations, funerals, and family reunions, is noteworthy among Illinois families; this often involves traveling long distances and considerable financial expenditure, as well as time and energy. A family living in a predominantly Black suburb had a tradition of large funerals, which took place in a local funeral parlor that had served many generations. The Baptist church, of which their ancestors were among the original founders, played an important role in the funerals. The family also celebrated birthdays, anniversaries, weddings, and other important life events with elaborate and well-attended ceremonies. Within the kindred, each of these celebrations activated different kin groups whose membership overlapped but which were clearly demarcated. Birthdays of children involved a household only; those of elders were celebrated by children and grandchildren. Weddings involved the father's side of the family more than the mother's, presumably since they were the "original" affinals. Reunions centered on the bilateral descendants of "Grandma and Grandpa Bibbs," although affinals were invited also. Other families, many of whose households and members still resided in the South, held reunions and funeral observances which large numbers of relatives traveled long distances to attend. When Ethel L.'s mother's mother died, five carloads of relatives from Chicago alone traveled to Mississippi and stayed for several days. Such celebrations serve to keep distant branches in touch as well as to reaffirm the importance of family and individual.

In Chicago and in southern Illinois, as in Holmes County and New Orleans, the church is important in maintaining family unity and identity. Even when individuals move from their home communities or neighborhoods, they frequently maintain their membership and interest in the home church; and many families have deacons and deaconesses among their elders who act as community leaders. In two instances, northern informants recalled grandfathers mainly in the role of deacon; and in one large extended family, based in a Chicago suburb, the church and church members played an important ritual and economic role in many family activities, especially funerals and anniversary celebrations.

The role variations of men in these families can be seen through memories about "grandfather." Besides as deacons, grandfathers were mentioned as landowners (in the South), as deserters and wanderers (also in two families from the South), and as inspiring children and grandchildren to become educated and "make something of themselves" (in two southern Illinois families originating in the South). Others remembered grandparents together as warm and supportive figures who visited or lived nearby and who took a hand in the care and upbringing of their grandchildren. Grandmother was often remembered as the center of the family, as mother is also characterized. Comparing the roles of male and female family members through the generations, in fact, one sees little variation. Father, like grandfather, can be the family support, active in the community and church; or absent as father, while active and supportive as son, uncle, stepfather, or boyfriend. These alternative roles depend on a number of economic and social factors and can in that sense be considered "adaptive." However, since these alternatives are built into the Black family structure and have existed for generations under differing conditions, they should not be considered *ad hoc* arrangements; likewise, variable household arrangements are an expression of the underlying strength of extended-family ties and not of a "loose" family structure.

There is some evidence that household membership may be more restricted in northern cities; however, the frequent presence of adopted children and of other relatives confirms the "elasticity" of arrangements noted by Powdermaker. In one family, a household included a husband, a wife, her children by a previous marriage, the couple's younger children, an unmarried daughter and her child, and a maternal sister's daughter, unmarried, with her children. The stepfather acted as father to all the children, although the children's own fathers took some responsibility. The adults worked at technical and sales jobs, except for the cousin and niece, who stayed home with the children. This family was economically stable and was integrated into the West Side neighborhood by other kinship and friendship ties. Other households, conjugal or matrifocal, clustered together with other domestic units in the extended group in apartment houses, duplexes and quadriplexes, and town houses. The family that owned the taverns, mentioned above, also owned a quadriplex where two sisters, a brother, and their mother's youngest brother all lived with their families. In many other instances, related family units were domiciled in the same apartment building. Matrifocal households, whether permanent or temporary, were generally nuclear units in the larger kin group; and even when households, whether conjugal or matrifocal, were not located near others in the family, close ties were maintained through telephoning, visiting, and participating in family celebrations.

CONCLUSION: THE COMMUNAL BASIS OF BLACK SOCIAL RESPONSIBILITY

Shimkin et al. (this volume) note a stress on family obligation, often at the expense of individual freedom, in Holmes County families. In Chicago, individualism is more stressed; however, an "independent attitude" does not preclude a strong sense of family obligation. Young (1971 [1970]) speaks of the "polarity" of "individualism and interrelatedness" in a southern community, pointing out that both elements are strong in the personality makeup. The freedom to come and go, to move in and out of households, encourages in Black families an individual mobility, supported by kinship arrangements, that has served them well in a quest for economic advancement. A concept of *collective* rather than *individual* responsibility (as vested primarily in husband and father) has been instrumental in maintaining the dignity and social responsiveness of the Black man under severe disadvantages and pressures, as well as ensuring the security of children. The effectiveness and support by male family members in various roles and capacities should not be underestimated; indeed, the present tendency to elect Black mayors may partly stem from the recognition of the Black man's ability to perform the impossible against great odds, because of his traditionally highly adaptable role. Far from being emasculated, the Black man, embedded in an extended-family system, has often avoided the worst consequences of failure in a restricted male role within the conjugal family setting and has maintained a position that is both supportive and supported.

The communal basis of Black social responsibility, authority, and power has served to mute the competitive, egotistic spirit that often pervades a scarcity economy. Poverty does not automatically lead to cooperation; it may result in violent conflict; one merely needs to look at studies of the ghettos, or read the newspapers, to realize this. The Black social system, based primarily on the family and secondarily on religious and other voluntary institutions, has survived despite, not merely because of, poverty conditions. The extended family has survived because it is economically more viable under such conditions; this does not imply that it has developed solely in response to poverty, or that it is not adaptable to other conditions. There is little indication in the Illinois families I have studied that economic stability, or length of stay in the city, results in lessening of extended-family ties; or that poverty either encourages or discourages them. I found extended families among middle-income groups in Chicago and in southern Illinois with much the same organization as among lower-income families. One large extended family in southern Illinois included many professionals among its members; yet they considered themselves one family, jointly supporting their oldest living member (in style), "passing on" (approving) potential mates of younger members, and taking responsibility for each other's children in the event of illness or death. I saw very little difference (other than economic status) between this family and a Chicago lower-income family, in which kinship responsibilities were undertaken with great expenditures of time, energy, and even money. In the latter family, two high-school-age members each gave ten dollars of their "school money" (intended for the purchase of clothing for the coming year) to a stepaunt on her birthday, after having traveled on the bus to St. Louis to attend her birthday celebration. This was a considerable expenditure for a poor family.

Marital ties, on the other hand, as noted above, may be greatly affected by economics. A Chicago woman's parents had survived many marital crises, largely because of the steady income earned by both of them. The daughter had broken up with her own husband, however, because he often refused to pay the rent or to give her adequate money for food. Another woman, on the verge of marrying her boyfriend, decided not to when she learned that she would have to continue to work full time. In the family owning the taverns, sons and sons-in-law worked hard at permanent jobs during the day as well as at the taverns at night, to support their families; in this extended family, households were predominantly conjugal in form.

The particular expressions which cooperation and mutual aid assume among extended-family households may and do differ with economic status and "life style"; however, even in those instances in which economic services are performed by relatives, one can see other alternatives which would be less costly. Foster homes, orphanages, day-care centers — these institutions take the place of extended families in White communities and are cheaper than the cost of an extra family member, raised from childhood. Obviously, the concept of "family" transcends purely economic considerations; it implies group responsibility to all members, as contrasted with individual responsibility within a nuclear unit only.

In my opinion, the continuities in Black family life far outweigh the differences. While there are class-related variations, such as the strength of the conjugal tie, the emphasis on "respectability," and the amount of economic aid among nuclear units, these differences need to be observed in the context of Black families in various settings, using a model other than that of the "ideal conjugal" family. The model which has been proposed and used in this discussion is that of the bilateral extended family. While it is undoubtedly more applicable in some instances than in others, the preponderance of evidence thus far indicates that it is more widely applicable to Black family organization than other models that have been used in the past.

REFERENCES

ASCHENBRENNER, JOYCE
    1973   Extended families among Black Americans. *Journal of Comparative Family Studies* 4: 257–268.

BILLINGSLEY, ANDREW
    1968   *Black families in White America.* Englewood Cliffs, N.J.: Prentice-Hall.

BOTT, ELIZABETH
    1957   *Family and social network.* London: Tavistock.

DAVIS, ALLISON, BURLEIGH B. GARDNER, MARY R. GARDNER
    1941   *Deep South.* Chicago: University of Chicago Press.

FRAZIER, E. FRANKLIN
    1939   *The Negro family in the United States.* Chicago: University of Chicago Press.

JOHNSON, CHARLES S.
    1934   *Shadow of the plantation.* Chicago: University of Chicago Press.

KUNKEL, PETER, SARA SUE KENNARD
    1971   *Spout Spring: a Black community.* New York: Holt, Rinehart and Winston.

LADNER, JOYCE
    1971   *Tomorrow's tomorrow: the Black woman.* Garden City, N.Y.: Doubleday.

LEWIS, HYLAN
    1955   *Blackways of Kent.* Chapel Hill: University of North Carolina Press.

LIEBOW, ELLIOT
    1967   *Tally's corner: a study of Negro streetcorner men.* Boston: Little, Brown.

LIU, WILLIAM, IRA W. HUTCHISON, LAWRENCE K. HONG
    1972   "The structural significance of conjugal power measures," in *Cross-national family life.* Edited by Marvin Sussman and Betty Caswell, 160–177. Leiden: Brill.

MOYNIHAN, DANIEL P.
    1965   *The Negro family: the case for national action.* Washington, D.C.: U.S. Government Printing Office.

POWDERMAKER, HORTENSE
    1939   *After freedom: a cultural study of the deep South.* New York: Viking.

RAINWATER, LEE
    1970   *Behind ghetto walls.* Chicago: Aldine.

RAWICK, GEORGE P.
    1972   *The American slave: from sundown to sunup, the making of a Black community.* Westport, Conn.: Greenwood.

SCANZONI, JOHN H.
1971   *The Black family in modern society*. Boston: Allyn and Bacon.
SMITH, RAYMOND THOMAS
1970   The nuclear family in Afro-American kinship. *Journal of Comparative Family Studies* 1: 55–70.
STACK, CAROL B.
1970   "The kindred of Viola Jackson: residence and family organization of an urban Black American family," in *Afro-American anthropology: contemporary perspectives*. Edited by Norman E. Whitten, Jr., and John F. Szwed, 303–311. New York: Free Press.
1972   Black kindreds: parenthood and personal kindreds among urban Blacks. *Journal of Comparative Family Studies* 3: 194–206.
1974   *All my kin*. New York: Harper and Row.
1975   "Who raises Black children: transactions of child givers and child receivers," in *Socialization and communication in primary groups*. Edited by Thomas R. Williams, 183–205. World Anthropology. The Hague: Mouton.
STAPLES, ROBERT
1971   "The myth of the Black matriarch," in *The Black family: essays and studies*. Edited by Robert Staples, 149–161. Belmont, Calif.: Wadsworth.
YOUNG, VIRGINIA HEYER
1970   Family and childhood in a southern Negro community. *American Anthropologist* 72: 269–288. (Reprinted 1971 in *Black matriarchy: myth or reality?* Edited by J. H. Bracey et al., 195–217. Belmont, Calif.: Wadsworth.)

The "Clan": Case Study of
a Black Extended Family in Chicago

REGINA E. HOLLOMAN and FANNIE E. LEWIS

ABSTRACT

This paper describes a Black extended family which is urban in origin and focus. Patterns of spatial clustering, fosterage, and mutual aid are discussed. The possible relationship between clustering and rates of neighborhood change is noted. Male–female relationships are examined in relation to family obligations. The study shows how kin, former mates, and present mate's family obligations cause stress on the husband–wife bond. A special feature of the study is that one of the informants was a fourteen-year-old girl, whose view of the family can be compared with that of adult informants.

INTRODUCTION

This study describes the structure, behavioral patterns, and values of an extended family of socioeconomically marginal Black people in Chicago. This family, self-designated "The Clan," shares many features with the "Mitchells" of rural Mississippi (Shimkin, Louie, and Frate, this volume) and the "Wesleys" of New Orleans (Jack, this volume). However, it has distinctive characteristics which are significant. The integration of the family and its persistence over time are not based in corporateness around property; there are no significant holdings in real or other property, no substantial amounts of money or important rights to be inherited. Yet the extended family has a substantive existence beyond that of a simple interlocking "network" of dyadic relationships. The family history shows frequent moves within and between areas of the city, with an entailed pattern of clustering and coordinated relocation. This "floating" quality contrasts sharply with the locational stability of the other cases. Finally, the study describes complexly related patterns of marriage, consensual unions, and child care. We regard these data as potentially the most important contribution of the study.

Underlying the presentation of the data are two general questions of importance for our understanding of family systems in urban environments: (1) Do people from different cultural backgrounds living in the same general urban environment behave as differently as they *say* they do? Are cross-cultural differences within urban populations mostly a matter of rhetoric, of deference to cultural tradition? Or are they either reflective of, or determinants of, genuine differences in intrafamilial behavior? And, (2) where behavioral differences are confirmed, can they be described as culturally determined? Or is what we call "cultural difference" simply a folk-abstraction from the differential impact on subpopulations (class, ethnic, and/or racial) of urban social processes? Although the case study does not resolve these issues, we do believe that it clarifies them. A good case study should produce a series of hypothetical statements suitable for testing in a larger population. This is what we have tried to do in our conclusions.

This article is the product of friendship and cooperation among three people: Holloman, an anthropologist; Lewis, a school teacher; and "Hannah Dorsey" — our pseudonym for a member of "The Clan" — Holloman's friend, and the aunt and adoptive mother of a child in Lewis's class. A request by a social worker for information about this troubled adolescent girl (whom we call "Feathers") initiated our case study. The social worker's questions were basic: Why does the child shift residence almost continually among three addresses? Where does she "really" live? And why are there so many people involved in her case? As we attempted to answer these questions, we realized that, in addition, Feathers's family merited an in-depth description as an excellent case of an urban Black extended family seeking to cope with major social stresses.

Our principal informants have been Feathers, her grandmother, Arlene, and especially, Mrs. Hannah Dorsey. Mrs. Dorsey, an intelligent woman with an inquiring mind, became an active participant in the research process and in its write-up. The testimony of three informants has provided a rather full, cohesive, and dynamic picture of family life as they see it. Weaknesses of the study include the lack of a male informant, of extensive direct observation, and of detailed quantitative and qualitative data on (a) money flows and (b) the flow of communications (visits and telephoning) between members. These latter data are essential to any final disentangling of the real from the ideal.

Our pseudonyms, throughout this paper, paraphrase the nicknames used by preference over given names by all of our informants. As a group, these nicknames have a definite style and flavor. They are similar to those collected by Abrahams (1970: 122) in toasts: Half-Head, Tough-Pen, Ninety-Proof, Struggle-Face, Whippy-Top, Sticky.

Our paper begins with an overview of the family, from the contrasting viewpoints of Feathers and Hannah. It then analyzes the principal structural features of the "Clan" — its core kin, subfamilies, and local clusterings and household compositions. It summarizes key attitudinal and behavioral features. It reviews mechanisms setting family boundaries and relating the family to the outside world. It then seeks to integrate these data, first, by proposing answers to the social worker's questions concerning Feathers, and, finally, by proposing working hypotheses which may be applicable not only to the "Clan" but to other urban, Black extended families. We believe that we are dealing here with a distinctive cultural tradition which does in fact produce different behavior in similar situations — in particular, we feel that the behavioral data with respect to child care support this conclusion. But we are also aware that socio-economic determinants are involved, and that work with higher-income families may show that some of the structural and behavioral properties which we have described are class-linked.

OVERVIEWS OF THE "CLAN": FEATHERS AND HANNAH

Feathers, although a troubled and purportedly "dull" child (she has been assigned to an educable mentally handicapped classroom), had a remarkable grasp of the core kin of her extended family. She provided the basic genealogical and marital data to which her aunt Hannah and grandmother Arlene made only moderate additions, clarifications, and revisions. Feathers was also familiar with the ages (sometimes to the half-year) of key family members, and with the locations and compositions of constituent households. Feathers's description is of the *empirical* extended family. She does not yet think in terms of cultural rules. By contrast, Hannah works with a rule set in mind. Tip-offs to the difference are her inclusion of deceased individuals, absentees who "would be" members "if" they were on the scene and chose to be so, and her omission of persons who apparently are being treated just like kin at the present time, but who do not fall under the rules for affiliation of pseudokin.[1]

In all, Feathers identified sixty-six persons, including herself, two fictive

---

[1] The manner in which Feathers's understanding of the concept "family" is developing is consistent with what Piaget has described for cognitive processes in general. The manner of abstracting from experience is not yet formal, in terms of a set of analytic rules.

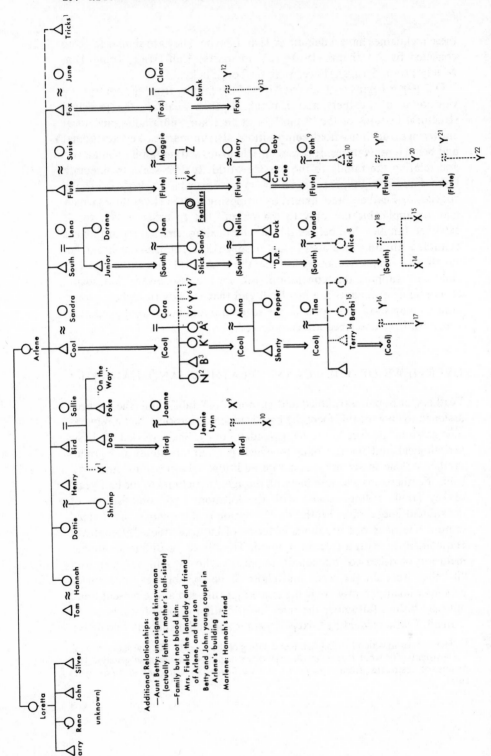

Additional Relationships:

—Aunt Betty: unassigned kinswoman
 (actually father's mother's half-sister)

—Family but not blood kin:
  Mrs. Field, the landlady and friend
   of Arlene, and her son
  Betty and John: young couple in
   Arlene's building

  Marlene: Hannah's friend

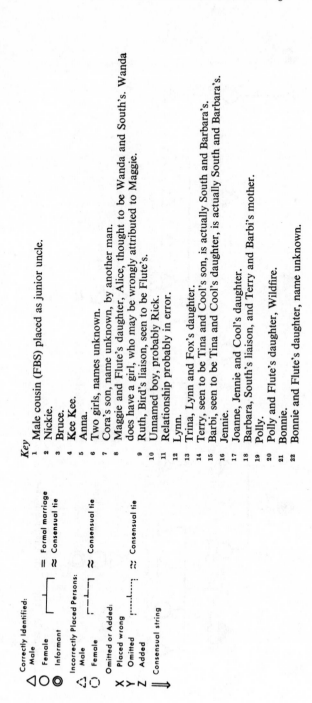

Correctly Identified:
△ Male
○ Female
◉ Informant

= Formal marriage
≀≀ Consensual tie

Incorrectly Placed Persons:
◁ Male
◯ Female

≀≀ Consensual tie

Omitted or Added:
X Placed wrong
Y Omitted
Z Added

≀≀ Consensual tie

⟹ Consensual string

Key
1 Male cousin (FBS) placed as junior uncle.
2 Nickie.
3 Bruce.
4 Kee Kee.
5 Anna.
6 Two girls, names unknown.
7 Cora's son, name unknown, by another man.
8 Maggie and Flute's daughter, Alice, thought to be Wanda and South's. Wanda does have a girl, who may be wrongly attributed to Maggie.
9 Ruth, Bird's liaison, seen to be Flute's.
10 Unnamed boy, probably Rick.
11 Relationship probably in error.
12 Lynn.
13 Trina, Lynn and Fox's daughter.
14 Terry, seen to be Tina and Cool's son, is actually South and Barbara's.
15 Barbi, seen to be Tina and Cool's daughter, is actually South and Barbara's.
16 Jennie.
17 Joanne, Jennie and Cool's daughter.
18 Barbara, South's liaison, and Terry and Barbi's mother.
19 Polly.
20 Polly and Flute's daughter, Wildfire.
21 Bonnie.
22 Bonnie and Flute's daughter, name unknown.

Figure 1. The "Clan": Feathers's view

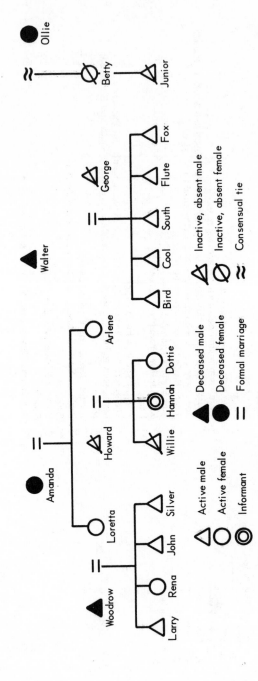

Figure 2.   The "Clan": Hannah's view — core kin

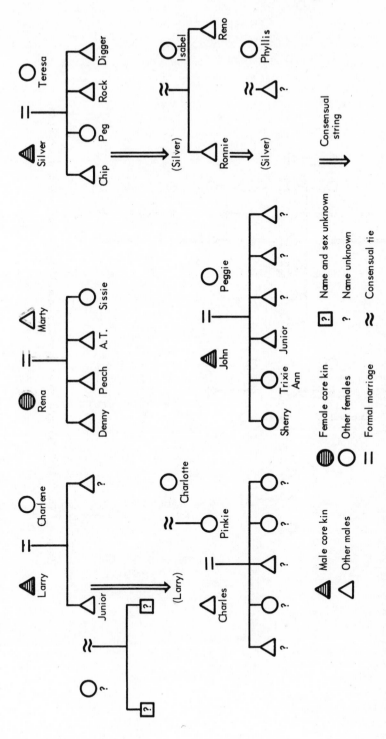

Figure 3. The "Clan": Hannah's view: Loretta's children and their subfamilies

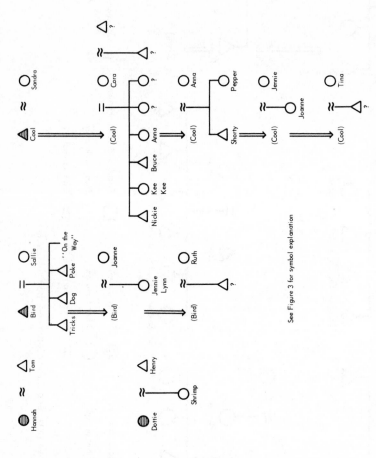

Figure 4. The "Clan": Hannah's view: Hannah, Dottie, Bird and Cool, and their subfamilies

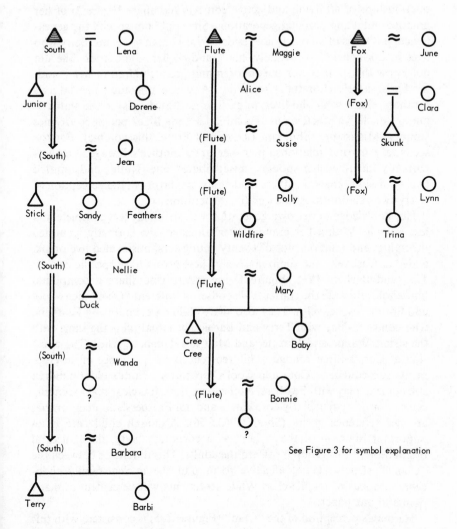

See Figure 3 for symbol explanation

Figure 5. The "Clan": Hannah's view: South, Flute and Fox, and their subfamilies

kin, and three friends, as "family" (Figure 1). She knew the names and relationships of all living and active core kin (compare Figure 2) of her grandparental and parental generations. She could not specify the genealogical positions of an older, nonresident kinswoman — "Aunt Betty who lives in Springfield" — actually, her grandmother's half sister. She did not know the spouses nor the children and grandchildren of her grandmother's sister's (Loretta's) offspring. And she upgraded her father's brother's eldest son (who lives, in part, in East St. Louis) to the status of junior "uncle," a practice not uncommon among Black people in Holmes County, Mississippi (Shimkin, Louie, and Frate, this volume). For the secondary marital relationship in her grandmother's lineage, Feathers correctly identified ten spouses, misattributed one (Ruth), and omitted five. Omissions apart, Feathers made only two errors in the perception of thirty-two relationships in ascending generations.

Her knowledge of her own generation was strikingly less complete and less reliable. Within her grandmother's lineage, she correctly identified the names and relationships of twenty youngsters, mislocated five or six, added at least two, and omitted seven. These errors have specific causes: Tina and Barbara (Y^{18}; Figure 1) are sisters who share a compound household; they are the consensual spouses of different "Clan" men (Cool and South, respectively). They also share child care, confusing Feathers, who comes to play with Terry and Barbi. The situation is the same with the sisters Wanda and Maggie, and Maggie's daughter, Alice. The omission of Cora's three youngest children reflects an ignorance of developments subsequent to Cora and Cool's separation; Cora's older children still come to play with Feathers. At the same time, it is clear that ascending generations — particularly core kin — and not Feathers's contemporaries are her reference group (Sherif 1963: 56). Although child care is an important function of the "Clan" as a corporate body, the structural orientation of this group is toward the adults. This difference between the "Clan's" structural and affective focus and the nuclear-family child-centered focus of middle-class White sentiments will be evident at many points in our paper.

Hannah's perception of the "Clan" (Figures 2–5) is consistent with this view. It comprises 114 persons, including four deceased and five absent members. Its structural segments, between lines of descent, and between core kin and subfamilies, are sharply defined. Yet the perception of descending generations is far less clear than the accounting of Hannah's elders and peers. Hannah does not know the names of 30 percent of the former, in contrast to one person (Cora's paramour), out of fifty-three in the latter group.

The "Clan" as perceived by both Hannah and Feathers is geographically restricted to Chicago, with only some minor exceptions. Tricks (son of Bird) is living in St. Louis, in contrast with "cousins" of Arlene. Arlene's half sister, Betty, lives in Springfield, Illinois. The whereabouts of Hannah's half brother, Willie, are unknown. Arlene has not seen her St. Louis cousins for five or six years; they are outside of Hannah's and Feathers's perceptions of the "Clan." Amanda and Walter (Figure 2) had originally come from Tennessee, and Loretta (now 66) and Arlene (now 63), as well as their older children, were born in Little Rock, Arkansas, in the wake of an early migration. They moved to Chicago in segments during World War II.

On the death of Amanda, the grandmother, in the early 1960's, family relations with Arkansas and St. Louis atrophied. However, as mentioned above, Arlene knows that her mother's cousins still live in St. Louis, although she has not seen them for five or six years. Hannah does not include these relatives within her family. Moreover, while Hannah regularly visits in Milwaukee with relatives of her stepfather, George, she refers to them as "my father's family," as distinguished from her own. Also, while Hannah had close relations with her godparents as a child, she did not include them in her perception of the "Clan."

THE GROUP OF CORE KIN

Structurally, the "Clan" comprises several sorts of subunits: a group of "core kin" (those children and grandchildren of *Walter* [Figure 2] who live near each other, and support each other through various acts of reciprocity); "consensual strings" (clusters of women and children whose relationship to one another is that they share claims of child support on the same "Clan" male); households, which show a marked tendency to cluster; and, finally, among the consensually linked females, several dyads of consanguineously related women. The core kin group is discussed in this section; the other units are discussed in the following section.

The core kin are a "group" in the sense that there is agreement among them as to who belongs; they recognize as heads of the group the elders, Loretta and Arlene; and they sometimes meet and act together as a unit. The core group is the focus of the more extensive network that comprises he extended family as a whole.[2]

[2] The terms "group" and "network" have been assigned various meanings by various authors. The problem thus created is discussed in Bott (1971 [1957]). The two terms are used here in the sense of Stack (1974: 93–94) and Bott.

History

The core in its present form began to take shape when Arlene came to Chicago to join her sister Loretta and her husband during World War II. Loretta, a widow, had a lasting formal marriage with Woodrow until his death in the mid-1960's. Her children, perhaps in reflection of this stability, have had relatively good educations and blue-collar employment. Larry, 47, who finished high school and trade school, is a machinist; Rena, 45, a high school graduate with some college attendance, cleans offices; John, 43, also a high school graduate, is a machinist; and Silver, 36, is a steelworker foreman, although he only completed the eleventh grade.

Arlene and her first husband, Howard, separated when she joined Loretta's family in Chicago. The marital breakup was evidently stormy. Willie remained with his father; no one in Chicago has heard from Willie for fifteen years. At the time of the breakup, Dottie was left with her father's sister in Little Rock, Arkansas. This was a secret kept from Dottie, who thought, until her aunt's death, that she was her mother; and from Arlene, who for years spent her vacations seeking her daughter in Arkansas. The reunion was effected only ten years or so ago, when Dottie was thirty years old or a little younger, with the help of a local minister. Because of the long separation, Dottie, while a full participant in the core kin group, retains some feeling of distance. "Dottie says she doesn't really feel like one of us because she wasn't raised with us."

Arlene took Hannah with her to Chicago. There Arlene soon remarried, to George Dorsey, by whom she had five sons: Bird, now 38; Cool, 35; South, 33; Flute, 30; and Fox, 28 (Figure 2). The second marriage also broke up, during the 1950's; George Dorsey remarried and broke contacts with his first family at his second wife's insistence. However, Hannah has maintained contacts with her stepfather's family in Milwaukee. Then, in July, 1974, Flute met his father by accident while in an unfamiliar part of Chicago. Shortly thereafter, George Dorsey came to stay at Hannah's apartment for several days, in order to see all of his first family. Hannah expects that her stepfather will now remain in touch.

Arlene's marital troubles may well have had adverse effects on her own family. In 1961, Hannah, in the wake of a bitter quarrel, killed her husband. Convicted of involuntary manslaughter, she has been unable to get more than domestic and other poor jobs since, although she is a high school graduate with some additional business education (see the following section). Dottie, also a high school graduate, is a teacher's aide. Among Arlene's and George's sons, Bird is a high school graduate and regularly employed as a mover. Cool, although he only finished the ninth grade, is "head of a group of private security guards" — which is a bit ambiguous. South, a tenth-grade dropout, is "unemployable due to a high school sports injury." Flute, also a tenth-grade dropout, is "a character — he works when he wants to." Fox, who went through the ninth grade, is a heroin addict, who supports his habit, at least in part, by pimping for June, his current liaison. Cool, Flute, and Fox are also part-time musicians, members of a group called "The Swingers."

The "Clan's" core kin are linked by consanguineous ties — "father, mother, brother, sister" (Shimkin, Louie, and Frate, this volume) — deeply valued throughout U.S. Black society. The experience of growing up together is also fundamental to the closeness of relationships in the core group. Hannah says that Silver, her cousin (Figure 2), is "just like a brother" because he was in school together with "the boys," her half brothers. Loretta's other children are not so close "because they are older." As mentioned earlier, Hannah has long ago lost contact with her full brother, Willie, and also feels some social distance from her long-separated sister, Dottie, neither of whom share the bond of corearing with her. Hannah is closest to her eldest half brother, Bird. According to her, "We feel like the father and mother. When my mother was working we kept care of the littler ones. We just kept on doing it." It is Hannah who telephones everyone to organize meetings and get-togethers, sometimes at Bird's suggestion.

The close interaction engendered by corearing can serve to incorporate other persons, kin and nonkin alike. Thus, Junior, the son of Arlene's half sister Betty (Figure 2), who lived with Arlene in 1963, would be included in the core group if he moved to Chicago and "began to act like a brother." Even nonkin who grew up with one can act as kin if they choose. Hannah talks about two men, Jerry and L.C., who are "just like brothers" although they are not related in any way. Jerry's mother was Arlene's close friend. When she died, Arlene took Jerry, then thirteen, and kept him for seven years. The case of L.C. is similar. Both men now live "across town" and have drifted away, but Hannah says that, if they chose to keep in close touch, they would be included in the group "because they are like brothers."

Interaction Patterns

For Hannah, frequent and intense interaction within the family is a basic value. She does not make the equation "good" = "stable." Rather, for her "good" = "close," in both a physical and a behavioral sense. "Good" is a property of the entire network of kin, not of a component household alone. "Everybody has stayed right here together; most families, some move away. Even those around may not see each other very often. We kept everyone in close."

Residential clustering, a major aspect of such interaction, is discussed below.

The purposes of interaction are many. During the time of this study, the core group came together many times for holidays, family events, and problem solving. These last events are of particular interest for understanding the group aspects of Black family behavior. The core kin group was facing two acute problems during this period; these were in reference to Fox and Feathers, respectively.

Fox, aged 28, the youngest brother, has been a heroin addict for five years; during this time he has had a history of arrests. He was separated from his wife, Clara (a White woman of Polish extraction), and their child, and lived across the street from them with a current girl friend, June. According to Feathers, he supported his habit by pimping, sending June down on the street to "turn a trick." Toward the end of this study, he moved several blocks away after a fight with the building janitor, who threatened to kill him. The core group has met several times to talk about how to help his wife, Clara; how to exert pressure on Fox to accept professional help; and what, in general, might be the best way to handle the situation.

The other recurrent problems have centered on Feathers, who is fourteen. She has had a history as a truant and runaway. She has been in trouble at school for fighting and for using drugs. In 1973 she disappeared for several days, so that Hannah had to file a missing-persons report. When she was found, the court appointed a caseworker on her behalf.

Feathers was unwanted by her mother, who attempted to abort her and continues to reject the child. Feathers has a malformed spine, which the family attribute to the botched abortion, and wears a body brace. It is clear that family fosterage, especially by Hannah, has been fraught with problems. And, while Feathers's social knowledge and understanding indicate intelligence, she is educationally retarded, a status which undoubtedly intensifies her feelings of rejection and hostility.

During the period of the study, members of the family met to discuss how to discipline Feathers. At one meeting, fifteen adults — members of the core group, and some spouses and girl friends — were present. Loretta and Arlene "dropped in" but did not stay for the entire discussion.[3] The group decided that Feathers and her older brother and sister (Figure 1) needed the influence of a man, and that Bird, Cool, South, and Flute would alternate weekends taking them somewhere and also "talking to them about how to behave." This was in fact done for a number of weeks. The group met again to arrive at a united position prior to a joint meeting with Feathers's social worker and a psychiatric consultant.

The core group can also be mobilized for such prosaic tasks as moving. In general, according to Hannah, "We call each other up at one, two, three in the morning if we need to. You can get three-fourths of them together at the drop of a hat." It should be stressed that the sheer size of the group is a basic social asset. There are always *enough* persons available to cope, somehow, with crises.

The self-designation of "Clan" and the system of nicknames paraphrased in our report are other markers of group identity. Moreover, while the group lacks either a rural or an urban base in real property, such as the "Yard" among the Wesleys of New Orleans (Jack, this volume) or a symbolic attachment to a historic family burial ground (see Aoyagi; Shimkin, Louie, and Frate; Frate and Logan, this volume), it does have a quasi-institutional identification rising out of an earlier period of greater church activity.

By tradition, the "Clan" is associated with "expressive" churches. At present, Loretta and Arlene are "mothers" in a Holiness church in West Side Chicago.[4] All of their children attended church. South, Cool, Flute, and Silver, who have been part-time professional musicians for many years, got their earliest musical training in the church. At present, however, only Dottie and South are regular attendants. Dottie goes to a neighborhood Holiness church — not her mother's — while South goes to church with his wife, a Jehovah's Witness. For a time, Hannah attended a Muslim temple with a man she was going with, but dropped this attendance when the relationship broke up. Thus, while past religious ties are significant, and religiosity is an orientation of several family members,

---

[3] Lewis speculates that Loretta and Arlene were doing their "fireside training" — i.e. it was not a token appearance. "Fireside training," a concept common to both Lewis's and the "Clan's" varieties of Black culture, involves value generation.
[4] In these churches older male leaders are deacons and older female leaders are "mothers." There is often more than one "reverend," and this particular church has male and female "reverends." Both Loretta and Arlene make regular use of a White faith healer who says that his entire practice is Black. Feathers's social worker was in the home on an occasion when he was there and witnessed him putting both women into trance states. On religious views among American Black people see also Grier and Cobbs (1971).

affiliations with a particular church are currently not significant as integrative mechanisms in the "Clan."

But a derivative occupational identification clearly is significant. When we first asked Hannah about the occupations of her half brothers, Cool, South, and Flute, she replied that they were musicians.[5] It was not until much later that we realized that very little of their present income comes from musical activities. Their musical group, which we call "The Swingers," includes three nonfamily members as well; Silver was also a member at one time. In the late 1960's "The Swingers" made a record for a major company and seemed to be on the verge of real commercial success. But listening tastes bypassed them, and Silver (apparently a leader) left the group.

At present, "The Swingers" are trying to change their style in the direction of "rock." They gave a performance recently which many family members, and indeed most of the former girl friends of the family's men, attended, bringing their children as well. According to Hannah, these people knew about this performance because of Arlene's role as a key communicator in the network: "They call my mother and she invited them."

Charles, Loretta's granddaughter's husband (Figure 3), is also a musician. During our study, Charles, Pinkie, and other members in his group left, in a van which held all their furniture, for an anticipated long-term engagement in Florida. The engagement fell through, and four families were reduced to living in a single room. Shortly thereafter, Loretta went to Florida and brought both her great-grandchildren back to live with her.

Although they are not economically successful, their music is a source of prestige and personal satisfaction for the family's men. It is clear that both Hannah and Feathers share in a sort of "reflected glory."

For its members, the "Clan" is more than a group of people; it is the social environment within which particular acts of assistance, and anticipated reciprocities, take place between individuals or small groups. This is especially true for child fosterage. Cree Cree, Flute's child by a consensual relation with Mary (Figure 5), is currently living with his grandmother, Arlene, because Mary is in jail. Horse, who is Cree Cree's maternal grandfather, i.e. Mary's father, visits him and contributes regularly to his support. (This instance warns us that we may be seriously understating male roles in this family because we have had no male informant.)

[5] For an insightful discussion of Black music and musicians, see Jones (1963: 175–236). For an excellent collection of lyrics of emotional expression and social aspiration, which are basic aspects of Black musicianship, see Nicholas (1971).

Aid within the family is neither altogether automatic nor free from social pressures and criticisms. Thus, Hannah states that she will give her mother "whatever she needs, but not money, because she just gives it to the boys, and I'm not going to support their [musical] records." It may be noted that, at the time of this study, Arlene was fostering five children, who were living with her full- or part-time. Loretta's fostering of Pinkie's children — her own great-grandchildren — initially without financial aid from their parents, who also came to share Loretta's apartment — aroused anger in Loretta's own children. They refused to contribute any money to her for these purposes.

Despite these occasional breakdowns, it is the system of reciprocal rights — equities giving access to psychological and social payoffs in return for past help given and future help promised — that motivates individual family members to remain within the network. Telephoning and dropping in ("keeping in touch") are the basic symbolic acknowledgements of reciprocal obligations and rights.

The attitudinal system of the "Clan" and how it both corresponds to and contrasts with the systems of customary family law in rural southern Black society is well expressed in the domain of funerals, wakes, and burials. In the rural South, and among urban migrants maintaining active ties with the South, funerals are the key occasion for demonstrating extended-family solidarity and respect for elders. Often the body of a family member will be returned from the North for burial in the family cemetery or plot, which is itself a visual symbol of solidarity (Shimkin, Louie, and Frate, this volume).

"Clan" funerals, by contrast, are deemed no more important than other family events. The largest funeral Hannah has attended was that of her maternal grandmother, Amanda (see Figure 2), in 1964. The grandmother had been living with Hannah at the time. There were no out-of-town participants, although Amanda had lived most of her life in Arkansas. Dottie did not attend the ceremony; as explained earlier, she had rejoined the family as an adult, and she said that "she did not know her grandmother well enough." The family disapproved of Dottie's absence but did not treat this failure as a serious breach of conduct. Bird attended the wake, which, like other "Clan" wakes, was held outside the home, but not the funeral, stating that "he didn't want to remember her like that." The only other event customarily connected with "Clan" deaths is a gathering in the home "to sort out the clothes," which are often the only legacy.

Despite their general economic situation, family members are much concerned with "proper" burial. "Who buried her or him?" is an important question, eliciting information about payment for the funeral. Public-aid burial is a disgrace; consequently, family members will pool funds to bury a kinsman who dies without burial insurance. The individual often carries his own insurance, and in that case, the identity of the beneficiary is often of intense family interest. Arlene carries her own policy, with Flute as the beneficiary. She also has paid-up policies for the burial expenses of South, Flute, and Fox. According to Hannah, Arlene could not afford to do this for her older children when they were little. In general, while death is less structured as an integrating force in the "Clan" than in many other extended Black families, it remains of substantial importance.

Summary

The group of core kin is strongly integrated, bounded in relation to more peripheral kin and the outside world. It is also a structured body with authority generally linked to age and past services. As mentioned earlier, Loretta and Arlene are, today, the "Clan's" recognized coheads. They serve as models, communicators, moral guides for young and adult members alike, and sources of shelter and support for members in trouble.

The basic sentiments[6] governing family attitudes toward Loretta and Arlene are well expressed in the lyrics of the song, "Grandma's Hands" (Bill Withers, LP, "Just as I am," SXBS 7006, Sussex Records):[7]

Grandma's hands
Clapped in church on Sunday mornin';
Grandma's hands
Played a tambourine so well;
Grandma's hands
Used to issue out a warning;
She'd say,
Billy, don't you run so fast,

---

[6]   Lewis, who was raised by her (great) grandmother until she was seven years old, because both of her parents were working, exemplifies intergenerational ties at their best. "I know my grandmother loved me. All my life, no matter what, I knew that security. My grandmother loved me." Lewis also notes that skills often skip a generation in Black families. "The grandmother teaches the granddaughter to sew. When her own daughter was small, she was working and didn't have time to teach her. So when that daughter is a grandmother she has nothing to teach, but it comes back in the next generation." This pattern compares closely to that observed in Holmes County, Mississippi (Frate and Logan, this volume).
[7]   Quoted by permission.

Might fall on a piece of glass,
Might be snakes there in that grass,
Grandma's hands.

Grandma's hands
Soothed a local unguen' mother;
Grandma's hands
Used to ache sometimes and swell;
Grandma's hands
Used to lift my face and tell her;
She'd say,
Baby, Grandma understands that you
   really love that man —
Put yourself in Jesus' hands;
Grandma's hands.

Grandma's hands
Used to hand me piece of candy;
Grandma's hands
Picked me up each time I fell;
Grandma's hands
Boy, they really came in handy;
She'd say,
Matty, don't you whip that boy,
What you want to spank him for?
He didn't drop no apple core.
But I don't have Grandma anymore;
If I get to heaven I'll look for
Grandma's hands.

As in other Black families, the high status of Loretta and Arlene within the "Clan" is brought out by a pattern of respect behavior.[8] At family dinners and picnics they are served first, with other adult men and women, and then children, following. How Arlene is addressed by family members varies with the closeness of relationships — core kin and the mothers of some "Clan" children calling her "Momma" and others "Mrs. Dorsey."

Hannah's and Bird's leadership roles do not appear, as yet, to be formally reinforced.

---

[8]   Lewis provides an example from her family: "We go every Mother's Day to see my husband's brother's wife's mother. She'd be insulted if we didn't come. On the Fourth of July we have to be somewhere else. We don't see them the rest of the year."

PERIPHERAL KIN: MARITAL RELATIONSHIPS AND SUBFAMILIES

The "Clan" is distinguished from other U.S. Black extended families thus far described by the number of consensual unions involved. (Whether this fact reflects difference in behavior or simply difference in reportage and observation is uncertain.) Seven of the eight resident married men of the family maintain from two to five active relationships, marital or consensual. By "active" we do not mean "sexually active." Rather, we refer to the fact that the man is in regular contact with his children and their mother. That the link is properly viewed as being *through the child* is witnessed by the fact that old relationships which didn't "come to something" (result in the birth of a child) had atrophied in every case, with the burning out of the physical attraction. The simultaneous existence of several mother–children groupings with child support rights (cultural and legal) on the same man creates what we have termed "consensual strings." The women involved do *not* share a cowife relationship, as they would in a polygynous system. But they do see each other at family events and often have conflicting contacts involving competition for shares in the man's available cash. Another sort of grouping within the "Clan" results from simultaneous relationships of consanguineously related women with pairs of "Clan" men. Most important to the structure of the whole is the extension of parental responsibilities through fosterage. Although each woman attempts to keep her children with her, in fact several "Clan" children are not living with either the biological father or the biological mother; several others for whom we have histories have lived with other members of the extended family in the past; some (Feathers is one) can properly be said to move regularly among component households. Active fosterage both reinforces relationships and replaces broken primary families.

In general, these features and correlated concepts (e.g. the definitions of full and half brother or sister) resemble patterns known in the Caribbean. But godparenthood, important in the Caribbean and linked with active or past Catholicism, is not a significant factor in "Clan" structure (although Hannah herself had a godmother).[9] The possibility of adaptive convergence remains.

---

[9] For an extensive treatment, see Laguerre, this volume; also Mintz and Wolf (1950).

Types of Marital Relationships

In the "Clan," despite its absence of holdings of real property and of status claims needing legitimization in the wider community, formal marriage is nevertheless distinguished from, and regarded as more valid than, consensual relationships. This is clear in the family's attitude toward Clara, Fox's deserted wife (see below), and in the pejorative concept of "Jody" — the archetypal adulterer — discussed in the next subsection. It is also evident in the family's rule that consensually based relationships are unextendable to other kin. The fact that X has a child by Y does not establish a relationship between X's and Y's extended families, even while the relationship is current, according to "Clan" views. This principle of nonextension is illustrated in the case of Cree Cree's maternal grandfather, Horse. Horse visits Cree Cree, who is fostered by Arlene, to whom he gives money regularly to help with Cree Cree's support (see previous section). However, Horse is not invited to "family" affairs. His tie is limited to the child. If Mary and Flute (see Figure 5) were married, Horse would be invited to such affairs, according to Hannah, since he is actively involved in "family" child keeping.

In some Black communities, sexual liaisons outside of marriage are regarded as private matters (Shimkin, Louie, and Frate; Aschenbrenner, this volume). For the "Clan," these are common knowledge. "Those that come to something" — that is, result in the birth of a child — do not, therefore, cause a sudden shift in relationships. At the same time, a distinction is drawn between sleeping with a woman and living with her. Hannah states that Flute has never lived with anyone but Maggie (see Figure 5). With the others, "He was just there. He wasn't living with her."[10]

A striking aspect of the consensual relationships is the high frequency with which they involve sisters, not in a form similar to "sororal polygyny," but in liaisons with two brothers.

This finding came about as follows: when Feathers was giving information on sexual unions, she would frequently interject that so-and-so was a sister or cousin of another woman in the family network (see Figure 1). This happened so frequently that we investigated the matter systematically. First we asked about preference rules: is it a good thing for two brothers to go with two sisters? Is it a good thing to go with a sister of a former girl friend? Our informants gave no indication that their culture encourages such relationships. Then we asked about actual relationships

[10] Lewis says that a man is not living with a woman until he is having his mail delivered there.

(excluding, as we did throughout our study, former girl friends who were not mothers of "Clan" children): with respect to every mother of a "Clan" child, does she have a sister or cousin who is or was a girl friend of another of the brothers or cousins? The results, presented below, show statistically most striking results. In five cases, pairs of brothers or male cousins had children by sisters or female cousins. In three cases, the kinswomen are presently living in a joint household.

Example A. Maggie and Wanda, who have children by Flute and South, respectively, are sisters who maintain a joint household (Figure 5).

Example B. Tina and Barbara are sisters, while Mary is their cousin. Tina and Mary had a joint household, upset during the study, by Mary's jailing (see previous section); Tina and Barbara had formerly shared one. Tina has a child by Cool; Barbara, two children by South; and Mary, two children by Flute (Figures 4 and 5).

Example C. Polly and Belle are sisters who live together. Polly has a child by Flute (Figure 4). Since Belle's child by South died, she is not included in the "Clan" roster (Figure 5).

Example D. Nellie and Isabel are sisters. Nellie has a child by South, and Isabel, a child by his cousin Silver (Figures 3 and 5).

Example E. Joanne and Bonnie are sisters, the former having a daughter by Bird; the latter, by Flute (Figures 4 and 5).

It does not appear that this pattern is deliberate; Hannah believes, "It just happened that way." However, it is an expression of the close ties between sisters characterizing, say, the "Bidwell" family in Holmes County and Chicago (Shimkin, Louie, and Frate, this volume). And there is some underlying relation to residential clustering by extended families. Note that, while Polly and Flute were "going together," Polly's mother lived next door to Arlene. "Because she was so close she was just naturally like family."

Once we had established the cultural rules for and the entailments of the two types of relationships, marital and consensual, we found ourselves left with the question: why do marriages occur at all? Why are not all unions consensual (as indeed they are in the case of Flute)? We believe with R. T. Smith that marriage is an act in the *status* system and has its meaning within that cultural context.[11] Marriage versus consensual union has implications for behavior in a very limited way (e.g. who, by extension, is invited to parties), but it does not appear to be related to support obligations. Nor do extensions through affinal links between kin groups appear to go beyond the level of socializing. The significance of marriage

[11]   Personal communication from Raymond T. Smith.

appears to be that it is a symbol of adulthood. Marriages tend to be made at an early age. If they do not occur then, it is likely (as in the case of Flute) that they will not occur at all. When we asked her why Flute never married, Hannah answered that he was "going to" but the girl's mother "wouldn't let her" and after that "he just never saw any point in it." This blocked marriage occurred at approximately the time he dropped out of school, and the matter dragged on for several years. By the time it was settled Flute was already acknowledged as an adult, and marriage, we believe, "no longer had any point" for him.

Sexuality, Infidelity, and Marital Conflict

In the "Clan," although some marital ties, such as Woodrow's and Loretta's, have been lifelong, expectations are strongly oriented toward instability. Marital bonds tend to be subordinate to the claims of kin, particularly of parents and siblings. Communication and lack of guardedness between the sexes is more often a component of the brother–sister relationship than of husband–wife relations. In our study of the "Clan," we were reminded of the Lozi saying, quoted by Gluckman:

Do not confide in your wife, confide in your sister. Tomorrow she may be someone else's wife; your sister is always your sister (Gluckman 1968: 454).

Hannah mentioned money, sex, and family problems as reasons for the breakup of marital and consensual unions. Cultural assumptions about sexuality and infidelity also seem to have their effect on the stability of husband–wife bonds. Strong sexual attraction is believed to be an overpowering but short-lived phenomenon. People under its power can't help themselves: "He had her nose so wide open you could drive a CTA bus in there." People who have been married for a long time may love each other, but they are not expected to be "in love."

Infidelity is generally thought to be the consequence of male initiative, framed in the stereotype of: "Jody's been here":[12]

A Jody is the man who comes in the minute you leave for work. He makes babies with your wife in your house while you're gone. He never works. He's a lover who makes his living from women. There are sneaky Jodies and those that

---

[12] The "Jody" material was provided initially by Lewis and verified by Hannah. For additional data on male–female relations in Black culture see Liebow (1967), de Coy (1967), Abrahams (1970), and Stack (1974). Both Hannah and Lewis feel that there is much more open discussion now than formerly of Black male images, as a result of recent trends in the movie industry.

operate in the open. It's a sneaky Jody who may end up hanging by his feet upside down from a manhole cover with his throat slit. But when a Jody operates in the open other men let him get away with it. That's what I can't understand. He'll stand up and grind on a girl and turn and smile at her father, better still her husband. He'll be talking with a woman, but he's standing much too close. You can tell a Jody by his clothes (like, a big hat, a real dude), by his words, his posture (he's got a "gangster lean" on the door of his car while he drives), and by trappings on his car — it's a big car, maybe white-on-white [white wall tires on white car], and it's got "pimp lights" [oversize].

Several popular songs deal with the "Jody" image. Hannah says that South and Flute cannot be described as Jodies because they avoid involvements with married women; the term is more appropriate for Fox.

Beyond infidelity, many factors which strengthen the bonds of a descent group weaken conjugal ties. For example, the ability and readiness to give money when it is needed are parts of extended-family reciprocity. Yet this may be at the cost of support for a formal or consensual spouse and one's own children.

In general, the study revealed a variety of conflict situations between marital and extended-family loyalties. We see them in the following analytic groupings:

1. Pressure may be brought on one partner by his or her mother or siblings (usually a sister) who dislike the spouse, especially a consensual one.

South wanted to marry Jean but her mother opposed it, so they didn't get married.[13] Now her mother stays out of it unless it concerns one of the children (Figure 5). Cool hasn't been living with Cora for six years. It was a mother-in-law problem. His wife was shy. She wanted to live with her mother, who ran Cool's house (Figure 4).

2. There is a structural tendency for kin groups to be competitive for the time and resources of men and women.

Here is the situation with Larry (Figure 3):

He lives close to Rena (his sister) and he used to *be* close, but it seems like he's drifting away. We thought it would be good when he married Charlene because he was really wild, but it seems like she's pulled him away. He's spending time with her people.

3. Pressure on a man and the woman he is living with may come from the mother of another of his children.

Of the men of the "Clan" only John (Figure 3) acknowledges children by only one woman. Many quarrels can be traced to resentment by a

---

[13]   Note that South is now married to Lena (Figure 5).

current spouse of those with earlier claims on her man. In 1961 Hannah killed her husband, Homer. Her account is as follows:

My husband had been married before. He had four kids. She'd call to demand clothes and things. She'd put his sister and his old girlfriends up to calling me. I was 10–12 years younger than he was. I was starting out working. We had to contribute 40 dollars per week. They felt that since I had a good job and he didn't, I should contribute. We paid the money but the kids would be all raggedy. I said I'd buy the clothes instead of giving them money. Then my husband came into some money. She wanted to cut me out of the settlement. They [his family] never liked me. They thought he would have gone back to her except for me, but it had been nine years. We had been fighting a lot, and he beat me up. That night he started for me and I picked up a paring knife and I hit him in the jugular vein. I was convicted of involuntary manslaughter. Since then, I can't get a good job. [She was given a suspended sentence.]

4. A man may resent having to contribute to the care of children not his own.

Loretta's second spouse, a relationship developed after Woodrow's death, left her after repeated warnings that he objected to the presence in their home of Pinkie's (Loretta's granddaughter's) small children. He said that he should be through with child raising. (See Figure 3; note that, currently, this former second spouse is not regarded as a member of the "Clan" because there are no children involved.)

Relationships through children by consensual unions depend not only on the relationship between the parents of the child but also on that between the mother of the child and the woman the man is living with at the time. South's wife, Lena, with whom he recently became reconciled, is extremely jealous of the mothers of his other children and does not want these children around (Figure 5). On the other hand, Sallie (Bird's wife) and Joanne (mother of another of his children) "have a beautiful relationship" (Figure 5). Joanne's child by Bird and Bird's wife, Sallie, "are about the same age, and Joanne is like Sallie's mother too." Joanne's daughter stays with Sallie and Bird every weekend.

Adults and Children

Children are greatly valued in U.S. Black society, as noted by Shimkin, Louie, and Frate (this volume) and eloquently phrased by Mrs. Fannie Hicks, Holloman's student:

Children bring adults together. Children are always wanted and always loved, so we know that the child will be just as well taken care of in one house as in another.

Correlated with strong pronatalism is aversion to birth control.[14] Thus, according to Hannah, Polly objected to Flute's use of birth-control devices, saying that she wanted his child. Hannah believes that she hoped to use the child to pull Flute away from Maggie, his most constant relationship. Furthermore, the use of contraceptives by one partner curtails the freedom of the other. It is "interference." Hannah expressed the idea that all forms of birth control in some way decrease the pleasure of intercourse.

A "Clan" woman is much more likely to have several children by her husband than by a consensual spouse. This contrast reflects the considerable ambivalence expressed by Hannah toward women's roles in illegitimacy. On the one hand, she states, "Men will be men." On the other, she deplores, "It didn't used to happen to women. Oh, maybe an accident. But it was wrong. There wasn't any of this just having somebody's baby."

Within this general framework, there is no question that, for the "Clan," the mother–child bond is primary. The sibling terminology reflects this descent principle. Note, however, that a *second* principle, reflecting the importance of corearing, is also reflected in the terminology. According to Hannah,[15] a *full* brother or sister is any child of your mother (whether that person grew up with you or not), or a child of your father (but *not* your mother) who grew up with you. A *half* brother or sister is a child of your father (but *not* your mother) who did *not* grow up with you.[16]

This terminological differentiation, although not hitherto reported from the United States, has extensive parallels on the West Indian island of Carriacou, where the society is based on legally outlawed polygyny. Thus,

. . . relations between the children of one man by two or three women resemble relations between the lawful descendants of two brothers more closely than siblingship, especially where the siblings are separated spatially. . . . Perhaps because of this, half-siblings are equated with just cousins and this difference of matrifiliation is sometimes expressed in generational terms (Smith 1962a: 293).

Hannah believes that the mother–child bond is not as strong as it traditionally has been. She says, "It used to be that the mother lived for

---

[14]   According to Lewis, Black women generally are under considerable social pressure neither to use contraceptives nor to have abortions. "If you love a man, you're supposed to want his baby."
[15]   Lewis agrees.
[16]   This sibling terminology touches on one of the oldest problems in the anthropological study of kinship — the relative importance of descent, marriage, and residence in the structure of kinship terminologies. For a recent review, see Buchler and Selby (1968: 10).

her kids. Now there are a lot of young girls — not all, but some — seems like they just want to dump them with whoever will take them. Seems like all they think about is having fun."

Since many unions are consensual, the acknowledgement of paternity by the father and the "Clan" as a body are important social acts. As indicated earlier, liaisons are rarely private, so that the facts are generally clear. Moreover, a child born while a man is married to and living with a woman bears his name and will be supported by him, even when there is good indication that the child is not his. Such a child is referred to as "caught in the net." Yet unresolved relationships do occur, as in the case of two "Clan" children, one of whom is recognized as a member by Arlene but not by the putative father, and the other who is recognized by the father but not by Arlene. Both children are members, *either* recognition apparently serving to validate membership.

All of the men in the "Clan" maintain an interest in all of their recognized children and take note of special occasions. "They're very busy on Christmas." They do not always provide regular support in the form of cash.

How the strains on male–female relations discussed earlier affect children is something which needs intensive study, but one example will suffice to indicate that the toll is probably great. Cool and his wife had planned a reconciliation. During the early part of the study they were buying furniture, preparatory to setting up a new apartment. Cool had agreed to accept her child by another man, born during the separation. However, one day he arrived to find that child's father in his wife's apartment. This ended the reconciliation. His oldest daughter, Nickie, was despondent and attempted suicide a few days later (Figure 4).

Under these circumstances, and under conditions of rejection as in Feathers's case, the supportive activities of the extended family are involved to help the affected children. The functionality of "child-keeping" (Stack 1974: Chapter 5) is obvious. When the parent(s) cannot keep a child for any reason, obligations of shared parentage within the extended family assure that someone will take — and love — the child, for a period or permanently. Placements out of necessity are always viewed as misfortunes. "A woman always tries to keep her kids together." However, a child may also be sent to stay with a relative for other reasons. These "purposive" placements, in Goody's terminology (this volume), take three forms in the "Clan's" practices:

1. A child may be sent to "do for" and keep company with an older member of the family who is living alone. This is an expression of respect and affection for that elder.

2. The child may be sent in order to intensify relationships between the parent and the fostering adult.[17]
3. The child may be sent away for his own good. Betty's son, Junior (Figure 2), came to live with Arlene because he had gotten into trouble in Springfield.

Fosterage in the "Clan," as in many other U.S. Black groups, involves a gradation of distinctions: "keeping," "raising," and "living with." A person who is *keeping* a child is usually contributing to his support economically. *Raising* refers to the transmission of moral standards and values. The person who raises you gives you your "fireside training" — a reference back to the time when a family would cluster around the fire in the evening to talk. This person transmits attitudes, e.g. in relation to sex, and culturally appropriate interpretations of events. In essence, "Who raised you?" asks an informant to select, from among all the people he has lived with and who have kept him, that one with whom he identifies so far as his inner self is concerned. *Living with* defines residence.

Many types of relatives and even fictive kin undertake fosterage. Hannah lived in the homes of two different sets of godparents, Arlene's friends, and also with her grandparents. According to her,

When I was little I liked it. They were always giving me things. My godfather sent me money all my life till he died. But when I was nine or ten I told my mother I didn't want to go anymore. After that, I didn't stay with my godparents anymore, but she said I had to go to my grandparents because they needed someone to do for them. But when I was twelve I just up and refused to go.

One of Hannah's godmothers was a cousin of her father; she called this couple "Mother" and "Daddy," and her biological mother, Arlene, "Moma." The other godmother was an unrelated friend of Arlene's — Hannah doesn't recall how she addressed her.

Only one type of fosterage is deplored, when a woman with children by former liaisons breaks her current relationship and "abandons" the children to the consensual stepfather.

All of these factors are involved in the questions raised at the very start of this study — to whom does a particular child (in this case, Feathers) "belong," and who is legitimately involved in decisions about him?

[17]   As an illustration, when Lewis's mother's half sister contacted her mother after a lapse of many years, Lewis's older sister was sent to stay with her aunt as a part of the relationship-building process.

RESIDENTIAL CLUSTERINGS AND HOUSEHOLD COMPOSITIONS

The central importance of face-to-face relationships in the functioning of the "Clan" has been emphasized throughout our study. We have also indicated that the "Clan" seeks, within its capabilities and resources, standard urban American goals; its members want good housing, good schools, a safe neighborhood, and enough money not to worry about money. One of the basic strategies employed by the "Clan" to meet these multiple requirements has been changing residences as better opportunities have appeared, or as adversities have required. In part, moving may also be an outlet for frustrations — a way for virtually powerless people to demonstrate some control over their environment. But in fact, the mobility achieved has been slow and uncertain at best.

Housing is a continuous problem for family members. The central cluster of households moved from the West Side ghetto to the somewhat more favorable uptown area of the North Side of Chicago in 1969 because Hannah heard about a good building, run by the Kate Maremont Foundation, which might be open to them. The building management screened tenants and sought to promote "a community". According to her, this was the best housing the family has had. Then the building was sold. Rents were raised and screening was discontinued. Since the building was large, it soon became unsafe, and the family moved.

Since then, Hannah and the central cluster of households have remained on the North Side, but with frequent moves (two in the last nine months) within a few blocks of each previous location. Such limited moves can be undertaken at low cost and with minimum disruption to the "floating community" of kin and pseudokin which provides the social environment of not only Blacks but blue-collar Whites, in the United States and England alike (see Adams 1967, 1970; Rosser and Harris 1965). Sometimes, however, a decision is made to abandon an area because of its progressive deterioration, or as a major effort toward upward mobility.

At the present time, Bird is trying to convince Hannah to move to Evanston, Illinois, a northern Chicago suburb far superior to their present neighborhood. Hannah is agreeable, and it is likely that the entire central cluster will relocate within a few months. In such a case, Bird and Hannah would lead; Arlene would move with them or shortly afterward. Within a few weeks, several other households would follow. This has been the pattern to date. Members move in and out of the central cluster but seldom live out of walking distance from at least one other member for more than a short while.

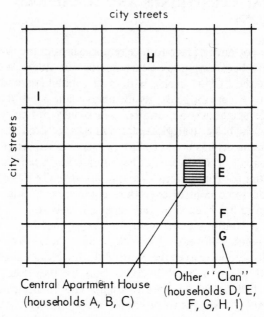

Figure 6.   The central cluster of "Clan" households

At present, nine households of the "Clan" are located within a maximum of seven blocks of each other, in the uptown area (Figure 6).

Three units of a small apartment house are occupied by "Clan" households: Unit A, on the second floor, includes Loretta and her granddaughter, Pinkie, with her husband, Charles, and their six children. Unit B, also on the second floor, is Arlene's, which she shares with five grandchildren, all offspring from consensual unions. They include Flute and Mary's son, Cree Cree; Cool and Anne's son, Shorty; and all three of South and Jean's children, Stick, Sandy, and Feathers. Feathers divides her time between the apartments of Arlene; her foster mother, Hannah; and her father. Unit C, on the third floor, is where Flute is staying with Susie. (Flute moved out during the time of the study.) Half a block away is another apartment house, with two "Clan" households. Unit D, on the second floor, is Hannah's and Tom's. Unit E, on the third floor, is where Bird, his pregnant wife Sallie, and their three children live.

Another block away is unit F, where Fox lives with his current liaison, June. They are across the street from unit G, the residence of Fox's wife, Clara, and their child. Barely four blocks from the central apartment house is unit H, where Dottie lives with her consensual husband, Henry, and their child. Farthest away, in this cluster, is unit I, the home of Silver, Teresa, and their four children.

Before the move uptown by those now in the central cluster, the entire "Clan" was located on the West Side of Chicago. Six households remain in three general locations, but not in the same buildings. The three locations are not within walking distance of one another. These groupings mark former locations of the central cluster and seem to be determined by the desires (and possibly the kin ties) of the women involved. Nevertheless, it is worth noting that whatever the combination of factors, the result is that those members of the core group who live away from the central cluster are still within walking distance of *one* other household: South and Lena live near John and Peggie; Rena and Marty live near Larry and Charlene; Cool and Sandra live near South and Nellie.

The life histories of the members of the core kin group show the fallacy of trying to arrive at statements about "prevailing household types." A variety of options exists. For a given person, the options vary from time to time during the adult phase of the life cycle. A woman may be living (over a period of years) with a husband, a consensual mate, a sister, a mother, alone with her children, with a different consensual mate, etc. The household, if spatially defined, is not an appropriate research focus for extended families structured like the "Clan." Several times we thought from Hannah's conversation that persons she spoke of lived in the same apartment when in truth they lived in different apartments in the same building. The nuance was unimportant to her. The important functions carried on by the family are not assigned to spatially defined units.[18]

THE CLAN AND ITS SOCIAL ENVIRONMENT: FRIENDS, ACQUAINTANCES, AND OFFICIALDOM

The low income level and the limited educational attainments of the family[19] lend considerable importance to its access to, and management of, external social resources. These can be grouped into two major categories — relationships with other nonkin within the Black ghetto, and relationships with public and private officials. Although the central cluster of the

[18] Lewis feels that one of the functions of clustering is exactly that it allows for ambiguity in assigning residence, e.g. Feathers can live simultaneously with Arlene and with Hannah because they live only a block apart.
[19] The educational attainments of the Clan's men are average for Black Chicago, among whom only 11 percent are professionals and managers; a fourth, in sales and clerical occupations; 10 percent, foremen and craftsmen; and more than half, apprentices and other blue-collar workers (U.S. Bureau of the Census 1972: 473, 504).

"Clan" is not living in a ghetto, their patterns of relationships do not seem to be significantly different from those described for ghettos. Probably these are traits which exist in any area lacking community organization. Uptown, a model-cities area is such a "noncommunity."

Within Black ghettos, two patterns of interpersonal, nonkin relationships have been described. Among the more successful migrants from the South, extreme cohesion persists. Daniel C. Thompson's observations are characteristic of much of Chicago's South Side:

Many [Black] people migrated from rural areas in Mississippi to northern cities and they have set up little enclaves. Sometimes you would think that they had moved from the South just last week, but the truth is that they have been there for years. They have been insulated within their little communities, and unless we study the communities from which they come, as well as the communities in which they are living in our large northern cities, we will be incapable of understanding the social context of some of their families (Thompson, in Kiser 1970: 314).

In contrast, the ghetto itself, with its stresses and anonymities, tends to generate casual and silent flows of persons who develop quick, sometimes intense, relationships, only to break them without a sign — and then reinstitute them, casually, at a later, almost random moment. Flute's encounter with his father in 1974 is illustrative. Overall, the pattern has been eloquently formulated by Abrahams (1970: 121) as follows:[20]

One of the strangest feelings for someone moving into a ghetto from a bourgeois background is the way in which friends will disappear for days, months, even years, without saying good bye, and will drift back with a minimum of comment and explanation. . . . Questions about this fluidity in interpersonal involvements will most commonly be answered by others in that person's (friendship) network with an incredulous giggle or a statement that indicates that this is the price of living life in terms of a series of crises. . . .

Arlene says that "Jesus is your only friend. You have associates, not friends." For her, there is no reason to expect closeness in a relationship outside the family. Hannah disagrees with this deep pessimism. "Ninety percent of the time it works out."
In fact, we discovered in the course of our study a graded pattern of relationships, identified by special vocabularies.

---

[20] Liebow's material (1967) is similar. The fragility of the ties is, in part, socioeconomically determined in our opinion. Nevertheless, given the structure of the extended family, we would expect family ties to be dominant over friendships and to find that clan friends become pseudo- or "play" kin (see Aschenbrenner, this volume), wherever the extended family is found.

Friend: The word "friend" apparently is used with less frequency than in White culture and usually has the connotation "best friend." "A friend is somebody you're up tight with, like with a cousin. You can go there anytime. You are as close as family. They are in your house, and you do lots together." Hannah, Belle (whose child by South is deceased), Clara (a former girl friend of Cool), and Marlene are friends. (Note that Feathers considers "Marlene" to be "family but not blood kin"; see Figure 1.) They are also a "running-buddy" group, which we discuss below. The fact that they are "like sisters" can also be seen in their relations, just cited, with Hannah's brothers.

Associate: Associates are people with whom you do "just certain things." If the interest is social and recreational, the individuals involved are *running buddies.*[21] Feathers once gave us a long list of "running-buddy" relationships for most of the female members of the family. Individuals who are kin may or may not also be "running buddies," e.g. hang out at the same bar together, and they may or may not also be "friends." A running buddy need not be a friend. "Your running buddy might never have been inside your house. He might, but he might not."[22] A *partner* is an associate in some economic or other purposeful undertaking.

Acquaintance: This is someone with whom you maintain a rather formal relationship.[23]

In general, while "friends" play kinlike roles in supportive and expressive relationships, the more distant categories of "running buddies," "associates," and "acquaintances" provide a setting for more selective ties, but ties still important for the integration of individuals at the local level. The communication of information is a common function of all levels of friendship.

Relations with Officialdom

As far as Hannah knows, no adult member of the family belongs to any organization other than a church, and only two of the active adults attend church regularly — Dottie and South, the latter because of his wife's insistence.

---

[21] The term "walking buddy," mentioned by Liebow (1967: 163), is probably a variation.

[22] Lewis says, "You know that it's possible while you and your buddy are sitting in the bar, one of your buddy's real friends might be robbing your house."

[23] Lewis says, "For example, if X invites me [just an acquaintance] to a party I know it's just because she needs a teacher."

Changes in the Chicago precinct system were reflected in the data. We asked Hannah about their political participation. She replied,

When David was the precinct captain he lived in the neighborhood. We saw him every day. We used to play whist a lot in my kitchen and we would talk a lot about politics. The main thing we talked about was police brutality. At that time [1970], there were only two Black policemen in Uptown. He wasn't happy with the way the Party [i.e. Daley's regular Democrats] was handling that. The precinct captain we have now lives outside the area. We only see him at election time.

Although Hannah talks about the importance of education and is herself a high school graduate (as are Loretta's four children and Bird), many members of the family have dropped out between the ninth and eleventh grades. Inquiries about the older children show no improvement. Barriers within schools are discouraging. Feathers goes to a school noted for its ethnic diversity. But it is the experience of both Holloman and Lewis, from working in the school, that the children's patterns of association follow ethnic lines of friendship and conflict. Moreover, there is no evidence in the family — nor among many Black experiences — that having a high school diploma is a job advantage. Other factors (Hannah's manslaughter conviction is an extreme case) have intervened all too often, with the result that graduates and dropouts work at the same level or are simply unemployed.

Living just above the poverty line and subject to many stresses, "Clan" members have had more than one adverse encounter with the law. They have also had to seek help from both welfare and private agencies, as noted in regard to the Kate Maremont Foundation and their housing. Skills in dealing with social agencies have developed, as in the case of Feathers, and with Legal Aid (where Hannah goes if she feels a lawyer's help is necessary). Holloman spoke with the head of Legal Aid in the area, and he stated that their clients represented the better-informed, more aggressive residents.

In general, the "Clan's" knowledge of available social resources is considerable. They told us that there is a systematic way to locate lost persons in the Chicago area. Globetrotter Company takes missing person announcements free of charge for broadcast over radio station WVON ("Voice of the Negro"). It was in this way that Hannah's grandmother, Amanda, located Arlene after contact was lost in the 1950's. According to Hannah, most cities with large Black populations have such a service; a study of them would be of considerable interest.

In summary, in the use of official resources, as in the location of housing and, especially, in the management of its internal affairs, the "Clan" exhibits considerable initiative, imagination, and constructive effort. It is the unity and social competence of the "Clan" as a structural entity that permits them to survive and to strive for the better as "Clan" people see it. An individual alone succeeds only if he is lucky or has a talent. Their way, in contrast, is the belief that "The Lord helps those who help themselves — but he helps those who help each other too."

Perhaps, moreover, there is a special grace for musicians.

FEATHERS AND THE "CLAN": SOME ANSWERS AND HYPOTHESES

Let us return to the social worker's questions. Feathers and her brother and sister, who have been rejected by their mother, are in the primary fosterage of her aunt and grandmother, with her father also taking responsibility as an explicit male role model and counselor. Feathers's home is within the "Clan," which loves her and supports her.

But the social worker's questions do not go far enough. It is true that Feathers is a troubled child, unhappy in school, supposedly dull, fleeing from her own insignificance. But in her activity as a social informant she exhibited capacities for extensive, correct observations, for social realism in her own milieu, that reflect considerable intelligence. Moreover, while the "Clan," as a decision-making body, perceived Feathers's case as one primarily of guidance and discipline, it is clearly a body seeking valid information, open to expert advice, and capable of understanding the ego needs of troubled children. Thus, what has emerged is a therapeutic opportunity to reassess Feathers's potential and to utilize her own family as a primary vehicle, and music as a basic medium, for activating her self-assurance and her latent abilities.

And there are many Featherses and many "Clans" in Black Chicago.

Let us go beyond this immediate set of problems and seek to view the implications of our study for the understanding of Black families, especially in the environment of the ghetto. The following points are submitted not as firm conclusions but as hypotheses for further testing.

1. Any study of Black family life must begin with the assumption that "family" in that subculture refers to the extended family, not the nuclear or matrifocal household unit.

The implications of this for both research design and public policy are clear. The Moynihan report, which proceeded on the assumption that "family" in Black culture is the same structural unit found in middle-class White culture, was able to conclude that the Black family is deteriorating because of an increase in illegitimacy, the fragility of the husband–wife bond, and the increase in matrifocal households (see Rainwater and Yancey 1967). The statistics are probably correct and clearly reflect *some* sort of change in Black society. However, they do *not* reflect structural deterioration of the extended family, which is the unit of maximum function. Indeed, the statistics may be contributing to its strengthening. What would serve as a valid indicator of change in the strength of extended-family structure? Certainly, the institution of fosterage is one vital extended-family function, and a decline in the rate or quality of foster age would indicate a weakening of the family system itself.

2. Black extended families in urban areas can develop and maintain strong structures.

The type of structure exemplified in this study includes a defined, titular leadership; a core group of active adults (the leaders' children); and an extensive network of subfamilies, based on both formal and consensual relationships.

3. The integration of the Black extended family is based on spatial clustering (especially where there is a central cluster containing the titular members), extensive fosterage, and the system of reciprocities related to rearing and other kin obligations.

a. Spatial clustering and relocation by cluster are important urban processes in Black communities, related to rate of population succession at the neighborhood level. They need to be measured.

b. Fosterage, like any cultural pattern concerned with child rearing, has implications for psychic development. Our limited data have shown both positive and negative aspects from the point of view of the child who experiences the shift.

c. Reciprocities of rearing are complementary, and those among adults are asymmetrical. The flows of money, goods and services, or supports need to be studied in detail. We suspect that the pattern of household financing among Blacks who are active participants in extended family networks differs significantly from those of persons whose households are coterminous with their (nuclear or matrifocal) families.

d. The extended family is viable under urban conditions. It is apparently not dependent for survival on patterns of corporateness around assets or a locality center (such as a common burial ground); this family has neither.

4. Systemic relationships among the various dyads existing in the extended family are such that considerable structural stress is placed on the bond between formal and consensual spouses quite apart from their relationship as individuals. These structural pressures result from

a. The favoring of kin over conjugal bonds in cases of conflict.

b. Competition for the individual's time between own and mate's kin group.

c. Competition between previous and present mate(s).

d. Presence in the house of present mate's children by a previous union.

5. The "Clan," as an example of Black extended family in an urban area, has roots in traditional Black culture. We have demonstrated that the cultural rules have behavioral correlates which we think are distinctive to this ethnic group. In particular, we regard the patterns of fosterage as sufficiently demonstrated and culturally distinct.

We suspect that other patterns of behavior also follow from the form of the extended family and that these too will be specific to the subculture, but we do not have the data to demonstrate them. Here, we refer particularly to patterns of money flows which we are assuming to be linked in part to fosterage. The difficulty of obtaining data of this sort for an extended family group is obvious.

6. Spatial clustering and relocation, although important processes in Black communities, are probably not culturally distinctive.

When Chicago's Greek Town underwent urban renewal, the population relocated in two communities, one north and one west, and kin ties were important in the relocation. It is simply that Blacks are forced to move more often than other ethnic groups.

REFERENCES

ABRAHAMS, ROGER D.
   1970   *Positively Black*. Englewood Cliffs, N.J.: Prentice-Hall.
ADAMS, BERT
   1967   *Kinship in an urban setting*. Chicago: Markham.
   1970   Isolation, function and beyond: American kinship in the 1960's. *Journal of Marriage and the Family* 32: 575–597.
BOTT, ELIZABETH
   1971 [1957]   *Family and social network*. London: Tavistock.
BUCHLER, IRA A., HENRY A. SELBY
   1968   *Kinship and social organization: an introduction to theory and method*. New York: Macmillan.
DE COY, R. H.
   1967   *The Nigger Bible*. Los Angeles: Holloway House.
GLUCKMAN, MAX
   1968   "Social beliefs and individual thinking in tribal society," in *Theory in anthropology*. Edited by Robert A. Manners and David Kaplan, 453–465. Chicago: Aldine.

GRIER, W. H., PRICE M. COBBS
1971   *The Jesus bag.* New York: McGraw-Hill.
JONES, LEROI
1963   *Blues people.* New York: William Morrow.
KISER, CLYDE V., *editor*
1970   Demographic aspects of the Black community. *Millbank Memorial Fund Quarterly* 48 (2, 2).
LIEBOW, ELLIOT
1967   *Tally's corner.* Boston: Little, Brown.
MINTZ, SIDNEY W., ERIC R. WOLF
1950   An analysis of ritual co-parenthood (*compadrazgo*). *Southwestern Journal of Anthropology* 6: 341–368.
NICHOLAS, A. X.
1971   *The poetry of soul.* New York: Bantam.
RAINWATER, LEE, WILLIAM L. YANCEY
1967   *The Moynihan report and the politics of controversy.* Cambridge, Mass.: M.I.T. Press.
ROSSER, COLIN, CHRISTOPHER HARRIS
1965   *The family and social change. A study of family and kinship in a south Wales town.* London: Routledge & Kegan Paul.
SHERIF, MUZAFER
1963   "Social psychology: problems and trends in interdisciplinary relationships," in *Psychology: a study of a science,* volume six. Edited by Sigmund Koch, 30–93. New York: McGraw-Hill.
SMITH, MICHAEL G.
1962a   *Kinship and community in Carriacou.* New Haven and London: Yale University Press.
1962b   *West Indian family structure.* Seattle: University of Washington Press.
STACK, CAROL B.
1974   *All our kin: strategies for survival in a Black community.* New York: Harper and Row.
U.S. BUREAU OF THE CENSUS
1972   *Census of population and housing: 1970. Census tracts.* Final Reports PHC (1)-43. Chicago, Ill., SMSA, parts one and two. Washington, D.C.: U.S. Government Printing Office.
WHITTEN, NORMAN E.
1965   *Class, kinship, and power in an Ecuadorian town.* Stanford, Calif.: Stanford University Press.

Kinship and Residential Propinquity in Black New Orleans: The Wesleys

LENUS JACK, JR.

ABSTRACT

The history of research on Black families has been dominated by inadequate conceptual frameworks emphasizing the independent, nuclear household and resultant social deterioration and ignoring the form, function, and critical importance of the extended family. As a social institution the Black extended family is prominent not only in rural America, but in urban areas as well.

The Wesley extended family in New Orleans, Louisiana, represents a five-generation kin network comprising a territorial as well as a consanguineous system. Territorially, the fifty-five individuals in fourteen households of the Wesley family are centered on a residential compound, called the "Yard." And both the residential unit and the larger kin network are linked through consanguineous ties in which matrilineal consanguinity is favored.

The Wesley family extends many benefits to its members, including residential security, ceremonial obligations, social ties, and economic cooperation. Though some of the specific forms of the Wesley extended family may not be typical for Black families as a whole, the structural underpinnings appear representative of Afro-Americans and in many instances resemble those of the West African extended families and lineages.

SPECULATION AND THE NEED FOR EMPIRICAL DATA ON THE BLACK FAMILY

A major problem of Black family historiography seems to be a lack of a viable conceptual framework. For the most part, research on the Black

The author is grateful for the advice of the following faculty members of the University of Pittsburgh: Mr. Clarence Turner, Black Studies Department; Dr. Arthur Tuden, Department of Anthropology; and Mr. Laurence Glasco, Department of History. Professor Demitri B. Shimkin, Department of Anthropology, University of Illinois at Urbana-Champaign, has also provided research suggestions and editorial help. Mr. James Bier and Mr. Dennis Frate, also of the University of Illinois, have been respon-

family in the United States has dealt with it from the viewpoint of the independent, nuclear household as the ideal. Frazier, Moynihan, and others all have made this conceptual mistake.

In particular, E. Franklin Frazier, in his pioneering work, *The Negro family in the United States* (1966 [1939]) deemphasized the significance of African survivals and argued for social deterioration as a principal force in Black family life. Frazier maintained that all vestiges of African culture were destroyed by the psychological shock of the slave trade, the "middle passage," and "seasoning." He further contended that the slave trade's selectivity toward young males lessened the chance of cultural survivals. With the successive bombardments of slavery, Reconstruction, migration, and urbanization, the Black family could not merit the title of an institution. Yet Frazier could see some potential strengths in the Black family; namely, a move from primitivism to Euro-American civilization (see also Frazier 1932, 1937).

It is true that Melville Herskovits (1941) debated Frazier on these issues. In Black America, Professor Herskovits felt that he could see African response patterns to the destabilizing forces of slavery and its consequences. The matrifocality of Black households and the peripheral family roles of Black men he saw as African traits. Polygyny, the preferred form of marriage in Africa (all monogamous households are potentially segments of polygynous ones), allows for a strong mother–child tie and a separate household for each wife. It is compatible with female-headed households and sequential marital relationships, which are thus seen as continuities rather than pathologies.

But Herskovits's arguments were largely rejected. Frazier's view of the Black family as a situational adaptation remained dominant. Another theory advanced was that of "incorrect" borrowing from White institutions; this was espoused by Johnson (1934) and Powdermaker (1939). More recently, there have been eclectic descriptions by Billingsley (1968), Hannerz (1969), and Young (1970). These have varied in merit, but none has been able to see the critical importance of the interhousehold relations and the suprahousehold functions of the Black extended family.

In fact, the most influential writer, Daniel P. Moynihan, has carried the Frazier theories to an extreme. In his well-known report and other writings (Moynihan 1965a, 1965b), he concluded that the underemployment and unemployment of the Black father and the "overemployment" of the Black mother have broken the will of Black people. This feeling

sible for the final layout and drafting of the figures. And last, the author wishes to express his gratitude to the Wesley family for their cooperation in collecting the material for this paper.

was so pervasive that Moynihan saw no immediate hope of disentangling the social "pathology" of the Black family.

This paper proceeds from a drastically different viewpoint. The author believes that careful, extensive, empirical research on Black family institutions must replace today's speculations. On the basis of his own life experiences and special studies, moreover, it is the author's hypothesis that the extended family matrix is of critical importance. In this amalgam of families, many Black people — men, women, and children — have their being. Each household maintains a separate and autonomous functioning, yet interrelates with and influences the others through the *network* of the extended family. Finally, the extended family, with its complex organization and many coordinating functions, is not just a rural phenomenon but one well established in American cities as well.[1]

The purpose of this paper is the careful description and analysis of an extended family in New Orleans, which has been given the pseudonym of "Wesley."[2] It has developed in its present site, a family compound called the "Yard," since the 1920's, and presently includes five generations. The extensiveness of the Wesley kin network resembles, in many ways, that of African extended families and lineages. Moreover, the Wesleys and their kin comprise a territorial as well as a consanguineous system.

While the representativeness of specific features of the Wesley extended family must as yet remain an open question even for Black New Orleans, the author submits that the complexities, functions, and interplay between networks of households such as these must be the direction taken by future study of the Black family system. Currently, the debate has been centered on the African or non-African origins, or the "pathological" or nonpathological nature, of the Black family, but until we know more about the nature and experience of the extended family in the Black community of the United States, debate of this sort will remain trivial.

THE WESLEY FAMILY: A CHARACTERIZATION

In general terms, the Wesley family of New Orleans is a multihousehold social entity, unified by consanguinity (especially matrilineal); by self-identification and by identification with a central figure of respect ("Mama"); by identification with a central site (the "Yard"), reinforced by the ownership and inheritance of real property; by mutual ceremonial

---

[1] This paper rejects the hypothesis of Talcott Parsons (1959: 241–274) that the extended family is dysfunctional in a mature, democratic, industrial society.

[2] All names mentioned in this paper are pseudonyms.

and other functional obligations (especially attendance at funerals); by extensive visiting and cooperation; and by perceived differences from more distant kin and unrelated neighbors. Some aspects of the Wesley family's life are perhaps not typical of Black families in New Orleans. Yet the very significant dimension of the interrelationship of kinship and residential propinquity is not limited to the Wesleys, nor would their case be an extreme of a continuum. Many of the spouses of the Wesleys have their relatives living near them. In fact, certain sections of New Orleans have family groups so large as to comprise half of their entire neighborhoods·

Structural Features

The Wesley family, as recognized by its members and by outsiders, comprises a group of fifty-five members in fourteen households resident in or near the "Yard" in New Orleans; a fifty-sixth member lives in California. All but one person in this group are related by blood or marriage. A much wider network of kin relationships is also recognized and functionally maintained by the Wesleys, but this is distinguished from the family proper.

Structurally, the Wesley family is made up of an "inner circle" of social adults of the great-grandparental, grandparental and parental generations, and of social dependents of the child and grandchild generations. This "inner circle" is comprised of Mrs. Lydia Laurent Wesley ("Mama"), her five daughters, two nieces (children of "Mama's" deceased brother and sister, respectively), a nephew (the son of another deceased sister), plus seven of "Mama's" grandchildren; all except "Mama" are the heads or the spouses of heads of households (Figure 1).

This "inner circle" developed as follows. In 1912, at the age of twelve, "Mama," her siblings, and her parents, the Laurents, moved to New Orleans. Although they had relatives living in the city, they did not settle nearby. Six years later "Mama," then eighteen years of age, married Robert Wesley, Jr., son of a family who were long-term residents of New Orleans. At first the couple lived in the "uptown" section of New Orleans, but after six years of marriage they bought a lot in the Delong area and build part of the house in which "Mama" still resides. (Robert died in 1926.) "Mama's" mother-in-law already owned two other adjacent houses; one eventually bought by "Mama" and the other inherited by "Mama's" five daughters. They, in turn, sold their share to their oldest sister and her husband. These adjacent lots and houses evolved into what is today referred to as the "Yard."

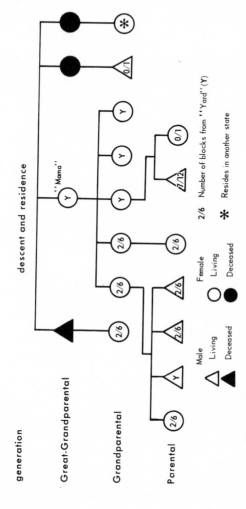

Figure 1. Genealogical relationships and residential patterns of the "inner circle" in the Wesley family

A succession of relatives and in-laws have lived in the "Yard." Today five of six households in the "Yard" are related. Other members of the Wesley family group live at varying distances from the "Yard." Eight other households in the block of the "Yard" are also related to the Wesleys in some way (Figure 2).

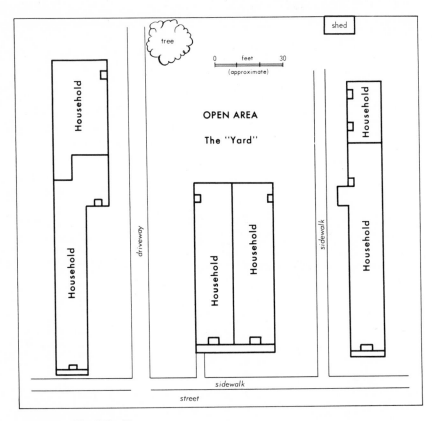

Figure 2. The "Yard"

Within the Wesley family, kinship and propinquity have basically influenced attitudes and behavior. In general, matrilineal consanguinity is favored. This is in part a demographic accident because many of the family's men have died at early ages. But it is also a social reality, not only in the "inner circle" but also in the wider kin network in which maternal relatives reside significantly closer to the "Yard" than do paternal ones (Tables 1, 2). The social interactions on the maternal side are correspondingly more extensive.[3] However, family members of the "child" generation do not have a matrilateral disparity in residence patterns. These "children" live residentially close to both sides of their families, although the content and intensity of their network relations seems to be more with their Wesley kin, whether male or female. Nevertheless, the morphological and interactional characteristics (following the terminology of Mitchell 1969: 12–29) of the network can be and are influenced by the women in-laws of the Wesleys.

KINSHIP DEFINITION AMONG THE WESLEYS. Kinship in this family is the social recognition of biological descent, either through the father or through the mother. *Step* relationships are handled descriptively. In such cases, one would hear a person speak of a kin's sibling, "X has a sister," and so on. Cousins are also blood relatives, though there are a few fictitious ones. A "cousin," first of all, begins with the children of siblings whether the siblings be any of the three possible pairs. The children of these siblings would be first cousins to each other. The first cousins of one's parents are called by the Wesleys that person's second cousins, and so on; but they must be related consanguineously. It is quite clear that, for instance, one's first cousin's first cousin is not actually one's cousin if that first cousin's first cousin is kin through a parent who is not kin consanguineously. Yet the personality of this specific nonconsanguineous individual could make him a fictitious cousin. Therefore, consanguinity is the essential characteristic of kinship which may still be augmented in particular cases.

Many of the Wesleys know their fourth, fifth, and sometimes even sixth cousins and how they are related.[4] Yet they are not considered as members of the Wesleys, which is an *exclusive* family group based on direct blood ties with "Mama's" daughters, their children (whether male or female), and their children's children. The Wesleys also include "Mama's" two nieces (daughters of her brother and sister) and nephew (son of another sister) but not any of their children. These children, and their children, along with a few affines would, however, be considered as members of a "family" network which is more inclusive.

---

[3] This pattern of residential propinquity of related women seems to be similar to that among other Black people. See Smith (1956) and Clignet (1970).
[4] This knowledge appears to be appreciably poorer for paternal kin, among whom names and residences may often be unknown.

Table 1. Spatial distribution from the "Yard" of members of the Wesley family "inner circle"[a]

Category	Number of persons	Residence In "Yard" or next door	Number of blocks distant				Outside New Orleans	
			0-1	2-6	7-12	13+	Other Louisiana city	Out of state
All Persons	16[b]	5[b]	2	7	1	0	0	1
Men	5	1	1	2	1	0	0	1
Women	11[b]	4[b]	1	5	0	0	0	0
Grandparental Generation: total	8	3	1	3	0	0	0	1
Men	1	0	1	0	0	0	0	0
Women	7	3	0	3	0	0	0	1
Parental Generation: total	7	1	1	4	1	0	0	0
Men	4	1	0	2	1	0	0	0
Women	3	0	1	2	0	0	0	0

Notes: [a] All adults who are heads or spouses of heads of households.
[b] Includes "Mama" in the great-grandparental generation.

Table 2. Spatial distribution from the "Yard" of the Wesleys and their kin network[a]

Category	Number of persons	Residence In "Yard" or next door	Number of blocks distant				Outside New Orleans Other Louisiana city	Out of state	Unknown
			0-1	2-6	7-12	13+			
All persons	61[a]	5	6	19	5	7	7	11	1
Members of "inner circle"	16	5	2	7	1	0	0	1	0
Paternal uncles of members of "inner circle"	4	0	0	0	1	0	3	0	0
Paternal aunts of members of "inner circle"	6	0	0	1	0	4	0	1	0
Maternal first cousins	21	0	4	8	2	1	0	6	0
Paternal first cousins	14	0	0	3	1	2	4	3	1

Note: [a] Living persons only.

RESIDENTIAL PROPINQUITY, HOUSEHOLD TYPES, AND PERCEIVED RECIPROCAL TIES. Residential propinquity is not significant in and of itself (compare Castillo et al. 1968: 15–16).[5] Yet it does facilitate extended family relations — especially with more distant kin. For it would seem that the closer the kin tie the farther one could be removed geographically without loss; and, perhaps, the further one is removed by kinship, the less likely that distance can be transcended. Three thousand miles of separation between close kin will almost never have a serious effect on their blood ties.

Within the Wesley family, "Mama" is the central unifying figure but other members of the older generations also play generic roles. At the same time, the family is partitioned into a variety of households — some nuclear, some multigenerational, some including unrelated as well as related persons;[6] and into differing intensities of personal relationships. An example of such "microextended" ties is as follows:

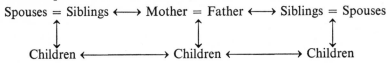

The arrows show reciprocal ties. A rank order of their perceived importance would generally be: first, parents to children; second, children to parents; third, between siblings; and fourth, between other relatives.[7]

[5] These authors ". . . use shared or contiguous residence or membership in the same household as a basic frame for anchoring their extended family." However, their critical definition of an extended family is independent of residence as such: ". . . looking at the ten elements of the ideal-type extended family and the optionality of shared residence, the absolute essentials for the existence of the extended family seem to be: recognition of kin relations beyond that of husband, wife, and unmarried children, shared responsibilities, and maintenance of expressive relations beyond the nuclear family. If these three elements are not present to any degree, then the extended family is non-existent, a phenomenon which probably remains to be well-evidenced in real life" (Castillo et al. 1968: 15–16).

[6] Considerable study is needed of the functional relations within these households, which are rarely evident from composition data alone. For example, whether particular persons in a given household constitute a subfamily or an autonomous nuclear family requires specific inquiry. The caution advanced by Castillo, Weisblat, and Villareal extends to the Wesley family, namely, ". . . the number of generations is a very inadequate basis for determining the extended character of a household . . . and perhaps it is not the lineality or collaterality of his relations which is important but rather the extent to which relations with such kin enter into the basic structure of relationships within the nuclear family" (Castillo et al. 1968: 15).

[7] In Sharp and Axelrod's study (1956: 433–439), about 70 percent of the Detroiters were engaged in some form of reciprocal aid that had this same rank order; "other relatives" played a limited part. In the Black extended family of "Viola Jackson," relations between siblings were more frequent and consistent (Stack 1970: 306). Extended family relations between adult siblings may take precedence under conditions of mobility. As of this moment, however, the data are inadequate to answer this question.

What must be stressed is that active behaviors encompassing all of these actors can and do exist at the same time.[8] These range into the "macroextended" family, the Wesleys, and even beyond into the broader kin network. Yet, in most cases, the ties of a more limited "microextended" family take priority in case of a dilemma. So closeness of blood tie normally transcends residential propinquity as the significant variable.

This perspective is essential to understanding the roles of "Mama" and other senior members of the Wesley family, and, finally, self-identifications by people as "Wesleys."

SOCIAL CONTROLS AS A SOURCE OF FAMILY IDENTITY. "Mama" is indeed a central figure in the family. She is one of the few links to the past, as well as the aunt, mother, grandmother, or great-grandmother of the family group. Respect for her emanates from each kin title held. Respect also accrues from old age. Yet "Mama" is not what one would consider a matriarch. Respect does not come from her power to command or demand. She cannot, nor would she, demand that her daughters ally themselves against all comers. Her influence comes from the advice a mother and grandmother has to give (such as about illnesses and child rearing), and persuasiveness in that what she has to say is right. "Mama" would have to be considered the spiritual leader of the group. She is a Mother of the Wesleys' church, which is the highest position women can hold in that church and is held by one person for the duration of her membership. "Mama" serves, also, as the conscience of the group and exerts her influence by cajoling family members to become active in their church and constantly inquiring when membership will be reinstated, if it has lapsed.

Generally "Mama's" influence is similar to that of the parents in "microextended" family relations. The rank order of extended family reciprocity for the "microextended" group reveals that a parent (or parents) is involved directly in the first two and indirectly in the third level described above: parents to children; children to parents; and between siblings. It must be specially stressed that the first order of reciprocity is from the parents to the children. Parents also encourage cooperation and congeniality among siblings, as well as with the "macroextended" family

---

[8] Most authors feel as Sussman (1959: 333) does: ". . . The extended American family system, for the married person, consists of three interlocking nuclear families; the family of procreation, the family of orientation, and the one of affinal relations (in-laws) whose interrelationships are determined by choice and residential proximity and not by culturally binding or legally enforced norms." Dotson (1951: 691) contends that the propinquity patterns of large families remain relatively unbroken in long-established cities such as New Haven.

network. This cooperation is noticeable in cleaning the "Yard," in mutual financial aid, in locating housing and in assistance in moving, in finding work, in giving advice, and in countless other things, such as taking pictures for special occasions.

Parents are looked to for solving family quarrels. Sometimes uncles are more influential than parents; or a woman's oldest brother or an oldest sister's husband may act as an authority figure and peacemaker. At times, age and high family status may confer the right to settle disputes.

The presence of common social controls despite residence in separate and autonomous, albeit nearby and cooperating, households, gives the Wesleys a single identity. This is intensified terminologically. When its members speak of the "Wesleys" or the "family" they are almost always speaking of the extended group and not any individual household. Friends, neighbors, and in-laws also recognize this close kin tie and clannish character, calling the group collectively "them Wesleys." Even small children in the Wesley family are cognizant of their affiliations, and this is demonstrable in a game in which they imitate each adult member of the group. This game, it might be added, is called the "Wesley."

In their environment, the Wesleys have a variable reputation. They are characterized by others as "a good family," "all for themselves," "all to themselves," "people to be like," "people not to be like," and "just plain crazy." They characterize themselves as "a good family," "comical," "like to have fun," "like to be with their own people" (which means their family), "no one like us" (unique), and "crazier than most."

The "Yard": Nature, Functions, and Influence

Since the 1920's, the "Yard" (see Figure 2) has been a traditional center of residence for the Wesleys. Five generations have grown up there; at least one representative of four of these generations is present in the "Yard" now. This site is a central area surrounded by three double houses owned by family members; in the past, there was another house in the "Yard." For the Wesleys, these houses are historically significant; many have been born and raised here, while the family's expanding members have been accommodated through additions to the original houses.

Although formal rules of residence in the "Yard" are absent, patterns of practice are evident.[9] One is that succession to housing is generally

---

[9]   As Stack (1970: 2) contends, "Residence, one of the dynamics of social organization, can only be understood if the basis for the active formation of households is understood."

restricted to family members. A second pattern is that family members generally are residents of the "Yard" all or much of their lives. Third, family members usually live in the "Yard" at the beginning of their careers as young adults, then move away, returning to live either in the "Yard" or nearby in later life.

The "Yard" is not only the Wesleys' traditional place of residence. It is also a recreation center, theater, meeting place, automobile shop, garden, day-care center, hotel, concert hall, a place for weddings, funerals, christenings, birthday parties, and suppers, or whatever activity some family member thinks of. It is a place of continuous socializing. To quote "Baby" Irma's succinct answers to a non-family-member:

QUESTION: Whom do you receive most often at your home?
ANSWER: How can you receive anybody if you are always over here?
QUESTION: Who makes the decision to visit relatives?
ANSWER: All of my relatives are here . . .

All Wesley family members have the right to use the "Yard," although in a strict sense there is not an *obligation* to aid one another in preparing it for whatever the occasion may be. Rather, it is felt that everyone helps because it has always been so; this is what one is *supposed* to do. This is something that family members feel cannot be explained to others.

Members do not knock at doors in the "Yard" but just walk in. There is no sense of boundary among them — except during quarrels, when a sense of territoriality emerges. At this time, everyone withdraws to his or her "side of the 'Yard'"; trespassers are blamed for any subsequent disturbances. Generally, these arguments are soon forgotten. In any case, the Wesleys may fight among themselves but will not tolerate attacks by outsiders. In most cases, there are few outsiders about, and they are treated with courtesy. Wesley members are upbraided for starting an argument with or picking on visitors, for this may embroil the family in a quarrel. The "Yard," however, is a fortress; no one dares attack Wesley people there. In contrast, differences between spouses are their own business.

Because of the central importance of the "Yard" in the life of the Wesley family and its broader kin network, many interrelationships in this social system are associated with residence in, near, or at a distance from, the "Yard." Analytically, a seven-point scale of propinquity has proven to be useful: in the "Yard" (either in the same house, or next door); 0–1 blocks away; 2–6 blocks away; 7–12 blocks away; thirteen or more blocks away; in another city in Louisiana; or in another state. Correspondingly, the Wesleys and their more extended network may be usefully grouped by social generation (including only the great-grand-

Table 3. Spatial distribution of living paternal uncles and aunts of the Wesley "inner circle": totals[a]

"Inner circle" category	Number of uncles and aunts				Residence										Outside New Orleans			
	Total		"Wesleys"		In "Yard" or next door		Number of blocks distant								Other Louisiana city		Out of state	
							0–1		2–6		7–12		13+					
	U[b]	A[c]	U[b]	A[c]	U[b]	A[c]	U[b]	A[c]	U[b]	A[c]	U[b]	A[c]	U[b]	A[c]	U[b]	A[c]	U[b]	A[c]
All persons:	6	9	4	6	0	0	0	0	0	1	2	0	0	8	6	0	0	1
Men with	4	1	4	2	0	0	0	0	0	0	1	0	0	1	4	0	0	0
Women with	2	8	4	6	0	0	0	0	0	1	1	0	0	7	2	0	0	1
Grandparental generation:																		
Total	0	6	0	2	0	0	0	0	0	1	0	0	0	5	0	0	0	0
Men with	0	0	0	0	0	0	0	0	0	0	0	0	0	0	0	0	0	0
Women with	0	6	0	2	0	0	0	0	0	1	0	0	0	5	0	0	0	0
Parental generation:																		
Total	6	3	4	4	0	0	0	0	0	0	2	0	0	3	6	0	0	1
Men with	4	1	4	2	0	0	0	0	0	0	1	0	0	1	4	0	0	0
Women with	2	2	4	4	0	0	0	0	0	0	1	0	0	2	2	0	0	1

Notes: [a] Totals may not add because of duplications.
[b] Uncles.
[c] Aunts.

parental, grandparental, and parental), by social centrality (contrasting the "inner circle" to more peripheral members), and by relationship to members of the "inner circle" (parent, sibling, maternal aunt, paternal aunt, paternal uncle, maternal first cousin, and paternal first cousin). It should be noted that there are no living maternal uncles for any member of the "inner circle."

The basic data on residence are presented in Figure 1 and Table 1 (pp. 243, 246). The first figure comprises all the parent, sibling, and maternal aunt relations of the "inner circle." The sixteen members of that group — eleven women and only five men — include one resident of California. The others live not more than twelve blocks away from the "Yard"; in

Table 4. Spatial distribution of living paternal uncles and aunts of the Wesley "inner circle": by member[a]

Member of "inner circle" by sex and generation	Number and residence of paternal uncles	aunts
Female grandparental	None	1 (13+)[b]
Female grandparental	None	1 (13+)[b]
Female grandparental	None	1 (13+)[b]
Female grandparental	None	1 (13+)[b]
Female grandparental	None	1 (13+)[b]
Female grandparental	None	1 (2/6)[b]
Female parental	{ 1 (6/12)[b] { 2 (other city)[c]	{ 1 (13+)[b] { 1 (n.a.)[d]
Female parental	None	{ 1 (13+)[b] { 1 (other state)[e] { 1 (n.a.)[d]
Male parental	{ 1 (6/12)[b] { 2 (other city)[c]	{ 1 (13+)[b] { 1 (n.a.)[d]
Male parental	1 (other city)[c]	None
Male parental	1 (other city)[c]	None
Male parental	1 (other city)[c]	None

Notes: [a] Includes duplications.
  [b] Distance in blocks from "Yard."
  [c] City in Louisiana other than New Orleans.
  [d] Data not available.
  [e] State other than Louisiana.

fact, within two blocks, on the average. For the entire body of sixty-one kinfolk (Table 2, p. 247), the median distance of residence away from the "Yard" is less than six blocks. Only eleven persons live out of state, while the residence of one is unknown. An mentioned earlier, maternal relatives live nearer to the "Yard" than do paternal ones. Overall, the majority of Wesleys and their kin live in such propinquity that even

Table 5. Spatial distribution of living maternal first cousins of the Wesley "inner circle": totals[a]

Members of "inner circle"		Number of maternal first cousins	Residence In "Yard" or next door	Number of blocks distant				Outside New Orleans	
Category	Number			0-1	2-6	7-12	13+	In another Louisiana city	Out of state
All persons:	15	21	0	8	12	6	1	0	8
Men	5	16	0	4	4	4	0	0	2
Women	10	21	0	4	8	2	1	0	7
Grandparental generation:									
Total	8	14	0	4	6	0	1	0	8
Men	1	9	0	1	1	0	0	0	2
Women	7	14	0	3	5	0	1	0	7
Parental generation:									
Total	7	7	0	4	6	6	0	0	0
Men	4	7	0	3	3	4	0	0	0
Women	3	7	0	1	3	2	0	0	0

Note: [a] Figures may not add because of duplications.

Table 6.   Spatial distribution of living maternal first cousins of the Wesley "inner circle": by member[a]

Member of "inner circle" by sex and generation	Number and residence of maternal first cousins
Female grandparental	1 (0/1)[b] 1 (2/6)[b] 2 (other states)[c]
Female grandparental	1 (0/1)[b] 1 (2/6)[b] 2 (other state)[c]
Female grandparental	1 (0/1)[b] 1 (2/6)[b] 2 (other state)[c]
Female grandparental	2 (2/6)[b] 2 (other state)[c]
Female grandparental	2 (2/6)[b] 2 (other state)[c]
Female grandparental	4 (13+)[b]
Female grandparental	8 (other state)[c]
Female parental	1 (0/1)[b] 4 (2/6)[b]
Female parental	3 (2/6)[b] 3 (7/12)[b]
Female parental	2 (2/6)[b] 1 (7/12)[b]
Male grandparental	3 (0/1)[b] 3 (2/6)[b] 2 (other state)[c]
Male parental	4 (7/12)[b] 1 (0/1)[b]
Male parental	1 (0/1)[b] 1 (2/6)[b] 1 (7/12)[b]
Male parental	2 (2/6)[b] 1 (7/12)[b]
Male parental	1 (0/1)[b] 1 (2/6)[b] 1 (7/12)[b]

Notes: [a] Includes duplications.
　　　 [b] Distance in blocks from "Yard."
　　　 [c] State other than Louisiana.

second and third cousins are no more than a fifteen-minute walk away.[10] The resemblance to contemporary patterns in Lagos, Nigeria is striking (see Marris 1960: 124).

[10] It must also be noted that relatives who are comparatively far away from the "Yard" are, in fact, close to each other. The man in the parental generation of the "inner circle" who lives farthest away (seven blocks; see Table 1) lives only a block away from his mother's sister.

Table 7. Spatial distribution of living paternal first cousins of the Wesley "inner circle"[a]

Members of "inner circle"		Number of paternal first cousins	Residence In "Yard" or next door	Number of blocks distant				Outside New Orleans	
Category	Number			0-1	2-6	7-12	13+	In other La. city	Out of state
All persons:	7	14	0	0	2	1	2	4	1
Men	4	7	0	0	0	1	1	3	0
Women	3	14	0	0	2	0.	1	1	1
Grandparental generation:									
Total	1	7	0	0	1	0	0	0	1
Men	0	0	0	0	0	0	0	0	1
Women	1	7	0	0	1	0	0	0	0
Parental generation:									
Total	6	7	0	0	1	1	2	4	0
Men	4	7	0	0	0	1	1	3	0
Women	2	7	0	0	1	0	1	1	0

Note: [a] Figures may not add because of duplications.

These residential patterns generate complex matrices of multiple kin relationships. In particular, paternal aunts and uncles linked twelve members of the "inner circle" with outlying parts of New Orleans and other cities in Louisiana (Tables 3 and 4). Every member of the "inner circle" except "Mama" had living maternal first cousins, most of whom resided nearby; nearly a third, however, lived out of state (Tables 5 and 6). Only seven persons had known paternal first cousins; they, like the paternal aunts and uncles, lived in more distant parts of New Orleans or in other Louisiana cities (Tables 7 and 8). In general, these wider relationships are important as means of broadening the range of communications and consequent socioeconomic opportunities open to the Wesleys. They in turn are reflections of earlier migrations, especially by women marrying into the Wesley family and then moving with their husbands to the proximity of the "Yard."[11]

To summarize, a high level of organization, residential propinquity, and high interaction rates, especially among maternal kin, are characteristic of the Wesley families. These features reinforce each other and lend a sedentary and clannish nature to this extended family. These findings are consistent with many other studies. In his study of the Black extended amily of the Boston Roxbury sample area, Feigin (1968: 663–664) has suggested that the closer relatives live to one another, the more intensive the interaction; or conversely, perhaps, the more intensive the interaction, the greater the propinquity of residence. He found that the greatest intensity of contacts was for relatives living within one block of the respondents. Sharp and Axelrod (1956: 434) also contend, from a study of a tract in metropolitan Detroit, that family functioning is facilitated by residential propinquity. This too is the opinion of Sussman (1959: 335). Moreover, Marris (1960: 123–128) has demonstrated that the frequency of expressive behaviors declined in central Lagos after the breakup of the traditional Yoruba residential pattern.

KIN OBLIGATIONS AND INTERACTIONS

For an understanding of the Wesley family, it is important to illustrate the kinds of functional relationship that occur at various distances, in terms of both kinship links and propinquity. A way of determining, to

[11] For "The kindred of Viola Jackson," Stack (1970: 3) states that among ninety-six family members who left the South between 1916 and 1967, "Two major patterns emerge from their life-histories: (1) Relatives tend to cluster in the same areas during similar periods; and (2) the most frequent and consistent alignment and cooperation appears to take place between siblings."

Table 8. Spatial distribution of living paternal first cousins of the Wesley "inner circle": by member[a]

Member of "inner circle" by sex and generation	Number and residence of paternal first cousins
Female grandparental	None
Female grandparental	None
Female grandparental	None
Female grandparental	None
Female grandparental	None
Female grandparental	None
Female grandparental	6 (2/6)[b] 1 (other city)[c]
Female parental	None
Female parental	2 (2/6)[b] 1 (13+)[b]
Female parental	3 (other city)[c]
Male grandparental	None
Male parental	1 (7/12)[b] 2 (13+)[b] 1 (n.a.)[d]
Male parental	3 (other city)[c]
Male parental	3 (other city)[c]
Male parental	3 (other state)[d]

Notes: [a] Includes duplications.
[b] Distance in blocks from the "Yard."
[c] City in Louisiana other than New Orleans.
[d] Data not available.

some extent, these functional relationships is to compare ceremonial and social functions such as funerals and weddings with day-to-day affairs and with emergencies. Hurricane Betsy, 1965, is probably the major crisis that the family had to overcome and is the best example of an emergency affair among kin.

Attendance at Funerals

It is significant that the funeral or the wake *must* be attended by all close consanguineous kin (at least up to the fourth cousin), no matter what the physical distance might be. Those who do not attend are subject to criticisms, gossip, and ill feelings. One *should* attend either the funeral or the wake of a residentially close relative, but there are not the same criticisms, gossip, and ill feelings if one does not attend. The significance of kin and whether one considers the deceased to be kin can be largely established by attendance and the excuses used for missing the event.

About the only acceptable excuses are the adverse effect attendance would have on a person's health, or on the health of an unborn child. The children of the deceased must at least view the body, no matter what health they are in. Paradoxically, it is a source of concern and conversation among the family and friends as to what effect the death and attendance will have on the child. The implication for relatives also is that attendance usually results in some adverse effect.

Attendance at Weddings

There is no imperative for attendance at weddings or wedding receptions. There is neither gossip nor criticism nor ill feeling because of absence. Usually, though, one will find brothers and sisters and other relatives in the entourage. Generally speaking, residentially close relatives will almost always attend. Those relatives who live at some distance (another city or state) and attend are usually grandparents, "uncles," and first cousins. It must be remembered that many of the kin of the Wesleys live in the same city.

Day-to-Day Interactions

It is this fact also that governs everyday affairs in the Wesleys' "Yard." Since one's maternal kin live close by, day-to-day activities are significantly directed toward these kin. The most frequent social grouping — an everyday affair for some — is of those members who live in the "Yard," to about two blocks away. Since all of the elementary school children of the Wesley family go to school around the corner from the "Yard," they stop to visit, many mornings, with children of other Wesley households prior to going to school. They regroup in the same place every evening before going home. These children are the carriers of information for their parents, who may live at a distance or who cannot meet with their kin that day. Those who comprise the most frequent adult grouping are Wesley daughters, a son (who works with one of the roofers in the block, and is the exception to the two-block physical distance limit), sisters, aunts, first cousins, and their husbands; some would be second cousins. The children range up to third cousins. The next group in frequency is usually non-Wesley-related individuals who live in the same block as the "Yard." Their kinship is either past fourth cousin, fictitious, or affinal. Then would come the Wesleys who live farther than two blocks away. They would, likewise, have some of the same links as the most frequent group. Just as important as proximity, if not more so, is that the frequency of day-to-day contacts is related to "microextended" family links.

Interactions in Emergencies

Just as important as the day-to-day contacts is the functional relationship of kinship groups that occurs in emergencies. The flood from Hurricane Betsy in 1965 caused much damage to the homes of many of the relatives who lived in the area. Some of the Wesleys who were affected by the floods moved in with "Mama's" sister immediately after evacuation from the school. Others stayed with a non-Wesley household in the same block as the "Yard" that had upstairs accommodations, or else in other Wesley households. From these relatives, they received food, clothing, and, of course, shelter. When the water receded, these relatives aided in cleaning up and repairing damage to the houses. Those relatives who were the first to return aided the late returners in straightening up their homes. All who were affected by the flood acted as information retrievers for sources of assistance to the flood victims. Those who were the first to get assistance from the government served as orientation counselors, so that many of the bureaucratic procedures were eliminated for their kinsmen. Furthermore, the information retrieval system was used to determine where family members could most advantageously use their money to replace their destroyed household property. Those relatives who lived in another city brought food, clothing, and financial aid upon learning the whereabouts of their kin. They were not a significant part of the information retrieval system because of their unfamiliarity with New Orleans and its structure and did not learn of their kinsfolk's return home in time to aid in the task of cleaning up. But they did use their skills in helping to repair cars. Furthermore, they gave even more money to the victims than did relatives who lived in the city. In this emergency, overall, the role of paternal kin was thus exceptionally great. Their remoter physical distance had, in a sense, given them the capacity to respond to a grave crisis.

THE WESLEYS AND THEIR NEIGHBORHOOD

The Wesleys live in a section of New Orleans which, because of its high unemployment and crime rates, might be regarded as an area illustrative of D. P. Moynihan's hypothesis of Black social decomposition (Moynihan

1965a, b). An Elliot Liebow (1967) might write about Black street corner men in the Wesley neighborhood, or it might even be termed another *Soulside* (Hannerz 1969).

Just how the block, of which the "Yard" is a part, compares statistically to the city of New Orleans in general can tell us something about the neighborhood involved. Forty-five percent of the population of New Orleans is Black. The block is all Black as compared to 89.6 percent of its census tract; 34 percent of the total population of New Orleans is under eighteen years of age and 14 percent is sixty-two years of age and over. The block statistics show similar age characteristics, with 33 percent under eighteen years of age, and 15 percent sixty-two years of age and over.

Some 53 percent of the houses on the block are owner-occupied, compared to 51 percent for the New Orleans Standard Metropolitan Statistical Area. The average number of rooms for owner-occupied housing units in New Orleans is 5.7, as compared to 5.1 for the block. The average value for owner-occupied homes in New Orleans is 25,000 dollars which is almost twice as much as for the block, 13,000 dollars. In terms of average number of rooms (3.7), renters in the block, when compared to the city average (3.8), fared better than homeowners, relatively speaking. Yet the average contract rent is fifty-eight dollars for the block, as compared to seventy-seven dollars for the city. The lower contract rent for the block is more of a result of relatives renting from other kin; probably, also, because there are a few long-time neighbors in the renters' group. There are, also, in the block, four one-person households, four female-headed households, and two households with either roomers or boarders. There are no group quarters in the block.

Among the Wesleys and their relatives on the block, the men are engaged in various occupations. Some work as bakers, casketmakers, laborers, or roofers. There are two roofing companies in the same block as the "Yard," which are owned and run by Wesley relatives, with most of the workers being kinspeople. Usually, the men are full-time employees with steady jobs — although seasonal and other vicissitudes of employment lay them off work at times. In job placement, relatives serve as a source of information as well as of reference. Employment for women has generally been in domestic service. Quite often, the women have replaced one another at work when illness struck.

From the clannishness of the Wesleys, one should not conclude that this is an isolated group in conflict with the rest of the community. Many of the neighboring households are dwelt in by kin and in-laws — thirteen in the block of the "Yard" alone. Neighbors do not regularly attend smaller Wesley family functions, though they are always welcome (there are no invitations given at these times). At the larger and more important affairs, such as funerals and wakes, weddings and receptions, and baby showers, neighbors are always present. With so many relatives in the neighborhood it is quite easy for relatives and in-laws to outnumber neighbors and friends. Although the Wesleys form the core of *their* family group, the geographical and kinship networks in which they are embedded are much larger.

THE WESLEY FAMILY: A GENERAL MODEL

The nature of the Wesley family may perhaps best be summarized by a systematic comparison with Queen and Habenstein's formulation (1967: 329–330), which purports to give the basic features of the Black urban extended family. The Wesley data indicate that husband–wife rather than mother–daughter relationships are fundamental in households; males are significant in family activities; residence is strongly determined by preexisting kin domiciles rather than being neolocal; and extended Black families are not "compromises" but rather fundamental, autonomous, and highly functional institutions.

The contrasts between the views of Queen and Habenstein and those of this author are, in detail, as follows:

QUEEN AND HABENSTEIN MODEL

1. A modified extended family built around the mother–daughter relationship and usually extending through three generations is the modal form of organization for the adaptive family.

2. . . . when looking across the broadest continuous segment of the family life cycle, one finds in the adaptive family one or more married daughters, sharing with the mother under a common roof the responsibility for support and socialization of the children. The father, in such a family, occasionally present, often itinerant or permanently absent, plays the weakest or most incidental role of all the adult principals.

3. Residence, in the long run, tends to follow the neolocal-matrilocal pattern. Ideally, the first resi-

dence of the married couple will be outside the wife's mother's household but not necessarily far from it. Children have great freedom and are encouraged frequently to visit aunts, grandmothers, great grandmothers.

4. Kin-related households, from two to possibly a dozen, form communication and interpersonal relationship networks that reflect both consanguinity and affinality. Core social relations will be those of mother–daughter and sister–sister, but sisters-in-law and mothers-in-law may also be participating members of "knots" in the kin network. These networks seem to proliferate where neighborhoods have a larger percentage of single dwellings and where husbands and wives, or wives and children, attempt to set up and main-

tain independent households. Here we may have a compromise form of family, residentially nuclear, but caught up in a network of matrilineal

ties which can serve to provide support and sociability to members of the elementary family units (Queen and Habenstein 1967: 329–330).

WESLEY FAMILY MODEL

1. Husband–wife with or without children is the modal family and household in the Wesley family group.

2. There is only one family in which a mother and her daughter (with or without a spouse) and child live in the same household. The daughter lives with her spouse who is the only working member of the household. To say that either the couple or the mother is in command of the household would be far from the truth. The male also plays an important role in family activities.

3. Not necessarily so; for of the seven non-consanguineous members of the "family" interviewed, only two had parents living. One, a male, said that "the average time, a man will pull more to his wife's people." He does live closer to his wife's parents (in the same block) than he does to his own parents (in the next block); but it is only a matter of degree. The mother of the other member (a female) lives in another state; but she was raised by her mother's mother who lives two blocks away and has a great-grandmother in the next block. She lives approximately seven blocks away from her husband's parents. These same seven members also have nine of twenty-two siblings living within twelve blocks (with one female having two sisters living in the next block); have one maternal aunt living within six blocks (one male has three aunts and two uncles living more than thirteen blocks away but who live around the corner from each other); have two paternal uncles and one paternal aunt within twelve

blocks; have eight of forty-six paternal first cousins living within twelve blocks (twenty-one of the remaining kin are those of one male who migrated to New Orleans and three others are kin to a female — either in another city or another state); and one maternal first cousin living within six blocks. Yet, sixty of the ninety-nine relatives (60.6 percent) in the above kinship category, excluding parents, are living within the same city as they are. When the male migrant is excluded from the statistics along with his twenty-three relatives, 75 percent of their relatives live in the same city. It is significant to note that the majority of the twenty-three relatives of that male live residentially close to one another whether it be in their rural nonfarm hometown or in Alaska. So for the Wesleys and their spouses, and they seem fairly representative of some families in the neighborhood, there is a high interrelationship between propinquity and kinship as dimensions of an extended family system. Therefore children can also visit and live with uncles, grandfathers, and great-grandfathers.

4. These households based on consanguinity, affinality, and fictitious kin (bringing in more kin) are large geographically as well as numerically. There are thirteen in the block of the "Yard," four of whom were not counted in the statistics on either the "Wesleys" or their spouses. The core social relations will be those of the "microextended" family: parent(s)-children, between siblings, and branching out to the "macroextended" family. There is no sex

differentiation; and no male is excluded whether he is kin by "blood," law, or classification. There are very serious doubts, borne out by the facts of the paper, about this being a compromise form of family. It appears that, ideally, the interrelated autonomous, and residentially close households are quite desired and actively pursued by various family members.

NEW RESEARCH PROBLEMS AND PROCEDURAL CAUTIONS

This paper demonstrates that the study of the Black extended family is a significant area of potential research in the fields of history, sociology, and anthropology. Possible research problems seem unlimited at this time. For example, work on some aspects of extended family interrelationships on a comparative basis might solve currently puzzling questions on the U.S. Black family, specifically.

The study of residence and housing patterns would be a logical, if not necessary, place to begin. One can also ask whether or not the residence and housing patterns have historical continuity. If so, why? Or, why not? One will find that, perhaps, this is a rural adaptation to the city, or, possibly, a phenomenon resulting from the vicissitudes of city life. The morphological and interactional characteristics of kin networks can be influenced by these patterns. The influence of the continuity or discontinuity of residence and housing patterns on such characteristics may also prove significant. Whether or not housing and residence patterns are a rural adaptation to the city or an urban phenomenon unrelated to the rural way of life could prove to make a difference in the nature of the basic social rationales. At the very least, social scientists should seek to give careful contemporary and, if possible, historic accounts of these important variables.

Such a study would necessarily involve evaluation of the significance of kin alignments. One should seek to determine why families become matrifocal, patrifocal, nuclear family oriented, or what might be called "multifocal" extended kin networks. So far as possible such a study must hold constant — or evaluate the degree of covariance of — important social variables such as race, class, and ethnicity, as well as the geographical variables of regional, urban, and rural settings. To this one may add the social, geographical, occupational, and real-property mobility of the group studied.

The morphological and interactional characteristics of kin networks are also very significant. Not only, as mentioned above, for their interrelationships with residence and housing patterns; but, more importantly, as guides to how families and households become intertwined and why one side of the family, or some particular relative or relatives, may become more significant in certain aspects of these morphological and interactional characteristics. To give an example, why would one's mother's kin be called by first names or nicknames and have few kin titles such as "aunt" or "uncle" — although living nearer than one's father's kin? And why would one's father's kin be called by their names preceded by a kin title, and why "promote" many more of one's father's kin to the rank of "uncle" or "aunt"? Does it mean that more people of one's father's kin must act according to the title given? Or is it a way of reinforcing kin ties that are not close either consanguineously or geographically or both? Maybe the functions change. It could well be that the network is used very differently in these different contexts.

Another area of possible research could be an analysis of comparative household and size structure in all interrelated households. Do such factors have an influence on the morphological and interactional characteristics of the network as a whole? What is the interrelationship between household size and structure with residence and housing patterns? It could be that structural-functionalism is important when the entire network is understood and studied. It could be that certain households, because of their size and structure, may tend to be more extended family oriented. Yet, to add another variable, the phase in the life-cycle of the households may be just as important; may, in fact, determine both size and structure.

The study of the Black extended family thus brings in demographically significant variables; the demographic characteristics of a kin network are, in some ways, of even greater importance than the cultural. In the case of the Wesleys the distribution of this social group by age and sex affects both morphology and interactions.

Investigators should be aware of the inadequacy of structural-functional analysis alone. Since social structure is an obvious manifestation of man's way of life, it is often looked to for indications of functional dynamics, especially when comparisons show similarities of form. This direction can lead to serious misconceptions.

A study using structure alone as an indicator of stability, or, conversely, of change over time, may give one the relative numbers of nuclear, extended, and augmented households. But the underlying networks of households may be either invisible, or seemingly noninfluential, or misunderstood by the researcher. It is the complexity and multidimensional structure of residence patterns and functions in the Black family that make it a viable institution.

The inadequacy of structural-functional analysis becomes especially evident when both structure and function are complex and multidimensional. This study demonstrates that, generally, the extended family among Blacks, and that of the Wesleys in particular, has various functions. The rules recognized by an individual family member correspond, moreover, to the relative closeness of blood ties and to the mutual recognition of relationships, as well as to residential propinquity. Yet these variables alone do not, nor can they, explain fully what acts are expected, by other members, of a person within the network. These variables cannot give one a formula for the proper or characteristic action of some kin. Other factors such as appropriate occasions also enter in. Functionalism is complex because of this combination of interrelated variables.

In addition, similarity of form does not necessitate similarity of meaning. Though there is a general pattern in the Wesley family for godparents to be blood kin and a willingness to have godparents for all children, these godparents do not have much influence or status as godparents. This is generally true except with the *very* young. In some other cultures, godparents are significant individuals for the godchild until early adulthood and, sometimes, throughout life.

More broadly, this study demonstrates a similarity of structure between Black (Wesley) and White society in that families live in separate and autonomous households in both, but it also proves there is a difference in the meaning of kin networks. The study further shows that Wesley households may be autonomous at some levels but interdependent at others. And, though some structures may be similar, the emphasis that Blacks may place on an aspect of family life may be different from that among Whites. These differences in emphasis provide important contradictions to viewing Black family life as a deprived version of an idealized Anglo-American model. Many Blacks, if all circumstances permitted, would want a nuclear family living in a separate household, but the interrelationship and residential propinquity of these nuclear households in a larger system is also considered a desirable situation.

Finally, warning must be given of biases in much writing about Black society. Some social scientists saturate their studies with political inferences. Some would like to entertain the idea that the trouble with Black America is its pathological family system: that unemployment, crime, delinquency, and other middle-class misconceptions about Black family life are products of its very existence. They look for and are disgusted to find a lack of the values and views of the "macrostructure" of the White society. For when they look at the structure of the Black family, they seek fault. When they find no fault with the structure, then they oppose the very meaning of Black lifeways.

In the same vein, many White researchers believe that Blacks are historically, passive *creatures*. Blacks do not make history; but, history makes Negroes. They *adapt*, but they do not *invent;* they *respond to* but do not *control* their environments. Further comment is not needed.

In summary, this paper demonstrates that the study of the extended family of Black people is a move in the right direction in historical, sociological, and anthropological research. It raises critical questions and offers theoretical and conceptual frameworks that research on the Black family should answer. Overall, structural-functional analysis is inadequate, but it should be pursued because it offers potential solutions for dealing with the multiple variables that exist within the Black community.

The study of the Black extended family encompasses both residence and housing patterns. These patterns and the process of locating houses for kin are definite characteristics of the extended family. Such studies would be likely to demonstrate, as this paper did with the Wesleys, that geographical and real-property mobility determine, to some extent, the matrifocality or patrifocality of a kin network and other morphological and interactional characteristics.

Once we know more about the nature and experience of the Black extended family, then, in the opinion of the author, the best possible research involving the Black family can be done: that is, a comparative study of Black American and African family systems. One must look to Africa, the Caribbean, and Central America to determine just what the Black cultural heritage is and what adaptations are more African than European or American Indian. One can and must find out what is southern (peculiar to Blacks and Whites of that region) and what is distinctively Black American, Caribbean, or African. Maybe, then — or concurrently — the historical developments and trends that have shaped many aspects of Black family life can be seen more clearly.

REFERENCES

BILLINGSLEY, ANDREW
    1968 *Black families in White America.* Englewood Cliffs, N.J.: Prentice-Hall.
CASTILLO, GELIA J., ABRAHAM M. WEISBLAT, FELICIDAD R. VILLAREAL
    1968 The concepts of nuclear and extended family: an exploration of empirical referents. *International Journal of Comparative Sociology* 9 (March): 15–16.

CLIGNET, RÉMI
   1970   *Many wives, many powers: authority and power in polygynous families.*
          Evanston, Ill.: Northwestern University Press.
DOTSON, FLOYD
   1951   Patterns of voluntary association among urban working-class families.
          American Sociological Review 16 (October): 687–693.
FEIGIN, JOE R.
   1968   The kinship ties of Negro urbanites. *Social Science Quarterly* 69:
          660–665.
FRAZIER, E. FRANKLIN
   1932   *The Negro family in Chicago.* Chicago: University of Chicago
          Press.
   1937   The impact of urban civilization upon Negro family life. *American
          Sociological Review* 2: 609–618.
   1966 [1939]   *The Negro family in the United States* (revised edition). Chicago:
          University of Chicago Press.
HANNERZ, ULF
   1969   *Soulside: inquiries into ghetto culture and community.* New York:
          Columbia University Press.
HERSKOVITS, M. J.
   1941   *The myth of the Negro past.* New York: Harper and Row.
JOHNSON, CHARLES S.
   1934   *The shadow of the plantation.* Chicago: University of Chicago
          Press.
LIEBOW, ELLIOT
   1967   *Tally's corner: a study of Negro street-corner men.* Boston: Little,
          Brown.
MARRIS, PETER
   1960   Slum clearance and family life in Lagos. *Human Organization* 19
          (Fall): 123–128.
MITCHELL, J. CLYDE
   1969   "The concept and use of social networks," in *Social networks in urban
          situations.* Edited by J. Clyde Mitchell, 12–29. Manchester, England:
          University of Manchester Press.
MOYNIHAN, DANIEL P.
   1965a   *The Negro family: the case for national action.* Washington, D.C.:
          U.S. Government Printing Office.
   1965b   Employment, income, and the ordeal of the Negro family. *Daedalus*
          94: 745–770.
PARSONS, TALCOTT
   1959   "The social structure of the family," in *The family: its function and
          destiny* (revised edition). Edited by Ruth N. Anshen, 241–274. New
          York: Harper. (Originally published 1949.)
POWDERMAKER, HORTENSE
   1939   *After freedom: a cultural study of the deep South.* New York: Viking
          Press.
QUEEN, STUART A., ROBERT W. HABENSTEIN
   1967   *The family in various cultures* (third edition). Philadelphia:
          Lippincott.

SHARP, HARRY, MORRIS AXELROD
  1956 "Mutual aid among relatives in an urban population," in *Principles of sociology*. Edited by Ronald Freedman et al., 433–439. New York: Holt, Rinehart and Winston.
SMITH, RAYMOND T.
  1956 *The Negro family in British Guiana. Family structure and social status in the village*. London: Routledge and Kegan Paul (in association with the Institute of Social and Economic Research, University College of the West Indies, Jamaica).
STACK, CAROL B.
  1970 "The kindred of Viola Jackson: residence and family organization of an urban Black American family," in *Afro-American anthropology; contemporary perspectives*. Edited by Norman E. Whitten, Jr., and John F. Szwed, 303–312. New York: Free Press. (Appeared originally 1969 in *Some views on Blacks and Black communities* (mimeographed). Edited by Susan H. S. Lorenzi, 1–11. University of Illinois, Urbana.)
SUSSMAN, MARVIN B.
  1959 The isolated nuclear family: fact or fiction. *Social Problems* 6 (Spring): 333–339.
YOUNG, VIRGINIA H.
  1970 Family and childhood in a southern Negro community. *American Anthropologist* 72 (April): 269–288.

Kinship and Friendship in Black Los Angeles: A Study of Migrants from Texas

KIYOTAKA AOYAGI

ABSTRACT

This paper describes five families who migrated from Texas to Los Angeles. "The home-town of the five families" presents the material necessary for understanding how a Black community in a small southern town differs from one in Los Angeles. With this knowledge in mind, I will proceed to the analysis of the migrants themselves from three viewpoints: on the background of their hometown, in the process of migration, and in the new environment. I will focus, first, on their interaction with their relatives in "The five families and their relatives"; second, on their interaction with fellow migrants from the same town in "The 'Middville' Club and its members"; and third, on their interaction with neighbors and friends in "Neighbors and friends of the five families in Los Angeles."

Migration involves a two-fold question; first, how and why do the migrants seek to maintain a relationship with their hometown? second, how do they adapt themselves to the new environment? Each of the sections has a bearing on these questions. In the last section, I will discuss the role of family and kinship as the basis for the Black way of life in urban living.

INTRODUCTION

This report focuses on the processes of urban adaptation among Black migrants to the city of Los Angeles and to other localities in Los Angeles County and its environs. The migrants, originating in a group of counties of northeast Texas — Harrison, Panola, Shelby, San Augustine, Nacogdoches and Smith — have also resided in a considerable number of other

First, I should like to acknowledge with gratitude the assistance of the American Council of Learned Societies in making possible my fieldwork in the United States in 1969 and 1970. Thanks also are due to Professor Philip Newman, then chairman of the Department of Anthropology, University of California at Los Angeles, who provided

places (Map 1). However, the field research on which this study is based was carried out in the city of Los Angeles, and in the migrants' primary hometown in Texas, given the pseudonym of "Middville" in "Toledo" County. This study describes, in particular, the nature of the relationships

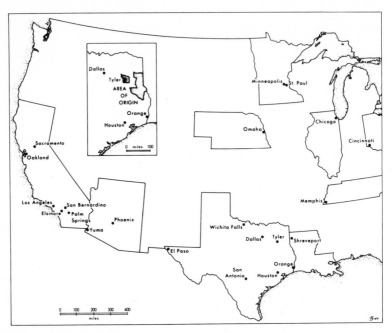

Map 1.   The five families: area of origin and urban destinations

the necessary facilities for my research project. To Reverend and Mrs. J. Sakakibara, Mr. and Mrs. Harry Ozawa, Reverend K. Sasaki, Reverend Herbersham, Mr. and Mrs. M. Honda, Mr. and Mrs. W. Morton, a special word of thanks is due for introductions and information facilitating my entry into fieldwork in Los Angeles. I regret that I can repay the members of the five families and some of their relatives only with the briefest acknowledgement, since without their patient cooperation and invaluable information, I would not have been able to write this report. Among my informants, I am particularly indebted to Mr. Alex Smith and Mrs. Helen Smith; Mrs. Mary Davis; Mr. C. D. Adams and Mrs. Valencia Adams; Mr. Joe Kennedy and Mrs. Jean Kennedy; Mr. J. Himes and Mrs. Eva Himes; and Mr. M. W. and Mrs. E. W., to use the pseudonyms mandatory for my paper. I am deeply indebted to Miss Yukie Ando, who spared time from her busy schedule to type the paper, and also to Mrs. Yuko Kobayashi, who corrected my English as a special favor at the last moment. Finally, I am also very grateful to the Department of Urban Affairs, which introduced me to the Model Cities Neighborhood Center in Compton; to Professor Viscount Nelson of the History Department who gave me useful suggestions; and to Mrs. Shirly L. Ross at the South Central Office of the Los Angeles County Department of Adoptions, who gave me the opportunity to learn of the problems involved in adoptions.

of the Black migrants with their kin and fictive kin, friends, and neighbors as a factor in urban adaptation processes. Emphasis has been placed upon careful reporting of life histories, sentiments, and relationships.[1]

A substantial segment of the southern Black population has been involved in migration to the West, particularly to California. The Black population of the city of Los Angeles increased from 1.5 percent (absolute number, 66) in 1860, to 17.9 percent (503,606 persons) in 1970, with an especially noticeable rise during the Second World War (de Graaf 1962: 262).

The first visible Black community appeared in Los Angeles sometime before World War I. It resembled "Mudtown" in the deep South (Bullock 1969: 12). At the present time, there are at least two major Black areas: one is in south-central Los Angeles, a vast area which is predominantly Black (and includes the Watts section); the other, Baldwin Hills, some distance from the south-central section, is rapidly becoming a Black area, although it was formerly regarded as an upper-class residential area. There are mixed communities between the two major areas.

Urban Adaptation and Kinship Ties

The relationship of Black migrants with their hometowns in the South has not yet been fully explored and remains obscure. This may be partially explained by the fact that Black migration in the United States generally has surged in successive waves on a massive scale. There have been studies of migration trends and patterns and studies of individual experiences underlying these patterns. Woodson (1918), Ross and Kennedy (1934), Florant (1942: 782–791), Myrdal (1944: 182–201), Shimkin (1971), and others have provided us with facts and theoretical issues of Black migration. Like many studies on Black migration, e.g. those by Woofter (1930), Kiser (1932), and Shimkin, Louie, and Frate (this volume), the present paper deals with the important theoretical relationship between migration and kinship. Besides studies of Black migration per se, a wide range of literature on Black people in the United States, from sociological studies to autobiography, also contains data on migration.

Many of the studies undertaken in both the South and the North tend to confine their descriptions to a certain locality. Yet some of them contain data useful for my specific concern, i.e. the relationship between the

---

[1] I should like to present the data ethnographically, that is, without theorizing too much. This ethnographic presentation will have the merit of providing good bases for discussion and for comparison with studies in other cities.

urbanites and their point of origin in the South: for example, recent studies of ghetto life in Washington, D.C., such as *Tally's corner* (Liebow 1967)[2] and *Soulside* (Hannerz 1969).[3]

The migrants come into an environment of different geographical as well as social arrangements, and migration creates new situations in friendships, fictive kinships, and kin relationships. This study, therefore, attempts to answer such questions as, do the migrants try to find home-towners as their friends in a new environment? If so, for what purpose? What happens to the status and role of a fictive kinsman whose "daughter" goes to live in a big city?[4] In what sense does she leave her natural family, and what ties are developed by her in newer kinship obligations? How much does distance affect kinship ties? What types of kin relationship are likely to be created and maintained in the new situation?

Understanding the impact of migration upon kinship relations should give us a clue to the nature of kinship, and such knowledge is crucial to our understanding of what is happening to Blacks in Los Angeles. In the value orientation of the migrants we have noted some elements of continuity and discontinuity that require further analyses. It is clear, however, that the Blacks' westward migration has been motivated by the desire for better economic opportunities and higher living standards or the wish to get away from the South or from their families. Some of their expectations have been unrealistic and have led to disappointment, but it is, after all, inevitable that such drastic changes should result in isolation, stress, and pain. It appears that the kin relationships, in particular, suffer from a high level of stress in migration.

[2] When Liebow (1967: 74, 75, 77) discusses the father–child relationship he often refers to a father visiting a child "back home" in the South and, in doing so, depicts aspects of the relationship between the urban dwellers and their relatives in the South, His explanation of patterns of man–woman and parent–child relationships could be more fully appreciated if the historical as well as the institutional background of the patterns had been taken into consideration.

[3] Hannerz (1969: 144–150), in his discussion of Soul — concept and content — mentions, in detail, southern heritage and Black experience in the South as essential elements of Soul. He seems to say that an understanding of southern background is indispensable to the better analysis of the behavior of city dwellers in the North:

Thus there is a "home country" not too many generations back, and ghetto dwellers recognize that they are still marked by it in many ways. They know that they are not only Black people surrounded by Whites but also southerners in a northern city. . . . From a southern background the ghetto dwellers have also derived one of the domains of most intense soul symbolism.

[4] Joyce Aschenbrenner (1971) describes the institution of "play-kin" relationships among her informants in Chicago as a cultural transplantation from the South. She makes an important contribution in describing this hitherto relatively unknown institution.

The Five Families: Genesis and Duration of Fieldwork

To explore these issues, the basic data were collected from the five families whose kin relationships (both consanguineous and fictive), friendships, and ties with their Texas hometown are described in this paper.[5] All the spouses of these families, except three husbands, came to Los Angeles directly or indirectly from a small city in upper East Texas, on the Louisiana border. They were mostly wartime migrants attracted by the defense industries in California; most arrived between 1940 and 1945.

I first met the five families in mid-December, 1969, and was in constant contact with them until mid-July, 1970. Then I went to their hometown in Texas for a month to meet their relatives.

A Definition of Adaptation

At this point, a definition of "adaptation" should be given. The migrant must find a job and living quarters, participate in churches and other institutions, and generally attempt to find "partners" of various kinds in the new environment. But in order to do these things, he cannot ignore his previous experiences, his knowledge of "what he has had." His kin ties in his hometown constitute one element of "what he has" as long as he maintains meaningful contact with them. He spends time and energy in maintaining these contacts which may significantly shape his life. One relative in the hometown may be more important than many cousins and aunts in the new setting, and the migrant may return to his hometown, even at a sacrifice. Essentially, therefore, the definition of adaptation has to do with the relationships the migrant has brought with him from his previous environment to his new situation. To use a biological analogy, I might define adaptation as the ability to tolerate selective forces in the environment in order to master environmental problems by developing effective structure, behavior, and forms of social organization.

---

[5] Fifty families were interviewed between March, 1970, and June of the same year in order to make comparisons with the five families. Most of these fifty families were living in Watts at the time of this survey. A questionnaire was used. I hope to present some of the findings from the fifty families as comparative data for discussion in the near future.

Arrangement of the Data on the Five Families

I shall arrange the data obtained on the five families as follows:

THE HOMETOWN OF THE FIVE FAMILIES. This section deals with the history of the Black community in "Middville," East Texas, based on genealogical records of pioneering Black families, as well as on the records of three Black churches. It also describes institutional arrangements and actual race relations. This general background on the hometown is indispensable for measuring the sociological distances the migrants have travelled.

THE FIVE FAMILIES AND THEIR RELATIVES. This section presents the family genealogies and the extensions of kinship among the five families. The extensions of kinship are substantiated by observation of the interactions of lineal or collateral relatives with the five families. At the same time, the nature of these interactions will be examined.

THE "MIDDVILLE" CLUB AND ITS MEMBERS. This section describes how the "Middville" Club was started, its character as revealed by an analysis of its main activities, and the relationship between the club and the five families.

FICTIVE KINFOLK AND FOSTERAGE OF NONKINFOLK. This section contains a discussion of the role of fictive kin, or "play relatives," as well as some examples of non kin fosterage among the five families.

NEIGHBORS AND FRIENDS OF THE FIVE FAMILIES IN LOS ANGELES. This section describes the geographical boundaries of each of the five families' neighborhoods, neighborhood relationships, and activities. It tries to show among whom and where the families have found their friends and the kinds of friendships made, and finally it evaluates the relative importance of the "Middville" Club compared with neighborhood relationships and friends.

SUMMARY. This section summarizes data on ties maintained by the five families with their relatives in both "Middville" and Los Angeles, as well as in other towns and cities in Texas and California. The extent of genealogical knowledge, family interaction, the persistence of fictive kinship, friendships with persons outside the "Middville" circle, and the role of the "Middville" Club are also summarized. The existence of other, similar, clubs in Los Angeles is touched upon. Finally, the implications, both positive and negative, for the future of the younger generation of the five families are considered.

THE STATISTICAL APPENDIX should be consulted for tabulations of the kinfolk and residences of the five families (Tables 1.1–1.5), *de facto* lines of descent (Figures 1.1–1.5), the components of family structure of the five families as an aggregate (Tables 2.1–2.6), and household composition in Texas and California, 1970 (Table 3).

THE HOMETOWN OF THE FIVE FAMILIES

"Middville" is located in the southeastern section of a small city of eastern Texas. The city itself is a county seat, with a population of a little over 5,000, 25 percent Black. In the midst of the square are the County Court House, District Clerk's Office, School Superintendent's Office, Welfare Office, library, and volunteer fire department. The grass-covered square surrounding these public buildings serves as an informal gathering place for townspeople, and also as a flat stand for a family or two, when they wish to sell their secondhand clothes and utensils. Cars flow into the square from all directions and circle it until they pull into the parking spaces just off the grass. On hot summer days a farmer may drive his truck in to sell farm produce such as watermelons.

"Middville" has two banks, a supermarket, a hardware store, a movie theater, a post office, a laundry, and several other stores for daily necessities. Prominent are automobile agencies, where Honda motor bicycles are neatly placed on display. The stores and business establishments are owned, without exception, by Whites. There are two newspaper offices and one local radio station; everyone follows local affairs closely. In the past, five papers used to serve this area, but at present only two remain in business, one of which has the longest history of any of the "Middville" papers, with its first edition going back as far as 1877. Beyond the square there continues, for about one-tenth of a mile, a line of stores of various kinds, including a spacious coin laundry. One is glaringly reminded that the laundry is for Whites only by the notice on the wall which reads: "We reserve the right to serve the White race...." Actually no Blacks dare to try it; they use either the Wash-Teria or the A.H. Wash-a-time in their own community.

The Black community is referred to as the "colored quarter" by some Whites. Passing an old cotton gin, one turns off the main road to get into the Black community. Crossing the Santa Fe railroad siding, one sees a

White cemetery on the left and houses on the right. The Wash-Teria, a barbershop, a cafe, a small filling station, and a supermarket form a little "square" exclusively for Blacks.

There are four churches: Mt. Zion Christian Methodist Episcopal Church, St. Paul Baptist Church, Bright Morning Star Baptist Church, and Church of God in Christ, the last of which attracts only a small congregation. In addition to these churches, other public or semipublic buildings include the Community Center, the Youth Club, and a mortuary. The private residences along the main road of the community look fairly nice; at least four of these houses are owned by a White and leased to Blacks, while others are owned by Blacks who lease them to Blacks. Here and there one will note houses left vacant by owners who have gone to Dallas or other large cities in Texas, or to the West.

Quite separate, and diagonally away from this community, there is a row of shacks occupied by Blacks; it is located in the northwestern corner of the city and is more secluded than the main body of the Black community.

In the White community one finds a keen interest in local history and family genealogy. For instance, there is a local historical club for Whites. One of its influential members has published records of hangings and marriages and a list of the deceased (White) residents since 1836. Some of the prominent White families have produced typewritten genealogical records while others have been preparing manuscripts. The newspapers share an interest in the genealogies of the prominent families by giving ample space to their backgrounds, especially if they are connected with local history. Among Blacks, there is no such interest in keeping family genealogies on record. The church records are the only common property available to them in connection with their community history. The African Methodist Episcopal Church, the predecessor of the Mt. Zion Christian Methodist Episcopal Church, was the first Black church organized in the city, but the year of its founding is not known. It moved from its first location, one and a half miles south of "Middville" to half a mile northeast of the city. Its present location is one mile southeast of the square. Att, Mary Davis' mother's father (see Appendix, Table 1.2), donated the land for the building of this church at its present site. St. Paul Baptist Church was the next church to come into being; its first site was in another town, about two miles west of the city. It moved from there to the northwest and then to the present site in the southeast. The Bright Morning Star Baptist Church was founded in 1908, by a pastor from another city in the same region. It was rebuilt in 1953. While it was being reconstructed, its members worshiped at the Church of God in Christ, the fourth church which was founded for Black residents. The Bright Morning Star Baptist Church does not seem to have moved as the others did; however, the fact that it had twenty pastors between 1908 and 1964 may have lessened the possibility of leaving an accurate official record.

A lodge to serve the Masons who had moved here was officially constituted by the District Deputy Grand Master in July, 1869. Its counterpart in the Black community began in 1945; it was organized by W. Hicks, the mortician, who acts as a Worshipful Master and offers his hall for meetings. There were seventy-two members in the beginning, but there are only fifty-six at present. The Heroines of Jericho, a women's auxiliary of Masonry, has a longer history, with its official opening dating back to 1923. At present it has eighteen members.[6] The Odessa Court of Caranthe has thirty-two members. The members gather on the first and third Friday of each month in the church cafeteria. The Knights of Pythias, a men's club, had sixty members about forty-five years ago, and used to have the annual sermon day on the fourth Sunday of March at Hick's Mortuary Hall; now it has only two members. W. Hicks said: "They don't want to be tied down nowadays." These clubs have emphasized either brotherhood and sisterhood, friendship, or good morals, institutional values which must have been cherished by people in this community, but it seems that their influence has been dwindling. The Lion's Club and a few other organizations which exist among Whites are not found in the Black community.

Educational institutions have been desegregated, while churches and fraternal organizations are separate and are tied in with each of the racial communities. There is a school in the Black community which was called C. H. Daniel High School. It was the school which the members of the five families found especially memorable and to which they made particular reference when they talked about their hometown. Originally a first to twelfth grade school, it was named after the principal, who died in 1950. Influenced by Daniel, R. H. Long became a teacher and later succeeded him as principal. The school's original buildings, built in 1928, 1950, and 1952, have been dismantled in recent years and new ones erected. In September, 1967, it was decided that Negroes from the ninth through the twelfth grade were to be integrated into White schools. Prior to the decision, a small group of White demonstrators marched in the square against integration, but open antagonism did not seem to continue long. Daniel High remained a first to eighth grade school until 1970, when it was changed into a junior high school for the seventh and eighth grades

---

[6] To become a member of this society one has to be of good moral character and have a male relative (brother, husband, or father) who is a member.

under the new name of "Middville" Junior High School. White students are daily bused to this Junior High in the Black community. Elementary, intermediate, and high school levels are all integrated. The Junior High School has 400 students, 70 percent of whom are White, and nine of the thirteen teachers are White. Another major change was the replacement of R. H. Long by a White principal in September, 1968; Long was made a counsellor. The move prompted Mary Davis to remark that his was a "jacket man's" job brought about by integration.

Higher education for the people in this general area is provided by Prairie View A & M College in Prairie View (northwest of Houston); Butler College in Tylor; Wiley College in Marshall (Harrison County); and a few other institutions (see Map 1). Prairie View started as a teacher training college, one of the seventeen Negro land grant colleges of the United States:

It was found in 1923 that 34 percent of the Negro teachers of the state were graduates at Prairie View. . . . [But the college later] has gone about so far toward the extreme in industrial education as the private Negro colleges have gone in cultural education . . . that the Texas Legislature has considered Prairie View as a branch of the Agricultural and Mechanical college is shown in the legislative enactment of 1915 (Davis 1934: 123, 124, 129).

Principal C. H. Daniel's three daughters went to Prairie View. Annie Reed went there with two of them. Jean Kennedy (see Appendix, Table 1.5) was one of the thirteen students who went to Prairie View in the same year. Mary Davis is also a graduate. Annie and Mary work as teachers, and Jean is an employee of the Los Angeles Post Office. It was with the encouragement of C. H. Daniel that they sought higher education. Mary was a teacher at Daniel High before she came to Los Angeles; Annie is teaching at "Middville" High School. Thus, this community has been receiving intellectual inflow from these schools.

The East "Middville" Community Club and the Youth Club are two of the self-help organizations which have appeared in recent years. The Community Club, with the vigorous support of the barber's wife, Ara Mae, now has forty members and works primarily toward improving general living conditions in areas such as health and sewage. The Youth Club, the brain child of J. W. Lee, a teacher at "Middville" Junior High School, was organized in 1969, with the aim of promoting an anti-delinquency program. One of Lee's major projects was to provide the young people with a place where they could meet socially on Saturdays and Sundays.

Five miles north of this community, there is a stretched-out community called "Africa Community." Most of the houses face a long, narrow, dusty, meandering street. Bushy cattle fields and woods provide most of the scenery in the far distance. C. D. Adams thinks that the designation "Africa Community" must have come from the fact that Blacks have lived there. Each of the thirty-two families in the community holds from ten to twenty acres of land. There are farmers, cattle raisers, a few teachers, and workers for local plywood companies and for poultry processing plants.[7] There are neither stores nor eating places. St. John Baptist Church, the only church in this community, has, according to its present pastor, about seventy members. There have been no records and minutes kept in the church, but an account book for successive years has been kept by one of the church members. According to some old settlers in the Black community of "Middville" there has been population movement between the two communities, particularly from the "Africa Community" to the Black community within the city; the indication is that the former has a longer history than the latter.

According to ninety-seven-year-old Agatha Osby, the oldest living authority on the historical background of the Black community, the Jennings, Richards, and Nobles are among the older families in "Middville." Their names appear as street names in the area. The pioneering families came to settle in this community in two ways. The ancestors of the Richards, Nobles, and Adamses had first settled in the "Africa Community" or its neighboring area and then moved into the present community. The other families, like the ancestors of Agatha Osby, came via communities other than the "Africa Community." Some of the earlier settlers purchased land from Whites or exchanged their land for that owned by Whites. Such land transactions laid the basis for the present community. The boundary of the developing community finally reached to the cemetery for Whites.

"Middville" is demographically and sociologically a biracial society; the population is dichotomous between Blacks and Whites, with residential segregation, different institutional arrangements, and different socioeconomic status according to race. The "Middville" Black community is to a large extent dependent on the White sector for commercial supply, job opportunities, banking, mass communications, and bureaucratic leadership. "Africa Community," less self-sufficient than the "Middville"

---

[7] After World War II, farmers in this region began to raise broilers commercially; today, the region is said to be the largest poultry-producing area in Texas. The production of cotton has declined. Using the by-products of the poultry industry, the farmers have improved the soil to establish pasture grasses, and today large herds of beef cattle graze where cotton and corn once grew. "Middville" is also located in the heart of the East Texas pine belt and is the site of sawmills and two plywood plants.

Black community, is not only dependent on the White sector for the same reasons, but also on the "Middville" Black Community for educational and certain community services, since there is only one church and no school. The "Middville" Black community is strategically better located than "Africa Community" for finding economic opportunities in the White sector; this has apparently encouraged part of the labor force of the "Africa Community" to move into the "Middville" Black community. There is also regular visiting between the "Africa Community" and the "Middville" Black community. Some "Middville" Blacks own part of the farmland, and some belong to the church in the "Africa Community."

THE FIVE FAMILIES AND THEIR RELATIVES

During my preliminary research, I was trying to find a small number of people with a relatively homogeneous southern background who would suit my purpose of studying "migration and kinship." One of my hypotheses was that Black urban culture could not be fully understood without taking into consideration the southern Black way of life. My strong assumption was that there would be social and cultural continuities on family and kinship levels among the southern Blacks who came and settled in Los Angeles.

After three months of the preliminary survey, I became acquainted with Lisa, first daughter of one of the five families, at the University of California at Los Angeles. She introduced me to her parents, who informed me of the existence of their hometown club and, in turn, introduced me to the other family members that belonged to the club. They were the *Smith, Davis, Adams, Miller,* and *Kennedy* families. Those who came from the "Middville" Black community were Helen Smith, Mary Davis, Valencia Adams, Sunny Miller, and Joe and Jean Kennedy. C. D. Adams was born in the "Africa Community." Alex Smith (Helen's husband) came from San Antonio, Texas; Charles Davis (Mary's husband) from Troupe [Smith County], Texas; and Richard Miller (Sunny's husband) from Marshall [Harrison County], Texas.

Family Rosters and Basic Statistical Data

In the appendix to this paper, which has been compiled from my data by Mr. Charles Williams, Jr. (see biographical notes), Tables 1.1 to 1.5 give, for each family, the roster of all recorded members. This roster identifies individuals by generation; patriline of descent; index number; name (where known); sex; race; status in 1970; relationships including parents, siblings, spouse (consensual or formal, continuing, divorced, separated), and offspring; and household affiliations in 1970.

Appendix Figures 1.1 to 1.5 graph the *de facto* lines of descent as indicated by the governing types of marriages — formal or consensual — and show considerable differences between the Smith, Davis, Adams, Miller, and Kennedy families over an extensive period of time. In the Smith family, consensual relationships in generations I through III were replaced by a predominance of formal relationships in generations IV through VI. Even more noticeable is the degree to which lines of descent have been truncated. Only one descent line reaches generation VII. In contrast, the Davis family has a continuous, strictly formal line of descent with only one divorce (generation IV); it is in essence patrilineal. The Adams family's chart resembles the Smiths', with both formal and consensual relationships, and in the truncation of branches. Its main line of descent is characterized by a distinctly formal set of relationships. In the Miller family figure, the distinctive features are an adoption in generation VI and truncation otherwise. The Kennedy family reflects a predominance of patrilineal descent, even though two consensual relations in generations I and II add a small degree of *de facto* matrilineal descent. Note the short-lived lines of descent between K16 and K42 (generations II to III) and between M19 and M46 (generations III to IV).

Tables 2.1 to 2.6 present basic statistics, first on the five families as an aggregate and then for each separately. The aggregate data present some points of interest. The sex of 402 out of more than 461 persons in the five families can be determined. It should be noted that males predominate in every generation, the overall sex ratio being 109 to 100, which indicates that these rosters are rather more complete than the usual census data, in which Black men are severely underenumerated. The pattern of marriages shows a sharp shift over time: in the first three generations, more than a third of the marriages were consensual. In generations IV, V and VI, this proportion drops to 6 percent. Again, while every recorded woman in the first three generations appears to have had at least one marriage, formal or consensual, the ratio for generations IV and V drops to less than 90 percent, and to less than 25 percent in the young sixth generation. For all marital relations, the proportion of divorces and separations, 16 percent, is quite low.

The life expectancies of the members of the five families have been low. By 1970, 30 percent, including all but one person in the first two genera-

Table 1. Biographical characteristics of focal persons in the five-family study

Name		Roster number[a]	Year of birth	Birthplace	Year of arrival in Los Angeles	Occupation[b]
Last	First					
Smith	Alex	J 46	1900	San Antonio (Texas)	1919	(Employee, Mobil Oil Co.)
	Helen	D 42	1910	"Middville"	1943	Domestic worker
Davis	Charles[c]	S 29	1897	Troupe (Texas)	1943	(Employee, Super Grate Open Flooring & Steel Co.)
	Mary	D 28	1907	"Middville"	1945	Head Start teacher
Adams	C. D.	N 40	1900	"Africa Community"	1935–6	(Employee, Union Pacific Railroad)
	Valencia	G 39	1901	"Middville"	1945	(Employee, Thrifty)
Miller	Richard	R 42	1896	Marshall (Texas)	1943–4	Junk collector
	Sunny	E 36	1906	"Middville"	1947	Domestic worker
Kennedy	Joe	O 49	1909	"Middville"	1941	Temporarily retired (employee, Continental Can Co.)
	Jean	E 50	1910	"Middville"	1943	Post office clerk

Notes: [a] Appendix, Tables 1.1 to 1.5. Roman numerals (generation markers) omitted above.
[b] Occupational descriptions in parentheses are former major jobs.
[c] Deceased, 1959.

tions, had died. Fertility has also been low, the offspring per woman rising from 1.8 in generation I (certainly, an incomplete figure), to 2.4 in II, and 2.5 in III. Then this average fell to 1.4 in IV, 1.1 in V, and 0.4 in VI. In other words, the families have not been replacing themselves, beginning with generation IV.

At the same time, the passing of generations has widened the span of relationships. In fact, by the sixth generation, second-cousin relations predominated over first cousin sets and even sibling sets: twenty-five, seventeen, and twenty-one, respectively; there were also fifteen sets of third cousins.

Table 3 summarizes information on twenty-one households in Texas and forty-eight households in California on which information as of 1970 is available; the data are for the five families as an aggregate. In Texas, husband–wife families predominate more decidedly than in California (58 percent). Conversely, the proportion of single-person households is even higher in California (29 percent) than in Texas (19 percent). This fact contributes to the small average size of households in both areas; however, even the largest types of households — couples with children (nuclear families) — average only 4.33 persons in Texas and 3.94 persons in California. In both areas, only 10 percent of the households are women-headed.

Focal Persons and Their Characteristics

The analysis of the five families rests upon a base plane — five married couples, one from generation IV of each family. Table 1 gives the key biographical characteristics of these ten focal persons. It should be noted that one of them, Charles Davis, died in 1959. It should also be noted that seven of this group — both Smiths, Mary Davis, both Adamses, and both Kennedys — are active or inactive members of the "Middville Club," an important integrating organization of the five families. Finally, it should be stressed that, while all ten of the focal persons are native Black Texans, and all the women are natives of "Middville," only one man is a native of this locality, and only one other is from the allied "Africa Community."

The Smith Family (Appendix, Table 1.1)

Lucindy, Helen Smith's maternal great-grandmother, was taken to Cincinnati, Ohio, by her owner, Mr. Moor, but she came back to Texas after his death. She had four children by him. One of them was Ealla, Helen's grandmother. Lucindy had two children by a Black man before she was taken to Cincinnati. Lucindy, who was half Cherokee Indian and had red skin, died at the age of seventy-seven or -eight. Ealla, Lucindy's daughter, had, in turn, two daughters by a White man, John Morrison. After Morrison died, Ealla married Arthur and had five children. Helen knows three of them. Ealla was born in Cincinnati and died at the age of twenty-five. Then Mandy, Helen Smith's grandmother on her father's side, took care of those five children. Beulah, Ealla's daughter by John Morrison, had two children, John and Anna, by a White man, and later married T. L., Sr. T. L., Sr., lives with his youngest daughter and her husband.

Helen knew Lucindy personally, but she had never met Sam, Mandy, Moor, and Ealla. It is notable that three White men appear on Helen's mother's side within the span of three generations. Viola, the daughter of one of Lucindy's sons by a Black man, had the experience of living with Lucindy, so that she knows more about Lucindy than Helen. Viola, now widowed, lives in Los Angeles. She has six children in Los Angeles, one in Sacramento, California, and two in Texas.

Helen's half brother, John, can almost pass for White. One of my White acquaintances told me emphatically that he was very White, but he was not "a White." His father was born in some place near Shelbyville, Texas, and moved from "Middville" to Beckville, Texas, when John was fairly small. He owned a farm in Carrolton, Texas, and was an overseer of a plantation of good size. John said,

I was born down below eight miles from Shelbyville in Todd Spring [Texas]. I got a [half] brother on my daddy's side. He lives in Shreveport [Louisiana]. I didn't know him until 1953. His name is Pete. Pete moved from here to Shreveport. Pete has a grocery store there. This man knew Pete is the son of the same father. I met Pete in Beckville in 1953. That was the last time I saw him. [Pete's mother, Fennie, was a native of "Middville."]

John once drove a school bus but he now owns three farms and fifty-one head of cattle. He bought the 107-acre farm in the "Africa Community" from his half brother T. L., Jr., when the latter went into military service in the 1940's. It is recorded in the deed that formerly this land had belonged to Beulah who had bought it for 2,215 dollars in 1946. T. L., Jr., son of Beulah, and his wife sold it to John and his wife, who paid 2,000 dollars. (Date of instrument is 1952. It appears that T. L., Jr., had priority of inheritance over John, who was Beulah's son by a White man.) John also purchased thirty-six acres of farmland in 1957 from a woman who migrated to California; another five acres of farmland were purchased in 1969. John has an additional income from the lease of houses he owns in his neighborhood. John and his wife appear quite wealthy.

John's sister Anna (also half sister to Helen) died when her daughter Shiela was only a child. (Anna's husband married a woman with three children about a year after her death.) Helen, who was by then living in Los Angeles, took care of Shiela, her half niece, for about ten years. During her stay at Helen's, Shiela met Kenneth, by whom she had a baby. She did not, however, marry Kenneth but Bobby, a butcher. Kenneth lives with his parents in Watts, while Bobby went to "Middville" with Shiela and her baby son (by Kenneth) to stay for a couple of months at her father's. Then she left for Houston and Bobby followed her, and now the three of them are in Los Angeles. Shiela and her son appear from time to time at Helen's.

Victoria, a younger full sister of Helen's, came to Los Angeles in order to get away from her alcoholic husband, who tried to abuse her when he was drunk. She had just had surgery and was too ill to put up with him. They have been separated for fourteen years, although not legally so. She does not intend to get divorced, since she is afraid that she would lose her property in Texas if she sought a divorce. Living with Victoria now are her first son, aged thirty-nine, divorced and out of a job, and her younger brother's (T. L., Jr.'s) first son, aged nineteen.

T. L., Jr., Helen's brother, divorced Florence because of her excessive drinking, which started after her sister committed suicide by throwing herself off the Golden Gate Bridge in San Francisco. The sister had been hospitalized several times before she killed herself. After the divorce, Florence moved to northern California with her eight-year-old daughter to live with a man she had known before she married T. L., Jr. The man is supposed to be working at an army post there. T. L., Jr., lives in an apartment with his second and third sons whom he supports by working in a market. Helen goes to his apartment almost every day to help with the household work and to take care of his second son, who is physically handicapped. When we were riding to his place she muttered to herself: "I have two families."

One may wonder why the first son of T. L., Jr., lives with Victoria instead of Helen. (Of T. L., Jr.'s siblings, Helen and Victoria live in Los Angeles and his youngest sister (E.W.) in "Middville.") Of course, Helen could take him into her family, but she does not feel up to taking care of another problem child after Shiela. While Shiela was with her, she quit one job after another; never able to hold on to a job, she caused Helen a great deal of anxiety. Helen is worried that T. L., Jr.'s first son is equally unstable psychologically, and might drop out of the city college and get into trouble. As for her own family, she has two girls, aged twenty-one and eighteen. The older daughter, Lisa, a university student, lives by herself, while the younger one lives at home.

Helen came to Los Angeles alone by train in 1943. She hoped to better her financial condition. She had had some teaching experience in "Middville," but she ". . . ended up working as a welder in the California Ship Building Company in Wilmington." At best she could earn ten dollars per day there. She met Alex, her cousin's friend, and married him.

Alex was born in San Antonio, Texas, in 1900. His father died when he was one and a half years old. About his father's father he only knows that he was said to be Mexican or Spanish and to have had a Spanish grant in San Antonio. He does not know his name. He guesses that his mother must have been born in San Antonio also, for all her children were born there. She moved to El Paso, Texas, with Alex and the other children when he was about four years old. His parents had considerable money at one time and were widely known in San Antonio.

The mother remarried a bartender in El Paso (Alex has a half sister, Lois, and a half brother, now deceased). In 1914 his mother sent him to Los Angeles to visit his "auntie," hoping that he would find a good job. According to Alex,

We had heard youngsters were making good living. That was a lie. Unless they were in motion picture business, the money was needed badly. I did not see any opportunity so far as work was concerned. So I left. [He stayed in Los Angeles for five weeks looking for a job.] I could get shoe shine boy, all that kind of stuff. At my age they make you go to school. If I went, I had no way to support myself. So I went back.

He apparently learned it was not easy to establish a life in a big city, and at the same time he was surprised to see the difference between the South and Los Angeles.

They were selling buttons with a picture of B. T. Washington at twenty-five cents in Los Angeles. I bought one. I kept it for years. Funny thing they did not sell those buttons around in El Paso. . . . I quit school for good in 1917. I had to leave here [his stepfather's home] between thirteen and fourteen years old. He could not support me. I moved out to Mrs. Butler's.

He said also that because he did not like this stepfather, he went to this Mrs. Butler's. He called her "his lady." Alex knew her through her child at school. She had a big family so she knew how to handle children, and she suggested that he stay with her.

When World War I broke out, he put his age up by one year, and went into Pullman service for the troops; he traveled through many states, which, he thinks, was very educational. After the War, he came to Tucson, Arizona, where he stayed a couple of months working at a club to make a little bit of money. Then he moved to Phoenix, Arizona, and tried in vain to find a job. He came to Los Angeles in November, 1919, and stayed in a hotel owned by a Japanese at 7th and Central. He recalls that the main part of the Negro Section was between 7th and 17th along Central Avenue at that time. Given a tip by his friends in El Paso, he moved from this hotel to a rooming house on 11th Street between Central and Stanford, but he didn't stay there long and changed his residence very often until he married in 1925. His first marriage lasted four years and five months. He admits that it was mostly his fault that the marriage broke up. Helen is his second wife. He mentioned, "We will have been married twenty-five years by March or April, this year. . . . I would not say she is the best woman, but she is a moral woman."

Renting a place at 21st and Hooper, he first opened a tobacco shop to sell cigars, cigarettes, and sundries, with space provided for playing cards and also for a shoe shine stand. This business lasted several years, after which he went to another part of California and bought a pool room there. It had space for playing social poker but not for gambling. Since business was not good except during the orchard harvest season, he sold it after one and a half years to come back to Los Angeles. Just before World War II, he worked for two plastering contractors and then for the Gilmore Oil Company. After three years at Gilmore Oil, he decided to open a coffee shop at 12th and Central, which he named the Blue Moon Café. He did the cooking and Helen waited on tables. However, within three or four months she became pregnant, which quickly led him to give up the business since he had no confidence in finding a good waitress to replace her. "You could not get a waitress to wait on table in that area. I decided to get out," he remarked. The third business of his own only lasted eleven months, so he went back to the Mobil Oil Company[8] to work in lubrication service in the department of transportation, and stayed there until 1960. He had to leave the company because of his alleged nervous breakdown, which he did not quite accept as the true reason. He has not had a

---

[8] The Mobil Oil Company incorporated Gilmore Oil in 1942, and employees of Gilmore were transferred to Mobil Oil. Since Alex had previously worked for Gilmore, he became an employee of Mobil Oil upon his return.

regular job since then; his wife is employed as a domestic worker in the White sections.

Once Helen's and Alex's family was established in Los Angeles, it provided a base for those relatives who came to Los Angeles.

The data from Helen's sister, Victoria, and her sons, Preston and Ronald, reveal the following facts. Preston started to visit Los Angeles in 1946; he stayed one year between 1946 and 1947; three months in 1951, when he came with a man from his town; three months in 1952, when he came alone; three months in 1953, when his aunt and uncle (Helen and Alex) took him on their way back home from a visit; and, finally, he came by himself to stay in 1953. He first lived with Helen and Alex at 54th and Broadway and later moved to his brothers' place at 54th and San Pedro. He stayed with Alex's family on each trip, including the three-month trips made during summer vacations.

Ronald lived one year in Los Angeles with Helen when he was six years old and attended first grade. Before moving to Los Angeles, he had visited two or three times. He came alone to stay in July, 1957, but returned to Texas in September and came back with his mother, Victoria. Victoria had previously come to Los Angeles for nine months in 1946, staying with her sister, Helen. Then in 1956, she came to stay, to get away from her husband. This time she lived with her sons, Willie and Tommy, both of whom had come to Los Angeles earlier than the two brothers Preston and Ronald. They lived in a four-bedroom house at 54th and San Pedro.

Helen's daughter, Lisa, interprets her mother's role as follows:

My mother has been the leader of our extended family here in Los Angeles. She takes care of the needs of our relatives. For example, you will notice that several members of the family are members of Freewill Missionary Baptist Church. It is my mother who got them involved in this church. When a friend of the family dies, it is usually my mother who represents the family at the funeral. She is usually instrumental in getting legal advice for the family, too. My father helps her in her role as the "leader." Note how my father helped some of the relatives to land on jobs. They all come to my parents for advice.

Helen actually took Preston and his wife, Margaret, and Victoria, who are now all members, to Freewill Missionary Baptist Church. Alex helped Victoria get her first job as a domestic worker at his employer's house in Los Angeles and also helped Preston get work as a parking and garage attendant when he arrived in the city.

The Davis Family (Appendix, Table 1.2)

Mary Davis's younger brother, Otis, passed away on a Sunday during the period of my fieldwork. The funeral was scheduled to be held on Thursday, the nineteenth of February. Mary planned to go to "Middville" but the doctor advised her not to travel because of her cough. I visited her place just a day before the funeral. The Church had given her a potted chrysanthemum which she was supposed to take with her to her hometown. It was conspicuous in the rather dark room where I was sitting. There were several telephone calls during my stay of about two hours; one was a long-distance call from one of her relatives and the other was from a coworker.

Mary is the oldest sister. The rest of her seven brothers and sisters are full brothers and sisters. Sharon and R. H. from Los Angeles; Curtis and his family; R. James (Jimmie's former husband's son), and Unit from Palm Springs, California; and Emeroy from Elsinore, California, all either flew or drove to the hometown for the funeral. Otis's brothers, Harry and R. H.; James Himes, husband of Eva; Otis's daughter's sons, Larry and Joel; and T. L., husband of Joe Ruth, who is the daughter of Otis's former wife, Vergie, were active pallbearers. The honorary pallbearers included R. H. Long, the high school principal, whose father is a cousin to James, and Oren Reed, W. D. Polley (see Appendix, Table 1.5, IV0.66), and three friends of the deceased's. The funeral took place at Mt. Zion Christian Methodist Episcopal Church, and the body was buried at St. John Cemetery in the backyard of St. John Baptist Church in "Africa Community." The floral bearers were the Odessa Court of Caranthe mentioned earlier.

Otis had been employed by the Chevrolet Company as a mechanic for more than twenty-five years. After he retired because of failing health, he moved to Prairie View (see Figure 1). His first wife, Vergie, was from the "Africa Community," and his second wife from a nearby town. Otis did not have any children by his second wife. Otis's sister, Katherine, whose husband died of cancer in 1954 or 1955, did not attend the funeral. Katherine currently lives with Emely, one of her daughters, and Emely's baby. Emely's husband is in military service. Mary has never seen him, nor the husband of Rachel, another daughter of Katherine's. It was notable that Emeroy, who is "not a whole brother" to Otis, attended the funeral.

Mary's mother, Sallie, aged eighty-six, has Indian features with high cheekbones, but her skin is brown. James, Sallie's father, was predominantly Indian in appearance, with high cheekbones and a large nose;

his skin color was gingercake brown.[9] He was a sharecropper. After he left the farm, he did truck farming: watermelons, peas, corn, and so on. He also cooked and sold barbecued foods on Saturdays or on special days such as June 'teenth.[10] James's wife Emely (Mary's grandmother) died when Mary was just a baby, so she does not remember her. However, she remembers having seen Emely's mother (Mary's mother's mother), also named Sallie, whom she presumes to have been a domestic slave by the way she talked. Sallie was light-skinned and had blue eyes. She raised Mary's mother and her mother's sister. Mary stated: "She lived with my parents and myself." Sallie's "partner," Fields, was also a slave, but he died before Mary was born.

Mary's knowledge about her father Osia and his family was rather limited (Appendix, Table 1.2, IIID.8). The father, who spent his entire life in "Middville," was a farmer, doing odd jobs, after harvest, at the brickyard owned by a White man. Att (Mary's father's father), unlike his son, was quite "Anglo," having long brown hair, blue eyes, and a long beard. She is not sure if Jane (her father's mother) married Att or not. According to her, Att used to have a large piece of land in the "colored quarters." Agatha Osby, who is the oldest lady in the community, remembers that Att had 300 acres. When he separated from his first wife, however, the land was divided between them; the part of the land where the houses belonging to Sallie (Mary's mother), Eva (Mary's sister), and the late Otis now stand was given away to the first wife, while the rest went to him. The deed kept in the District Clerk Office evidences that Att witnessed the seventh of June, 1893, that she was entitled to an equal one-half of the eighty-seven acres of their community estate. Actually, forty acres out of the eighty-seven acres were transferred to her. Since then some of his land was conveyed to the Gulf Beaumont and Great Northern Railway Company, and about twenty acres were sold to several individuals. These transactions were made between 1906 and 1913.

There are three houses in the spacious residential area in "Middville": Sallie lives alone in one of them; Eva's family shares the largest one with the family of her daughter, Patricia; the family of the late Otis used to live in the remaining one. Patricia, her husband, and their daughter will soon move into a new house which is under construction in the same

[9]   Mary's color scale ranges from fair through light brown, olive brown, medium brown, brown, gingercake brown, dark brown, velvet dark brown, and dark; she describes her relatives and friends in these terms.
[10]   Besides the fact that Mary has happy memories of June 'teenth (Texas Independence Day), she referred to a gathering held by a secret fraternity in the community. The house was built by a Black man.

residential area. Patricia often goes to Sallie's house to stay overnight, taking care of her. Sallie seems happy when she is surrounded by her daughters. Homecoming at the Mt. Zion Church provides a rare opportunity for the reunion of mother and daughters. Mary, Eva, and Jimmie came home this summer but Katherine did not. Homecoming took place on the second of August. Mary came from Los Angeles on the last day of July. She was kept quite busy making cakes for Homecoming, as she was last year. For the past two years, she has been all the busier because she has had to do Eva's share of the work since Eva is diabetic. Jimmie joined the group from Palm Springs. Mary and Jimmie stayed with their mother. There were over fifty persons at Homecoming. There was a big feast early in the afternoon in the annex of the church; the food was supplied by several families. After the feast, the homecomers were introduced one by one; this was followed by a Homecoming sermon by the pastor of St. Paul Baptist Church and a worship sermon by the pastor of Mt. Zion Christian Methodist Episcopal Church. There was special organ music played by C. T., who came back from Prairie View with his family (see Appendix, Table 1.4, VT.52).

The fact that the invited speaker was from the Baptist Church and people like Annie Reed who belong to other churches were present indicates that Homecoming is a social affair which stimulates mutual visiting among members of various churches. It seems more important to share the Homecoming spirit, food, and socializing than to draw a strict boundary between the sects. Mary went back to Los Angeles on the eleventh, and Jimmie returned to Palm Springs on the thirteenth.

Mary was born in "Middville" in 1907, finished the tenth grade by 1926, and then proceeded to Prairie View College. After one year of study there, she received an elementary teaching certificate valid for kindergarten through sixth grade. She came back to "Middville" to teach third, fourth, and fifth grades at Daniel High. That opportunity was granted to her. She was paid fifty "whole" dollars a month, out of which she gave twenty dollars a month for nine months to her mother's younger sister's daughter to help her earn her "little certificate." She said, "This girl, Ida, was living with us," since her mother had died. Ida started to teach in St. Augustine's.

Reflecting upon her school days, Mary said, "I always wanted to go to school." She continued her college education by going to summer school. When the extension school of Prairie View was set up in Nacogdoches, Texas, on Saturdays, she attended that until 1933. But she grew tired of continuing her education in an on-and-off manner, and finally went back to college to finish. In May of 1936,

I came back with a B.A. degree to "Middville," Texas! [But] I felt like crying, because nobody cared for nothing. But, the principal and his wife and a teacher from our high school came for my commencement. I was so glad somebody came from home. W. C. Polley, brother of Joe Kennedy [see Appendix, Table 1.5, IV0.49], also came down and brought me back to "Middville." . . . I read books and books at school. I was determined to get a B.A. I was the second woman to have received a B.A. in "Toledo" County.

She had wanted to take English but majored in home economics with her minor in English and education, because the high school principal and other colleagues suggested that she take home economics. She taught at Daniel High from 1936 to 1945.

Mary and Charles were married in Yuma, Arizona, in 1945. He had visited Mary in his capacity as an insurance man, and a year later, at their second meeting, he proposed to her. She first thought it was a joke, for she knew she was not pretty to look at. She described herself: "My hair is black and straight and I am very dark."

As Charles had been in Los Angeles since 1943, the newly married couple took the train to Los Angeles the day after their wedding to settle in his niece's house in Watts. They stayed there until 1951 when they moved to the Baptist Church on Avalon to take care of the Church property. Charles was already a member and later Mary joined. Charles worked at Super Grate Open Flooring and Steel Company from 1943 to 1959, at about forty-eight dollars a week. He also had a sideline job at the Brown Cornell Insurance Company from 1954 to 1955. Toward the end of September, 1959, he died of a heart attack while driving. Mary was informed of his sudden death by a policeman. His body had been taken to the county morgue. The sad news was communicated to the relatives on her side through Jimmie in Palm Springs, whom Mary phoned. Since Charles's two brothers in the city were both dead, Mary contacted one of his nieces in Los Angeles.

Twenty-nine people viewed his body at the church. Apart from relatives there were also some representatives from his work; church members; friends of either his or Mary's, or their mutual friends; people from the "Middville" Club, or from the Southeast Interracial Council; a person from an art, charity, and literary club to which Mary belongs; and a couple representing Jewish Women's Clubs of Los Angeles. R. H. (see Appendix, Table 1.2, IVD.10) and his wife were the only relatives from Mary's side who gathered to mourn. The deacons and some active members of the church acted as pallbearers, but none of the relatives. Probably this was because there were no proper male relatives on his side; his only living brother, who lives in Kilgore, is blind, and the deceased man had no children.

The Adams Family (Appendix, Table 1.3)

Po and Mo lived during the time of slavery. Their daughter, Mary, seems to have been born in Orange, Texas, and died around 1864. Po and Mo, Jake (Mary's husband), Mary, and little Florence and Kizai (their daughters) moved from Orange to a rented farm in East Hamilton, Texas. Later Kizai and her husband, Elix, bought this farm. One of their children, Narsis, and Narsis's daughter and her family still live on this farm. Valencia has rather a stronger attachment to East Hamilton than to "Middville." Showing a picture of Narsis's house and yard with a fish pond, she said, "When I go home to Texas, I mean Narsis's house in East Hamilton, I go there." The picture also showed a hog hanging up and ready to be butchered.

When Mary died, Jake returned to Vermont, Texas, his hometown, and Florence and Kizai lost contact with their father. Later, however, when they located him, he had remarried and had become wealthy dealing in real estate. Mo raised Florence and Kizai.

Florence, Valencia's mother, worked for twenty-seven years for a White family, while she raised her children; she was well paid and raised her children in a two-room house on the employers' property. After she had moved to California, Valencia used to drop by this house whenever she went back to "Middville." The children played and slept with the R.s' children. Mr. R. protected Florence's children from malign White children, by saying, "Don't bother Florence's kids!" Looking back upon her childhood, Valencia said, "When Mama died, all of them were at the funeral. . . . I call him [Mr. R.] when I need him."

Judy Dixon (Mary's sister and Florence's and Kizai's aunt) also lived in the days of slavery. She lived longer than anybody else and was the "captain" of the family. Her daughter, Cora, outlived her own daughter, Elja. Cora took care of Elja's children, and she used to ask Valencia and her sister, Allean, to take care of Joelynn and Allean (Valencia calls her "little Allean" to distinguish her from her own sister, who is called "big Allean"). When Cora died, Valencia brought Joelynn to Los Angeles. After a year and a half, she sent Joelynn back to Texas to bring her sister Allean to Los Angeles. Valencia took care of Joelynn, while little Allean was taken to stay at big Allean's house, which is just across the street from Valencia's. This place had been found by Valencia, who suggested Allean live there. At that time Allean was living alone, separated from her husband, and working as a beautician in Pico, California. She felt the house was too close to Valencia's but moved in on the condition that she would not be interfered with.

Living with big Allean, little Allean finished school and then left the house for married life. Little Allean lives with her family in one of the apartment houses on the same street. Meanwhile, Joelynn moved from Valencia's to big Allean's, because, as Valencia put it, "her husband made his presence felt in her house."

The twenty-fourth of January, 1970 was a big occasion for Valencia. Joelynn was married on that day at the Black church on West Adams Boulevard, which has the largest congregation in Los Angeles. Valencia helped make her wedding dress and paid for the wedding cake and for miscellaneous food and drink for the reception. The wedding guests included Katherine; Claude and Kay from Sacramento; big Allean; Elenora and her husband; George, former husband of the first daughter of Joe and Jean Kennedy; Joe and Jean Kennedy, their daughter and granddaughter; C. D. Adams's elder sister's son and his wife; and C. D.'s younger sister and her husband. Valencia feels greatly relieved now, as her remaining charge is a boy, Joelynn's brother Edmond, who may not require as much cost and care as the girl did. Edmond lives next door, willingly or unwillingly, under Valencia's eye. She said: "I put him there to watch."

Claude, son of big Allean, visited Japan three times during the Korean War; during this time he met Kay, a Japanese girl, and married her. He works as head therapist at a hospital in Sacramento. Kyle, their son, who was fair when he was a baby, said, "When I was a baby, I was a Japanese, but now I am *Kokujin* [Black man]." Valencia speaks well of Kay, who is sweet-tempered and keeps the house clean. Kay pleases Valencia by giving her gifts such as a beautiful tapestry which she embroidered herself. Big Allean and Katherine (the wife of Valencia's nephew, Floyd) are also on good terms with Kay. Allean and Kay talk on the phone often, and Katherine and Kay invite each other's families to big dinners. Katherine's husband Floyd was raised by Valencia and C. D. after Erna (Valencia's sister) died. His wedding ceremony was held at his aunt's house. Valencia pointed to the table in the living room, saying, "The reception was held right here." Only five or six years ago Floyd and his family left for Sacramento, where he works as an electrician for the Southern Pacific Railroad. His wife and two children come down to Los Angeles to spend a good portion of the summer at his aunt's almost every year. Auntie and her husband also go up to Floyd's place in July and sometimes bring the children back to Los Angeles.

According to Valencia, nowadays kinfolk seldom get together except for July Fourth, Thanksgiving, and Christmas, when many families exchange visits with their relatives. Valencia says, "We are too far apart," but she and her husband regularly go to Texas in the summer for a five- or six-week stay. Claude and Floyd have never gone back to their home-town since they experienced military life; they know they can no longer get along with people "down there." As for C. D., he likes to talk about going to Texas or how many hours it took him to go down there last time.

The role of Valencia Adams among her relatives is not minor. She is a central figure like Helen Smith. Valencia tells that she has taken care of Joelynn, Allean, and Edmond because she has no children of her own. She also says with pride, "Floyd and Claude are never arrested at all, never get into trouble." Her sense of responsibility for her younger rela-tives is really strong.

C. D. Adams's great-grandfather on his father's side was Irish. His father's mother, Bean (Appendix, Table 1.3, IIE.16), was a slave, and her husband, Dan, was almost a full-blooded Indian. On his mother's side, his mother's mother's father, Nelson S., was of German origin; James, his mother's father, was also White. C. D. never saw Nelson or his Irish great-grandfather, His mother's mother, Mary, was a slave. Nancy, daughter of Mary and James, was C. D.'s mother. Mary's other daughter, Viola, by her marriage to a Black man, has never married but has two sons.

C. D.'s father, Tuck, was born just outside "Middville" and had 311 acres of land. Tuck and Nancy, C. D.'s parents, had thirteen children, who helped their father on the farm.

C. D., the ninth child, was born in July, 1900 in the "Africa Com-munity." At the age of sixteen he started to work with a section gang on the railroad and stayed in one job for about a year. "Most of the young-sters who left home no doubt end up with this type of work. I could say it was the best opportunity, but I did not stay longer." He recalls those days with some bitterness, for it was the kangaroo court which prompted him to give up the job. He was given a few lashes for small offenses, such as leaving dirty shoes in the cabin. After that experience he went to Nacog-doches and worked for the Texaco Oil Company. His job was to fill the tanks for vehicles in the yard; he was paid 3.60 dollars a day. Then he moved to Greenville, Texas, and back to his hometown. In 1919, he left for Omaha, Nebraska. His older brothers, Bill and Quincy, were already there. His younger sister, Mary, later followed them after she was separated from Eugene, a White husband. After working at a packing company and driving a taxi for nine months, he went to the Union Pacific as a dining-car waiter, the same job Quincy had. He was on and off the job between 1922 and 1924 and was finally laid off. Then he went on the Burlington (known as the C.B. & Q.) to work as a dining-car waiter.

While working there he heard "the boys" talking about Minneapolis. In 1925 he decided to go there and got a job as a dining-car waiter on the Sioux Line. His experience in Minneapolis as well as in Canada, where his work took him frequently, brought him in contact with an atmosphere quite different from that of the South. Quitting his waiter's job, he became a redcap at the Milwaukee station. In 1932, he worked as a washroom attendant at the Chicago World's Fair under the supervision of a Jewish boss. After the fair was over, he continued to work under him in the washrooms of hotels and night clubs in which the boss had connections. At the suggestion of his friends in Chicago, he tried a dining-car job on the Sea Board Airline Railroad, but soon left it to move back to Chicago around 1935. He did not stay there long either, and returned to Omaha, where he again worked for the Union Pacific. He was on the regular run from Omaha to Los Angeles and decided to move in with his brother Bill, who had arrived in Los Angeles in 1925 and was renting a house on East 43rd Street. After a year, when Florence, his first wife, came from Omaha to join him, he moved out and rented another place a block away. He had married Florence in 1932 in St. Paul, Minnesota. He was Florence's third husband. He had known her first and second husbands slightly. Florence now lives on the west side of Los Angeles with her divorced son, Maurice, who bears the name of her second husband, Magee, although actually Maurice is the son neither of Magee nor of her first husband. Maurice works now as a waiter in a club.

C. D. and Florence moved from 43rd to a nearby street, then to 42nd Street where they stayed until 1942, when they separated. He said, recalling their desperate need for money at the time, "We ran up bills. To pay those bills, my wife worked, her son who was with us worked, too." His fifth residence was located on 51st Boulevard; he stayed there for about six months. During this time, he married Valencia, who was staying in Oakland.

Valencia was sixty-eight years old in 1969. She reminisced:

When I became big size, I went to school [Daniel High]. When I was in eleventh or twelfth grade, Mama moved to East Hamilton. She had some cattles there. She took a break and stayed down there. I stayed in town with Judy [Dixon] and Cora. Then, I started sparking my husband [C. D.]. I was sixteen and he was nineteen years old. But he went away. He had a brother in Nebraska. His parents asked him to go. I was so disappointed . . . I decided to see Mama in East Hamilton. Mama's friend was there. She [the friend] said Mama would let Valencia go home with her to Shreveport [Louisiana].

Valencia was supposed to stay only a few days but remained fifteen years. She married a man from Mississippi but got divorced very soon because he was jealous and drank a lot. She operated a cafe for fifteen years and also cooked barbecued food for ten years.

Her nephews, Claude and Floyd, stayed with her there. Floyd went into the army at the age of eighteen. Meanwhile her sister Allean came to Shreveport and started a beauty shop in Valencia's shop. Valencia then left for Oakland, California, where she put Claude into school and worked as a top welder in a shipyard for about two years. Allean also left Shreveport to come to Los Angeles in 1943. As suggested by C. D.'s brother, who visited Valencia in Oakland and who knew that C. D. was separated, she came to Los Angeles and started to work in a Thrifty store. This was just before the end of the War. Determined to stay in Los Angeles, Valencia returned to Shreveport to dispose of a houseful of furniture. After a month she came back to Los Angeles to resume her work at Thrifty. Shortly afterwards she married C. D. in the courthouse of San Bernardino, California, in the presence of two witnesses; one of them was a friend of the bridegroom's who worked on the same job.

The new couple had their living quarters on 51st Street. They moved from there to a place ten blocks east of Western Avenue, and then to the house of William L. on East 53rd Street. He, too, was from the "Africa Community." C. D. said, "We were raised together." Therefore C. D. could count on William for a place to stay. C. D. recalled, "In those days we could hardly find a house for rent." Soon William's sister came to Los Angeles and moved into the same house. C. D.'s family was compelled to move out since the house did not have enough space. They rented a room on West 41st Place, where they stayed until 1947. Their present house cost them 13,700 dollars; they paid for it in ten years.

The Miller Family (Appendix, Table 1.4)

Sarah (Sunny Miller's mother's mother's mother), who remained a domestic slave all her life, died at the age of ninety-five in "Middville." She was brought to the United States as a slave, but Sunny does not know her point of origin. Leah was her daughter by O Masta. Sunny remembers Leah as a beautiful woman who had bright color and long black hair. Leah died at the age of fifty-four. Bowden, Leah's husband and Minnie's father, had Indian blood and a reddish complexion. He was born in the town and did farming work for different people. He died in 1919. Minnie, Sunny's mother, survives her ten sisters and two brothers and still lives in this community. Sunny's father, Bob, who was a White man, was born somewhere in "Toledo" County and is now deceased. He was an independent farmer. Minnie, who should be eighty-five years old by now, naturally can add a little more information about her ancestry. Her father's mother was a slave; she was probably from Alabama, although Minnie is not too sure. Bowden, Minnie's father, also a slave, worked for the L. family after he had been liberated. He made Minnie work with him and Leah in the fields although she was only fourteen or fifteen years old. Minnie was kept at it for five years, and recalls, "My father was a little mean."

Leah was born in the time of slavery, but escaped slave status because of her young age. She died of breast cancer at the approximate age of fifty-seven (Sunny said fifty-four).

When working in L.'s fields, they stayed at the place of an old lady named Betty Morrison. It had two or three rooms where there were four or five beds and some chairs but no other furniture. There was a wood stove and coal oil lamp. They used homemade quilts instead of blankets, and Minnie still has a fine homemade quilt. For sheets, they stitched up nine white cotton flour sacks to make one sheet. They ate beans, peas, greens, pork, and chicken, and drank cow's milk.

Minnie remembers she moved from Shelbyville (Texas) to "Middville" to find "a better opportunity" in 1910. By this she meant a better opportunity to work for White families. Her grandmother took care of her three children while she was at work. She worked for five White families for four years.[11] However, as the day's work brought her only "four bits," she decided to return to the "Africa Community," where she and Sweaden (Appendix, Table 1.4, IIIN. 15) rented thirty-five acres of land from a White man, a big landowner of the Good Hope community. They grew vegetables, potatoes, and cotton. There were three cotton gins; they went to the one by the Santa Fe railroad, mentioned earlier. The other two were located out of town.[12]

It was in 1914 or 1915 that Minnie married Sweaden, who was born in the "Africa Community." Meanwhile her grandmother, Sarah, died in the "Africa Community" and was buried in Rather cemetery near Shelbyville. Sweaden wanted to move to "Middville," so they went there in 1928 and bought their present place of three and a half acres. Now one of his brothers, his baby sister, and one nephew live on the same street.

Sunny was born in 1906 in "Middville." She married a man from Tenaha (Texas) in 1928 and moved to Marshall, where he worked as a

[11]   These five White families included the family of the mother of the present manager of a big food store in the square and another family which is connected with the owner of a drug store, the only one in the square.
[12]   According to John, there was one in Arcadia and another in Artfork. The operation of these cotton gins was discontinued about thirty years ago.

hotel porter. They were divorced in 1940 or 1941 because of his involvement with another woman. His second wife died two years ago, leaving him childless as he had no child by either marriage. Sunny paid a visit to his house only once, when his second wife died and his sister came to visit him. At present, he lives in Gardena, Los Angeles County, and works as a longshoreman. Sunny came to Los Angeles with a friend in 1947 and stayed a month at this friend's mother's house. She found the climate better for her asthma, so she went back to Texas to pack for settling down in Los Angeles. In Los Angeles, she got two or three domestic jobs. At present, she works for a Russian Jewish couple in Beverly Hills; she has worked for twenty-two consecutive years for this family, starting at a dollar an hour; lately she makes fifteen dollars a day and works two days a week.

Richard, her second husband, has three daughters by his previous marriage. He had been separated for ten years when he met Sunny in a cafe one morning. In order to marry her he got a legal divorce. He has little knowledge about his ancestry, because his parents died when he was young. His memory does not stretch beyond his father. But he does know that both of his grandparents on his mother's side were born in Marshall, Texas, and that their daughter Georgia, his mother, married Eric and had four sons.

When Richard was in Marshall, he drove a taxi. He drove alone all the way to Los Angeles in 1943 or 1944, where he stayed at Mozell's, one of his daughters. He worked in the packing house of the United Dressed Beef Company in the Bernon district. His job was to wash cattle, and he kept the job for sixteen years until he retired in 1961 at the age of sixty-five. By now he should be seventy-seven years old.

Richard barely finished three years of schooling. Sunny says, "He doesn't read well and doesn't write." It is her role to pay household bills and to read the papers for him. They subscribe to the *Stars and Stripes*; the *Torch*; a veterans' publication; a weekly paper, the *Los Angeles Citizen*; and an official publication of the Los Angeles County Federation of Labor, which is free. I also noted on the table a copy of the *Butcher Workman*, a January–February, 1970, issue put out by the Amalgamated Meat Cutters and Butcher Workmen of North America.

Encouraged by the fact that Rev. Philip, one of his tenants, attends an adult education program held in the evening at Washington High School, Richard has started to take reading lessons, four nights a week, at a cost of twenty-five cents for three months. He tries to read now. Apparently influenced by her husband, Sunny is also thinking about going to night school.

Since his retirement, Richard has taken on the job of picking up junk, mostly newspapers, using his own truck, which has been his since the days when he worked in the packing house. He works for a couple of hours in the evening, and if he is telephoned, he goes to collect waste materials from a certain number of homes. He has a list of these homes. He earns from twenty-five to thirty dollars a month on the average by selling used papers and other junk to two junk dealers, on Alameda Street and in Gardena.

It has been mentioned earlier that Valencia Adams and Mary Davis extended helping hands to their relatives by taking some of them into their homes or raising their small children. Sunny mentions such joint effort and care directed toward C. T., the son of her half brother, Earl, and Christine. As is shown in the Appendix (Table 1.4), C. T. is related to Sunny as the grandson of Ted and Minnie, while he is related to Mary Davis (Appendix, Table 1.2) on his mother's side: Christine's mother's father and Jane, Mary's father's mother, were half siblings. Therefore, Sunny's family and Mary's family, together with his own parents, made up a "big family" for him and helped him go to school. Even Sunny's mother pitched in and saw to his general welfare. Sunny says, "We've been all good to him," and points out "all togetherness" as a specific source of satisfaction gained from being a member of the big family. C. T.'s mother, Christine, lives in "Middville" with Earl, who is her second husband. He is a native of "Middville" as her late husband was. According to Annie (Appendix, Table 1.4, IVE. 34), C. T.'s father, Earl, was born in Shelbyville and came to "Middville" in 1910 where he stayed several years working in the hotel in the square. Fifteen years ago he went to Tyler, where he works as a barber.

Mary Davis was C. T.'s first teacher at Daniel High School. Sunny says,

That is why they feel close. She was kind of responsible [for him]. My sister [Annie] taught him music. He is good at either piano or organ; he goes from piano to organ when he grows tired of playing on the piano, or the other way around. No drinking, no smoking.

C. T. corresponds with Mary regularly. He always starts his letters, "My dearest coz Mary." He does not hide his strong attachment to her in his letters and tells her she is his "next mother." She is not embarrassed by being told so. He tells her what's going on in the hometown: which relatives he met, how he could not get to see her parent [Sallie] this time, and so on, as if to renew his closeness to her. He expected to receive a Ph.D. in 1971, the third Black with that degree in Earth Science. He asked her to pray for his success in this very difficult task. He was eventually awarded the degree, which was an honor not only to him but to his family, which remained in Texas for economic reasons while he was completing his course at a midwestern university. His success also brought a particular gratification to his "big family," especially to its devoted member, Mary.

C. T.'s wife is from Houston, Texas. They have adopted a Korean child and given him the surname of a Japanese prime minister. Either Sunny or Mary must have mistaken him for a Japanese child.

While Sunny has some relatives to talk about, her husband Richard has few relatives on his side. His only surviving brother lives in Dallas, Texas, and the other two brothers lived and died in Dallas. As already mentioned, he knows only his parents and the names and the jobs of his mother's parents. Those relatives who keep regular contact with him are his three daughters by his previous marriage, who live near each other. The youngest daughter lives with her mother, while the second one, married and since separated, lives with her forty-year-old daughter. Two or three times a year, particularly at Christmas time, they all visit their father and Sunny with a present for each. He goes to see them once every two or three months. His former wife does not come around to see him.

The Kennedy Family (Appendix, Table 1.5)

Jean Kennedy knew her great-grandmother, Lucy. She assumes Lucy would have come from Sexton, Texas, but does not know about Lucy's "partner," except that he was White. Jean's grandfather, Bill Polly, was White and lived with Iva, Lucy's daughter, and their four children in the same house, a fact well known in the community. Bill did not have a White wife, and Iva was known as his housekeeper. People called this family "Mrs. Lucy's people" or "Mr. Cliff's people." Bill lived in Sexton and was a big landowner when he died. Jean's father, Cliff, son of Iva and Bill, moved to "Middville." He worked for a local car agency and a cotton-processing company and also as a gardener.

Jean remembers three older generations on her maternal side, though she cannot recall the names of her mother's grandparents. According to Jean's mother, Tiny, her own father, Burke (Appendix, Table 1.5, IID.9), his two children (Tiny and her brother), and their grandparents came to "Middville" in the summer of 1901. Tiny's mother, Ida, had come earlier. Tiny's husband, Cliff, as mentioned above, came here in 1907 and married Tiny in 1909. The house where Tiny now lives was built in 1923. Next door is her youngest daughter's house. Tiny's memory of her ancestry is a little more accurate than her daughter Jean's. However, their knowledge does not go beyond the second generation above Tiny on either side.

Jim, Joe Kennedy's mother's father, was an independent farmer with fifty acres of land, raising cotton, corn, hogs, and cows. Flour and sugar were the goods his family had to buy. Joe never saw his grandfather's first wife. (Jim's second and third wives were both from Timpson in eastern Texas.) Joe's father, Plue, washed and greased cars for his living. He never joined the church and was never out of town. Joe does not know his grandparents on his father's side at all; for some reason, he does not talk about his mother either.

Joe's wife, Jean, was born in "Middville" in 1910. Her memory of her girlhood is closely associated with Bright Morning Star Baptist Church. Burke, her mother's father, was a deacon of the church. Her mother carried her to the church when she was a baby, where she was put into a crib during the service. At the age of twelve she was baptized.

Jean went both to high school and to Prairie View College with Mary Davis. The high school principal, who had also taught her mother, encouraged her to obtain a higher education. Jean was fifteen years old when she went to college. After finishing the regular term of one year, her married life compelled her to prolong her schedule of college education and she was able to go only to summer school every year until she became thirty-two.

In 1943 she came to Los Angeles. Her husband was already there. She had been teaching public school in a small town near "Middville" and had to wait until the term was over. Soon after her arrival, she went to an employment agency in Hollywood, which directed her to Lockheed Aircraft, in Burbank, where she was employed as an assembler at ninety cents an hour. She was one of the many who were laid off at the termination of World War II in 1945. Next year she took a Civil Service clerk's examination. She has been working at the post office since 1948, and presently she earns 8,000 dollars a year.

Unlike Jean, who has held the same job for more than twenty years, Joe has shifted from job to job. He went from Daniel High School in 1926 to Henderson Business College in Memphis, Tennessee. He dropped out after one year, not because of financial problems but because of homesickness, and returned to "Middville." He started working for the railroad as a tie stenciller. After a year and a half, he shifted to driving a truck for a grocery company. He held that job until around 1941 when he went to Los Angeles on his aunt Beulah's suggestion. He knew that there was a great demand for labor in the defense industries in California. He went to the Consolidated Steel Company and got janitorial work in the company's shipyard. After three months of this work, he went to the company's welding school, which assured him a position as a welder. However, the shipyard closed down in August, 1945. He then had various janitorial jobs in an electric fan company on Alameda Street and in the Rowan Company downtown; he was a shipping clerk in a garment company and a porter in the Prudential Drugstore on Wilshire Boulevard; and finally, since 1952, he has had a job with Continental Can Company. He is temporarily away from the company because of a bad leg.

THE "MIDDVILLE" CLUB AND ITS MEMBERS

At the outset, I will list the names of the people among the five families and their relatives who belong to the "Middville" Club. Active members are indicated by italics.

The Smith Family: Alex; Helen; T. L., Jr. (Helen's younger brother) and his wife; M. H. (Helen's mother's half brother's son) and his wife; *W. L.* (Helen's younger sister's former husband's older brother) and his wife; Victoria (Helen's younger sister); Ronald (Victoria's son) and his wife. Preston (Victoria's son) and his wife do not belong to the club but go to the picnics sponsored by the club.

The Davis Family: Charles (deceased); *Mary*; R. H. (Mary's younger brother) and his wife.

The Adams Family: C. D.; Bob (C. D.'s older sister's son) and his wife; *Valencia*; Allean (Valencia's younger sister).

The Miller Family: Richard and Sunny do not belong to the club.

The Kennedy Family: Joe; Juanita (Joe's father's younger brother's daughter); *Jean*; A. G. (Jean's younger sister) and her husband.

The people listed above constitute about half the total club membership. It is important to note that not all relatives of the five families in Los Angeles belong to the club. Helen represents the Smith family although she has become inactive, while Joe and Jean Kennedy cooperate in keeping the club active. On the other hand, Richard and Sunny Miller do not belong to the club.

Helen Smith recalls the motive for forming the "Middville" Club as follows:

A young lady from "Middville" came down with cancer, and she passed away very soon, which prompted us to form a club for mutual help in 1954. Every member pays fifty cents a month, and the Club uses the money to contribute fifteen dollars to a sick person.

Joe Kennedy, former president, confirms Helen's remark: "There was a couple out from 'Middville.' Mrs. had cancer and died. Three kids were left behind." The immediate motive therefore was to give financial assistance to surviving children. Valencia Adams, on the other hand, emphasizes the social nature of the club, saying that from its beginning the club put aside, knowingly or unknowingly, the more serious objective of giving aid to the needy for the enjoyment of social activities. It was Valencia who hit on the idea of getting together for a cozy talk and exchanges of news. The meeting materialized after she kept herself busy on the phone, and thirty-six people showed up at her house the following Sunday. She said there was no problem in contacting people from "Middville," because she knew the names of so many people.

The Club has bylaws and minutes, which suggests a little more formal nature than a merely social one. It is stated in the bylaws that the object shall be charity and social benefit for the members; a member must be from "Middville" or a relative of someone from "Middville"; regular meetings shall be held on the second Sunday in each month; and the annual meeting will be held on the second Sunday in April. There are various committees, including a welfare committee, a social committee, a sunshine committee, and a sick committee. The social committee handles social affairs, such as Christmas parties and an annual picnic. The sunshine committee sends get-well cards to sick persons and condolence cards to bereaved families. A member of the sick committee calls on the sick. The entrance fee is one dollar, and the monthly dues are fifty cents. Meetings are held at the homes of the members from a list made by month of birth. A member will be dropped if he fails to come to meetings for three consecutive months, or if he does not pay his dues. The club will give a member five dollars a month for sickness for a maximum of three months. When a member dies, the club will call a special meeting and give the deceased family fifty dollars. The club will send flowers to the immediate family of the deceased, and fifteen dollars will be contributed for a wreath or spray

The minutes have been kept for the period from September, 1955 to January, 1965. According to the minutes, Valencia Adams was the first president. Joe Kennedy took over the position in 1956 and remained in office until 1959, when Ennis became president. In April, 1962, Jean Kennedy became president. The records of major activities and votes given in the minutes are literally as follows:

Date of Minutes   *Actions and Votes*
Sept. 11, 1955   A wedding gift for Mr. E.: $2.74. Voted to send Mrs. K., who is sick, $10.00.

Oct. 9, 1955	Voted to have a potluck dinner on the next meeting.
Dec. 11, 1955	Mrs. B. be paid for the two weeks. She was ill due to fractured ribs and that Mrs. J. be paid for three weeks. She was ill due to operation. The Christmas party was the new business taken up.
Feb. 12, 1956	Plan for a chittling dinner on March 3.
Apr. 8, 1956	Voted to go to church together the 2nd Sunday in May at the church of Miss P. in Pasadena and have dinner at Clifton afterwards with the club paying the expenses.
June 10, 1956	Mr. E. K. was given $10 for the time that he was sick. Plan for the picnic for the 4th Sunday in July.
Aug. 12, 1956	Plan for a scholarship to a desiring student. Report on the meeting of the Sears Foundation for community improvement. Introduction of the visitors from "Middville," Texas. Sent Miss J. J. $10: She is recovering from an operation at the university hospital. Plan for the "Middville" Club annual picnic on Sunday, July 28, 1957 at Lincoln Park.
Sept. 9, 1956	Sent Mr. L. sick benefit of $5.00; Miss J. sick benefit of $5.00 and a free will offering of $5.50. Mr. L. C. joined the club.
Oct. 14, 1956	New member — Mr. & Mrs. W. and daughter.
Feb. 10, 1957	Mr. & Mrs. A. J. C. joined in with us.
May 11, 1958	Mrs. L. was paid $6.24 for the wreath for Mr. W.
July 13, 1958	Mr. & Mrs. S. guests.
May 10, 1959	Report on the money collected in community club award drive, $615. The money to send Diana to Summer Camp to be decided at the next meeting.
Aug. 9, 1959	Mrs. A. made a report on her trip to Texas.
Oct. 11, 1959	Plan for a rummage sale for the 1st Saturday in Dec.
Mar. 13, 1960	Resignation of Miss J. J. as of June 1, 1960.
July 10, 1960	It was motioned and seconded to give Mrs. W. M. J. $25.
Oct. 9, 1960	The club would have a Halloween Party Oct. 29. All club members were asked to bring 2 cans of canned food to the next meeting for Christmas basket.
Dec. 11, 1960	Discuss the New Year Party to [be] held Dec. 31, 1960.
Mar. 12, 1961	Expense paid Mrs. K. $5.00 for illness.
Nov. 12, 1961	The sum of $243.45 drawn out of the Bank of America and loan to Mrs. H.
Feb. 11, 1962	Report on Mrs. M. to pay her the maximum for the illness $15.
Aug. 12, 1962	The club was very sorry to have Mrs. A. resign the club.
Oct. 13, 1962	Mr. & Mrs. R. H. were the visitors to the club. They joined the club.
Sept. 1963	It was motioned and seconded that we would give ten Christmas baskets to the needy which will be given through the welfare committee. Also each member will be required to bring a donation to go in the Christmas basket for the next three months.

Mar. 8, 1964   The resignation of Mrs. T. L. and Mrs. S. M.
June 14, 1964   Send Mr. C. P. $15, who is ill, as a gift plus 30 cents for a
                money order.

The above excerpts do not include minutes of the repeated regular meetings or parties such as the Christmas party and the annual picnic. It is clear from this list that the most frequent action taken is in connection with the contribution of money to sick members, which seems to reflect the advanced age of many members. Although there is no article in the bylaws regarding "congratulatory" presents of money, there was such a case in 1955. It can also be noted that the members sometimes enjoy having a potluck dinner, a chittling dinner, or dinner at a restaurant. They welcome visitors from their hometown or reports on trips to the hometown.

The bylaws state that a member shall be from "Middville," Texas, or a relative of someone from "Middville." Checking the hometowns of the majority of the members revealed that the exclusive nature of the club in this sense is well maintained. Among the members there are a number of affinal or consanguineous kin to the Kennedy, Adams, Davis, and Smith families. The Miller family, as already noted, does not belong to the club. The Smith family is represented by Helen, although Alex does not come to the meetings, and Helen apparently lost interest in the club and stopped going to meetings several years ago. The membership has declined slowly. Probably one reason for the declining activity of the club is that the second generation of the families are only marginal members of the club. Concrete examples are the two daughters of the Smith family; two daughters of the Kennedy family and their families; and Preston and Ronald, the two sons of Victoria (Helen's younger sister), who may join recreational activities but do not belong to the club. Thus, the club seems to be very much an association for the migrants of the first generation. The members of the second generation seem more skillful in adapting themselves to urban living, and they seem to have a potential for upward social mobility. If so, these factors would tend to weaken the direct ties already established between "Middville" and their parents.

FICTIVE KINFOLK AND FOSTERAGE OF NONKINFOLK

Fictive Kinships

It may be appropriate to introduce here briefly data about "play-relatives," since the role of "play-relatives" seems to be intermediate between that of relatives and that of friends. They are fictive, i.e. non-consanguineous, relatives without serious obligations to fulfill. "One claims the other as one's play-relative," or "one is claimed by the other as the other's play-relative." However, J. Aschenbrenner describes such obligations in this manner:

The playful aspect of the relationship was reflected in the nature of the obligations: a girl merely "played" at being a daughter, giving only token services; the woman made light demands as an excuse to give her "playdaughter" gifts when she so desired (Aschenbrenner 1971: 11).

Mary Davis claims Earnestine as her play-daughter. Earnestine was her assistant teacher at the Head Start school at 69th and Compton. As a play-mother, Mary gave her a gift and donated money. In return, Earnestine remembers Mary's birthday. A daughter of Bertha claims Mary is her "mother." Bertha, who was her assistant teacher at another Head Start site, used to bring her little daughter of nineteen months with her every day because she could not afford a baby-sitter. Mary recalls, "Everybody took care of this baby at the site. She started to call me 'Mama.'" She still calls Mary "Mama." Mary will give her money on her birthday, Christmas, or Easter.

Mary once claimed Lena, a widow living with her own daughter, as her "mother." Mary says, "She was such kind of a motherly person. It was sixteen or seventeen years ago. She showed sympathy when Charles and I needed sympathy." On Lena's last birthday Mary bought a plate as a present to her. Mary calls her "my mammy Kirk."

For Mary the custom of claiming play-relatives is not a new one. It was twenty-eight years ago that Lola claimed her as her "daughter." Lola was a neighbor living across the street in the "Middville" Black community. Mary said, "Whenever she baked something like plain cake or pie she gave it to me." Mary returned similar things when she baked them. Mary will send cards to or reminisce with her play-mother as she does with her real mother, back in her hometown at Christmas or Easter, or on her birthday.

Sunny Miller has a play-daughter whom she claims as hers. She found this child living miserably in her neighborhood and took pity on her. Helen Smith has no play-relatives in Los Angeles. She only remembers that one of her classmates at Daniel High in "Middville" claimed her as a play-relative.

One can gather from these data that patterns of fictive kin relationship still persist in the new environment, but for the families in Los Angeles such relationships could also be categorized as friendships.

Fosterage of Nonkinfolk

Before Charles died, Mary Davis decided to help Ruthy, a member of her church, out of her predicament. Young and unmarried, Ruthy needed someone to look after her one-year-old baby until she finished school and got a job. Mary offered her help out of sheer pity for the baby, who looked very ill. The baby began to call Charles "Papa," Mary "Big Mama," and its own mother "Ruthy." During the two years they kept this girl, the father came to see her several times. Mary suspected, however, that this man would not go near the child once they had taken it back to Ruthy, because he had married another woman and would not want to get involved financially or otherwise; and if the child was no longer under the care of a stable family, he could be forced to assume an unwelcome obligation. Mary knows Ruthy works in a public place but does not know where she lives. Once Ruthy gave Mary her telephone number, but it was disconnected soon afterward. Ruthy's girl should be sixteen years old by now.

Mary and Charles also took care of two little boys of one of Charles's colleagues who lived next door. Their mother was working also. When Mary and Charles moved to their present place, they took the boys with them. The boys stayed with them for about a year between 1954 and 1955. Today, Mary has no contact with either the boys or their parents.

If these two examples of fosterage of nonkinfolk are typical, they seem to indicate that in Los Angeles fosterage constitutes only a tenuous and temporary tie, as opposed, for instance, to Valencia Adams's continued relationship with Mr. R., her mother's employer in "Middville," in whose household she was brought up.

NEIGHBORS AND FRIENDS OF THE FIVE FAMILIES IN LOS ANGELES

Wherever newcomers settle, they will necessarily be involved in a relationship with their neighbors. One of my major objectives here has been to find out how often the newcomers have consciously tried to find relatives and other migrants from the same town or region as neighbors and friends. These five families have found friends in the "Middville" Club, through fictive kinships, in churches, in places of work, and, to a lesser extent, in their neighborhoods.

Neighborhood Relationships

The neighborhood is different from the other organizations mentioned above since it is an aggregate of people with less-structured communication channels, where consensus is rarely attained, and where people do not necessarily share common interests. This may have something to do with the fact that the neighborhood has been a minor source of friends for the five families. Neighborhood relationships, however, vary among the five families.

The Smiths own a small, well-kept house on an old street, narrow and poorly paved, at least in its Black section. Helen Smith considers her neighborhood as extending over an area two blocks long and one block wide. Her knowledge about her neighbors is uneven; there are some neighbors about whom she knows almost nothing. For instance, she had not known that the house next door held twenty-two persons (said to be from Mississippi) until it burned down in the 1960's. Helen collects condolence money from the neighbors when a death occurs, as was the case when the wife of the White couple next door to her died recently. Apparently, however, the Smiths do not have personal friends among their neighbors.

The Adams family exchanges greetings with their immediate neighbors on either side and across the street. Valencia and her sister Allean visit freely with two elderly women who live with a couple in the house to the left. These two women, the couple they live with, another woman, and two families across the road were invited to Joellean's wedding reception and gave presents.

The Kennedys live the farthest from Watts. Through the 46th Block Improvement Club (which includes two White families) Joe and his wife know a number of neighbors quite closely. Joe appreciates the friendship of one neighbor whom he met four years ago through the club and who fixed the top of his garage without charging him. Another one with whom he became close a few years ago has since died, but Joe still talks about him. They used to talk with each other in the yard very often. According to Joe, this man was "a big talker." About a third neighbor, whom he has known for twelve years, he says, "He is just a neighbor. He visits me. He is a regular guy. We like football and baseball. We have things in common." Of all the neighbors, however, Mr. and Mrs. L. are the ones the Kennedy family feels closest to: "Mr. L. is *a large brother to me.* He married a girl of my home [town]. We were good friends [of hers while in "Middville"]. We have known him eight years." Joe also pointed out that Mrs. L. came from a suburb of "Middville."

Mary Davis has lived alone in her own house since her husband died. She sounded rather sad about her neighborhood: "I don't like the neighborhood. There are people who are not desirable. They are loud, noisy, take possession. They may be fighting. That is why they are so loud and noisy. They use four-letter words, all kinds of words." What she means by "take possession" is that someone uses the curb in front of her house as a garage. She complains, "A car has been left there since last Monday. One family with four cars monopolizes the curb."

She knows two of her neighbors well; one lives behind her house and works as an interior decorator as well as a painter. The other lives next door. She calls them her friends but she would not call other neighbors so.

The Millers' neighborhood is a run-down area with widespread property damage. Sunny confides that among the neighbors she knows personally there are some bad ones but also a certain number of good ones she "can go with."

Joe and Jean Kennedy seem to have more friends in their neighborhood than the other four families. Perhaps this is due to the fact that they have gotten to know their neighbors through the 46th Block Improvement Club. Referring to one of the differences between her hometown and Los Angeles, Jean mentioned the lack of closeness in Los Angeles; people have no concern for their neighbors, and there are no tangible signs of friendly feeling there. Although she likes her neighborhood in Los Angeles, she is not sure how much friendliness or closeness she should offer, or how much friendliness she can expect of her neighbors. She will talk to neighbors if she happens to see them, but she is not certain how far she can go in initiating friendly chats. If a "talk over the fence" expresses one of the typical neighborhood relationships, it fittingly represents the psychological attitude she has towards her neighbors.

Mary Davis can call two of her neighbors her friends, but they do not invite each other into their homes. Sunny Miller and Helen Smith mentioned that there was no exchange of visits with their neighborhood friends. It is only Valencia Adams who associates with her neighbors socially: she invites two elderly women neighbors to her house, and they in turn invite her to their home.

Friendships Through Work and Church Organizations

Mary Davis has two friends at Head Start; one is a Jewish coworker who lives near Santa Monica. Mary was invited to her house for her birthday this year. The other friend is her assistant teacher. The fictive kinships arising through her Head Start work have already been described in the previous section.

Sunny Miller belongs to a World War I Veterans' Auxiliary which meets on the first Friday of each month at Compton Park. Meetings include a roll call, "penny march," and potluck dinner to which everybody brings a covered dish. Members' birthdays are celebrated and other social activities are connected with the meetings.

Among the five families, church ties vary in closeness and duration. For a person like C. D. Adams, who goes to his wife's church three times a year at most, the chances of forming friendships are slim. Since last year, however, he has become a member of Mt. Zion Church in "Middville," which he attends more than twice a year. He chose this hometown church because "most of his relatives go there," and he makes an annual contribution of twenty-five dollars because "I thought the church needed my support."

Valencia Adams has been a regular member of McCoy Memorial Baptist Church, where she once served as an usher, since 1946. She picked this church because Reverend Anderson is her longtime friend. He comes from Shreveport, Louisiana, where he began his ministerial career at Jubilee Baptist Church; Valencia belonged to its choir. The pamphlet report of envelope contributions in 1969 shows contributions from 604 persons on an individual basis, ranging from 10 to 824 dollars, with the highest contribution made by Reverend Anderson himself. Valencia is well in the upper ranks.

Sunny Miller has been a regular member of St. John Baptist Church for twenty-one years. The minister has been her friend for twenty-three or -four years, and among the church members there are two couples who have been her friends for more than twenty years. Her husband went from the Pilgrim Baptist Church on the East Side to St. John Baptist Church on the West Side about ten years ago for the sake of convenience. Unlike C. D., he has no attachment to his hometown nor any commitment to any civic or political organization.

Helen Smith goes to the Freewill Missionary Baptist Church. The minister comes from a small Texas town, and many members are also from Texas. As already mentioned, she introduced some of her relatives into this church, so that she now has both friends and relatives there. Alex, however, apparently does not go to church at all.

SUMMARY

Each of the five families has close relatives back in their hometown and still keeps in touch with them in various ways, such as visiting, telephone calls, and greetings of various forms through the "Middville" Club. Members of the five families travel over one thousand miles to participate in church or family reunions, to attend funerals, to see their relatives, or to take vacation trips. Visiting is not only in one direction. On and off people from "Middville" visit Los Angeles, giving their relatives and friends opportunities to welcome them and to hear the hometown news.

Most relatives of Helen Smith, Jean Kennedy, and Sunny Miller are located either in "Middville" or in Los Angeles, while the relatives of Mary Davis, Valencia Adams, and C. D. Adams are more dispersed. For Mary there is an intermediate stepping stone at Palm Springs, where her younger sister's family and her younger brother live, while Mary's mother, younger sister, and other relatives live in "Middville." Valencia and C. D. interact with the families of her nephews in Sacramento and with her relatives in "Middville" and in East Hamilton, Texas. Alex Smith has only a few relatives on his side, one of whom is living in Los Angeles. He shares with his wife, Helen, a strong sentiment toward "Middville" rather than San Antonio, his birthplace. The same is true of Richard Miller, who has no relatives in his hometown, Marshall, Texas, since the death of his younger brother. He interacts only with his three daughters in Los Angeles occasionally. For Joe Kennedy, relatives on his side are dispersed in Texas and Michigan. He feels close to and keeps in contact with his younger sister in Wichita Falls, Texas. One of his cousins on his father's side, and the family of his deceased older brother's son live in Los Angeles.

In the distribution of relatives living in Los Angeles, there is residential propinquity among many but not all the siblings; for example, Helen and her younger brother, T. L., Jr.; Valencia and her younger sister, Allean; the Kennedys' two adult daughters; and the three daughters of Richard by his previous wife. In the case of both the Kennedys and the Smiths, parents and adult children live apart from each other.

Genealogical knowledge among the five families often goes back to the days of slavery, and some informants could describe their slave ancestors from their direct personal knowledge. It is noticeable that they generally possess more detailed knowledge of genealogy on the maternal side than on the paternal side. Also, data in their family genealogies lead us to assume that interracial unions between Black and White, or between Black and Indian, have been of no small significance in "Middville."

A matrifocal tendency exists in two cases (Smith, Adams) but not so unequivocally in other cases. Interaction between parents (regardless of marital status) and their adult children and between adult siblings is frequently observable, while it seems that there is very little interaction between paternal and maternal kin. Informal family get-togethers of parents, children, and grandchildren are a frequent practice, particularly on special occasions such as Thanksgiving, Christmas, New Year's, Easter, and Independence Day. Extension of kinship is not just descriptive knowledge but has a real and substantial meaning to those concerned. It sometimes includes even the second cousin's children as in the case of Valencia's relationship with her mother's mother's sister's daughter's daughter's children (Appendix, Table 1.3) or C. T.'s relationship with Mary Davis (Appendix, Tables 1.2 and 1.3). By "real and substantial meaning" is meant aid of various forms among the relatives. We have already noted examples of monetary aid, shared living space, and help by doing domestic work, finding jobs, or fostering a child.

As for fictive kinship, it seems that the fact of migration has not cut off fictive kin relationships which existed between play-relatives in their hometown. A fictive partner (play-daughter) will send cards or reminisce with her fictive relative (play-mother) as much as with her real mother. The data from the five families show that patterns of fictive kin relationship still persist in the new environment; a few members of the five families, for instance, Mary Davis and Sunny Miller, both childless, have found their play-relatives among neighbors and friends.

As for friendships, the migrants have formed a hometown club in the new environment and found their friends among people from the same locality. But this does not mean that they have not found other friends. The "Middville" Club has played an important role; it has renewed the otherwise weakening ties between the migrants and their hometown, and it has strengthened social relationships among the members by expressing sympathy, in the form of money or by other means, toward its members and their relatives, both in Los Angeles and "Middville," in cases of illness or death.

During my research I found that there are other groups similar to the "Middville" Club among the Los Angeles Black residents. One such group is called the Timpson Club, named after a small city in eastern Texas. Another group, called the Better Mississippian, is composed of Black professionals in the area. The former, a hometown association, seems to be more akin to the "Middville" Club in its nature, while the latter seems to emphasize the professional ties of its members. However, an analysis of these two groups is yet to be made. A Black newspaper occasionally mentions a Chicago Club, of which very little is known to me except that it is larger than the "Middville" Club or the Timpson Club.

The result of the interviews with the fifty families (see Note 5) living in the area at the time of my research also indicates that there are several other groups of the hometown-association type. These groups, varied in size, are not organized formally enough to have names as such, but they provide a meeting place for people from the same town. The groups provide much-needed opportunities to get together, to eat and drink, to play cards, to have fun by exchanging gifts on special occasions. The members take turns in opening their homes for meetings, at frequencies ranging from once a month to once or twice a year. The smallest of the groups consists of only three families, while larger ones have from twenty to twenty-five people. Although they are all social in nature, there are interesting differences. For instance, one group makes each meeting an occasion to enjoy food prepared by its members, while another promotes friendly ties among its members by encouraging them to bring their children to the meetings. Yet another, composed of friends close since grammar school days, meets simply to have a good time.

Finally, a brief reference should be made to the possible implications of what has been described in this chapter for the next generation of the migrants. There are negative as well as positive implications. Negative implications are related to the basic attitudes which the migrants from the South have formed in urban adaptation, either toward their own race or toward Whites. Such basic attitudes will be transmitted to the generation to come on the family level. Positive implications are related to certain aspects of the Black way of life, for example, mutual aid among relatives and friends.

The children of the five families are now in a position to observe from some distance the interplay between their parents and their relatives. Lisa, the eldest daughter of the Smiths, says that, because she is not too deeply involved in such interactions, she can see them more objectively and thus form a better understanding of the Black way of life. Lisa is aware of the existence of the spirit of mutual help among her folks, of her mother's important and prominent role in maintaining family solidarity. She feels that these features are necessary and positive aspects of the Black way of life, and that they will become a foundation for better appreciation of Black culture in urban life.

APPENDIX: STATISTICAL INFORMATION (Compiled by Charles Williams from the data of Dr. Kiyotaka Aoyagi)

Table 1.1. The Smith family: kinfolk and residences

Generation	Index number	Name First	Name Last	1970 Status Sex	Race	Alive	Age	Location	Relationships Parents	Siblings	Spouse(s)	Children	Divorced or separated	Household affiliation(s)
I	IA.1	Lucindy[a]	-	F	B	†	-	-	-	-	IB.2(CL?); IC.3(CL)	IIA.5, 6; IIA.7–10	-	IB.2?; IC.3
	IB.2	-	-	M	B	†	-	-	-	-	IA.1(CL?)	IIA.5, 6	-	IA.1(CL?)
	IC.3	-	-	M	W	†	-	-	-	-	IA.1(CL)	IIA.7–10	-	IA.1(CL)
	ID.4	Sam[b]	Moor	M	B	†	-	-	-	-	-	IID.14	-	-
II	IIA.5	-	-	M	B	†	-	-	IA.1; IB.2	IIA.6 (IIA.7–10)	-	IIIA.18	-	-
	IIA.6	-	-	M	B	†	-	-	IA.1; IB.2	IIA.5 (IIA.7–10)	-	-	-	-
	IIA.7	-	-	F	B	†	-	-	IA.1; IC.3	IIA.8–10 (IIA.5, 6)	-	-	-	-
	IIA.8	Ealla[c]	-	F	B	†	-	-	IA.1; IC.3	IIA.7, 9, 10 (IIA.5, 6)	IIE.11(CL)	IIIA.24, 25; IIIF.19–23	-	IIE.11; IIF.12
	IIA.9	-	-	M	B	†	-	-	IA.1; IC.3	IIA.7, 8, 10 (IIA.5, 6)	-	-	-	-
	IIA.10	-	-	M	B	†	-	-	IA.1; IC.3	IIA.7–9 (IIA.5, 6)	-	-	-	-
	IIE.11	John	Morrison	M	W	†	-	-	-	-	IIA.8 (CL)	IIIA.24, 25	-	IIA.8(CL)
	IIF.12	Arthur	-	M	B	†	-	-	-	-	IIA.8	IIIF.19–23	-	IIA.8
	IIG.13	Mandy	-	F	B	†	-	-	-	-	IID.14	IIID.26	-	IID.14
	IID.14	Joe	-	M	S?	†	-	-	ID.4; -	-	IIG.13	IIID.26	-	IID.14
	IIH.15[d]	-	-	M	B	†	-	-	-	-	IIJ.16(CL)	IIIJ.28	-	IIJ.16(CL)
	IIJ.16	-	-	F	B	†	-	-	-	-	IIH.15(CL)	IIIJ.28	-	IIH.15(CL)
	IIK.17	-	-	F	B	1	-	-	-	-	IIIA.18	IVK.31–39	Deceased	IIIA.18
III	IIIA.18	Viola	-	F	B	1	-	L.A.	IIA.5; ?	-	IIK.17	IVK.31–39	Widowed	IIIA.18
	IIIF.19	-	-			1	-	-	IIA.8; IIF.12	IIIF.20–23 (IIIA.24, 25)	-	-	-	-
	IIIF.20	-	-	F	B	1	-	-	IIA.8; IIF.12	IIIF.19–23 (IIIA.24, 25)	-	-	-	-
	IIIF.21	-	-	F	B	1	-	-	IIA.8; IIF.12	IIIF.19, 20, 22, 23 (IIIA.24, 25)	-	-	-	-

Table 1.1. The Smith family: kinfolk and residences *continued*

Genera-tion	Index number	Name First	Last	1970 Status Sex	Race	Alive	Age	Location	Relationships Parents	Siblings	Spouse(s)	Children	Divorced or separated	Household affiliation(s)
	IIIF.22	-	-	F	B	1	-	-	IIA.8; IIF.12	IIIF.19–23 (IIIA.24, 25)	-	-	-	-
	IIIF.23	-	-	F	B	1	-	-	IIA.8; IIF.12	IIIF.19–22 (IIIA.24, 25)	-	-		-
	IIIA.24	-	-	F	B	†	-	-	IIA.8; IIE.11	IIIA.25 (IIIF.19–23)	-	-		-
	IIIA.25	Beulah	-	F	B	†	-	-	IIA.8; IIE.11	IIIA.24 (IIIF.19–23)	IIID.26 IIIL.27(CL)	IVA.40, 41; IVD.42–45	-	IIIL.27(CL) IIID.26 IIIA.25
	IIID.26	T.	L.SR.	M	B	1	-	Midd.	IID.14; IIG.13	-	IIIA.25	IVD.42–45	-	IIIA.25
	IIIL.27	-	-	M	W	1	-	-	-	-	IIIA.25 (CL?)	IVA.40, 41	Separated	IIIA.25
	IIIJ.28	-	Smith	M	B	†	-	-	IIJ.16; IIH.15	-	IIIM.29	IVJ.46	-	IIIM.29
	IIIM.29	-	-	F	B	†	-	-	-	-	IIIJ.28; IIIN.30	IVJ.46; IVN.47, 48	-	IIIJ.28; IIIN.30
	IIIN.30	-	-	M	B	†	-	-	-	-	IIIM.29	IVN.47, 48	-	IIIM.29
IV	IVK.31e	-	-	?	B	1	-	Tex. ?	-	IVK.32–39	?	?	?	?
	IVK.32		-	?	B	1		Tex. ?	IIIK.17; IIIA.18	IVK.31, 33–34	?	?	?	?
	IVK.33	-		?	B	1		Sacra., Calif.	IIIK.17; IIIA.18	IVK.31, 32, 34–39	?	?	?	IVK.33
	IVK.34			?	B	1		L.A.	IIIK.17; IIIA.18	IVK.31–33, 35–39	?	?	?	IIIA.18
	IVK.35		-	?	B	1		L.A.	IIIK.17; IIIA.18	IVK.31–34, 36–39	?	?	?	IIIA.18
	IVK.36		-	?	B	1		L.A.	IIIK.17; IIIA.18	IVK.31–35, 37–39	?	?	?	IIIA.18
	IVK.37	-	-	?	B	1		L.A.	IIIK.17; IIIA.18	IVK.31–36, 38–39	?	?	?	IIIA.18
	IVK.38	-	-	?	B	1		L.A.	IIIK.17; IIIA.18	IVK.31–37, 39	?	?	?	IIIA.18
	IVK.39	-	-	?	B	1		L.A.	IIIK.17; IIIA.18; IIIA.1	IVK.31–38	?	?	?	IIIA.18

Table 1.1.   The Smith family: kinfolk and residences *continued*

Genera-tion	Index number	Name		1970 Status					Relationships					Household affiliation(s)
		First	Last	Sex	Race	Alive	Age	Loca-tion	Parents	Siblings	Spouse(s)	Children	Divorced or separated	
IV	IVA.40	John[f]	-	M	B	1	-	Midd.	IIIA.25; IIIL.27	IVA.41 (IVD.42-45)	IVO.49	-		IVO.49
	IVA.41	Anna[f]	-	F	B	†	-	-	IIIA.25; IIIL.27	IVA.40 (IVD.42-45)	IVP.50	VP.56		IVP.50
	IVD.42	Helen	Smith	F	B	1	60	L.A.	IIIA.25; IIID.26	IVD.43-45 (IVA.40 41)	IVI.46	VI.58, 59	-	IVI.46
	IVD.43	Victoria	-	F	B	1	-	L.A.	IIIA.25; IIID.26	IVD.42, 44, 45 (IVA.40, 41)	IVQ.51	VQ.61-64	Separated	IVD.43
	IVD.44	T.	L. JR.	M	B	1	-	L.A.	IIIA.25; IIID.26	IVD.42, 43, 45 (IVA.40, 41)	IVR.52	VD.69-72	Separated	IVR.52
	IVD.45	E.	W.	F	B	1	-	Midd.	IIIA.25; IIID.26	IVD.42-44 (IVA.40, 41)	IVS.53	-		IVS.53
	IVJ.46	Alex	Smith	M	B	1	70	L.A.	IIIJ.28; IIIM.29	IVN.47, 48	IVD.42	VI.58, 59		IVD.42
	IVN.47	Lois	-	F	B	1	-	L.A.	IIIN.30; IIIM.29	IVN.48 (IVJ.46)	IVT.54			IVN.47
	IVN.48	-	-	M	B	†	-	-	IIIN.30; IIIM.29	IVN.47 (IVJ.46)	-			
	IVO.49	-	-	F	B	1	-	Midd.	-	-	IVA.40	-	-	IVA.40
	IVP.50	-	-	M	B	1	-	Midd.	-	-	IVA.41	VP.56	-	IVP.50
	IVQ.51	-	-	M	B	1	-		-	-	IVD.43	VQ.61-64; VR.73	Separated	IVD.43
	IVR.52	Florence	L.	F	B	1	-	N. Calif.	-	-	IVD.44	VD.69-72; VR.73	Divorced	IVR.52
	IVS.53	M.	W.	M	B	1	-	Midd.	-	-	IVD.45	-		IVS.53
	IVT.54	-	-	M	B	†	-	-	-	-	IVN.47	-		
V	VU.55	Kenneth	-	M	B	1	-	(Watts) L.A.	IVP.50; IVA.41	?	VP.56(CL)	VIP.74	Separated	VU.55(CL
	VP.56	Shiela	-	F	B	1	-	L.A.			VV.57; VU.55(CL)	VIP.74		VV.57
	VV.57	Bobby	-	M	B	1	-	L.A.	IVI.46; IVD.42	VJ.59	VP.56			VV.57
	VJ.58	Lisa	Smith	F	B	1	21	L.A.	IVI.46; IVD.42	VJ.59				VJ.58

Table 1.1. The Smith family: kinfolk and residences *continued*

Genera-tion	Index number	Name First	Name Last	1970 Status Sex	Race	Alive	Age	Loca-tion	Relationships Parents	Siblings	Spouse(s)	Children	Divorced or separated	Household affiliation(s)
	VJ.59	-	Smith	F	B	1	18	L.A.	IVJ.46; IVD.42	VJ.58	-	-	-	IVJ.46
	VW.60	-	-	F	B	1	-	L.A.	-	-	VQ.61	VIQ.76, 77	Divorced	VIYY.75; VIQ.76
	VQ.61	Willie	-	M	B	1	39	L.A.	IVQ.51; IVD.43	VQ.62–64	VW.60	VIQ.76, 77	Divorced	IVD.43
	VQ.62	Tommy	-	M	B	1	-	L.A.	IVQ.51; IVD.43	VQ.61, 63, 64	VX.65	VIQ.77–80	-	VQ.62
	VQ.63	Preston	-	M	B	1	-	L.A.	IVQ.51; IVD.43	VQ.61, 62, 64	VY.66	-	-	VQ.63
	VQ.64	Ronald	-	M	B	1	-	L.A.	IVQ.51; IVD.43	VQ.61–63	VZ.68	VIQ.84	-	VQ.64
	VX.65	Margaret	-	F	B	1	-	L.A.	-	-	VQ.62	VIQ.77–80	-	VQ.64
	VY.66	-	-	F	B	1	-	L.A.	-	-	VQ.63; VXX.67	VIXX.82, 83	Divorced	VQ.63
	VXX.67	-	-	M	B	1	-	-	-	-	VY.66	VIXX.82, 83	Divorced	VXX.67
	VZ.68	-	-	F	B	1	-	L.A.	-	-	VQ.64	VIQ.84	-	VQ.64
	VD.69	-	-	M	B	1	19	-	IVD.44; IVR.52	VD.70–72 (VR.73)	-	-	-	IVD.43
	VD.70	-	-	M	B	1	-	L.A.	IVD.44; IVR.52	VD.69, 71, 72 (VR.73)	-	-	-	IVD.44
	VD.71	-	-	M	B	1	-	L.A.	IVD.44; IVR.52	VD.69, 70, 72 (VR.73)	-	-	-	IVD.44
	VD.72	-	-	F	B	1	8	N. Calif.	IVD.44; IVR.52	VD.69–71 (VR.73)	-	-	-	-
	VR.73	-	-	M	B	1	-	-	IVR.52; ?	-	-	-	-	-
VI	VIP.74	-	-	M	B	1	-	L.A.	VP.56; VU.55	-	-	-	-	-
	VIYY.75	-	-	M	B	1	-	L.A.	-	-	VIQ.76	VIYY.85	-	VIYY.75
	VIQ.76	-	-	F	B	1	-	L.A.	VQ.61; VW.60	VIQ.77	VIYY.75	VIYY.85	-	VIYY.75

Table 1.1. The Smith family: kinfolk and residences *continued*

Genera-tion	Index number	Name First	Name Last	Sex	Race	Alive	Age	Loca-tion	Parents	Siblings	Spouse(s)	Children	Divorced or separated	Household affiliation(s)
	VIQ.77	-	-	F	B	1	-	L.A.	VQ.61; VW.60	VIQ.76	-	-	-	VW.60
	VIQ.78	-	-	F	B	1	-	L.A.	VQ.62; VX.65	VIQ.79–81	-	-	-	VQ.62
	VIQ.79	-	-	M	B	1	-	L.A.	VQ.62; VX.65	VIQ.78, 80, 81	-	-	-	VQ.62
	VIQ.80	-	-	M	B	1	-	L.A.	VQ.62; VX.65	VIQ.78, 79, 81	-	-	-	VQ.62
	VIQ.81	-	-	M	B	1	-	L.A.	VQ.62; VX.65	VIQ.78, 80, 81	-	-	-	VQ.62
	VIXX.82	-	-	M	B	1	-	L.A.	VXX.67; VY.66	VIXX.83	-		-	VQ.63
	VIXX.83	-	-	M	B	1	-	L.A.	VXX.67; VY.66	VIXX.82	-			VQ.63
	VIQ.84	-	-	M	B	1	-	L.A.	VQ.64; VZ.68	-	-			VQ.64
VII	VIIYY.85	-	-	M	B	1	-	L.A.	VIYY.75; VIQ.76	-	-			VIIYY.75

Key to Tables 1.1–1.5:

M = Male
F = Female
B = Black
W = White

1 = Living
† = Deceased
Midd = "Middville," Texas
L.A. = Los Angeles, California

(CL) = Common law
O = Half sibling
- = Unknown or inapplicable
? = Information lacking

Note: 1970 status (alive, age, location) inapplicable for all deceased members; capital letter I omitted throughout to avoid confusion with Roman numeral I.

[a] Lucindy was a slave and reportedly half Cherokee Indian; age at death, 77–78; see text.
[b] Sam, Helen's father's father, was an ex-slave.
[c] Ealla reportedly died at age 25.
[p] Alex Smith's ancestry begins with his grandfather, believed to have been Spanish or Mexican.
[p] Further information on Viola's children (IVK.31–39) lacking.
* John and Anna also shared a half brother, Pete; see text.

Table 1.2.   The Davis family: kinfolk and residences

Genera-tion	Index number	Name First	Name Last	1970 Status Sex	Race	Alive	Age	Loca-tion	Relationships Parents	Siblings	Spouse(s)	Children	Divorced or separated	Household affiliation(s)
I	IA.1	-	Fields	M	B	†	-	-	-	-	IB.2	IIA.3	-	IA.1
	IB.2	Sallie	Fields	F	B	†	-	-	-	-	IA.1	IIA.3	-	IA.1
II	IIA.3	Emely	-	F	B	†	-	-	IA.1; IB.2	-	IIC.4	IIIC.7	-	IIC.4
	IIC.4	James	-	M	B	†	-	-	-	-	IIA.3	IIIC.7	-	IIC.4
	IID.5	Jane	-	F	B	†	-	-	-	-	IIE.6(CL?)	IIID.8	-	IIE.6(CL)
	IIE.6	Att	-	M	B	†	-	-	-	-	IID.5(CL?)	IIID.8	-	IID.5(CL)
III	IIIC.7	Sallie	-	F	B	1	86	Midd.	IIC.4; IIA.3	?a	IID.8	IVD.10, 13, 15, 18, 20, 23, 26, 28	-	IIID.8
	IIID.8	Osia	-	M	B	†	-	Midd.	IID.5; IIE.6	-	IIIC.7; IIIF.9	IVD.10, 13, 15, 18, 20, 23, 26, 28	-	IIIC.7; IIIF.9
	IIIF.9	-	-	F	B	†	-	-	-	-	IIID.8	IVD.30, 32	-	IIID.8
IV	IVD.10	R.H.	-	M	B	1	-	L.A.	IIID.8; IIIC.7	IVD.13, 15, 18, 20, 23, 26, 28	IVG.11	VD.34, 35	-	IVD.10
	IVG.11	-	-	F	B	1	-	L.A.	-	-	IVD.10	VD.34, 35	-	IVH.12
	IVH.12	Curtis	-	M	B	1	-	Palm Sp., Calif.	-	-	IVD.13	VH.36, 37, 39	-	IVH.12
	IVD.13	Jimmie	-	F	B	1	-	Palm Sp., Calif.	IIID.8; IIIC.7	IVD.10, 15, 18, 20, 23, 26, 28 (IVD.30, 32)	IVH.12; IVJ.14	VH.36, 37, 39; VD.41	•	IVH.12; IVJ.14
	IVJ.14	-	-	M	B	†	-	-	-	-	IVD.13 (CL)	VD.41	•	IVD.13(CL)
	IVD.15	Eva	-	F	B	1	-	Midd.	IIID.8; IIIC.7	IVD.10, 13, 18, 20, 23, 26, 28 (IVD.30, 32)	IVK.16	VK.43-45, 46, 47, 49	•	IVK.16
	IVK.16	James	Himes	M	B	1	-	Midd.	-	-	IVD.15	VK.43-45, 46, 47, 49	•	IVK.16
	IVL.17	-	-	F	B	1	-	-	-	-	IVD.18	VK.43-47, 49	•	IVD.18

Table 1.2. The Davis family: kinfolk and residences *continued*

Genera-tion	Index number	Name		1970 Status					Relationships				Divorced or separated	Household affiliation(s)
		First	Last	Sex	Race	Alive	Age	Location	Parents	Siblings	Spouse(s)	Children		
	IVD.18	Harry	-	M	B	1	-	-	IIID.8; IIIC.7	IVD.10, 13, 15, 20, 23, 26, 28 (IVD.30, 32)	IVL.17	-	-	IVD.18
	IVM.19	Katherine	-	F	B	1	-	-	-	-	IVD.18	VM.51	Divorced	IVM.19
	IVD.20		-	F	B	1	-	-	IIID.8; IIIC.7	IVD.10, 13, 15, 18, 23, 26, 28 (IVD.30, 32)	IVN.21	VN.53, 55, 56	-	VSS.54
	IVN.21			M	B	+		-	-	-	IVD.20	VN.53, 55, 56	-	IVN.21
	IVO.22	Otis[b]	-	F	B	1	-	-	-	-	IVD.23	-	-	IVD.23
	IVD.23		-	M	B	+	-	-	IIID.8; IIIC.7	IVD.10, 13, 15, 18, 20, 26, 28 (IVD.30, 32)	IVO.22; IVP.24	VD.58, 60, 62	Divorced	IVD.23
	IVP.24	Vergie	-	F	B	1	-	-	-	-	IVD.23	VD.58, 60, 62	Divorced	IVP.24
	IVQ.25	Unit	-	F	B	1	-	-	IIID.8; IIIC.7	-	IVD.26	VD.64–66	Separated	IVQ.25
	IVD.26		-	M	B	1	-	Palm Sp., Calif.		IVD.10, 13, 15, 18, 20, 23, 28 (IVD.30, 32)	IVQ.25; IVR.27	VD.64–66	Divorced	IVD.26
	IVR.27	Mary	-	F	B	1	-	-	IIID.8; IIIC.7	-	IVD.26	VD.66	Divorced	IVR.27
	IVD.28		Davis	F	B	1	63	L.A.		IVD.10, 13, 15, 18, 20, 23, 26 (IVD.30, 32)	IVS.29	-	-	IVD.28
	IVS.29	Charles	Davis[c]	M	B	+	-	L.A.	IIID.8; IIIC.7	?	IVD.28	-	-	IVS.29
	IVD.30	Emeroy	-	M	B	1	73	Elsinore, Calif.	IIID.8; IIIF.9	IVD.32 (IVD.10, 13, 15, 18, 20, 23, 26, 28)	IVT.31	-	-	IVD.30

Table 1.2. The Davis family: kinfolk and residences *continued*

Generation	Index number	Name: First	Last	Sex	Race	Alive	Age	Location	Parents	Siblings	Spouse(s)	Children	Divorced or separated	Household affiliation(s)
	IVT.31	-	-	F	B	1	-	Elsinore, Calif.	-	-	IVD.30	-	-	IVD.30
	IVD.32	-	-	M	B	†	-	-	IIID.8; IIIF.9	IVD.30 (IVD.10, 13, 15, 18, 20, 23, 28)	IVU.30	VD.68, 69	-	IVD.32
V	IVU.33	-	-	F	B	1	-	L.A.	-	-	IVD.32	VD.68, 69	-	IVD.32
	VD.34	-	-	M	B	1	-	L.A.	IVD.10; IVG.11	VD.35	-	-	-	IVD.10
	VD.35	-	-	F	B	1	-	L.A.	IVD.10; IVG.11	VD.34	-	-	-	IVD.10
	VH.36	-	-	M	B	1	-	-	IVH.12; IVD.13	VH.37, 39 (VD.41)	-	-	-	?
	VH.37	Sharon	-	F	B	1	-	L.A.	IVH.12; IVD.13	VH.36, 39 (VD.41)	VV.38	-	-	VV.38
	VV.38	-	-	M	B	1	·	-	-	-	VH.37	VIH.71, 72, 73	-	VV.38
	VH.39	-	-	M	B	1	-	-	IVH.12; IVD.13	VH.36, 37	VW.40	VIH.71, 72, 73	-	VH.39
	VW.40	-	-	F	B	1	-	-	-	-	VH.39	-	-	VH.39
	VD.41	R. James	-	M	B	1	-	-	IVD.13; IVJ.14	(VH.36, 37, 39)	VX.42	VID.74, 75	Divorced	VD.41
	VX.42	-	-	F	B	1	-	-	-	-	VD.41	VID.74, 75	Divorced	VX.42
	VK.43	-	-	F	B	1	-	Midd.	IVK.16; IVD.15	VK.44-47, 49	-	-	-	IVK.16
	VK.44	-	-	F	B	1	-	Midd.	IVK.16; IVD.15	VK.43, 45-47, 49	-	-	-	IVK.16
	VK.45	-	-	M	B	1	-	Midd.	IVK.16; IVD.15	VK.43, 44, 46, 47, 49	-	-	-	IVK.16
	VK.46	-	-	M	B	1	-	Midd.	IVK.16; IVD.15	VK.43-45, 47, 49	-	-	-	IVK.16
	VK.47	Patricia	-	F	B	1	-	Midd.	IVK.16; IVD.15	VK.43-46, 49	VY.48	VIY.76	-	VY.48
	VY.48	-	-	M	B	1	-	Midd.	-	-	VK.47	VIY.76	-	VY.48

Table 1.2. The Davis family: kinfolk and residences *continued*

Genera-tion	Index number	Name First	Last	Sex	Race	Alive	Age	Loca-tion	Parents	Siblings	Spouse(s)	Children	Divorced or separated	Household affiliation(s)
	VK.49	-	-	M	B	1	-	-	IVK.16; IVD.15	VK.43-47	VZ.50	.	-	VK.49
	VZ.50	-	-	F	B	1	-	-	-	-	VK.49	VIRR.77, 78	-	VK.49
	VD.51	-	-	F	B	1	-	-	IVM.19; IVD.18	-	VRR.52	VIRR.77, 78	-	VRR.52
	VRR.52	-	-	M	B	1	-	-	-	-	VD.51	-	-	VRR.52
	VN.53	-	-	F	B	1	-	-	IVN.21; IVD.20	VN.55, 56	-	.	-	.
	VSS.54	-	-	M	B	1	-	Midd.	-	-	VN.55	VISS.79	-	VSS.54
	VN.55	Emely	-	F	B	1	-	Midd.	IVN.21; IVD.20	VN.53, 56	VSS.54	VISS.79	-	VSS.54
	VN.56	Rachel		F	B	1	-	-	IVN.21; IVD.20	VN.53, 55	VTT.57	VITT.80-82	-	VTT.57
	VTT.57	-	-	M	B	1	-	-	-	-	VN.56	VITT.80-82	-	VTT.57
	VD.58	Uzetta		F	B	1	-	-	IVD.23; IVP.24	VD.60, 62	VUU.59	VIUU.83, 84	-	VUU.59
	VUU.59	-	-	M	B	1	-	-	-	-	VD.58	VIUU.83, 84	-	VUU.59
	VD.60	-	-	M	B	1	-	-	IVD.23; IVP.24	VD.58, 62	?	VID.85-87	?	? Information lacking on wife
	VVV.61	T.	L.	M	B	1	-	Midd.	-	-	VD.62	VIVV.88, 89	-	VVV.61
	VD.62	Joe Ruth	-	F	B	1	-	Midd.	IVD.23; IVP.24	VD.58, 60	VVV.61	VIVV.88, 89	-	VVV.61
	VWW.63	-	-	M	W	1	-	-	-	-	VD.64	VIWW.90, 91	-	VWW.63
	VD.64	-	-	F	B	1	-	-	IVD.26; IVQ.25	VD.65 (VD.66)	VWW.63	VIWW.90, 91	-	VWW.63
	VD.65	-	-	M	B	1	-	-	IVD.26; IVQ.25	VD.64 (VD.66)	-	-	-	?
	VD.66	-	-	F	B	1	-	-	IVD.26; IVR.27	(VD.64, 65)	VXX.67	-	-	VD.66

1970 Status

Table 1.2. The Davis family: kinfolk and residences *continued*

Genera-tion	Index number	Name		1970 Status					Relationships					Household affiliation(s)
		First	Last	Sex	Race	Alive	Age	Loca-tion	Parents	Siblings	Spouse(s)	Children	Divorced or separated	
	VXX.67	-	-	M	B	1	-	-	-	-	VD.66	-	-	VXX.
	VD.68	-	-	F	B	1	-	-	IVD.32; IVU.33	VD.69	-	-	-	?
	VD.69	-	-	M	B	1	-	Midd.	IVD.32; IVU.33	VD.68	VZZ.70	-	-	VD.69
	VZZ.70	-	-	F	B	1	-	Midd.	-	-	VD.69	-	-	VD.69
VI	VIH.71	-	-	?	B	1	-	-	VH.39; VW.40	VIH.72, 73	-	-	-	?
	VIH.72	-	-	?	B	1	-	-	VH.39; VW.40	VIH.71, 73	-	-	-	?
	VIH.73	-	-	?	B	1	-	-	VH.39; VW.40	VIH.71, 72	-	-	-	?
	VID.74	-	-	M	B	1	-	-	VX.41; VX.42	VID.75	-	-	-	?
	VID.75	-	-	F	B	1	-	-	VD.41; VX.42	VID.74	-	-	-	?
	VIY.76	-	-	F	B	1	-	Midd.	VY.48; VK.47		-	-	-	VY.48
	VIRR.77	-	-	F	B	1	-	-	VRR.52; VM.51	VIRR.78	-	-	-	?
	VIRR.78	-	-	F	B	1	-	-	VRR.52; VM.51	VIRR.79	-	-	-	?
	VISS.79	"Baby"	-	F?	B	1	-	-	VSS.54; VN.55		-	-	-	VSS.54
	VITT.80	-	-	?	B	1	-	-	VTT.57; VN.56	VITT.81, 82	-	-	-	VTT.57
	VITT.81	-	-	?	B	1	-	-	VTT.57; VN.56	VITT.80, 82	-	-		VTT.57
	VITT.82	-	-	?	B	1	-	-	VTT.57; VN.56	VITT.81, 80	-	-	-	VTT.57
	VIUU.83	Larry	-	M	B	1	-	-	VUU.59; VD.58	VIUU.84	-	-	-	VUU.59
	VIUU.84	Joel	-	M	B	1	-	-	VUU.59; VD.58	VIUU.83	-	-	-	VUU.59
	VID.85	-	-	?	B	1	-	-	VD.60; ?	VID.86, 87	-	-	-	?

Table 1.2. The Davis family: kinfolk and residences *continued*

Genera-tion	Index number	Name		1970 Status					Relationships					Household affiliation(s)
		First	Last	Sex	Race	Alive	Age	Loca-tion	Parents	Siblings	Spouse(s)	Children	Divorced or separated	
	VID.86	-	-	?	B	1	-	-	VD.60; ?	VID.85, 87	-	-	-	?
	VID.87	-	-	?	B	1	-	-	VD.60; ?	VID.85, 86	-	-	-	?
	VIVV.88	-	-	F	B	1	-	Midd.	VVV.61; VD.62	VIVV.89	-	-	-	VVV.61
	VIVV.89	-	-	M	B	1	-	Midd.	VVV.61; VD.62	VIVV.88	-			VVV.61
	VIWW.90	-	-	?	B	1	-	-	VWW.63; VD.64	VIWW.91	-			?
	VIWW.91	-	-	?	B	1	-	-	VWW.63; VD.64	VIWW.90	-			?

a Sallie (Mary Davis's mother) had a younger sister whose daughter was named Ida; see text.
b Otis died in February, 1970.
c Charles Davis died September, 1959; he left one living brother in Kilgore; two deceased brothers lived in Los Angeles; see text.

Table 1.3. The Adams family: kinfolk and residences

Genera-tion	Index number	Name		1970 Status					Relationships					Household affiliation(s)
		First	Last	Sex	Race	Alive	Age	Loca-tion	Parents	Siblings	Spouse(s)	Children	Divorced or separated	
I	IA.1	"Po"a	-	M	B	†	-	-	-	-	IB.2	IIA.10, 11	-	IA.1
	IB.2	"Mo"a	-	F	B	†	-	-	-	-	IA.1	IIA.10, 11	-	IA.1
	IC.3	-	-	F	B	†	-	-	-	-	ID.4(CL)	IIC.14	-	ID.4(CL)
	ID.4	Nelson	-	M	W	†	-	-	-	-	IC.3(CL)	IIC.14	-	IC.3(CL)
	IE.5	-	-	F	B	†	-	-	-	-	IF.6(CL)	IIE.16	-	IF.6(CL)
	IF.6	-	-	M	W	†	-	-	-	-	IE.5(CL)	IIE.16	-	IE.5(CL)
II	IIG.7	-	-	M	B	†	-	-	-	-	IIH.8	IIIG.18, 20	-	IIG.7
	IIH.8	-	-	F	B	†	-	-	-	-	IIG.7	IIIG.18, 20	-	IIG.7
	IIJ.9	Jake	-	M	B	†	-	Vermont, Texas	-	-	IIA.10	IIIJ.21, 22	-	IIJ.9

Table 1.3.   The Adams family: kinfolk and residences *continued*

Genera- tion	Index number	Name		1970 Status					Relationships				Divorced or separated	Household affiliation(s)
		First	Last	Sex	Race	Alive	Age	Loca- tion	Parents	Siblings	Spouse(s)	Children		
	IIA.10	Mary[b]	-	F	B	†	·	·	IA.1; IB.2	IIA.11	IIJ.9	IIIJ.21, 22	·	IIJ.9
	IIA.11	Judy	Dixon	F	B	†	·	·	IA.1; IB.2	IIA.10	IIK.12	IIIK.25, 27	·	IIK.12
	IIK.12	-	-	M	B	†	·	·			IIA.11	IIIK.25, 27	·	IIK.12
	IIL.13	-	-	M	B	†	·	·			IIC.14	IIIL.28, 29	·	IIL.13
	IIC.14	Mary[c]	-	F	B	†	·	·	IC.3; ID.4		IIL.13; IIM.15	IIIL.28, 29; IIIC.31	·	IIL.13/ IIM.15
	IIM.15	James	-	M	W	†	·	·	IE.5; IF.6		IIC.14(CL)	IIIC.31	·	IIC.14(CL)
	IIE.16	"Bean"[d]	-	F	B	†	·	·			IIN.17	IIIN.32	·	IIN.17
	IIN.17	Dan	-	M	I[e]	†	·	·			IIE.16	IIIN.32	·	IIN.17
III	IIIG.18	-	-	M	B	†	·	·	IIG.7; IIH.8	IIIG.20	IIIO.19 (CL)	IVO.33	·	IIIO.19(CL)
	IIIO.19	-	-	F	B	†	·	·			IIIG.18 (CL)	IVO.33	·	IIIG.18 (CL)
	IIIG.20	Elija	-	M	B	†	·	·	IIG.7; IIH.8	IIIG.18	IIIJ.21	IVG.35, 37, 39	Separated	IIIG.20
	IIIJ.21	Florence	-	F	B	†	·	·	IIJ.9; IIA.10	IIIJ.22	IIIG.20	IVG.35, 37, 39	Separated	IIIG.18
	IIIJ.22	Kizai	-	M	B	†	·	·	IIJ.9; IIA.10	IIIJ.21	IIIP.23	IVP.41, 42, 44-48	·	IIIP.23
	IIIP.23	Elix	-	F	B	†	·	·			IIIJ.22	IVP.41, 42, 44-48	·	IIIP.23
	IIIQ.24	-	-	M	B	†	·	·			IIIK.25 (CL)	IVK.50	·	IIIK.25 (CL)
	IIIK.25	Cora	-	F	B	†	·	·	IIK.12; IIA.11	IIIK.27	IIIQ.24 (CL)	IVK.50	·	IIIQ.24 (CL)
	IIIR.26	-	-	M	B	†	·	·			IIIK.27 (CL)	IVK.51	·	IIIK.27 (CL)
	IIIK.27	Sally	-	F	B	†	·	·	IIK.17; IIA.11	IIIK.25	IIIR.26 (CL)	IVK.51	·	IIIR.26 (CL)
	IIIL.28	-	-	M	B	l	·	·	IIL.13; IIC.14	IIIL.29			·	?
	IIIL.29	Viola	-	F	B	l	·	·	IIL.13; IIC.14	IIIL.28	IIIS.30(CL)	IVL.53, 54	·	IIIL.29
	IIIS.30	-	-	M	B	l	·	·			IIIL.29(CL)	IVL.53, 54	·	IIIS.30

Table 1.3. The Adams family: kinfolk and residences *continued*

Genera-tion	Index number	Name First	Name Last	1970 Status Sex	Race	Alive	Age	Location	Relationships Parents	Siblings	Spouse(s)	Children	Divorced or separated	Household affiliation(s)
	IIIC.31	Nancy	-	F	B	†	-		IIC.14; IIM.15	-	IIIN.32	IVN.40, 55	-	IIIN.32
	IIIN.32	Tuck	-	M	B	†	•	-	IIN.17; IIE.16	-	IIIC.31	IVN.40, 55	-	IIIN.32
IV	IVO.33	Eleanora	-	F	B	1	-	L.A.	IIIO.19; IIIG.18	-	IVT.34	-	-	IVT.34
	IVT.34	-	-	M	B	1	-	L.A.	-	-	IVO.33	-	-	IVT.34
	IVG.35	Allean	-	F	B	1	-	-	IIIG.20; IIIJ.21	IVG.37, 39	IVU.36	VU.58	Divorced	IVG.35
	IVU.36	-	-	M	B	1	-	-	IIIG.20; IIIJ.21	-	IVG.35	VU.58	Divorced	IVU.36
	IVG.37	Erna	-	F	B	†	-	-		IVG.35, 39	IVV.38	VV.59	-	IVV.38
	IVV.38	-	-	M	B	1	-	-	IIIG.20; IIIJ.21	-	IVG.37	VV.59	-	IVV.38
	IVG.39	Valencia	Adams	F	B	1	69	-	IIIG.20; IIIJ.21	IVG.35, 37	IVN.40	-	-	IVN.40
	IVN.40	C.D.	Adams	M	B	1	70	-	IIIN.32; IIIC.31	IVN.55	IVG.39	-	-	IVN.40
	IVP.41	-	-	M	B	†	-	-	IIIP.23; IIIJ.22	IVP.42, 44–48	-	-	-	IVP.41
	IVP.42	Narsis	-	F	B	1	-	E. Hamilton, Texas	IIIP.23; IIIJ.22	IVP.41, 44–48	IVW.43	VW.61	-	IVP.42
	IVW.43	-	-	M	B	†	-	-	-	-	IVP.42	VW.61	-	IVW.43
	IVP.44	-	-	M	B	1	-	-	IIIP.23; IIIJ.22	IVP.41, 42, 45–48	-	-	-	?
	IVP.45	-	-	F	B	†	-	-	IIIP.23; IIIJ.22	IVP.41, 42, 44, 46–48	-	-	-	•
	IVP.46	-	-	F	B	†	-	-	IIIP.23; IIIJ.22	IVP.41, 42, 44, 45, 47, 48	-	-	-	•
	IVP.47	-	-	F	B	†	-	-	IIIP.23; IIIJ.22	IVP.41, 42, 44–46, 48	-	-	-	•
	IVP.48	-	-	F	B	†	-	-	IIIP.23; IIIJ.22	IVP.41, 42, 44–47	-	-	-	•

Table 1.3. The Adams family: kinfolk and residences *continued*

Genera-tion	Index number	Name First	Name Last	1970 Status Sex	Race	Alive	Age	Loca-tion	Relationships Parents	Siblings	Spouse(s)	Children	Divorced or separated	Household affiliation(s)
	IVX.49	-	-	M	B	?	-	-	-	-	IVK.50 (CL)	VK.64, 65, 67, 68	-	IVX.49
	IVK.50	Elja	-	F	B	†	-	-	IIIK.25; IIIQ.24	-	IVX.49	VK.64, 65, 67, 68	-	IVK.50
	IVK.51	-	-	F	B	†	-	-	IIIK.27; IIIR.26	-	IVY.52	-	-	IVY.52
	IVY.52	-	-	M	B	1	-	-	IIIL.29; IIIS.30	IVL.54	IVK.51	-	-	IVY.52
	IVL.53	-	-	M	B	1	-	-	IIIL.29; IIIS.30	IVL.53	-	-	-	IIIL.29
	IVL.54	-	-	M	B	1	-	-		IVL.53		-	-	IIIL.29
	IVN.55	McNeal	Adams	M	B	1	-	-	IIIN.32; IIIC.31	IVN.40	IVZ.56	-	-	IVN.55
	IVZ.56	Mabel	Adams	F	B	†	-	-	-	-	IVN.55		-	IVN.55
V	VRR.57	Kay	-	F	J	1	-	Sacra-mento, Calif.	-	-	VU.58	VIU.70	-	VU.58
	VU.58	Claude	-	M	B	1	-	Sacra-mento, Calif.	IVU.36; IVG.35	-	VRR.57	VIU.70	-	VU.58
	VV.59	Floyd	-	M	B	1	-	Sacra-mento, Calif.	IVV.38; IVG.37	-	VSS.60	VIV.71, 72	-	VV.59
	VSS.60	Katherine	-	F	B	1	-	Sacra-mento, Calif.	-	-	VV.59	VIV.71, 72	-	VV.59
	VW.61	-	-	F	B	1	-	-	IVW.43; IVP.42	-	VTT.62	VITT.74, 75	-	IVP.42
	VTT.62	-	-	M	B	1	-	-	-	-	VW.61	VITT.74, 75	-	IVP.42
	VUU.63	-	-	M	B	1	-	L.A.	-	-	VK.64	VIUU.77, 78	-	VUU.63
	VK.64	Allean	-	F	B	1	-	L.A.	IVK.50; IVX.49	VK.65, 67, 68	VUU.63	VIUU.77, 78	-	VUU.63

Table 1.3. The Adams family: kinfolk and residences *continued*

Genera-tion	Index number	Name		1970 Status					Relationships				Divorced or separated	Household affiliation(s)
		First	Last	Sex	Race	Alive	Age	Loca-tion	Parents	Siblings	Spouse(s)	Children		
	VK.65	Edmond	-	M	B	1	-	L.A.	IVK.50; IVX.49	VK.64, 67, 68	-	-	-	?
	VVV.66	-	-	M	B	1	-	L.A.	-	-	VK.67	-	-	VVV.66
	VK.67	Joelynn	-	F	B	1	-	L.A.	IVK.50; IVX.49	VK.64, 65, 68	VVV.66	-	-	VVV.66
	VK.68	-	-	M	B	1	-	Midd.	IVK.50; IVX.49	VK.64, 65, 67	VWW.69	VIK.79, 80	Separated	VK.68
	VWW.69	-	-	F	B	1	-	Midd.	VU.58; VRR.57	-	VK.68	VIK.79, 80	Separated	VWW.69
VI	VIU.70	Kyle	-	M	B	1	-	Sacra-mento, Calif.	-	-	-	-	-	VU.58
	VIV.71	Evette	-	F	B	1	-	-	VV.59; VSS.60	-	-	-	-	?
	VIV.72	Benita	-	F	B	1	-	-	VV.59; VSS.60	-	-	-	-	?
	VIXX.73	-	-	F	B	1	-	-	-	-	VITT.74	VIITT. 81–83	-	VITT.74
	VITT.74	-	-	M	B	1	-	-	VTT.62; VW.61	VITT.75	VIXX.73	VIITT. 81–83	-	VITT.74
	VITT.75	-	-	M	B	1	-	-	VTT.62; VW.61	VITT.74	VIYY.76	VIITT. 84–87	-	VITT.75
	VIYY.76	-	-	F	B	1	-	-	-	-	VITT.75	VIITT. 84–87	-	VITT.75
	VIUU.77	-	-	M	B	1	-	L.A.	VUU.63; VK.64	VIUU.78	-	-	-	VUU.63
	VIUU.78	-	-	F	B	1	-	L.A.	VUU.63; VK.64	VIUU.77	-	-	-	VUU.63
	VIK.79	-	-	F	B	1	-	Midd.	VK.68; VWW.69	VIK.80	-	-	-	?
	VIK.80	-	-	M	B	1	-	Midd.	VK.68; VWW.69	IVK.79	-	-	-	?
VII	VIITT.81	-	-	M	B	1	-	-	VITT.74; VIXX.73	VIITT.82, 83	-	-	-	VIITT.74
	VIITT.82	-	-	M	B	1	-	-	VITT.74; VIXX.73	VIITT.83, 84	-	-	-	VITT.74

Table 1.3.   The Adams family: kinfolk and residences *continued*

Genera-tion	Index number	Name First	Name Last	Sex	Race	Alive	Age	Loca-tion	Parents	Siblings	Spouse(s)	Children	Divorced or separated	Household affiliation(s)
	VIITT.83	-		F	B	1			VIITT.74; VIXX.73	VIITT.82, 84	-		-	VIIT.74
	VIITT.84	-	-	F	B	1			VIITT.75; VIYY.76	VIITT. 85–87	-	-	-	VIIT.75
	VIITT.85	-	-	F	B	1	-		VIITT.75; VIYY.76	VIITT.84, 86, 87	-	-	-	VIIT.75
	VIITT.86	-		F	B	1	-		VIITT.75; VIYY.76	VIITT.84, 85, 87	-	-	-	VIIT.75
	VIITT.87	-		M	B	1	-		VIITT.75; VIYY.76	VIITT. 84–86	-	-	-	VIIT.75

[a] Po and Mo were slaves.
[b] Mary, daughter of Po and Mo, reportedly died in 1864.
[c] Mary, C. D. Adams's mother's mother, was a slave.
[d] "Bean," C. D. Adams's father's mother, was a slave.
[e] Dan, C. D. Adams's father's father, was a nearly full-blooded Indian; see text.

Table 1.4.   The Miller family: kinfolk and residences

Genera-tion	Index number	Name First	Name Last	Sex	Race	Alive	Age	Loca-tion	Parents	Siblings	Spouse(s)	Children	Divorced or separated	Household affiliation(s)
I	IA.1	Sarah[a]	"	F	B	†	95	-	-	-	IB.2	IIA.5	-	IB.2(CL)
	IB.2	"O Masta"	"	M	W	†	-	-	-	-	IA.1(CL)	IIA.5	-	IA.1(CL)
	IIC.3	-	-	F	W	†	-	-	-	-	IID.4	IIID.18	-	IID.4
	IID.4	John	Morrison	M	W	†	-	-	-	-	IIC.3; IIL.13(CL)	IIID.18	-	IIC.3
II	IIA.5	Leah	-	F	B	†	57[b]	-	IA.1; IB.2		IIE.6	IIIE.16, 19, 21[c]	-	IIE.6

Table 1.4. The Miller family: kinfolk and residences

Genera-tion	Index number	Name		1970 Status					Relationships				Divorced or separated	Household affiliation(s)
		First	Last	Sex	Race	Alive	Age	Location	Parents	Siblings	Spouse(s)	Children		
	IIE.6	Bowden[d]	-	M	B	†	-	-	-	-	IIA.5	IIIE.16, 19, 21[c]	-	IIE.6
	IIF.7	-	-	F	B	†			-	-	IIG.8	IIIG.23	-	IIG.8
	IIG.8	-	-	M	B	†			-	-	IIF.7	IIIG.23	-	IIG.8
	IIH.9	Jane	-	F	B	†			-	-	IIH.11	IIJ.10(CL)	IIIH.26	-	IIJ.10(CL)
	IIJ.10	-	-	M	B	†			-	-	-	IIH.9(CL)	IIIH.26	-	IIH.9(CL)
	IIH.11	-	-	M	B	†			-	IIH.9	IIK.12	IIIH.27	-	IIH.11
	IIK.12	-	-	F	B	†			-	-	IIH.11	IIIH.27	-	IIH.11
	IIL.13	Ealla	-	F	B	1			-	-	IIC.3(CL)	IIIL.29	-	IIC.3(CL)
III	IIIM.14	Ted	-	M	B	†			-	-	IIIE.16	IVE.32	-	IIIE.16(CL)
	IIIN.15	Sweaden[e]	-	M	B	†	-	Midd.	-	-	IIIE.16	-	-	IIIE.16
	IIIE.16	Minnie	-	F	B	1	-	Midd.	IIE.6; IIA.5	IIIE.19, 21	IIIN.15; IIIM.14 (CL); IIIO.17 (CL); IIID.18 (CL)	IVE.32; IVE.34; IVE.36	-	IIIN.15; IIIE.16
	IIIO.17	-	-	M	B	1			IID.4; IIC.3	-	IIIE.16 (CL)	IVE.34	-	IIIE.16(CL)
	IIID.18	Bob	Morrison	M	W	†	85	Midd.	-	-	IIIE.16 (CL)	IVE.36	-	IIIE.16(CL)
	IIIE.19	-	-	M	B	†			IIE.6; IIA.5	IIIE.16, 21	IIIP.20 (CL)	IVP.37	-	IIIP.20(CL)
	IIIP.20	-	-	F	B	?			-	-	IIIE.19 (CL)	IVP.37	-	IIIE.19(CL)
	IIIE.21	-	-	M	B	†			IIE.6; IIA.5	IIIE.16, 19	IIIQ.22	IVQ.39	-	IIIQ.22
	IIIQ.22	Georgia	Miller	F	B	†			-	-	IIIE.21	IVQ.39	-	IIIQ.22
	IIIG.23	Eric	Miller	M	B	†			IIG.8; IIF.7	-	IIIR.24	IVR.41, 42, 44, 46	-	IIIR.24
	IIIR.24	-	-	F	B	†			-	-	IIIG.23	IVR.41, 42, 44, 46	-	IIIR.24
	IIIS.25	Sallie	-	F	B	1			-	-	IIIH.26	IVH.48	-	IIIS.25
	IIIH.26	Osia	-	M	B	†			IIH.9; IIJ.10	-	IIIS.25	IVH.48	-	IIIH.26

Table 1.4.   The Miller family: kinfolk and residences *continued*

Genera-tion	Index number	Name First	Name Last	1970 Status Sex	Race	Alive	Age	Location	Relationships Parents	Siblings	Spouse(s)	Children	Divorced or separated	Household affiliation(s)
	IIIH.27	-	-	F	B	1	-	-	IIH.11; IIK.12	-	IIIT.28	IVT.31	-	IIIT.28
	IIIT.28	Beaula	-	M	B	1	-	Midd.	-	-	IIIH.27	IVT.31	-	IIIT.28
	IIIL.29	-	-	F	B	†	-	-	IIL.13; IID.4	-	IIIU.30	IVU.50	-	IIIU.30
IV	IIIU.30	T. L.	-	M	B	1	-	Midd.	-	-	IIIL.29	IVU.50	-	IIIU.30
	IVT.31	Christine	-	F	B	1	-	Midd.	IIIT.28; IIIH.27	(IVE.34, 36)	IVE.32(CL)	VT.52	-	IVT.31
	IVE.32	Earl	-	M	B	1	-	Midd.	IIIE.16; IIIM.14	(IVE.34, 36)	IVT.31(CL)	VT.52	-	IVE.32
	IVV.33	-	-	F	B	†?	-	-	-	-	IVE.32	-	●	IVW.35
	IVE.34	Annie	-	F	B	1	-	Midd.	IIIE.16; IIIO.17	(IVE.32, 36)	IVW.35	VW.54	-	IVW.35
	IVW.35	Sunny	Miller	M	B	1	-	Midd.	IIIE.16; IIID.18	(IVE.32, 34)	IVE.34	VW.54	-	IVW.35
	IVE.36	-	-	F	B	1	64	L.A.	IIIP.20; IIIE.19	-	IVR.42	-	-	IVR.42
	IVP.37	Jeff	-	M	B	1	-	Palm Sp., Calif.		-	IVX.38	VP.56-61	-	IVP.37
	IVX.38	-	-	F	B	1	-	Palm Sp., Calif.		-	IVP.37	VP.56-61	●	IVP.37
	IVQ.39	-	-	F	B	1	-	L.A.	IIIQ.22; IIIE.21	-	IVY.40	-	●	IVY.40
	IVY.40	-	-	M	B	1	-	L.A.	-	-	IVQ.39	-	●	IVY.40
	IVR.41	-	Miller	M	B	†	-	-	IIIR.24; IIIG.23	IVR.42, 44, 46	-	-	●	-
	IVR.42	Richard	Miller	M	B	1	74	L.A.	IIIR.24; IIIG.23	IVR.41, 44, 46	IVE.36	VR.62, 63, 65	-	IVR.42
	IVZ.43	-	Miller	F	B	1	-	L.A.	-	-	IVR.42	VR.62, 63, 65	Divorced	IVZ.43
	IVR.44	-	Miller	M	B	1	-	-	IIIR.24; IIIG.23	IVR.41, 42, 46	IVSS.45	-	-	IVR.44
	IVSS.45	-	Miller	F	B	†	-	-	-	-	IVR.44	-	-	IVR.44

Table 1.4. The Miller family: kinfolk and residences continued

Genera-tion	Index number	Name		1970 Status					Relationships				Divorced or separated	Household affiliation(s)
		First	Last	Sex	Race	Alive	Age	Loca-tion	Parents	Siblings	Spouse(s)	Children		
	IVR.46	-	Miller	M	B	†	-	-	IIIR.24; IIIG.23	IVR.41, 42, 44	IVT.47	VR.66	-	IVR.46
	IVT.47	-	Miller	F	B	†	-	-	IIIH.26; IIIS.25	-	IVR.46	VR.66	-	IVR.46
	IVH.48	Mary	Davis	F	B	1	-	L.A.	-	-	IVUU.49	-	-	IVVV.49
	IVUU.49	Charles	Davis	M	B	†	-	L.A.	IIIU.30; IIIL.29	-	IVH.48	-	-	IVUU.49
	IVU.50	Helen	Smith	F	B	1	-	L.A.	-	-	IVVV.51	-	-	IVVV.51
>	IVVV.51	Alex	Smith	M	B	1	-	L.A.	IVT.31; IVE.32	-	IVV.50	VIT.68 Adopted	-	IVVV.51
	VT.52	C.T.	-	M	B	1	-	-	-	-	VWW.53	VIT.68 Adopted	-	VT.52
	VWW.53	-	-	F	B	1	-	-	-	-	VT.52	-	-	VT.52
	VW.54	Wylma	-	F	B	1	-	-	IVW.35; IVE.34	-	VXX.55	-	-	VXX.55
	VXX.55	-	-	M	B	1	-	L.A.	IVP.37; IVX.38	-	VW.54	-	-	VXX.55
	VP.56	-	-	?	B	1	-	L.A.	IVP.37; IVX.38	VP.57-61	-	-	-	IVP.37
	VP.57	-	-	?	B	1	-	L.A.	IVP.37; IVX.38	VP.56, 58-61	-	-	-	IVP.37
	VP.58	-	-	?	B	1	-	L.A.	IVP.37; IVX.38	VP.56, 57, 59-61	-	-	-	IVP.37
	VP.59	-	-	?	B	1	-	L.A.	IVP.37; IVX.38	VP.56-58, 60, 61	-	-	-	IVP.37
	VP.60	-	-	?	B	1	-	L.A.	IVP.37; IVX.38	VP.56-59, 61	-	-	-	IVP.37
	VP.61	-	-	?	B	1	-	L.A.	IVP.37; IVX.38	VP.56-60	-	-	-	IVP.37
	VR.62	-	-	F	B	1	-	L.A.	IVR.42; IVE.36	VR.63, 65	-	-	-	IVZ.43
	VR.63	-	-	F	B	1	-	L.A.	IVR.42; IVE.36	VR.62, 65	VYY.64	VIR.69	-	VYY.64
	VYY.64	-	-	M	B	1	-	L.A.	-	-	VR.63	VIR.69	-	VR.63
	VR.65	-	-	F	B	1	-	L.A.	IVR.42; IVE.36	VR.62, 63	-	-	-	?

Table 1.4. The Miller family: kinfolk and residences *continued*

Genera-tion	Index number	Name First	Name Last	Sex	Race	Alive	Age	Loca-tion	Parents	Siblings	Spouse(s)	Children	Divorced or separated	Household affiliation(s)
	VR.66	-	-	M	B	1	-	-	IVR.46; IVTT.47	-	VZZ.67	-	-	VR.66
VI	VZZ.67	-	-	F	B	1	-	-	VT.52; VWW.53	-	VR.66	-	-	VR.66
	VIT.68 (Adopted)	-	-	M	K	1	-	-	-	-	-	-	-	VT.52
	VIR.69	-	-	F	B	1	-	-	VR.63; VYY.64	-	-	-	-	VR.63

a Sarah, Sunny Miller's maternal great-grandmother, was a slave; she died in "Middville" at age 95.
b Leah died at age 54 according to text.
c Leah and Bowden reportedly had 13 children (see text); information available on 3 only.
d Bowden died in 1919.
e Sweaden died in 1973.

Table 1.5. The Kennedy family: kinfolk and residences

Genera-tion	Index number	Name First	Name Last	Sex	Race	Alive	Age	Loca-tion	Parents	Siblings	Spouse(s)	Children	Divorced or separated	Household affiliation(s)
	IA.1	-	-	F	B	†	-	-	-	-	IB.2	IIB.10	-	IB.2
I	IB.2	A.B.	-	M	B	†	-	-	-	-	IA.1	IIB.10	-	IB.2
	IC.3	-	-	F	B	†	-	-	-	-	ID.4	IID.9	-	ID.4
	ID.4	-	-	M	B	†	-	-	-	-	IC.3	IID.9	-	ID.4
	IE.5	Lucy	-	F	W	†	-	-	-	-	IF.6(CL)	IIE.8	-	IE.5(CL)
	IF.6	-	-	M	W	†	-	-	-	-	IE.5(CL)	IIE.8	-	IE.5(CL)
	IIG.7	Bill	Polly	M	B	†	-	-	-	-	IIE.8(CL)	IIE.18, 20, 22, 23	-	IIE.8(CL)
II	IIE.8	Iva	-	F	B	†	-	-	-	-	IIG.7(CL)	IIE.18, 20, 22, 23	-	IIE.8(CL)

Table 1.5. The Kennedy family: kinfolk and residences

Genera- tion	Index number	Name		1970 Status					Relationships				Divorced or separated	Household affiliation(s)
		First	Last	Sex	Race	Alive	Age	Loca- tion	Parents	Siblings	Spouse(s)	Children		
	IID.9	Burke	–	M	B	+	–	–	ID.4; IC.3	–	IIB.10	IIID.24, 25	–	IID.9
	IIB.10	Ida	–	F	B	+	–	–	IB.2; IA.1		IID.9	IIID.24, 25	–	IID.9
	IIH.11	Jim	–	M	B	+	–	–		IIJ.13–15	IIJ.12	IIIH.37–39	–	IIH.11
	IIJ.12	Mary	–	F	B	+	–	–		IIJ.12, 14, 15	IIH.11	IIIH.37–39	–	IIH.11
	IIJ.13	–	–	F	B	+	–	–		IIJ.12, 13, 15			–	
	IIJ.14	–	–	F	B	+	–	–					–	
III	IIJ.15	–	–	F	B	1	–	–		IIJ.12–14	IIK.16	IIK.42, 43	–	IIK.16
	IIK.16	–	–	M	B	+	–	–		IIJ.12–14	IIJ.15	IIK.42, 43	–	IIK.16
	IIL.17	–	–	M	B	+	–	–			IIIE.18	IVL.45	–	IIIE.18
	IIIE.18	–	–	F	B	1	–	Midd.	IIE.8; IIG.7	IIIE.20, 22, 23	IIIM.19; IIIL.17	IVL.45; IVM.46	–	IIIM.19; IIIL.17
	IIIM.19	Mable	–	M	B	+	–	–			IIIE.18	IVM.46, 48	–	IIIE.18
	IIIE.20	–	–	F	B	+	–	–	IIE.8; IIG.7	IIIE.18, 22, 23	IIN.21		–	IIN.21
	IIN.21	McNeal	–	M	B	1	–	–			IIIE.20		–	IIN.21
	IIE.22	–	–	M	B	+	–	–	IIE.8; IIG.7	IIIE.18, 20, 23			–	
	IIIE.23	Cliff	–	M	B	+	–	–	IIE.8; IIG.7	IIIE.18, 20, 22	IIID.24	IVE.50, 52, 54, 56	Divorced	IIIE.23
	IID.24	Tiny	–	F	B	1	–	Midd.	IID.9; IIB.10	IIID.25	IIIE.23	IVE.50, 52, 54, 56	Divorced	IIID.24
	IIID.25	–	–	M	B	+	–	–	IID.9; IIB.10	IIID.24			–	
	IIIO.26	–	–	F	B	+	–	–		IIIO.28, 30, 32, 35, 36	IIIP.27		–	IIIP.27
	IIIP.27	–	–	M	B	1	–	–			IIIO.26		–	IIIP.27
	IIIO.28	–	–	M	B	1	–	–		IIIO.26, 30, 32, 35, 36	IIIQ.29	IVO.58	Divorced	IIIQ.28
	IIIQ.29	–	–	F	B	+	–	–			IIIO.28	IVO.58	Divorced	IIIQ.29
	IIIO.30	–	–	M	B	+	–	–		IIIO.26, 28, 32, 35, 36			–	IIIQ.29
	IIIR.31	–	–	F	B	1	–	–		–	IIIO.32		–	IIIO.32

Table 1.5.   The Kennedy family: kinfolk and residences *continued*

Genera-tion	Index number	Name First	Last	Sex	Race	Alive	Age	Loca-tion	Parents	Siblings	Spouse(s)	Children	Divorced or separated	Household affiliation(s)
	IIIO.32	-	-	M	B	1	-	-	-	IIIO.26, 28, 30, 35, 36	IIR.31; IIIS.33	-	-	IIIO.32
	IIIS.33	-	-	F	B	†	-	-	-	-	IIIO.32	-	-	IIIO.32
	IIIT.34	-	-	F	B	1	-	-	-	-	IIIO.35	IVO.59–63	-	IIIO.35
	IIIO.35	-	-	M	B	1	-	-	-	IIIO.26, 28, 30, 32, 36	IIIT.34	IVO.59–63	-	IIIO.35
	IIIO.36	Plue	Kennedy	M	B	†	-	-	-	IIIO.26, 28, 30, 32, 35	IIIH.37	IVO.64, 49, 66	-	IIIO.36
	IIIH.37	-	Kennedy	F	B	†	-	-	IIH.11; IIJ.12	IIIH.38, 39	IIIO.36	IVO.64, 49, 66	-	IIIO.36
	IIIH.38	-	-	F	B	†	-	-	IIH.11; IIJ.12	IIIH.37, 39	-	-	-	-
	IIIH.39	Beulah	-	F	B	1	-	L.A.	IIH.11; IIJ.12	IIIH.37, 38	IIIU.40	-	-	IIIU.40
	IIIU.40	-	-	M	B	1	-	L.A.	-	-	IIIH.39	-	-	IIIU.40
	IIIV.41	-	-	M	B	1	-	-	IIK.16; IIJ.15	-	IIIK.42	-	-	IIIV.41
	IIIK.42	-	-	F	B	1	-	-	IIK.16; IIJ.15	IIIK.43	IIIV.41	-	-	IIIV.41
	IIIK.43	-	-	F	B	1	-	-	IIK.16; IIJ.15	IIIK.42	-	-	-	-
IV	IVW.44	-	-	M	B	1	-	Midd.	IIIL.17; IIIE.18	(IVM.46, 48)	IVL.45	?(Children)	-	IVW.44
	IVL.45	-	-	F	B	1	-	Midd.	-	-	IVW.44	?(Children)	-	IVW.44
	IVM.46	-	-	M	B	1	-	Midd.	IIIM.19; IIIE.18	IVM.48 (IVL.45)	IVX.47	-	-	IVM.46
	IVX.47	-	-	F	B	1	-	Midd.	-	-	IVM.46	-	-	IVM.46
	IVM.48	-	-	F	B	1	-	-	IIIM.19; IIIE.18	IVM.46 (IVL.45)	IVY.68 (CL)	VM.70–82	-	IVY.68 (CL)
	IVY.68	-	-	M	B	?	-	-	-	-	IVM.48 (CL)	VM.70–82	-	IVM.48 (CL)
	IVO.49	Joe	Kennedy	M	B	1	61	L.A.	IIIO.36; IIIH.37	IVO.64, 66	IVE.50	VO.84, 85	-	IVO.49
	IVE.50	Jean	Kennedy	F	B	1	60	L.A.	IIIE.23; IIID.24	IVE.52, 54, 56	IVO.49	VO.84, 85	-	IVO.49
	IVZ.51	-	-	M	B	1	-	L.A.	-	-	IVE.52	-	-	IVZ.51

Table 1.5. The Kennedy family: kinfolk and residences *continued*

Generation	Index number	Name — First	Name — Last	1970 Status — Sex	Race	Alive	Age	Location	Relationships — Parents	Siblings	Spouse(s)	Children	Divorced or separated	Household affiliation(s)
	IVE.52	A.G.	-	F	B	1	-	L.A.	IIIE.23; IIID.24	IVE.50, 54, 56	IVZ.51; IVMM.53	VMM.87	-	IVZ.51 IVMM.53
	IVMM.53	-	-	M	B	1	-	-	-	-	IVE.52	VMM.87	Divorced	IVMM.53
	IVE.54	-	-	M	B	1	-	Midd.	IIIE.23; IIID.24	IVE.50, 52, 56	IVNN.55	VE.90, 92, 93	Divorced	IVMM.53 IVE.54
	IVNN.55	-	-	F	B	1	-	Midd.	-	-	IVE.54	VE.90, 92, 93	-	IVE.54
	IVE.56	-	-	F	B	1	-	Midd.	IIIE.23; IIID.24	IVE.50, 52, 54	IVOO.57	-	-	IVOO.57
	IVOO.57	-	-	M	B	1	-	Midd.	-	-	IVE.56	-	-	IVOO.57
	IVO.58	Juanita	Kennedy	F	B	1	-	L.A.	IIIO.28; IIIQ.29	-	-	-	-	IVOO.57 IVO.58
	IVO.59	-	Kennedy	F	B	1	-	-	IIIO.35; IIIT.34	IVO.60-63	-	-	-	?
	IVO.60	-	Kennedy	M	B	1	-	-	IIIO.35; IIIT.34	IVO.59, 61, 62, 63	-	-	-	?
	IVO.61	-	Kennedy	F	B	1	-	-	IIIO.35; IIIT.34	IVO.59, 60, 62, 63	-	-	-	?
	IVO.62	-	Kennedy	F	B	1	-	-	IIIO.35; IIIT.34	IVO.59, 60, 61, 63	-	-	-	?
	IVO.63	-	Kennedy	M	B	1	-	-	IIIO.35; IIIT.34	IVO.59-62	-	-	-	?
	IVO.64	-	-	F	B	1	-	Wichita Falls, Texas	IIIO.36; IIIH.37	IVO.49, 66	IVPP.65	VPP.96, 98	-	IVPP.65
	IVPP.65	-	-	M	B	1	-	Wichita Falls, Texas	-	-	IVO.64	VPP.96, 98	-	IVPP.65
	IVO.66	W.C.	Polley	M	B	†	-	Midd.	IIIO.36; IIIH.37	IVO.49, 64	IVQQ.67	VO.100, 101, 103, 105, 106	-	IVO.66
	IVQQ.67	-	-	F	B	1	-	Midd.	-	-	IVO.66	VO.100, 101, 103, 105, 106	-	IVQQ.67
V	VW.69	-	-	?	B	?	-	Midd.	IVW.44; IVL.45	?	?	?	?	IVW.44

Table 1.5.   The Kennedy family: kinfolk and residences *continued*

Genera-tion	Index number	Name		1970 Status					Relationships				Divorced or separated	Household affiliation(s)
		First	Last	Sex	Race	Alive	Age	Loca-tion	Parents	Siblings	Spouse(s)	Children		
	VM.70	-	-	?	B	?	-	-	IVM.48; IVY.68	VM.71–82	?	?	?	?
	VM.71	-	-	?	B	?	-	-	IVM.48; IVY.68	VM.70, 72–82	?	?	?	?
	VM.72	-	-	?	B	?	-	-	IVM.48; IVY.68	VM.70, 71, 73–82	?	?	?	?
	VM.73	-	-	?	B	?	-	-	IVM.48; IVY.68	VM.70–72, 74–82	?	?	?	?
	VM.74	-	-	?	B	?	-	-	IVM.48; IVY.68	VM.70–73, 75–82	?	?	?	?
	VM.75	-	-	?	B	?	-	-	IVM.48; IVY.68	VM.70–74, 76–82	?	?	?	?
	VM.76	-	-	?	B	?	-	-	IVM.48; IVY.68	VM.70–75, 77–82	?	?	?	?
	VM.77	-	-	?	B	?	-	-	IVM.48; IVY.68	VM.70–76, 78–82	?	?	?	?
	VM.78	-	-	?	B	?	-	-	IVM.48; IVY.68	VM.70–77, 79–82	?	?	?	?
	VM.79	-	-	?	B	?	-	-	IVM.48; IVY.68	VM.70–78, 80–82	?	?	?	?
	VM.80	-	-	?	B	?	-	-	IVM.48; IVY.68	VM.70–79, 81–82	?	?	?	?
	VM.81	-	-	?	B	?	-	-	IVM.48; IVY.68	VM.70–80, 82	?	?	?	?
	VM.82	-	-	?	B	?	-	-	IVM.48; IVY.68	VM.70–81	?	?	?	?
	VRR.83	George	-	M	B	1	-	L.A.	-	-	VO.84	VIRR. 115–116	Separated	VRR.83
	VO.84	-	-	F	B	1	-	L.A.	IVO.49; IVE.50	VO.85	VRR.83	VIRR. 115–116	Separated	VO.84
	VO.85	-	-	M	B	1	-	L.A.	IVO.49; IVE.50	VO.84	VSS.86	VIO. 117–118	-	VO.85
	VSS.86	-	-	F	B	1	-	L.A.	-	-	VO.85	VIO. 117–118	-	VO.85
	VMM.87	-	-	M	B	1	-	L.A.	IVMM.53; IVE.52	-	VTT.88	VIMM. 119–120	-	VMM.87

Table 1.5. The Kennedy family: kinfolk and residences *continued*

Genera-tion	Index number	Name		1970 Status					Relationships				Divorced or separated	Household affiliation(s)
		First	Last	Sex	Race	Alive	Age	Loca-tion	Parents	Siblings	Spouse(s)	Children		
	VTT.88	-	-	F	B	1	-	L.A.	-	-	VMM.87	VIMM.119–120	-	VMM.87
	VUU.89	-	-	M	B	1	-	L.A.	IVE.54; IVNN.55	VE.92, 93	VE.90	VIUU.121	-	VUU.89
	VE.90	-	-	F	B	1	-	L.A.	IVE.54; IVNN.55	VE.92, 93	VUU.89	VIUU.121	-	VUU.89
	VVV.91	-	-	F	B	1	-	-	IVE.54; IVNN.55	VE.90, 93	VE.92	VIE.122	Divorced	VVV.91
	VE.92	-	-	M	B	1	-	L.A.	IVE.54; IVNN.55	VE.90, 93	VVV.91	VIE.122	Divorced	VE.92
	VE.93	-	-	F	B	1	-	Midd.	IVE.54; IVNN.55	VE.90, 92	VWW.94	VIWW.123	-	VWW.94
	VWW.94	-	-	M	B	1	-	Midd.	-	-	VE.93	VIWW.123	-	VWW.94
	VXX.95	-	-	M	B	1	-	-	IVPP.65; IVO.64	VPP.98	VPP.96	-	-	VXX.95
	VPP.96	-	-	F	B	1	-	-	IVPP.65; IVO.64	VPP.98	VXX.95	-	-	VXX.95
	VYY.97	-	-	M	B	1	-	-	IVPP.65; IVO.64	VPP.96	VPP.98	-	Divorced	VYY.97
	VPP.98	-	-	F	B	1	-	-	IVPP.65; IVO.64	VPP.96	VYY.97; VZZ.99	-	Divorced	VYY.97
	VZZ.99	-	-	M	B	1	-	-	IVO.66; IVQQ.67	VO.101, 103, 105, 106	VPP.98	-	-	VZZ.99
	VO.100	-	-	M	B	1	-	Midd.	IVO.66; IVQQ.67	VO.101, 103, 105, 106	-	-	-	IVQQ.67
	VO.101	-	-	F	B	1	-	-	IVO.66; IVQQ.67	VO.100, 103, 105, 106	VRRR.102	VIRRR.108, 109	-	VRRR.102
	VRRR.102	-	-	M	B	1	-	-	-	-	VO.101	VIRRR.108, 109	-	VRRR.102
	VO.103	-	-	F	B	1	-	L.A.	IVO.66; IVQQ.67	VO.100, 101, 105, 106	VSSS.104	VISSS.110, 111	-	VSSS.104
	VSSS.104	-	-	M	B	1	-	L.A.	-	-	VO.103	VISSS.110, 111	-	VSSS.104
	VO.105	-	-	M	B	1	-	L.A.	IVO.66; IVQQ.67	VO.100, 101, 103, 106	-	-	-	VO.105
	VO.106	-	-	F	B	1	-	L.A.	IVO.66; IVQQ.67	VO.100, 101, 103, 105	VTTT.107	VITTT.112	-	VTTT.107

Table 1.5. The Kennedy family: kinfolk and residences *continued*

Genera- tion	Index number	Name First	Last	1970 Status Sex	Race	Alive	Age	Loca- tion	Relationships Parents	Siblings	Spouse(s)	Children	Divorced or separated	Household affiliation(s)
VI	VTTT.107	-	-	M	B	1	-	L.A.	-	VIRRR.109	VO.106	VITTT.112	-	VTTT.107
	VIRRR. 108	-	-	M	B	1	-	-	VRRR.102; VO.101	VIRRR.108	-		-	VRRR. 102?
	VIRRR. 109	-	-	M	B	1	-	-	VRRR.102; VO.101	VIRRR.108	-		-	VRRRR.102
	VISSS.110	-	-	F	B	1	-	L.A.	VSSS.104; VO.103	VISSS.111	-	-	-	VSSS.104
	VISSS.111	-	-	F	B	1	-	L.A.	VSSS.104; VO.103	VISSS.110	-	-	-	VSSS.104
	VITTT.112	-	-	F	B	1	-	L.A.	VITTT.107; VO.106		VIUUU. 113	-	Divorced	VTTT.107
	VIUUU. 113	-	-	M	B	1	-	-	-		VITTT.112	-	Divorced	VIUUU. 113
	VIVVV.114	-	-	F	B	1	-	L.A.	VRR.83; VO.84		VIRR.115	VIRR.124	-	VIRR.115
	VIRR.115	-	-	M	B	1	-	L.A.	VRR.83; VO.84	VIRR.116	VIVVV.114	VIRR.124	-	VIRR.115
	VIRR.116	-	-	F	B	1	-	L.A.	VRR.83; VO.84	VIRR.115	-	-	-	VO.84
	VIO.117	-	-	M	B	1	-	L.A.	VO.85; VSS.86	VIO.118	-	-	-	VO.85
	VIO.118	-	-	M	B	1	-	L.A.	VO.85; VSS.86	VIO.117	-	-	-	VO.85
	VIMM.119	-	-	M	B	1	-	L.A.	VMM.87; VTT.88	VIMM.120	-	-	-	VMM.87
	VIMM.120	-	-	M	B	1	-	L.A.	VMM.87; VTT.88	VIMM.119	-	-	-	VMM.87
	VIUU.121	-	-	F	B	1	-	L.A.	VUU.89; VE.90	-	-	-	-	VUU.89
	VIE.122	-	-	M	B	1	-	-	VVV.91; VE.92	-	-	-	-	?
	VIWW.123	-	-	M	B	1	-	Midd.	VWW.94; VE.93	-	-	-	-	VWW.94
VII	VIIRR.124	-	-	M	B	1	-	L.A.	VIRR.115; VIVVV. 114	-	-	-	-	VIRR.115

Table 2.1. Components of family structure: the five families as an aggregate

Generation	Persons			Marriages			Stability		Present status		Offspring		Span of relationships (kinfolk)										
													Sibling		Half sibling		1st cousin		2nd cousin		3rd cousin	
	Total	Male	Female	Total	Formal	Consensual	Divorced	Separ.	Alive	Dead	Sets	Pers.	Sets	Pers.	Sets	Pers.	Sets	Pers.	Sets	Pers.	Sets	Pers.
I	20	9	11	11	4	7	0	0	0	20	11	16	N/A	N/A	N/A	N/A	N/A	N/A	N/A	N/A	N/A	N/A
II	43	20	23	20	14	6	0	0	1	42	20	48	5	13	1	6	0	0	N/A	N/A	N/A	N/A
III	79	33+	36+	33	24	9	2	4	30	49	26	82	14	47	2	10	9	17	0	0	0	0
IV	127	56+	52+	51	46	5	7	3	103	24	31	80	15	71	6	26	18	49	6	21	0	0
V	122+	49+	55+	42	41	1	7	2	121	1	31	56	19	70	3	12	27	68	12	34	6	14
VI	61	21+	28+	5	5	0	1	0	61	0	4	9	21	46	1	3	17	41	25	45	15	25
VII	9	4	5	0	0	0	0	0	9	0	0	0	2	7	0	0	2	7	2	2	4	9
Total	461+	192+	210+	162	134	28	17	9	325	136	123	291	76	254	13	57	73	182	45	102	25	48

Definitions for Tables 2.1–2.6:

FORMAL: Marriage by law or ceremony (religious).

OFFSPRING: Children produced from a union whether formal or consensual.

CONSENSUAL: Any union less than formal; not by law or religious ceremony. A union held together only by the consent of two individuals (male and female).

SPAN OF RELATIONSHIPS (Kinfolk): Refers to siblings; half siblings; 1st, 2nd and 3rd cousins.

PERSONS: The total number of offspring in the total number of sets.

SIBLING: Those offsprings who are full sister or brother (same parents).

HALF SIBLING: Brother or sister with one common parent.

SETS: Those offspring with the same parents (mother and father).

1ST COUSIN: The son or daughter of an uncle or aunt.

2ND COUSIN: The son or daughter of a first cousin.

3RD COUSIN: The son or daughter of a second cousin.

PERSONS: Even though total number of individuals could be determined per family, the data were not lucid enough to determine the sex of all members in each family (e.g., Viola [Smith Roster] had nine children but their sex was not given). Because of the lack of information, the sign (+) was used to show that the particular figure may be larger than noted.

MARRIAGES: There is a possibility that in several of these families (Smith and Davis, see text) between the 1st and 4th generations, some persons maintained consensual-consensual or formal-consensual relationships simultaneously. This was more the case during slavery than afterwards.

PRESENT STATUS (1970): Refers to the conditions of each person (living or dead) in his respective generation as of 1970. That was the year in which Dr. Aoyagi prepared his investigation of the five Black families that migrated from Texas to Los Angeles between 1940 and 1945. Ages, when they are given, are also relative to the year 1970.

N/A: Not available.

Table 2.2.   Components of the family structure: the Smith family

Genera-tion	Persons			Marriages			Stability		Present status (1970)		Span of relationships (kinfolk)												
											Offspring		Sibling		Half sibling		1st cousin		2nd cousin		3rd cousin	
	Total	Male	Fe-male	Total	For-mal	Con-sen.	Divor-ced	Separ.	Alive	Dead	Sets	Pers.	Sets	Pers.	Sets	Pers.	Sets	Pers.	Sets	Pers.	Sets	Pers.
I	4	3	1	3	0	3	0	0	0	4	3	7	0	0	0	0	0	0	0	0	0	0
II	12	8	4	5	2	3	0	0	0	12	5	10	3	7	1	6	0	0	0	0	0	0
III	14	5	9	5	4	1	0	2	8	6	5	18	2	7	1	7	3	8	2	6	0	0
IV	26	9+	8+	9	8	1	1	2	24	2	5	12	5	18	2	9	2	0	0	0	0	0
V	19	11	8	7	6	1	2	0	19	0	5	10	3	10	1	5	4	11	5	10	0	0
VI	11	8	3	1	1	0	0	0	11	0	1	1	4	9	1	3	4	9	1	1	1	1
VII	1	1	0	0	0	0	0	0	1	0	0	0	0	0	0	0	0	0	0	0	1	1
Total	87	45+	33+	30	21	9	3	2	63	24	24	58	17	51	6	30	11	28	8	17	1	1

Table 2.3.   Components of the family structure: the Miller family

Genera-tion	Persons			Marriages			Stability		Present status (1970)		Span of relationships (kinfolk)												
											Offspring		Sibling		Half sibling		1st cousin		2nd cousin		3rd cousin	
	Total	Male	Fe-male	Total	For-mal	Con-sen.	Divor-ced	Separ.	Alive	Dead	Sets	Pers.	Sets	Pers.	Sets	Pers.	Sets	Pers.	Sets	Pers.	Sets	Pers.
I	2	1	1	1	0	1	N/A	N/A	0	2	1	1	0	0	0	0	0	0	0	0	0	0
II	6	3	3+	3	3	0	0	0	0	6	3	15	0	0	0	0	0	0	0	0	0	0
III	20	7+	10	7	3	4	0	3	4	16	6	9	1	13	0	0	5	5	0	0	0	0
IV	18	8	6+	10	10	0	1	0	13	5	5	12	1	4	1	3	4	6	3	8	0	0
V	16	4+	1	4	4	0	2	0	16	0	2	2	2	9	0	0	0	0	2	2	1	1
VI	2	1		0	0	0	0	0	2	0	0	0	0	0	0	0	0	0	0	0	0	0
Total	64	24+	24+	25	20	5	3	3	35	29	17	39	4	26	1	3	9	11	5	10	1	1

Table 2.4. Components of the family structure: the Adams family

Genera-tion	Persons			Marriages			Stability		Present status (1970)		Offspring		Span of relationships (kinfolk)									
													Sibling		Half sibling		1st cousin		2nd cousin		3rd cousin	
	Total	Male	Fe-male	Total	For-mal	Con-sen.	Divor-ced	Separ.	Alive	Dead	Sets	Pers.	Sets	Pers.	Sets	Pers.	Sets	Pers.	Sets	Pers.	Sets	Pers.
I	6	3	3	3	1	2	0	0	0	6	3	4	0	0	0	0	0	0	0	0	0	0
II	11	6	5	6	5	1	0	0	0	11	6	10	1	2	0	0	0	0	0	0	0	0
III	15	9	6	7	3	4	1	1	3	12	7	29	4	8	1	3	2	4	3	12	0	0
IV	34	12+	12+	8	6	2	0	0	23	11	4	7	4	25	0	0	7	28	4	8	4	7
V	13	7	6	6	6	0	0	1	13	0	5	9	1	4	0	0	2	2	2	3	5	9
VI	11	5	6	2	2	0	0	0	11	0	2	7	4	8	0	0	2	4	0	0	2	7
VII	7	3	4	0	0	0	0	0	7	0	0	0	2	7	0	0	2	7	0	0	0	0
Total	97	45+	42+	32	23	9	1	2	57	40	27	66	16	54	1	3	15	45	9	23	11	23

Table 2.5. Components of the family structure: the Davis family

Genera-tion	Persons			Marriages			Stability		Present status (1970)		Offspring		Span of relationships (kinfolk)									
													Sibling		Half sibling		1st cousin		2nd cousin		3rd cousin	
	Total	Male	Fe-male	Total	For-mal	Con-sen.	Divor-ced	Separ.	Alive	Dead	Sets	Pers.	Sets	Pers.	Sets	Pers.	Sets	Pers.	Sets	Pers.	Sets	Pers.
I	2	1	1	1	1	0	0	0	0	2	1	1	0	0	0	0	0	0	0	0	0	0
II	4	2	2	2	1	1	0	0	0	4	2	2	0	0	0	0	0	0	0	0	0	0
III	3	1	2	2	2	0	0	1	1	2	2	10	2	2	0	0	0	0	0	0	0	0
IV	24	11	13	14	13	1	3	0	19	5	10	24	2	10	2	10	0	0	0	0	0	0
V	37	19	18	13	13	0	1	0	36	1	10	21	7	22	2	7	10	24	0	0	0	0
VII	21	4+	5+	0	0	0	0	0	21	0	0	0	8	19	0	0	3	16	10	21	0	0
Total	91	38+	41+	32	30	2	4	1	77	14	25	58	19	53	4	17	13	40	10	21	0	0

Table 2.6. Components of the family structure: the Kennedy family

Genera-tion	Persons			Marriages			Stability		Present status (1970)		Offspring		Span of relationships (kinfolk)										
													Sibling		Half sibling		1st cousin		2nd cousin		3rd cousin		
	Total	Male	Fe-male	Total	For-mal	Con-sen.	Divor-ced	Separ.	Alive	Dead	Sets	Pers.	Sets	Pers.	Sets	Pers.	Sets	Pers.	Sets	Pers.	Sets	Pers.		
I	6	3	3	3	2	1	0	0	0	6	3	3	0	0	0	0	0	0	0	0	0	0		
II	10	4	6	4	3	1	0	0	1	9	4	11	1	4	0	0	0	0	0	0	0	0		
III	27	14	13	12	12	0	2	0	14	13	6	16	5	17	0	0	2	5	1	3	0	0		
IV	25	12	13	10	9	1	1	0	24	1	7	25+	4	14	1	4	6	16	5	18	2	7		
V	37+	14+	11+	12	12	0	2	1	37+	0	9	14	6	25+	0	0	7	25+	6	9	9	15		
VI	16	10	6	2	2	0	1	0	16	0	1	1	5	10	0	0	8	12	1	1	1	1		
VII	1	1	0	0	0	0	0	0	1	0	0	1	0	0	0	0	0	0	0	0	0	0		
Total	122	58+	52+	39	40	3	6	1	93+	29	30	70+	21	70+	1	4	23	58	13	31	12	23		

Table 3. Household compositions in Texas and California, 1970

Household type and characteristic	Texas[a]			California[b]		
	Frequency			Frequency		
	Number	Percent of total	Average size (persons)	Number	Percent of total	Average size (persons)
All households	21	100.0	2.76	48	100.0	2.64
Families	17	81.0	3.18	34	71.0	3.32
Husband–wife:	15	71.0	3.20	28	58.0	3.32
Conjugal couple	6	29.0	2.00	9	19.0	2.00
Couple with children only	6	29.0	4.33	19	40.0	3.94
Extended:	3	14.0	3.33	0	0	—
Single generation	0	0	—	0	0	—
Two generation	2	10.0	3.00	0	0	—
Multiple generation	1	5.0	4.00	0	0	—
Woman-headed:	2	10.0	2.50	5	10.0	3.20
Mother–children	2	10.0	2.50	4	8.0	3.25
Grandmother–children–grandchildren	0	0	—	0	0	—
Other	0	0	—	1	2.0	3.00
Male-headed (father–children)	0	0	—	1	2.0	3.00
Single individuals	4	19.0	1.00	14	29.0	1.00

[a] Includes 20 households in "Middville" and 1 household in East Hamilton.
[b] Includes 41 households in Los Angeles, 3 households in Palm Springs, 2 households in Sacramento, 1 household in northern California, and 1 household in Elsinore.

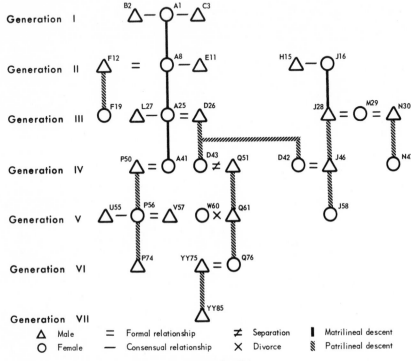

Figure 1.1. *De facto* lines of descent (Smith family)

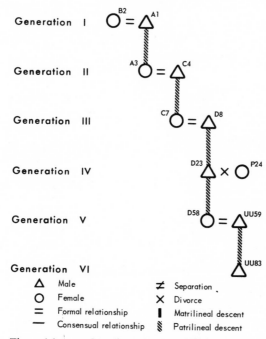

Figure 1.2. *De facto* lines of descent (Davis family)

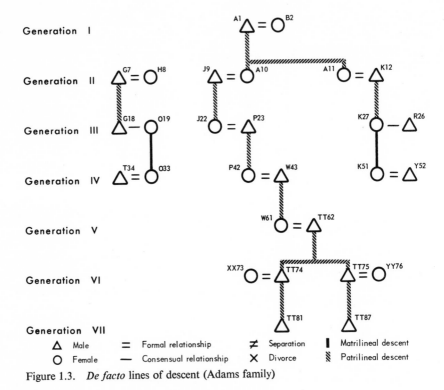

Generation I

Generation II

Generation III

Generation IV

Generation V

Generation VI

Generation VII

| △ Male | = Formal relationship | ≠ Separation | ▮ Matrilineal descent |
| ○ Female | — Consensual relationship | ✕ Divorce | ░ Patrilineal descent |

Figure 1.3. *De facto* lines of descent (Adams family)

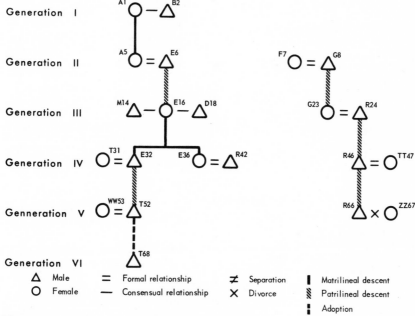

Figure 1.4. *De facto* lines of descent (Miller family)

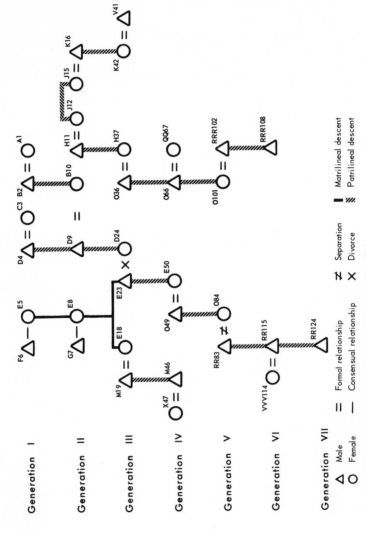

Figure 1.5. *De facto* lines of descent (Kennedy family)

REFERENCES

ASCHENBRENNER, JOYCE
  1971   "Black culture: South to North." Paper read at annual meeting of the
         American Society for Ethnohistory, Athens, Georgia. October.
BULLOCK, PAUL, *editor*
  1969   *Watts: the aftermath, by the people of Watts.* New York: Grove Press.
DAVIS, WILLIAM R.
  1934   *The development and present status of Negro education in East Texas.*
         New York: Teachers College, Columbia University, Bureau of
         Publications.
DE GRAAF, LAWRENCE BROOKS
  1962   *Negro migration to Los Angeles, 1930 to 1950.* Unpublished Ph.D.
         thesis, University of California, Los Angeles.
FLORANT, LYONEL C.
  1942   Negro internal migration. *American Sociological Review* 7: 782–791.
HANNERZ, ULF
  1969   *Soulside: inquiries into ghetto culture and community.* New York:
         Columbia University Press.
KISER, CLYDE V.
  1932   *Sea island to city. A study of St. Helena islanders in Harlem and other
         urban centers.* New York: Columbia University Press.
LIEBOW, ELLIOT
  1967   *Tally's corner: a study of Negro street-corner men.* Boston: Little,
         Brown.
MYRDAL, GUNNAR
  1944   *The American dilemma.* New York: Harper and Bros.
ROSS, F. A., L. V. KENNEDY
  1934   *A bibliography of Negro migration.* New York: Columbia University
         Press.
SHIMKIN, D. B.
  1971   "Black migration and the struggle for equity: a hundred-year survey,"
         in *Migration and social welfare.* Edited by Joseph W. Eaton, 77–116.
         New York: National Association of Social Workers.
WOODSON, C. G.
  1918   *A century of Negro migration.* Washington, D.C.: Association for the
         Study of Negro Life and History.
WOOFTER, T. J., JR.
  1930   *Black yeomanry.* New York: Henry Holt.

Familialism in Texas: A Texan View

M. JOURDAN ATKINSON

ABSTRACT

Not only is Texas different from the rest of the United States, but regions within Texas have differed, geographically and historically, since Indian times — the eastern timberland, versus the western plains and prairies, versus the Rio Grande valley.

For historical reasons the Black population of Texas has been concentrated in East, South, and lower Central Texas. Dallas and Houston are both on the edge of East Texas and still reflect these historical continuities. Since World War II, Black migration has been rural to urban within the state, rather than out-of-state. And the Texas Black today is notable for his independence of outlook, especially toward bureaucracy.

Black families in Texas have extensive knowledge of their ancestors, both Black and White. White families in Texas likewise know their genealogies and cousins several degrees removed. Hence, the extended family in Texas should be regarded as a "southernity" rather than a distinctive ethnic trait. Attendance at funerals is regarded as obligatory in both White and Black families, and burial in the "home place" is desired by Texans whatever their ethnic origins and social class.

GEOGRAPHICAL AND HISTORICAL REASONS WHY TEXAS IS "DIFFERENT"

The Past

Even in Indian times, the timberland easteners and the plains and prairie westerners held themselves to be culturally different, the latter considering the ambush facilities of the former to be particularly dreadful. Neither Spanish nor Anglo-Black overlays have changed the feeling that one part of Texas is different from the other, and that both are different from the rest of the United States. People from both regions are distinctly aware of being Texans and southwesterners, but all Texans will admit that East

Texas is much more a part of the South, partly because of proximity and partly because of the lumber interests (the old ambush factor) that tie in with those of western Louisiana and southern Arkansas.

It is a historical fact that southerners, thinking they might be overrun by Federals during the Civil War, rushed their Blacks into East Texas — that is, into the timbered area of concealment (again, the old ambush factor) — and hid them there until the war was over. The Blacks were then turned loose to fend for themselves as best they could. Meanwhile, thirty East Texas courthouses were burned, ahead of the arrival of the Freedman's Bureau, to destroy slave records and so on. This is why research stops in certain counties at that time.

After the Civil War, White southerners overran Texas to take public land given up by the Comanches after the destruction of the buffalo. Old Texans had proposed to settle their ex-slaves on these lands, but the newcomers put up their signs: "Nigger, don't let the sun go down on you here," so the Texan ex-masters left their Black ex-slaves land in the old plantation area, in South and lower Central Texas. Consequently this is where Texas's Black population is concentrated, except for the few Blacks who "went West with the cattle."

The Present

Both Dallas and Houston are on the edge of East Texas. One catches a reflection of historical and cultural differences when listening to Blacks plan their conventions: to Fort Worth, to San Antonio, and now to Houston, but not to Dallas or Waco. To the east lies old Ku Klux Klan country, and the east begins beyond Dallas. Waco has been a Ku Klux Klan headquarters; North and West Texas have nothing to offer.

Houston, along with its "gilded ghettos,"[1] has its "Bottom" where the poor, many on welfare, live in shotgun houses without air conditioning,[2] but whatever the situation in any Texas city, the state has no county that can be compared with Holmes County, Mississippi, as far as conditions for Blacks are concerned.

Of 254 counties, only three, Harrison, Marion, and San Jacinto, had Black majorities just before World War II. Harrison, by far the largest, east of Dallas on the Louisiana border, had a population of 51,000,

---

[1]   An expression applied to well-to-do Black areas in Houston, as compared with the "Bottom."
[2]   The folk expression "shotgun house" implies a single-room width, so that one might stand at the front door and shoot through all the rooms straight out the back door.

approximately three-fifths Black.[3] Harrison is described as a rural area. Marshall, the county seat, acquired a Black Methodist College, Wiley, in 1873, and a Black Baptist College, Bishop, in 1881. (St. Mary's, the non-Black Catholic academy, was founded in 1917.)

In 1970, the Census gives the county population as 45,000. Despite the increase in property values between World War II and the present, together with the establishment of some industry and development of oil and lumber interests, the population (that was, politically speaking, all Black) has been reduced by a tenth: in the three decades 1940–1970, Black numbers have decreased nearly one-half while non-Blacks have increased nearly a third.

Meanwhile, the total Black population of Texas, which was less than a million in 1940, is now a million and a half, and more than a fifth of Texas's Blacks live in Harris County where Houston is the county seat. These figures indicate that the Black flow has been rural to urban, not out-of-state but to local cities, and that it probably has been augmented by inflow from other states.

Perhaps the reason for not going out-of-state is inherent in the angry question a Black woman raised a few nights back on a radio talk show. She said [paraphrased],

I don't know why these social workers don't want to talk to you soon as they find out you're a Texan. If you're on welfare and from Arkansas or Louisiana they like you fine, but they don't want to hear nothing you got to say if you're from somewhere in Texas!

The history of the Texas Black is not the history of other Blacks, politically or economically,[4] so he differs psychologically and therefore reacts differently to bureaucratic agents — less "meaching" of manner. He may live in the "Bottom" and be on welfare, but he sees that as no reason to be "looked down on" or spoken to abruptly and without feeling. In his opinion, anyone is due courtesy from all "public servants."

[3] All statistics in this paper are from the *Texas Almanac* 1945–1946 and 1972–1973. Round numbers are used in the text.
[4] Unlike freedmen in the South, Texas freedmen had an economy. Texas emancipation waited on Appomattox, so the postwar Freedmen's Bureau assessed an indemnity to be paid in cash for years of bondage after the official Emancipation Proclamation. Moreover, many plantation masters left land heritages to their Black children, and some, simply out of gratitude for services performed — as witness the will of Mary Doyle, Travis County, who left all cattle and land to the family Blacks.

GENEALOGICAL KNOWLEDGE AND THE CULTURAL
EFFECTS OF TEXAS'S DISTINCTIVENESS

An interesting aspect of Professor Aoyagi's paper (this volume) is the number of references to interethnic marital and extramarital unions. Although birth statistics and records may be scanty, almost all Texas Blacks seem to have handed-down information about their genealogies that is reliable. If they don't know exactly, they will say so, contrary to the kind of information they may give about other private affairs. If the manner of asking hurts their feelings, they, will simply say "I don't know," rather than making up an answer.

If one walks along the street in Texas and talks with Black children, or with Black people and one says to a Black child, "What is your name?," the child will say, "Mary," and one will say, "Spell it for me," and the child will say, "Mar-r-r-y." This is a Spanish pronunciation, and almost any Black child on almost any street is going to flutter that "r." This is just one cultural trait symptomatic of the fact that the Spanish Black was in Texas long before the Anglo Black. The Spanish Blacks were there a hundred years earlier, as a matter of fact, and the influence is still extremely strong. The family situation in Spanish colonial times was entirely different from what it was under under the French. Today, French influences extend as as far south and west as Houston; until World War I, however, the region south of San Antonio was entirely Spanish-speaking.

John Webber, a distinguished and quite well-to-do White man, had probably arrived in Texas by the 1820's. In the 1850 United States Census of Population, his name is listed in Travis County; his wife is listed as "Negro" and his children, eight of them, as "Mulattos." This is, perhaps, the only family listed in the United States Census which indicates a legally recognized ethnic intermarriage in Texas. Nevertheless, it is the writer's experience in doing research (her own family has been in Texas since Texas was part of Mexico) that families in Texas are as aware of their White and Indian ancestry as of their Black ancestry, whether the relationship was legal, common law, or merely casual concubinage.

In 1909, the writer's uncle, J. C. Maxwell (a White planter), gave a barbecue for the descendants of the Maxwell Black family that came to Texas from Virginia with their owners not long before the Civil War brought slavery to a close:

A reunion which, for its uniqueness, is probably without a parallel in the history of the south, was held on the J. C. Maxwell farm near Sprinkle yesterday afternoon. The participants in the reunion were the ex-slaves of Mr. Maxwell and their families. The reunion was the celebration of the fifty-first anniversary of the coming to Texas of Mr. Maxwell and the slaves he brought with him. . . .

The idea was original with Mr. Maxwell, as probably no other reunion of the kind was ever held in this country. Mr. Maxwell came to Texas with his father in 1858, bringing with them twenty-five slaves. Of this number but seven of the original twenty-five were present at the reunion yesterday.

The families of these have multiplied rapidly, however, and at the reunion Uncle Mose Fraction, the senior of the ex-slaves counted the children, grandchildren and great grandchildren of the "family" and estimated there were 148 in all. Of this number about 50 were present at the reunion yesterday. The others have scattered, many of them going to Oklahoma, when the territory was opened. . . .

Barbecue Was Ample

A table was prepared and on this was spread ample barbecued steer and pig. The negroes stood around a table some 50 feet in length, the juicy pieces of meat being prepared as only meat can be by those experienced in this line of culinary.

"You folks will have to wait for the second table," announced Mr. Maxwell to the half dozen White guests who had been invited on the occasion. "This is the negroes' day and they will come first."

One of the most interesting of the old slaves was Aunt Fanny Tucker, who was Mr. Maxwell's nurse. She brought with her the old family Bible, which was owned by her grandmother. On the blank pages between the Old and New Testaments is recorded the birth of her mother in 1812. Aunt Fanny's birth is recorded there in 1828 and her sister, Jinny's, some time later. From there on the family tree has more numerous branches and is more complete. For a woman 81 years of age Aunt Fanny is remarkably preserved and she was the center of attraction, as she sat smoking her clay pipe among the younger negroes. The old mammy convulsed with laughter when some one spoke of her youthful appearance, saying she didn't have a gray hair in her head, when it was discovered she wore a wig. . . .

The seven negroes at the barbecue who came from Virginia with the Maxwells are Fanny Tucker, Mose Fraction, Thomas Madison, William Shanks, Louis Allen, Jack Black and Amy Shanks. All are over 70 years of age, the majority of them being in their 80's. This group was photographed, as were other groups of the negroes. . . .

The slaves were freed in June of 1865, but they remained with their former owners until the end of the year. For this they were guaranteed enough food and clothing to start out in their new life of freedom. The Maxwell negroes were treated well, most of them being allowed to rent small tracts of land on which they could make a living. The old negroes have all settled about Sprinkle and have done well there. They never forget their places. They are treated with kindness and give kindness in return.

Mr. Maxwell believes he has been successful in transferring the negroes from slaves into free people, a problem which puzzled all slave holders (*Austin American* 1909).

THE EXTENDED FAMILY AS A "SOUTHERNITY"

The concept of the extended family covers Texas like as laprobe when a norther blows, or like the hot sunshine in July and August. It is no more Black than it is Latino, Anglo, or central European, and perhaps it should be referred to as a "southernity" rather than as a distinctive ethnic trait. Several not-unusual incidents evidence this intimate coverall, the basis of which is recognition of one's kin and one's "family friends."

When the writer's daughter was small she was overheard saying,

I never know whether grown-ups are my daddy's sisters and brothers or my mother's sisters and brothers or my grown-up cousins or just their (my parents') friends, because I call them all "aunt" and "uncle."

She was, of course, taught the finer distinctions with time. But the bond thus closely knit would remain for a lifetime — unless, as noted by Shimkin, Louie, and Frate (this volume), severed by a real cause for enmity.

Again, a local ship's pilot (Anglo) once came with a problem; he had a Texas pilot's license but he wanted a federal license also. (Houston is a port city.)

To acquire the Texas license, it had been necessary only for another Texan to declare that he (whose great-grandfather's name is inscribed on the San Jacinto Monument)[5] was born a United States citizen. The swearer need not have been more than five years old at the time of the remembered birth. But the federal requirement was for the swearer to have been at least fourteen years old at that time and unrelated "by blood or marriage."

"Any five-year-old," the pilot observed with considerable scorn for federal child psychology, "would be more impressed than a harumscarum teenager by the arrival of a new baby!" But that was not the problem. The problem was that this man, who was a fourth-generation Texan, could find nobody who had known him in his youth who was less closely related than a fifth cousin.

This dilemma was explained to a judge: "Folks up North who made the law very likely have never 'counted kin' beyond second cousins." The judge, probably knowing his own family tree to the tips of its branches, said: "Let him come on into my court with a fifth cousin — I'll grant him a license."

[5] A monolith slightly taller than the Washington Monument, topped with a Texas star, on the battlefield of San Jacinto outside Houston, where Texas independence from Mexico was won in 1836. The monument bears the names of Sam Houston's Army of the Republic of Texas.

The style and expense of a Texas funeral symbolizes the importance both of the deceased and of those who sponsor the funeral. Sometimes there is no other occasion on which a family ne'er-do-well may put himself forward. Or one's presence may signal a silent claim to estate or heirlooms. But, whatever the funeral complications within the family, "outsiders" will critically estimate evidence of grief, of good or bad faith, and of common sense: Were the wishes of the deceased carried out in the funeral arrangement? Was the expenditure over-modest or over-lavish? And, above all, how great was the expression of loss by the community at large?

Recently the mother of a Black next-door neighbor, a retired school principal, "passed on." Born in Houston ninety-three years ago, she was the oldest member of Antioch Baptist Church. A landmark, Antioch is today shadowed by downtown skyscrapers. (Its congregation has so far resisted offers of a million dollars from those wishing to replace it with an office building or a hotel.)

The body was held at a funeral parlor from Sunday morning until 11 a.m. Saturday, for relatives who were flying in from New York, California, and Oklahoma City, plus those driving from Texas towns.

Because it is unsafe to leave a house closed when the family is known to be absent (long obituaries had been in the papers) and because remembrances would continue to pour in, the writer stayed at the son's home through the burial hour.

Nine carloads of family left the house at quarter to eleven, preceded by a motorcycle policeman. They would find the congregation waiting at Antioch.

More than twenty potted plants were received and arranged (sprays and "designs" went to the grave), and kitchen and dining room were so full of prepared food that one lost track of who sent what.

When the church ceremony was concluded and a procession formed that would escort the body to the cemetery, three Missionary Women (a formal organization) came to the house instead. They got the food ready and were there to serve the throng that gathered for dinner, after which everyone drifted away. The long week was over.

When a brother died in Austin, the writer was out-of-state. Arriving worn from the night's travel, she found his daughter's house overflowing with food and goodwill.

The concept of the "home place" where one's body should find "eternal rest" is, like the concept of the dignity of death, common to Texans of whatever ethnic distinction. Asked where he is "from," a Texan may very well reply that he is from Austin, or San Antonio, or

Nacogdoches, or wherever, but that he lives in Del Rio or some other town.

This doubly informative answer (giving both the place where the speaker "grew up" and his present place of residence) will, nine times out of ten, elicit a response that the questioner's grandfather "came from there," too; or that he has an uncle or a brother in the place of residence. So within minutes, the consultants may establish a bond of social intimacy due to discovery of mutual friends, mutual in-laws or mutual "blood kin."

At this point, one gets the feel of the ancient mystique, autochthony. Born on the soil where his dead are buried, the "native" has a pure pride in his own being. In Texas's ethnic mixture, except for a handful of not very politically minded Indians, the Blacks are the oldest element. They came here with the Spanish before Anglo or central European colonists, and here they will stay.

This is the "home place" where Blacks not only are part of the past but where they have a stake in the future — as recent elections of Blacks to judicial, legislative, and administrative positions in Dallas, San Antonio, and Galveston, as well as in Houston, show.

Politically on his way, the Black is not the mere representative of the diluted "African blood" that more or less darkens his complexion. He is the representative of all those people whose "blood" (actually genes) pulses in his veins. Sometimes quite literally, they are his "extended family."

REFERENCES

Austin American
    1909   "Barbecue for his ex-slaves." *Austin American* (now *American Statesman*). Austin, Texas.
Texas Almanac
    1945–1946; 1972–1973   Dallas: Belo.

Texas Indeed Is Different: Some Historical and Demographic Observations

DEMITRI B. SHIMKIN

ABSTRACT

Historically, Texas has been a culturally distinctive region, its distinctiveness arising from complex origins — Spanish-American, Southern, Frontier, and German — and from its geographic and demographic isolation. Prior to the Civil War, Texas's ethnic composition included Anglo-American settlers, both slave-holding planters and Appalachian in-migrants. The "colored" population was concentrated in eastern Texas, while the "Mexicans" predominated along the Rio Grande, up the Gulf Coast beyond Corpus Christi, and in the San Antonio region. "German" minorities were found in Galveston and in the Guadalupe and Colorado valleys. Slaves were imported both from the Old South and from Africa, and free Negroes were often enslaved. Consequently, the "colored" population comprised 30 percent of the state total by 1860.

The Civil War had little effect upon Texas, except for accelerated White in-migration from mountain areas of the South. By 1880, the eastern counties of Texas had made advances in educational facilities for Blacks, while the Mexican population remained the object of White prejudice.

The period of World War II and subsequent years saw massive intrastate urbanization of Texas's Black population, primarily for economic reasons, in contrast to a lack of mobility among Anglo-Americans and Anglo-Germans, probably accounted for by the strength of local and familial ties. Nevertheless, the basic pattern of ethnic distribution in Texas persisted from 1850 through 1970.

THE COMPLEX ORIGINS OF TEXAN CULTURE

The cultural distinctiveness of Texas, within the framework of American society, which has already been indicated in Dr. M. J. Atkinson's commentary (this volume), needs to be emphasized. This distinctiveness has arisen from the complex origins of that culture — in part Spanish-American, in part southern, in part German, in part Frontier — and from the relative isolation of Texas, geographically and demographically. For example, the migrants from Texas to Los Angeles studied by Dr. K. Aoyagi (this volume) represent a selective movement, with the predominant shift of the Texas Black population during World War II being intrastate urbanization. This contrasts sharply with the wholesale transfer of Black populations from Mississippi to Chicago, Detroit, and elsewhere. In consequence, the contextual framework of the migratory flows is different, and subtle institutional and behavioral contrasts must, accordingly, be expected. Above all, much research is needed to identify the characteristic features and variations of the extended family and other elements of Black culture in Texas, historically and today.

The basis of these generalizations is reviewed here to augment the Aoyagi and Atkinson data, and to provide guides to further work. Table 1

Table 1. The Negro population of Texas and other former Confederate States, 1870–1970

	Texas			Other states		
Year	Persons	Index[a]	Negro/total ($\times$ 100)	Persons	Index	Texas/all Confederate States ($\times$ 100)
1870	253,475	100	31.0	3,685,525	100	6.9
1880	393,384	155	24.7	4,966,616	135	7.3
1890	488,171	193	21.8	6,698,829	182	6.8
1900	620,722	245	20.4	5,498,780	149	10.1
1910	690,049	272	17.7	7,237,951	196	8.7
1920	741,694	293	15.9	7,314,306	198	9.2
1930	854,964	337	14.7	7,552,036	205	10.2
1940	924,391	365	14.4	7,954,609	216	10.4
1950	977,458	386	12.7	8,071,542	219	10.8
1960	1,187,125	468	12.4	8,462,995	230	12.0
1970	1,419,677	560	12.7	8,834,122	240	13.8

Sources: U.S. Bureau of the Census 1969: 245–247; 1971; 1973. The states covered are Alabama, Arkansas, Florida, Georgia, Louisiana, Mississippi, North Carolina, South Carolina, Tennessee, Texas, and Virginia.

[a]   1870 equals 100.

shows the great difference between a consistant absolute growth of the Black population in Texas, 1870–1970, and its far slower expansion — with an actual decline during the terrible years of the 1890's (Woodward 1953) — in the other states of the former Confederacy. The contrast for the period 1950–1970 is especially telling: an increase of 45 percent compared to one of less than 10 percent. Otherwise stated, Black people have remained in Texas, brief periods of out-migration (1900–1910; 1935–1945) apart; elsewhere in the once-Confederate South, out-migration has predominated.

Prior to the Civil War, Texas was a multiethnic society, dominated by southern Anglo-American settlers (slave-holding planters from the lowlands and "yeoman farmers" from the mountains) (Jordan 1969). In 1850, Texas included "Texan" (Anglo-American), "German," "French," and "Mexican" populations, a variety of Indian tribes in the unsettled western areas, and a rapidly growing "colored" population, largely slaves (Table 2). Withal, Texas society was loosely structured, for the

Table 2.   The ethnic composition of Texas, 1850 and 1970

	Thousand persons			Percent distribution		
	1850		1970	1850		1970
Ethnic group	A[a]	B[b]		A[a]	B[b]	
Total population	212.6	(250.1)	11,197	100.0	100.0	100.0
"Texan" (Anglo)[c]	130.2	(133.2)	7,555	61.2	(53.3)	67.5
"German"[d]	11.5	11.5	238	5.4	4.6	2.1
"French"[e]	1.1	1.1	110	0.5	0.4	1.0
"Mexican"[f]	11.2	(21.2)	1,793	5.3	(8.5)	16.0
"Colored"[g]	58.6	58.6	1,420	27.5	23.4	12.7
Other[h]		24.5	81		9.8	0.7

Sources: Olmsted 1857: 165, 428, 473–474; Jordan 1969; U.S. Bureau of the Census 1973; Schoolcraft 1853, I: 538.

[a] Coverage of Census area only. [b] Includes reported Indian population, Schoolcraft (1853), and estimates for "Anglo" and "Mexican" persons in areas not covered by the Census (Olmsted 1857: 165; map opposite p. 42). [c] Includes, in 1850 and 1970, all persons not covered in Notes a–h. [d] German surnames in 1850 (Jordan 1969); Olmsted's estimate of the German-born comes to the same figure (calculated from p. 428n); in 1970, persons with German as a mother tongue. [e] In 1850, persons with a French surname; in 1970, those with French as a mother tongue, including 19,109 Negroes. [f] In 1850, persons with Spanish surnames; in 1970, those with Spanish as a mother tongue. [g] In 1850, includes both slave and free persons. [h] In 1850, includes 15,000 Comanches, 4,000 Apache, 1,200 Caddo, 1,500 Kiowa, 1,000 Wichita, and 1,800 other Indians; in 1970, includes 17,957 Indians (almost all, recent in-migrants), 7,635 Chinese, 6,537 Japanese, 3,442 Filipinos, and 45,026 "others."

dispersing effects of a thinly settled frontier limited conflicts as it promoted local variations, movements, and accommodations.

The "Mexicans" predominated along the Rio Grande, up the Gulf Coast to beyond Corpus Christi, and in Bexar County (San Antonio).

"Germans," many of them refugees from the abortive revolutionary uprisings of 1848, were a large minority in Galveston, then the largest town in Texas, with a population of 4,177 persons, White and Black (Olmsted 1857: 474; Fornell 1961: 125–139). They were also farmers and, more rarely, slave-holding planters, in the Guadalupe and Colorado valleys; three-fourths of the population of Victoria County was "Ger-

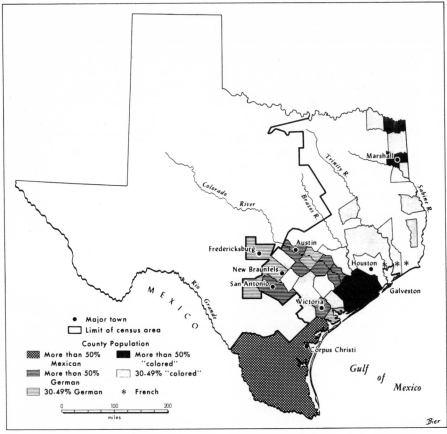

Map 1.   Ethnic minorities in Texas. Census counties, 1850. *Source:* Olmsted 1857:
165, 428, 473–474; map opposite p. 42

man." In the West Texas of that day, Comal, Gillespie, and Medina
counties were almost totally "German," including both farmers and
substantial numbers of craftsmen in the towns of Neu Braunfels and
Fredericksburg.

The "colored" were most numerous in the plantation areas of the
Lower Colorado, Brazos, and Trinity valleys, and in the swampy forests
of northeast Texas and the Sabine River (Map 1). In the latter areas
there were free Negroes as well as slaves. Frederick Olmsted (1857: 386)
found the following at the time of his visit in 1856:

We inquired about the free negroes of whom they were speaking, and were told
that there were a number in the county [evidently Sabine County], all mulattoes,

who had come from Louisiana. Some of them owned many negroes, and large stocks. There were some white people, good-for-nothing people, that married in with them, but they couldn't live in Texas after it; all went over into Louisiana. They knew of no law excluding free negroes from the State; if there were any such law, no one here cared for it.

SLAVERY IN TEXAS

Throughout the pre-Civil War period, the importation of slaves from the Old South and Africa, and the enslavement of free Negroes, which Texas law facilitated, were intensely stimulated by the enormous profits to be gained through growing cotton with cheap labor (DuBois 1969: 180 and *passim*; Fornell 1961: 230–264). In consequence, the "colored" population, which numbered some 12,000 in 1840, according to the incomplete census of the Republic of Texas (White 1966: Foreword), had risen to 182,921, or 30 percent of the state total, by 1860 (U.S. Bureau of the Census 1943: 762).

The conditions of slavery varied. In many respects, they were least onerous for the hired-out urban slaves; in Galveston, which in some respects aped Charleston, South Carolina, house slaves were integral parts of wealthy households. In certain instances, most likely cases of concubinage, legal measures were taken to provide for the security of certain slaves by means of wills:

In such circumstances certain lawyers in the city, who customarily acted as executors in liquidating estates often became in effect the guardians of the "household" or merchant-employed slaves who belonged among the properties of their deceased clients. In situations where property was inherited by persons not living on the Island [of Galveston] or by heirs who had no particular wish to be kind to strange Negroes with whom they had no particular concern or affection, the executors often became actual advocates for the rights of Negro slaves who had been protected by the stipulations of a will. In this curious circumstance, the "legal rights of slaves" on the Island were in many cases more to be desired than the legal rights enjoyed by free Negroes. These particular rights were not "human rights" but rather rights which came to the slave primarily because he was property and thus had to be respected as such in accord with the provisions of a will. The legal rights of the free Negro were very few indeed, and his position so untenable during the late fifties that he sometimes chose voluntarily to reenter slavery (Fornell 1961: 117–118).

Most often slavery was harsh. Migration was difficult, even when plantations moved as units:

Before you come upon them you hear, ringing through the woods, the fierce cries and blows with which they urge on their jaded cattle. Then the stragglers appear, lean dogs or fainting negroes, ragged and spiritless. An old granny, hauling on, by the hand, a weak boy — too old to ride and too young to keep up. An old man, heavily loaded, with a rifle. Then the white covers of the wagons, jerking up and down as they mount over a root or plunge into a rut, disappearing, one after another, where the road descends. Then the active and cheery prime negroes, not yet exhausted, with a joke and a suggestion about tobacco. Then the black pickinninnies, staring, in a confused heap, out at the back of the wagon, more and more of their eyes to be made out among the table legs and bedding as you get near; behind them, further in, the old people and young mothers, whose turn it is to ride. As you get by, the white mother and babies, and the tall, frequently ill-humored master on horseback, or walking with his gun, urging up the black driver and his oxen. As a scout ahead is a brother, or an intelligent slave, with the best gun, on the look-out for a deer or a turkey (Olmsted 1857: 55–56).

Slave-trade consignments endured even greater hardships. On the coast, near Victoria (Map 1), Olmsted met

... a gang of negroes, three men, two women, and two boys, under guard of a white man and a very large yellow mastiff. The negroes each had some article to carry, one an ax, another a rifle, another a kettle, a fourth led a horse, to whose saddle were fastened a ham, a coffee-pot, and a buffalo robe. This last, undoubtedly, would be the white man's covering at night, the negroes having no extra clothing. They were evidently slaves consigned to some planter in the interior, probably by his factor in New Orleans, as part of the proceeds of his crop. . . . They were much fagged, and sullen with their day's walk. The prospect before them was a boundless flat prairie, with a cold north wind, and rain threatening (Olmsted 1857: 240).

The sales and transfers of slaves were common within Texas as well. For example, in Liberty County, north of Galveston, were many Creole French, old migrants from Louisiana. Many had fallen into poverty, selling their slaves to merchants in Galveston (Olmsted 1857: 374). In general, dislocations were common among "the restless, almost nomadic, small proprietors" (Olmsted 1857: 92).

These physical difficulties were intensified by frequent hostility toward slaves:

"Dam 'em, give 'em hell," frequent expressions of the ruder planters toward their negroes, appeared to be used as if with a meaning — a threat to make their life infernal if they did not submit abjectly and constantly. There seemed to be the consciousness of a wrong relation and determination to face conscience down and continue it; to work up the "damned niggers," with sole eye to selfish profit, cash down, in this world . . . (Olmsted 1857: 123).

The presence of free Negroes in eastern Texas, near the Sabine River (Olmsted 1857: 386–388), of Germans unsympathetic to slavery in the West (Olmsted 1857: 432), and especially of antislavery "Mexicans" gave rise to continual flights to freedom by slaves, and to ensuing conflicts between Anglo-Texans and other ethnic groups. Olmsted observed that the "Mexicans"

... consort freely with the negroes, making no distinction from pride of race. A few, of old Spanish blood, have purchased negro servants, but most of them regard slavery with abhorrence. . . . They are regarded by slaveholders with great contempt and suspicion, for their intimacy with slaves, and their competition with plantation labor (Olmsted 1857: 163).

Slaveholding, in general, divided Texas society, with the planters in opposition not only to the "Mexicans" and "Germans" but to the small farmers and herdsmen of southern mountain origin as well:

The manners and ideals of the Texans and of the Germans are hopelessly divergent, and the two races have made little acquaintance, observing one another apart with unfeigned curiosity, often tempered with mutual contempt. The Americans have the prestige of preoccupation, of accustomed dominance over Mexicans and slaves, of language, capital, political power, and vociferous assumption. The Germans, quiet and engrossed in their own business, by nature law-abiding and patient, submit to be governed with little murmuring.

A large proportion of the emigrants have remained apart, in German communities, and have contented themselves with . . . their own little public affairs . . . (Olmsted 1857: 431).

The presence of this incongruous foreign element of Mexicans and Germans tends, as may be conceived, to hinder any rapid and extensive settlement of Western Texas by planters. . . . Planters have consequently settled in masses, almost exclusively upon the Colorado and Lower Guadalupe bottoms [Figure 1], leaving the great remaining western pasture regions to their more natural occupation of huntsmen and small farmers.

The herdsmen have no use for slaves, which are only adapted for working in gangs under constant supervision, and cannot be trusted in an employment requiring isolation and discretion. And both herdsmen and farmers find in the proximity and society of planters, a mutual incompatibility (Olmsted 1857: 440–441).

THE EFFECTS OF THE CIVIL WAR

The Civil War had little effect on Texas, a refuge area where slaveholders moved in some 200,000 slaves during the four years of conflict (Connor 1971: 209). In addition, the war seemed to accelerate migration from mountain areas of the Old South to the hill area of Central Texas (Jordan 1970). These hunters, gatherers, and subsistence farmers introduced an "Appalachian" culture which blocked the westward movement of ethnic minorities, even after the end of slavery and the expulsion of Indian tribal remnants. Until the rise of the oil industry after World War I, Texas remained very rural, isolated externally and internally. Marked local differences prevailed.

As early as 1880, the eastern counties, with old traditions of Negro freedom, had made advances in education for Black people. Thus, in Bowie County there were forty-eight public free schools, "including those for colored children" (Commissioner of Insurance, Statistics, and History 1882: 33). Cass County, "38½ percent colored," had fifty-eight white and thirty-one colored public free schools (1882: 53–55). In Harrison County, two-thirds Black,

The colored population have two academies, well endowed, provided with substantial brick buildings, and under the management of white teachers. There are also in the county public free schools provided for a scholastic population of 5,171, besides 906 in the city schools of Marshall, the schools being apportioned between white and colored pupils according to their respective numbers. All the leading religious denominations have commodious houses of worship in Marshall, and churches are found in every neighborhood, both for the white and colored (Commissioner of Insurance, Statistics, and History 1882: 140–141).

The best of the old plantation counties was Waller, west of Houston, the site of

. . . Prairie View Normal school, an institution supported by the State for the education of colored teachers for the public free schools, in which 45 students are furnished board, books, and tuition without charge (Commissioner of Insurance, Statistics, and History 1882: 327).

More characteristic, however, was the comment for Wharton County, northeast of Victoria:

The relation of the two races is entirely harmonious, but the preponderance in numbers of the colored element has operated to retard the development of its natural resources (Commissioner of Insurance, Statistics, and History 1882: 334).

In contrast to the moderate improvement of race relationships evidenced in these data, Texas attitudes toward the Spanish-speaking population appeared to harden. For example, in Hidalgo County, along the lower Rio Grande, educational conditions were assessed as follows:

The scholastic population, organized into school communities in the year 1881–82, was 294, for which there were 11 public free schools, which were taught four and a quarter months. About 90 percent of the inhabitants are Mexicans, who are indifferent to education, and indisposed to patronize the public schools (Commissioner of Insurance, Statistics, and History 1882: 147).

The intensity of prejudice in Hidalgo County is shown in a later document on Protestant churches in Texas. During the 1920's, sectarian conflicts had caused an original Union church to break up into separate denominations. At the same time, White (1928: 29) reported,

One part of the cooperative arrangement is still in existence. That is the Mexican mission. It is frankly a Methodist enterprise. It is not self-supporting. While the Methodists are more interested in it than the other denominations, because it belongs to their denomination, both Baptists and Presbyterians contribute money and occasionally service to its maintenance. In connection with the Mexican mission a school for Mexican children was established, and it is supported by all the Protestant churches. These activities receive united support, because they are directed at the Roman Catholic Church which from the start was accepted as a common enemy. Each denomination is not "strong enough" to maintain its own mission and school. Hence they work together.

The extreme conservatism of Texas society prior to World War II (oil booms notwithstanding) is well discussed by Goodwyn (1955). It is underscored by the persistence of Negro lynchings — at least three a year between 1889 and 1922: 20 in 1895, 23 in 1897, 16 in 1922; a total of 345 between 1882 and 1936 (Connor 1971: 378). It is revealed graphically by comparing the distribution of the state's Negro population in 1940 with that of the "colored" in 1850 (Maps 1 and 2). It is revealed statistically by the fact that, in 1940, only 45 percent of both White and Negro populations was urban (U.S. Bureau of the Census 1943: 763; 1973: 103). This demographic rigidity was, in part, the result of explicit laws — city ordinances and subdivision restrictions — which established legal barriers to Negro settlement outside of defined areas (Connor 1971: 378).

THE EFFECTS OF WORLD WAR II

World War II initiated extremely rapid changes, which were accelerated during the 1950's by Supreme Court actions on school desegregation — and subsequent White reactions. While significant out-migration took place during the 1940's — a net loss of 101,000 "non-White" persons during that decade (Shryock 1964: 111) — the most fundamental change for the Negro population of Texas, 1940-1970, was intrastate urbanization. Massive shifts of population took place from previously rural areas in the eastern prairies to largely metropolitan counties near the Gulf Coast and along the Balcone escarpment (the line, roughly, of Dallas–San Antonio) (Map 3). A simple comparison shows the nature of this change. In 1940, the four urban counties with 25,000 or more Negroes (Harris, Dallas, Jefferson, and Tarrant) domiciled 227,638 Negro persons, or one-fourth of the state total (U.S. Bureau of the Census 1943: 792–805). In 1970, the seven urban counties with 25,000 or more Negroes

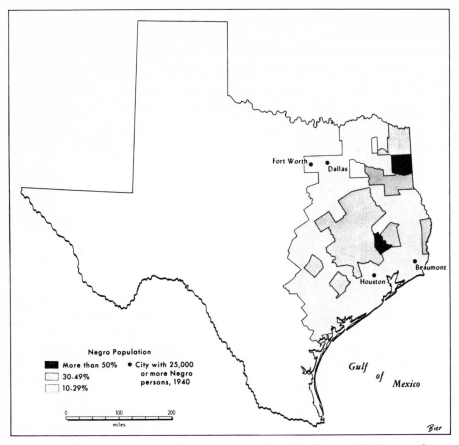

Map 2.   Negro population in Texas. Focal counties, 1940. *Source:* U.S. Bureau of
the Census 1943: 760, 792–806

(Harris, Dallas, Tarrant, Bexar, Jefferson, Travis, and Galveston) had
835,119, or almost four times as many Negro residents as earlier; they
constituted 60 percent of the state total U.S. Bureau of the Census [May]
1973: 275–330).

PRESENT-DAY ETHNIC DISTRIBUTIONS AND MIGRATION

It is remarkable that, in spite of these changes, the basic pattern of ethnic
distribution established by 1850 was still evident in 1970 (Maps 1, 4).
Fragmentary evidence is available to explain this persistence. Stapleton's

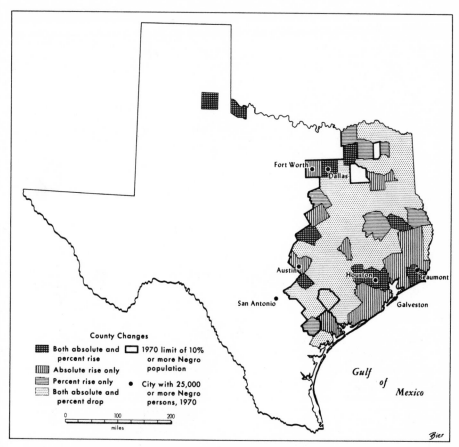

Map 3. Negro population in Texas. Distributional changes, 1940–1970. *Sources:* U.S. Bureau of the Census 1943: 760, 792–806; 1973: 264–271

analysis (1969) of White, male, rural migration originating near Lubbock, Texas, shows that of 236 high-school graduates over the years 1953–1963, 30 remained in their home communities, 34 migrated and then returned, while 172 left (Stapleton 1969: 97). Of the last, 67 went to small urban places and the remainder to metropolitan centers; of the entire group, 194 persons remained within 200 miles of Lubbock. Twenty-five were in Dallas, four in Houston, and thirteen out-of-state (Stapleton 1969: 91). For the entire group, the choices of residence were based on the following: "my family lived in area," 25.8 percent; "wife's family lived in area," 10.6 percent; "job and people," 15.7 percent; "liked town or city," 12.7 percent; "liked climate," 11.4 percent; "other," 23.7 percent (Stapleton

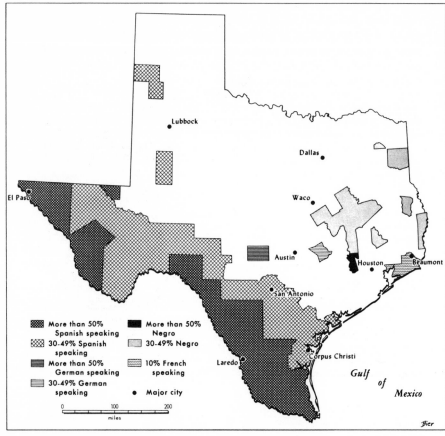

Map 4. Ethnic minorities in Texas. Focal counties, 1970. *Source:* U.S. Bureau of the Census 1973: 264–271, 435, 907–927

1969: 103). At the same time, the perceived reasons for possible future moves were rather different: "pay" was cited by 50.9 percent; "new occupation," by 15.4 percent, "climate," by 13.2 percent; and "family ties and opportunity to farm," by only 10.1 percent; "other," by 10.5 percent (Stapleton 1969: 106). Father's occupation and the migrant's own level of education were the major sociological determinants (Stapleton 1969: 107, 122). In general, Stapleton concluded that

. . . occupational inheritance in farming and, conversely, mobility from agriculture is much greater and less respectively in the South Plains than throughout the United States in general (Stapleton 1969: 122).

The intense nature of familial, local, and ethnic ties within the German-American population of Texas has been eloquently described by Vera Flach, a Chicagoan of Welsh extraction, who married into this community. Her experiences in the 1920's and 1960's sketch the essential continuities and changes (Flach 1973). When she first married into the German-American community, she

... learned that the German-American people had one great central creed. It was woven into the very fabric of their being. All other characteristics stemmed from it. It motivated everything they did. This central theme was *Family*.

From the first I was intrigued by the large families. The small telephone book sometimes had a whole page of the same name. I got used to hearing, "She is my third cousin." "He is Mother's uncle by marriage." ... The center and symbol of the Family Cult is "Geburtstag" (birthday). ...

This devout interest in *Family* spread itself to include all persons and projects of German origin. These people were Americans, but the Fatherland, its language, its triumphs in literature, music and science were always of paramount interest (Flach 1973: 6–7).

The German-American community had become a little less isolated by the 1960's:

Sometimes a new family is accepted and assimilated easily. Others find the nucleus of old German families difficult to penetrate and are unhappy about it. ... There are no statistics but an educated guess would be that much less German is spoken now than forty years ago. In some families small children are still bilingual. In others English has been used for years. Nearly all business is conducted in English but there is always someone who can speak the old language (Flach 1973: 107).

The effects of social change and continuity on the structure and functioning of Black families in Texas need detailed study. The five families investigated by Dr. K. Aoyagi (this volume) reveal patterns of discontinuity which stand in contrast to the extreme familialism referred to by Dr. M. J. Atkinson (this volume) and confirmed in the data on Anglo-American and German-American families cited above. Yet there is at least one clue that familialism may be less significant today for Texas Black people than for the Anglo-Americans or the Spanish-speaking Texans — although still more important than for the U.S. Black population as a whole.

A recent statistical analysis for the United States as a whole interprets "non-White" migration patterns as follows:

As a group the economic incentives are the most important. Areas with high average income levels strongly attract blacks on net balance, suggesting that the chance to earn a higher income is very important to blacks. Median income is significant at the 99% confidence level in the regression on all SEA's [Standard Economic Areas] and rural SEA's, although only significant at the 90% level in the one on urban SEA's (Askin 1970: 53–54).

Data from Texas yield different results. For the forty-eight counties that were 20 percent or more Negro in the 1970 Census, no correlation was observable between per capita income in 1969 and rate of migratory gain, 1960–1970 (r = −0.03).[1] Moreover for the fifty-one counties with 30 percent or more Spanish-speaking population, the correlation was negative (r = −0.26). For forty-two counties with less than 5 percent Black or Spanish-speaking, i.e. strongly "Anglo" counties, the correlation was even more negative (r = −0.43). Otherwise stated, in-migration correlated with poverty to an increasing degree in heavily Black, Chicano, and, especially, Anglo counties. For the first two, extreme poverty below the level permitting out-migration might be a factor; for the Anglo population, and in lesser degree for Chicanos and Blacks, the intensity of local, family ties among the least educated and the poorest must be the predominant force accounting for this anomaly.

In summary, historically and currently, Texas must be regarded as a culturally distinct part of the United States, one in which familial institutions retain especial strength, above all in poorer, rural areas.

[1]   The relevant counties are as follows: (a) 20 percent or more Negro: Anderson, Austin, Bastrop, Bowie, Burleson, Caldwell, Camp, Cass, Chambers, Cherokee, Colorado, Falls, Freestone, Galveston, Grimes, Harris, Harrison, Houston, Jasper, Jefferson, Kaufman, Lee, Leon, Liberty, Limestone, Madison, Marion, Matagorda, Morris, Nacogdoches, Navarro, Newton, Panola, Polk, Red River, Robertson, Rusk, Sabine, San Augustine, San Jacinto, Shelby, Smith, Trinity, Upshur, Walker, Waller, Washington, and Wharton; (b) 30 percent or more Spanish-speaking: Aransas, Atascosa, Bee, Bexar, Brewster, Brooks, Calhoun, Cameron, Castro, Crockett, Culberson, Dawson, Deaf-Smith, Dimmit, Duval, Edwards, El Paso, Frio, Goliad, Hidalgo, Hudspeth, Jeff Davis, Jim Hogg, Jim Wells, Karnes, Kenedy, Kinney, Kleberg, LaSalle, Live Oak, Loving, Martin, Maverick, McMullen, Medina, Nueces, Pecos, Presidio, Reeves, Refugio, San Patricio, Starr, Sutton, Terrell, Uvalde, Val Verde, Webb, Willacy, Wilson, Zapata, and Zavala; (c) less than 5 percent minorities (the "Anglo" counties): Archer, Armstrong, Baylor, Basque, Brown, Callahan, Carson, Childress, Clay, Cooke, Denton, Donley, Eastland, Erath, Franklin, Gray, Grayson, Hamilton, Hartley, Hemphill, Hutchinson, Jack, King, Lipscomb, Llano, Lynne, McCullock, Montague, Ochiltree, Oldham, Palo, Pinto, Parkes, Randall, Roberts, Shackleford, Stephens, Stonewall, VanZandt, Wheeler, Wichita, Wise, and Young. Source: U.S. Bureau of the Census 1973. Statistics on migratory gains (or losses) by county, 1960–1970, are from Texas Office of Economic Opportunity 1972: XII: 2–6; on 1969 per capita incomes by County from Texas Office of Economic Opportunity 1972: A: 14–28 (correlations calculated by Mr. Stanley Hyland).

REFERENCES

ASKIN, A. BRADLEY
1970 "An economic analysis of Black migration." Unpublished Ph.D. thesis, Department of Economics, M.I.T., Cambridge, Mass.

DUBOIS, W. E. B.
1969 *The suppression of the African slave-trade.* New York: Schocken. (Originally published 1896.)

COMMISSIONER OF INSURANCE, STATISTICS, AND HISTORY
1882 *The resources, soil, and climate of Texas.* Galveston: Belo.

CONNOR, SEYMOUR V.
1971 *Texas. A history.* New York: Thomas Y. Crowell.

FLACH, VERA
1973 *A Yankee in German-America.* San Antonio, Texas: Naylor.

FORNELL, EARL WESLEY
1961 *A profile of Galveston,* part one: *The Texas crescent on the eve of secession.* Austin: University of Texas Press.

GOODWYN, FRANK
1955 *Lone-star land: twentieth-century Texas in perspective.* New York: Knopf.

JORDAN, TERRY G.
1969 Population origins in Texas, 1850. *Geographical Review* 59 (1): 83–103.
1970 The Texan Appalachia. *Annals of the Association of American Geographers* 60 (3): 409–427.

OLMSTED, FREDERICK LAW
1857 *A journey through Texas; or, a saddle-trip on the southwestern frontier: with a statistical appendix.* New York: Dix, Edwards.

SCHOOLCRAFT, HENRY R.
1853 *History, condition, and prospects of the Indian tribes of the United States,* part one. Collected and prepared under the direction of the Bureau of Indian Affairs, per Act of Congress of March 3, 1847. Philadelphia: Lippincott, Grambo.

SHRYOCK, HENRY S., JR.
1964 *Population mobility within the United States.* Chicago: Community and Family Study Center, University of Chicago.

STAPLETON, RICHARD C.
1969 *An analysis of rural manpower migration patterns in the south plains region of Texas.* Washington, D.C.: U.S. Department of Commerce/ National Bureau of Standards. August. (Reproduced by the Clearinghouse for Federal Scientific and Technical Information, Springfield, Va. 22151.)

TEXAS OFFICE OF ECONOMIC OPPORTUNITY
1972 *Poverty in Texas.* Austin, Texas: Department of Community Affairs.

U.S. BUREAU OF THE CENSUS
1943 *Sixteenth census of the United States: 1940. Population,* volume two: *Characteristics of the population. Pennsylvania, Texas.* Washington, D.C.: U.S. Government Printing Office.

1952   Census of population: 1950, volume two: Characteristics of the population. Texas. Washington, D.C.: U.S. Government Printing Office.
1969   Changing characteristics of the Negro population, by Daniel O. Price. 1960 Census Monograph. Washington, D.C.: U.S. Government Printing Office.
1971   General demographic trends for metropolitan areas, 1960–1970. Texas. PHC(2)-45. Washington, D.C.: U.S. Government Printing Office.
1973   1970 census of population, volume one: Characteristics of the population. Texas. Washington, D.C.: U.S. Government Printing Office.
WHITE, GIFFORD, editor
1966   The 1840 census of the Republic of Texas. Austin: Pemberton.
WHITE, REVEL CLYDE
1928   Denominationalism in certain rural communities in Texas. Indianapolis: The Training Course for Social Work of Indiana University.
WOODWARD, C. VANN
1953   The strange career of Jim Crow. New York: Oxford University Press.

The Black Extended Family in the United States:
Some Research Suggestions

VERA M. GREEN

ABSTRACT

The contributions and limitations of the chapters by Demitri B. Shimkin, Gloria J. Louie, and Dennis A. Frate, and by Lenus Jack, Jr., are reviewed in these comments. Both studies initiate efforts in the much wider research still needed, including more precise hypotheses and evaluations of "situational adaptations," as well as studies of White cultural variations in the South. Further study is also needed on Black perceptions of "strong" and "weak" as applied to individuals and families and even entire communities, and the relationship of these perceptions to status stratifications, ability or inability to enforce behavioral standards, and toleration of "weakness" as the price of social functioning.

Finally, in research on Black people, insufficient attention has been given to the existence of "cultural–ecological areas" within the United States. A preliminary formulation includes nine separate areas.

This paper seeks to review the contributions and limitations of the Shimkin–Louie–Frate and the Jack studies on the Black extended family in this volume, with particular reference to delineating areas of needed and fruitful future research. Both works contain data which can potentially increase the understanding of this country's Black families in academic and administrative circles. The families presented in both studies represent one type of extended family which is also frequently encountered in other parts of the South and in northern ghetto areas as well. The Shimkin–Louie–Frate and Jack studies indicate the importance, among other things, of adult adoption and the extension of fictive kinship ties, the significance of which has only recently been understood by welfare and public agency officials. Although the studies reviewed focus primarily on kinship ties, the importance of nonkin and nonkin household units should also be stressed.

To my knowledge, Shimkin, Louie, and Frate are among the few to discuss feuding in relation to southern Black families. According to my own Mississippi informants, feuds often erupted into shoot-outs on or in the vicinity of the church or picnic grounds, or near other areas where large numbers of people gathered for social occasions. One might suspect that the attitudes that tolerate this type of behavior (and the contexts for its expression) might be the same that tolerate gang-related behavior in the urban ghettos.

Conversely, I am concerned about the absence of situational definition in both studies, as the data presented do not appear to rule out situational factors completely.

In Louisiana, both English and French varieties of American Black culture can be found. Jack's families bear French (e.g. Laurent) and English (e.g. Wesley) names. Was this done deliberately to give some indication of a blending of the two traditions, as frequently occurs? If so, to what extent might the comparative lack of knowledge of paternal kin be related to this type of "cultural" division among the families? It is implied that other household groups or "yards" on the same and adjacent blocks contain other extended families. Are they predominantly of French or of English background, or are they various mixtures of the two? I feel that these are important questions. The answers to them would help in starting to delineate areas of cultural overlapping as well as distinctiveness among Blacks in the United States. Studies of Blacks of all classes, both rural and urban, who are descendants of five or six generations of birthright Catholics are needed for comparison with those in similar socioeconomic conditions who are birthright Baptists and Methodists. This would help us to determine the relative effects of exposure to Catholic versus Baptist and Methodist traditions on Black family patterns.

Above all, it must be recognized that these studies are only the initial efforts of a much larger task, both analytical and comparative. Further research is required in order to more sharply define situational and processual models so that the possible effects of "situational adaptation" can be precisely hypothesized and evaluated. Also needed are intensive studies of equivalent types of southern White families in Holmes County and New Orleans, as well as other areas, so that the distinctions and common points of Black and White southern cultures can be accurately stated. This is a vital issue for, as Pearsall states, the important variations which exist within southern White cultures also have been, and continue to be, ignored (Pearsall 1966: 129). In this context I would draw attention to the need for identifying "African" traits in White, as well as in Black, cultures.

Beyond these general suggestions, I feel that work in depth is needed on the situations, behaviors, and values associated with attributions of "strength" and "weakness." Also I feel that a systematic "culture area" approach to U.S. Black studies is essential. Below, I address these matters in detail.

THE ISSUES OF "STRONG" AND "WEAK"

The importance of distinctive family reputations as "strong" or "weak" has been initially explored in the Shimkin–Louie–Frate study, and this has constituted a contribution to the often-ignored problem of stratification within Black folk or traditional rural communities. Academics should especially note that informants divided families into the two categories, indicating that "strong" was neither necessarily identified with "middle class" nor correlated with wealth. It may be important to note that the old expression "respectable" or "nice" is replaced by "strong" when, in the eyes of community members, the former terms are taken over by Whites to indicate accommodative or nonradical tendencies. Yet I would argue that the essential concept remains the same: it expresses a common striving, in the authors' words, for "moral rightness, mutual concern, and economic betterment ('improving') maintained despite the inevitable adversities, the surface compromises, the humiliations, and the periodic human failings of Black life in a savagely hostile White world" (Shimkin et al., this volume). I would also insist that this quality is respected even by those who are themselves "weak." In fact serious problems occur when misguided outsiders are overly sympathetic to the latter, who conform more closely to the stereotypic view of Black behavior, while ignoring or considering as "middle class" — or worse, as "White" — those who are "strong." This is especially true when the "strong" require assistance from outside sources and agencies.

In the further study of "strong" and "weak" as basic keys to understanding the subtle systems of stratification in Black communities, the reputations of entire communities may be usefully examined. The folklore surrounding Mound Bayou in Bolivar County, Mississippi,[1] as

---

[1] Mound Bayou was established in 1887 by Isaiah T. Montgomery, a former slave of Jefferson Davis, the Confederate President, as an independent all-Negro community. In 1965, 37,000 acres of Black-owned land bolstered the independence of this small town (Rose 1965: 363–376). Overshadowed by Cleveland, the seat of Bolivar County, as a center of civil rights activity at this time, Mound Bayou later was the site of a major health program developed by Jack Geiger, M.D., (then of Tufts University Medical School) and now community controlled.

gathered from Mississippians in Chicago who came primarily from Madison and Yazoo Counties,[2] is as follows: the community is "run by Blacks for Blacks," the male inhabitants are "men," that is, they do not tolerate undue interference by Whites. Whites, accordingly, do not "mess" with those from Mound Bayou. My informants indicated that the people from this locality were not "bad niggers" in the sense of a recent song:

Bad, Bad, Leroy Brown, Baddest man in the whole damn town,
    badder than ole King Kong,
    meaner than a junk yard dog . . .[3]

which expresses one type of toughness for the poorer Black masses and ghetto youths.

Rather, the men of Mound Bayou were considered tough in the sense of "strong" as used by the Holmes County informants. That is, they respected themselves and would stand up for their rights.

The force of this folklore was evident when a professional person from Mound Bayou came to Chicago to start practice in the fifties. His office was plastered with signs indicating militant civil rights activity in Mound Bayou, and his practice grew to overflowing virtually overnight. From the comments I heard from the clients, the critical connection made by them was not that he was especially good in his profession, but rather that he was from Mound Bayou.

In view of the importance given Mound Bayou by Mississippi Blacks it would be interesting to investigate comprehensively the structure of family and community in this town.

Although Holmes County is apparently without class stratification as such, status differences — e.g. between Black landowners and domestic workers, at the extremes — are reported by Shimkin et al. I would emphasize the need for studying status differences in folk or traditional rural communities such as these. My information from Yazoo County in Mississippi indicates that there can be subtle but meaningful status differences even between Black tenant farmers and Black sharecroppers, especially when the families have been sharecropping for several generations.

[2] Madison County, just northeast of Jackson, Mississippi, although predominantly Black, is in the clay and prairie-soil regions and much less agricultural than Bolivar, Holmes, or Yazoo counties. The county seat, Canton, was the scene of severe repressions against civil rights efforts during the 1960's (Moody 1968: 256–310). In Yazoo County, which, like Holmes County, is both "Hill" and "Delta," the Black majority is smaller and little organized. Studies of migration from Yazoo County to Chicago and of the adaptation of migrants have been conducted under the direction of Daniel Price (Kiser 1970: 61–63).
[3] Words and music by Jim Croce; Blendingwell Music and American Broadcasting Music. Used by permission.

Low status and special social vulnerability have been associated in these communities, especially in the past, with "weak" conduct that is tolerated but not necessarily condoned (Young 1970: 273). Few scholars have bothered to note that illegitimacy in the rural South can result from conditions carrying various degrees of disapproval by the Black community (Johnson 1934). Still fewer have attempted to place this "tolerance of lapses" in socioeconomic perspective.

The problem is, how often have members of Black communities been in a position to enforce their own standards? How often might a Black woman carrying an illegitimate child by a powerful White or even a landowning Black father be "ostracized" in the rural South? Often, the institution with this responsibility is the local church. This, in rural areas, is frequently on the land of a White plantation owner. Until very recent years at best, were good workers on influential Whites' plantations jailed for killing even other Blacks? On the basis of informants' statements in Yazoo and Madison counties and the literature, I conclude, not often.

The foregoing types of situational context often result in an environment in which many southern Blacks then attempt to solve personal and community problems extralegally, which in some instances results in violence and leads to feuding, or they simply passively accept their "fates."

My own exploratory research in Houston, Texas, and personal experience in New York City and Chicago confirm Drake and Cayton's (1945) observation that older Black neighborhoods are generally multistatus and multiclass. In them, families of all types live in close proximity. Note that the family studied by Jack lives in a section with high unemployment and crime rates. This factor is relevant to the statement of Shimkin et al. regarding Black tolerance of "lapses" — "moral correctness" is the ideal, but "weakness" is tolerated as the price of keeping heterogeneous neighborhoods functioning.

Finally, I must stress that in an area where males are very restricted in terms of their adult roles, wenching and fighting become important indicators of manhood. Fathering and giving birth to children are frequently considered to constitute an end of adolescence. I have heard the following expressions: "she's a woman now," or "he looks like a boy but he's got a baby by X's daughter . . ." Another factor is the southern rural Black folk belief that sexual intercourse has therapeutic value. Youngsters past puberty with skin disorders, nervousness, or stomach ailments, as well as girls with menstrual problems, have been told: "That'll go 'way when you get married," or, "You need you a boy- [or girl-]friend."

I feel, in all, that the study of "strong" and "weak" families is part of a larger set of questions in Black culture.

THE "CULTURAL–ECOLOGICAL AREAS" APPROACH TO BLACK CULTURE

To date, studies of Black culture in the United States have tended to be primarily those of "folk" Blacks, predominantly in the rural areas of the deep South or in the slums of urban ghettos. Moreover, there are large geographical areas of the United States where no sector of the Black population has been studied. A grave danger of biases exists in our present unsystematic knowledge, especially as we *insist* upon generalizing to the whole "Black community" on the basis of two or three of the many lifestyles found among U.S. Blacks of different classes and geographical locations.

As a tool for future research, and on the basis of readings; social work and work in public housing; anthropological fieldwork; family and friendship ties; and residence for a year or more in Iowa, Illinois, Arizona, Texas, New York, New Jersey, and Mississippi, I propose nine "cultural–ecological areas" for the American Black population. I should point out that this proposed grouping takes into account historical, economic, social, and environmental factors[4] and also responds to recent migrations and cultural changes, thus building upon older classifications, such as Frazier's (1957). Although easy movement and communications may be reducing local variations, especially among the younger generation, in some parts of the country, there has been remarkable continuity in other areas since the early 1700's.

The proposed preliminary and broad classification is as follows:[5]

1. Southern Tidewater–Piedmont (for example, eastern Maryland, Virginia, and North Carolina). High percentage of landownership, higher percentage of "patriarchal" family types; class and color stratified, especially in the cities; large numbers of birthright Episcopalians even among the lower classes and rural people.

2. (A) Coastal Southeast (South Carolina and eastern Georgia, often referred to as the "Gullah" area). English "Creole" culture, strongly class-structured, especially in the cities, which have long traditions of free as well as slave "people of color," and free Negroes.[6] In rural areas, weakly structured but cohesive communities (Wagley 1960);

---

[4] "Cultural–ecological" is used in a general sense, attempting to combine the approaches of Steward (1955) and Vayda and Rappaport (1967).

[5] It should be noted that not all parts of the United States have been covered, and that the groupings are based on cultural distinctiveness, not population size. The relationships between them and the culture regions applicable to the White population need further study (Green 1975).

[6] The distinction between "people of color" and "Negro" made in the older U.S. statistics was between persons believed to have appreciable White or Indian blood, versus those with little or none.

(B) Lower Atlantic coastal plains. "Black yeomanry" (Woofter 1930) with a noticeable percentage of Black landownership.

3. Lowland southern areas: Black Belt.[7] Central and western Georgia, Alabama, Mississippi (except southwestern counties); parts of Tennessee, Kentucky, Arkansas, and Missouri; extensions, via pre-Civil War migrations, to English Louisiana and Texas. Less class-structured than in areas 1 and 2, especially among rural people. Greater percentage of intermixing between phenotypically darker individuals and mulatto types. Strong familialism, including feuding, among both Whites and Blacks.

4. Areas of French tradition (for example, southwestern Mississippi, Louisiana, eastern coastal Texas). Historically, large numbers of free "people of color" and free Negroes (Roussève 1937). Sharp divisions along class and color gradients. Large numbers of birthright Catholics. Creole and Cajun French spoken.

5. (A) Areas of Indian influence (Oklahoma; and parts of Arkansas and Kansas). Reciprocal influences with former southeastern tribes (especially Choctaw);

(B) Tri-racial areas (parts of New York, New Jersey, Tennessee).

6. Southwestern areas (West Texas, New Mexico, Arizona, and California). Least class-stratified; birthright Catholics, Baptists, Methodists; number of old settlers in small farms and ranching.

7. Old eastern colonial areas (New Jersey, Pennsylvania, New York, Massachusetts). Rural, urban, and seafaring communities; historical importance of family ties; numerous phenotypically darker persons with "old family" connections.

8. Midwestern and far western areas (Illinois west to Washington state). Less class-structured; greater evidence of nuclear families, although other kin ties remain important.

9. Post-1920 metropolitan North and West ghetto constellations (major inner cities, e.g. New York, Detroit, Chicago, San Francisco). Ghetto cultures drawn from the above areas, but especially the southern ones (Rose 1969: 4).

The bulk of research on Blacks to date has focused primarily on areas 3 and 9. It is hoped that an awareness of the existence of other types of community would induce scholars to study total Black communities in other areas. Consequently, I would suggest that such a classification of "cultural–ecological areas" be used and further elaborated so that we may avoid stereotyping all American Blacks in terms of poorly understood

[7] "Black Belt" refers to counties in the cotton-growing, lowland regions of Virginia, South Carolina, Georgia, Mississippi, Arkansas, and Louisiana that were, up to the time of recent migrations, 60 percent or more Black. See, for example, Calef and Nelson (1956: 88).

and potentially pernicious polar opposites. Such an endeavor should prove useful for the continuing study of Black family types as well as for investigation of other aspects of contemporary U.S. Black culture.

REFERENCES

CALEF, WESLEY C., HOWARD J. NELSON
   1956   Distribution of Negro population in the United States. *Geographical Review* 46: 82–97.
DRAKE, ST. CLAIR, HORACE CAYTON
   1945   *Black metropolis*. New York: Harcourt, Brace.
FRAZIER, E. FRANKLIN
   1957   "The cultural background of southern Negroes," in *Institute on cultural patterns of newcomers*, 11–15. Chicago: Welfare Council of Metropolitan Chicago.
GREEN, VERA M.
   1975   "Racial vs. ethnic factors in Afro-American and Afro-Caribbean migration," in *Migration and development*. Edited by H. I. Safa and B. M. du Toit, 83–96. World Anthropology. The Hague: Mouton.
JOHNSON, CHARLES
   1934   *The shadow of the plantation*. Chicago: University of Chicago Press.
KISER, CLYDE V., *editor*
   1970   Demographic aspects of the Black community. *Milbank Memorial Fund Quarterly* 48 (2, 2).
MOODY, ANNE
   1968   *Coming of age in Mississippi*. New York: Dial Press.
PEARSALL, MARION
   1966   Cultures of the American South. *Anthropological Quarterly* 39 (2).
ROSE, HAROLD M.
   1965   The all-Negro town: its evolution and function. *Geographical Review* 55: 362–381.
   1969   "Social processes in the city. Race and urban residential choice." Research Paper 6. Association of American Geographers. Washington, D.C.
ROUSSÈVE, CHARLES B.
   1937   *The Negro in Louisiana. Aspects of his history and his literature*. New Orleans: Xavier University Press.
STEWARD, JULIAN
   1955   *Theory of culture change*. Urbana: University of Illinois Press.
VAYDA, ANDREW P., ROY A. RAPPAPORT
   1967   "Ecology, cultural and non-cultural," in *Introduction to cultural anthropology*. Edited by James Clifton, 477–497. Boston: Houghton Mifflin.
WAGLEY, CHARLES
   1960   "Plantation America: a culture sphere," in *Caribbean studies: a symposium*. Edited by Vera Rubin, 3–13. Seattle: University of Washington Press.

WOOFTER, T. J., JR.
1930 *Black yeomanry.* New York: Henry Holt.
YOUNG, VIRGINIA H.
1970 Family and childhood in a southern Negro community. *American Anthropologist* 72: 269–288.

SECTION FOUR

Afro-American Perspectives on the Extended Family

Persistence, Borrowing, and Adaptive Changes in Black Kinship Systems: Some Issues and Their Significance

DEMITRI B. SHIMKIN and VICTOR UCHENDU

ABSTRACT

This chapter first examines the evidence for defining the Afro-American family as reported in parts of the United States, the Caribbean, and Central and South America, as a single institution. Then follow Uchendu's thirteen basic propositions summarizing the structural and functional characteristics of the African extended family. These structural characteristics, replicated in the Americas, as illustrated in the chapters by Shimkin, Louie, and Frate; Green; Goody; and Laguerre, are compared and contrasted with those of peasant Europe and their British and American derivatives.

The possible processes which have been involved in the development of Afro-American extended families are examined. In so doing, the authors find a reaffirmation of Herskovits's theories of the West African origin of a number of New World Black social features. The similarities between Bush Negro and Haitian kinship are detailed; so are certain parallels with Jamaican and Holmes County, Mississippi, viewpoints. European features in Afro-American kinship systems must be examined critically in order to elicit transformations altering the initial institutions, for example, god-parenthood in Haiti. Likewise, there are evident weaknesses in explaining Afro-American kinship solely as adaptive changes related to slavery and "plantation culture."

The present status of social analysis of Afro-American family systems is still inadequate. The authors make five suggestions for improving the study of these systems. These include formulations of systematic theories of institutional characteristics; field studies corresponding to valid representations of the models used; special attention to migratory streams; detailed local histories of families, communities, and institutions; and comparative frameworks essential to the understanding of social phenomena.

Finally, the study and understanding of the extended family as part of the Afro-American cultural tradition will provide correctives to often misguided social policies both in the United States and in emerging states.

AFRO-AMERICAN EXTENDED FAMILIES: A SINGLE INSTITUTION?

Extended families — corporate or quasicorporate descent groups comprising a number of households under elderly leadership and undertaking tasks of mutual aid, emotional support, and social regulation — are widespread throughout much of the Afro-American world. Previous chapters in this book have described such extended families within the United States, in Mississippi, Illinois, Louisiana, Texas, and, in attenuated form, California. The older literature has indicated their presence in much of the rural South, notably in the Sea Islands of South Carolina (Woofter 1930; Kiser 1932).[1]

Elsewhere in the New World, the extended family is of basic importance in Haiti (Herskovits 1937; Simpson 1942; Bastien 1961; and, especially, Laguerre, this volume). It is also well developed on the small island of Carriacou, north of Grenada in the Lesser Antilles (M. G. Smith 1962). William Davenport's data on Jamaica, which are concentrated on the "lower class," display many of the structural and behavioral characteristics of the extended family. For example, distinctions are made between a "hard core" of "near family" (parents, parents' siblings, first cousins, children, siblings' children, and grandchildren) and more distant relatives. Within this grouping, "loving" sentiments and reciprocal support are supposed to prevail; disputes are almost always settled without recourse to the police or the law. With propinquity, there came "constant exchanges of assistance and favors." In fact, "some persons are so kin-oriented as to believe that close friendship should be maintained only between close relatives, never between unrelated persons." And "sexual relationships between a person and anyone of his kindred are generally considered to be incestuous . . ." (Davenport 1961: 422–423). Yet Davenport denies that these kindreds are corporate groups. It appears to us to be likely, however, that in Jamaica, genuine extended families characterize stable, landowning peasant communities such as "Orange Grove" and "Mocca" (Clarke 1957: 33–72 and *passim*).

The "nonunilineal descent groups," reinforced by a type of ancestor worship, which are found among the Black Carib of Central America (Solien 1959) also appear to be extended families, in the usage of this volume. The matrilineages of the South American Bush Negroes, which

[1]   Researches on Sea Island culture, including Afro-American persistences, are being conducted by J. Herman Blake (Oakes College, University of California at Santa Cruz) and his associates. Otterbein's data, although quite incomplete, indicate strongly that in familial patterns, as in many other cultural realms, the Bahamas closely resemble South Carolina (Otterbein 1966, 34–37, and 111, 128–130).

are of considerable importance to our argument, will be discussed in more detail in the next section.

For other American areas currently available data are either negative or ambiguous.[2] Nevertheless, it appears probable, as Laguerre's work shows, that new studies oriented to kin functions beyond "mating" and child care will discover other, well-defined instances.[3]

The extensive African data can be summarized, in Victor Uchendu's opinion, in the form of thirteen basic propositions:[4]

1. The extended family is the most pervasive and most durable corporate structure in the African kinship system. Even in African societies where marital relations tend to be fragile and corporate clans and lineages are absent or weakly developed, the extended family tends to enjoy viability.

2. The central feature of the extended family is its *structural extension* through which a number of features or attributes of the system can be explained.

3. The extended family is a multifunctional institution which is capable of and known to be adaptable to a wide range of activities. The African extended families perform more than the traditional functions of the family (reproduction, status placement, biological maintenance, socialization, and sexual control). Among their modern roles are (a) to help their members to acquire an education, (b) to improve their skills, both technical and industrial, (c) to accumulate investment capital, and (d) to adjust to new, urban environments.

4. While *structurally* all human societies possess the capability of developing and maintaining an extended family, it appears, however, that the extended family system tends to be most viable in social environments where face-to-face interaction can be maintained and property and security needs can be fostered and protected.

5. The African extended family is often conceived of and treated, in

---

[2] Kottak's data on Arembepe, a small fishing village 60 km. north of Salvador, the capital of Bahía, indicate a very feeble development of extended kinship, in contrast to the Brazilian elite pattern (Kottak 1966, 78–99 and *passim*). How representative this may be of Black Brazilians remains an open question. For Ecuador, in the small coastal town of San Lorenzo, Whitten found only "personal kindred"; however, his case study of the "Arisala" family indicates that these may on occasion approximate true corporate bodies, i.e. extended families as defined here (Whitten 1965: 136–142, 148–163).
[3] A likely case is Providencia, an English-tradition Colombian island 400 miles southwest of Jamaica (Wilson 1961).
[4] For an earlier analysis of the structural features of African extended families and their adaptive capacities in the process of urbanization and social mobility, see Uchendu (1971). The relations of African kinship structures to "stateless" political organization (Horton 1972) and to native urbanization (Krapf-Askari 1969) illustrate other aspects of the adaptive capacities of African extended families.

political terms, as a "power center." Differences in political power among extended families translate into such folk categorizations as "strong" and "weak" families.

6. Historical studies reveal that "strong families" are strong because of the qualities of their leadership. Very few families have retained their reputation as "strong families" (*ndi ike*) for more than three or four generations. The cycles of dynamic leadership therefore correlate with the cycles of growth and decline of the extended family.

7. African extended families manifest a primacy of descent ties over marital ties. It follows therefore that this extended family as a system is threatened by any change in marital value that regards husband–wife emphasis as a focal value.

8. Tensions and contradictions within the extended family are cushioned by a number of structural devices, e.g. the alliance between the individual and the grandparental generation; and the structural balance between the individual and his or her father's extended family, on the one hand, and his or her mother's extended family, on the other — a balance of rights in one and of privilege in the other (i.e. contrasts between patrilineal and matrilineal systems).

9. The most viable extended families under conditions of rapid, externally induced change, tend to be those which continually reinforce their membership in terms of resource and emotional support and which are in turn supported by their migrant membership.

10. Emotional commitment to and sharing of the success goals of members and understanding of the frustrated goals tend to be unifying factors.

11. Respect for the elders, which is symbolically carried over to respect for ancestors, is a common value. Elders and ancestors are not only symbols of authority, but are moral authorities.

12. Primacy of descent system makes fosterage the only viable system of incorporation within the extended family. Legal adoption has failed woefully.

13. The extended family shows its resilience in crisis situations and paradoxically uses its success in such situations to reinforce its stability.

These structural and functional characteristics are replicated in the American instances. The "strong" versus "weak" contrast has been noted by Shimkin, Louie, and Frate for Holmes County, and emphasized as a general feature of U.S. Black society by Vera Green. Dr. Esther Goody's comparative study of fosterage shows the fundamental nature of a practice repeatedly discussed in the chapters on the United States. Moreover, in the United States and in Haiti (see Laguerre, this volume), as well as in

Africa, it is the grandparent–grandchild relationship which is specifically central in fosterage and in derivative reciprocal obligations. Finally, there are no incompatibilities noted between the pattern adumbrated for Africa and the American data.

Comparisons with the extended families of peasant Europe (Thomas and Znaniecki 1927; Arensberg and Kimball 1968; Maraspini 1968), and their derivatives in urban Britain (Rosser and Harris 1965), the United States (Adams 1970), and Latin America (Fals-Borda 1955) do show basic structural contrasts. Families of the European tradition are based primarily on marital ties, often legally indissoluble and generally reinforced by formal familial agreements, property transfers, and major ceremonials. The families, moreover, are primarily sets of sharply delimited households with strong male authority and rights of membership often limited to legitimate offspring. While interhousehold economic cooperation, crisis support, and social visiting are extensive, fosterage is uncommon; affiliation with a household through marriage or adoption supersedes antecedent ties. Sharp distinctions are made between dominant norms and deviant behavior, which is usually subject to explicit sanctions; alternative "weak" and "strong" modalities are absent.

Without minimizing structural, functional, and attitudinal features, such as the extreme importance attached to family unity, that are common to both Euro-American and Afro-American types of extended families, the configurational differences cited appear to us to be basic (see for example, Thomas and Znaniecki 1927: 89; Arensberg and Kimball 1968: 61–61, 72–75; Maraspini 1968: 142, 167, 193). What is more, the close comparison of familial norms and behavior shows repeated differences in nuance between the Euro-American and Afro-American configurations. In the first, family leadership is characteristically a question of power over persons and resources; in the second, it is a moral influence, often with religious overtones. In one case, the central ceremonial which marks the obligatory gathering of the widest kin is the marriage of family members; in the others, it is the funeral of a respected adult.

These considerations lead us to regard the Afro-American extended family as a single type of institution, albeit with much local and situational variability, sharing many common elements with Euro-American and other types of extended families, but also with a distinctiveness that is identifiable and analytically meaningful. Specifically, we feel that interpretations and predictions developed from the comparison of one Afro-American extended family with another have special validity and power.

POSSIBLE PROCESSES IN THE DEVELOPMENT OF AFRO-AMERICAN EXTENDED FAMILIES

A tentative evaluation of the nature and relative significance of persistence, borrowing, and adaptive changes in Afro-American kinship systems is essential both to strengthen our hypothesis of the unitary nature of the Afro-American extended family and to reinterpret phenomena which have been variously categorized, i.e. as local inventions of the "poor" (Stack 1974: 27–31). Such reinterpretations have, we feel, major implications for policy. (See also the next section.)

Herskovits's Position Reaffirmed

It is our belief that Melville Herskovits's theories of the West African origin of a number of New World Black social features, notably the extended family and the "matrifocal" household, are correct, as is his analysis of the relative intensity of these retentions — the progression from Guiana (Bush Negroes) to Haiti, Brazil, and so forth (Herskovits 1941: 167–186, 1966: 43–61; and Mintz 1964 for an appreciation). We are aware both of sharp criticisms of Herskovits's position (M. G. Smith 1960) and of recent supporting investigations on religion (Simpson 1972) and music (Handler and Frisbie 1972). We believe, moreover, that studies by Hurault (1961) and Köbben (1967) have greatly improved the case for Africanisms (of course, modified by slavery, plantation life, and secondary syncretisms), for Bush Negro social structure. They have also brought the Bush Negro picture much closer to other New World Black systems, particularly the Haitian, than was evident from the earlier literature.[5]

Concretely, the following similarities between Bush Negro and Haitian kinship (as described in Laguerre, this volume) appear to be significant:

1. The social foundation is a multigeneration, multihousehold, localized descent group (*bee*, among the Boni) conscious of genealogy and united by inherited spirits, to which a "chapel" on the kin group's lands is dedicated, and by annual ceremonies in which all kin join.

2. Group leadership (*lo*, or extended lineage, among the Boni and Djuka) has priestly associations.

3. The kin group is exogamous.

4. Polygyny is regularly practiced, but with each wife always having a separate residence.

5. Marriage, as opposed to liaisons, involves a formal proposal to be approved by the bride's older kinspeople, a bridal gift (*prix de la virginité*

[5] For a critical bibliography on the Bush Negroes, see Price (1972).

among the Boni, see Hurault 1961: 147), and presentation of the couple to their ancestors.

6. Purposive fosterage (Goody, this volume) for the education of both boys and girls is extensively practiced. In such fosterage, grandparents have a specially important role. Note for the Boni, that "If the maternal grandmother insists upon raising a child, the mother cannot refuse . . ." (Hurault 1961: 127).

7. Twins are believed to have special supernatural power.

8. Young children are buried separately from adults, with little ceremony, and close to the kin group's dwellings.

Two major differences between the Bush Negroes and the Haitians can be ascribed to European influences among the latter, i.e. the sharp distinction between formal marriages and *plaçage*, and the complex of godparenthood. The strong patrilineal, patrilocal emphasis of the Haitians contrasts with Bush Negro matrilineality. However, the significance of the paternal line is clear in a number of ways among the latter. For example, among the Boni, food taboos (and associated exogamy) and personal values are inherited patrilineally (Hurault 1961: 32–33, 125). Among the Djuka, the descendants of men constitute a corporate group in each village distinct from both matrilineal descendants and in-migrant affines (Köbben 1967: 12). Moreover, inheritance is not limited to matrilineal kin:

Sons who live in their father's village and have worked with him, as happens in a minority of cases, will receive the largest portions, but in other cases the sons get less or even nothing at all (Köbben 1967: 29).

Finally, it must be emphasized that neither the Haitians nor the Bush Negroes make terminological distinctions between maternal and paternal kin. In all, the two systems may represent varying stresses upon a "double unilateral organization" of the type described for the Umor of Nigeria (Forde 1939).

Striking similarities to Bush Negro kinship are not limited to Haiti. A number of resemblances to other New World Black societies may be cited. For example, Boni concepts of the integrity of lineage land and the usufruct character of individual holdings (Hurault 1961: 77–82) have broad resemblances to Jamaican concepts of "family land" (Clarke 1957: 448, 451) and to those of Holmes Countians in Mississippi (Logan and Frate, this volume).

Again, numerous parallels are present in U.S. Black society to the tenor of work organization and authority of the Boni:

The group comprised within an agricultural settlement (*habitation de culture*) is tied together by mutual affinities, and is burdened by a hierarchy other than that which derives from kinship ties: the authority of the mother over her daughter; the authority of the "uncles" over the "nephews."[6]

The grouping which conforms most clearly to the matrilineal structure of the Refugee Blacks [i.e. the Boni], consists of an elderly woman, her unmarried sons, her daughters and the daughters of her daughter, with their husbands coming to support land clearance but not forming part of the group. Often, it is this old woman who leads the settlement, but often it is also an older uncle, her classificatory brother, who has long worked with her. Sometimes this elderly woman has installed herself and her daughters in a settlement founded by her husband . . .

For relatively numerous groups united more by mutual affinities than [even] by kinship ties, the minimum of authority needed for good understanding and work organization is exercised by the founder . . . (Hurault 1961: 102–103).

This could well be a description of the Mitchells of Holmes County (Shimkin, Louie, and Frate, this volume).

Particularistic, situational explanations of "matrifocal" behavior need to be reexamined in the light of the following description for the Boni, whose men are certainly not "castrated" in any social or economic sense:

Family life as we understand it does not exist. . . . The man builds a house for his wife in her natal village, but he does not come to live with her; he makes her and his other wives several-day visits during which he provides her with imported objects (salt, gasoline, cloth, etc.) of which she has need, lends her assistance with heavy work while she, on her side, provides him with products from the clearing. The rest of the time he lives as a bachelor in his mother's village, where he has built his own house. . . .

The man's life and the woman's remain entirely separate, and their union has more the character of a temporary association founded on material interests, than of a marriage. For each, family life remains entirely oriented toward his matrilineage (Hurault 1961: 35).

In general, we feel that the evidence for a common New World type of kinship organization stemming out of African origins is massive. The question today is no longer one of principle, but rather of defining the magnitude and distribution of this basic heritage.

Borrowings

We feel that theories ascribing features of Afro-American kinship systems to borrowings from outside sources must be examined critically. A great deal of both the older and more recent literature contributing to this

---

[6]   "Uncles" are all male persons of the ascending generation from Ego; "nephews" are both males and females of the descending generation from Ego (Hurault 1961: 31–34).

effect, e.g. Greenfield's on Barbados (1966), appears to us to be speculative. In contrast, de Granda's impressive review (1973) exemplifies the type of documentary mobilization which needs to be done to define European impacts and their consequences upon Black societies.

The subject is immense, and it appears best to limit discussion to a few salient points. The evidence for borrowings from European cultures is indisputable in three major aspects of kinship: kinship terminologies, church-and-state recognized marriages (with their correlates in wifely status and "legitimacy" for offspring), and, in areas of Catholic influence, the complex of godparental relationships.

In examining these borrowings, it seems important to us to watch for recurrent transformations which may, in fact, alter profoundly — in logic and in function — the initial institutions. A case in point is the godparental complex which in its European and Latin American forms is basically a relation between a child's parents and its godparents (Mintz and Wolf 1950) but which is viewed primarily as a mechanism of purposive fostering in Haiti (Laguerre, this volume). Some of these transformations present complicated problems of analysis. An illustration is the general, single term "niece" for siblings' children of both sexes in Jamaica (Davenport 1961: 422) and the Boni Bush Negro practice assimilating the entire descending generation to "nephew" (Hurault 1961: 31). Again, we can note that the common practice of Holmes Countians and other Black people in the United States of the children of a multigeneration household calling its female head "Mama" and their own mother by name is exactly replicated in Trinidad and in Guiana (Shimkin, Louie, and Frate, this volume; Herskovits and Herskovits 1947: 109; R. T. Smith 1956: 160–162). Clearly, some interesting questions of transmission versus parallel innovation need to be resolved in these instances.

We would also like to stress the potential significance of transmittals of features of European origin back to Africa by way of mixed-blood, especially part-Portuguese, colonists in West Africa. Many were large-scale slavers with close ties to the King of Dahomey; some intermarried with Black royalty. Some maintained true harems, despite their formal Catholicism. Other migrants from America were returned slaves, including some born in Africa. Verger's survey (1953) yields tantalizing hints of the social patterns and influence of these people; a thorough study would be invaluable.

Adaptive Changes

By and large, the explanatory hypotheses in studies of Afro-American kinship have been vague and weak. It is unclear either how slavery could have totally extirpated cultures or how its effects persisted for generations after its end. The attribution of social similarities among New World Black people to a "plantation culture" (Wagley 1960) also is unconvincing. New World plantations have varied greatly in product, size, and organization; they have ranged from manors to factories, as it were. How could their effects be uniform? Nor does this theory explain the difference between Negro and East Indian family systems in the same environment in Trinidad (Freilich 1963). It must be emphasized too that the institutions of Blacks in plantation areas are closely paralleled by those of Blacks in areas always devoted to mining, forestry, and subsistence agriculture, e.g. on the Pacific Coast Lowland of South America (West 1957: 126–204; Whitten 1965). And why did plantations in the East Indies fail to produce "plantation cultures"?

It is also difficult to attribute explanatory force even to the best static descriptions. R. T. Smith's interpretation of family structure and functioning in British Guiana (1956) is very sensitive. His model of changes during the course of marriage that are associated with a "redistribution of power" (R. T. Smith 1956: 148) in the household are psychologically convincing, and not for that area alone. But the processes described seem to have no necessary correlation to "low social status in a stratified society" (R. T. Smith 1956: 253). What is more, they have abundant analogues among the unstratified Bush Negroes, as particularly discussed by Köbben (1967). In contrast, a study of Italian culture would have disclosed an entire armament of social mechanisms keeping males dominant despite their "low social status in a stratified society" (Maraspini 1968: 151–155, 228, 252).

We must then raise the question of what is to be explained. On a worldwide basis, and with any reasonable model of human sexuality, it is indeed the rigid marital structure of Western society that needs understanding. This structure, functional primarily to control property and access to status, remains dominant in large part because of its reinforcement by the apparatus of established church or analogous political parties within nation-states which are controlled by this very property-holding and high-status group. In this view, it would be the position and culture of the elite in, say, Barbados, not those of the common folk, that need explanation (M. G. Smith 1965: 235–242).

In general, we feel that the present status of social analysis in regard to

Afro-American family systems is still inadequate for viable generalizations. The need is for much better designed research. Specifically, we suggest the following:

1.   As the foundations of research, systematic theories of institutional characteristics, impacting phenomena, and end results need to be formulated. R. T. Smith's inventory of basic household activities (child care, sexual services, domestic services, economic support, managerial functions, status-defining functions) is a case in point (R. T. Smith 1960: 67–68). It contrasts sharply with the inherent sterility of Stack's restrictive definition (1974: 31) of families as those "providing domestic needs of children and assuring their survival." Dynamically Uchendu's formulation (1971) of the potential impacts of industrial employment and social mobility upon African extended families is a first step toward testable hypotheses.

2.   The basis of field studies must correspond to a valid representation of the models used. In particular, as Laguerre's study shows, it is the interdependence of households and the complex cooperation between those of low and high status that gives Haitian extended families particular social strength. By the same token, handling different household types as social isolates and truncating research to some arbitrary category of "poverty" simply insures biased data and faulty analysis.

3.   Special attention is needed, in order to define social adaptations, to the study of migratory streams from communities of origin to those of destination (Shimkin 1971; Fried et al. 1971). Most of the phenomena associated with "matrifocality" appear to be more convincingly explained as migratory changes imposed upon systems of an Afro-American type (Otterbein 1965).

4.   Wherever possible, detailed local histories of families, communities, and institutions need to be undertaken to gain concrete bases for evaluating social adaptation. To this day, studies such as Eggan's classic investigation of the impact of White social norms upon Choctaw kinship remain models for emulation (Eggan 1937; 1966: 15–44).

5.   Comparative frameworks are essential to the understanding of social phenomena. Studies are needed both in the variations of a particular complex such as fostering and in the "controlled comparisons" (Eggan 1954) of total societies. Fruitful controlled comparisons would, for example, be detailed studies of slave society in the United States and in Brazil.

SOME IMPLICATIONS FOR POLICY

We believe that familial institutions and, particularly, the complex comprised in a special type of extended family, are part of an extensive, living, Afro-American cultural tradition. The essence of this tradition is a set of postulates and behavioral rules, a "deep structure,"[7] which permits a range of specific forms, adapted to particular circumstances via "strong" and "weak" options. This formulation does not attribute institutions of this type to all Black societies nor, above all, to all Black people.

We believe also that further well-designed research will substantially expand the geographical occurrence and range of features involved in this tradition and will clarify the mechanics of change and abandonment. However, even at present, the evidence is sufficient to add the extended family to the inventory of those features which make for a sense of pride and identity, for a common underlying language, in the Afro-American world.

The implications of this finding, especially for Black people in the United States, have been lucidly stated by Blauner (1970: 361):

The stronger that Negro ethnic culture becomes the greater the possibility for black people to utilize *both* group power and individual mobility to take what they can and give what will be accepted from this basically racist society — a process that in time will contribute to the transformation of this society and its racism. For in American life, ethnic culture is identity, and there is no individual or group progress without a clear sense of who one is, where one came from, and where one is going.

Insistence upon the reality, functionality, and strength of Black familial institutions is also essential as a corrective to the often misguided social policies of modern societies, not only of the United States but also of emerging states anxious to be "modern" and "progressive." This point was well made years ago, by Thomas and Znaniecki (1927: 48–49) in regard to Polish peasants in the United States:

American social institutions try by a continuous supervision and interference, to develop a strong marriage-group [i.e. nuclear family] organization among the Polish immigrants who begin to show certain signs of decay of family life or among whom the relation between husband and wife and children does not come up to American standards in certain respects. The results of this activity are quite baffling. Far from being constructive of new values, the interference proves rather destructive in a great majority of cases in spite of the best efforts of the most intelligent social workers. . . . The whole misunderstanding comes from the lack of realization that the Polish immigrants here, though scattered

[7]   For a brilliant use of "deep structural" analysis for modern Indonesian culture, see Wessing (1974).

and losing most of their social coherence, are still not entirely devoid of this coherence and constitute vague and changing but as yet, in some measure, real communities, and that these communities have brought from the old country several social institutions, among which the most important is the family institution. . . . As far as the family organization is concerned, any interference of external powers — political or social authorities — must act dissolvingly upon it, because it affects the fundamental principle of the family as a social institution — the principle of solidarity.

Even more important, in our opinion, is the need for a rethinking, in terms of a widening gamut of cultural experiences, and in terms of a broader and deeper grasp of human psychology, of the validity of accepted norms and labelled "pathologies." Clearly, there are manifold needs, often in conflict, which can be met only by some type of familial system. Clearly, too, every system has its rewards and its costs, its strengths and its weaknesses. In a changing world bound increasingly by the powerful constraints of nation-state controls, meeting changing human needs will require positive and active "social engineering" (Gorecki 1973). Black extended-family systems need, we feel, to be comprised within, and to contribute to, the humanization of modern societies through ethically valid "social engineering."

REFERENCES

ADAMS, BERT N.
  1970 Isolation, function and beyond: American kinship in the 1960's. *Journal of Marriage and the Family* 32: 575–597.
ARENSBERG, CONRAD M., SOLON T. KIMBALL
  1968 *Family and community in Ireland* (second edition). Cambridge, Mass.: Harvard University Press.
BASTIEN, RÉMY
  1961 Haitian rural family organization. *Social and Economic Studies* 10: 478–510.
BLAUNER, ROBERT
  1970 "Black culture: myth or reality?" in *Afro-American Anthropology*. Edited by Norman E. Whitten, Jr., and John F. Szwed, 347–366. New York: Free Press.
CLARKE, EDITH
  1957 *My mother who fathered me. A study of the family in three selected communities in Jamaica.* London: George Allen and Unwin.
DAVENPORT, WILLIAM
  1961 The family system of Jamaica. *Social and Economic Studies* 10: 420–454.
DE GRANDA, GERMAN
  1973 Materials for the sociohistorical study of the Afro-American linguistic elements in Spanish-speaking areas. *Caribbean Studies* 13: 110–130.

EGGAN, FRED
1937   Historical changes in the Choctaw kinship system. *American Anthropologist* 39: 34–52.
1954   Social anthropology and the method of controlled comparison. *American Anthropologist* 56: 743–763.
1966   *The American Indian: perspective for the study of social change.* Chicago: Aldine.

FALS-BORDA, ORLANDO
1955   *Peasant society in the Colombian Andes: a sociological study of Saucio.* Gainesville: University of Florida Press.

FORDE, C. DARYLL
1939   Kinship in Umor — double unilateral organization in a semi-Bantu society. *American Anthropologist* 41: 523–553.

FREILICH, MORRIS
1963   The natural experiment, ecology and culture. *Southwestern Journal of Anthropology* 19: 21–39. .

FRIED, MARC, *et al.*
1971   "Patterns of migration and adjustment: a comparative analysis," in *Migration and Social Welfare.* Edited by J. W. Eaton, 117–141. New York: National Association of Social Workers.

GORECKI, JAN
1973   Illegitimacy and social engineering. *Journal of Comparative Family Studies* 4: 269–275.

GREENFIELD, SIDNEY M.
1966   *English rustics in black skin.* New Haven, Conn.: College and University Press.

HANDLER, JEROME S., CHARLOTTE J. FRISBIE
1972   Aspects of slave life in Barbados: music and its cultural context. *Caribbean Studies* 11: 5–46.

HERSKOVITS, MELVILLE
1937   *Life in a Haitian valley.* New York: Alfred A. Knopf.
1941   *The myth of the Negro past.* New York: Harper and Row.
1966   *The New World Negro.* Edited by Frances S. Herskovits. Bloomington, Ind.: Indiana University Press.

HERSKOVITS, MELVILLE, FRANCES S. HERSKOVITS
1947   *Trinidad village.* New York: Alfred A. Knopf.

HORTON, ROBIN
1972   "Stateless societies in the history of West Africa," in *History of West Africa*, volume one. Edited by J. F. A. Ajayi and Michael Crowder, 78–119. New York: Columbia University Press.

HURAULT, JEAN
1961   *Les noirs réfugiés Boni de la Guyane française* [The Boni, fugitive Blacks of French Guiana]. Dakar: Institut français d'Afrique noir.

KISER, CLYDE V.
1932   *Sea Island to city. A study of St. Helena islanders in Harlem and other urban centers.* New York: Columbia University Press.

KÖBBEN, A. J. F.
1967   Unity and disunity — Cottica Djuka as a kinship system. *Bijdragen tot de Taal- Land- en Volkenkunde* 123: 10–52.

KOTTAK, CONRAD P.
1966   *The structure of equality in a Brazilian fishing community.* Ann Arbor, Mich.: University Microfilms.

KRAPF-ASKARI, EVA
1969   *Yoruba towns and cities.* Oxford: Clarendon Press.

MARASPINI, A. L.
1968   *The study of an Italian village.* The Hague: Mouton.

MINTZ, SIDNEY W.
1964   Melville J. Herskovits and Caribbean studies: a retrospective tribute. *Caribbean Studies* 4: 42–51.

MINTZ, SIDNEY W., ERIC R. WOLF
1950   An analysis of ritual co-parenthood (compadrazgo). *Southwestern Journal of Anthropology* 6: 341–368.

OTTERBEIN, KEITH F.
1965   Caribbean family organization: a comparative analysis. *American Anthropologist* 67: 66–79.
1966   *The Andros islanders. A study of family organization in the Bahamas.* University of Kansas Social Science Studies 14. Lawrence, Kans.: University of Kansas Press.

PRICE, RICHARD
1972   The Guiana maroons: changing perspectives in "Bush Negro" studies. *Caribbean Studies* 11: 82–105.

ROSSER, COLIN, CHROSTOPHER HARRIS
1965   *The family and social change. A study of family and kinships in a south Wales town.* London: Routledge and Kegan Paul.

SHIMKIN, D. B.
1971   "Black migration and the struggle for equity: a hundred-year survey," in *Migration and social welfare.* Edited by Joseph W. Eaton, 77–116. New York: National Association of Social Workers.

SIMPSON, GEORGE E.
1942   Sexual and familial institutions in northern Haiti. *American Anthropologist* 44: 655–674.
1972   Afro-American religions and religious behavior. *Caribbean Studies* 12: 5–30.

SMITH, MICHAEL G.
1960   "The African heritage in the Caribbean," in *Caribbean studies: a symposium* (second edition). Edited by Vera Rubin, 34–46. Seattle: University of Washington Press.
1962   *Kinship and community in Carriacou.* New Haven and London: Yale University Press.
1965   *Stratification in Grenada.* Berkeley and Los Angeles: University of California Press.

SMITH, RAYMOND T.
1956   *The Negro family in British Guiana. Family structure and social status in the villages.* London: Routledge and Kegal Paul.
1960   "The family in the Caribbean," in *Caribbean studies: a symposium* (second edition). Edited by Vera Rubin, 67–75. Seattle: University of Washington Press.

SOLIEN, NANCIE L.
1959   The nonunilinear descent group in the Caribbean and Central America. *American Anthropologist* 61: 578–583.

STACK, CAROL B.
1974   *All our kin: strategies for survival in a Black community.* New York: Harper and Row.

THOMAS, WILLIAM I., FLORIAN ZNANIECKI
1927   *The Polish peasant in Europe and America,* two volumes. New York: Knopf.

UCHENDU, VICTOR C.
1971   "The extended family and employment," in *The challenge of unemployment to development and the role of training and research institutes in development,* 181–193. Paris: Development Centre of the Organization for Economic Co-operation and Development.

VERGER, PIERRE
1953   "Influence du Bresil au Golfe du Benin" [The influence of Brazil on the Gulf of Benin], in *Les Afro-Américains* [The Afro-Americans]. Edited by Th. Monod. Mémoires de l'Institut français d'Afrique noir 27: 11–104. Dakar: Institut fundamental d'Afrique noir. (Reprinted 1968. Amsterdam: Swets and Zeitlinger.)

WAGLEY, CHARLES
1960   "Plantation-America: a culture sphere," in *Caribbean studies: a symposium* (second edition). Edited by Vera Rubin, 3–13. Seattle: University of Washington Press.

WESSING, ROBERT
1974   "Cosmology and social behavior in a West Javanese settlement." Ph.D. thesis, University of Illinois, Urbana.

WEST, ROBERT C.
1957   *The Pacific lowlands of Colombia.* Louisiana State University Studies Social Science Series 8. Baton Rouge: Louisiana State University Press.

WHITTEN, NORMAN E., JR.
1965   *Class, kinship and power in an Ecuadorian town.* Stanford, Calif.: Stanford University Press.

WILSON, PETER J.
1961   Household and family in Providencia. *Social and Economic Studies* 10: 511–527.

WOOFTER, THOMAS J., JR.
1930   *Black yeomanry: life on St. Helena Island.* New York: Henry Holt.

Ticouloute and His Kinfolk: The Study of a Haitian Extended Family

MICHEL LAGUERRE

ABSTRACT

This study analyzes the structure and functioning of a Haitian extended family, relating these phenomena both to individual characteristics and to the historical development of Haitian family patterns. This study differs from previous research, which has dealt primarily with rural families in the context of the *lakou*, or kin-based compound, by considering diverse social environments and their correlates in the households of a single large family.

I have chosen a sample of ten households, all linked by kinship. They were located in four environments: fully rural, village, urban (Port-au-Prince), and U.S. (Brooklyn). To delineate the variations and interconnections operative, I have combined biographical, structural, and functional approaches.

My basic conclusions are (1) that the Haitian extended family is kept together by consanguineous, legal, and customary affinal, ritual, and fictive kinship bonds; (2) that, as a corporate body, it promotes both survival and socioeconomic mobility for its members through mutual aid, economic sharing, and social solidarity reinforced by religious sanctions; and (3) that the slave-plantation system, the rise and decline of the *lakou*, and local and international migration all have modified the extended family — a dynamic, adapting part of Haiti's African legacy.

INTRODUCTION

This essay seeks to augment previous studies on Haitian kinship through the examination of the history, structure, and functioning of an extended family. By extended family, I refer not only to a cluster of patrilineal joint

This paper was written under a grant from the University of Illinois Research Board. I have been helped by the guidance and advice of Professor Norman Whitten. I am very grateful to Professor Demitri Shimkin for his invitation to write this chapter, and for his helpful suggestions, insightful comments, and editorial assistance. I am grateful to Professor Victor Uchendu, also of the University of Illinois, and to Dr. Jean Baptiste Romain, Dean, Faculté d'Ethnologie, Université d'État d'Haiti, with whom I have discussed aspects of this chapter during a reconnaissance trip to Haiti in the

families, associated with a rural residential and landholding unit (*lakou*),[1] but to a network including many other members. These are linked to each other through consanguineous, legal, and customary affinal, ritual, and fictive kinship; and through sharing rights and obligations pertaining to the socioeconomic and religious well-being of the whole network, i.e. the extended family. I feel, as a native Haitian, that the extended family in this sense is an institution of major importance. It permits the effective use of limited local resources in peasant economies, facilitates linkages across rural–urban and class divisions, and supports wider mobility, including migration to the United States. And, through the interdependence of households, it provides safeguards and stability for the highly diverse residential, reproductive, and support arrangements of individual family members.

My study refers to one family (given the pseudonym of Ticouloute)[2] with which I have been acquainted for over fifteen years. In addition, during the winter of 1973–1974 I made a field trip to Haiti, recording extensive structured and unstructured interviews with members of this extended family. On my return to the United States, I interviewed several other members who now live in New York and Chicago.

The characteristics of this one extended family include, of course, much that is unique. This is brought out, in particular, in Ticouloute's personal history. In general, the family has been better educated and more successful socioeconomically than many. Yet I would submit, from my own Haitian life experience, that there are many "Ticouloute"-type families and that their careful description and understanding is indeed important for an effective approach to the basic unity and coping capacity of Haitian society.

In this essay, I shall discuss the literature of Haitian kinship and then sketch Ticouloute's familial biography and the histories of ten households in the family. I shall summarize the more general institutional features of

---

winter of 1973–1974. The responsibility for interpreting those materials of course remains with me, the author.

In writing Creole words in this chapter, I have chosen not to use the Laubach orthography so commonly used in recent years by Haitian scholars. Instead, and in order to alert nonspecialist readers to the links between French and Haitian terminologies, I have followed the traditional French way of spelling Creole words.

[1] The *lakou*, a little community within a geographical unit, is a compound in which the father, by providing land segments to his sons, allows them to live close by, with their wives and children. Consanguineous, legal, fictive, and ritual kinship ties link the *lakou* (Laguerre 1973c).

[2] All names and all local places in Haiti associated with the "Ticouloute" family are pseudonyms.

the Ticouloute family, relating them to traits previously noted in Haitian ethnographic reports. I will seek to interpret my findings historically and processually. Finally, I will suggest research needed to gain a sound picture of Haitian kinship, including the extended family.

HAITIAN KINSHIP: A STILL UNSOLVED PROBLEM

To date, virtually all the publications dealing with Haitian kinship have been devoted to peasant households within the context of the *lakou*. These have made important contributions, reviewed below. However, the bulk of the work has been done in the countryside within thirty miles (as the crow flies) of Port-au-Prince, with a little research in that city (Legerman 1969) and in northeast Haiti (Simpson 1942). Almost all the work has been descriptive, qualitative, and static; the statistical studies of Comhaire-Sylvain (1958, 1961) and de Ronceray (1969), while very useful, have conceptual limitations. And actual family and household histories have been ignored.

The pioneering ethnographic study of Haiti, Dr. Jean Price-Mars's *Ainsi parla l'oncle* [Thus spake the uncle] (1928 [1954]) sought to develop popular pride during the period of occupation by the U.S. Marines by revealing the richness of our heritage. Chapter VIII is devoted to peasant customary marriage and the family. It sketches the setting and processes of family formation: the superior status of a married man, *un habitant notable* (Price-Mars 1928 [1954]: 206); the distinction between premarital adventures and courting (pp. 206–209); love magic (pp. 210–211); formal engagement via the *lettre de demande en mariage* (pp. 210–216); the bridal gift (p. 216); the invocation of protection for the young couple by family deities and the dead (pp. 216–217); and the young couple's neolocal residence (p. 217).

Dr. Price-Mars's writings and aid stimulated professional field study, at Mirebalais, some twenty-five miles northeast of Port-au-Prince, by Melville Herskovits (1937). This investigation clarified many elements of family organization and functioning:

The word "family" as employed in Haiti can be understood only in terms of a broader meaning than is given it in Europe and America, where it describes only the most immediate relationship group. Though in Haiti this type of organization, consisting of mother, father, and children, lies at the base of its structure, the Haitian "family" includes a wide range of relatives, direct and collateral, on the sides of both parents. The immediate family is thus but a part of a larger group, to which it is in many instances subordinate.

rger relationship grouping originates in the immediate family, and the
of new extended families is a continuing arc. Characteristically, the
gins when a man leaves the habitation of his father and with his wife,
~~settles on~~ and somewhat remote from the dwellings of either his people or those
of his wife. As the sons of this couple grow up and marry, they make their
homes near that of their father, so that in time a group of immediate families
related in the paternal line clusters about the dwelling of the original settler,
forming a habitation . . . [i.e. a *lakou*].

. . . In accordance with this rule of residence, only rarely will a man settle on the
property of his wife's parents. . . . When this does occur, it is probably because
of a serious quarrel with his own people. In such a case, if his marriage endures,
he becomes a quasi-member of his wife's family, but unless he has committed
some extremely grave offense, such as publicly insulting or striking a parent or
grandparent, he does not forfeit membership in his own group . . .

. . . The deities of the *vodun* cult are believed to be inherited in family lines, a
tradition that gives the larger family one of its most pronouncedly African
traits . . . (Herskovits 1937: 122–125).

The oldest male member of the extended family is its head, who must
live in the "ancestral habitation." He has a quasi-priestly role: ". . . his is
the important voice in the worship of the ancestors and the family gods"
(1937: 125). "All elders may punish by beating, though the oldest member
of the family exercises that right most freely and may chastise those who
are themselves grown men and women" (Herskovits 1937: 127).

These extracts give the flavor of Herskovits's contributions. But he also
made some mistakes. For him, the peasants have two types of marriage:
plaçage and church-sanctioned marriage. He omits the *mariage civil* as a
legal form which allows both spouses and their children rights to inheritance.

Professor Herskovits's findings were largely confirmed and extended by
George Simpson's researches in northeast Haiti. He too stressed the
significance of extended kinship:

Even when sons and daughters leave the family land, the bonds of kinship are
not shattered; and family pride and family solidarity are manifested in such
ways as the ability to recite genealogy, the eagerness to establish some familial
connection with a visitor or new acquaintance, and the reciprocal obligations
of kinsmen (Simpson 1942: 655).[3]

But he drew family boundaries out much farther than Herskovits:

. . . The Haitian family includes not only the ascending and descending relatives of all degrees, but also the farthest removed collateral kin whose lineage is

[3] In a later work, Simpson has stated, "Since the extended family is still the most
important basis of social organization in non-urban areas, activities which maintain or
strengthen kinship bonds contribute to the perpetuation of the Haitian peasant culture
pattern and the Haitian social structure" (Simpson 1971: 512–513).

almost lost in the dim past. Sometimes even godfathers, godmothers, and god-children are counted as members of the family group. These latter are often as important in family affairs as blood relatives themselves. It is not unusual to hear an individual say about another man: "He is my brother because we have the same godfather." Frequently, a godson claims a part of the estate of his godfather, and the legitimate heirs often consider this as quite natural (Simpson 1942: 661).

His specific contributions, e.g. on *plaçage* and on *ti-moune*, the custom of sending rural children to live with town families (for education or, often, exploitation), are also noteworthy.

However, it is Rémy Bastien (1951, 1961) who has studied Haitian rural family organization most extensively. He gathered his data in the Marbial Valley, twenty-five miles southwest of Port-au-Prince, while working with Alfred Métraux in 1948 for the UNESCO Pilot Project in Fundamental Education. In contrast to Herskovits's emphasis on African origins, Bastien felt that slavery and the wars of 1791–1803 had "obliterated" family ties in Haiti (1961: 479). He attributed the rise of Haiti's "small property system" to reforms initiated by Jean Jacques Dessalines, Haiti's first native ruler, in 1804–1806. These permitted the development of a rural social system ". . . which, while adding little to the agricultural technique of colonial times expressed a deep cohesion, an effective use of available labor and a popular religious tradition" (Bastien 1961: 479).

Bastien further clarifies the *lakou*, noting the regular presence of its graveyard; the reinforcement of ties between adult brothers and, often, cousins, through frequent exchanges of cooked food; the obligation of family solidarity in case of disaster; and the role of land as the great element of both "union and disruption" (1961: 481–486). He tested genealogical knowledge — one informant displaying precise acquaintance with 167 relatives (*parents*) over five generations — as a basis of ascertaining kinship terminology, especially consanguineous, and kinship roles. For example,

. . . the grandparents exercise authority equal to the parents over the grand-children in matters of socialization and behaviour, and commonly children fear the sternness of the grandfather more than that of the parents. . . . Cousins of both sexes are ideal playmates in Marbial where children are not encouraged to form gangs and roam the countryside . . . (Bastien 1961: 488, 489).

Bastien's treatment of affinal kin, however, is weak.

Bastien's contributions include major insights into behavioral motivations. The key to the very extensive development and use of godparental links by the Haitian peasant is a search for advantage and security for himself and his children: "When you choose godparents you must do so with a view to extend the family" (Bastien 1961: 491). In analyzing the basic functions of the Haitian family, the authoritarian nature of marriage and *plaçage* and the formal nature of husband–wife relations are stressed by Rémy Bastien. Virginity and faithfulness are required only of women; moreover,

Not long ago the male's superiority manifested itself further in the eating habits — all adult men of a *lakou* ate first, being attended by one or two "dames." When they were through, the "dames," whatever their age or status, had their meal with the children. In the case of a nuclear family, the man sat down to eat while his wife or concubine stood at the door . . . A couple, whether *placé* or married, seldom show tenderness and love even in front of their kin. They may praise mutually their kindness and devotion but hardly ever will they sit within touching distance of each other (Bastien 1961: 506, 507).

In 1937–1939, and again in 1956–1957, Suzanne Comhaire-Sylvain resided in the Kenscoff district, fifteen miles southeast of Port-au-Prince, where Dr. Price-Mars had conducted his pioneering family study years earlier. She was able to confirm and expand Price-Mars's original observations on peasant marriage. She verified that ". . . boys have the initiative in choosing their sweethearts. Any girl who dared to press her preference openly would thereby ruin her reputation . . ." (Comhaire-Sylvain 1958: 217). She discovered some feuds, which inhibited courtships. Marriage prohibitions were associated with family illnesses and with degrees of relationship. None could take place ". . . between members of the same direct line and among kinsfolk of the following categories, including affines; uncle and niece, aunt and nephew, godfather and goddaughter, godmother and godson . . ." (1958: 218).

Particularly interesting are her statistics. Among 261 legally unmarried men, 10 percent were *plaçage* polygamists; among 387 legally married men, the frequency of polygamous *plaçage* was almost 20 percent (1958: 229). There was also much local variation, with 20 percent of the men in Kenscoff *bourg* being polygamists, compared to less than 6 percent in the region of Furcy. Underlying polygamy were considerations of economic status: ". . . men take great pride in having many farm holdings in different localities, and tradition teaches them to believe that they need a "wife" in each locality or on each holding to take care for their fields or property" (1958: 231). The desire for children is another incentive. So is prestige, to be the "'big man,' [with] most land, most animals, most children and most 'wives' . . ." (1958: 231–232).

Comhaire-Sylvain's 1961 study of households in the Kenscoff region is drawn from a somewhat larger sample than used in her 1958 report. The data as presented are difficult to use; Table 1, compiled and generously provided by Dr. D. B. Shimkin, presents them in somewhat clearer form.

The predominance of husband–wife families, the substantial proportion of polygamous families, and the low proportion of woman-headed families are notable. This is a strongly patrilateral group.

These data are also limited. They do not indicate dynamic perspectives, such as household histories using Fortes's developmental-cycle model could generate (Fortes 1958). Also, there is no indication of interhousehold interactions, of key importance in the *lakou* context and partly reinstituted in more recent ". . . clusters of houses belonging to the same family (father and children, mother and children, brothers and sisters) and built on a property originally owned by the father or the mother . . ." (Comhaire-Sylvain 1961: 197).

Paul Moral, a French geographer, complements previous researchers on peasant families in Haiti in two ways. First, he clarifies the notion of *plaçage* by differentiating *plaçage honnête*, which is monogamous in nature, from bigamous or polygamous *plaçage*. Second, he explains why the *lakou* system is declining: ". . . the rapid increase of the population, the extension of cleared land, the repeated successoral land holdings have caused the disintegration of old familial cores" (Moral 1961: 170 [translated by M.L.]).

With this slow disappearance of the *lakou*, some recent writers have concentrated their attention on households outside the *lakou* system. Thus, Legerman (1969: 81) has concluded from an analysis of family life in three settings that there is more of a tendency toward matrifocality on plantations and in urban slums than among southern Haitian peasants. In another study (Legerman 1971 [1962]), there was noted the variability and importance of kin ties (cognatic, affinal, and ritual) among poultry saleswomen in Port-au-Prince. This is a unique study, for Haiti, of kinship and occupation. De Ronceray (1969: 1–34), studying changes in attitudes in Haitian families, also concludes that women in urban families have more power and are less conservative than their rural counterparts.

Also significant from a different angle is Stycos's study (1964) on Haitian attitudes toward family size which finds that

. . . family size is a matter of very low salience for most Haitian men and women . . . norms concerning appropriate family size seem nonexistent and inappropriate for most subjects . . . an attitude of religious fatalism about the number of children is characteristic . . . (Stycos 1964: 47).

The studies reviewed above provide a significant foundation of knowledge on the Haitian family, particularly households within and, recently, outside of the *lakou*. But little attention has been paid to delineating kinship networks, and to the ways in which households are linked to each other through structural and functional ties. And we do not know

Table 1.   Household compositions in the Kenscoff region[a]

Type of household ("Wife" includes placée)	Frequency		Population included		Persons per household
	Number	Percent	Number	Percent	
All households	917	100.0	4,888	100.0	5.33
I 0 Nuclear family (H-Wi-Ch)	530	57.8	3,340	68.3	6.30
1 With children of both only	499	54.4	—	—	—
2 With other children[b]	20	2.2	—	—	—
3 With nonkin[c]	11	1.2	—	—	—
II 0 Nuclear(H-Wi-Ch)-extended	63	6.9	482	9.9	7.65
1 With husband's parents only	3	0.3	—	—	—
2 With husband's mother only	6	0.7	—	—	—
3 With husband's siblings only	3	0.3	—	—	—
4 With wife's parents only	1	0.1	—	—	—
5 With wife's mother only	11	1.2	—	—	—
6 With wife's siblings only	4	0.4	—	—	—
7 With grandchildren only	9	1.0	—	—	—
8 With other kin	22	2.4	—	—	—
9 With nonkin[d]	4	0.4	—	—	—
III 0 Conjugal couples (H-Wi)	71	7.7	155	3.2	2.18
1 Alone[e]	55	6.0	—	—	—
2 With kin only[f]	11	1.2	—	—	—
3 With nonkin[g]	5	0.5	—	—	—
IV 0 Polygamous and allied Subfamilies	88	9.6	420	8.6	4.77
1 Polygamous:[h]	75	8.2	—	—	—
Mother–child only	66	7.2	—	—	—
Mother–child and others	9	1.0	—	—	—
2 One spouse away[i]	13	1.4	—	—	—

Table 1 *continued*

Type of household ("Wife" includes *placée*)	Frequency		Population included		Persons per household
	Number	Percent	Number	Percent	
V 0 Other	165	18.0	491	10.0	2.98
1 Childless *placée* wives[j]	22	2.4	—	—	—
2 Woman–headed families	78	8.5	—	—	—
Mother–child only	44	4.8	—	—	—
Grandmother–grandchildren only	14	1.5	—	—	—
Grandmother–mother–grandchildren	10	1.1	—	—	—
Other	10	1.1	—	—	—
3 Single women	17	1.9	—	—	—
4 Women and women friends	2	0.2	—	—	—
5 Male–headed families	10	1.1	—	—	—
Father–child only	2	0.2	—	—	—
Grandfather–grandchildren only	5	0.5	—	—	—
Grandfather–father–grandchildren	1	0.1	—	—	—
Other	2	0.2	—	—	—
6 Single men	31	3.4	—	—	—
7 Men and male nonkin[k]	5	0.5	—	—	—
All families[l]	862	94.0	—	—	—
All husband–wife families[m]	664	72.4	3,977	81.4	5.99
All polygamous families[n]	97	10.6	—	—	—

a Compiled by Demitri B. Shimkin from Comhaire-Sylvain (1961).
b Husband's or wife's children (18 cases); adopted children (2 cases).
c Servants and employees (10 cases); boarded children (1 case).
d Servants.
e Includes 15 cases with children living elsewhere.
f Grandchildren (6 cases); siblings (3 cases); husband's nephews (2 cases).
g Servants (4 cases); apprentice (1 case).
h Father of children lives with other wife (or *placée*).
i Working in other place or living elsewhere.
j Presumably polygamous [DBS].
k Servants (4 cases); friends (1 case).
l Items V. 3, 4, 6, and 7 are excluded.
m Items I, II, and III.
n Items IV. 1 and V. 1.

anything about the developmental histories of households. Again, with the disappearance of the *lakou* as a geographical unit, what is happening so far as the extended family is concerned? Can we consider the extended family and the way in which it functions, moreover, as adaptive mechanisms for coping with poverty? What roles do ritual kinship and voodoo play in the functioning of the extended family? What roles does the extended family play in local-level politics?

These questions are still unsolved. This essay on the history and functioning of Ticouloute's extended family will help in answering some of them.

THE ORIGINS AND RISE OF A FAMILY LEADER: TICOULOUTE

Ticouloute, a man of sixty-nine in 1973, is the most influential member of his extended family, which, in that year, included some thirty households and perhaps 150 living persons residing in the central plateau of Haiti (about fifty to sixty miles northeast of Port-au-Prince), and in lesser numbers in Port-au-Prince, New York, and Chicago. All are descendants of four deceased couples in the generation of Ticouloute's paternal grand father: that person and his wife; Ticouloute's wife's paternal grandfather and his wife; Ticouloute's wife's paternal grandfather's sister and her husband; and Ticouloute's wife's paternal grandmother's brother and his wife.

Ticouloute's prominence comes from his father's role in the struggle against U.S. intervention, from his family's means, and from his personal characteristics and conduct. Literate, stably married, concerned with his kinsfolk, and aided by strong relations with his wife's family, he is now the sole survivor of four brothers and the family's informal leader.

When the United States Marines came to Haiti in 1915, Ticouloute was ten years old. His father, André, a guerrilla leader, fought against the Marines on the side of the *Kako* leader, Charlemagne Péralte.[4] André was killed in an ambush in 1918; later in the same year, Ticouloute's mother died.

---

[4] The American intervention at Port-au-Prince on July 28, 1915, to "protect American and foreign interests" during a Haitian revolutionary crisis, was followed immediately by Admiral William Capertons's policy of repression. His dispatch of August 2, 1915, to the Secretary of the Navy stated, "Large number Haitian revolutions, largely due existing professional soldiers called cacos, organized in bands under lawless, irresponsible chiefs, who fight on side offering greatest inducement but nominally recognize the government. Stable government not possible in Haiti until cacos are disbanded and power broken.

Such action imperative at Port-au-Prince if United States desires to negotiate treaty for financial control of Haiti . . ." (Davis 1936: 168–170).

Despite these provocative policies, substantial armed resistance to the United States

The year after, the four brothers and their sister — Timano, Ticouloute, Boukman, Bouch Fobo, and Nirvana Grodada (in order of age and sex) — left "Nancongo" to escape the continual harassment of marines looking for weapons and *Kako* sympathizers. They went to "Ziltic," where their father had bought a house some time before the American occupation. They settled in "Ziltic" but went back and forth to visit with their relatives on certain occasions. For example, they went once a year during November for the annual voodoo *manger-les-morts*, food offerings in memory of the dead (see Herskovits 1937: 212–213, 259).

They did so for five consecutive years. After that, they lost contact with their relatives in "Nancongo" because of the death of one of the uncles who used to pay for the *manger-les-morts*. Also, because of continual raids by marines in search of *Kakos*, much risk was attached to this kind of venture. Later, because of the acute economic crisis the island was passing through during the decade 1930–1940, Ticouloute and his brothers and sister were not able to pay for the trip.

In "Ziltic," the brothers and sister lived in the same house. The oldest brother, Timano, worked to pay for the rent and the schooling of the younger brothers and sister. The sister, Nirvana Grodada, cooked for them. Every night before going to bed, they assembled in front of the oratory of their home to pray. They prayed for their dead ancestors as well as for their living relatives, including their godparents. The evening prayer was like a kind of litany, in which a long list of dead and living relatives was cited.

Marines developed only in the central plateau and the north in the summer of 1918, in the wake of illegal road building (*corvées*) with many abuses. At that time, Charlemagne Péralte, allegedly a "caco chief of Hinche" in central Haiti (Davis 1936: 218), escaped *gendarme* custody and began an uprising. This reached its peak in 1919, when 5,000–6,000 *cacos* were believed to be in the field. Péralte was assassinated on October 31, 1919, by *gendarmerie* infiltrators. Benoit Battraville, his major lieutenant, succeeded Péralte and maintained major operations, culminating in an attack upon Port-au-Prince on January 15, 1920. Battraville was killed in May, 1920, and Haitian resistance collapsed thereafter. Reports of atrocities by United States Marines culminated in an allegation by Brigadier General George Barnett, U.S.M.C. that "practically indiscriminate killing of natives has been going on for some time" (Davis 1936: 225). This allegation was rejected by a naval court of inquiry in October, 1920 (Davis 1936: 226). See also Millspaugh (1931).

The "unrelenting war" of United States-controlled authorities against the voodoo religion in 1915–1920 must also be noted. Simpson (1971: 516) specifies that "*Houmforts* [temples] were destroyed and the *houngans* [voodoo priests] were sentenced to hard labor or given heavy fines. For a time it seemed that *vodun* would disappear."

The final departure of the United States Marines in 1934 was celebrated in later years as the "Festival of the Second Independence" which Herskovits (1937: 11) found to be ". . . marked by the 'illumination' of all houses the night before and a solemn discourse from the mayor after a *Te Deum* has been sung in church" [D. B. Shimkin].

About 1930, Timano married and left to establish his own house. Ticouloute, who had received his elementary school diploma (*Certificat d'Études Primaires*), then took on the responsibility of running the house for himself, his younger brothers, and his sister. He paid for their schooling. At the same time, they went to Timano's house every week to eat a meal, alternated in helping him with his corn and rice fields, and worked together whenever he organized a *coumbite*, or field-clearing bee (see Herskovits 1937: 70–76; Métraux 1971).

In 1932, when Ticouloute got married, his next younger brother, Boukman, started work to pay rent for the house where the youngest three were living. When Boukman was unable to make ends meet, he, Bouch Fobo, and Nirvana Grodada went to stay and eat at their older brothers' homes. A few years later, they were all married.

Ticouloute's wife grew up in "Mangots," twelve miles from "Ziltic." Her father used to be *Chef-de-section*[5] of this rural area, and a plantation owner. She left her family compound to gain her elementary school diploma in "Ziltic," where she lived with her godmother and met Ticouloute.

In the *lakou* where Ticouloute's wife was brought up, there resided, besides her father, mother, and brothers, her grandfather, Sonson, and two of her father's brothers with their wives and children. In the center was a voodoo house,[6] from which paths led to the grandfather's and sons' houses. Nearby was a *mappou* or kapok tree[7] which was considered as a *poteau-mitan* or "center pole" linking the living to the dead and to the *loa* or voodoo spirit (see also Herskovits 1937: 309–319; Simpson 1971: 491–521), protectors of the *lakou* (Figure 1). The *lakou* people as well as other relatives gathered once a year, on November second, around the *mappou* tree, holding voodoo ceremonies for the dead and the spirit protectors of the *lakou*.

During the first phase of his marriage, much interaction occurred between Ticouloute and his wife's primary kin and between the young couple and their godparents. There were many reciprocal visits. It should be noted that Ticouloute's wife's cousins had migrated around 1930 from "Mangots" to "Ziltic." The oldest cousin, Brenor, bought land there and built a house. Later, he gave a portion of the land to his youngest brother.

Under the Constitution of 1889, 531 *sections* were the smallest rural administrative divisions of Haiti (Dorsinville 1969: 454).

cording to Herskovits (1937: 155–156), such houses usually have two rooms, one ated to the voodoo deities (*loa*), the other to the spirits of twins and family dead. *pentandra* (L.): common throughout the island in forests and along stream scoso 1943: 369). On the relation of the *mappou* tree to voodoo sacrifice, in e uprising of 1791 see also Price-Mars (1928 [1954]: 42); Laguerre (1974a). pment of voodoo during the French colonial period see Laguerre (1974b).

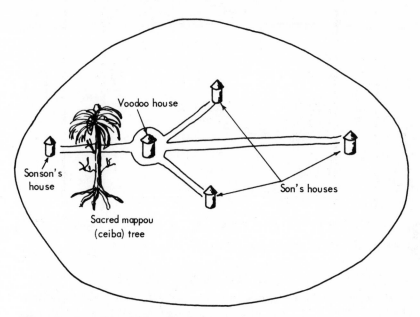

Figure 1. A traditional *lakou*: Sonson's

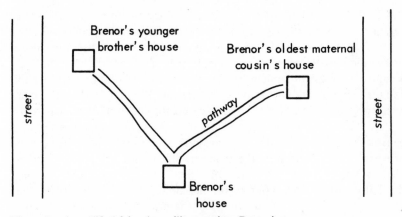

Figure 2. A modified *lakou* in a village setting: Brenor's

And, finally, he sold another portion to his oldest maternal cousin. The households of these three men and their wives and children formed a kind of *lakou* (Figure 2).

Ticouloute's brother-in-law, Klo, had also built a house in "Ziltic." He built it in the *lakou* of his great-aunt Acacia. A peculiarity of this *lakou*

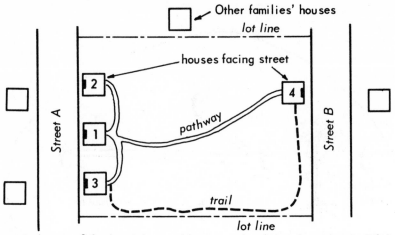

1   Acacia's house   2,3 Acacia's sons' houses   4   Acacia's nephew's (Klo's) house

Figure 3.   A modified *lakou* in a village setting: Acacia's

was that there was no voodoo house in the center. In addition, the *lakou*, bounded by two streets, was rectangular rather than circular. The houses of Acacia and her two sons faced one way; Klo's house was on the next street, facing the other way (Figure 3).

Ticouloute's first child was a daughter, who died at three. Eight days after her birth, she was *andoyée*, i.e. baptized according to nonvoodoo folk rites. A young woman friend of the family was chosen as godmother, and the son of Ticouloute's closest neighbor as godfather. Two months later, the child was given Christian baptism by the village priest. At that time, the child had the mayor of the village as godfather, and the village bakery's woman owner as godmother. These two people were the better off than the parents.

It is the village midwife who delivers babies. Six months prior to a delivery, she gives clinical advice, prescribing various kinds of tea for the prospective mother. After the delivery, she buries the placenta in the kitchen house, under the ashes, thus preventing anyone from harming the baby. Three days after birth, she presents the baby to the four cardinal points, that is, to the supernatural forces. As Ticouloute's second daughter died four days after birth, *andoyée* but without Christian baptism, she was buried in the garden in front of Ticouloute's house.

All the other Ticouloute children were *andoyés* and then formally baptized. With each new baby, Ticouloute played a transaction game to make the most advantageous choice possible, for godparents are expected to help their godchild in every way. The godparents, for their part, expect their godchildren to take care of them in old age if they have no children of their own. Moreover, if these godparents are politicians or vendors, they expect the parents and the godchildren to help during electoral campaigns or to trade with them.

Thus, Ticouloute, desiring good educations for his children, managed to draw on people in the upper and middle classes of his village for godparents for his children. This allowed him to have contacts, through these godparents, with other people in key positions in Port-au-Prince. When a child had to go to Port-au-Prince to finish high school, Ticouloute would get a letter from his *compè* (see Bastien 1961 : 493), or mayor of the village, and bring this letter to the principal of the lycée. This was enough for his sons to be admitted. Correspondingly, during elections, Ticouloute would do his best to make his extended family vote for his *compè*. Such are the reciprocal prices of godparenthood transactions.

Timano, Ticouloute's oldest brother, a blacksmith, died years ago. His wife had died earlier, and he had no children. Before his death, he gave his house to his sister, Nirvana Grodada.

Ticouloute's second brother, Boukman, moved to another locality, "Troucoucou." However, when he separated from his first *placée*, he took their daughter to her sister's house in "Ziltic." Later, his son from a second *placée* stayed with Ticouloute, until Boukman married the mother so that his son might be accepted in the village Catholic school. And, at the time of corn and rice harvests, he always sent some from his fields as gifts to his brothers and sister. The brothers, in their turn, preferred to buy their rice from Boukman. Boukman died in the mid-1960s.

Bouch Fobo, Ticouloute's youngest brother, who died in 1969, had especially close relations with his sister, Nirvana Grodada, later Madame Gromosso. She fostered his three boys from two *plaçages*, paying for their schooling. For a time, after his first *placée* died, Bouch Fobo stayed with the Gromosso family. His oldest son went on to Port-au-Prince, staying with a godmother, to finish high school there. He is today working at a dry cleaner's in Port-au-Prince, helping support his younger brother, his half brother, one cousin, and the Gromossos, who fostered him in earlier years.

Gromosso is a tailor and loves children, although he and his wife, Nirvana Grodada, have none. She is a merchant and a *mambo*, second in importance after a voodoo priest. As a *mambo*, she had spiritually married Loko, a *loa habitant*.[8] For protection from Loko, when one of Boukman's boys was sick, she asked the voodoo priest to baptize him; thus the boy has voodoo as well as Christian godparents. When Ticouloute's children were sick, he would usually ask a medical doctor for help. In cases when

---

[8]   The *mambo*, or voodoo priestess, is especially a healer and a diviner, like the priest or *houngan*, according to Herskovits (1937: 151–152).

this did not help, Nirvana Grodada would take the child to a voodoo priest, paying his bill. She also played an important role for the extended family in organizing *manger-les-morts* for the dead. She and Gromosso are very much concerned about the well-being of every member of the extended family.

A similar pattern of solidarity can be seen between Ticouloute and his wife's kindred. When his brother-in-law Klo was widowed, Klo's son was fostered in Ticouloute's house. Later, Klo was converted to the Baptist Church and married a second wife, who bore him a daughter and a son. Klo died in 1972, and his daughter stayed with her uncle Ticouloute until she got married.

When they were young, Ticouloute's children ate either at their father's home or at any relative's. In fact, they spent no more time in their own home than in kinsfolk's and godparents' homes, especially during the summer months, when they did not have to study or take care of those still younger.

Today (1973), Ticouloute has five surviving children, two sons and three daughters. None are living with him.

His oldest daughter is married and living in Port-au-Prince. Earlier, however, when her husband Decius had lost his job, they moved into the household of his *bopè*, or father-in-law, Ticouloute. They have six children of school age; a godchild and two relatives of hers are also living with them.

Ticouloute's older son has gone to Canada. His school expenses had been paid by his godmother. When he started working, he began to send money regularly to his parents and other relatives. He also paid for his younger brother's and, later, a younger sister's, passage to New York. This sister, Ticouloute's second-oldest living daughter, Josée, stayed in New York with an "aunt" (actually, a cousin once removed) until she got married in 1973. This "aunt" had migrated to New York in 1957 and was able to buy a building with ten apartments in it. Here she lived with her children and her sister's nuclear family, plus a few nephews and more distant relatives.

Most recently, Josée, now married to Venance, has paid for the passage to New York of the youngest of Ticouloute's daughters.

Every month Ticouloute receives some money from his children, who also send money to their cousins, aunts, and other relatives. The children's strategy is to help with passage to New York for relatives, so that less will have to be sent (for subsistence rather than opportunity) to Haiti. Migration to New York is now the major point at which the Ticouloute extended family is manifesting its solidarity.

Ticouloute and his wife, now that their children are in Port-au-Prince or out of Haiti, are strengthening their ties with relatives still living in the village, and Ticouloute and his wife also want to finish their lives on good terms with their relatives: nephews, nieces, cousins, godchildren, and children. If they should be sick, these relatives would be the first to help them.

Some of these people come to Ticouloute when they want advice. And, since he receives some money from his children in New York, some come to ask for financial help.

DIVERSITY AND INTERDEPENDENCE: TEN HOUSEHOLD HISTORIES IN THE TICOULOUTE EXTENDED FAMILY

The Ticouloute extended family is composed of kinsmen related consanguineously, affinally, by folk adoption, and ritually (godparents and godchildren). It also encompasses dead ancestors and a voodoo spirit. As the familial biography of Ticouloute has shown, it is also a corporate body composed of interdependent households which work together to solve problems of survival, satisfaction, and social mobility.

To analyze the dynamic features of the family diachronically and structurally, ten households have been selected for historical review. These households, about one-third of the family total, are believed to be representative in the varieties of social environment, duration, type,

Table 2.   Characteristics of illustrative households in the Ticouloute extended family

Number	Name of head	Social environment	Duration: date of formation	disso-lution	Type of household[a]	General level of stability[b]	Number of structural phases
1.	Sonson	*Lakou*	1890	1925	Nuc Ext	H	5
2.	Boukman	Open rural	1937	(1964)	Nuc Poly	L	6
3.	Bouch Fobo	Open rural	1943 (1951)	(1950) 1969	Nuc/WH	I	8
4.	Ticouloute	Village	1932	—	Nuc Ext	H	9
5.	Gromosso	Village	1945	—	Conj C Ext	H	6
6.	Klo	Village	1932 1958	(1945) 1972	Nuc Ext	I	6
7.	Irene	Village	1945	1958	Nuc/WH	I	3
8.	Decius	Urban[c]	1957	—	Nuc Ext	H	5
9.	Agatha	Urban[c]	1960 1965	1963 —	Nuc/WH	L	6
10.	Venance	U.S.A.[d]	1969	—	Nuc Ext	H	3

Approximate dates are in parentheses.

[a] Nuc Ext (nuclear extended, i.e. husband, wife, children, kin, and/or nonkin); Nuc Poly (nuclear polygamous); WH (woman headed); Conj C Ext (conjugal couple extended, i.e. husband, wife, kin, and/or nonkin other than own children). "Wife" here includes *placée*.

[b] H: High; I: Intermediate; L: Low.   [c] Port-au-Prince.   [d] Brooklyn.

general level of stability, and number of structural phases to be found in that family (Table 2). The heads of households covered include Ticouloute's father-in-law; two brothers and Ticouloute himself; his sister's husband; his wife's two brothers; one son-in-law; his wife's brother's daughter; and his other son-in-law. The household histories are summaries of more extensive data, emphasizing structurally significant phases, and are analyzed in terms of each household rather than in terms of a mechanical household development-cycle theory.

Sonson's Household; Lakou *Context; Monogamous*

Structural phase	Composition				
	Husband	Wife	Children	Nephews/Nieces	Godchildren
A	+	+	−	−	−
B	+	+	−	0	−
C	+	+	+	0	−
D	+	+	−	0	−
E	+	+	−	−	+

Symbols: + = full-time resident; 0 = part-time resident; − = absent. (Used for all households.)

STRUCTURAL PHASES

A.   About 1890, Sonson, later to be Ticouloute's father-in-law, got married and built a house in his father's compound. Adding a new member involved a kind of symbolic interaction with *lakou* members. One cannot become a full member of a *lakou* in one day. This is a slow process of integration and adaptation in which the new wife *fait l'apprentissage* on the plane on which her participation in communal activities is to be. She needs to develop strategies to be able to compete with other households so that hers may appear to be the most harmonious. This is not an economic competition, but an attempt to avoid behavior to be condemned as the *bête noire* or "black sheep" of the *lakou.* Yet the adaptation is more or less difficult depending on whether the *lakou* is rich or poor, according to peasant standards, and on whether the newcomer comes from a rich or poor family.

B.   The couple temporarily received a nephew into their household; this young relative was placed with them for two months during harvest. At that time his parents were in their fields, so that he had to be fostered.

C.   The couple began to have children, while continuing the temporary fosterage of nephews and nieces as needed. From this grew a communal feeling — brotherhood — between the children and their first cousins. (Compare Bastien 1961: 489–490.)

D. The children started leaving the household, moving to an aunt in "Ziltic" to finish elementary school. Their mother came to "Ziltic" village every other Saturday to sell farm products at the public market and bring food to the children. Temporary fosterage of one nephew continued.

E. On marriage, the children, nephews and nieces left the compound. Sonson and his wife then adopted a godchild, who helped them and other people, particularly as a communications channel with the young married people who had left. The godchild was able to read messages or letters that his *paren* [godfather] and *marin'n* [godmother] received.

Boukman's Households; Troucoucou Village: Also "Far Away" Rural; Polygamous

	Composition					
		Polygamous households				
		First		Second		Third
Structural phase	Husband	*Placée*	Children	*Placée*/Wife	Children	*Placée*
A	+	+	−	−	−	−
B	+	+	+	−	−	−
C	+	−	−	+	−	−
D	+	−	−	+	+	−
E	+	+	+	+	+	−
F	+	+	+	+	+	+

STRUCTURAL PHASES

A. Boukman and his first *placée* started living together in 1937.

B. They had a daughter.

C. They separated and their daughter was fostered in "Ziltic." Boukman then took a second *placée*.

D. Boukman and the second *placée* had a son.

E. He resumed relationships with his first *placée*, his son being fostered by Ticouloute. But, in order to have his son accepted by the village school, which was run by the Catholic archdiocese, he had to marry his son's mother, and reincorporate his son in that household.

F.   Boukman continued living with his wife and his first *placée*; both bore more children. Then he bought land "far from home," spending a week to a month every time he went there. He built a house on this land for his third *placée*; this relationship was childless since she is barren. Boukman died about 1964.

Bouch Fobo's Households; "Ziltic" Village; Serial Plaçage

Structural phase	Composition				
		Serial households First		Second	
	Husband	*Placée*	Children	*Placée*	Children
A	+	+	−	−	−
B	+	+	+	−	−
C	+	−	+	−	−
D	0	−	−	0	−
E	+	−	−	+	−
F	+	−	−	+	+
G	−	−	−	+	+
H	−	−	−	+	−

STRUCTURAL PHASES

A.   In 1943, Bouch Fobo started living with his first *placée*. No legal contract was signed, precluding inheritance by either from the other.

B.   The couple had two boys, who were given their father's name. As he had legally recognized them, they were eligible to inherit from him and from their mother.

C.   His *placée* having died, Bouch Fobo tried to maintain a household for the two boys for six months. Then he placed them for fosterage with Gromosso, his brother-in-law.

D.   Bouch Fobo alternated half-time between his own house and Gromosso's. When home, he was "visited" by his *placée*-to-be.

E.   He started living on a permanent basis with his second *placée*. The boys had the option of moving to their father's house or remaining with their aunt and uncle. They preferred the latter.

F.   His second *placée* bore Bouch Fobo a son, whom he recognized legally.

G.   In 1969, Bouch Fobo died; his second *placée* remained in his house with their son.

H.   Because of her lack of financial resources to provide this son with a good education, she placed him in fosterage with Gromosso. She remained alone in Bouch Fobo's house, which now legally belonged to her son.

Ticouloute's Household; "Ziltic" Village; Monogamous

Structural phase	Composition						
	Husband	Wife	Servant	Niece/ nephew	Children	Son-in-law's nuclear family	Godchild
A	+	+	+	−	−	−	−
B	+	+	+	+	+	−	−
C	+	+	+	−	−	−	−
D	+	+	+	+	+	−	−
E	+	+	+	−	+	−	−
F	+	+	−	−	+	+	−
G	+	+	−	+	+	−	−
H	+	+	−	−	−	−	−
I	+	+	−	−	−	−	+

STRUCTURAL PHASES

A.   In 1932 Ticouloute married; a young servant lived with them. An unrelated orphan was taken in by Ticouloute; he nevertheless called Ticouloute *mon-onk* and his wife *ma-tante*.

B.   They had one daughter; another lived only four days. Ticouloute's brother-in-law, Klo, brought his son to the house. It is current practice in Haiti that, when a child's mother dies, its father's sister is most likely to care for the child until the father remarries.

C.   In 1935 Ticouloute's daughter died. Klo's son returned to his father's household. The servant remained with the Ticouloutes.

D.   The servant remained. Children were born to the Ticouloutes. Klo's daughter from his second marriage lived with them so she might go to school.

E.   The niece returned home to Klo. She had failed twice in school and could not go on. The household was reduced to Ticouloute, his wife, his children, and the servant.

F.   The servant got married, with Ticouloute's wife serving as a god-mother for the marriage. Ticouloute gave the servant a portion of land where he could build a home and live with his wife. Ticouloute's oldest living daughter married a military man in 1957. After his release from the army, Decius, the son-in-law, and his family lived with the Ticouloutes until the younger man was able to get a job in Port-au-Prince in 1962.

G. After Klo's death in 1972, his daughter was incorporated into Ticouloute's household. His older son, who had been studying in Port-au-Prince, migrated to Montreal, Canada.

H. All the children left; the niece was also married. Ticouloute and his wife were alone for the first time in the history of their household.

I. In 1973, they adopted one of their godchildren.

Gromosso's Household; "Ziltic" Village; Monogamous; Childless

Structural phase	Composition			Wife's brother's children	
	Husband	Wife	Wife's brother	By first *placée*	By second *placée*
A	+	+	−	−	−
B	+	+	−	+	−
C	+	+	0	+	−
D	+	+	−	+	−
E	+	+	−	+	+
F	+	+	−	−	+

STRUCTURAL PHASES

A. Gromosso and Nirvana Grodada married in 1945. He was a tailor for all members of the extended family and she was a merchant; thus the Gromossos were among the family's richest members.

B. Upon the death of Bouch Fobo's *placée*, the Gromossos fostered their two nephews.

C. Bouch Fobo also moved in, as a part-time resident, until he got his second *placée*. During this time, he helped pay for the food and schooling of his children.

D. Bouch Fobo left, leaving the boys with their aunt and uncle. They preferred staying there rather than with their stepmother.

E. When Bouch Fobo died, his son by his second *placée* came into the Gromosso household, joining the two other boys.

F.   The boys of the first *plaçage* left Gromosso's home in 1967. One got a *placée*. The other was fostered in Port-au-Prince by his godmother, finished high school, and went to work. The remaining nephew remained with Gromosso and his wife.

Klo's Household; "Ziltic" Village; Serial Monogamy

Structural phase	Composition					
		First marriage		Second marriage		
	Husband	Wife	Children	Wife	Children	Godchild
A	+	+	−	−	−	−
B	+	+	+	−	−	−
C	+	−	0	−	−	−
D	+	−	+	+	−	−
E	+	−	+	+	+	+
F	−	−	−	+	+	+

STRUCTURAL PHASES

A.   In 1932 Klo, Ticouloute's brother-in-law, married.

B.   They had a boy.

C.   His wife died. Their son stayed partly with Klo but most of the time with Ticouloute and his wife, Klo's sister.

D.   In 1958 Klo remarried and his son rejoined him permanently.

E.   Klo and his second wife had a son and daughter. His older son as well as a godchild also lived with them.

F.   Klo died in 1972, and his daughter was given in fosterage at Ticouloute's house. His widow became head of the household, which consisted of her, her son, and a godchild.

Irene's Household; "Ziltic" Village; Monogamous Plaçage

Structural phase	Composition		
	Husband	*Placée*	Daughter
A	+	+	−
B	+	+	+
C	−	+	+

STRUCTURAL PHASES

A.   In 1945, Irene, Ticouloute's other brother-in-law, set up a *plaçage*.

B.   Irene and his *placée* had a daughter, Agatha, whom he recognized legally.

C.   In 1958 he died, and his widow became head of the household; Agatha left her in 1960. In 1963, she moved in with Agatha.

Decius's Household; Port-au-Prince; Monogamous

Structural phase	Composition					
	Husband	Wife	Children	Wife's sister	Husband's sister	Cousin and distant relative
A	+	+	−	−	−	−
B	+	+	+	−	−	−
C	+	+	+	+	−	−
D	+	+	+	+	+	−
E	+	+	+	−	+	+

STRUCTURAL PHASES

A.   Decius married Ticouloute's daughter in 1957.

B.   They had children. On Decius's release from military service, he and his family stayed with Ticouloute until Decius could find a job in Port-au-Prince.

C.   In Port-au-Prince, another of Ticouloute's daughters, Josée, joined them.

D.   Decius's sister also came to live with them.

E.   Josée left for New York. A cousin and a distant relative came to stay, however, in order to go to school in Port-au-Prince.

Agatha's Households; Port-au-Prince; Matrifocal

	Composition								
		Successive households							
	Woman of house	First (*plaçage*)			Second (marriage)			Third	
Structural phase		Man	Child	Mother	Husband	Child	Stepsons	Cousins	Godchild
A	+	+	−	−	−	−	−	−	−
B	+	+	+	−	−	−	−	−	−
C	+	−	+	+	−	−	−	−	−
D	+	−	+	+	+	+	−	−	−
E	+	−	+	+	+	+	+	−	−
F	+	−	+	+	−	+	−	+	+

STRUCTURAL PHASES

A.   Agatha was taken into *plaçage* in 1960.

B.   She had a daughter.

C.   Her man died in 1963, and her mother moved in with her.

D.   She married a sergeant and had another child. Agatha's daughter and mother continued living with them.

E.   Adeka, the husband, brought his two sons (Agatha's stepsons), the issues of an earlier affair, into the household.

F.   Adeka and the two stepsons left. Agatha, her two children, and her mother were joined by two second cousins and a godchild in the household. These children and those of Decius, who lives nearby, are close; there is frequent food sharing and sleeping back and forth between the two households.

Venance's Household; Brooklyn, U.S.A.; Monogamous

Structural phase	Composition				
	Husband	Wife	Son	Wife's sister	Cousin
A	+	+	−	−	−
B	+	+	+	−	−
C	+	+	+	+	+

STRUCTURAL PHASES

A. Josée, Ticouloute's daughter, migrated to Brooklyn in 1969. At first she was single and stayed at an "aunt's" apartment house. She and Venance were married in 1973. They remained in this "aunt's" building, taking an apartment.

B. They had a son.

C. Josée's young sister and a cousin of Venance's migrated to New York and took up residence with them.

This review of household histories in the Ticouloute extended family leads to the following observations:

1. Despite a considerable range of social environments and a long span of time, the households of this family seem to express variants of a single pattern.

2. This pattern has two alternatives, stable husband–wife relations (usually marital, more rarely *placée*), or unstable serial or polygamous ones. In the first case, married couples soon become nuclear families and then nuclear-extended families. In the second case, households break up; the incorporation of children and others into allied nuclear-extended families and a terminal stage as woman-headed families are the expectable sequences.

3. High death rates and early mortalities have also been important sources of household instability.

4. The types and frequencies of households noted in the Ticouloute extended family correspond well to the general pattern noted by Comhaire-Sylvain (1961) (see Table 1).

5. The structural and dynamic features of the households can, however, be understood adequately only in terms of extensive interhousehold relationships, which influence behavior at all levels, from responses to disaster to facilitating education and upward social mobility.

6. The structures and histories shown above are considerably simplified, with the network of godparent–godchild relationships, in particular, being another level of familial integration.

THE INSTITUTIONAL SETTING OF THE TICOULOUTE EXTENDED FAMILY: STRUCTURAL FEATURES, RULES OF BEHAVIOR, AND INTEGRATING VALUES

Haitian extended families interrelate individuals of differing characteristics and personalities with continuing social structures and their associate rule systems and values. In this essay we have shown the immense roles of Ticouloute and his sister, Nirvana Grodada (later, Madame Gromosso) in the development and functioning of their family. Then we have sketched the varying consequences, ranging from polygamous to matrifocal households, of differing choices by various members of the extended family. In this section, structural features, rules of behavior, and integrating values governing Ticouloute's family (and many other Haitian extended families) are explored.

Family Structure and Kinship Terminology

Haitian Creole terms cover five categories of kinship — by blood, by legal marriage, by folk marriage, by folk adoption (and fosterage), and by ritual act. The Haitian kinship terminology has borrowed most of its terms from the French, but the usages in Haitian and French society are often different (compare Bastien 1961: 486–496). In particular, Haitian families accentuate (by upgrading and otherwise) clusters of relationships which may be of special importance to their households at given phases of household history. Certain relatives may be needed, for example, at the birth, or in case of the illness, or to aid the schooling, of a child.

Ticouloute and his wife, being a legally married couple, interact as *mari* [husband] and *madam* [wife]. Others refer to them as *missié* [Monsieur, or Mr.] and *madam* [Madame, or Mrs.]. In common-law relations, the man refers to his *placée* as *ménage* [girl friend], while she refers to her common-law husband as *mouchem* [boy friend]. In *plaçages* such as Bouch Fobo's households, his friends would ask him about his *tifem* [woman], while they would call her *manzè* ["mam'selle"] (plus her name). Brothers-in-law always call each other by their first names.

Ticouloute today has two *gason* [boys] and three *fi* [girls]. In terms of their relations to each other, these *gason* and *fi* are *frè* and *sè* [brother and sister]. They call their father *papa* and their mother *manmam*. Ticouloute himself refers to his grandfather as *granpapa* and to his grandmother as *granmanmam*; to his great-grandfather as *grangranpapa*, and to his great-grandmother as *grangranmanmam*.

Ticouloute's children refer to uncles and aunts as *mon-onk* or *tonton*, and *ma-tante*, respectively. They refer to their nephews as *neve*; to their nieces as *nies*. Parallel and cross first cousins are known as *cousin gemin* or simply *cousin* or *cousine*, depending upon sex. Second cousins are termed *cousin sougemin* or *cousin loin* or *fanmi* (i.e. *famille*). Respected older cousins are equated with uncles and aunts. The terms *cousin loin*, or "distant cousin," and *fanmi loin* are frequently used for other blood relatives.

In the Ticouloute extended family, as among many other Haitians, twins are referred to as *marassa*. Their parents take special care of them because *marassa* are supposed to have special, supernatural powers. In fact, there is within voodoo a cult of twins (see Herskovits 1937: 144).

Children taken in through folk adoption and fosterage are considered *fanmi, fanmi loin*, or *ti fanmi* (*"petite famille"*) [little family.]

Ticouloute refers to his brothers-in-law as *bofrè* (*beau-frère*) and his sisters-in-law as *belsè* (*belle-soeur*). The children identify the wife of their mother's or father's brother as *ma-tante-par-alliance*; the husband of their father's or mother's sister, correspondingly is *mon-onk-par-alliance*. Ticouloute's father-in-law is his *bopè* (*beau-père*); his mother-in-law is his *belmè* (*belle-mère*). They refer to him as their *bofis* (*beau-fils*); Ticouloute's father and mother might have referred, had they lived, to his wife as their *belfi* (*belle-fille*).

Ritual kinship is sometimes nominal and sometimes carries true responsibilities. Children who share the same godparents are considered as *frè-batem* or *sè-batem*. The godchild and the children of his godparents are also considered to be *frè-* or *sè-batem*. The couple who share the same godparents with another couple are considered *frè-* or *sè-mariage*. For their first communion, children are paired and they are thus *frè-communion* or *sè-communion* to each other. They are all "kin" by nominal ties. *Paren andoyé* and *marin'n andoyé* are the godfather and godmother, respectively, of children who have passed through the *andoyage* baptism. With Christian baptism, the children receive new *paren* and *marin'n*. The godparents refer to their godchildren as *fiel*. The godfather refers to the godmother and the mother of his godchild as *comè*, and to the father as *compè*. The godmother refers to the godfather and the father of her godchild as *compè* and to the mother as *comè*. The father and mother of the child refer to the godmother as *comè*, and to the godfather as *compè*.

Ritual Kinship

As this essay has mentioned repeatedly, ritual kinship, or, better, kinship by "coparenthood" (the *compadrazgo* of the Latin world), can generate strong bonds. There are five forms of ritual kinship which usually carry effective responsibilities.

These can be identified as follows: (a) The *baptême andoyé*. Before Christian baptism of the child, a folk baptism is accomplished. The officiant may be a bush priest[9] or any third person except the father or the mother. The child is given a godfather and godmother, usually young folks or friendly neighbors of humble economic conditions. These *paren andoyés* and *marin'n andoyées* are expected to help the child through his childhood, so far as baby-sitting is concerned, and to render some little services from time to time to the parents. After the child has reached adolescence, he may cut his linkage with his *paren* and *marin'n andoyées* to avoid the derision of other boys. (b) At his Christian baptism, the child is given a godfather and a godmother. They may be of better economic conditions or have the same status as the parents of the child. Those godparents are chosen in anticipation of the child's future. In case of need, they will pay his schooling, board, and room and may have him stay with them. They may help pay the expenses of his marriage or of a trip to New York. The links go beyond mere affection; they meet the child's economic needs. (c) For their wedding, the couple has godparents. They are for moral support and for strenghtening existing friendships. (d) Voodoo baptism takes place at any time after Christian baptism. By this baptism, the child receives a *loa-mait-tête* [literally, a Master of the Head *Loa*][10] and is given voodoo godparents. This is the first stage in voodoo initiation. The role of the *loa-mait-tête* is to guide and protect the child. The role of the godparents is to make sure that the engagement they have taken on behalf of the child is being followed from year to year. (e) When the child becomes an adult, he may want to spiritually marry a spirit in order to gain upward mobility in the voodoo hierarchy. On this occasion he also gets voodoo godparents. This accentuates friendship and solidarity between the godchild and his voodoo godparents.

Certain events and rites of passages are voodoo or Catholic/Protestant church domains. Sometimes Catholic and voodoo rites are used in parallel for the event. Table 3 shows the separation and the intermingling of voodoo/Catholic/Protestant domains.

Some domains such as *plaçage* and sickness of a supernatural origin may be entirely voodoo, while First Communion and Confirmation are solely Catholic domains. The Catholic and the voodoo baptism are two domains emically but one etically, or, to restate this in nontechnical terminology, in terms of native perceptions as opposed to external forms. However, Catholic marriage is formally different from voodoo marriage; we are dealing here with two distinct types of marital tie.

[9] A layman who is able to read prayers and chant litanies; see also Herskovits 1937: 144. On folk priests in colonial Haiti see Laguerre 1973d.

[10] Compare Herskovits's discussion of the Afro-Brazilian *candomble*, especially the rituals of initiation (Herskovits 1966: 232–235). In these rituals the tutelary deity possesses the novice as the "master of the head." [E.M.S.]

. Religious domains

Ritual event	Voodoo	Catholic	Protestant
1. Baptism	+	+	+
2. First Communion	−	+	−
3. Confirmation	−	+	−
4. Marriage	+	+	+
5. *Plaçage*	+	−	−
6. Funeral	+	+	+
7. Illness	+	−	−
8. Memorial	+	+	−
9. Novena	+	+	−

Rules of Familial Behavior

Well-defined customs and, in part, accepted formal law, govern many aspects of Haitian family behavior.

The pattern of marriage throughout rural Haiti is most often between people of the same village who are not related by known consanguineous, legal (affinal), or fictional (ritual) ties. Parents take great care not to let daughters marry an outsider whose past they do not know. They would avoid having a daughter marry someone who already has a *placée*. Although exogamy, the avoidance of marriage with traceable kin, is the rule, among certain groups of mulattos, especially in the far southwest of Haiti, there is some tendency toward endogamy.

Legal marriage and *plaçage* followed by a legal acknowledgement of paternity generate bilateral kin ties. Legitimate and formally recognized children take their father's name. In other cases, and particularly in relationships where the father is married to someone other than the mother, matrilateral ties predominate. The "unrecognized" children socialize more with their maternal cousins than with their half brothers and sisters.

In the *lakou*, patrilocal residence was customary; it required much adaptation from young wives. Elsewhere it is most commonly neolocal. In the *lakou* and village, occupations were commonly transmitted from father to son (folk physician, blacksmith, shoemaker, etc.) and from mother to daughter (midwife).

In general, the extended family is bilateral, and children pay equal attention to the relatives of their father and to those of their mother. However, authority in the household rests in the husband's hands whether or not he is a regular resident (see Comhaire-Sylvain 1961: 203–

205). He is the head, even though he might not be the breadwinner. His consent is needed for any major decision concerning his wife and the children. Usually, he provides his wife with money to run a small business.

Conflicts between husband and wife are resolved within the extended family whenever possible. Their godparents or any relative living close by would come and give them some advice, seeking reconciliation. Most often, conflicts stop at this level. If not, a brother or an uncle will be called upon to settle the matter.

According to customary law, when there is an internal family conflict, three possibilities are open to solve it: to call upon older folks; to call upon a folk lawyer (emphasis is put on reconciliation and unity of the extended family); or to go to the village court. When there is an external conflict, elders from both sides meet. If they cannot reach a conclusion, they go to the village court.

In matters of inheritance, the brothers and sisters get together and divide the legacy among themselves. If they cannot come to a decision, they call upon uncles, aunts, and other older relatives to solve their dilemma. If they still cannot reach a conclusion, they go to the village court; however, this will cause jealousies and divisions within the extended family (see also Bastien 1961: 484–486).

In the household, daughters are expected to help their mother and to care for younger brothers and sisters, while sons help in the fields. Both sexes learn expected behavior at home. Sisters pass on dresses to younger sisters; if they are the same size they wear each other's dresses. The same happens among brothers. If a couple has only one child, or two children of opposite sex, they pass on outgrown clothes to a younger cousin or godchild.

Within each household, parents or godparents do whatever they can to pay for the schooling of boys. They pay less attention to the education of girls, unless the couple is economically very capable. The boy is considered the prospective head of the household if the father dies. Through his education he can get a better job with a good salary — and he is expected to help the younger brothers and sisters. Since there is no Bureau of Welfare in Haiti, sons are expected to take care of their parents during their old age. If their godparents have no children, they are expected to help them also. The parents expect that the daughter may help if her husband allows it. But in the case of the sons, there is no *if*.

The patterns of coresidence, particularly child fosterage, are shaped by cultural tradition but initiated by needed mobility for schooling or in the wake of a parent's death. Most economically capable families foster a young relative or godchild, as we have already illustrated in detail. In fosterage for mobility, parents in rural areas place their children of school age, as a first stage, at their sister's, brother's, aunt's, cousin's, uncle's, godparent's, or any other relative's home so they may go to village elementary schools. At high school age, these same children will be placed at some relative's home in Port-au-Prince. By tradition, the house of a relative is the house of any other relative ("*kay fanmim, se kay moin*"). This is why one would feel free to move into a relative's home if one were incapable of renting a house. A cousin or any relative may also stay at a relative's when he moves to a city looking for a job, without having to pay anything for his room. By custom, the host would not accept any money from a relative. However, that person is expected to pay for food if he can.

It was customary for peasants to bury their dead in the garden or family plot. Since the American occupation, under state and church encouragement, people now bury their dead in the cemetery. Unbaptized children are still buried in the garden or family plot.

Integrating Values: Reciprocities and Religious Reinforcements

Haitian extended families, such as Ticouloute's, are effective corporate bodies not only through well-defined structures and rules of behavior but also through the influence of paramount integrating values. Three are most significant.

What holds the whole family together is not merely a simple question of coresidence and propinquity but primarily the obligations that one feels toward one's kinsmen. Close residence certainly plays an important role, in that it allows relatives to meet and help each other on an everyday basis. Close residence also allows children to eat and sleep at their relatives' homes from time to time; and consequently they learn to care about their relatives and to strengthen their kinship ties with them.

Economic solidarity also keeps the family together. This consists of financial aid as well as the sharing of food, clothes, and other resources. To work land and to organize a *coumbite* (see Herskovits 1937: 70–76; also Métraux 1971), one gets help from other members of the family. This solidarity has different patterns. For example, a peasant would expect his relative who is living in Port-au-Prince to take care of his child of high-school age. The relative in Port-au-Prince expects his relative in New York to help pay the bill if one of his children is sick. Peasants expect their peasant relatives to help in the *coumbite* or in harvesting the products of their fields. The peasant is expected to buy his produce from his relatives rather than from someone else. This solidarity is strengthened by reciprocal help: for example, support at the time of an electoral campaign.

Religious faith plays an important role in family unity even when its members espouse different beliefs. Grandmothers and mothers are church-goers. Both Christians and voodooists celebrate the memory of the dead annually. They pay for a mass during November which most relatives attend. The voodooists additionally hold a *manger-les-morts*. Both pray daily for the dead and for living relatives, for the young and the old, for those who are living in the rural areas as well as for those who are living in cities, for those who are living in Haiti as well as for those who are living outside the island. By such daily prayer, they represent symbolically, to themselves, the image of a united extended family; they express, in this way, their solidarity with other members of their extended family.

HISTORICAL AND SITUATIONAL FACTORS IN THE HAITIAN EXTENDED FAMILY

The study of Ticouloute's extended family has revealed great cultural complexity. It has illustrated the workings of an institution of pervasive importance to Haitians.

This institution cannot be understood in synchronic terms alone; conversely, its traditional elements have meaning only as they function within contemporary situations. For these reasons and also to reinterpret our heritage in Jean Price-Mars's terms, I will sketch a developmental theory of the Haitian extended family.

In my opinion, its forms and functions are the result of an ongoing Creolization process of African slaves, starting with the ecology of the slave-plantation system (Laguerre 1970: 48–65). Even though we know that the slaves came from Africa, which country provided the most slaves is still a matter of controversy. There is, however, some linguistic evidence pertaining to the persistence of remnants of the Fon language in the Haitian Creole dialect. Montilus, after doing fieldwork in Haiti and spending five years in Dahomey, suggests that the cult of the dead within the *lakou* context is of Dahomean origin (Montilus 1973).

The Africans brought with them their world view but could hardly, and in fact did not, reproduce their family systems trait by trait. Even the *maroons*, or fugitives from the slave plantations, because of the shortage of women and the peculiar conditions under which they conducted guerrilla warfare, were forced to develop new strategies as far as family organization was concerned (Laguerre 1973a). Their West African cultural heritage, slavery, and the ecology of the plantation system shaped the development of the Black family structure day by day. Nevertheless, the slaves retained some cultural aspects of their African heritage such as voodoo and, more particularly, ancestor worship and their solidarity with their kinsmen.

The lack of women and the sharing of Black women with colonists and indentured servants reduced to a minimum the extension of polygamy. The most common mating forms were monogamous *plaçage*, church marriage (mainly among slaves belonging to the plantations of religious orders), and polygamous *plaçage*, which was restricted mainly to Black overseers, medicine men, some skilled slaves, and voodoo priests (cf. Laguerre 1973b: 113).

The plantation formed the matrix within which the extended family could function. Most often some members of the same extended family belonged to the same plantation owner (Trouillot 1957: 29). Within the same geographical unit, they could exercise and manifest their solidarity toward each other. For example, the grandmother unable to do fieldwork stayed in her hut and took care of the children. Dutertre (1667: 518) remarked that, in the slave quarter, the slaves tended to build their huts close to their relatives' huts. There was a common practice also for slaves to let kinfolk, especially young relatives, godchildren, and old relatives, live with them.

Godparenthood is an institution which was developed during the colonial period. The godparents were either friends or relatives and usually had a higher status in the slave community than the parents. When the master decided to sell a husband and wife to different masters, one of the godparents would take care of the child. Then the child would have a suitable place to stay. The godparents were recognized as having some power in the slave community, or as having good relations with the master. Indeed, some of the godparents were free men.

The institution of *andoyage* is also a remnant of the colonial heritage. In this plantation society, the priests were not always available for the sacrament of baptism. So the children were first baptised by a folk priest (*pè savan*) a slave who was able to imitate as closely as he could the Christian baptismal rite. As some of the slave children could not be baptized before they were eight to ten years old, they had *andoyé* god-parents which, in those circumstances, had functions similar to those of the godparents of Christian baptism.

Close neighbors and friends were considered as *fanmi loin*. Their existence and incorporation as *fanmi loin* is attested by Labat (1742: Vol. 4, p. 186). They are among people consulted at the occasion of the marriage of a member of the family. The godparents are also consulted on this occasion.

After Independence, agrarian reform took place (Bastien 1961: 478–480). On the land the peasants received, they developed — perhaps reinstituted — a kind of familial settlement similar to existing patterns in Dahomey. The comparison of this pattern with the Dahomean pattern has been studied by Guerin Montilus (1973: 42). The *lakou* was composed of the households of a father and his sons. The houses formed a circle with the voodoo temple in the middle. The authority of the patriarch was respected. The *lakou* provided a geographical unit within which primary blood-related kin could interact. The annual voodoo service for the dead strengthened the functional unity of the extended family.

This *lakou* system has been declining since the beginning of the century because of continuing divisions of the land. Lack of land has forced children to move out. By buying land far from the original settlement, and by a continual migration to villages and cities, families dispersed, so that the *lakou* is slowly disappearing. But those raised in a *lakou*, despite the disappearance of the *lakou* as a geographical unit, kept their ties with their *lakou*-mates. Once every year, all of them would assemble in the *lakou* for the commemorative service known as *manger-les-morts*, at the base of the biggest tree (usually the *mappou*), the link between the living and the dead.

Purposeful migrations to the cities have provided the extended family with a larger spatial setting than the *lakou* and stimulated other kinds of solidarity. Those who migrated to cities acted as hosts to their relatives when the latter came in their turn. They would also provide a place for young relatives who came to the cities in order to pursue secondary and even university educations. The city people are consulted by their country relatives on the choice of a physician or a lawyer.

Migration from rural areas to cities has caused the development of a household pattern in which the father is often absent. This does not mean matrifocality, however; rather, the husband stays in the rural area to work his land and comes once every week or two to his home. He still provides money and food, and his authority is unbroken. The wife is usually sent to stay in a city or village to take care of the children while they are in school, or to start a small business. Sometimes the arrangement is polygamous.

In Port-au-Prince, some genuine matrifocality is observable.

Most recently, migration overseas has provided a new challenge to family solidarity, which has, however, persisted to a remarkable degree. The migrants' remittances help pay for the migrations of relatives and for the support of their kinfolk in Haiti.

FINDINGS AND NEEDS FOR FURTHER RESEARCH

In summary, the Haitian extended family, as indicated by prior study and through this essay on Ticouloute and his kinfolk, is a body of consanguineous, affinal, and ritual relatives, usually bilateral. Historically associated with a particular geographical unit, the *lakou*, which is now disappearing, the extended family continues to be of pervasive functional importance. It is a vehicle of mutual aid, reinforced by ritual and religious sentiments, which operates effectively both in rural settings and in urban ones.

Various factors have affected the development and functioning of the extended family in Haiti: the West African cultural heritage of the slaves, the slavery system itself, the ecology of plantations, agrarian reforms after Independence, the ambiguous status of voodoo, the socioeconomic exploitation of the peasants by national ruling elites, and domestic and foreign migration. Despite these manifold forces, the Haitian extended family has remained a functioning, integrated, and situationally adaptive institution.

Much remains to be done to understand the extended family, and to utilize this understanding to meet Haiti's problems of chronic underdevelopment.

First, a series of monographic studies of extended families in different parts of Haiti and in different social strata is essential. The approach of this essay, combining biographical, household-historical, statistical, structural, and functional data, indicates what needs to be done systematically.

Second, the detailed analyses of particular family functions need investigation on the basis of concrete case material. What are the actual ways in which economic production is organized by families? What are the patterns, the strengths, and the problems of child care? What are the actual procedures through which family conflicts are resolved?

Third, special attention is needed to examine variability and change in these institutions. To what extent does urban slum life create new patterns? Conversely, what functions do urban extended families play in generating employment, entrepreneurship, and business management? How have contacts with Port-au-Prince and New York affected women's attitudes toward the authority of husbands, or toward birth control?

Fourth, the interrelationships between familial and other major folk institutions in Haiti need systematic study. In particular, a careful examination of voodoo ritual kinship would give a better understanding of voodoo communities.

And finally, the relations between actual family institutions, familial behavior, governmental laws and practices, and Haiti's immense economic and social needs have to be examined carefully. For example, a study of the social contexts and folk techniques for avoiding pregnancy is an essential prerequisite for any systematic family planning concomitant with Haiti's economic development. It is hoped that this may yield useful guides to policy and practice for the Haitian people.

REFERENCES

BASTIEN, RÉMY
   1951   *La familia rural Haitiana* [The Haitian rural family]. Mexico City: Libra.
   1961   Haitian rural family organization. *Social and Economic Studies* 10: 478–510.
COMHAIRE-SYLVAIN, SUZANNE
   1958   Courtship, marriage and *plasaj* at Kenscoff, Haiti. *Social and Economic Studies* 7: 210–233.
   1961   The household at Kenscoff, Haiti. *Social and Economic Studies* 10: 192–222.
DAVIS, HAROLD P.
   1936   *Black democracy. The story of Haiti* (revised edition). New York: Dodge.
DE RONCERAY, HUBERT
   1969   Le changement social dans les familles haïtiennes: familles urbaines [Social change in Haitian families: urban families]. *Les cahiers du centre d'investigations en sciences sociales* 3 (4): 1–34.
DORSINVILLE, MAX H.
   1969   "Haïti et ses institutions (de l'époque coloniale à 1957) [Haiti and its institutions (from the colonial period to 1957)]," in *Papers of the Conference on Research and Resources of Haiti*. Edited by Richard P. Schaedel, 441–485. New York: Research Institute for the Study of Man.
DUTERTRE, JEAN BAPTISTE
   1667   *Histoire générale des Antilles habitées par les Français* [General history of the French-inhabited Antilles]. Paris: Tijolly.
FORTES, MEYER
   1958   "Introduction," in *The developmental cycle in domestic groups*. Edited by Jack Goody, 1–14. Papers in Social Anthropology 1. Cambridge: Cambridge University Press.
HERSKOVITS, MELVILLE
   1937   *Life in a Haitian valley*. New York: Knopf.
   1966   *The New World Negro*. Edited by Frances S. Herskovits. Bloomington: Indiana University Press.
LABAT, JEAN BAPTISTE
   1742   *Nouveau voyage aux isles de l'Amérique* [New voyage to the American islands], volume four. Paris: G. Cavelier.

LAGUERRE, MICHEL
1970 Brassages ethniques et émergence de la culture haïtienne [Ethnic admixtures and the emergence of Haitian culture]. *Laurentian University Review* 3 (2): 48–65.
1973a "Anatomy of the Haitian maroon communities: maroons as a cultural and political force." Paper presented at the IXth International Congress of Ethnological and Anthropological Sciences, Chicago.
1973b "Nativism in Haiti: the politics of voodoo." Unpublished M.A. thesis, Roosevelt University, Chicago.
1973c The place of voodoo in the social structure of Haiti. *Caribbean Quarterly* 19 (3).
1973d The failure of Christianity among the slaves (in Haiti). *Freeing the Spirit* 2 (4): 10–24. Washington, D.C.
1974a An ecological approach to voodoo. *Freeing the Spirit* 3 (1): 4–12. Washington, D.C.
1974b Voodoo as religious and revolutionary ideology. *Freeing the Spirit* 3 (1): 23–28. Washington, D.C.
LEGERMAN, CAROLINE J.
1969 "Haitian peasant, plantation and urban lower-class family and kinship organizations: observations and comments," in *Papers of the Conference on Research and Resources of Haiti*. Edited by Richard P. Schaedel, 71–84. New York: Research Institute for the Study of Man.
1971 [1962] "Kin groups in a Haitian market," in *Peoples and cultures of the Caribbean*. Edited by Michael M. Horowitz, 382–399. Garden City, N.Y.: Natural History Press. (Originally published 1962 in *Man* 62: 145–149.)
MÉTRAUX, ALFRED
1971 "Cooperative labor groups in Haiti," in *Peoples and cultures of the Caribbean*. Edited by Michael M. Horowitz, 318–339. Garden City, N.Y.: Natural History Press. (Originally published 1951 in *Making of a living in the Marbial Valley (Haiti)*, by A. Métraux, 67–86. Educational Clearing House Occasional Paper in Education. Paris: United Nations Educational, Scientific and Cultural Organization.)
MILLSPAUGH, ARTHUR C.
1931 *Haiti under American control. 1915–1930.* Boston: World Peace Foundation.
MONTILUS, GUERIN
1973 "Mythes, écologie, acculturation en Haïti [Myths, ecology, and acculturation in Haiti]." Unpublished Ph.D. thesis, University of Zurich, Zurich.
MORAL, PAUL
1961 *Le paysan haïtien: étude sur la vie rurale en Haïti* [The Haitian peasant: a study of rural life in Haiti]. Paris: G. P. Maisonneuve et Larose.
MOSCOSO, R. M.
1943 *Catologus florae domingensis*, parte I: *spermatophyta* [Catalogue of Dominican flora, part one: spermatophytes]. New York: Universidad de Santo Domingo.

PRICE-MARS, JEAN
1928 [1954] *Ainsi parla l'oncle* [Thus spake the uncle]. New York: Parapsychology Foundation. (Authorized facsimile of 1928 edition produced 1972 by University Microfilms, Ann Arbor, Mich.)

SIMPSON, GEORGE E.
1942 Sexual and familial institutions in northern Haiti. *American Anthropologist* 44: 655–674.
1971 "The belief system of Haitian *vodun*," in *Peoples and cultures of the Caribbean*. Edited by Michael M. Horowitz, 491–521. Garden City, N.Y.: Natural History Press. (Originally published 1945 in *American Anthropologist* 47: 35–59.)

STYCOS, MAYONE J.
1964 Haitian attitudes toward family size. *Human Organization* 23: 42–47.

TROUILLOT, HENOCK
1957 La condition de la femme de couleur à Saint Domingue [The condition of women of color in Santo Domingo]. *Revue de la société haïtienne d'histoire, de géographie, et de géologie* 103 (January–February).

Delegation of Parental Roles in West Africa and the West Indies

ESTHER N. GOODY

ABSTRACT

This paper discusses an important aspect of family behavior in Black societies. It deals with contemporary patterns of child fostering, with both kin and nonkin, with *crisis* fostering distinguished from *purposive* fostering. The geographical areas within which these contemporary patterns are considered are West Africa (northern and southern Ghana) and the West Indies and Caribbean region (Jamaica, Dominica, and British Honduras), with comparisons between these two general areas. Most foster parents in the West Indies are in the grandparental generation (lineal kin), and in West Africa in the parental generation (collateral kin). Male foster parents are common in West Africa and rare in the West Indies. The paper also includes a discussion of fostering and "daily minding" of children among West African and West Indian parents resident in England.

There are divergences in the rationales for fostering between West African and West Indian parents, both at home and abroad. In the West Indies, fostering, usually beginning in infancy, involves the transfer of emotional loyalties, whereas in West Africa, fostering of an older child involves kinship reciprocities and often also provides consciously sought educational or economic benefits to the child, especially when it is fostered by nonkin.

INTRODUCTION

The ethnographic literature on West Africa contains many references to the sending of children to kin to grow up away from their own parents (Skinner 1964; Oppong 1965; Cohen 1969; Azu 1974; Goody 1961, 1966, 1969, 1971a, 1973; Muir and Goody 1972). A number of "explanations" have been offered for this widespread practice, which can never be seen solely as an economic, micropolitical, or kinship institution, and often seems to share aspects of all of these. In all the societies for which it is reported, the fostering of children by kin also provides proxy parents in cases where the family of orientation has been scattered by death or divorce of the parents. Such a rescue operation may be termed *crisis fostering* to distinguish it from *purposive fostering* arranged while the family is intact, which is entered into with the intention of securing some benefit to the child, his parents, the foster parents, or perhaps to all.

Many reports on West Indian domestic and kinship organization also include a reference to sending children to kin to be looked after. Typically an infant goes to his mother's mother or perhaps to a mother's sister and is often brought up to regard this foster mother as his mother, using "mother" as a term of address for her and calling his own mother by whatever term her siblings use (see R. T. Smith 1956: 143; Clarke 1966: 142, 179; Spens 1969: 278 ff.). These accounts suggest that the rearing of children by kin in the West Indies tends to be the result of the inability of the parents to provide proper care (whether because they have no joint home or because the mother must work full time), a situation that I have called crisis fostering in discussing the West African material. However, there are also hints of purposive fostering in the West Indies; Clarke speaks of "schoolchildren" who are ostensibly taken into a household to help in exchange for food, clothing, and a chance to go to school. One such child she encountered was treated much like the other children in the house — all of whom helped with chores — but she alone did not go to school (Clarke 1966: 177). Among the Black Carib of Guatemala, Gonzalez describes the sending of young boys to families in town, where they take an increasing share of jobs around the house and learn both literate skills and town ways (Gonzalez 1969: 54 ff.). Again, Horowitz refers more than once to children staying with kin in cases where their parents are living together on Martinique (1967: 49). But on the whole the picture is one of fostering as a means of coping with children of dissolved or nonresidential unions. Indeed, M. G. Smith (1962b: 80) writes as though this was the only circumstance under which children would be sent to be reared by kin and treats fostering in the way he does household composition, as a reflex of the mating forms.

In both West Africa and the West Indies, then, children are sent to be reared by kin when the family of orientation cannot, for some reason, manage. And in both areas, fostering is used as a means of widening the education of a child, of providing relatives with companionship and assistance, and of strengthening ties with kin who are relatively well off. In the West Indies it appears to be *crisis fostering* which is most prominent, while in West Africa *purposive fostering* is probably more important.

The question of whether the West Indian institution is a "survival" from West Africa via the slaves brought to Caribbean plantations is not relevant at this point. I am concerned with analyzing the present constraints and supports of behavior, whatever their origin.

Although people from these two regions seem to have very similar institutions with respect to child rearing by kin, they behave very differently when they come as immigrants to the United Kingdom. In a recent study in four London boroughs, we have documented the very high percentage of West African children sent to English foster parents (Goody and Muir 1972). Less direct information from several sources indicates that West Indians virtually never send their children to English foster parents (though the local authority may occasionally place children of disturbed or broken homes with their own foster parents as a welfare measure). Instead, West Indian mothers prefer to send their young children to a "nanny" who takes several children into her home from early morning until six in the evening. Payment is on either an hourly or a weekly basis, and the mother is expected to do all laundry for the child and must often provide food. These women are also known as "daily minders." Probably the large majority of women who do daily minding are themselves West Indian, and it appears likely (though reliable figures are not available) that the majority of children sent to them are also West Indian.

The problem I wish to pose here is this: why should two groups with apparently similar institutions at home for coping with children outside the natal family of orientation react in such different ways to the constraints of living in an urban environment abroad? In order to be able to answer such a question, we must look more closely at both traditional and contemporary fostering in these two areas, as well as at the circumstances of life in London for both groups of immigrants. It may be that the parents of each group are seeking different goals in coming to England and, more immediately, have different reasons for delegating the care of their children to others. Or the choice between forms of child care may simply be one of economics: one mode or the other may be more expensive and require more resources. Or it may be that we have been over hasty in seeing the traditional forms as they appear in West Africa and the West Indies as essentially similar. Perhaps they function rather differently at a basic level, and in the immigrant situation this difference gives rise to the variations in adaptations to the new environment which we have found.

FOSTERING IN WEST AFRICA

Despite the relatively small number of West African societies for which there are detailed, numerical data on frequency and distribution of foster children, it is becoming clear that this is a pan-West Africa phenomenon for which no locally appropriate functional explanation will suffice. While it is perfectly true that fostering "fits" stratified societies such as the Hausa and Bornu because it is one avenue for the establishment of client relationships, it also appears between commoners in Gonja and among the relatively egalitarian Ga. Similarly, where wives are kept in seclusion by well-to-do Muslims, the need to have a child as a link between households and with the market is pressing; it is neatly met for those without children of their own by their taking a foster child. But fostering is also common among pagan and Christian Yoruba, where no such explanation is appropriate. Or again, in contemporary towns and cities, one often comes across children staying with kin, helping in the house and attending school. But African fostering cannot have arisen as a means of avoiding expensive boarding-school fees. I myself first came upon fostering among the Gonja of northern Ghana in a town with no school, and where indeed few children, and scarcely any adults, had had a chance to attend one. The Dagomba, also of northern Ghana, make use of fostering to train a daughter's child in the traditional skill of the paternal *dang* (Oppong 1965). The neighboring Gonja have many of the same skills and a high incidence of fostering, but only rarely do they use the institution as the basis of apprenticeship. In the west of the kingdom, the Gonja do, however, see the sending of a son to grow up with his mother's brother as one form of arranging for the mother's care when she eventually returns in old age to her natal kin. The son already there can give her a home and can farm for her, in addition to the support which her brother is morally obliged to contribute. The spatial distribution of marriages is narrower in eastern Gonja, and a wife's "retirement" less likely to mean her departure to a distant village. Perhaps for this reason, the fostering of a son with his mother's brother is much less common in the eastern divisions.

One could go on citing similarities and differences between local variations of fostering in West Africa. The general point should be clear — there are a wide range of specific "reasons" or "functions," each of which makes excellent sense in its own context, but no one (or, indeed, several) of which can be made to "account" for the widespread occurrence of institutionalized fostering of children by kin in West Africa.

Yet if one considers other culture areas, this practice is strange enough to warrant some kind of "explanation."[1] Few Europeans or Americans would readily take a sibling's or cousin's child into their home for several years, or send their own son or daughter to an aunt or grandparent from the age of five until they were grown up. Purposive fostering, the placing of children with kin to fulfill one's obligations and at the same time gain for them the opportunity to grow up in a different family, often in a different town, does not seem to occur in Indo-European societies. There are partial equivalents of a functional kind (*compadrazgo* and other forms of fictional kinship) but not the actual removal of a boy or girl for the whole of childhood and adolescence, as we commonly find in West African societies.

Why is there this very general difference between the two sets of societies? What kind of underlying factor is common to all the various West African groups which have different particular reasons for fostering their children?[2] It must be a very general factor, because these groups differ widely in language, social structure, political organization, and religious institutions. The simple answer is that fostering reflects the claims, rights, and obligations of members of an extended kin group. Given the norm that kin have to share rights and obligations over resources, the fostering of children becomes only a special case of such sharing.

Fostering Among the Gonja of Northern Ghana

This is entirely explicit for the Gonja of northern Ghana. Rights of siblings over one another's children are expressed in two models. One model allocates the first daughter of a marriage to the father's sister as a foster daughter, in recognition of her role in establishing the bride in her new home. The father's sister will be informed of the birth of this first daughter and should send *kola*[3] to the naming ceremony and provide waist beads for the little girl. When the child has reached the "age of

---

[1] Though it is by no means unique; see studies of fostering and adoption in Eastern Oceania in V. Carroll, editor, 1970, as well as the Caribbean material.

[2] There is another, equally important, question, with which I am not concerned here: what accounts for the fact that fostering is institutionalized in some West African societies, while it appears to be absent from others? This question is more difficult than might appear, because our work in London suggests that even those groups which do not foster in West Africa are prepared to do so in the United Kingdom. In other words, the underlying factor is present in these ostensibly nonfostering groups too, but there appears to be some alternative institution which takes the place of fostering within the traditional system. But all the prerequisites are there, in both types of West African Society.

[3] Seed of the Kola tree (genus Cola).

sense" (*e kø kinyesheng*), the father's sister comes with a gift of cloth for the mother and for the child and takes the little girl home with her. She will remain with her aunt until she is ready to marry, suitors paying their respects to both the foster mother and the true parents. There is a term of reference for female foster parent, *tchepe*, but the child uses the term for father's sister in addressing her.[4] She never calls the father's sister "mother" nor ceases to call her own mother by the familiar *maa* form for "mother."

The other model for Gonja fostering designates the second or third son as a foster child of the mother's brother. A man who wishes to insure his rights over a sister's son may insist on paying the expenses of the naming ceremony which takes place seven days after birth. Otherwise he will come to "beg" for the child some time during its infancy or early childhood. As with a female foster child, the boy does not join his foster parent until he is considered old enough to "have sense," which means around the age of six or seven. Once a boy has joined his foster father he should remain until old enough to marry, learning from him the skills of farming, hunting, and house building which are necessary for all adult men. The foster father ought to help the youth to marry, or he may offer him a horse or a gun rather than a wife. Thereafter the boy may either remain with his mother's brother or return to his father; among Muslims and members of the ruling estate, men virtually always return in the end to their father's town, but commoners may opt to remain with a mother's brother. The term of reference for male foster parent is *nyinipe*, but in address the appropriate kinship term is used and not the term for father, which continues to be applied to the real father.

In practice, a wide range of relatives serve as foster parents in Gonja, but these two models are the stated forms that act as charters for other claims. Siblings all say that they "own" (*wø*) each other's children, which means both that they are responsible for them and that they have claims over them. Unless there is some reason why the parents cannot manage their children, perhaps through poverty, lack of discipline, or the breakup of the natal family of orientation, the initiative in arranging fostering is usually left to the would-be foster parent. Only when he or she presses his or her rightful claim will the child actually be sent. Occasionally a child is sent to an officeholder or to a Koranic teacher. In these cases it is more likely to be the ends of the parent which are the critical factors.

It is characteristic of West African societies that the "sibling group" is not thought of as confined to children of the same mother and father. This inclusiveness is usually reflected in the terminology, which designates

4   Or, if with another relative, the kin term ordinarily used for that person.

the children of sisters (in matrilineal systems), or of brothers (in patrilineal systems), or of brothers and sisters (among the bilateral Gonja) as themselves siblings. For instance, Fortes (1949) writes of Tallensi brothers (*sunzøp*) as in some contexts including all male members of the agnatic lineage of a man's own generation. In Gonja, *all* of a person's relatives of the same generation are either "older sibling" or "younger sibling." Claims on the children of classificatory siblings are also success-fully made in Gonja, though only rarely when the relationship is more distant than that of first cousins. It would seem to be in those cases where the terminology is open-ended and the norms of siblings' rights and obligations very generally phrased that the recognition of claims over children serves to define the limits of effective obligation. Rearing a sibling's child has this function because, in addition to the formal moral obligation of kinship, the fostering relationship itself creates what I have elsewhere called the "reciprocities of rearing" (Goody 1971b). That is, specific, reciprocal, obligations of care and support are built up during childhood; the foster parent is seen as looking after the child and feeding and training it, and these acts create a debt which the child must later be prepared to repay. Thus, where second- or third-order relationships might cease to be considered binding in and of themselves, when they are reinforced by fostering a second set of obligations comes into play which is compelling in its own right. Furthermore, the fostered child grows up in a household of classificatory siblings (the foster parents' children) with whom he or she is on effective terms of full sibship, rather than the more distant relationship which exists between distant kin who meet only occasionally.

In traditional West African societies, then, fostering depended on claims made against and honored by kin. At the same time, the sending of foster children between elementary families served to strengthen the bonds between kin by superimposing specific claims on the more general ones which tend to define the roles of distant relatives. An illuminating comparison might be with systematically practiced cross-cousin marriage; indeed the diagram Yalman (1967: 154) uses to indicate the claims of cross-cousin marriage in a Kandyan Sinhalese village would serve equally well to illustrate the claims of fostering (Figure 1). As with cross-cousin marriage, it would be a mistake to expect that fostering will always occur between the children of primary kin (see Goody 1973).

In Table 1 data on relationship of foster parents are given from four different studies, representing in all seven communities from eastern, central, and western Gonja. The sex of the fostered child is given in parentheses for each study. Several points emerge from these figures.

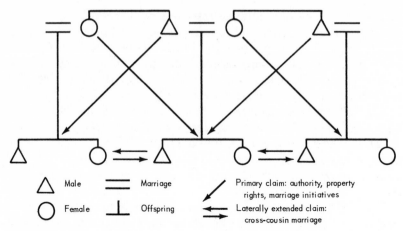

Figure 1. The interconnections and lateral extensions of customary claims: Kandvan Sinhalese. (Modified from Yalman 1967)

First, in all the studies, a very substantial proportion of foster parents come from the parental generation (between 39 and 59 percent). This should be borne in mind for comparison with the West Indian pattern of fostering. Next, if we compare the proportion of male and female foster children resident with a grandparent (real or classificatory), we find that it is the girls who are much more likely to be sent to someone in their grandparents' generation (50 percent), while for boys this only happened 20 percent of the time. This same pattern is found in some of the southern Ghana samples. The sending of girls to a "grandmother" fits with their training in a domestic role, for they are expected to take over household tasks as well as provide companionship for the old women. Old men, on the other hand, are fed and looked after by their daughters or daughters-in-law, and a boy cannot be expected to fill a man's economic role. Finally, only in the men's marriage survey (sample 4) were there children sent to foster parents who were not kin. Indeed, only in two of the three communities represented in the men's marriage survey did this occur. These boys went either to the household of a chief (six cases) or to a Koranic teacher (five cases, all in western Gonja). No girls went to nonkin in any of the communities studied.

Table 1. Gonja, northern Ghana: generation of foster parent for four samples

Sample	Total		Source of foster parents							
			Grandparents' generation		Parents' generation		Child's generation		Nonkin	
	Number	Percent	Number	Percent	Number	Percent	Number	Percent	Number	Percent
Buipe census (children: m and f)[a]	34	100.0	13	38.0	20	59.0	1	3.0	0	—
Kpembe core sample (children: m and f)[b]	31	100.0	15	48.0	12	39.0	4	13.0	0	—
Bole/Daboya sample (adults: f)[c]	77	100.0	39	51.0	35	45.0	3	4.0	0	—
Men's marriage survey (adults: m)[d]	65	100.0	13	20.0	37	57.0	4	6.0	11	17.0

[a] Old Buipe (1956).

[b] These are all the fostered children in two sections of the divisional capital of Kpembe (eastern Gonja) (1964).

[c] The Bole sample consisted of all adult women in randomly selected compounds in the western Gonja divisional capital of Bole; the Daboya sample consisted of all the adult women in nine selected compounds in the central Gonja divisional capital of Daboya (1965).

[d] This survey was carried out in three divisional capitals of eastern, central, and western Gonja and in surrounding villages. The informants were all adult men in selected compounds (1966).

Fostering in Southern Ghana

I must stress at the outset that most of my own work in West Africa has been with a relatively remote group, the Gonja, on whom the industrial age has hardly begun to make an impact. The coastal peoples to the south have, on the other hand, been within the orbit of European trade and all that this implies since the beginning of the seaborne trade with Europe in the late fifteenth century. I have been able to do little work directly with coastal peoples apart from making brief surveys in four communities representing three different language groups in southern Ghana. The following remarks draw on these surveys as well as on interviews with West Africans in London and on two current books: Dr. C. Oppong's *Marriage in a matrilineal elite* (1974) and Gladys Azu's *The Ga family and social change* (1974). Although the documentation for the coastal areas is incomplete, the picture is fairly clear.

Briefly, there appears to be a tendency to shift from fostering by kin to the arrangement of "fostering" with strangers who can provide either training in modern skills or a chance to gain familiarity with urban, Western ways. In the Ewe, Krobo, and Fanti communities which I looked at briefly in southern Ghana, daughters were sent to live with and "serve" women who baked bread for sale, seamstresses, and traders; sons went to fishermen, carpenters, fitters, and masons. Where such teachers were available within the kin group they were selected for preference, but in a number of cases they were not, and an arrangement was made with a friend or someone of good reputation who could train the child. My impression was that availability of a suitable "master" could determine the choice of skill to which the child would be apprenticed. For Ga boys, there appears to be a similar pattern of choice between a kinsman or a local expert of good repute (Azu 1974).

For girls, in addition to skills in sewing, baking, and trading, there has evolved the institution of the "housemaid." I say evolved, because there does not appear to have been anything similar in the traditional societies of West Africa, with the possible exception of girls who were lent to a creditor as surety for a debt.[5] These children (they might also be boys, though apparently this was less common) are referred to in the classical ethnographic literature as having been "pawned," and there seems to be a word in many if not all of the West African languages to distinguish this

---

[5] A further possible exception may have occurred in traditional Yoruba society. Informants on the London survey sometimes distinguished between a relative sent as a foster child (*alagbato*) and an unrelated child (*omodo*), who was considered of inferior status, likened by a few informants to that of a slave.

practice.[6] Such pawns worked in the household of the creditor until the debt was redeemed. There might ultimately be an agreement to let the girl be married there in exchange for cancelling the debt, but casual sexual relations between the girl and her master were usually specifically forbidden.

The modern housemaid may be a relative of her master or mistress. This is preferred and is common (Oppong 1974). However, many appear to be unrelated and to come for a sum of a few pounds paid monthly or annually to the parents of a young girl or, when she is older, to the girl herself.[7] Such girls tend to stay only a few years and then either marry or move on to some form of more remunerative employment, perhaps to an apprenticeship where they can learn a more saleable skill than housekeeping. There is a definite pattern of recruiting girls in rural areas to work as "housemaids" in the cities of Ghana.

It would seem that as the skills and experiences which parents desire for their children become more diversified, they begin to look beyond their kin to find someone to train them. Fostering by kin is gradually transformed into various forms of apprenticeship and domestic service. At the same time that kin are proving less able to meet these needs, there is a movement toward limiting the acknowledgment of kinship claims by those whose own education has led to a standard of living far above that of most of their relatives. While there is evidence that parents and full siblings still successfully request assistance in regular and substantial amounts, among the educated elite there is no longer the same pattern of honoring the claims of distant kin, even when made according to traditional norms (Oppong 1969a).

The data in Tables 2 and 3 come from three very brief surveys in southern Ghana. The purpose of the surveys was to discover whether the Gonja were unusual in giving such weight to fostering by kin in the rearing of their children, or whether similar practices might be found in other West African societies. Time and resources did not allow me to spend more than a few days in either the Ewe or the Fanti community, while the Krobo survey was conducted through local assistants after I had returned to England. The main weakness of the material lies in its narrow focus. The interviews with Ewe and Fanti were necessarily conducted through an interpreter, and the central question, once the constitution of the informant's sibling group had been established, was, "Who reared . . .

[6] In *Gbanyito* the verb is *terma*, while the verb which applies to fostering is *belo* [to rear or bring up].
[7] Ages can be guessed only very roughly from Busia 1950, my main source on this point. The youngest girls may be ten or twelve years old.

Table 2.   Relationship between child and foster parent in three southern Ghana societies: boys

Society[a]	Total		Source of foster parents							
			Grandparents' generation		Parents' generation		Child's generation		Nonkin	
	Number	Percent	Number	Percent	Number	Percent	Number	Percent	Number	Percent
Total:	135	100.0	3	2.0	99	73.0	24	18.0	9	7.0
Fanti	52	100.0	0	—	39	75.0	11	21.0	2	4.0
Ewe	11	100.0	2	18.0	7	64.0	2	18.0	0	—
Krobo	72	100.0	1	1.0	53	74.0	11	15.0	7	10.0

[a] These data for Tables 2 and 3 are based on interviews in which the rearing histories of all members of the informant's full sibling group were recorded. In Ewe and Fanti communities, the informants were selected from people known to my sponsors and form what can only be described as an arbitrary sample. The Krobo sample consists of all adults in every tenth compound on selected streets of the two largest Krobo towns. The figures exclude 56 cases in which the generation of the foster parent could not be determined, although he or she was stated to be a relative.

Table 3.   Relationship between child and foster parent in three southern Ghana societies: girls

Society[a]	Total		Source of foster parents							
			Grandparents' generation		Parents' generation		Child's generation		Nonkin	
	Number	Percent	Number	Percent	Number	Percent	Number	Percent	Number	Percent
Total:	144	99.0	16	11.0	77	53.0	23	16.0	28	19.0
Fanti	48	100.0	8	17.0	26	54.0	6	12.0	8	17.0
Ewe	26	100.0	6	23.0	10	38.0	7	27.0	3	12.0
Krobo	70	101.0	2	3.0	41	60.0	10	14.0	17	24.0

[a] See note to Table 2.

(each sibling in turn)?" Although this was further broken down by periods in infancy, childhood, and adolescence, a full exploration of the rearing situation was not possible. I am persuaded that the Krobo interviewers confined themselves almost entirely to the formal interview schedule. Informants were adults, and the information thus refers to childhood of from twenty to sixty years ago (1972). What I did not anticipate in planning these surveys was the shift from kinship to nonkin fostering. Hence when exploring the vocabulary of child rearing in the vernacular in order to standardize the questions prior to interviewing, I did not ask about how such apprentice fostering was referred to. The figures in Table 2 particularly, on the nonkin fostering of boys, do not fit with observations on the sending of boys to learn such skills as carpentry, driving, "fitting" (automotive mechanics), and so on. While this may be a very recent pattern, it seems more likely that informants did not consider these apprenticeships as "rearing" when the "master" was not a kinsman. Those few cases which do appear in Table 2 may be the ones in which a change of residence occurred in the context of apprenticeship, thus more closely approximating the kinship fostering pattern, in which the foster parent expects to have the domestic services of the child as part of the relationship.

In these southern Ghana samples a substantially higher proportion of girls than boys is sent to nonkin foster parents. Some of these girls are learning trades like baking or sewing, while others are acting as "housemaids." The fact that they were considered as being "reared" by their mistresses may be related to the domestic nature of the skills they were learning and to the undoubted fact that their training involved helping their mistresses in her household work and also in some cases learning a particular skill.

Both boys and girls in the southern Ghana samples are sent relatively infrequently to grandparents to rear. The contrast with the figures for Gonja (northern Ghana) is pronounced, and the difference between this pattern and that of the West Indian samples is extreme. There are some divergences between the different southern Ghana samples in frequency of fostering by the grandparental generation on which I cannot comment here. There is a regular tendency for girls in all samples to go more frequently to their grandmothers than boys to their grandfathers. This, as I suggested in discussing the Gonja data, seems likely to be related to the domestic nature of the fostered girl's training.

The great majority of the boys in the southern Ghana samples went to a "sibling" of either the father or the mother (73 percent). This preference for a foster parent of the parental generation appeared in some of the

Gonja samples and is much clearer here. For the girls in the southern Ghana sample also, the parental generation provided by far the largest class of foster parents (53 percent), with the next largest group being unrelated (19 percent). A substantial minority of both boys and girls (18 percent and 16 percent respectively) went to an elder sibling (own or classificatory). These proportions are much higher than the 6 percent average for the Gonja samples and probably reflect the fact that older siblings who are educated or have learned a trade are more likely to be seen as able to contribute to a child's development than older siblings in the preindustrial, prebureaucratic world of northern Ghana in the first half of the twentieth century.

Comparison of Fostering in Northern and Southern Ghana

While both northern and southern Ghanaian samples reflect a preference for selecting foster parents from the parents' own generation, there is a relatively greater emphasis in the north on sending a child to a grandparent and in the south on making use of siblings and unrelated foster parents (Table 4). At the time these children were being fostered, between 1910 and 1950, northern Ghana scarcely participated in the economic differentiation and educational stratification of modern society. The south, on the other hand, had begun to enter the age of technology with all that this involves. In seeking to understand the shift away from grandparents as foster parents in favor of siblings and strangers, the critical factor is the balance between fostering as a reflection of rights vested in kinship roles and fostering as a mode of education. Both these aspects coexist in traditional Gonja fostering (see Goody 1973). However, with a shift to sibling and nonkin fostering, the element of kinship rights becomes secondary to the educational functions of fostering. A child is not sent to an elder sibling (and certainly not to a stranger) because they have a *right* to a lien on its labor and companionship. On the other hand, this was a significant element in the request for a foster child in traditional Gonja. It would appear that in the modern world of southern Ghana, rights vested in kinship roles have become less compelling than the need to help children to make their way in the new occupational and social milieu. Indeed, the shift probably reflects the diminishing role played by the senior generation in helping youth to become established in the adult world. Instead of age in itself leading to positions of importance, relatively restricted skills, especially those based on advanced education, become the critical factor. In all the Ghanaian samples there is a pronounced emphasis

Table 4. Generation of foster parent: comparison of northern and southern Ghana: combined samples

Sample groups	Total		Source of foster parents							
			Grandparents' generation		Parents' generation		Child's generation		Nonkin	
	Number	Percent	Number	Percent	Number	Percent	Number	Percent	Number	Percent
Gonja, northern Ghana	207	100.0	80	39.0	104	50.0	12	6.0	11	5.0
Southern Ghana	279	100.0	19	7.0	176	63.0	47	17.0	37	13.0

on fostering by parents' siblings. This emphasis reflects reciprocal rights and obligations acknowledged between both full and classificatory siblings.

I have argued thus far that traditional fostering by kin, while it fulfilled many specific functions which varied with the form of each society, also reflected the strength of claims which members of a kin group could successfully make on one another. As the skills demanded for full participation in an increasingly diversified economy grow more complex, with success in school of growing importance on the one hand and mastery of many new crafts on the other, it is no longer possible for just any adult to provide the model and the training which are necessary for the child to take his place in society. Where no kinsman is available, an arrangement for the child's education must be made on another basis. The usual pattern is that the child's labor over a period of several years pays for the training he receives, though a lump sum may be given to the teacher at the beginning or at the end of the training period. In this transformation of the traditional institutions of fostering we see two aspects emphasized: the experience is sought for the child as a way of helping prepare him for a more successful adulthood; the labor of the child is a major part of the recompense for the training received, but money may pass either to the "teacher" or to the parents in lieu of the kinship obligation which would once have sufficed. If there is a highly educated member of the family — a teacher, a clergyman, or one who is in another kind of important job — he will often be asked to take on children, since it is felt that he is in a position to give them better training than others would be; it is not only specific skills which are sought but a facility with the written and spoken word and with Westernized ways.

Fostering by West Africans in London

How is all this related to the fostering of children by West Africans in London? There are many practical reasons why fostering might appeal to this group: they often live in cramped conditions and do not have room for small children. The mother may need to work full time to help support the father's studies; often, the mother is herself trying to train in addition to her job, and thus needs to be free in the evenings. Many mothers are training as nurses and need to be free for night duty or even to live in the hospital. The father is usually studying as well as working and needs a quiet home in which to read. Yet English or American parents in a similar situation would simply not consider fostering a child with strangers as an appropriate solution. It should be made clear that West African parents are often distressed to have to part with their very young children to foster parents, and they take elaborate pains to insure that the families to whom they go are clean and kind and that they feed and care for them properly. But basic assumptions of the two cultures differ. A cultural paradigm as to the appropriateness of delegating child rearing underlies West African thinking on this subject which, though there is evidence that Europe once shared at least some of the same ideas,[8] has ceased with the writings of psychologists from Freud to Bowlby to seem credible to the West. One part of the explanation of the high incidence of fostering by West Africans in London, then, is that parents who are trying to fill several other roles as well share a cultural view of parenthood which approves of delegating certain aspects of this role.

Another aspect of the explanation lies in the traditional definition of fostering as character building, an educational process. This educational side of fostering has been increasingly emphasized in recent years as the institution has been adapted to modern conditions. When faced with a child-care problem in England, the West African parent asks, how can I arrange both for the care and for the education of my child? Since it is very young children who constitute the main problem,[9] language and domestic culture are the main things the child is expected to learn. A number of parents in our intensive study commented explicitly on the advantage they hoped their children would gain at school from having spoken English as a first language. A different sort of light is shed on this aspect of fostering in England by a question which we asked the parents on the extensive survey: "If you were living in West Africa now, or when you go back, would you consider fostering your child?" While some parents replied that they would have to do so if a relative was in need, the great majority said that there were no circumstances under which they would do this. And by far the most common reason given was, "there is no one there better able to rear him than we are." That is, relative to their kin and the people they knew, these budding elites did not feel there was

[8] Morgan (1944), in writing about the Puritan family in seventeenth century New England, records the placing of daughters in the houses of relatives and friends to learn housecraft, while male apprenticeship began at eleven or twelve and lasted for a minimum of seven years, with the master having complete control over the movements of the youth, in and out of working hours. See also Aries (1962: 374) on the prevalence of sending children out to wet nurses in France in the seventeenth century. Systematic searching would almost certainly reveal many more examples from a period when the boundaries of the family were not yet so tightly drawn as they are in our society today.
[9] See Muir and Goody (1972) and Goody and Muir (1972) for a discussion of the developmental cycle of West African immigrant families and the resulting high incidence of births among student parents.

anyone who could train their children any better than they could them-selves. Yet this judgment apparently does not apply in the United Kingdom, for while living in London 50 percent of this sample of nearly 300 couples had either previously fostered a child with an English family (25 percent) or were currently doing so (25 percent). Their firm rejection of fostering in West Africa ostensibly included "all circumstances" and thus ought to be comparable with the situation of very real objective strain under which many lived in London. But even allowing for a certain amount of idealization, it is clear that West African parents feel they are getting something of worth through fostering their children with English parents which fostering in West Africa would not secure. This is mainly seen as greater facility with the language and a greater ease with Western institutions, both of prime importance to a highly upwardly mobile group.

Summary: West African Fostering in Different Contexts

I have very briefly considered the distribution of children in fosterage in three very different West African contexts: first, we saw that in Gonja society, where education and occupational differentiation are very little affected by industrialization, children almost always go to kin. Exceptions are found only among boys, who are sometimes sent to Koranic teachers and occasionally to officeholders. Forty percent of the children go to a foster parent of the grandparental generation, while about half go to kin of the parental generation — that is, to a parent's real or classificatory sibling.

The second context was contemporary southern Ghana, where apprentice fostering is becoming important. Here "masters" are still sought among kin for preference, but differentiation of skills may make this impossible. Apprentice fostering affects both boys and girls but exists side-by-side with fostering for more diffuse objectives. Children are also sent to educated relatives in the hope that they may receive both an improved education and perhaps advantages in securing work later. Here foster parents are seldom of the grandparental generation, and children most often go to a "sibling" of the parent, or, in a substantial number of cases, to nonkin.

The final situation in which we have found fostering of children by West African parents is among the temporary immigrants in London. Here the children are much younger, reflecting the absence of domestic help or relatives in the household to assist with the care of infants and toddlers. There are no relatives available to serve as foster parents in

London,[10] and children all go to strangers, and indeed to non-West African couples, who care for them in exchange for a weekly payment.

These data reflect a clear progression from fostering by kin to fostering by strangers which shows a close similarity to apprenticeship. They also suggest a decreasing reliance on the grandparental generation in situations in which fostering is viewed as a means of securing skills or advantage for the child. Admittedly the situation of immigrants in London is an extreme one but perhaps all the more revealing for that, especially when contrasted with the response of West Indians to objectively similar circumstances.

FOSTERING IN THE WEST INDIES

Crisis and Purposive Fostering

There are a few references in the ethnographic literature on the West Indies to the sending of children to live with kin even though their natal family of orientation is still intact and forms a coresidential unit. Gonzalez writes of the "loaning" of children between compounds as sometimes being based on kinship ties, and this seems to include children of intact families (1969: 52–53). Sanford also refers to "loaning" of children and it seems likely that in some of these cases the parents are living together (1971: 100). Horowitz specifically mentions that parents may send a child to a relative from an intact conjugal household (1967: 49). There are also clear indications that children are sent to stay with nonkin who are in a position to offer them a better start in life than their own parents. Edith Clarke's data (1966) from three very different communities in Jamaica show a substantial proportion of children living with neither parent; over the three communities the average is 18 percent (see Table 5). Nearly one-third of these fostered children are living with nonrelatives. In the poorest community (Mocca) almost half the fostered children are with nonkin, while nearly all those from prosperous Orange Grove are with relatives. But although Orange Grove children are seldom sent out to live with nonkin, Clarke reports that more unrelated children come to live in Orange Grove homes than was the case in the other communities studied (1966: 178).

The sending of children to middle and upper-class White and Creole families in the hope that they will receive an education and assistance in

---

[10] In fact a surprising number of West African couples do have one or two relatives in the United Kingdom, but as they are also in the United Kingdom in order to study and must work to support themselves, they are not available as foster parents.

Table 5.   Fostered children living with kin and nonkin in three Jamaican communities[a]

Community	All children		Fostered children							Percent of all children who are fostered[b]		
	Number	Percent	Total		Living with kin		Living with nonkin				By kin	By nonkin
			Number	Percent	Number	Percent	Number	Percent				
Combined total including:	747	100.0	138	100.0	99	100.0	39	100.0		18.5	13.3	5.2
Orange Grove	296	39.6	22	16.0	20	20.0	2	5.0		7.4	6.7	0.7
Sugar Town	318	42.6	90	65.0	65	66.0	25	64.0		28.3	20.4	7.9
Mocca	133	17.8	26	19.0	14	14.0	12	31.0		19.5	10.5	9.0

[a] Clarke 1966: Appendix 5.
[b] It is not clear from Clarke (1966: Appendix 5) whether the children enumerated are those in each community or all the children born to adults living in each community. I nevertheless include the comparison to give some indication of the proportions of children being reared by relatives and nonkin.

finding a secure occupational niche is also reported by Gonzalez for the Black Caribs of Guatemala (1969: 53 ff) and Sanford for the Carib and Creole population of a British Honduras community (1971: 94–95).

Yet despite these references, purposive fostering with kin and with strangers seems to account for a relatively small proportion of the children who are reared apart from both their parents in the Caribbean area. Again from Sanford's figures, 59 percent of her instances of "child keeping" (205 cases) I would classify as crisis fostering, with another 13 percent (46 cases) as probable crisis fostering. If we include the latter group, then something like 72 percent of her cases were due to the inability of the parents to rear the child themselves (Sanford 1971: 82). As Sanford points out, this classification is based on reasons given "after the fact" and undoubtedly represents bias of some sort. Unfortunately there are few figures of which I am aware which enable a distinction to be drawn between crisis and voluntary fostering in the Caribbean area.[11]

Although additional figures are lacking, the burden of the descriptive material on the West Indian area is clearly that children are most often placed with a proparent because their parents have no home in which to care for them. These may be children of transient unions, "outside" children whose presence in a conjugal household is not welcome, or children whose parent or parents must work in a city or abroad and cannot care for them as well; but for some such reason the parents cannot cope and some proparental figure has to be found.

Divergence from West African Pattern

The multifunctional quality of fostering in the West Indies is precisely what we find in traditional West African societies, and the adaptations in West Africa to Western industrial changes are echoed in those described for the Caribbean. Yet the working out of the pattern is subtly different. Not only does a relatively higher proportion of crisis fostering seem to characterize this area, but fostering among kin seems more likely to mean the rearing of a child by a parent's own parent rather than, as in West Africa, by a wide range of classificatory relatives, particularly parents' siblings.

It is in societies based on cognatic descent systems or with weak unilineal descent groups that fostering appears to flourish in West Africa.

[11]   To do so on the basis of whether or not the child's parents are living together at the time of inquiry is not satisfactory, since in at least some cases the family of orientation is likely to have dispersed following the fostering arrangement.

West Indian societies are cognatic, with a few weakly unilineal (e.g. M. G. Smith 1962a). Despite this similarity, the range of kin which participates is wider in West Africa than in the West Indies. What is interesting for the comparison of fostering in the two areas is that these collateral kin are, in West Africa, seen as having a claim on children to foster. Furthermore, they are ready to acknowledge requests to take children which are phrased in terms of kinship ties.

Sanford (1971: 108) refers to anxiety over dependability of kinship bonds among the Creole and Carib peoples of British Honduras. But the bonds of which she is speaking are those linking primary kin, that is, full and half siblings and parents and children. And given the dispersal of half siblings in different households in the town, and the extended absence of fathers and the periodic absence of many mothers, this is perhaps not surprising. It is a case of a dispersed core, with very little in the way of backup institutions. The comparable situation in West Africa finds the paternal half siblings usually located in a single compound (this will be the case with maternal half siblings in a matrilineal system like Ashanti). The same compounds contain a number of elementary families, linked by senior members of a kin group, who usually recognize one person as their formal head. This person in turn represents the compound to the community, acting on behalf of the individual members on such public occasions as life crisis rituals or serious litigation.[12] Should the child's own family of orientation break up, there is a double safety net — on the one hand there are the two ongoing residential groups in which the parents have birth status rights, into either of which he will be welcomed, and on the other there are the kinsfolk living elsewhere who have a claim on him and an obligation to care for him if this becomes necessary. Fostering does sometimes occur within a residential complex of several domestic groups. In Gonja, this happens most often when an elderly mother is assigned one of her granddaughters as a companion and a runner-of-errands. But on the whole fostering occurs between compounds, and very often between villages. By this I mean that the parents are living in a different compound or village from that of the foster parent, and that these are their regular homes. In Gonja, and I believe in other West African societies too, the fostered child moves between fixed points (domestic groups, though not necessarily based on a conjugal unit), and these fixed points are embedded in a nexus of wider institutions, kinship, jural, ritual, and political, into which the child is introduced in a systematic way and as a member of his residential group.

[12]   See Fortes (1969: Chapters 9 and 10) for an especially clear account of the compound as a mediating structure in Ashanti.

To an outsider, it seems as though the fostered child in the West Indies has only his foster home as a secure base.[13] And further, that, however strong the bonds between parent, child, and foster parent, this foster home is in effect an isolated unit. Even where domestic groups are gathered into larger aggregates (as among Black Caribs in Guatemala [Gonzalez 1969]), there is not the pattern of extradomestic institutions into which these larger groups are integrated.

Thus fostering in West Africa leads the child out from the domestic and local group of the parents, but this remains his primary base and he (or she) remains the child of this compound, of this village, of these particular parents. One minor index of this continuity in Gonja is that kinship terminology does not alter with fostering. The child and the foster parent use the same kin terms as before, and the child continues to call only his own parents by the fond terms for "mother" and "father." The major index of the lack of change in status through fostering is that a man is eligible for no new offices by virtue of residence with his foster parent, and remains eligible for whatever offices were open to him in his natal community; inheritance is not altered by fostering relationships, though a fond foster parent may give gifts *inter vivos* to a foster child.

In contrast, there seem to be two themes in West Indian fostering. First, the child may be sent "outside" to unrelated foster parents, usually in a quasi-servant role, but with the intention that he learn urban middle class ways and get an education. If this is successful, then as an adult he will be in a good position to support his parents. There may be a breaking of ties with natal kin and an attempt to "pass" into middle class society. If the child fails to secure an education or effective occupational skills, he will be thrown back onto his own kin and class.

The second theme is the fostering grandmother. Here the child is returned to the mother's home, which may or may not still be her primary base. If the mother has established a separate conjugal household, it is likely to be with a man who is not the child's father, and the majority of writers on the West Indies seem to agree that "outside" children are not welcome in the conjugal home (see especially Clarke 1966: 174). If, as in Sanford's community in British Honduras, the parents are both away working, there *is* no conjugal home to which the child can relate. The

[13]   This is partly a function of the age at which a child is sent to foster parents. In West Africa this tends to be at around age five to seven, often referred to as the time when a child begins to "have sense." In the West Indies, on the other hand, the pattern seems to be to place an infant with a foster mother in order that the mother can work to support herself and the child and can be free to try to form a stable union. In the latter case, the child knows no other home than that of the foster parent, though the mother may visit it regularly.

result appears to be a very strong relationship with the fostering mother. Several authorities have noted that she is apt to be called "mother," while the real mother is referred to by her name and treated as a "sister." Sanford suggests that it can go much farther than this. Writing of a woman who reared a younger brother and sister, she says,

This woman receives from her younger siblings the reverence and the regular acquiescence to her authority over them that a mother would receive. . . . Their attitudes are almost a caricature of the respect for authority which is a strongly evidenced characteristic of social relations in Stann Creek. No matter that they are both quite old and responsible themselves, their sister is the elder and she is loved, feared, and obeyed in all respects as if they were children. She is their psychic mother (Sanford 1971: 133–134).

Yet Sanford insists that the "keeping" of children by Creole and Carib peoples in British Honduras is not a form of adoption, and gives as evidence the fact that the mother's right to reclaim her child is recognized as overriding any promise she might have made to the fostering parent (Sanford 1971: 92–94, 125). Interestingly enough, this is discussed in the context of the treatment of parent and foster parent by the grown foster child. A girl who sent gifts only to her foster mother and not to her real mother was criticized for forgetting the woman who bore her and looked after her in infancy. Sanford remarks that she would not have been able to withstand these criticisms if she had been living in the community, but as she was working abroad they did not affect her. Another woman affirmed that if either of the two boys she had reared should turn out well (i.e. become well off), she would see to it that the mother shared in her good fortune. As these examples suggest, it appears to be the fostering mother in the first instance who benefits from the assistance of grown children, but the mother is seen as having a residual claim, though this may be difficult to enforce and may depend on the goodwill of the foster parent.

Such dual responsibility can be seen as arising, on the one hand, from the moral obligation which links genetrix (and genitor) and offspring, regardless of their subsequent relationship, and on the other from the reciprocities of rearing which arise from the dependency of infancy and childhood and the emotional and moral claims made on the child in adulthood. The same dual obligations exist for the West African foster child, but there are two important differences in their form. First, the moral obligations towards his biological parents are augmented by the fact that they also provide him with his place in adult society, since this is (or was in traditional times) implicit in birth status. This very strong pull back to one's natal kin is recognized by the Gonja, who say that a son will always return eventually to live with his father. Anyone could provide instances of this happening, even in middle age. The rights and obligations arising out of bestowal of birth status may be seen as *status reciprocities*.

Secondly, there seems to be much less emphasis on children as a form of security in old age in West Africa. With Sanford, I suspect that this may be because of the insecurity of the West Indian situation, rather than because West African parents do not look to their children for comfort in old age. But in the African context there is a wider range of relatives with whom one may find support; and, perhaps more important, old age in many societies is a time when both men and women are highly respected for their wisdom and skill.[14] Nor, in most traditional societies, were adult sons likely to disappear regularly for the major part of their working lives. In the West Indies both the migration of young adults out of the country or to distant centers of employment and the absence of a strong extended kin group leave the older folk without a sure means of support and companionship in old age.

In the West Indies, then, the fostering of children appears to be associated with a narrower range of kin ties; the foster child is often without an alternative home and grows up very strongly identified with his foster mother. Her home is his home; there is little to pull the foster child back to his own parents, although he owes them respect and support too; and finally, adults, particularly women, may depend very greatly in old age on the support of their youngest "child," who is very likely to be a foster child. Indeed, it would seem that by fostering her daughters' children, a woman can effectively so extend her own period of child rearing that it lasts not until middle age but through to old age. Sanford speaks of women "building their empires as mothers" by appropriating their daughters' children (1971: 99; see also Clarke 1966: 180–181).

The importance of the grandmother as foster parent in the Caribbean can be seen in Table 6. The figures for British Honduras and Jamaica also reflect the pattern of sending children to nonkin, presumably in apprentice fostering. The other point to note from Table 6 is the very low proportion of foster parents of the parents' own generation. There are some cases in each sample, but the figures are very low in comparison with those for grandparents.

[14] The coming of Western technology and education is altering this rapidly. When wisdom is learned at school, the elders are at an increasing disadvantage.

Table 6.   Caribbean fostering relationships by generation

| | | | Source of foster parents | | | | | | |
| | Total | | Grandparents' generation | | Parents' generation | | Child's generation | | Nonkin | |
Sample	Number	Percent	Number	Percent	Number	Percent	Number	Percent	Number	Percent
Total:	567	100.0	360	64.0	65	11.0	8	1.0	134	24.0
Dominican rural village[a]	146	100.0	130	89.0	10	7.0	—	—	6	4.0
British Honduran coastal village[b]	285	100.0	156	55.0	34	12.0	6	2.0	89	31.0
Three Jamaican communities[c]	136	99.0	74	54.0	21	15.0	2	1.0	39	29.0

[a] Spens 1969.
[b] Sanford 1971. I have omitted category "other kin" (N = 64) in calculating percentages, as this could not be assigned to any generation. The figures in Table 6 thus represent percentages of those classifiable by generation from Sanford's data.
[c] Clarke 1966: Appendix 5. I have considered only children living with neither parent. Two cases have been omitted as they could not be classified by generation.

West Indians in London

These comments are based on a pilot study carried out with Dr. T. Spens and a West Indian assistant in a district of London where there is a small enclave from an island in the Lesser Antilles. They draw also on reading of West Indian ethnography and on Dr. Spens' close knowledge of this particular island. They must, however, be considered as tentative findings rather than as the results of a full-scale study.

The trip to England is in a sense but a further extension of the emigration in search of work which takes West Indians from the farm to the local sugar plantation, on to the towns and cities, or perhaps to the fruit, tobacco, or sugar estates on other islands or the mainland of Central America. Puerto Ricans (who are U.S. citizens) go to the United States in search of work. Those from the ex-British colonies come, or used to come, to England. Many, both men and women, leave a child behind with a mother or sister, and some men come promising to bring over wives and children. Those who reunite their families in England often add to them, while others find a spouse and start a family. The jobs they are able to get are those which English workers avoid: as railwaymen or bus conductors, or in industrial cleaning, or in unskilled and semiskilled factory work — jobs which pay poorly and require few skills. Since both husband and wife are almost certainly committed to sending money home regularly, both must work.

The pattern of illegitimate first (and often second) pregnancies is very clear among the families in the pilot study. Seven out of nine women had borne their first child before marriage, and three were still not married several years later. Illegitimacy of the firstborn is not equally characteristic of all these women, however. Again and again these women explain that they came to England because they had a child (or several children) to support, and they could not do this successfully on their home island. Thus emigrants to London appear to be selected from those who have difficulty meeting their responsibilities under the conditions of low wages and high unemployment on the home island. Mothers of illegitimate children are prominent in this group and probably account for the large majority of single women who come to work in England. All those in the pilot sample had left their illegitimate children with kin in the home island. One of the women had come with her husband, but again for much the same reason — to work and secure a better standard of living. This couple left their first child behind with the wife's mother so that they could both work full time. This is exactly the reasoning given by single women for leaving a child with its grandmother: "If I had to look after the child I couldn't work so much, and that is why I came to England."

But for the single woman with a child to support, work has an added meaning: she must send money to the woman in whose care she has left the child. This person is almost always the mother's mother. The money is seen as fulfilling two obligations. In the first place, the care of her child places an extra burden on the grandmother. And secondly, the daughter feels responsible for helping the mother herself with cash if she possibly can. There is, however, a subtler pressure on a woman to contribute to her child's support: if she is the one who provides money for daily necessities and for such extra expenses as the clothes and celebration of First Communion, then she has a much clearer claim to the child's affection and loyalty later on. She has been a proper mother, even though circumstances forced her to leave the child to be reared by others. This is of very great importance in the mother's eyes. One woman, whose mother died just before she left for England, had left her daughter with the child's godmother. She did this very reluctantly, and insists that she has always continued to send money for her support, because the godmother would like to adopt the girl, and she does not want to lose her. In another case the mother had sent money for the maintenance of her son while he was being looked after by his father's mother. She was careful to continue these payments in order to retain her rights in the child, and later was able to take him to live with her.

A woman feels differently about the child she has left with her own mother. My impression is that this is usually a temporary arrangement in the beginning — "until I am able to send for the child in England." Whether the grandmother views it in this way is unclear. Significantly, two of the women in our sample had encountered serious resistance from their mothers when seeking to bring to England the child left in their care. Both had left the child for some time longer, and one ended by having to return to the West Indies to resolve the matter there. Thus the mothers do not from the first consider that they are turning a child over to its grand-mother "for good." However, this is often the outcome of fostering by the maternal grandmother, either because she effectively resists returning the child, or because the mother is never in a position to send for it.

The grandmother's position is very much strengthened by the fact that a child left with her in infancy grows up knowing her as its mother and calling her "Mama," while calling its own mother by her first name and often treating her like an older sibling. Interestingly enough, this even happens when the mother is present in the household. One of the women in the London district studied had lived with her mother after the birth of her first child, going out to work while the grandmother looked after the baby. The child grew up calling the grandmother "Mama" as its mother did, and calling the mother by her first name as the grandmother did. The mother describes the situation as "like I was the big sister." It didn't worry her at the time, and after some years she left her son with his grandmother to come to England where she married and had two more children. When the boy joined her in England he still refused to call her "Mama"; at this time she minded very much and tried unsuccessfully to change the pattern which had been established in his infancy. There is another instance in our small pilot sample of this same pattern — a son who grew up calling his grandmother "Mama" and who in this case refused to admit that his own mother *was* his mother.

Women are very ambivalent about "losing" a child to their mother in this way. On the one hand they feel extremely grateful that the grandmother was able to care for the child at a time when they could not do so. This places the mother doubly in her own mother's debt: first, there are the reciprocities of rearing built up during her own infancy and childhood; now there is a second set which links child, mother, and grandmother. In this situation the continued residence of the child with its grandmother in adolescence and adulthood is seen as one way of looking after the grandmother in her old age, one way of fulfilling the obligation felt towards her. One of the women in the pilot study, still unmarried and with four children, said that she sometimes regrets having had so many children: "No man will marry you with four children. They are scared of the responsibility." However, she went on to say that whenever she thinks like this, she remembers her mother and how she needs the children and what a help they are to her. The eldest boy is now seventeen and has a job, and in addition makes a vegetable garden for his grandmother. The others fetch wood and water and run errands. She expects them to look after her mother in her old age. So she is glad she had the children, since her mother needs them. "But," she added, "they must also give me some sort of respect as well."

And here is the crux of the matter. A child who feels primary obligations toward his grandmother and treats his mother "like a big sister" cannot be depended on by the mother in her later years in the same way as one she has reared herself.

The reciprocities of rearing are laid down between child and grandparent, not between parent and child. And concern about whether children will care for their parents in old age is very real.[15] Mrs. M.'s first child was born in the West Indies and acknowledged by the father, who could not marry the mother as her family was "lower" than his. The girl

[15] It was Dr. Spens who made me realize the depth of this.

has been raised by a sister of Mrs. M.'s mother, and even now is staying with her since Mrs. M.'s husband does not want the child in their home. Mrs. M. is pleased that her daughter shows great fondness and respect for her foster mother, but she only hopes "that she will not neglect me in my old age, when she is bigger and able to help herself." The West Indian interviewer comments that in her opinion the girl will not let Mrs. M. down because she is conscious of her mother's goodness toward her. The interviewer is here referring to the fact that Mrs. M. has always sent money to help with her daughter's maintenance and has kept in touch with her.

The concern over whether a child will feel obliged to care for a parent in old age when reared by someone else is most clearly seen when the foster parent is not the maternal grandmother. This is probably because the mother feels a strong obligation toward her own mother, which she can fulfill through her child, and also because the bond between mother and grandmother is close enough so that the child identifies the two and can reasonably be expected to give the mother too "some respect when she is old." But when the foster parent is a stepmother or godmother, then women become really anxious that they will lose their right to the child's sense of obligation in old age. In one of the sample families, the husband and wife had virtually separated but still occupied the same house. The mother was determined to try to maintain this arrangement as otherwise she feared she would lose her children. She wants to look after them when they are small so that they can care for her when she is old. She thinks they will do this, except perhaps the eldest girl, who is against her.

None of the West Indian children in the pilot study had been sent to English foster parents, and indeed informants from this London district specifically deny that they would ever do this. Sending very young children to a "nanny," that is, a woman who looks after them locally during the day, is a fairly common practice. Ideally women prefer to stay at home when their children are very young, but this is not always possible. Some who must work manage by taking an evening job when the husband can be at home with the children. Others make use of either West Indian or English daily minders ("nannies") with whom they leave the children from early in the morning until five or six in the evening. School-age children are often "latchkey" children, who return to an empty house and may even be expected to start the supper for a working mother.

To what extent is the preference of West Indian parents for daily minding rather than fostering with English families a matter of economic necessity? The range of costs for daily minding in London (at 1970 prices) starts below that for fostering, but there is an area of overlap. The less expensive foster parents charge no more than the more expensive daily minders. There are additional costs in both forms of care: for daily minding, food (usually supplied by the parents), laundry, twice-daily fares on bus or underground, and, of course, clothing; for fostering, occasional lump sums for clothes, new shoes, etc., and the expense of visits.

It is worth noting that although the West Africans in London are on the whole much better educated than the West Indians, the jobs they are able to find are very often the same. Both tend to take unskilled or semiskilled jobs in transport, the post office, or factories. Hence many West Africans are not materially better off than West Indians. Although virtually *all* West Africans are in London as students, only 11 percent of the extensive sample were mainly supported by either loans, student grants, or money from home. The families in one of the two groups in the intensive phase of the West African Immigrants Study, the Ibo, were receiving no money from home and were instead trying to send money to kin who had lost homes and jobs as a result of the Biafran war. Overall, the Ibo families tended to delegate their parental roles less frequently than the others, but this applied equally to fostering and daily minding. Despite their financial straits, there were Ibo families who fostered their children in English homes.

When discussing the relative advantages of fostering and daily minding with West Africans, the choice generally turned on factors other than expense. Daily minding was preferred because parents could check up on the minder's standard of care, and because of convenience if there was a good minder near the mother's place of work. It was disliked because of crowded conditions, poor care, and constant travel. Fostering was disliked because of the difficulty of checking on the foster parents' care of the children (parents are expected to give notice of visits beforehand), and because of the difficulty and expense of frequent visits. Fostering was preferred to daily minding because of the "home atmosphere" — the children were thought to get more attention and be treated more like own children by a foster parent; there was no need to take and fetch the children every day (often in the dark and cold); and the mother was free in the evenings to study or work the night shift.

Fostering can be considerably more expensive than daily minding, and a few West African families are undoubtedly better off than virtually all West Indians. Yet these differences do leave a considerable area of overlap, since there are West Africans who are as hard up as the typical West Indian family, but who still prefer to foster their children rather than send them to a daily minder. While there is probably an economic element in the choice between the two modes of care, even impoverished West African parents foster their children. Nor can the economic factor entirely account for the explicit rejection of English foster homes by West Indian parents.

COMPARATIVE ANALYSIS

Comparison of Contemporary Patterns of Fostering in West Africa and the West Indies

We noted that there were two themes, one dominant and one subordinate, in West Indian fostering. The main theme is the caring for a child by the maternal grandmother when the mother is for some reason unable to do so herself. The secondary theme is the sending of a child to nonrelatives in apprentice fosterage. Both are reflected in the summary figures for the West Indies in Table 7 (drawn from the totals of Tables 4 and 6), where by far the majority of foster parents are found in the grandparental generation, while the next largest category consists of nonkin. This pattern contrasts strongly with the relative lack of emphasis on the mother–daughter–granddaughter chain in West Africa. If we take the southern Ghana situation as reflecting a degree of occupational and social differentiation roughly equivalent to that in the West Indies,[16] we find that the great majority of related foster parents are in the parents' generation, that is, they are collateral rather than lineal kin. While the figures suggest that resorting to nonkin in apprentice fosterage is less pronounced in the Ghanaian samples, observations do not entirely support this finding. This may be because nonkin fostering is increasing rapidly at present, while the figures refer to the childhood of informants who were adults in the mid-1960's. Fostering by nonkin is definitely more common in southern Ghana than in the north, where several samples had no instances, and the overall incidence is substantially below that in the south and markedly lower than the figures for the West Indies. We have suggested that this is probably related to the greater occupational and social differentiation in the south, itself a response to increasing urbanization and industrialization.

But why should there be such a striking contrast between the West Indian preference for fostering by maternal grandmothers and the West

[16] Southern Ghana lacks, of course, the racial differentiation which plays such a central part in West Indian stratification. I would not wish to imply that this is not of great importance in determining the available avenues of social mobility in the two culture areas, but the West Indian data come from Black and colored populations, and thus the discussion is necessarily limited to this stratum.

Table 7. Comparison of fostering relationships, by generation of foster parent, in northern Ghana, southern Ghana, and the Caribbean: from totals of Tables 4 and 6

Sample groups	Total		Source of foster parents							
			Grandparents' generation		Parents' generation		Child's generation		Nonkin	
	Number	Percent	Number	Percent	Number	Percent	Number	Percent	Number	Percent
Northern Ghana	207	100.0	80	39.0	104	50.0	12	6.0	11	5.0
Southern Ghana	279	100.0	19	7.0	176	63.0	47	17.0	37	13.0
Caribbean	567	100.0	360	64.0	65	11.0	8	1.0	134	24.0

African pattern of sending children to collateral kin of both parents? The analysis of West African material has indicated that two factors are critical in accounting for this bias. On the one hand, mothers are very often in need of someone to care for an infant while they work or establish a stable conjugal union. The woman on whom a mother has the strongest claim for such service is her own mother. On the other hand, older women are extremely anxious about what will become of them in old age, and one kind of provision they can make is to continue "mothering" children after their own period of childbearing has ended. The children they have the strongest claim to are premarital children of their daughters (and less often, of their sons). Finally, the needs of mother and daughter coincide: the former is seeking to gain an additional child, the latter to delegate the care of an infant.

The dynamics behind the sending of children to be reared by their parents' siblings in West Africa is entirely different. Parents believe that they are likely to spoil their own child, while a relative will be more demanding. The purpose of noncrisis fostering is the education of the child as well as the fulfillment of kinship obligations recognized between full and often between classificatory siblings. To the extent that foster parents in the grandparental generation are seeking domestic services rather than supplying training in adult skills,[17] then the preference for collateral kin also reflects the educational aspect of fosterage.

Finally, it should be emphasized that only very rarely are men stipulated as foster parents (or "keepers") in the West Indies, while the West African data show a rough balance between male and female foster parents. This I take to reflect the essentially *nurturant* role of West Indian fosterage except where older children are sent to nonkin. The utilization of male foster parents in West Africa corresponds to their function in training boys in both adult skills and manly virtues.

The differences reflected in Table 7 result in a distinctive "shape" to fostering in West Africa and in the West Indies which may be summarized as follows:

West Africa	*West Indies*
1. Strong element of purposive fostering by kin	1. Emphasis on crisis fostering by kin; purposive fostering by nonkin

[17] This assumption is only partly warranted in a West African context. A father's father may still be relatively young and actively engaged in his trade. On the other hand, many grandparents are sent foster children to provide companionship and small services when they become old and infirm.

2. Most foster parents are in parents' generation (i.e. collateral kin)
3. Male foster parents common
4. Model of fostering stresses the claims of foster parent
5. Fostering kin are not necessarily primary kin of parents
6. Fostering links siblings' children (lateral linkage)

7. Fostering does not change birth status identity; status reciprocities unaltered

2. Most foster parents are in grandparental generation (i.e. lineal kin)
3. Male foster parents rare
4. Model of fostering stresses the needs of parent and child
5. Fostering kin tend to be primary kin of parents
6. Fostering links generations (lineal linkage merging mother and her siblings with their children)

7. Fostering may change birth status identity informally; no status reciprocities operate

Comparison of Child Care Arrangements by West Africans and West Indians in London

What, then, can we say about the observed difference between the West Indians, who refuse to consider placing their children with English foster parents while in England, and the West Africans, who favor this form of arrangement? We have seen that both groups must make some arrangement for their young children to allow them to pursue the goals for which they have traveled so far. And, while economic factors would favor a higher incidence of fostering among West Africans than among West Indians, these factors are not sufficient to account for the complete rejection of English foster parents by the latter group. Further, it is clear that both groups share the premise that delegation of some aspects of the parents' roles may be in the best interests of both parent and child.

I would suggest that the difference lies in the cultural meaning of fostering to the two groups. For *West Indians*, the rearing of a young child by another woman involves the transfer of at least some (if not all) aspects of "motherhood," with all the loyalties and obligations that arise out of child care in the early years. So long as this transfer is used to reinforce the ties between a woman and her own mother, it is tolerated as necessary, though we have seen that feelings here may also be ambivalent. But to risk the loss of a child to a complete stranger — which is the implication of sending it to live with another family — is simply unthinkable. The care offered by English foster parents is not seen as offering any advantages to compensate for the threat to ties which the child will feel obliged to honor as an adult.

For *West Africans*, the meaning of fostering is different. Traditionally children were not sent away as infants, and a foster parent is not seen as a substitute mother but rather as someone providing character training and instruction. Where fostering occurs between kin, it is recognized as fulfilling (and creating) rights and obligations, but these in turn reinforce existing ties of a secondary nature rather than create a new set of primary ties (as happens between the West Indian child and the foster parent who becomes a "psychic mother"). The delay of fostering in West Africa until the child "has sense" at six or seven is consistent with this pattern of augmenting existing ties rather than creating a new set of primary bonds. Early rearing reciprocities are already established between the mother and child and reinforced by status reciprocities linking the child to both parents. Only the later reciprocities of rearing based on training in adult skills remain as a basis of bonding. When the parental roles are under strain in an immigrant situation, the West African response is also consistent with the traditional pattern. The roles of father and mother are seen as firmly established and not as vulnerable to threat in a caretaking situation. The fostering experience is perceived as providing a service to parents and their children and as being primarily educational and custodial in function (since no kinship obligations are involved in fostering by strangers).

Conclusions

In West Africa, kinship fostering is evolving into apprenticeship on the one hand and residential formal education on the other. To end with a speculation, I suggest that much the same pattern may have occurred in Western Europe with the development of a more complex division of labor. The relevant factor in occupational differentiation is that it becomes increasingly difficult to find a master of the required trade among one's kin. Apprenticeship then becomes an obvious alternative and is clearly associated with movement into the city and away from kin. Where trades are restricted to a closed group, especially a kin group, the picture would obviously be altered, and information from caste-based societies would be critical here. Again, the centralizing of advanced literate skills in religious foundations which exclude family life (and hence cannot supply their own recruits) is another critical case which would reward study in the context of educational fostering. Like apprenticeship, formal education takes over some of the functions of fostering in less complex societies, functions which themselves include the provision of a link between the nuclear family and wider structures beyond.

REFERENCES

ARIES, PHILLIPE
1962 *Centuries of childhood: a social history of family life.* Translated by R. Baldick. New York: Knopf.
AZU, GLADYS
1974 *The Ga family and social change.* African Social Research Documents. Leiden: Afrika Studie-Centrum.
BUSIA, K. A.
1950 *Report on a social survey of Sekondi-Takoradi.* Accra: Government Printer.
CARROLL, V., *editor*
1970 *Adoption in eastern Oceania.* Honolulu: Bishop Museum.
CLARKE, EDITH
1966 *My mother who fathered me: a study of the family in three selected communities in Jamaica* (second edition). London: Allen and Unwin.
COHEN, A.
1969 *Custom and politics in urban Africa.* London: Routledge and Kegan Paul.
FORTES, M. F.
1949 *The web of kinship among the Tallensi: the second part of an analysis of the social structure of a trans-Volta tribe.* London: Oxford University Press for the International African Institute.
1969 *Kinship and the social order: the legacy of Lewis Henry Morgan.* Chicago: Aldine.
GONZALEZ, NANCIE S.
1969 *Black Carib household structure.* American Ethnological Society Monographs 48. Seattle: University of Washington Press.
GOODY, ESTHER N.
1961 "Kinship, marriage and the developmental cycle among the Gonja of northern Ghana." Unpublished Ph.D. thesis, University of Cambridge, Cambridge.
1966 Fostering of children in Ghana: a preliminary report. *Ghana Journal of Sociology* 2: 26–33.
1969 "Kinship fostering in Gonja: deprivation or advantage?" in *Socialization: the approach from social anthropology.* Edited by Philip Mayer, 51–74. Association of Social Anthropologists Monographs 8. London: Tavistock.
1970 "The Kpembe study: a comparison of fostered and non-fostered children in eastern Gonja." Manuscript report, Social Science Research Council, London.
1971a Varieties of fostering. *New Society* 18: 237–239.
1971b "Forms of pro-parenthood: the sharing and substitution of parental roles," in *Kinship: selected readings.* Edited by Jack Goody, 331–345. London: Penguin Books.

GOODY, ESTHER N. (*cont.*)
  1973 *Contexts of kinship: an essay in the family sociology of the Gonja of northern Ghana.* Cambridge Studies in Social Anthropology 7. Cambridge: Cambridge University Press.

GOODY, ESTHER N., C. L. MUIR
  1972 "Factors related to the delegation of parental roles among West Africans in London." Manuscript report, Social Science Research Council, London.

HOROWITZ, MICHAEL M.
  1967 *Morne-paysan: peasant village in Martinique.* New York: Holt, Rinehart and Winston.

MORGAN, EDMUND S.
  1944 *The Puritan family, religion and domestic relations in seventeenth-century New England.* Boston: The Trustees of the Public Library.

MUIR, C. L., ESTHER N. GOODY
  1972 Student parents: West African families in London. *Race* 13: 329–336.

OPPONG, C.
  1965 "Some sociological aspects of education in Dagbon." Unpublished M.A. thesis, Institute of African Studies, Legon, Ghana.
  1969a Education of relatives' children by senior civil servants in Accra. *Ghana Journal of Child Development* 2 (2).
  1969b A preliminary account of the role and recruitment of drummers in Dagbon. *Research Review* 6: 38–51.
  1974 *Marriage in a matrilineal elite.* Cambridge: Cambridge University Press.

SANFORD, MARGARET S.
  1971 "Disruption of the mother–child relationship in conjunction with matrifocality: a study of child-keeping among the Carib and Creole of British Honduras." Unpublished Ph.D. thesis, Catholic University of America, Washington, D.C.

SKINNER, E. P.
  1964 Intergenerational conflict among the Mossi: father and son. *Journal of Conflict Resolution* 5: 55–60.

SMITH, MICHAEL GARFIELD
  1962a *Kinship and community in Carriacou.* Caribbean Series 5. New Haven: Yale University Press.
  1962b *West Indian family structure.* American Ethnological Society Publications. Seattle: University of Washington Press.

SMITH, RAYMOND THOMAS
  1956 *The Negro family in British Guiana: family structure and social status in the village.* London: Routledge and Kegan Paul (in association with Institute of Social and Economic Research, University College of the West Indies, Jamaica, 1956).

SPENS, T.
  1969 "Family structure in a Dominican village." Unpublished Ph.D. thesis, University of Cambridge, Cambridge.

YALMAN, N.
  1967 *Under the Bo Tree: studies in caste, kinship, and marriage in the interior of Ceylon.* Berkeley: University of California Press.

SECTION FIVE

Implications for Policy

Black Institutions and Potential Social Change in the United States

LEONARD D. BORMAN

ABSTRACT

This volume continues the pattern of the discussion session on the Black extended family held at the IXth International Congress of Anthropological and Ethnological Sciences in Chicago in September, 1973, in which anthropologists and their findings are at the service of the community, with the collaborative effort under *community control*. This approach in the social sciences has great significance for social change. Furthermore, "outsider" and minority groups today question the effectiveness and ethics of traditional social science research, rejecting what is often viewed as an exploitative approach. The work of Shimkin and his associates in Holmes County Mississippi, and in many other current self-help and community-aid projects indicates the ability and readiness of individuals and groups to solve their own problems and should be recognized and supported nationally.

When the basic papers of this volume were presented at the IXth International Congress of Anthropological and Ethnological Sciences in Chicago in September, 1973, Shimkin and his associates organized a session that was remarkably different from many of the other scholarly sessions. It was chaired by Mr. Eddie W. Logan, the Black indigenous research director of the Milton Olive III Memorial Corporation, of Holmes County, Mississippi, who wrote the introduction to this volume. Sitting on the dais along with him were members of the community of Holmes County, Mississippi, including Honorable Robert G. Clark, Jr., the Black State Legislator, to whose penetrating comments on the policy significance of the Black family work I will refer below. The scientists whose research and comments are also reported in this volume were seated in the first row of the audience. It was obvious that the community was running the session, as their members responded fully, while the chairman frequently implored the anthropologist-discussants to keep their remarks within a five-minute limit.

This volume continues that pattern, which clearly puts anthropologists and their findings at the disposal of the community, rather than on the scholarly shelf. Moreover, it exemplifies a collaborative relationship between researchers and community that has existed since the first actions and studies were initiated by the Milton Olive III Memorial Corporation of Holmes County. It is the nature of this collaboration, what it signifies and possibly foreshadows for policy development and social change, that I would like to comment upon.

Anthropology, as one of the human sciences, is probably less bound to the models of the natural sciences than our related sister disciplines. One of the major guiding practices underlying sociology, psychology, and social psychology is the drawing of clear and sharp distinctions between the scientist and his subjects or respondents. Laboratory like objectivity becomes a sacred guideline as individuals, groups, and communities are seen as objects to be described, observed, counted, or manipulated in terms of some research design or academic problem that the scientist has in mind. Since this pattern of pursuing scientific activities follows the early mathematical models of physics, there has been a natural separation of the scientist from his object of study.

The scientific enterprise, moreover, has been guided by a series of practices and preferences that include an emphasis on quantitative measurement; the division of nature into arbitrary, analytic parts to be pursued piecemeal by separate disciplines; and the development of a series of esoteric languages for each discipline involved. Accordingly, most scientists, including social scientists, have had a tendency to separate themselves both from the specific communities of their concern and from the general public. As with most professional organizations, including branches of learning, there has been a tendency among social scientists to remove themselves from the purview of the public and be guided solely by the competence and counsel of colleagues. Even the publication of their findings has meant mainly communicating with their professional peers — and not with the general public.

But even physics, which was the classic model for many of the social sciences, has been changing. Steve Pratt and Jay Tooley, in their brilliant monograph on action psychology (which was stimulated in part by action anthropology) review some of these developments in physics:

After three hundred years of expunging such notions [of the scientist as a participant observer], physics has in one decade found that it must get back into physics a plural approach to exploration including the idea of methodological pluralism, of totality, wholeness, individuality, degrees-of-freedom of and from determinacy, conditional causality, the nature of the surprise in

nature, "the subtle relation of what is seen to how it is seen . . . the insepara-
bility of what we are studying and the means that are used to study it, the
organic connection of the object with the observer" (Robert Oppenheimer)
(Pratt and Tooley 1967: 159).

While many physicists have raised basic questions about their traditional assumptions, including the ways in which their findings are used by
society, most social scientists have continued in a traditional pattern
which separates scientist from citizen, pure science from applied. Universities, as primary employers of social scientists, have contributed to this
gap; there the scientist sees himself primarily as a teacher–researcher and
his primary clients become his students. The results of this division on the
development of priorities in policy for society have been, to say the least,
disastrous. All too often, this arbitrary, traditional division has served to
trivialize the workings of science (learning more about less and less) and
to denigrate the work of the citizen and the practitioner. In the vacuum,
of course, working toward the development of priorities as to what should
be done with material and human resources, have been pressures and
forces based on vested self-interest, power, and prejudice. Subgroups such
as Blacks, who observed social and cultural practices that diverged from
the prevailing pattern, lacked the wherewithal for recognition or legitimization.

The collaborative work between Shimkin and his associates and the
Holmes County Black community, described in part in this volume,[1]
clearly moves in the direction of overcoming the traditional distinctions
between the pure and the applied sciences. Collaboration clearly means
cooperation, copartners, coresearchers in advancing science and at the
same time human well-being. Some major scientific findings are presented
in this volume. The importance of the bilateral extended family with
reciprocal obligations for the Black community of Holmes County and
for those members who have migrated elsewhere emerges clearly as a
significant finding in our understanding of the viable support network
underlying Black communities in the United States. The pattern that has
emerged on the role of such extended families in fosterage, economics,
health, education, housing, and indeed almost every area of human
well-being is just beginning to be understood.

Moreover, such basic understandings and insights could not be known
without cooperation and copartnership between the researchers and the
community. Through the nutritional survey undertaken by the Holmes

[1] A fuller review is given in Eckenfels and Schoenberger 1974. Over the history of the
Holmes County effort more than twenty medical, social science, and other specialists
have contributed at least ten man-years of voluntary effort.

County Health Research Project, led by elected representatives of the
Black community, with an indigenous educator (Bernice Montgomery)
serving as the Principal Investigator, with a staff consisting of local people,
and with Shimkin and his associates serving as unpaid professional
consultants, significant helping–learning projects were inaugurated. And I
reiterate that the learnings have not been trivial findings but major
contributions, as this volume indicates, about the Black family and its
cooperating households in the United States and abroad. One project,
designed for the control of hypertension, demonstrated the endemic
nature of hypertension for Blacks in the County:

Mass community screening yielded over 4,000 blood pressure readings from
people of all ages in a door-to-door survey. This full-scale effort confirmed the
grave findings on the prevalence and intensity of hypertension indicated by our
earlier Nutrition Survey [41 percent of all adults] . . . and predicted by the high
frequencies of disability recorded in our initial Population Census.

The results of the community screening uncovered a high number of juveniles
with elevated blood pressures. While there was a strong direct relationship of
age to mean systolic blood pressure, significant differentials also became evident. Particularly at risk are heads of households and their spouses; . . . in-
migrants from surrounding localities to Holmes County; and Delta as opposed
to Hill residents. . . . The first two factors are likely to be of sociopsychological
origin and the third of physical deprivation (Eckenfels and Schoenberger
1974: 3).

This project was successful in its case findings and in its demonstration
that a community with limited professional support could control this
killing disease. It was, tragically, unsuccessful in the search for funds to
save more functioning lives.

In one sense, Shimkin and his colleagues epitomize the modern-day
"action anthropologists" who, in Sol Tax's terms, "eschew pure science,"
as they pursue two coordinate objectives: helping a group of people to
solve a problem and learning something in the process.

For one thing his work requires that he not use people for an end not related to
their own welfare; people are not rats and ought not be treated like them. Not
only should we not hurt people; we should not use them for our own ends.
Community research is thus justifiable only to the degree that the results are
eminently useful to the community and easily outweigh the disturbance to it.
When the theoretical anthropologist publishes his report of the literate community, he changes the name and disguises it as well as he can — perhaps keeps
away from the place. The townspeople may resent his having used them for
some purpose not their own. Sometimes they suppose he has made millions off
them. The action anthropologist on the other hand characteristically would not
only not publish anonymously but his report is likely to be part of the program
itself, participated in by the community. In any case, he has moral justification

for expecting that the community would glean from his scholarship to help in the development of new knowledge that may be used to help others. One may characterize action anthropology by saying that the community in which it works is not only its subject to study but also its object (Tax 1952).

It is clear that the entire Holmes County team can be seen as operating in the tradition of action anthropology. But more than that, they are serving to reconnect the social or behavioral sciences to the interest and concerns of specific communities and of the public at large. In so doing, they are revitalizing the most potentially productive strength of their discipline, which is the public's concern with their findings. In the terms of Pratt and Tooley, this team, which once worked under conditions of real danger, has revived the concepts of concern, involvement, significance, purpose, and passion — all once thoroughly exorcised in the earlier delimited views of science.

Moreover, this powerful collaborative role with the community moves the scientists to engage in matters of policy formulation, execution, and evaluation at all levels. At least two efforts in this direction have come to my attention. One is the ongoing effort on the part of the Black community and its supporting team to help the Milton Olive III Memorial Corporation of Holmes County acquire stable funding for viable services and supporting research. Another is a brilliant report prepared by Shimkin entitled "Black problems and potentials in rural development" (Shimkin 1974). This report outlines what well might become a national strategy for improving socioeconomic conditions among the Black, primarily rural population of the United States. In this paper, Shimkin points out the necessity for a dual approach to Black economic needs:

The central cities do, indeed, provide the arenas of major efforts to gain breakthroughs via political force, consumer pressures, and labor organization; but the rural areas and the small towns appear to be the best for Black entrepreneurship. . . . [Moreover], measures to maintain or strengthen the Black economy are fundamentally tasks of the Black population itself; even the most benign actions of the White majority cannot replace these essential initiatives. Within this setting, three positive roles can be played by White people — safeguarding equality under the law, increasing access to resources, and providing technical assistance. In all cases, supportive activities are effective — as long experience has shown, only insofar as they are worked out in collaboration with those who are to be helped; based on accurate information; technically sound; dispassionately evaluated and corrected as needed; and continued for needed, but self-terminating periods (Shimkin 1974: 62, 63).

The terms "anthropologist" or "scholar" could be substituted for "White" in Shimkin's analysis. In Tax's terms, if the scholar can expect the community to cooperate in contributing to knowledge, the community can expect the scholar to cooperate in developing important and viable policies for their well-being and, indeed, survival. Community collaboration as described and advocated here can open a whole host of new productive and significant activities undreamed of through traditional frameworks. It may provide opportunities to reinvent new roles, relationships, and responsibilities for anthropologists, and other behavioral scientists, that move far beyond the closely circumscribed cocoon — which Hymes (1972) sees more as a coffin — in which most currently find themselves. The conservatism of most traditional scholarly departments, operating under sacrosanct scientism, may erect barriers to discourage this direction. If so, anthropologists and other behavioral scientists may find themselves increasingly being denied access to peoples and places of the world that find no conceivable uses for such scientists. The American Indians have raised serious questions about the work of archaeologists and the function of museums. Given the large number of monographs written about them they feel they have derived little benefit from the work of ethnologists and cultural anthropologists. The recent symposium on *Anthropology and the American Indian,* published in 1973, indicates that anthropologists have much to be modest about in their impact on public policy toward American Indians in the United States. The recent writings of Vine Deloria (1970) have criticized the self-serving interests of many anthropologists who have conducted studies among Indian tribes. Moreover, the Spiegels (1973), in their review of twenty-four outsider and minority groups in the United States, questioned both the effectiveness and the ethics of much social scientific research that rests on "rational" strategies alone. Such strategies have ". . . assumed that man tends to act rationally on the basis of the best information available to him and that ignorance and superstition are the prime foes of change and progress" (Spiegel and Spiegel 1973: 605).

Other assumptions about the nature of man call for diverse social change efforts. These include reeducation strategies, often requiring close, continuous involvement from community development activities to small-group therapy. My own activities with the Kalmuk Buddhist Mongols, pastoral nomads who resettled as displaced persons in Philadelphia and New Jersey, allowed me to develop a whole repertoire of relationships through acting as a cultural interpreter, a soccer team organizer, and an amanuensis. (See Roche 1954; Gearing 1956; Borman 1971.)

The third approach elaborated by the Spiegels is one that frightens many scholars and scientists and yet may be one of the most important underlying determinants of what gets done. This is the strategy that focuses on economic, political, and other dimensions of institutional power. Pratt and Tooley elaborate this orientation as

... participant-social-action-research [that] gives full weight to other aspects of organizational structure (political and socio-economic) involving reality-based conflict of interests, vested interests, coercive hierarchies and power arrangements. Here, kinds of power are differentiated: pseudo-power, psychological power, bestowed, earned, status-derived, assigned or delegated power, positive power (enforceable in the legal sense), and coercive power as contrasted with influence in a limited psychological sense. The question of power, defined as the capacity to affect (or effect) outcomes, is central to change-agentry, particularly in dealing with the facilitators and obstructors of change (Pratt and Tooley 1967: 145).

Collaboration with the community, reengaging social science to social action, should lead down some of these productive — even if harrowing — paths. Mr. Logan's incisive introduction to this volume provides a characteristic challenge to the courageous persons who might follow such paths.

One significant area has already emerged in which the findings from the Holmes County action study parallel developments in other related spheres. In their efforts to help the Black community "achieve self-realization and strengthen self-identities," Shimkin and his associates have tapped the natural, cohesive capacity within the Black community so often ignored by official service systems. This capacity, reinforced by scientific gathering, can lead to important insights by Black leaders. Illustrative are Representative Clark's valuable definition of the areas of Mississippi law — in regard to housing, care of the aged and the chronically ill, taxation, insurance benefits, and the protection of children — where reforms are needed to provide equitable treatment of Black, as opposed to White, familial institutions.

In general, the recent work of other social and behavioral scientists and professional practitioners examining a great variety of indigenous, natural human support systems, including self-help and mutual aid groups, indicates the great readiness and effectiveness of ordinary "people-powered" activities operating outside the aegis of traditional care-giving institutions.

There appears to be a veritable explosion of such activities, which were reported on recently (June, 1974) in the Self-Help Exploratory Workshop held in Chicago (Borman 1974). Voluntary, consumer-oriented groups, clubs, associations — cross-cutting every imaginable condition — have proliferated at an astounding rate in recent years. Gussow and Tracy, who have been studying self-help health groups, find that the community of the "similarly-afflicted" provides needed peer-group support to sustain even the most severely incapacitated (Gussow and Tracy 1974). Nathan Hurvitz is convinced that "peer self-help psychotherapy groups," such as Alcoholics Anonymous, Recovery, Inc., Synanon, Gamblers Anonymous, etc., are not only more effective than professional treatment in helping their members overcome their problems but provide a continuing fellowship network to prevent backsliding (Hurvitz 1974). The recent work of Caplan (1974), Gartner and Reissman (1974), and many others following the earlier writings of Mowrer (1964), are opening new vistas in our recognition of the importance of kin and other support networks in our society.

The systems of self-reliance that Shimkin and his associates have described for the Black community, as with the other indigenous developments, need to be recognized, encouraged, and supported through a major national effort to strengthen the local capacity of people to solve their own problems. But it may very. well be that the current structures of bureaucracies, agencies, and professionals are unable to reform themselves in these new and needed directions. They may need to be subjected to all of the change strategies outlined above. And while the essential initiatives must lie with the people themselves, as Logan, for example, points out, they can be assisted immeasurably in developing more sophisticated methods and techniques for problem solving and policy development. This brings us full circle in advocating the role of anthropology and the other human sciences as the study of man, in the service of man . . . with the community always on the dais.

REFERENCES

Anthropology and the American Indian
    1973   San Francisco: Indian Historian Press.
BORMAN, LEONARD D.
    1971   Melting pots, vanishing Americans and other myths. *Library Trends* 20 (2): 210–222.
    1974   *Proceedings of self-help exploratory workshop*. June, 1974. Chicago: W. Clement and Jessie V. Stone Foundation.
CAPLAN, GERALD
    1974   *Support systems and community mental health*. New York: Behavioral Publications.
DELORIA, VINE, JR.
    1970   *We talk, you listen*. New York: Dell.
ECKENFELS, EDWARD J., JAMES A. SCHOENBERGER
    1974   "The endemic nature of hypertension and the pilot program for community control: from research to service." Mimeographed manuscript. American Public Health Association, 102nd Annual Meeting, Community Health Planning Section. October 24th. New Orleans.

GARTNER, ALAN, FRANK REISSMAN
1974 *The service society and the consumer vanguard.* New York: Harper and Row.

GEARING, FRED
1956 "First, they listen." *University of Chicago Magazine.* May: 5–7.

GUSSOW, ZACHARY, GEORGE S. TRACY
1974 *Voluntary self-help health organizations: a study in human support systems.* March. Chicago: Report to the W. Clement & Jessie V. Stone Foundation.

HURVITZ, NATHAN
1974 "Peer self-help psychotherapy groups: psychotherapy without psychotherapists," in *Sociology of psychotherapy.* Edited by Paul M. Roman and Harrison M. Trice. New York: Jason Aronson.

HYMES, DELL
1972 *Reinventing anthropology* (first edition). New York: Pantheon.

MOWRER, O. HOBART
1964 *The new group therapy.* Princeton, N.J.: D. Van Nostrand.

OPPENHEIMER, ROBERT
1956 Analogy in science. *American Psychologist* 11: 128.

PRATT, STEVE, JAY TOOLEY
1967 Action psychology. *Journal of Psychological Studies* 15 (3): 137–231.

ROCHE, MARY
1954 "Philadelphia's lost tribe." *Harper's Magazine.* August: 53–59.

SHIMKIN, DEMITRI B.
1974 "Black problems and potentials in rural development," in *Rural community and regional development: perspectives and prospects,* 53–73. Urbana-Champaign: Department of Agricultural Economics, University of Illinois.

SPIEGEL, DON, PATRICIA KEITH-SPIEGEL
1973 *Outsiders, USA.* San Francisco: Rinehart.

TAX, SOL
1952 Action anthropology. *America Indigena* 12 (2): 103–109.

Biographical Notes

BERT N. ADAMS received his B.A. in Voice from William Jewell College (Liberty, Mo.) in 1954, his B.D. and Th.M. from the Southern Baptist Seminary in 1960, and his Ph.D. in Sociology from the University of North Carolina (Chapel Hill) in 1965. From 1970 to 1972, he was Senior Lecturer in Sociology at Makarere University, Uganda; he is currently Professor of Sociology at the University of Wisconsin, Madison. He has done research on U.S. family structures, on mobility and kinship, and on Ugandan Asians in Africa, Great Britain, Canada, and India. He is the author of *Kinship in an urban setting* (Markham, 1968) and *The American family: a sociological interpretation* (Markham, 1970) and coauthor of *Readings on the sociology of the family* (Markham, 1971).

KIYOTAKA AOYAGI did his graduate study at Tokyo Toritsu University and is now Associate Professor of Anthropology at the International Christian University, Tokyo. He has done fieldwork on the acculturation of Japanese-Canadians in British Columbia, Negro businessmen in Nashville, Tennessee, Black families in Texas and California, village life in South Korea, and the social structure of Okinawa, Japan. He is coauthor of *The Japanese village that crossed the sea* and *Anthropology*.

JOYCE ASCHENBRENNER received her B.A. from Newcomb College (Tulane University) in 1954 and her Ph.D. in Anthropology from the University of Minnesota in 1967. She was Assistant Professor of Sociology at the University of Minnesota from 1967 to 1970, and from 1970 to the present has been Assistant/Associate Professor of Anthropology at Southern Illinois University (Edwardsville). She has done research on Muslim families in the Indian subcontinent, urban Chippewa, and Black families in Chicago and is the author of several papers.

MARY JOURDAN ATKINSON received her Ed.D. from the Division of Social Sciences, Texas Southern University, Houston. Granddaughter of a slave-holding Texas pioneer and great-granddaughter of a Cherokee Indian, she is a social historian of East Texas and is author of the popular *Indians of the Southwest* (fourth edition, 1963).

JAMES A. BIER received his B.S. in Geology from Case-Western Reserve University, Cleveland, in 1953 and his M.S. in Geography from the University of Illinois at Urbana in 1957. He is presently Staff Cartographer in the Department of Geography, University of Illinois at Urbana. His cartographic publications include: *Atlas of Illinois resources*, six volumes (State of Illinois, 1958–1964), *Campground atlas of the U.S. and Canada* (Alpine Geographical Press, 1960–1971), *The cable car in America* (Howell-North Books, 1971) and *Atlas of Hawaii* (University of Hawaii, 1973). He was also a contributor to *National atlas of the United States* (U.S. Geological Survey, 1970).

FANNEY BOOKER attended college for two years. She is the owner of the Fanney Booker Home for the Elderly in Lexington, Mississippi, and is active in the Freedom Democratic Party, the Holmes County Community Center, and the Methodist Church. At one time, she was also with the former Providence Cooperative Farm. She was born in Holmes County, Mississippi, in 1906.

LEONARD BORMAN received his M.A. and Ph.D. (both in Anthropology) from the University of Chicago in 1965. He is currently Research Associate at the Center for Urban Affairs, Northwestern University (Evanston, Ill.). From 1958 to 1965, he was Chief of the Anthropology Section, V.A. Hospital, Downey, Ill.; from 1966 to 1970 he was the Director of Program Development, Stone-Brandel Center (Chicago); and from 1970 to 1974 he was Program Director at the W. Clement and Jessie V. Stone Foundation. His interests include applied anthropology, mental health, and self-help groups. Dr. Borman has done field research on the Penobscot and Passamaquody Indians (1951), on the Kalmuk Mongols in the U.S. (1952–1956), and on U.S. mental hospitals (1958–1965). He is the author of many papers.

J. MATILDA BURNS is a college graduate and has been a schoolteacher since 1959. Since 1967, she has been active in the Freedom Democratic Party, the Robert F. Kennedy Civic Improvement Association, and the Parent–Teachers Association. She is a member of the Holmes County School Board and a Community Representative for the Milton Olive III Memorial Corporation. She was born in Greenwood, Leflore County, Mississippi, in 1938.

ROBERT G. CLARK received his B.S. from Jackson State University in 1953, his M.A. from Michigan State University in 1959, and his L.L.D. from Mary Holmes College (West Point, Miss.) in 1968. A Mississippi State Representative from 1967 to the present, he is a former health-education teacher and football coach as well as the owner of the House of Clark Furniture Store. He has been active politically since 1965, has functioned as Chairman of the Holmes County Regular Democratic and Loyal Democratic Parties, as President of the Holmes County Teachers Association, and as President of the Black Elected Officials of Mississippi, and has worked with the Freedom Democratic Party and the Robert F. Kennedy Civic Improvement Association. He was born in Holmes County, Mississippi, in 1929.

DENNIS A. FRATE received his B.A. in Anthropology from Miami University, Oxford, Ohio; did graduate study in Geography and Anthropology at Louisiana State University, Baton Rouge, Louisiana, 1970–1972; and is now a Ph.D. candidate in Anthropology at the University of Illinois at Urbana. He is also a Research Associate at the Center for Advanced Computation, University of Illinois. His field-work has been done on the Old Order Amish (Berne, Indiana; 1970) and on nutrition, geophagy, and family structure in Holmes County, Mississippi (1971 to the present). He is author of several technical papers on geophagy. He was born in Cleveland, Ohio, in 1948.

ESTHER N. GOODY received her B.A. in Sociology from Antioch College, Ohio, in 1954 and her Ph.D. in Social Anthropology from Cambridge University in 1961. She is a Fellow of New Hall, Cambridge, and a Lecturer in Social Anthropology at the University of Cambridge. Her fieldwork includes research in Ghana (1956–1957, 1964–1966, and 1974) and in London. She is the author of *Contexts of kinship* (1973) and many papers.

VERA GREEN received her B.A. from Roosevelt University, her M.A. from Columbia University, and her Ph.D. from the University of Arizona. Presently, she is Educateuse Fondamentale with UNESCO and Associate Professor of Anthropology at Livingston College, Rutgers University (New Brunswick, N.J.). Formerly, she was at the University of Iowa (Anthropology) and at the University of Houston (Anthropology). She has done field research on Puerto Ricans, U.S. Blacks, and West Indians in New York City and in Puerto Rico; on community development in Michoacan, Mexico; on voluntary associations in Aruba, Curaçao, and South India. She is the author of *Migrants in Aruba* (1974) and several papers.

REGINA E. HOLLOMAN received her M.A. in Sociology and Anthropology and her Ph.D. in Anthropology from Northwestern University (Evanston, Ill.). She is presently Associate Professor of Anthropology at Roosevelt University (Chicago, Ill.). She has done research on cognitive development, California self-help groups, and multiethnic communities in Chicago and has carried out fieldwork among the San Blas Cuna Indians in Panama. She is the author of several papers.

LENUS JACK, JR. received his B.A. from Southern University in New Orleans and his M.A. from the University of Pittsburgh. He is an instructor in History at Louisiana State University and Director of Research at Xavier University (New Orleans, La.). He is the author of *Gert Town: a preliminary land-use study*.

NADINE RANDLE JONES received her B.A. in Sociology from Jackson State University (Miss.) in 1971. Currently Survey Interviewing Supervisor of the Holmes County Health Research Project, she was born in Holmes County, Mississippi, in 1946.

MICHEL LAGUERRE studied at the Collège Saint Martial, Port-au-Prince, Haiti; he received his B.A. in Philosophy from the Université du Quebec and his M.A. in Anthropology from Roosevelt University (Chicago) in 1973. Presently, he is a Ph.D. Candidate in Anthropology at the University of Illinois at Urbana and a Fellow of the Institut d'Ethnologie d'Haiti. He has done field research in Haiti, among West Indians in Montreal, and among U.S. Blacks in New Orleans and Chicago. He is now working on a book, *Black power in Haiti: the politics of voodoo*, and has published several papers.

FANNIE E. LEWIS received her B.A. and M.A. in Special Education from Northeastern University (Boston, Mass.). Now a Chicago public school teacher, she was born in Tuskegee, Alabama, where her father was a member of the faculty.

EDDIE W. LOGAN received his B.A. in Science from Jackson State University (Miss.) in 1962 and his M.A. in Science Education from Fisk University (Nashville, Tenn.) in 1967. Director of the Holmes County Health Research Project from 1969 to the present, he is also a part-time cattle and hog farmer. He was a science teacher at the Durant Attendance Center (1962–1965) and at Tyston High School, Kosciusko, Mississippi (1967–1969) and a part-time instructor at Saints Junior College, Lexington, Mississippi (1967–1972). He moved to Holmes County in 1962 and ran for Holmes County Superintendent of Education in 1971. He was born in Winston County, Mississippi, in 1933.

GLORIA JEAN LOUIE is a student in anthropology at the University of Illinois at Urbana. Her primary interest is in medical anthropology. She was born in Holmes County, Mississippi, in 1950.

REV. LEON E. ROBINSON has been a Th.D. Minister since 1952 and a resident of Holmes County since 1946. Active politically since 1959, he is a member of the Freedom Democratic Party and of Grass Roots People of America. He was born in Greenville, Mississippi, in 1912.

RUBYE G. ROBINSON received her B.A. and has been a schoolteacher since 1932. She has been active politically since 1959 and is a member of the Freedom Democratic Party. She was born in Holmes County, Mississippi, in 1912.

DEMITRI B. SHIMKIN received his B.A. and Ph.D. in Anthropology from the University of California at Berkeley in 1939. He is also a graduate of the Command and General Staff College of the U.S. Army (1944). He has been Professor of Anthropology and of Geography at the University of Illinois at Urbana from 1960 to the present. He was in the U.S. Army, 1941–1947, where he became a Lt. Colonel. Other positions include Instructor, National War College, 1946–1947; Member, Institute for Advanced Studies (Princeton), 1947–1948; Research Associate, Russian Research Center, Harvard University, 1948–1953; and Senior Research Specialist, U.S. Bureau of the Census, 1953–1960. Field research includes Wyoming (Shoshone), 1937–1940, 1966; Alaska

(Ft. Yukon), 1949; Southern Illinois (1963); and Mississippi (1966 to the present). He is the author of *Minerals: a key to Soviet power* (1953) and many papers, as well as coauthor of *Process and pattern in culture* (1964) and *The classic Maya collapse* (1973).

EDITH M. SHIMKIN received her B.A. in English from George Washington University (Washington, D.C.) in 1934. She has done advanced studies at George Washington University in Political Science and at the University of Illinois in Slavics. She is presently an Associate of the Russian and East European Center at the University of Illinois, and was formerly with the National Geographic Society and War Department General Staff (1941–1943). She is coeditor of *Law and the Soviet society* (1964) and has written several papers on U.S.S.R. archaeology.

VICTOR UCHENDU received his Senior Teacher's Diploma from the Nigerian Ministry of Education in 1959, his B.Sc. from the University of Ibadan in 1962, and his M.A. and Ph.D. in Anthropology from Northwestern University (Evanston, Ill.) in 1965. He has been Professor of Anthropology and Director of the African Studies Center, University of Illinois at Urbana, from 1971 to the present. Formerly, he was with Stanford University (1966–1969) and Makarere University, Uganda (1966–1971). He has done research on tropical African agriculture, economic development, food habits, and religious systems, and is the author of *The Igbo of southeastern Nigeria* (Holt, 1965) as well as of numerous papers.

CHARLES WILLIAMS, JR., received his B.A. in Social and Political Sciences from Rust College (Miss.) in 1969 and was a graduate student and Teaching Assistant in Anthropology at the University of Illinois at Urbana. He was a Social Studies teacher, 1968–1969, and was in the U.S. Army, 1971–1974. His main research interest is in political anthropology. He was born in Columbus, Mississippi, in 1946.

Index of Names

Abrahams, Roger D., 203, 223 n, 232
Adams, Bert N., 33, 137, 138, 165, 173–179, 229, 395, 497
Adams, C. D., 281
Adams, Walter A., 124
Ajayi, J. R. A., 26 n
Allen, Louis, 359
Aoyagi, Kiyotaka, 215, 271–352, 358, 364, 375, 497
Arensberg, Conrad M., 395
Aries, Phillipe, 463 n 8
Aschenbrenner, Joyce, 181–199, 184, 194, 221, 232 n, 274 n 4, 309, 497–498
Atkinson, Mary Jourdan, 355–362, 363, 364, 375, 498
Axelrod, Morris, 248 n 7, 257
Azu, Gladys, 447, 456; *The Ga family and social change*, 456

Bagdikian, Ben H., 77 n, 122
Bailey, H. T., 47, 66
Barnett, Brig. Gen. George, 417 n
Bastien, Rémy, 392, 411–412, 421, 424, 433, 437, 443
Battraville, Benoit, 417 n
Bell, Robert R., 137
Bernard, G., 74 n
Bier, James, 498
Billingsley, Andrew, 74 n, 127, 174–175, 176, 182, 240; *Black Families in White America*, 174–176, 192–193
Bims, Hamilton, 178
Black, Jack, 359
Blake, J. Herman, 392 n
Blassingame, Y. W., 131

Blauner, Robert, 402
Blood, R. O., 71 n, 137
Blumberg, Leonard, 137
Bond, Horace M., 126
Booker, Fanney, 8 n 3, 150, 151, 152–153, 158, 159–160, 167, 498
Borman, Leonard D., 487–494, 498
Bott, Elizabeth, 185, 211 n
Bowlby, John, 463
Brannon Smith, Hazel, 8 n 3
Brimmer, Andrew, 136–137
Brown, James S., 137
Bruce, Philip A., 135
Buchler, Ira A., 226 n
Buford, H. Junker, 124
Bullock, Paul, 273
Burns, J. Matilda, 150, 151, 155, 157, 158, 163–164, 499
Busia, K. A., 457 n 7

Calef, Wesley C., 385 n
Calloway, Rev. Marsh, 8 n
Caperton, Adm. William, 416 n
Caplan, Gerald, 494
Carmichael, Stokely, 7 n 1
Carroll, V., 451 n 1
Carter, Hodding, III, 8 n 3
Castillo, Gelia J., 248 and n 5
Cayton, Horace, 124, 140, 383
Clarke, Edith, 392, 397, 448, 465, 466, 469, 471, 472
Clark, Robert G., Jr., 9, 10 n, 12, 150, 159, 165–168, 169, 487, 493, 499
Clark family, 66–67
Clignet, Rémi, 245 n

Cobbs, Price M., 215 n
Cohen, A., 447
Comhaire-Sylvain, Suzanne, 409, 412, 413, 415, 432, 436–437
Connor, Seymour V., 369, 371
Coombs, Orde, 127
Cox, A. E., 8 n 3
Croce, Jim, 382 n 3

Daniel, C. H., 279, 280
Davenport, William, 392, 399
Davis, A., 70 n, 73 n, 119–121, 135, 188; *Children of bondage*, 119 n; *Deep South*, 120–121, 188–189
Davis, Harold P., 416 n–417 n
Davis, Jefferson, 381 n
Davis, William R., 280
De Coy, R. H., 223 n
De Graaf, Lawrence Brooks, 273
De Granda, German, 399
Deloria, Vine, Jr., 492
De Ronceray, Hubert, 409, 413
Dessalines, Jean Jacques, 411
Divine, Father, 129
Dixon, Vernon J., 33
Dollard, John, 67 n 12, *Children of bondage*, 119 n
Dorsinville, Max H., 418 n 5
Dotson, Floyd, 249 n
Douglas, Stephen A., 133
Doyle, Mary, 357 n 4
Drake, St Claire, 124, 140, 383
Dubois, W. E. B., 74 n, 113–115, 133, 367
Dutertre, Jean Baptiste, 440

Eckenfels, Edward J., 27 n, 30, 489 n, 490
Edwards, Harry, 129
Edwards, Ozzie, 31
Eggan, Fred, 401
Epps, Willie, 8 n
Evans, R., 33

Fals-Borda, Orlando, 395
Farber, B., 26 n
Feigin, Joe R., 257
Flach, Vera, 375
Florant, Lyonel C., 273
Forde, C. Daryll, 397
Fornell, Earl Wesley, 365, 367
Fortes, Meyer, 413, 468 n, 483
Fraction, Mose, 359
Frate, Dennis A., 3–19, 23–24, 25–147, 149–169, 176, 177, 178, 187, 188, 194, 197, 201, 210, 213, 215, 217, 218 n,

221, 222, 225, 273, 360, 379, 380, 381, 382, 383, 394, 397, 398, 399, 499
Frazier, E. Franklin, 73 n, 75, 124, 127, 129, 173–174, 175, 179, 182, 189, 384; *The Negro family in the United States*, 240
Freilich, Morris, 400
Freud, Sigmund, 463
Friar, Samuel, 26 n
Frisbie, Charlotte J., 396

Gardner, Burleigh B., 70 n, 73 n, 119–121, 135, 188; *Deep South*, 120–121, 188–189
Gardner, Mary R., 70 n, 73 n, 119–121, 135, 188; *Deep South*, 120–121, 188–189
Gartner, Alan, 494
Gearing, Frederick, 492
Geiger, Jack, 381 n
Gibson, Count, Jr., 33 n
Gluckman, Max, 223
Golodetz, Arnold, 33
Gonzalez, Nancie S., 448, 465, 467, 469
Goodwyn, Frank, 371
Goody, Esther N., 227, 394, 397, 447–483, 499
Gorecki, Jan, 403
Gratham, Rev., 7
Green, Vera M., 379–386, 394, 500
Greenfield, Sidney M., 399
Grier, W. H., 215 n
Gussow, Zachary, 493–494

Habenstein, Robert W., 262–263
Haley, Alex, *Roots*, 176
Halpern, Joel M., 28
Hamer, Fannie Lou, 28 n 2, 74, 121
Hamilton, Charles V., 7 n 1
Handler, Jerome S., 396
Hannerz, Ulf, 240, 261, 274 and n 3
Harris, Christopher, 229, 395
Hays, William C., 177
Heinnitz, G., 33
Heiss, Jerold, 175
Henry, H. M., 134
Herskovits, Frances S., 399
Herskovits, Melville J., 130–131, 137, 240, 392, 396, 399, 409–410, 417 and n, 418 and n 6, 421 n, 434, 435 n 9, 435 n 10, 438
Hicks, Fannie, 225
Hicks, W., 279
Hill, Reuben, 137 n
Holloman, Regina E., 201–237, 500

Holt, Len, 8 n 3
Hong, Lawrence K., 184
Horowitz, Michael M., 448, 465
Horton, Robin, 393 n 4
Hughes, Langston, 34 n
Hurault, Jean, 396, 397–398, 399
Hurvitz, Nathan, 494
Hutchison, Ira W., 184
Hyland, Stanley, 376
Hymes, Dell, 492

Jack, Lenus, Jr., 187, 194, 201, 215, 239–267, 379, 380, 383, 500
Jackson, Jacquelyne, 175
Johnson, Charles S., 119 n, 189, 240, 383
Johnson, Guion G., 134 n, 135, 136
Jones, Leroi, 216 n
Jones, Nadine Randle, 150, 158, 162, 500
Jordan, Terry G., 365, 369

Kennard, Sara Sue, 188
Kennedy, L. V., 273
Kimball, Solon T., 395
Kimble, foreman of Bonanza plantation, 6–7
King, Rev. Martin Luther, 9
Kiser, Clyde V., 117–119, 232, 273, 382 n 2, 392
Köbben, A. J. F., 396, 397, 400
Kottak, Conrad P., 393 n 2
Krapf-Askari, Eva, 393 n 4
Kunkel, Peter, 188

Labat, Jean Baptiste, 440
Ladd, William, 124–125
Ladner, Joyce, 178, 191; *Tomorrow's tomorrow*, 176–177
Laguerre, Michel, 220 n, 392, 393, 394, 396, 399, 401, 407–443, 500
Lashoff, J., *Preliminary report on patterns of medical and health care in poverty areas of Chicago*, 78 n
Lee, J. W., 280
Legerman, Caroline J., 409, 413
Leichter, Hope J., 33
Lepper, M., *Preliminary report on patterns of medical and health care in poverty areas of Chicago*, 78 n
Lewis, Fannie E., 201–237, 501
Lewis, Hylan, 123–124; *Blackways of Kent*, 190
Liebow, Elliot, 194, 223 n, 232 n, 233 n, 261, 274 and n 2
Litwak, Eugene, 137, 138
Liu, William, 184

Logan, Eddie W., 3–19, 30, 149–169, 215, 218 n, 397, 487, 493, 494, 501
Long, R. H., 279, 280, 291
Lopata, Helena, 175
Lorenzi, Henry, 5–6, 7, 9, 27 n, 30, 57
Lorenzi, Susan H. S., 5–6, 7, 9, 27 n, 57
Louie, Gloria Jean, 25–147, 150, 151, 165, 167, 168, 169, 176, 177, 178, 187, 188, 194, 197, 201, 210, 213, 215, 217, 221, 222, 225, 273, 360, 379, 380, 381, 382, 383, 394, 398, 399, 501
Love, Edgar, 8 n 3, 9
Loventhal, Milton, 7 n 1
Lynch, William O., 48

Madison, Thomas, 359
Mae, Ara, 280
Mair, L. P., 131–132
Maraspini, A. L., 395, 400
Marc, Fried, 401
Marris, Peter, 255, 257
Masher, Shirley, 28 n 2
Maxwell, J. C., 358–359
McCracken, Hugh Thomas, 27 n, 57
McDowell, Jennifer, 7 n 1
McGee, Lillie, 28 n 2, 31
Meredith Coleman, Hazel, 28 n 2
Métraux, Alfred, 411, 418, 438
Millspaugh, Arthur C., 417 n
Mindel, Charles H., 177
Minter, D. R., 8 n
Mintz, Sidney W., 220 n, 396, 399
Mitchell, J. Clyde, 245
Mitchell, William E., 33
Montgomery, Bernice, 7, 9, 26 n, 28 n 2, 490
Montgomery, Eugene, 28 n 2
Montgomery family, 66
Montgomery, Isaiah T., 381 n
Montilus, Guerin, 439, 443
Moody, Anne, 382 n 2
Moore, William, Jr., 126
Moral, Paul, 413
Morgalla, Michael M., 47
Morgan, Edmund S., 463 n 8
Moscoso, R. M., 418 n 7
Moses, Robert, 92
Mowrer, O. Hobart, 494
Moynihan, Daniel P., 138, 174, 175, 179, 182, 240, 260; report, 235, 240
Mueller, Eva, 124–125
Muir, C. L., 447, 449, 463 n 9
Myrdal, Gunnar, 273

Nelson, Howard J., 385
Nicholas, A. X., 216 n
Nukunya, G. K., 132–133

Olive, Milton, Sr., 29
Olmsted, Frederick Law, 134–135, 365, 366–367, 368–369
Oppenheimer, Robert, 489
Oppong, C., 447, 457; *Marriage in a matrilineal elite*, 456
Osby, Agatha, 281, 292
Ostfeld, Adrian, 4, 10
Otterbein, Keith F., 392 n, 401

Parsons, Talcott, 241 n
Pearsall, Marion, 380
Péralte, Charlemagne, 416, 417 n
Piaget, J., 203 n
Pitchford, Mary, viii
Pock, Erma Jean, 4
Powdermaker, Hortense, 69 n, 119 n, 121, 190, 196, 240
Pratt, Steve, 488–489, 491, 493
Price, Daniel, 382 n 2
Price-Mars, Jean, 409, 412, 418 n 7, 439
Price, Richard, 396 n

Queen, Stuart A., 262–263

Rainwater, Lee, 68 n 5, 72 n, 125–126, 141, 177, 182, 185, 236
Randle family, of Holmes County, 162, 169
Rappaport, Roy A., 384 n 4
Rawick, George P., 194
Redman, Estelle, 168
Reid, Ira de A., 138 n
Reissman, Frank, 494
Rice, Ann, 10 n 6, 30, 31, 47, 48, 52, 53, 54, 64, 65 n 9, 71, 77
Robinson, Rev. Leon E., 150, 151–157, 158, 160–162, 501
Robinson, Rubye G., 150, 158, 160, 168, 501
Roche, Mary, 492
Rockefeller family, 185
Rose, Harold M., 381 n, 385
Rosser, Colin, 229, 395
Ross, F. A., 273
Rousséve, Charles B., 385
Rushing, P. V., 75
Rushing, Rev. Philip, 150, 159, 164–165
Russell, Rev., 7

Saffold, Emily, 159
Sanford, Margaret S., 465, 467, 468, 469–470, 471, 472
San Juan, Pedro, 28
Scanzoni, John H., 126, 136, 175, 178, 182, 183
Schneider, David M., 71
Schoenberger, James A., 489 n, 490
Schoolcraft, Henry R., 365
Selby, Henry A., 226
Shanks, Amy, 359
Shanks, William, 359
Sharp, Harry, 248 n 7, 257
Sherif, Muzafer, 210
Shimkin, Alexander D., 9, 11
Shimkin, Demitri B., 4, 8 n 3, 8 n 4, 10 n 6, 11, 16, 25–147, and 149, 150, 151, 164, 165, 167, 168, 169, 176, 177, 178, 187, 188, 194, 197, 201, 210, 213, 215, 217, 221, 222, 225, 273, 360, 363–376, 379, 380, 381, 382, 383, 391–403, 412, 415, 417 n, 487, 489, 490, 493, 494, 501–502; 'Black problems and potentialities in rural development', 491
Shimkin, Edith M., 502
Shryock, Henry S., Jr., 371
Simpson, George E., 392, 396, 409, 410–411, 417 n, 418
Skinner, E. P., 447
Skrygley, F. D., 134 n
Smith, Michael Garfield, 226, 392, 396, 400, 448, 468
Smith, Raymond Thomas, 191–192, 222, 245 n, 399, 400, 401, 448
Solien, Nancie L., 392
Spens, T., 448, 472, 473, 475 n
Spiegel, Don, 492
Spiegel, Patricia Keith, 492
Stack, Carol B., 121 and n, 186, 191, 194, 211, 223 n, 227, 248, 250 n, 257 n, 396, 401; *All my kin*, 186 n
Staples, Robert, 176, 184
Stapleton, Richard C., 373–374
Steward, Julian, 384
Stewart, Isaac, 159
Stewart, Robert, 31
Stycos, Mayone J., 413
Sussman, Marvin B., 249 n, 257
Sweetser, Dorrian Apple, 138
Sydnor, Charles S., 133, 134 and n, 135
Szelenyi, Ivan, 138

Talpalor, Morris, 133–134, 135
Tax, Sol, 490–491
Thomas, Joe, 159

Thomas, William I., 28, 395, 402–403
Thompson, Daniel C., 232
Tooley, Jay, 488–489, 491, 493
Tracy, George S., 493–494
Trouillot, Henock, 440
Tucker, Fanny, 359

Uchendu, Victor C., 391–403, 502

Vayda, Andrew P., 384 n 4
Verger, Pierre, 399
Vermeer, Donald, 132
Villareal, Felicidad R., 248 and n

Wade, Richard C., 134
Wagley, Charles, 384, 400
Warner, W. Lloyd, 124
Webber, John, 358
Weisblat, Abraham M., 248 and n
Weld, Theodore D., 133, 135
Wessing, Robert, 402 n
West, Robert C., 400
White, Gifford, 367

White, Revel Clyde, 371
Whitten, Norman E., Jr., 393 n 2, 400
'William' (of Holmes County, 1968), 68
Williams, Charles, Jr., 28 n 2, 79 n, 282, 317, 502
Wilson, Peter J., 393 n 3
Withers, Bill, 218
Wolf, Eric R., 220 n, 399
Wolfe, D. M., 71 n, 137
Woodson, C. G., 273
Woodward, C. Vann, 364
Woofter, Thomas J., Jr., 115–116, 119, 273, 385, 392
Wright, Allie Mae, 9
Wright, Jerry, 127–129, 178
Wright, Willie Mae, 152 and n

Yalman, N., 453, 454
Yancey, William L., 236
Young (of Long Branch), 14–15
Young, Virginia Heyer, 122–123, 190, 197, 240, 383

Znaniecki, Florian, 28, 395, 402–403

Index of Subjects

Accountability, public, of social research, 150

Adams family, of 'Middville', study of, 283, 314, 315; characteristics of focal persons, 284, 285, 295–299; family structure, 343, 345; fictive kin, 310; hometown, 282, 314; household compositions, 347; and residences, 314, 327–332; lines of descent, 350; and 'Middville' club, 305; neighbors and friends, 311, 313

'Adaptation', situational, effects of, 380

'Adaptation', urban, definition of, 275

'Adaptive' approach, in research on Black family, 181–182, 186–187, 196, 240

Adolescents; girl, in Chicago, problems of, 201, 202–211, 214–215, 235; in Holmes County, 70

Adolescent sexuality, 122, 128, 383

Adoption, 122; adult, 67, 379; in Africa, 132, 394; laws regarding, 32; in North United States, 194; in South United States, 189, 190. See also Fosterage

Adult: adoption, 67, 379; fosterage, 110, 111

Adult education, 11, 26, 293–294, 301, 304

Adulthood, entrance into, in Holmes County, 60

Africa: families in, 131, 141, 393–395; marriage in, 130–131, 132; slave imports from, 133–136. See also Africa, West

Africa Community', E. Texas, 280–282, 285, 286, 297, 300

African origins of Black culture, 32, 113, 114, 130–133, 138, 141, 239–240, 267, 396–398, 439–441; necculture, 28

Africa, West: child fostering in, 447–448, 449, 450–465, 478–483; by Bornu, 450; by Ga, 450; by Gonja, 450, 451–456, 460–462, 464, 468, 469, 473–478; by Hausa, 450; by Ibo, 477; in South Ghana, 456–462, 464 and n, 478, 479: colonists in, 399; women of, 130–131, 132

Africans, West; immigrants to London, child fostering among, 449, 451 n 2, 456 and n, 462–464, 464–465, 477-478, 481–482

Afro-American extended families: cultural tradition, 402; possible processes in the development of, 396–401; a single institution, 392–395

Age: grades, 59–60, of Holmes County population, 49–50, 56, 65 n, 86; of husbands and wives, relative, 52; life expectancy, Black, 65, 86, 283–285; of migrants from Holmes County, 54, 55, 86. See also Old people

Age status, 128. See also Elders

Agriculture. See Farmers; Farming; Plantations

Alabama, Macon County, tenant farmers in, 189

Alaska, migrants in, 263

Alcohol, 62, 75; in affluent families, 183

All my kin (Stack), 186 n

'America', concept of, 6

Ancestors: in Africa, 394; in Haiti, 423; slaves, 126. *See also* Genealogy

Ancestor worship, 397, 440

Anthropology, role of, 488–494; 'action', 490–491

Anthropology and the American Indian, (symposium), 492

Appreciation' ceremonies, 67 and n 11

Apprenticeship, 482; in 17th century, 463 n 8; and fostering, 456, 457, 459, 464, 471, 480, 482; in Ghana, 456

Archaeology, questions re, 492

Arembepe village, Bahia, 393 n 2

Arkansas, 121; migrants from, 127, 211, 212, 217

Art, Black experience in, 33–34

Attala County, Mississippi, Head Start in, 10 n 6

Austin American, 358–359

'Austin' family, from Bolivar County, study of, 122

Authority, in the family, 120, 122, 123, 155–157, 158, 189; in Africa, 133, 394, 395; and Boni work organization, 398; in Chicago, 211, 218; in Europe, 395; 'founder', 109–110; in Haiti, 410, 436–437, 441; in South United States, 190; spokesman, senior, 73. *See also* Female-headed households; Male-headed households

Bahamas, 392

Bankhead-Jones Farm Tenant Act, 47

Baptism: in Haiti 433–434, 440. *See also* Godparenthood

Baptist Church: Antioch, Houston, 361; of Blacks in United States, 93, 101, 102, 154, 380; and other denominations, 128, 154, 380; funerals of, 195, 291; in Haiti, 422; in Holmes County, 86, 89, 93; in Illinois, 96, 97, 195; Jerusalem, 86, 89; in Los Angeles, 290, 294, 313; and slaves, 135; in Texas, 278–279, 281, 291, 293, 304

Barbados, 399, 400

Bay City, Michigan, 99

Bee, Boni descent group, 396

Beef Cattle Project, Holmes County, 10–11, 48

Bible, guides to behavior, 28, 61, 74

'Bidwell' family of Chicago, study of, 29, 76, 77–103, 138, 140, 178, 222; components of family structure, 79;

family lifeways, 87–103; as migratory network, 77–86; *tabulated*, 79–85

Bilateral descent, 23, 66–67

Birth: in hospital, 59; midwives, 59, 66, 420

Birth ceremonies, 452. *See also* Baptism

Birthdays: among German Americans, 375; celebrations, in Illinois, 195, 198

Birth rate, in Holmes County, 52–53

'Black Belt', United States, 385 n

Black Community. *See* Community, Black

Black culture: 'deculturation' of Black family, 181–182; ecological approach to, 384–386; and family structure, 139–142, 178–179, 182, 186, 237; heritage of, 267; history of, 130–136; and identity, 176, 178, 402; misperceived by Whites, 182, 235–236, 239–240; neo-African, 28; studies of, 112–130; varieties of, in Louisiana, 380. *See also* Blacks, of Holmes County; Research, into Black culture

Black families in White America (Billingsley), 174–176, 192–193

Black Muslims, 113, 129, 141, 215

Black Panthers, 128 and n, 141

'Black problems and potentials in rural development' (Shimkin), 491

Black P. Stone Nation, 140

Blacks, of Holmes County, Mississippi, 3–4, 25–34, 139–142; age grades of, 59–60; and Civil Rights movement, 5–10; community, organizing, *1962–1967*, 5–10; *1967–1971*, 10–12; *1971–1974*, 12–19; daily life and change, 62–64; discuss anthropological issues, 150–169, 487; domestic workers, 58; landowners, 7, 47, 57, 58, 117; relations with Whites, 5–9, 47, 57, 58, 59, 63, 70 and n, 73, 74; shopkeepers and craftsmen, 59; social institutions and values, 57–62; teachers, 7, 59; university education, 11. *See also under* Families, extended Black; Holmes County, Mississippi; Migration

Blackways of Kent (Lewis), 190

Boni, Bush Negroes: extended families of, 396–398; 'nephews', 399

Boston, Mass., medical care in, 33; migration to, 115, 118; Roxbury study in, 256

Boycotts, 15–16

Boys: education of, 123, 480 (*see also* Apprenticeship); fostered, in Ghana,

Boys (*cont.*)
452, 456, 458, 480; in Haiti, 437; household role, in Ghana, 454; household tasks of, in Holmes County, 63; relations with parents, 125. *See also* Brothers
Brazil, 393 n 2, 396
Britain: extended families in, 395; *See also* London
British Guiana, 400
British Honduras, fostering in, 467, 468, 469, 470, 471, 472
Brothers: in Finland, 138; 'go for', 194–195; -in-law, 70; 'just like', 213; in polygynous societies, 226–227; relations between, 70; and sisters, 70–71, 133; terminology re, 226. *See also* Consanguineous ties; Siblings
Burial of the dead: in California, 128–129; children, 65 n 9, 67 n 13, 397, 438; in Haiti, 438; in Holmes County, 30–31, 67 n 13, 73; in hometown, 30–31, 217; payment for, 217–218. *See also* Funerals
Bush Negroes: Boni, 396–398; Djuka, 396, 397; of Guiana, 131, 396–398, 399, 400; South American, 392

California: kin in, 242, 253; migration to, 50 n 7, 113, 121, 127–129, 141, 153, 273; study of Black families in, 178. *See also* Los Angeles
Canada, immigrants to, 422
Canton, Mississippi, Civil rights repression in, 382 n 2
Capital, industrial, lack of Black, 136–137
Caribbean: Black cultural heritage from, 267; Catholicism in, 220; fostering in the, 465–472, 479; peripheral kin in, 220. *See also* Haiti; Jamaica; West Indian
Carib, the, of Central America, 392; of Guatemala, 448, 467
Carolina: Piedmont, mill town study, 123–124. *See also* 'Kent'; South Carolina
Carriacou island, W. Indies, 226, 392
Catholicism: and Black families, 380, 399; in the Caribbean, 220; in Haiti, 435; in Mississippi, 64, 153–154; in Texas, 371
Catholic Schools, 101, 371; in Haiti, 421, 425

Central Mississippi, Inc., and Head Start, 13 n
Ceremonial functions: relative importance of, 24, 395. *See also* Funerals; Weddings
Charleston, S. Carolina, 116, 135
Chevrolet Company, 291
Chicago, Illinois: Black extended family in, 177; church in, 100, 195, 215 and n, 233; early studies of, 124–125; economic effect on families in, 197–198; Greek town, 237; precinct system, 234; social agencies, 231–235
Chicago, Southern migrants in, 298, 382 (*See also* 'Bidwell' family of Chicago, study of the); age distribution of, 55, economic behavior of, 164–165, 168–169, family organisations of, 189–190, 193–194, 197, 232; fictive kin of, 194–195, 274 n 4; Haitians, 408, 416; *1969*, study of Holmes Countians, 31–33; from Holmes County, 50–52, 54, 55, 76–77, 139, 140, 150, 151, 152–153, 160, 164–165, 168–169; return home for funerals, 195. *See also* 'Clan', the, Chicago family study
'Chicago club', in Los Angeles, 316
Chicago Housing Authority, unpaid rent to, 164–165
Chicago Today (newspaper), 94, 96, 99
Child care: in Chicago, Black, 203, 210, 227–228; White institutional, 198, 449, 476–477. *See also* Fosterage
'Child-keeping', in Chicago, 227
Child rearing: Black, in United States, 183; and class, 119 n; effects of slavery on, 173–174; and household, Holmes County, 110; and neighborhood, St Helena, 117
Children: African, 130, 132; of consensual unions, 224–225, 226–228; deaths of, 54, 65 n 9, 67 n 13, 397, 438; of deceased, 259; in Ghana, 'pawned', 456–457; in Haiti, 411, 422, 437; in Holmes County, 60, 63, 69–70, 72, 139, 155–156; illegitimate, 53, 67, 122, 473–475; length of time regarded as, 128; and male kinsmen, 122; of migrants to California, 127, 128; Milton Olive III Memorial Program for, 9, 13, 60; of Muslims, 450; naming, 68, 452; school attendance, 162, 164, 166–167, 166 n, 169; Southern attitude to, 189, 190; urban Black, case material on, 119 n; value set on, 176, 225–226; of

Children (*cont.*)
  Wesley family, as information carriers
  259. *See also* Boys; Brothers; Daughters; Education; Fostering; Girls;
  Head Start; Infants; Parents; Sisters
Children of bondage (Davis and Dollard),
  119 n
Chinese, in Texas, 365
Christianity: and African codes, 138;
  and baptism, in Haiti, 434–435; and
  Black Muslims, 129; and Blacks, 153,
  155, 161; and Civil Rights movement
  6, 99, 155; Southern Christian Leadership Conference, 99. *See also* Church;
  Godparenthood; Religion
Church: in California, 128; in Chicago,
  100, 195, 215 and n, 233; and Civil
  Rights, 155, 158; as community, 44–
  46, 58, 61, 71 and n 18, 139, 154 and
  n, 161 (*See also* Holmes County
  Church communities); different denominations, 153–154, 293, 371 (*See
  also* Baptist Church; Methodist
  Church); decline of, 154–155, 158;
  and enforcement of standards, 383; in
  Holmes County, 44–46, 58, 61, 67 n
  11, 71, 73, 86, 89, 93, 161 and n (*See
  also* Holmes County Church communities); Homecoming, 293; in Los
  Angeles, 290, 294, 313; maintaining
  family unity, 195, 215–216; and
  migrants, 128; ministers, 61, 67, 74 n
  25, 155, 158, 161; monthly service, 108;
  'shouting' in, 158 n; and slaves, 115–
  116; as social centre, 90, 97, 98, 99,
  112, 114, 128, 161; support from, 152;
  in Texas, 278–279, 291, 293, 370–371;
  -trials, 117; women in, 60, 61, 249.
  See also Baptist Church; Catholicism;
  Christianity; Methodist Church; Protestant Church; Religion
Church of God in Christ, 154, 278–279
Cinema, effect of, 223 n
Civil Rights Movement, in Holmes
  County: *1962–1967*, 5–10, 34, 58, 92;
  and the church, 155, 158; and
  morality, 6; and violence, 6; voter
  registration drive, 5–8, 9, 10, 11–12,
  99, 163 n 45
Civil War: effect on Texas, 356, 369–371;
  and slaves, 135–136, 173
'Clan', the, Chicago family study, 201–
  237; educational attainments, 231 n
  19, 234; 'Feathers', 202, 214–215,
  235; group of core kin, 211–219; group

of peripheral kin, 220–228; household
  compositions, 229–231; identifying
  members, 203–211; social environment, 231–235
Class, social: and behavior, 203; and
  Black family, 62, 120–121, 141; Black
  upper, 121; in California, 128; and
  child rearing, 119 n; confused with
  race, 175; and relations with Whites,
  192; and sexual role segregation, 185
Cleveland, Mississippi, 381 n
Clubs and societies: in California, 128;
  hometown, of migrants, 315–316; in
  Holmes County, 60–61; in Los
  Angeles, 311, 312–313, 315–316;
  'Middville Club', 276, 285, 305–308;
  in Texas, 'Middville', 276, 279, 280
Clustering, residential, 229–231, 236,
  237, 257 n
Code of *1705*, 133–134
Cognitive processes, 203 n
Colonial period, in Haiti, 440
Colonists, French, of West Africa,
  399
'Color, people of', 384 n 6, 478 n
Columbus, Mississippi, 141
'Common-law' relationship, 115, 130
Communications: of Chicago family,
  213–218; by children, 259; in emergencies, 260; in Holmes County, 64,
  73; between households, 108–109, 112,
  140, 259, 260, 262. *See also* Interaction, social
Communities, Church. *See* Holmes
  County Church communities
Community Action Program, 60
Community, Black: and accountability
  of research, 150; cohesive capacity
  of, 493–494; organizing, in Holmes
  County, 5–19, 57, 63; and research
  workers, 487–494; supportive, 151–
  153, 494
Community centers, secular, 154, 158; in
  Texas, 280
Community control projects: in Holmes
  County, 17–18. *See also* Public
  Programs
Community Health Improvement Program, Holmes County, 11, 12, 73
Conflicts, marital: in Chicago, 224–225;
  in Haiti, 437
Conjugal relationships. *See* Marital
  relationships; Marital ties; Marriage
Consanguineous ties: in Chicago, 213,
  223, 224; and conjugal ties, 71–72,

Consanguineous ties (*cont.*)
133, 188, 194, 223, 224; households
based on, 190, 191; matrilateral, 184,
188, 436; matrilineal, 244–245, 262–
263, 265, 283, 392-393, 397, 398. *See
also* Siblings
Consensual unions: in Chicago, 193,
220, 221–225, 236–237; children of,
226–227, 237; 'Common-law', 115,
130; in Holmes County, 51, 53, 72; in
Los Angeles, 283; in Philadelphia, 115
Consolidated Steel Co., 305
Contraception, use of, 86, 226 and n 14;
in Haiti, 443; by St Helena natives,
118; and religious groups, 129
Coparenthood (*compadrazgo*), in Haiti,
434–435. *See also* Godparenthood
Cotton gins, 300 and n 12
County, in Mississippi, importance of,
58
Courts: church trials, 117; village, in
Haiti, 437; White law, 117
Covington, Georgia, 114
Creole: culture, 384; French slaves, 368;
terminology, in Haiti, 433, 439
Creoles, in West Indies, 465, 467, 468,
470
Crisis situations: in Africa, 394; foster-
ing in, 448, 467, 480; in Holmes
County, and status difference, 67; in
'Kent', 123; in New Orleans family,
258, 260
Cultural difference, in urban environ-
ments, 202–203
Cultural-ecological areas, approach to
Black culture, 384–386
Cultural pluralism, of United States, 177,
178
Culture, Black. *See* Black culture; Re-
search into Black culture

Dahomey, W. Africa: colonists and,
399; family in, 131; and Haiti, 439,
441
Daily News, (Chicago), 98, 100
Dallas, Texas, 356, 362, 373
Daughters: first, in Ghana, 451–452;
fostered, in Ghana, 456, 457; in Los
Angeles migrant family, 316; and
mothers, Black, 125, 262, 263
Davis family, of 'Middville', study of,
285, 314; characteristics of focal persons, 284, 285, 291–294; family
structure, 343, 345; fictive kin, 308–
310, 315; hometown, 280, 282, 314;

household compositions, 347; kinfolk
and residences, 314, 322–327; lines of
descent, 349; and 'Middville' club,
305; neighbors and friends, 312
Deacons for Defense, 128 n
Dead, the, cult of in Haiti, 439, 441
Death customs: and children, 259; con-
dolence money, 311. *See also* Burial;
Funerals
Death rate: in Holmes County, 53, 65;
infant mortality, 12, 34, 53, 54, 65
Death, significance of: in Chicago, 218;
in Holmes County, 54. *See also*
Burial; Funerals
'Deculturation' of Black family, 181–182
Deep South (Davis, Gardner and Gardner), 120–121, 188–189
Descent, bilateral, 23, 66–67
Descent groups, Boni *bees*, 396
Descent lines, of five Texan families, 314,
348–352
Descent ties: African primacy of, 394;
and marital, 394; matrilineal, 392–
393, 397, 398; patrilineal, 283, 394,
397. *See also* Consanguineous ties
Detroit, Michigan: marital relations in,
71 n 19; migrants in, 78, 80, 86, 88,
127, 140; migration to, 54, 76; resi-
dential propinquity in, 257; study of
blue-collar families in, 137, 248 n 7;
visitors from, 28
Discrimination, racial: greater in United
States than Europe, 178, 179; in
Texas, 277–278; in West Indies, 478
n. *See also* Ku Klux Klan
Divine, Father, 129
Divorce: in Africa, 132; in Holmes
County, 72; in Texas, 283; in U.S.A.,
183
Djuka Bush Negroes, 396, 397
Domestic workers, Black: low status of
in United States, 58, 70, 300, 301, 382;
training of, in Ghana, 456, 457, 459
Dominance, male/female, 60; in house-
hold. *See* Authority, in the family;
Female-headed households; Male-
headed households
Dominica, fostering in, 472
Dorsey family, of Chicago. *See* 'Clan'
the, Chicago family study

Earnings: children's, 70; in Holmes
County, 65; 'side', in St Helena, 118.
See also Income
East Indies, 400

Ebony (magazine), 102
Economic behavior, of Black families:
African, 132; aid, within family, 217, 236, 237; co-operation, 103–108, 109, 112, 121–122, 140, 151, 158, 160, 162, 165, 178; and family values, 33, 73, 197–198; of Holmes County household, 155–156; of migrants, 164–165, 168–169; in St Helena, 117–118; solidarity, in Haiti, 438–439. *See also* Farming; Poverty
Economic opportunity: and family life, 182, 184, 185–186; lack of Black in United States business, 136–137. *See also* Poverty
Economic position of Blacks in United States, how to improve, 491
Economy, of Holmes County, 46–48; earnings, 65
Ecuador, 'personal kindred' in, 393 n 2
Education: adult, 11, 26, 293–294, 301, 304; effect on Africa, 471 n; -al attainments of Blacks, 53, 231 n 19; of Blacks, 32, 160, 163–164; Black students at University of Illinois, 11; of 'The Clan', Chicago, 234; and fostering, 437–438, 448, 458, 460, 462, 463, 464, 469, 480, 482–483; in Haiti, 421, 437; in Holmes County, 48, 63–64; and kinship obligations, 457, 462; legislation re, 166–167; money provided for, 160; Project Grass Roots, 11, 26; and religion, 154–155; sex differences in, 437; and status, 123; in Texas, 279–280, 293–294, 370; value set on, 162, 163. *See also* Apprenticeship; Head Start Program; Schools; Teachers
Elders: in Africa, 394, 471 and n; in Haiti, 410; in Holmes County, 60, in United States, age-status, 128. *See also* Old people
Elections: Black groups in, 14, 16; of mayors, 197; *1967* Mississippi, 9; *1971* general, 11–12, 14, 16. *See also* Voter registration
Employment: in Chicago, 86; in England, of immigrants, 473, 477; in Holmes County, 48, 58–59; in New Orleans, types of, 261; and status, 58–59. *See also* Unemployment
Episcopalian Church, 128
Ethnic identity, 176, 178, 402
Ethnocentrism, value, 177

European: extended families, 395; influences, 397, 399, 440; marital ties, 395; peasant societies, 28 and n 3, 34; serfdom, 28 n 3, 33–34, 141. *See also* French; Spanish
Evanston, Illinois, 229
Ewe Clan, of Ghana, 132–133
Extended family in Black Societies, The, (Shimkin, Shimkin and Frate), 3–4

Families, extended Black: African, 130–133, 141; basic features of, 66–76, 262; and Black culture in United States, 139–142, 182, 186, 237; and class structure, 120–121; concept of, 66–68; as corporate body, 73–74, 151–152, 158, 162; corporate economic systems of, 58, 103–108, 109, 112; economic behavior of, 33; in Haiti, 423, 433–443; historical continuity and, 130–136, 141; in Holmes County, 4, 18, 23–24, 27, 32, 66–76, 139–141; and household, distinguished, 109–110; ideal type of, 187–188, 239; identifying members of, 203–211; and Italian-American, 23–24; and kinship networks, 112–130; and legislation, 165–168; and marriage tie, 71–72, 188; models compared, 262–264; observation of, 23–24; organization and functioning, in North and South United States, 188–196; parents in, 72; and politics, 27; reunions of, 159–160, 195, 358–359; rights and obligations of, 68–71; situational adaption of, 136–137, 141; and slavery, 133–136; social interaction of, 112; in S. Texas, 360–362; stereotypes, 175, 179; 'strong' and 'weak', 74–75, 87, 381–383; structural characteristics of, 187–188, 343–346, 433–438; studies of, 27–34; supportive behavior of, 151–152, 164–165; types of organization, 192; compared with White, 136–137, 141, 142, 175, 176–177, 185–186, 266. *See also* Kinship; Migrants
Family: concept of, 66–68; ideal type of, 187–188
Family life, supposed standard American, 182–186
Fanney Booker Home for the Elderly, 159, 160
Farmers: Black landowners, 7, 47, 57, 58, 117; a family of sedentary subsistence, 103–112; Mileston Farmers'

Farmers (*cont.*)
    Cooperative, 27, 47, 60; tenant, kin-
    ship relations among, 188–189; in
    Texas, 281 n, 286–287. *See also* Farm-
    ing
Farmers' Home Administration, Holmes
    County, 167
Farming: in Holmes County, 46–47, 65;
    and migration, 47, 374; on St Helena
    island, 117–118. *See also* Farmers;
    Plantations
Farm Report, 93
Farm Tenant Act, Bankhead-Jones, 47
Fathers: 'absentee' U.S., 183; acknow-
    ledgement of paternity, 53, 67, 227;
    African, 130, 133; in Chicago, 193–
    194, 227; children's relations with, 69,
    190, 227, 274 n 2; in consensual
    unions, 53, 227; dispersed relation-
    ship, 193–194; foster-, 480; in Haiti,
    441; in Holmes County, 69; of
    illegitimate children, 67, 122; patri-
    archal families, 73 n 22, 120, 121, 189,
    190, 193; patrilateral system, 184,
    413; patrilineal system, 283, 394, 397;
    patrilocal residence, 436; polygynous,
    226, 227; in Pruitt-Igoe, 125–126; role
    of, 69, 130, 174; status of, 69, 383.
    See also Men, family role of; Parents
Female-headed households, Black, 184;
    in Africa, 133, 240; in Haiti, 432; in
    Holmes County, 50, 51, 52, 133, 155–
    157; and polygyny, 240. *See also*
    Matriarchal families; Matrifocality
Feuds: in Black families, 58, 68, 360; and
    White influences, 136
Fictive Kin ('play-kin'), 23, 128, 141,
    274 n, 379, 451; in Chicago, 194–195;
    compadrazgo, 434–435, 451; 'go for
    brother', 194–195; in Los Angeles,
    308–309, 315. *See also* Godparenthood
Filipinos, in Texas, 365
Finland, adult siblings in, 138
Fire, danger, in Holmes County, 34, 151
    and n
'Fireside training', 216 n 3, 228
'Floating community', 229
Florida: musical group visit, 216; slave
    trade, 133
Food stamp Program, U.S., 47, 48, 52,
    107, 167, 168
Fosterage: in Black extended family, 24,
    67, 72, 86, 110–111, 139, 235, 236, 237;
    in Carolina, 123; in Chicago, 216–217,
    220, 227–228; crisis and purposive,

448, 451, 467, 480; by grandparents,
    395, 397, 454, 459, 460, 469-470, 471,
    473–476, 478–480; in Haiti, 411, 434,
    437–438; and Italian-American family,
    24; keeping, raising and living with,
    227, 228; in Los Angeles, 310; by men,
    480; in 17th century, 463 n 8. *See also*
    Adoption; Africa, West; Africans,
    West; Foster-parents; London, child
    fosterage in; West Indian; West
    Indians
Foster-parents, relations with: in Ghana,
    458, 469; in Holmes County, 69, of
    real mother, 470, 471, 473–476; in
    West Indies, 448, 469–471, 473–476
'Founder' of family, 109–110
France, 17th century, fostering in, 463
    n 8
Freedman's Bureau, 356, 357 n 4
Freedman's Relief Association, 135–136
French: colonists of West Africa, 399;
    Creole slaves, 368; culture, 64, 380;
    influence, 358, 365, 433; tradition,
    areas of, 385
Friendship, among Blacks, 137; in
    Chicago, 231–233; in Los Angeles,
    309, 310–312, 315; networks, 232. *See
    also* Fictive Kin; Neighbors
Funerals: children at, 259; deceased
    returned to Hometown for burial, 30,
    217; in Holmes County, 30–31, 54,
    67, 68, 69; in Illinois, 195, 217–218;
    in Italian-American family, 24; in Los
    Angeles, 294; in New Orleans, 262;
    payment for, 218; in St Helena, 119;
    significance of, to Blacks, 24, 54, 114,
    187, 195, 393; in Texas, 291, 361.
    See also Burial of the dead; Funerals,
    attendance at
Funerals, attendance at obligatory: in
    Holmes County, 54, 67, 68, 69; in
    New Orleans, 258–259; time off work
    for, 69, 168; travelling to, 24, 30–31,
    119, 189, 195, 291, 361

Ga family and social change, The, (Azu),
    456
Galveston, Texas, population of, 365;
    slavery in, 367, 368
Gambia River Valley, West Africa, 176
Genealogy, awareness of, 278, 314,
    358–359, 396; in Haiti, 411
Generalization, on geographical basis,
    384; in research, 175, 179, 185
Geophagy, 23, 29, 63, 132

Georgia, 119, 141; landowners of, 189; slave trade, 133

'Georgiatown', study of, migrants to, 122–123

Germans, in Texas, 365–366, 368, 369, 375

Ghana, fostering in, 478, 479: Ashanti, 468 n; by Dagomba, 450; by Ewe clan, 132–133, 456, 457, 458; by Fanti, 456, 457, 458; among the Gonja, 450, 451–456, 460–462, 464, 468, 469, 470–478; by Krobo, 456, 457, 459; in Southern Ghana, 456–462, 464, 478 and n, 479. *See also* Africans, West

Ghettoes, urban, 138, 174, 186, 197, 235, 274 n 3; compartmentalized, 140; of Houston, 356; in Philadelphia, 115; relationships within, 232, 380; in Washington, 274

Girls: in Chicago, problems of one, 201, 202–211, 214–215, 235; domestic training of, in Ghana, 456, 457, 459; education of, 123; first daughters, in Ghana, 451–452; fostered, in Ghana, 456, 457; and grandmothers, 69, 454, 459; in Haiti, 437; household role of, 63; migrant, in Los Angeles, 316; relations with mothers, 125, 262, 263; relations with foster-parents, 69, 458. *See also* Daughters; Sisters

Globetrotter Company, 234

Godparenthood: in Caribbean, 220; Catholic origins of, 399; in colonial period, 440; in Haiti, 397, 399, 411, 420–421, 425, 432, 434–435, 437

Godparents: in Chicago, 228; as foster-parents, W. Indian, 474; in New Orleans, 266; *padrino*, Italian-American godfather, 24

Gonja, tribe of Ghana, fostering among, 450, 451–456, 460–462, 464, 468, 469, 470–471

Grandfathers: in Northern U.S., 195–196; relations with, 69. *See also* Grandparents

Grandmothers, Black, 189, 218 n; in Chicago, 218–219; foster girls, in Ghana, 454, 459, 478–480; foster girls in West Indies, 469–470, 471, 473–476, 478–480; relations with girls, 69, 454, 459. *See also* Grandparents

Grandparents: in Africa, 394, 395, 454, 459, 460; in the Caribbean, 472; in Chicago, 228; and fosterage, 395, 397, 454, 459, 460, 472; in Haiti, 411; in Holmes County, 166–167, 168; in

Italian-American family, 24; in North U.S., 195–196; in South U.S., 190. *See also* Grandfathers; Grandmothers

Greenwood, Mississippi, 92, 163 and n 45

Guatemala, Black Carib of, 448, 467, 469

Guiana, 399; Bush Negroes of, 131, 396–398

Haiti: European inuflence in, 397; extended family in, 392, 394, 396–397, 401, 407–416, 423, 433–438; god-parenthood in, 399; historical and situational factors, 439–442; households of, ten, 423–432; integrating values, 438–439; Kenscoff, 412–414; *lakou*, 408 and n 1, 409, 410, 411, 413, 416, 419, 420, 424, 436; Marbial Valley, 411; marriage in, 397, 409, 410, 412, 413; migration from, 422, 441; Mirebalais, 409; Port-au-Prince, 409, 413, 416 and n 4, 421, 430, 441; research suggestions re, 442–443; U.S. Landings, *1915*, 416 n. *See also* 'Ticouloute' and his family, in Haiti, study of

Head of family. *See* Authority, in the family

Head Start Program: in Holmes County, 5, 9, 10, 10 n 6, 13 and n, 47, 48, 56, 59, 63, 99, 110–111; instructors, 59, 93, 95; in Los Angeles, 309, 312–313

Health: hypertension, 4, 12 n, 26, 490; infant mortality, 12, 34, 53, 54, 65; medical care, 33, 48, 65, 167; poor conditions of Holmes County, 53; problems in Holmes County, 4, 9–10. *See also* Holmes County, Health Research Project

Heroines of Jericho, 279

Holmes County, Mississippi, 34–66, 139–142; and Black Mississippi, 64–65, 80, 139; Church in, 44–46, 58, 61, 67 n 11, 71, 73, 86, 89, 93, 161 and n (*See also* Holmes County Church Communities); compared with Africa, 131, 132–133, 135; compared with other districts, 137, 138, 140, 141; daily life and change in, 62–64; Delta and Hills regions of, 43–46, 58, 139; economy of, 46–48; health conditions in, 4, 9–10, 53, in-migrants of, 56–57; *maps of*, 43, 45; physical setting, 34–

Holmes County (*cont.*)
46; plantations, 6–7; population, 48–
57; size of, 16, 18; social institutions
and values, 57–62; study in, 489–490,
493; subsistence farming family of,
103–112; workshop in, *1973*, 150–158.
See also Blacks, of Holmes County;
Migration; Mileston Community;
Mitchell family, of Holmes County,
study of
Holmes County, Church communities,
44–46, 58, 61, 71 and n 18, 139, 161;
Balance due, 9, 58, 71 n 18; Coxburg,
45; Durant, 8, 44, 46, 49; Fox Run,
91; Howard, 45; Lexington, 44, 49,
58, 159–160; Long Branch, 14; Mount
Eaton, 103–104, 106, 112; Mount Olive,
58, 71 n 18; Paul Williams, 88; Pecan
Grove, 58; Pleasant View, 86, 87, 88,
89, 90, 91, 93, 100, 102; Plum Creek,
87; Randletown, 162; Second Pilgrim's Rest 7 and n 1; Sequoia, 94, 98,
100, 102; Strongheart, 92, 93, 98, 102;
Tchula, 8 n 4, 44, 49, 56; Tin Cup, 71 n
18; Tipton, 103–108, 112
Holmes County Health Research Program, 4, 9–10, 11, 12, 13, 17, 30, 48–
49, 167, 489–490
Homecoming, celebrations, Church, 293
Hometowns, association with migrants:
return to for burials, 30–31, 189, 195,
217, 314; clubs, 315–316; send money
to, 164–165, 168–169
Hospitality, importance of, 31
Hospitals, Holmes County, 59
Household: African, 133, 468–469; basic
activities of, 401; in California, 285;
in Chicago, 50–52, 229–231; clustering, 229–231, 236, 237, 257 n; compositions, 50–57, 347; daily life of,
in Holmes County, 63; economics of,
33, 155–156; and family, distinct from,
23, 109–110, 186–187, 191; forms, of
North and South U.S., 190–193, 196;
in Haiti, 412–416, 422, 423–432, 437,
441; in New Orleans, 248 and n, 250,
261, 263–264; one-parent, 184; and
residential propinquity, 248 and n 5,
249, 250; research into structure of,
265, 266; on St Helena, 116; sexual
roles in, 61–62; of sharing subsistence
farmers, 103–112; in Texas, 285; West
African and West Indian, 468–469.
See also Female-headed households;
Male-headed households

Housing: in Chicago, 164, 168–169, 229;
high density public, 125; in Holmes
County, 30, 63, 65, 104; in Houston,
356; New Orleans, 261; problems,
167, 169; Pruitt-Igoe development,
St Louis, 68 n 14, 72, 125–126, 140–
141, 177
Houston, Texas, 303, 356, 357, 358, 360,
362, 373, 383; San Jacinto monument,
360 and n
Hurricane Betsy, *1965*, 258, 260
Hypertension, 4, 12 n, 26, 490

Ibo families, West Africa, 477
Identity, Black, 162, 169, 176, 178, 402;
of family, and social controls, 249–
250; group, makers of 215
Ideologies: effect on research, 174–175;
an overview of current, 173–179
Illegitimacy: attitude to, in Chicago,
226; among West Indians in London,
473–475; Whites' attitude to, 175, 177,
182, 183, 383. *See also* Illegitimate
children
Illegitimate children: cared for by male
kinsmen, 122; in Georgiatown, 122;
in Holmes County, 53, 67
Illinois: church in, 195; economic effects
on families in, 197–198; migration to,
77 and n 26, 121, 122, 228; ritual
occasions in, 195; South, fictive kin in,
194. *See also* Chicago; Springfield
Illinois Central Railroad, 46, 47, 87, 159
n 32
Immigrants: to London (*see* London,
England, child fosterage in). *See also*
Migrants
Income: earnings, 65, 70, 118; effect on
family life, 182–184, 191, 197, 416. *See
also* Economic behavior; Unemployment
Indianapolis, study of Blacks in, 126,
136, 175, 178
Indians, American: and archaeology,
492; Choctaw, 64, 401; Chickasaw,
64; Comanches, 356, 365; families of,
73 n 21, 114; influence, areas of, 385;
systems of kinship and marriage, 136;
in Texas, 355, 356, 362, 365
Indonesia, 402 n
Industry, Black participation in, 136–137
Infancy, in Holmes County, 60
Infant mortality, Black, 12, 34, 53, 54,
65
Infants, burial of, 67 n 13

Infidelity: in 'Clan', Chicago, 223–224
Inheritance: African, 397, 469; disputes over, 70; in Haiti, 437. *See also* Property
'Institutional' (cultural) approach to research on Black family, 182, 186, 187–188, 240
Institutions: child-care, 198, 449, 476–477; of ghettoes, 140; Kate Maremont Foundation, 229, 234; for old people, 167, 169; power of, 493; White, borrowing from, 240
Insurance: burial, 218; laws, and extended family, 168, 169
Interaction, social, of extended families: in Holmes County, 57–62, 67, 112; in Los Angeles, 315; in New Orleans, kinship patterns, 257–260, 264–265; lack of, 112. *See also* Communications
International Congress of Anthropological and Ethnological Sciences, IXth, 150, 158, 176, 487
Interstate, 46, 48, 55
Italian-American families, 23–24
Italian culture, males in, 400

Jackson, Mississippi: Health Improvement Project in, 12; and Holmes County, 46, 65 n 9; migrants to, 54, 76, 78, 80, 86, 88, 90, 101, 102, 103; at reconstruction, 67
Jamaica: extended family in, 392; 'family' land, 397; fostering in, 465, 466, 471, 472; 'nieces', 399
Japanese, in Texas, 365
Jehovah's Witnesses, 215
Jerusalem Baptist Church, in Holmes County, 86, 89
Jet (magazine), 94, 96, 99, 102
Jews, kin groups of, 33
'Jody', concept of adulterer, 221, 223–224
Journal of Marriage and the Family, 176

Kalmuk Buddhist mongols, 492
Kandyan Sinhalese, customary claims of, 454
Kate Maremont Foundation, Chicago, 229, 234
Kennedy family, of 'Middville', study of, 283, 314; characteristics of focal persons, 283, 285, 303–305; components of family structure, 343, 346; hometown, 280, 282, 314; household compositions, 347; kinfolk and residences, 314, 336–342; lines of descent, 352; and 'Middville' Club, 305, 306, 308; neighbors and friends, 296, 311, 312
'Kent', town in the Carolinas, study of Blacks in, 113, 123–124, 135, 190
Kentucky, E., 141
Kinfolk and residences, of five Texan families, 317–342
Kinship: definition, in New Orleans, 245; obligations and interactions, 257–260; relations, effect of migration on, 274. *See also* Terminology, Kinship
Kinship networks, 177; in California, 127–129; demographic characteristics of, 264–265, 266, 267; ego-centred, 186; 'Georgiatown', 122–123; in Holmes County, 57–58, 66–68; 'Kent', 123–124; Natchez, 119–121; Pruitt-Igoe, 125–126; and religion, 129; in rural and urban United States, 112–130; St Helena, 115–119; series of groups, 186; Sunflower County, 121. *See also* 'Bidwell' family; Mitchell family
Korea, children from, adopted, 303
Korean war, 296
Ku Klux Klan, 128 n; in Mississippi, 8, 92, 163 n 45; in Texas 356

Lagos, Nigeria, residence patterns in, 255, 257
Lakou, Haitian compound, 408 and n 1, 409, 410, 411, 413, 416, 419, 420, 424, 436; after independence, 441, 442
Land: 'family' in Jamaica, 397; family disputes over, 70; in Haiti, 411; held by Blacks, in Holmes County, 73, 75, 105, 117; leasing, family, 104–112; slaves bound to, 133–134; slaves allowed to buy, 117; transferred to descendants of Whites, 67 n 12. *See also* Farming; Landowners; Plantations
Land, lineage, African, 397
Landowners: in Holmes County, Black, 7, 47, 57, 58, 117; Mileston Farmers' Co-operative, 27, 47, 60; White, 47, 105, 135. *See also* Farmers; Farming
Language, *See* Terminology, kinship
Latin America: culture of, 141; extended families in, 395; godparenthood in, 399. *See also* South America

Law: re adoption, 32; and Black culture, 32; Black customary, 32; Courts, 117. *See also* Legislation

Leadership: in African families, 394; family spokesman, senior, 73; among Negroes, 126–127. *See also* Authority, in the family; Female-headed households; Male-headed households

Legal Aid, 234

Legislation: supporting for Blacks, need for, 165–168, 169, 177, 179, 493

Levirate, 136

Lexington Advertiser, 8 n 3, 52 n, 54, 67, 89, 93

Life expectancy, Black, 65, 86; death rate, U.S., 53, 65; infant mortality, 12, 34, 53, 54, 65; in Texas, 283–285

Literature, Black experience in, 33–34

Little Rock, Arkansas, migration from, 211, 212

Lo, Boni extended lineage, 396

Locality, family centre, 141, 215, 236; African, 133; clustering, 229–231, 231 n, 236; locational stability, 201; 'the Yard' of the 'Wesleys', 250–257, 259, 260. *See also* Neighborhoods; Residence; Residence patterns; Residences; Residential propinquity

London, England, child fosterage in: of West African parents, 449, 451 n 2, 456 and n, 462–464, 464–465, 477–478, 481–483; West Indians, 449, 473–478, 481–482

Look (magazine), 96

Los Angeles, California: Baldwin Hills, 273; 'Middville Club', 276, 285, 305–308, 310, 314, 315; migrants to, 54, 76, 127, 271–273, 274, 275; (*See also* Adams family; Davis family; Kennedy family; Miller family; Smith family); neighborhoods of, 310–312; social organizations of, 312–313, 315–316

Louisiana: migrants from, 128; migrants to, 153, 163 n 47, 246, 247, 251, 252, 253, 254, 255, 256, 257, 258, 367, 368; varieties of Black culture in, 380. *See also* New Orleans; Wesley family, of New Orleans, study of

Lozi, the, saying of, 223

Lying, 28

Lynching; in Holmes County, 6, 57, 63; in Texas, 371

Madison County, Mississippi, 64, 163, 382 n 2, 383

Male-headed households, Black, 174–175; in Haiti, 410, 436–437. *See also* Fathers; Men, Black

Male kinsmen, and care of children, 122. *See also* Brothers; Fathers; Men; Sons

Marital relationships: of 'The Clan', Chicago, 220–225; conflicts, 224–225, 437; 'segregate', 192. *See also* Marital ties; Marriage

Marital ties: and consanguineous ties, 71–72, 133, 188, 194, 223, 224; and descent ties, 394; European, 395. *See also* Marital relationships; Marriage

Marriage: in Africa, 130–131, 132, 396–397, 453; approval of relatives necessary for, 193, 224; Black, supposed unstable by Whites, 173, 175, 177, 182, 185, 193; 'common law', 115, 130; cross-cousin, 453; dissolution of, 72, 132, 183, 283; and economic factors, 193, 198; endogamous and exogamous, 24, 141, 436; ethnic inter-, 314, 358; in 'Georgiatown', 122–123; in ghettoes, 115; in Haiti, 397, 409, 412, 435, 436, 440; in Holmes County, 49, 52, 53, 71–72, 75, 76; in Italian-American family, 24; in 'Kent', 124; polyandry, 113; polygamy, 113, 136, 425, 432, 440; polygyny, 226, 240, 396, 412; prohibitions re, 412, 136; significance of, in Chicago, 222–223; and slavery, 113–114, 115, 134, 136, 173, 175, 439–440; and status system, 222; in Sunflower County, 121; of Texan families, 283, 358; in Western Society, 400. *See also* Consensual unions; Marital relationships; Marital ties; Weddings

Marriage in a matrilineal elite, (Oppong), 456

Martinique, children stay with kin, on, 448

Masons, 61; in Texas, 279

Matriarchal families, 184; in Chicago, 190; in Natchez, 120; in South U.S., 189, 190. *See also* Female-headed households

Matrifocality, 184, 401; in Africa, 398; in Haiti, 413, 441; in Los Angeles, 314–315; in New Orleans, 249; in Northern U.S., 194, 196, 264, 265, 267; West African origins of, 396. *See also* Female-headed households

Matrilateral ties, Black, 184, 188; in Haiti, 436

Matrilineage, of South American Bush Negroes, 392–393, 397, 398

Matrilineal consanguinity, 244–245, 262–263, 265

Matrilineal descent system, 283, 394, 397

Mayors, election of Black, 197

Medical care: in Boston, 33; faith healing, 215 n 4; hospitals, in Holmes County, 59; long-term, in Holmes County, 33; midwives, 59, 66, 420; in Mississippi, 65; of old people, 167. *See also* Health

Medicare, in Holmes County, 48

Memphis, Tennessee, 46, 76, 304; slave trade in, 133

Men, Black: dominance by, 60; educational attainments of, 231 n 19; fosterage by, 480; households headed by, 174–175, 410, 436–437; image of, 184, 223 n; model for, 183; proportion of in Holmes County, 49–50; status of, 383. *See also* Brothers; Fathers; Men, family role of

Men, family role of, 197; in Chicago, 193–194, 195, 196; in Ghana, 454; in Holmes County, 24, 69, 71, 122, 155–156, 158, 183, 184–185; in St Helena, 116; in West Indies, 192. *See also* Brothers; Fathers; Male-headed households

Methodist church, Blacks and, 96, 97, 154, 380; in California, 128; Episcopal Church, 278, 291; in Texas, 371

Mexican-Americans, extended families among, 141

Mexicans, in Texas, 365, 368–369, 370, 371; mission, 371

Michigan, 121. *See also* Detroit

'Middville', East Texas, 277–282; 'Africa Community' in, 280–282, 285, 286, 297, 300; High School, 279–280, 293, 302, 304; 'Middville Club', in Los Angeles, 276, 285, 305–308, 310, 314, 315; research in, 272, 276; study of five families from (*See* Adams family; Davis family; Kennedy family; Miller family; Smith family)

Midwives: Black U.S., 59, 66; in Haiti, 420

Migrant Farmer Program, Mississippi, 11

Migrants: African, 133 (*See also* Slaves); in California, 127–129 (*See also* Adams family; Davis family; Kennedy family; Miller family; Smith family); in Chicago, (*See* 'Bidwell' family of Chicago); children of, 316; in Detroit, 78, 80, 86, 88, 127, 140; hometown clubs of, 315–316; and hometowns, 140, 151, 152–153, 158, 159, 161, 164–165, 168–169, 273–274, 314; in Iowa, 159; in London (*see* London); return to hometowns, 30–31, 77, 189, 195, 217, 314; from St Helena, 118–119; studies of, 125; urban adaptation of, 275. *See also* Migration

Migration: Black perception of, 158; to California, 127–129, 141; to 'Georgiatown', 122; from Haiti, 422, 441; help in, 151, 152–153, 161; into Holmes County, 48, 49–50, 54, 56–57, 77; out of Holmes County, 26, 46, 47–48, 49–50, 54–56, 71 n 18, 76–77, 78, 108–109, 139–140, 151; in 'Kent', 124; effect on kinship, 108–109, 139–140, 159 n, 161, 274; from St Helena, 118; song re, 153; study of, 382, 401; in Texas, 357, 364, 371–376; to the West, waves of, 273–274; early White, 48. *See also* Migrants

Migratory family network. *See* 'Bidwell' family of Chicago

Mileston Community, Mississippi, Black, 44, 47; Civil Rights Movement in, 6, 7, 7 n 2, 9; Farmers' Co-operative, 27, 47, 60; Plantations of, 7 n 2

Military service, 76, 78, 80, 86, 88, 91

Miller family, of 'Middville', study of, 283, 314, 315; characteristics of focal persons of, 284, 299–303; family structure, 343, 344; fictive kin, 309, 315; hometown, 282, 314; household compositions, 347; kinfolk and residences, 314, 332–336; lines of descent, 351; and 'Middville' Club, 305, 308; neighbors and friends, 312, 313

Milton Olive III Memorial Corporation, 25–29, 60, 487, 488, 491; Board of, 17; chartered purposes, 10 n 5; founded, 9–10; program for children, 9, 13, 60

Milwaukee, 298; relatives in, 211, 212

Minneapolis: migration to, 50 n 7, 77, 298; new colony in, 30

Mississippi: Black, Holmes County, 64–65; Central Mississippi Inc., 13 n; Counties of, 58; Pilot Project for Black Education, 11; rural, 113, 151; Slavery in, 133, 134–135; State Health Department, 13; State House, 9; White planters of, 135; Bolivar County, 64, 77 n 26, 122; Claiborne, 49; Columbus, 62; Humphreys, 64, 163; Jefferson, 49, 64; Leflore, 64, 163 and n 45; Madison, 64, 163, 382 n 2, 383; Marshall, 64, 133; Sunflower, 64, 121; Tunica, 49, 64. *See also* Holmes County, Mississippi

Mississippi Freedom Democratic Party, in Holmes County, 7 and n 1, 9, 12, 15–16, 27, 60; Voice of the Working People, 15

Mitchell family, of Holmes County, sedentary subsistence farmers, study of, 23–24, 29, 76, 103–112, 138, 140, 178, 201, 398; child and adult fosterage, 110–111; communications patterns, 108–109; family relationships, 104–105; household/family dichotomy, 109–110; resource base, 105–108; social interactions of, 112

Mobil Oil Co., 289 and n

Mormons, 129

Motherhood, Black perception of, 176, 191

Mother: Black, importance of role of, 189, 249; and daughters, 125, 262, 263; discipline by, 72 n 20; and foster mothers, 470, 474–476; relations with, 69 and n, 226–227; terminology re, 399; unmarried, 53, 122, 473–475 (*see also* Illegitimacy); working Black, 186. *See also* Grandmothers; Matriarchal Families; Matrifocality; Matrilateral ties; Matrilineage; Matrilineal Consanguinity

Mother's Day, 219 n

Mound Bayou, Mississippi, 381–382, 381 n

Moundville, Mississippi, 94, 99

Moynihan report, the, 235–236, 240

'Mudtown', deep South U.S., 273

Music, 396; Black, 216 n; groups, 216; Soul, 274 n 3

Muslims, family life of, 450, 452

Naming children, 68; ceremonies, in Ghana, 452. *See also* Baptism

Natchez, Mississippi, 119–121

Nation of Islam, 129

Negro family in the United States, The (Frazier), 240

Neighborhoods: in New York City, older Black, 383; secular community centers, 154, 158, 280. *See also* Ghettoes, urban; Holmes County Church communities; Residence; Residences; Residential propinquity

Neighbors, relations with: in Los Angeles, 276, 310–312, 315; in New Orleans, 260–262. *See also* Friendship

Nephews, Boni, 399

New Haven, 249 n

New Orleans, Louisiana, 54, 187, 260–262; church in, 195. *See also* 'Wesley' family of New Orleans, study of

New York City: Brooklyn, 431–432; Haitians in, 408, 416, 422–423; migrants to, 76, 78, 82, 91, 115, 116, 118, 124, 127, 140; older black neighborhoods in, 383; St Helenians, 118, 119

Nicknames, 202–203, 215, 265

'Nieces' in Jamaica, 399

Noble family (of 'Middville'), 281

Norms, accepted, 403; ideal type of Black family, 187–188; stereotype of U.S. family, 182–186

Northern cities of U.S.A., Black families in, 191–196. *See also* Chicago; Detroit; New York

Nuclear family: Black, in California, 178; dominant urban type, 178; White 190, 210; wrongly taken as the ideal, 239

Obligations of kinship: and fostering, 67, 451, 470–471, 475, 480; in Ghana, re siblings' children, 452–453, 460–462, 480; in Haiti, 438; in Holmes County, 67, 68–71; in New Orleans, 257–260, 266

Occupational status, Holmes County, 58–59

Oil industry, 369, 371

Oklahoma, 359

Old Age Assistance, 47, 48

Old people: attitude to, in South United States, 190; care of, in Ghana, 454, 471; care of, in Haiti, 437; and fostering, 475–476, 480 and n; provision for, in Holmes County, 50 n 6, 70, 167–168, 169; sexual roles of, 175; in West Indies, 471. *See also* Elders; Grandparents

Operation Breadbasket, 140
'Opportunity system', American, 183

Parents: deaths of, in Holmes County, 54; one-parent homes, 184; relations with, in Holmes County, 69, 72, 155–156; in St Louis, 125–126; as social controls, 249–250. *See also* Fathers; Mothers
'Pathological' approach, in research on Black family life, 138, 174–175, 178, 181–186, 191, 240, 241, 266–267; 'pathologies', 403
'Patriarchal' family, 73 n 22, 120, 121, 193; in South U.S., 189, 190. *See also* Fathers
Patrilateral system, 184; in Haiti, 413
Patrilineal descent, 283, 394, 397
Patrilocal residence, in Haiti, 397, 436
'Pawned' children, in Ghana, 456–457
Philadelphia, Pennsylvania: ghetto study in, 115; migration to, 115, 116, 124; religious community in, 129
Physics, developments in, 488–489
Piedmont, Carolina, mill town study in, 123–124
Plantations: African elements in life on, 131; replace African culture, 113; in Haiti, 439–440; in Holmes County, 6–7, 8, 9, 44, 58, 75; kinship system on, 194; moved as units, with slaves, 367–368; 'New World', 400; 17–18th century, 134–135; Slavery on, 28 n 4, 113–114, 173, 367–368; voting registration on, 6–7; White, and enforcement of Black standards, 383; White extended families of, 135. *See also* Slavery; Slaves
'Play-kin'. *See* Fictive kin
Police, in Chicago, 234
Polish, peasants in United States, 402–403
Politics: in Chicago, participation in, 234; in Holmes County, organization of Blacks: *1962–1967*, 5–10; *1967–1971*, 10–12; *1971–1974*, 12–19, 57, 63; lack of participation in, 112; and sexual dominance, 60
Polyandry, Black, in United States, 113
Polygamy: in Haiti, 425, 432, 440; in United States, Black, 113, 136
Polygyny: in Africa, 240, 396; in Haiti, 412; in W. Indies, 226
Population: of Holmes County, 30, 48–57; sex ratio, 49–50, 86, 283; of Texas, 283–285, 357, 367, 371, 372, 373, 374;

1870–1970 Negro Texas, 364; U.S. Censuses, 30, 50, 358
Poverty, effects on family life, 182–184, 191, 197, 416; in St Helena, 117. *See also* Unemployment
Power, institutional, 493
Prairie View College, Texas, 280, 293, 304
Prairie View Normal School, 370
Preliminary report on patterns of medical and health care in poverty areas of Chicago, (Lepper and Lashoff) 78 n
Professional: members of Illinois family, 198; workers, club for Black, 315
Project Grass Roots (re adult education), 11, 26
Property, held by Blacks, 136–137. *See also* Land
Protestant church: in Haiti, 435–436; in South United States, 153 n 14; in Texas, 370–371
Providence Co-operative Farm, Mississippi, 8 n 3
Providencia island, 393 n 3
Pruitt-Igoe housing development, St Louis, research on, 68 n 14, 72, 125–126, 140–141, 177
Public programs: Black cultures as bases for, 142; Foodstamps, 47, 48, 52, 107, 167, 168; Grass Roots, Project, 11, 26; in Holmes County, 5, 9–13, 17–18, 48. *See also* Head Start Program; Holmes County Health Research Program
Puerto Ricans, 473
Puritans, in New England, fostering among, 463 n 8

Racial differentiation, in W. Indies, 478 n
Racism, of modern America, 402
Radio, station WVON, 234
Reconstruction, effect on slaves, 136, 240
Religion: and Black Muslims, 129; and Civil Rights Movement, 155, 158; faith healing, 215 n 4; in Haiti, 439; in Holmes County, 61, 74 n 25, 139, 153–155, 158, 160–161; in 'Kent', 124; Providence Co-operative Farm, 8 n 3; social reconstruction through, 129. *See also* Christianity; Church
Research, into Black culture: accountability of, 150; 'adaptive' approach, 181–182, 186–187, 196, 240; current, an overview of, 173–179, 186–187, 239–241; generalization in, 175; in Haiti, 442–443; and ideology, 174–

Research (*cont.*)
175; 'institutional' approach, 182, 186, 187–188, 240; new problems in, 264–267; 'pathological' approach, 138, 174–175, 178, 181–186, 191, 240, 241, 266–267, 403; relations with community studied, 487–494; 'similarity' perspective, 175, 179; studies conducted, 112–130; suggestions for, 379–386, 401, 402, 442–443

Residence, 250 and n. *See also* Housing; Locality; Neighborhoods; Residence patterns; Residences; Residential propinquity

Residence patterns: in Black urban extended family, 262, 264, 265, 267; in Haiti, 410, 436, 438 (*See also* Lakou). *See also* Residences; Residential propinquity

Residences: changing and clustering, 229–231, 257 n; kinfolk and, of five Texan families, 317–342

Residential propinquity, of extended families: in Los Angeles, 314; in New Orleans, 248 and n 5, 249–257, 258, 262, 263–264, 266

Responsibility, Black social, collective and individual, 197–199

Reunions, family, 314, 315; in Illinois, 195; in Mississippi, 159–160; in Texas, 358–359. *See also* Funerals

Richards family (of 'Middville'), 281

Ritual kinship: in Haiti, 434. *See also* Godparenthood

Ritual occasions, observance of: in Haiti, 435–436; in Illinois, 195. *See also* Funerals; Weddings

Robert Francis Kennedy Civic Association, 60

Roots, (Haley), 176

Russian serfdom, 28 n 3, 33–34, 141

St Helena, island off S. Carolina, study of Blacks of, 115–119

St Louis, Missouri; migration to, 54, 76, 78, 80, 90, 210, 211; poor Black women in, 191; Pruitt-Igoe housing development, 68 n 14, 72, 125–126, 140–141, 177

San Antonio, Texas, 314, 356, 362

Savannah, Georgia, 115, 116, 118

Schools, Black: age limits, 162; attendance, 162, 164, 166–167, 169; and Civil Rights, 99; in Chicago, 234; funds for, 160; in Holmes County, 59,
160–167, 169; laws re, 166–167; in Texas, 279–280, 293, 302, 304, 370, 371. *See also* Education; Head Start Program; Teachers

Scientists, social: and general public, 488, 489–494. *See also* Research

Sea Islands, off South Carolina, 32, 113, 129, 392 and n; and Holmes County, 32, 140; St Helena, 115–119; slavery in, 135, 136

Security, in Black family, 190, 191

Selective buying campaign, 15–16

Self-Help Exploratory Workshop, *1974*, 493

Self-help groups, 493–494

Selma, Alabama, 9, 62, 141

Sex discrimination, in education, in Haiti, 437

Sex ratio, in Black United States families, 86; in Holmes County, 49–50; in Texan families, 283

Sexual behavior: in St Helena, 116; permissiveness of Blacks, 176, 177; White double standard, 176, 177. *See also* Consensual unions

Sexuality: in 'The Clan', Chicago, 223–224; rural Black attitude to, 383. *See also* Illegitimacy

Sexual relationships: adolescent, 122, 128, 383; in kin group, Jamaican, 392; and religious group, 129; in St Helena, 116; effect of slavery on, 173. *See also* Consensual unions; Marital relationships; Marriage

Sexual roles, Black, 176–177; of ageing Blacks, 175; in Holmes County, 155–157, 158; in North United States, 196; and religious groups, 129; segregation of, 184–185, 193. *See also* Fathers; Female-headed households; Male-headed households; Men, Black; Men, family role of; Mothers; Women

Shakers, 129

Siblings: adult, 248 and n 7; foster each others' children, 452–453, 459–462; in Ghana, 452–453, 459–462; relations between, 70, 249; terminlogy for, 226 and n, 245, 452–453. *See also* Brothers; Consanguineous ties; Sisters

'Similarity' perspective re Black family, in research, 175, 179

Sisters: and brothers, 70, 220, 221–222; bring up own siblings, 70, 470; in Haiti, 437; in Holmes County, 70;

Sisters (*cont.*)
-in-law, 70; relations between, 70, 87, 262. *See also* Consanguineous ties; Siblings
Size of Black family: in Haiti, 413; in Holmes County, 53; urban, 115
Slavery: 17–18th century, 134–135; in Civil War, 135–136, 356; free Negroes during, 366–367; effects on Black personality and society, 173–174, 181–182, 240, 399, 400, 439–441; ending of, 173, 357 n 4, 359; in Haiti, 411, 439–441; on plantations, 28 n 3, 113–114, 173 (*See also* Plantations); on St Helena, 115; in Texas, 300, 367–369. *See also* Slaves
Slaves: as ancestors, 126; imported from Africa, 133–134; bound to land, 133–134; after Civil War, 356, 359; ex-slaves, allowed to buy land, 117; brought to Holmes County, 48; return to Africa, 399; reunion of descendants of, 358–359; trade in, 133, 368; trading by prohibited, 132. *See also* Slavery
Slave trade, 133, 368
Smith family, of 'Middville', study of, 283, 314, 315, 316; characteristics of focal persons, 284, 285–290; family structure, 343, 344; fictive kin, 309; hometown, 282, 314; household compositions, 347; kinfolk and residences, 314, 317–321; lines of descent, 348; and 'Middville' club, 305, 306, 308; neighbors and friends, 311, 312, 313; young daughter of, 282, 316
S.N.C.C., 92
Social controls, and family identity, 249–250
'Social engineering', 403
Social interaction. *See* Interaction, social
Socialization of children, 183; in the South, 190
Social reconstruction, and religion, 129
Social resources, of the 'Clan', Chicago, 231–235
Social responsibility, communal basis of Black, 197–199
Social scientists: bias of, 185; and Holmes County projects, 16–17. *See also* Research, into Black culture
Social welfare: exclusion from, 152; effect on extended families, 33, 125, 138, 165, 167–168; Foodstamps, 47, 48, 52, 107, 167, 168
Social workers, in Chicago, 202, 203
Society of United States, supposed uniformity in, 181–186
Songs, Black, 153, 216 n, 218–219, 224, 382
Sons: and fathers, 133. *See also* Boys
Soul, 274 n 3
Soulside (Hannerz), 261, 274
South American: Bush Negroes, 392; Lowland, 400. *See also* Latin American
South Carolina, 66, 141; Church in, 161 n 38; St Helena, 115–119; Sea Islands, 32, 113, 129, 135, 136, 140, 392 and n; slavery in, 134; white planters of, 135
Southern Christian Leadership Conference, 99
Spanish, in Texas, 355, 358, 362, 365, 370, 376 and n. *See also* Mexican
Spiegel Catalog Co., 97, 98, 100
Springfield, Illinois, 121, 210, 211, 228
Starkville, Mississippi, 66
Statistical information: fallacious re Blacks, 175; for Holmes County, 30; on Texan families, 283. *See also* Population
Status: differences, 382–383; differences in families, and interaction, 67; of families, 123, 124, 126–127; marriage and, 222; and occupations, 58–59; in the South, 190. *See also* 'Strong' traits and 'weakness'
Stereotypes, family, 73 n 2; of Black family, 87, 175, 179, 381; of United States family norm, 183
'Strong' traits and 'weakness', 381–383; African concepts of, 394, 402; in Holmes County families, 62, 74–75, 87
Sun-Times (Chicago newspaper), 94, 96, 98, 101
Support, mutual, 151–153. *See also* Economic behavior, of Black families

Taboos, of the Boni, 397
Tally's corner (Liebow), 274
Tax laws, and Blacks, 167, 169
Teachers, Black; and Civil Rights Movement, 7; salaries of, 160, 168; status of, 59; in Texas, 280, 293
Tennessee, migrants from, 211
Terminology, kinship, 133, 399; fosterage, 69; of Ghana, 452–453, 469; of Haiti, 433–434; in Holmes County,

Terminlogy (*cont.*)
67; for mothers, 399; for siblings, 226 and n, 245, 452–453
Texaco Oil Co., 297
Texas: 'Appalachian' culture, 369; Black culture in, 113; Black population, 364; cultural distinctiveness, 355–356, 363–367; effects of Civil War, 369–371; ethnic distribution, 372–377; familialism in, 355–362, 375–376; Harrison County, 271, 356–357, 370, 371–372; *map*, 272; migrants from, 127, 271–352, 364; the past, 355–356, 363–367; slavery in, 133, 367–369; World War II, 371–372. *See also* 'Middville'
Texas Almanac, 357 n 3
Texas Office of Economic Opportunity, 376
'Ticouloute' and his family, in Haiti, study of, 408–409, 416–434, 438, 439; historical and situational factors, 439–442; ten household histories, 423–432; institutional setting of, 432–439
Tidewater, Virginia, 66
Timpson Club, Los Angeles, 315
Tomorrow's tomorrow (Ladner), 176–177
Trading, by women, 132
Traditionalism, in Holmes County, 63
Trinidad, 399, 400
Twins: African, 397; in Haiti, 434

U.S. Army, 76, 88, 91, 101
U.S. Census of Population: *1850*, 358; *1960*, 50; *1970*, 30
U.S. Commission on Civil Rights, 8 n 4
U.S. Department of Agriculture: Food-stamps, 47, 48, 52, 107, 167, 168
U.S. Department of Health, Education and Welfare, 53, 65 n 10
U.S. Farm Security Administration, 7 n 2
U.S. Federal Government: and Holmes County community control projects, 17; and Holmes County employment, 48; and hospitals and schools, 59; and slavery, 135–136
U.S. Marines, in Haiti, 409, 416 and n 4, 417
U.S. Supreme Court, 371
Universities, role of, 489
University of Illinois: admits Black students, 11; study by, 31
University of Mississippi, Health Improvement Program, 11

Unmarried mothers: in 'Georgiatown', 122; in Holmes County, 53; West Indian immigrants, 473–475
Umor, the, of Nigeria, 397
Unemployment: and Black family life, 240; in Holmes County, 47–48, 50–52, 65, 167
Union Pacific Railway, 297, 298
Union Steel Company, 95, 97
'Uniqueness' position, in regarding Black culture, 175–176, 178, 179
United Kingdom: extended families in, 395; immigrants to, employment of, 473, 477. *See also* London, child fosterage in
Urban adaptation of migrants, definition of, 275; hometown clubs, 315–316; and kinship ties, in Los Angeles, 273–274, 308, 316
Urban environments, family systems in, 202, 236; life in Black, 174, 178. *See also* 'Clan, the', Chicago family study; Ghettoes, urban
Urbanization, of African extended families, 393 n 4

Value ethnocentrism, 177
Values, integrating, in Haiti, 438–439
Vicksburg, Mississippi, slave trade, 133
Vietnam, war in, 98–99
Violence: and Civil Rights movement, 6, 8, 8 n 3, 8 n 4; in Holmes County, 6, 57, 63; lynchings, 6, 57, 63, 371. *See also* Ku Klux Klan
Virginia: extended Black family in, 131; slavery in, 133–134, 159, 358–359; White planters of, 135
Voice of the Working People (Mississippi), 15
Voodoo, in Haiti, 418 and n, 435–436, 440, 441; baptism, 435; -godparents, 435; twins and, 434
Voter registration: drive in Holmes County, 5–8, 9, 10, 11–12, 163 n 45; Southern Christian Leadership Conference, 99

Waco, Texas, 356
'Wanderer' (slaving ship), 133
Washington: ghetto life in, 274; migrants to, 124, 153
Waterloo, Iowa, 76; migrants to, 159 and n 32
Watts, survey in. 275 n

'Weakness', concept of family, 62, 74, 75, 381–383, 394, 402

Weddings: European, 395; in Haiti, 435; in Holmes County, 24, 70, 96; in Illinois, 195; in Italian-American family, 24; in Los Angeles, 296; Negro U.S., 114; in New Orleans, 259, 262

Welfare, social, in United States: effect on extended families, 33, 125, 138, 165, 167–168; exclusion from, 152; Food-stamps, 47, 48, 52, 107, 167, 168

'Wesley' family, of New Orleans, study of, 201, 215, 241–267, 380; as general model, 262–264; kin obligations and interactions, 257–260; kinship definition among, 245–248; 'Mama', 242, 248, 249; neighborhood of, 260–262; residential propinquity and ties, 248–249, 252, 254, 256; social controls and, 249–250; structural features, 242–245; the 'Yard', 250–257, 259, 260

West Africa. *See* Africa, West

West Africans. *See* Africans, West

West Indian: child fosterage, 448–449, 465–482; family structure, 191–192; marriage, 130; migration, 471, 473; old people, 471; women, 130, 131. *See also* Caribbean; Haiti; Jamaica

West Indians: in London, 449, 473–478, 481–482; in U.S. cities, 138 n

White, 'passing for', 286

White families: Black perception of, 142, 176–177; children of, 72, 210; compared with Black, 136–137, 141, 142, 175, 176–177, 185–186, 266; morality of, 177; need for study of, 380; nuclear, 72, 210; of planter society, Southern U.S., 135

White Life Table for South Eastern United States, 53

Whites: Black attitudes to, 117, 382; Black descendants of, 67 n 12; Blacks copy ways of, and status, 121, 165, 381; distorted perception of Blacks, 32, 142, 173–176, 185, 267; in Holmes County, relations with Blacks, 5–9, 47, 57, 58, 59, 63, 70 and n, 73, 74; influences on Negroes, 136, 141, 165,

176–177; landowners, in Holmes County, 47, 105, 135; law courts, 117; sexual standards of, 176, 177; and slaves, 134 (*see also* Slavery); supportive role towards Blacks, 491; in Texas, 278, 279. *See also* Ku Klux Klan; Research, into Black culture; White families

Widows, isolation of, 175

Wisconsin, 121

Women, Black: African, 130–131, 132; behavior prescribed by religious groups, 129; community role, in Holmes County, 71, 74, 75; dominance of, in Holmes County, 60, 61; fertility rates, 52–53; in Ghana, 454; in Haiti, 412, 413; in Holmes County, numbers of, 49; Muslim wives, 450; power of, 183, 184–185; related, 245 and n 3, 262–263 (*see also* Daughters; Mothers; Matrilineal ties; Sisters); role of, 176–177; in St Helena, 116; in St Louis, 191; self-sufficient, 130–131; trading by, 132. *See also* Women, family role of

Women, family role of: in Detroit, 137; in 'Georgiatown', 122, 123; in Holmes County, 24, 61–62, 71, 155–157, 158; in New Orleans, 249. *See also* Daughters; Female-headed households; Matriarchal families; Matrifocality; Matrilateral ties; Matrilineage; Matrilineal consanguinity; Mothers; Sisters

Women's Liberation Movement, 156–157, 158

Woodlawn Organization, 140

Work: Boni organization of, 397–398; and status, in Holmes County, 58–59. *See also* Employment

World War I, effects of, 78, 163, 289

World War II; economic effect of, 46, 304; effects on Texas, 371–372; migration in, 273, 364

Yazoo County, Mississippi, 382 and n 2, 383

Yoruba, African tribe: child fostering 450, 456 n; residential pattern, 257